Medieval Music

The Library of Essays on Music Performance Practice.
Series Editor: Mary Cyr

Titles in the Series:

Medieval Music
Honey Meconi

Renaissance Music
Kenneth Kreitner

Baroque Music
Peter Walls

Classical and Romantic Music
David Milsom

Medieval Music

Edited by

Honey Meconi
University of Rochester, USA

ASHGATE

© Honey Meconi 2011. For copyright of individual articles please refer to the Acknowledgements.

All rights reserved. No part of this publication may be reproduced, stored in a retrieval system or transmitted in any form or by any means, electronic, mechanical, photocopying, recording or otherwise without the prior permission of the publisher.

Wherever possible, these reprints are made from a copy of the original printing, but these can themselves be of very variable quality. Whilst the publisher has made every effort to ensure the quality of the reprint, some variability may inevitably remain.

Published by
Ashgate Publishing Limited
Wey Court East
Union Road
Farnham
Surrey GU9 7PT
England

Ashgate Publishing Company
Suite 420
101 Cherry Street
Burlington
VT 05401-4405
USA

www.ashgate.com

British Library Cataloguing in Publication Data
Medieval music. – (The library of essays on music
  performance practice)
  1. Performance practice (Music)–History–To 1500.
  I. Series II. Meconi, Honey.
  781.4'3'0902-dc22

Library of Congress Control Number: 2010940356

ISBN: 9780754628514

Printed and bound in Great Britain by
TJ International Ltd, Padstow, Cornwall.

Contents

Acknowledgements vii
Series Preface ix
Introduction xi

PART I PLAINCHANT

1 Lance W. Brunner (1982), 'The Performance of Plainchant: Some Preliminary Observations of the New Era', *Early Music*, **19**, pp. 316–28.   3
2 Katarina Livljanić (2002), 'Giving Voice to Gregorian Chant or: Coping with Modern Orthodoxies', *Basler Jahrbuch für historische Musikpraxis*, **26**, pp. 47–58.   15

PART II SECULAR MONOPHONY

3 Hans Tischler (1974–1976), 'Rhythm, Meter, and Melodic Organization in Medieval Songs', *Revue belge de musicologie*, **28–30**, pp. 5–23.   29
4 Hendrik van der Werf (1988), 'The "Not-So-Precisely Measured" Music of the Middle Ages', *Performance Practice Review*, **1**, pp. 42–60.   49
5 Sylvia Huot (1989), 'Voices and Instruments in Medieval French Secular Music: On the Use of Literary Texts as Evidence for Performance Practice', *Musica Disciplina*, **43**, pp. 63–113.   69
6 Christopher Page (1993), 'Johannes de Grocheio on Secular Music: A Corrected Text and a New Translation', *Plainsong and Medieval Music*, **2**, pp. 17–41.   121

PART III POLYPHONY TO 1300

7 Edward Roesner (1979), 'The Performance of Parisian Organum', *Early Music*, **7**, pp. 174–89.   149
8 Charles M. Atkinson (1989), 'Franco of Cologne on the Rhythm of Organum Purum', *Early Music History*, **9**, pp. 1–26.   165
9 Jeremy Yudkin (1980), 'The *Copula* According to Johannes de Garlandia', *Musica Disciplina*, **34**, pp. 67–84.   191
10 Ernest H. Sanders (1985), 'Conductus and Modal Rhythm', *Journal of the American Musicological Society*, **38**, pp. 439–69.   209
11 Christopher Page (1988), 'The Performance of Ars Antiqua Motets', *Early Music*, **16**, pp. 147–64.   241

PART IV MASS AND MOTET AFTER 1300

12 James W. McKinnon (1978), 'Representations of the Mass in Medieval and
    Renaissance Art', *Journal of the American Musicological Society*, **31**, pp. 21–52.   261
13 Roger Bowers (1983), 'The Performing Ensemble for English Church Polyphony,
    c. 1320–*c.* 1390', in Stanley Boorman (ed.), *Studies in the Performance of Late
    Mediaeval Music*, Cambridge: Cambridge University Press, pp. 161–92.   293
14 Gilbert Reaney (1969), 'Text Underlay in Early Fifteenth-Century Musical
    Manuscripts', in Gustave Reese and Robert J. Snow (eds), *Essays in Musicology
    in Honor of Dragan Plamenac on His 70th Birthday*, Pittsburgh: University of
    Pittsburgh Press, pp. 245–51.   325

PART V THE POLYPHONIC CHANSON

15 Christopher Page (1977), 'Machaut's "Pupil" Deschamps on the Performance of
    Music: Voices or Instruments in the 14th-Century Chanson', *Early Music*, **5**,
    pp. 484–91.   335
16 Christopher Page (1982), 'The Performance of Songs in Late Medieval France:
    A New Source', *Early Music*, **10**, pp. 441–50.   343
17 Lawrence Earp (1991), 'Texting in 15th-Century French Chansons: A Look
    Ahead from the 14th Century', *Early Music*, **19**, pp. 194–210.   353
18 David Fallows (1990), 'Embellishment and Urtext in the Fifteenth-Century Song
    Repertories', *Basler Jahrbuch für historische Musikpraxis*, **14**, pp. 59–85.   365

PART VI OTHER MATTERS

19 Margaret Bent (1972), 'Musica Recta and Musica Ficta', *Musica Disciplina*, **26**,
    pp. 73–100.   395
20 Anna Maria Busse Berger (1988), 'The Origin and Early History of Proportion Signs',
    Journal of the American Musicological Society, **41**, pp. 403–33.   423
21 Christopher Page (1979), 'Jerome of Moravia on the *Rubeba* and *Viella*',
    Galpin Society Journal, **32**, pp. 77–98.   455
22 Shai Burstyn (1990), 'The "Arabian Influence" Thesis Revisited', *Current
    Musicology*, **46**, pp. 119–46.   481

Series Bibliography   509
Name Index   513

Acknowledgements

The editor and publishers wish to thank the following for permission to use copyright material.

Amadeus for the essays: Katarina Livljanić (2002), 'Giving Voice to Gregorian Chant or: Coping with Modern Orthodoxies', *Basler Jahrbuch für historische Musikpraxis*, **26**, pp. 47–58; David Fallows (1990), 'Embellishment and Urtext in the Fifteenth-Century Song Repertories', *Basler Jahrbuch für historische Musikpraxis*, **14**, pp. 59–85.

Cambridge University Press for the essays: Christopher Page (1993), 'Johannes de Grocheio on Secular Music: A Corrected Text and a New Translation', *Plainsong and Medieval Music*, **2**, pp. 17–41. Copyright © 1993 Cambridge University Press; Charles M. Atkinson (1989), 'Franco of Cologne on the Rhythm of Organum Purum', *Early Music History*, **9**, pp. 1–26. Copyright © 1989 Cambridge University Press; Roger Bowers (1983), 'The Performing Ensemble for English Church Polyphony, c. 1320–c. 1390', in Stanley Boorman (ed.), *Studies in the Performance of Late Mediaeval Music*, Cambridge: Cambridge University Press, pp. 161–92. Copyright © 1983 Cambridge University Press.

Claremont Graduate University for the essay: Hendrik van der Werf (1988), 'The "Not-So-Precisely Measured" Music of the Middle Ages', *Performance Practice Review*, **1**, pp. 42–60.

Colorado College Music Press for the essays: Sylvia Huot (1989), 'Voices and Instruments in Medieval French Secular Music: On the Use of Literary Texts as Evidence for Performance Practice', *Musica Disciplina*, **43**, pp. 63–113; Jeremy Yudkin (1980), 'The *Copula* According to Johannes de Garlandia', *Musica Disciplina*, **34**, pp. 67–84. Copyright © 1981 American Institute of Musicology; Margaret Bent (1972), 'Musica Recta and Musica Ficta', *Musica Disciplina*, **26**, pp. 73–100.

Current Musicology for the essay: Shai Burstyn (1990), 'The "Arabian Influence" Thesis Revisited', *Current Musicology*, **46**, pp. 119–46. Copyright © 1990 The Trustees of Columbia University in City of New York.

The Galpin Society and Christopher Page for the essay: Christopher Page (1979), 'Jerome of Moravia on the *Rubeba* and *Viella*', *Galpin Society Journal*, **32**, pp. 77–98.

Oxford University Press for the essays: Lance W. Brunner (1982), 'The Performance of Plainchant: Some Preliminary Observations of the New Era', *Early Music*, **19**, pp. 316–28. Copyright © 1982 Oxford University Press; Edward Roesner (1979), 'The Performance of Parisian Organum', *Early Music*, **7**, pp. 174–89. Copyright © 1979 Oxford University Press; Christopher Page (1988), 'The Performance of Ars Antiqua Motets', *Early Music*, **16**, pp. 147–64. Copyright © 1988 Oxford University Press; Christopher Page (1977), 'Machaut's "Pupil" Deschamps on the Performance of Music: Voices or Instruments in the 14th-Century Chanson', *Early Music*, **5**, pp. 484–91. Copyright © 1988 Oxford University Press; Christopher

Page (1982), 'The Performance of Songs in Late Medieval France: A New Source', *Early Music*, **10**, pp. 441–50. Copyright © 1982 Oxford University Press; Lawrence Earp (1991), 'Texting in 15th-Century French Chansons: A Look Ahead from the 14th Century', *Early Music*, **19**, pp. 194–210. Copyright © 1991 Oxford University Press.

University of California Press for the essays: Ernest H. Sanders (1985), 'Conductus and Modal Rhythm', *Journal of the American Musicological Society*, **38**, pp. 439–69; James W. McKinnon (1978), 'Representations of the Mass in Medieval and Renaissance Art', *Journal of the American Musicological Society*, **31**, pp. 21–52; Anna Maria Busse Berger (1988), 'The Origin and Early History of Proportion Signs', *Journal of the American Musicological Society*, **41**, pp. 403–33.

University of Pittsburgh Press for the essay: Gilbert Reaney (1969), 'Text Underlay in Early Fifteenth-Century Musical Manuscripts', in Gustave Reese and Robert J. Snow (eds), *Essays in Musicology in Honor of Dragan Plamenac on His 70th Birthday*, Pittsburgh: University of Pittsburgh Press, pp. 245–51. Copyright © 1969 University of Pittsburgh Press.

Every effort has been made to trace all the copyright holders, but if any have been inadvertently overlooked the publishers will be pleased to make the necessary arrangement at the first opportunity.

Series Preface

The four volumes that comprise the *Library of Essays on Music Performance Practice* are divided according to the traditional boundaries of the historical periods in music: Medieval, Renaissance, Baroque, and Classical/Romantic. Musical style and common approaches to composition within these four periods offer a way of unifying the writings, and each volume features a coherent selection of essays about how music was performed before the modern era of recorded sound. The essays are arranged within topics that draw readers' attention to areas of special interest and facilitate investigating a specific line of inquiry through several related essays. The topics vary according to the contents of each volume, but some areas of investigation also cross the temporal boundaries of individual volumes, making the series as a whole well worth consulting for anyone who wishes to understand more about how music of the past was performed. Issues such as the size and configuration of performing forces (choral versus solo voices and small versus large instrumental ensembles), pitch, vibrato, inexact rhythmic notation, and improvisation have often given rise to scholarly debate and revisionist thinking that has changed the direction of future research and performance. Many of the essays chosen for inclusion here demonstrate methods and approaches that have proven especially valuable as models for future research. The repertoire represented ranges broadly across Western art music, both secular and sacred, and each volume addresses issues that arise in both vocal and instrumental music. The geographical area covered also extends well beyond Europe.

Each volume includes a substantial introduction written by an editor who is a recognized authority in the field of performance practice and who has made significant contributions to research, teaching, and performing early music within the period in question. The editor's introduction offers an authoritative overview of the issues and controversies that have dominated performance practice research within a particular historical period and how the results of that research have changed the way the music is now performed and understood. Drawing on his or her own extensive research and personal experience, the editor is well-situated to provide a context for readers and to assist them in gaining a deeper understanding of the issues and controversies that hold particular importance. A select bibliography in each volume directs readers toward additional essays and books that amplify topics represented within the volume and also identifies other issues that warrant further study.

One of the paradoxes within the field of performance practice is that the desire of scholars, performers, and listeners today to understand how old instruments sounded, how music was sung and by whom, and how musical symbols were interpreted is itself a relatively new concept. Whether one investigates how music was performed in the past in order to create an 'authentic' performance (this term now having been generally abandoned in favour of descriptors such as a 'historically-informed' or 'historically-inspired' performance), the quest to understand more about the past can be traced to a revival of interest in early instruments that began about a hundred years ago. Since that time, the field has expanded greatly to include vocal as well as instrumental techniques and to embrace not only scholarly research and editing but also the practical knowledge that instrument builders, performers, and conductors are able to contribute. The results of research in performance practice, especially essays written within the past thirty years or so, have fundamentally changed the way that early music is performed today. *The Library of Essays in Music Performance Practice* offers fertile ground for students, scholars, performers, instrument builders, and listeners who wish to review these research results and for anyone who wishes to gain new insights about how studies in performance practice have brought about greater understanding and appreciation for music of the past and the directions that such research may take in the future.

MARY CYR
Series Editor
University of Guelph, Canada

Introduction

A decade into the twenty-first century, the performance of medieval music – and the study of that performance – holds a curious position in the musical and scholarly world. The surviving repertoire is vast and covers a longer chronological span than any other era in Western music. Wildly different genres offer dramatic contrasts in style, and performers range from cloistered nuns and monks to professional string quartets (for example, the Kronos Quartet). The modern student has more material for perusal than ever before, today's listener has an unrivalled smorgasbord of recordings from which to choose and the contemporary performer has decades of predecessors, both professional and amateur, as guides and models. Yet performers of medieval music now face challenges of a kind not experienced by earlier generations, challenges arising in part from decades of exciting scholarship.

Performers and scholars have many sources of evidence on which to draw to learn about performance of the time. The notated music itself is a starting point; theoretical treatises can supply additional information, as can archival records, chronicles and literary accounts of music-making. Surviving musical instruments and iconographical evidence play a role as well. How much modern performance itself can tell us about medieval practice remains controversial, with (not surprisingly) active performers more confident about this source of information than those who are primarily scholars.

Various books and other resources provide overviews or in-depth looks at medieval performance issues. A starting point is the entry on 'Performing Practice' in *New Grove* (Brown et al., 2001). Books on the subject include *Performance Practice: Music before 1600* edited by Howard Mayer Brown and Stanley Sadie (1989); *A Performer's Guide to Medieval Music* edited by Ross Duffin (2000); *Companion to Medieval and Renaissance Music* edited by Tess Knighton and David Fallows (1992); *Medieval and Renaissance Music: A Performer's Guide* by Timothy McGee (1985); and *Performing Medieval and Renaissance Music: An Introductory Guide* by Elizabeth Phillips and John-Paul Christopher Jackson (1986), with the first of these presenting the most scholarly perspective and the last the most overtly 'how to' approach.[1] An annotated bibliography of selected material to 1988 appears in Roland Jackson's *Performance Practice, Medieval to Contemporary: A Bibliographic Guide*,[2] and the proceedings of an important conference were published as *Studies in the Performance of Late Mediaeval Music*, edited by Stanley Boorman (1983). Full-length studies by Christopher Page include *Voices and Instruments of the Middle Ages: Instrumental Practice and Songs in France, 1100–1300* (1987) as well as *The Owl and the Nightingale: Musical Life and Ideas in France, 1100–1300* (1989a). Bernard Sherman's *Inside Early Music: Conversations with Performers* presents views of leading professionals Marcel Pérès, Susan Hellauer, Christopher Page, and the late Barbara Thornton in its medieval part.

---

[1] See the Bibliography and Series Bibliography for full citations of all sources given in the Introduction.
[2] The earlier Vinquist and Zaslaw bibliography has much less material on music before 1600.

Several journals are devoted to or address performance practice, including *Early Music* and the *Basler Jahrbuch für historische Musikpraxis*. *Plainsong and Medieval Music* includes essays as well as an annual liturgical chant bibliography whose index directs the reader to publications on performance practice. *Historical Performance* (the journal of Early Music America) and *Performance Practice Review* appeared first in print and now have an on-line presence, while the *Journal of the American Musical Instrument Society* and the venerable *Galpin Society Journal* present some essays on early instruments.

This plethora of material makes it easy to overlook the staggering number of obstacles that scholars and performers face in dealing with medieval music. The challenges begin with trying to define what qualifies as medieval in the first place, and it hardly needs saying that period designations are typically used more for convenience than anything else. A frequently used starting date for the Middle Ages is 476, the 'end' of the Western Roman empire, though musical sources only appear centuries later. The 'ending' date is more problematic and ultimately arbitrary. It is no accident that most of the books mentioned previously treat medieval and Renaissance music together, for the dividing line is hardly clear. Is it 1400? 1500? Somewhere in between? Both this volume and the Renaissance volume in the series include essays that could easily have appeared in their sister volumes, and a certain amount of horse-trading between editors determined the ultimate situation of several contributions. Readers interested in either medieval or Renaissance music should thus consult both volumes.

Far more serious challenges appear the instant we turn our attention from the dates defining the Middle Ages to the material that survives. Things we take for granted in dealing with later music – pitch, rhythm, performing forces – remain uncertain or unknowable for large segments of the repertoire. Pitch, for instance, is not clarified until the development of a workable staff in the early eleventh century. Before that, notation appears to have served as a reminder to singers who basically already knew a melody, with the notational symbols known as neumes presented, at best, positioned roughly higher or lower depending on where they stood within a melody.

The staff was not immediately adopted throughout Europe and in any event did not solve all problems involving pitch. There exist a bevy of neumes known as 'ornamental' whose precise interpretation remains controversial. Some of these may have designated the use of microtones. If so, this important element of performance disappeared with the move from neumatic notation to square notation in the thirteenth century, for the combination of staves and square noteheads rendered impossible the presentation of microtones.

Even this seeming nailing down of pitch did not necessarily capture the basic melodic line, for performers routinely altered this line in some genres by raising or lowering an individual pitch by a half step, depending on context. The precise application of these altered notes, known variously as 'performers' accidentals' or 'musica ficta', remains highly problematic, though it is some small consolation to know that even contemporaries disagreed as to when the written pitch should be varied.

Problems of pitch are, if anything, exceeded by those concerning rhythm, whether we are dealing with monophony or polyphony. In terms of sacred monophony, many believe that when chant was first written down some sort of rhythmicized performance was intended. There is no agreement on just what that was, though, for the earliest notation keeps its rhythmic secrets to itself. By the thirteenth century theorists tell us that chant was normally performed in even note values, but when that became the standard (with the move to square notation?) is unknown.

Clearer indications of rhythm begin to show up in the twelfth century, when polyphony starts to get complex and requires a careful co-ordination among parts that leads to the codification of the rhythmic modes. Yet again, however, the notation is open to many different interpretations, and it is only in the early fourteenth century that rhythmic notation is finally clarified through the adoption of the mensural system. Even then, though, problems are not over, for difficulties arise both in the notationally complex and innovative music of the *ars subtilior*, and, more enduringly, in the proportion signs used within a work. Finally, secular monophony has been plagued as well with questions about the applicability of modal rhythms to its song melodies, with fierce arguments on both sides of the issue.

In addition to the problems involving pitch and rhythm, the question of which performing forces to use looms large over medieval music. Before the late sixteenth century, performing forces were not typically indicated in music, with instrumental tablature the main exception. For everything except plainchant, the questions of what kind of instruments as well as how and when (or if) to use them have been major ones; for voices, which type and how many have also come under scrutiny (male or female? adult or child? soloists or multiple singers per part?) Polyphonic chansons have presented a major battleground for this issue. Over all of this lies the question of whether this lack of guidance means that there is a best solution if only we can find it, or whether the works were intended to be highly flexible in this component, with anything (within reason) acceptable. Finally, many other components of execution remain wide open for medieval music, including tempo, dynamics, phrasing, articulation, balance, tone quality and expression.

Even if we somehow had complete agreement on the pitch, rhythm and performing forces required for this music, we would still face the huge question of just what it is that the manuscripts have transmitted to us. We confront all the questions that any manuscript source of early music presents: was the manuscript intended for performance, or as a reference copy, or as an archive of outdated music, or as a luxury object for display and the generation of envy and respect, or some combination of the above, or something else entirely? Is a piece of medieval music a 'piece' in the same way that we think of, say, a song by Brahms, or is it a snapshot of a single performance, or is it a blueprint for experimentation? How should the predominantly oral culture of the Middle Ages influence how we perform a written work? Is the written melodic line the complete melody, or does the piece require improvisation and ornamentation to come alive? When something unusual is marked, should all analogous passages be treated the same way? Did the work's composer intend for it to sound a certain way that we should try to discover? Or was each work truly created anew each time it was performed? Did the work have a 'composer' at all, or is what was notated the result of a collaborative process?

Contemporary material for information about the many questions raised above is not nearly as helpful as we would like. Very few actual instruments survive. With iconographical depictions, and with literary descriptions of music-making, the messages are often difficult to decipher, and we always must question how true-to-life the representation is. We have none of the 'how to' instrumental manuals that begin to appear in the sixteenth century, and little material for voice.[3] Once we get beyond notation in theoretical treatises, we are typically

---

[3] One important resource is the *Summa musice*; see the edition and translation by Page (1991). A much later but also valuable source is the late fifteenth-century treatise discussed in Dyer (1978).

left without much guidance in practical matters.[4] And the music that survives, though our starting point, represents an indeterminate fraction of what must have existed, with anything improvised gone forever, and only the merest trace left of non-liturgical music for anyone besides the very highest social class.

Still other challenges face the performer and scholar of early music today, and to look at these we must take a brief turn through the history of performance practice and the early music revival, which are related but not identical. The revival of music from the past (that is, music no longer in the active repertoire) has been going on for centuries, but, initially at least, the music revived was performed unquestioningly according to the practices of the time of its revival rather than of origin, for example, Bach was played on the piano in the nineteenth century. Performance practice has instead asked how music was played when it originated, and then attempted to recreate that practice.

The nineteenth-century revival emphasized Baroque music, with some Renaissance and even medieval music tossed in as well. As the twentieth century unrolled, each decade brought more scholarship and more performance, with an explosion of interest in the 1960s, carrying through the 1970s and into the 1980s.[5] By then the principle behind performance practice had been extended far beyond music that had lain dormant for centuries and was beginning to be applied to works that had never left the repertoire, for example, Beethoven and others still later in the nineteenth century. The twentieth century is now considered fair game as well.

Neither performances nor the philosophy behind them escaped scrutiny; as the movement snowballed, so did inquiries into its means and ends. Not long before the expansion of the 1960s, for instance, Donald Grout (1957) took up the issue in 'On Historical Authenticity in the Performance of Old Music'. His essay stated immediately that: 'An ideal performance is one that perfectly realizes the composer's intentions' (1957, p. 341). He noted that:

> Historical Musicology, like Original Sin, has given everybody a bad conscience: we worry about historical authenticity in the performance of old music, which is to say that we fear lest we interpret the notation in accordance with the wrong tradition. (1957, pp. 342–43)

He went on to confront three basic assumptions by asking whether there was one correct way to perform a specific piece or whether the performer had some latitude; whether we can truly discover what past traditions were; and whether, assuming we could uncover a past tradition, we had the resources to match those of the composer and thus recreate that tradition, concluding that:

> It is evident that a completely authentic modern performance of old music is, at least in the overwhelming majority of cases, an impossibility. Attempts at such performances succeed only by virtue of compromise, reckoning not on certainties but on probabilities, taking into account the variable factors of the original tradition, confessing but when necessary disregarding the imperfect

---

[4] An important exception is the work of Jerome of Moravia; see Page's essay on him reprinted here (Chapter 21). Lists of theoretical treatises with information on performing matters can be found in both Brown and Sadie (1989, pp. 267–68), and in McGee (1998, pp. 155–83); McGee provides Latin originals of the appropriate passages.

[5] Harry Haskell provided an overview of this process in *The Early Music Revival* (1988), and since then scholars have focused more intensively on various components of the revival; see, for example, James Garratt, *Palestrina and the German Romantic Imagination*.

state of our knowledge, and ignoring the anachronisms that result from the unavailability of the correct media or the disappearance of older techniques. (1957, p. 345)[6]

The next two decades or so saw an upsurge in performance of early music – including medieval works – and impressive works of scholarship. The major journals *Early Music* and *Basler Jahrbuch für historische Musikpraxis* were founded in 1973 and 1977 respectively, for example, and Stanley Boorman organized an important conference on the performance of late medieval music in 1981 (with proceedings published two years later). But rumblings about authenticity and its associated issues kept popping up. Jeremy Montagu (1975, p. 242) wondered why, if there were so many 'authentic' performances of works, 'all differ so widely'; Michael Morrow (1978, p. 245) stated: 'Authenticity can only mean the real thing; and no modern performance of any music of the past can sustain such a claim'.

Then, in the 1980s, the issue exploded. Essays such as 'On Letting the Music Speak for Itself' (Taruskin, 1982) and 'The Limits of Authenticity' (Taruskin *et al.*, 1984) raised major and vociferous objections to the whole cult of authenticity, creating a new meaning for the Scarlet Letter and leading to substitution of the soon equally reviled phrase 'historically informed performance'. A conference on authenticity generated the critical volume *Authenticity and Early Music* (Kenyon, 1988). In essays or books, scholars, performers and scholar-performers jumped on the bandwagon or rose to the defence of current performing practices, with even Pierre Boulez chiming in. Taruskin returned to the topic with sufficient frequency to generate a book's worth of essays, *Text and Act* (1996). Major criticisms included the following: (1) attempting to realize 'the composer's intentions' is a foolish goal, as composers themselves are and were flexible in what they expect from performance; (2) our supposedly 'authentic' performances reflect instead twentieth-century modernist aesthetics (and thus, though no-one stated it explicitly, we are presenting a twentieth-century equivalent of playing Bach on the piano); and (3) our recreation of contemporary practice (for example, pitch, instruments) is simply preparation for the true work of bringing the music alive through the performer's interpretation and vivid imagination. The problems for authenticity, of course, are gravest with the Middle Ages, the period where we have the least information in all of early music.[7]

Where does all of this leave the scholar and performer, and the reader of this volume? Grout (1957, p. 346) himself wrote, more than fifty years ago, '[o]ne is tempted at this point to speculate as to whether we have any business to be performing old music at all'. Yet both scholar and performer continue to explore medieval music and its performance issues. And well they might, for the music is fascinating, engaging, frequently complex, often staggeringly beautiful and always challenging, sometimes maddeningly so.

Grout, who believed in the ideal of authentic performance and realizing the composer's intentions, recognized the impossibility of realizing that ideal and thus asked why we should pursue it at all. His response was that striving for that ideal provides information (still true) and generates better performances (a subjective response but not one that can be rejected outright, simply because our reaction to any performance is subjective). But he went on to

---

[6] Putnam Aldrich discussed 'The "Authentic" Performance of Baroque Music' in the same volume; note the use of scare quotes. Aldrich (p. 170) concluded that 'true authenticity is obviously a chimera'.

[7] The extent of these problems led Daniel Leech-Wilkinson (2002) to title his book *The Modern Invention of Medieval Music*; he claims we are inventing rather than re-creating medieval music.

acknowledge that: '[t]he only danger in the ideal would seem to be that it could mislead one into regarding knowledge of the past as a substitute for imagination in the present, rather than as food for it' (1957, pp. 346–47), a statement completely in keeping with later critics of 'authenticity' and presented more than two decades earlier.

With the recognition that medieval music still continues – and will continue – to exert its pull on scholars and performers, this volume pulls together a selection of representative English-language essays on various aspects of medieval performance practice. The bibliography, not intended to be complete, lists numerous other works, also in English. Virtually all of the pieces given here in full or listed in the bibliography direct the interested reader to earlier work as well as to contributions in other languages. The issues covered are discussed briefly below; although they are fitted into specific categories, a certain amount of crossover takes place nonetheless.

Plainchant[8]

In contrast to all other medieval music, plainchant has been performed continuously since it was created, in some instances centuries before it was first written down. Seizing on this longevity, recordings are quick to advertise plainchant as 'timeless', 'unchanging' or 'eternal'. Yet this choice of adjectives could hardly be further from the truth, for it would be difficult to find another genre that has undergone so much change in its performance style. By the nineteenth century, recognition of the distance chant had travelled since its origins prompted serious research into those origins, thus leading to the plainchant revival – the attempted rediscovery or recreation of chant in its earliest forms, accompanied by a consequent major shift in the way it was performed.[9] The influence of this revival still dominates performance today.

The notational challenges outlined earlier guaranteed that rhythm would remain a major problem in attempting to recreate chant's original performance; indeed, William Dalglish (1978, p. 10) has described chant rhythm as 'musical scholarship's ... bête noire'. An overview of the issues is found in John Rayburn (1964), *Gregorian Chant*. The problems begin with the earliest complete chant manuscripts. These collections, from the vicinities of St Gall, Laon and elsewhere in the late tenth and early eleventh centuries, are written with neumes indicating elements of expression, including some that influence rhythm or tempo (for example, using the letter 'c' to indicate *celeriter*, quickly). Although the notation is ambiguous in many respects, 'mensuralist' scholars have proposed proportional or metric performance of varying kinds, citing both manuscript evidence and their interpretations of medieval theorists. These scholars include such major figures as Hugo Riemann, Peter Wagner, Ewald Jammers and many others. An especially strong proponent of proportional rhythm is J.W.A. Vollaerts (1960), whose views appear in *Rhythmic Proportions in Early Medieval Ecclesiastical Chant*.

In contrast, a very different style based on these earliest sources was advocated by the monks of the Solesmes monastery in France, the guiding hands behind the practicalities of the chant revival. This style uses a basic foundation of equal notes but adds subtle changes in stress and value, with different interpretations of this basic style championed by different

---

[8] An excellent overview of the issues is found in David Hiley (1989).
[9] See Kenneth Levy *et al.* (2001) for a survey of the later history of chant.

editors. Major figures in the defining (and redefining) of this style include Prosper Guéranger and Joseph Pothier, André Mocquereau and Joseph Gajard, and most recently Eugène Cardine and his disciples. Cardine's (1982) *Gregorian Semiology*, first published in Italian in 1968 as *Semiologia gregoriana*, is a major reference here.[10]

The performance of chant scarcely remained static through the Middle Ages. By the time of Aribo (ca. 1070), the use of durational nuance (however defined) was said to be long gone (Planchart, 1989, p. 128), and certainly the manuscripts presented chant differently. The norm of equal note values is attested by Jerome of Moravia and other writers in the thirteenth century; Jerome lists a mere five exceptions to this standard (see Hiley, 1989, p. 44). But by this time we also have chant that uses rhymed metric verse, from which some scholars have adduced a corresponding metric performance. Further, from the fourteenth century on some chant (though by no means all) is clearly written in mensural notation, which obviously suggests the use of mensural rhythms. The issue is thus complex and ultimately undecided, and does not even begin to consider the variations that must have occurred between different regions and different times. Regardless of such challenges, most scholars these days favour the use of equal note values, and performers are more likely to follow that preference than utilize proportional rhythms; this preference is at least in part a result of the huge influence of the Solesmes tradition. Rather less agreement exists on vocal style, including the performance of the so-called 'ornamental neumes', for example, the quilisma, oriscus and various liquescent neumes.[11]

Two complementary essays, published twenty years apart, underscore the difficulties facing the performer of chant today. Lance Brunner's 'The Performance of Plainchant: Some Preliminary Observations of the New Era' (Chapter 1) presents an excellent overview of the rhythmic issues, including a distinction between the various Solesmes-inspired solutions. Brunner touches as well on the problems of ornamental neumes and the timidity with which most performers approach them, with important additional observations on the ways in which the aesthetic of Solesmes and the liturgical function of chant have tended to restrict exploration of certain aspects of chant performance. The prevalence of Solesmes-inspired performances has certainly worked against the kind of exuberant singing attested to by various medieval writers, and Brunner recommends, too, greater collaboration between ethnomusicologists and modern chant performers. Experimentation in the realm of microtones is called for as well. Certainly the monophonic music of most of the rest of the world has greater vocal flexibility than that of the majority of chant performances, at least when Brunner was writing. Interestingly, since the time of Brunner's essay the realm of chant that has received the most attention (and variety) in performance has been the music of Hildegard of Bingen, who was only just beginning to reach mainstream early music consciousness in 1982.

Chapter 2, by scholar/performer Katarina Livljanić, provides a thoughtful overview of the ultimate unknowingness of chant performance, underscoring the privileged position given to the notational practices of St Gall and Metz by Cardine, the recognition by Cardine himself of the elasticity of his prescriptions and the different interpretations of exactly the same rule on different recordings. Livljanić discusses shifts in interpretation since the nineteenth century

---

[10] Cardine's work has inspired an enthusiastic following; some of the results of his pupils' work are described in Albarosa (1983).

[11] The most dramatic interpretations are given by Timothy McGee (1996, 1998).

and the difficulties posed in looking towards traditional musics as an aid to performance, while highlighting the basic problem of chant performance: just what is it that we are trying to recreate?

Secular Monophony

The performance of secular monophony presents some new problems. Most manuscripts of the repertoire are relatively late, copied decades after the heyday of the music they contain. The late date of the written record, as well as the large number of variant versions of melodies, suggests a predominantly oral transmission of the repertoire, thus engendering the standard questions about the stripped-down nature of what survives (for example, have we received the song in its entirety or simply a blueprint?) Other questions include whether pieces in different languages would have been performed in similar ways, and whether works in different genres of the same language would have the same performance tradition. In addition, as with plainchant, rhythm remains a huge issue, and far more than with plainchant, the question of whether or which instruments to use looms large.

Most melodies were transmitted in non-mensural square chant notation, without any indication of rhythm, though some songs survive in mensural notation. Scholars have proposed wildly different rhythmic interpretations of the melodies, sometimes with complete disregard for the actual notation of a song. One group of musicologists argues that performances should utilize measured rhythm, most typically the modal rhythms that characterize polyphonic music of the same time period. This group of scholars, dating back more than a century, includes Pierre Aubry, Jean-Baptiste Beck, Friedrich Gennrich, Hubert Heinen, Heinrich Husmann, Friedrich Ludwig, J.E. Maddrell and more recently Hans Tischler. As with the application of rhythmic values to chant, there is disagreement within this cadre of musicologists as to exactly how rhythmic patterns should be applied.

A contrasting school argues for performance using a mostly free or declamatory rhythm (again, with varying interpretations as to just how free the rhythm should be). Proponents include Ewald Jammers, Raffaello Monterosso, Antonio Restori and Hendrik van der Werf. Despite a somewhat shorter scholarly pedigree, this school of performance tends to be more prevalent among today's musicians.

A third method is that of isosyllabic performance, most recently advocated by John Stevens. In this interpretation, each syllable of text is granted roughly the same amount of time; melismas, for example, become rapid ornamental flourishes.

Finally, some suggest that genre determines rhythm (see, for example, Page, 1987, pp. 73ff), with measured rhythms required for pieces in what has been called 'low style', for example, dances and pastoral songs, and rhythmic freedom reserved for works in 'high style', that is, courtly or aristocratic pieces (though scholars also disagree as to how valid such style distinctions are in the first place).

The role of instruments is another area of controversy. Literary sources and numerous images – including some in the songs' manuscripts themselves – suggest that instruments played a significant part in performance, but there is almost no evidence as to just what instruments should be used with what kind of works, what they should play (doubling? drones? improvisation?), or when they should play (throughout? before and after? between strophes?). Two leading scholars have questioned the role of instruments altogether: Hendrik van der

Werf, who considers the evidence for their use to be weak (see Chapter 4), and Christopher Page, who suggest that their use should be restricted to the genres of 'low style', with 'high style' music unaccompanied. Page's (1987) *Voices and Instruments of the Middle Ages* is an especially important exposition of this interpretation.

Other elements of monophonic performance remain largely unexplored: should songs with two narrators be sung by two singers? Should refrains be choral? Should the accidentals that appear in some sources be more widely applied?

The four essays included here provide starting points for further investigation of the problems. Hans Tischler's essay, 'Rhythm, Meter, and Melodic Organization in Medieval Songs' (Chapter 3), lays out one interpretation of the problem of rhythm in the major repertoires of secular monophony. Acknowledging that more than one interpretation may be possible, he believes that 'interpreting the poetry and the music for the potential user' is the responsibility of the scholar, even if that interpretation is definite rather than definitive (p. 30–31). As a primary proponent of the application of measured rhythm to the repertoire, Tischler cites the medieval preoccupation with number as well as the metric structure of poetry itself, which shifts to rhymed free verse at precisely the time that the music of the trouvères was itself fading away.

In a contrasting approach, Hendrik van der Werf's 'The "Not-So-Precisely Measured" Music of the Middle Ages' (Chapter 4) produces a pithy summary of the views of a leading scholar on the issue of rhythm in the secular monophonic repertoire. Van der Werf gives a quick overview of the sources, their notation, and the question of meter. Arguing that the varied readings of the same song in different manuscripts reflect different performances, he suggests that this variation must be based on an essentially equal-note rhythm, with text and melody of commensurate importance in a song. Van der Werf discusses as well some of the trouvère songs that survive with precisely notated rhythm, and touches also on the difficulty of devising specific rules vis-à-vis the application of musica ficta. He concludes with cautionary notes on the evidence (or lack thereof) for the specific use of instruments in performing this repertoire.

The question of instrument use is taken up at length in Chapter 5, Sylvia Huot's 'Voices and Instruments in Medieval French Secular Music: On the Use of Literary Texts as Evidence for Performance Practice'. Huot provides thoughtful guidelines for evaluating the material about music in literary sources, noting ambiguities in transmission and examining the function of musical references within individual narratives.[12]

Chapter 6, 'Johannes de Grocheio on Secular Music: A Corrected Text and a New Translation', by Christopher Page, treats one of the most important of all medieval theoretical treatises, the *De musica* of Johannes de Grocheio, the only one to address secular monophony and to connect instruments specifically to the genre. As such, Grocheio is the author cited regularly to support interpretations of performance practice (for example, Maddrell, 1970, 1971). Grocheio's significance had already been attested to by a full critical edition as well as a complete English translation, but Page returns to the original manuscripts to provide a revised text and a fresh translation of the key part pertaining to secular music. As such it forms a foundation for all later work.

---

[12] Important work by other scholars utilizing literary sources is that of Elizabeth Aubrey and especially Christopher Page.

Polyphony to 1300

The rise of complex polyphony in the twelfth century[13] demanded the development of a system of rhythmic notation; performers needed some way to co-ordinate the different parts. Questions surrounding the modal rhythm eventually generated 'have been the most hotly debated of all aspects of *ars antiqua* scholarship,' as Edward Roesner (2009, p. xiv) notes. Major English-language scholars contributing to the debate include Roesner himself as well as William Waite, Richard Crocker, Theodore Karp, Leo Treitler, Hans Tischler, Gordon Anderson, Gilbert Reaney, Ernest Sanders, Janet Knapp, Sarah Fuller, Jeremy Yudkin and Charles Atkinson.[14] Although issues of rhythm are far from settled – some acknowledge the impossibility of ever uncovering full answers (Karp, 1999, p. 21) – many scholars now believe that the system evolved gradually, that multiple interpretations may in fact be correct and that flexibility rather than rigidity vis-à-vis the rhythm is called for in approaching this repertoire.

For the earliest layer of the repertoire, the twelfth-century polyphony cultivated in Aquitaine and appearing in the Codex Calixtinus and the so-called 'St Martial' manuscripts, the move has been away from the strict modal interpretation argued by Theodore Karp and others and towards the greater flexibility advocated by, for example, Sarah Fuller. For the music sometimes called 'Notre Dame polyphony' – music in reality both disseminated and created outside of Paris as well as within – rhythm has again remained the key focus in performance. One of the primary sources of information is the theorist Johannes de Garlandia, but as Edward Roesner (1982, p. 132) observes,

> No two scholars agree on exactly what Garlandia's words mean, and over the past thirty years in particular the text has generated a body of commentary reminiscent of medieval scriptural exegesis in the subtlety of its arguments, the diversity of the conclusions drawn, and the heat with which these contributions have been attacked and defended.

And with the Notre Dame repertoire we have again a source situation equivalent to that of the troubadours, with surviving manuscripts all later than the period in which the music originated.

It would be child's play to fill an entire volume with essays debating various approaches to the rhythms used for pre-1300 polyphony, but almost all who treat the subject say little about performance beyond rhythm, and, as indicated, disagreement is rife. The essay by Edward Roesner reprinted here, 'The Performance of Parisian Organum' (Chapter 7), is noteworthy for looking at additional performance issues besides rhythm.[15] Roesner pulls together statements on performance from a variety of theoretical treatises, generating a convincing case for all-vocal performance of the repertoire;[16] earlier scholarship tended to accept the use of instruments, especially for the performance of chant tenors. Roesner discusses a bevy of other topics as well, including the use of elongated initial notes, potential places for

---

[13] For the earlier body of polyphony found in the Winchester Troper of ca. 1000, Alejandro Planchart freely admits that 'the performer needs to "invent" his or her performance' (see Planchart, 2000, p. 29).

[14] An overview of much of the research is found in Yudkin (1983).

[15] But see Chapter 11 for the correct understanding of copula. Another important reference for the performance of Notre Dame polyphony is Craig Wright (1989, pp. 317–54).

[16] Even though theorist Anonymous IV provides a cryptic comment concerning a stringed instrument in connection with organum purum; see Page (1989b, p. 92).

embellishment, tempo, the treatment of currentes, ad libitum performance of rests and the ornamental interpretation of 'longa florata', 'florificatio vocis' and 'in floratura'.

Not all would agree with Roesner's (Chapter 7) remarks or interpretive choices; his statement '*Organum purum* is conceived in "modal rhythm"' (p. 159) and the resulting transcriptions are but one manifestation of a controversial approach. Chapter 8 by Charles Atkinson, 'Franco of Cologne on Organum Purum,' is included as a thoughtful and well-argued example of an alternative interpretation of some of the same material, including rhythm as well as the problematic 'longa florata'. Roesner's and Atkinson's essays thus provide a sample of the ongoing debates that have fuelled so much *Ars antiqua* scholarship.

Chapter 9, 'The *Copula* According to Johannes de Garlandia', by Jeremy Yudkin, is significant for providing a clear solution to the formerly problematic term 'copula'. Again working with Johannes de Garlandia, Yudkin demonstrates that copula occupies the realm in between organum purum and discant, sharing the long held tenor notes that characterize the former while giving the upper voice the clear rhythmic patterns of the latter.

The conductus, a major genre of the period (albeit one whose function is uncertain), has received considerably less attention than organum. Much of the research has focused, not surprisingly, on its rhythm, with a good portion of the debate played out in the pages of the *Journal of the American Musicological Society*. The essay included here, Ernest Sanders's 'Conductus and Modal Rhythm' (Chapter 10), is an argument for greater flexibility in the treatment of rhythm than advocated by preceding work, with a call for isosyllabic treatment of *cum littera* parts. For contrasting views, see, for example, the work of Anderson, Reaney and Knapp listed in the bibliography.

As with the conductus, relatively little work has appeared on the performance of another major genre of the *Ars antiqua*, the motet. Christopher Page is one of the few to have approached the subject; his essay 'The Performance of Ars Antiqua Motets' (Chapter 11), provides an excellent overview of some of the main issues. Page argues for performance by nearly identical adult male voices in, generally, the high tenor range, with a vocalized tenor and an emphasis on changes in rhythmic mode. Individual motet voices can be performed on their own as well, and solo vocal rather than instrumental performance overall is likely. Drawing on his own extensive experience with performance, Page further recommends attention to full rhythmic values, historical pronunciation, careful Pythagorean tuning without the use of vibrato, strict tempo and various other details to generate the most effective performance.

Mass and Motet after 1300

The question as to which performing forces were intended for the polyphony of the fourteenth and fifteenth centuries has been a musicological issue for more than a century; the history of the debate is covered thoroughly in Daniel Leech-Wilkinson (2002), *The Invention of Medieval Music*. A major component of the question is the treatment of untexted or partially texted lines of both sacred and secular polyphony. Early research, which heavily favoured the use of instruments (even at times for texted lines), was conducted primarily in German (the dominant language of musicology for many decades), but English-language questioning of some of the assumptions appeared in works such as Leonard Ellinwood's (1936) 'Francesco Landini and His Music' and in Lloyd Hibberd's (1946) chronologically wide-ranging 'On

"Instrumental Style" in Early Melody'. The debate heated up in the 1970s,[17] exploded in the 1980s, peaked in the early 1990s and has been largely dormant since then – a trajectory impressively similar to the debate surrounding authenticity. More than one scholar has remarked rather sadly on the fallout of the proceedings.[18]

Generally speaking, the prevailing view has changed from one that accepted the possibility of all-vocal performance but viewed as the norm performance that combined voices and instruments, to the opposite conclusion: that all-vocal renditions were the norm (or at least the ideal) but that some performances incorporated instruments. The growing body of scholarship supporting this conclusion[19] coincided with the rise of important professional groups that followed these basic tenets, such as (to name just two) the Hilliard Ensemble and Gothic Voices. As various scholars have noted, the sheer beauty of the musical result was convincing in its own right.

The three essays reprinted in this sacred music part approach the question of performing forces from very different angles. James McKinnon deals with the mass, the major liturgical rite of the Catholic Church during the Middle Ages. His 'Representations of the Mass in Medieval and Renaissance Art' (Chapter 12) is one of a series of essays he wrote detailing the results of his research using iconographical sources of the period (see especially McKinnon, 1968, 1983). The driving question behind this essay was the '*a cappella*' question: was sacred music, specifically the mass, performed without instrumental accompaniment? The question could apply to either monophony or polyphony, as it is typically not possible to tell from an illustration which is being performed. McKinnon (Chapter 12) begins by tracing the history of the *a cappella* issue, specifically the nineteenth-century glorification of the concept, followed by the contrary view held through most of the twentieth century. He then demonstrates that 'the vast majority of medieval musical iconography is biblical illustration, not depiction of medieval liturgy' (p. 265). Those images that do depict the mass uniformly do so without showing any musical instruments, at least in the Middle Ages and early Renaissance, though instrumental representation increases the later we get chronologically.[20] McKinnon drew on archival records as well to support his findings, leading to his important conclusion that *a cappella* performance for the period in question was the norm, even if not the absolute.[21]

A completely different approach is taken by Gilbert Reaney in Chapter 14, 'Text Underlay in Early Fifteenth-Century Musical Manuscripts'. While Reaney (Chapter 14) states immediately that he is 'not trying to suggest that instruments did not perform the lower parts of late medieval polyphonic music,' (p. 326) he also notes that 'we do tend to assume that

---

[17] Important forerunners in the previous decades include Frank L. Harrison (1966/1978), and the work of Edmund Bowles.

[18] Fallows (1997, p. 565); Kreitner (1998, *passim*); Leech-Wilkinson (2002, pp. 132–40 and *passim*); and Fallows again (2005, pp. 161–62). Both Fallows and Leech-Wilkinson were directly involved in changing the paradigm of performance.

[19] Important essays dealing mostly, though not exclusively, with later fifteenth-century music include Wright (1981) and Fallows (1983).

[20] Specific instances of instrumental participation in the liturgy can be found in Polk (1969), Rastall (1970–71), Fallows (1983) and Korrick (1990), among other places.

[21] Important forerunners to McKinnon's work include Bowles (1957) and Harrison (1966/1978). On p. 331 of the latter Harrison argues that even parts given 'tuba' or 'trompette' indications were performed vocally.

all textless parts are not vocal, when perhaps we should add the upper voice text to the lower parts'. He then marshals a variety of evidence that does indeed suggest vocal performance of untexted or partly texted voices in sacred music: the increasing use of texting for these lower parts in the early fifteenth century (in contrast to the fourteenth century), the different texting practices for the same piece in different manuscripts, the use of textual incipits that mark imitative parts and so on. Division of longer note values into shorter ones makes it relatively easy to adapt text to parts transmitted with few or no words.[22]

A third methodology is followed by Roger Bowers in Chapter 13, 'The Performing Ensemble for English Church Polyphony, c. 1320–c. 1390'. Working carefully through the available repertoire, supplementing the musical evidence with archival data, Bowers demonstrates that for the period in question, four unaccompanied adult male singers consisting of two altos, one tenor and one baritone were the performance norm, with the music accordingly composed to meet this standard.[23] With these three essays, then, iconography, scribal practice, archives and musical structure combine to support *a cappella* practice.

The Polyphonic Chanson

If anything, the use of instruments for the performance of polyphonic chansons seemed even more certain than the use of instruments in sacred music. Chansons of the fourteenth century were routinely described by musicologists as being for voice with instrumental accompaniment, owing to the lack of text in the lower parts, and the same practice was said to apply to the fifteenth-century chanson as well. While all-vocal performance was admitted as at least a possibility, the many different instrumental combinations depicted in contemporary illustrations seemed to certify a colourful and widely varying performance of these small gems. Two essays by Howard Mayer Brown express the standard view of secular performance in the mid-1970s: his succinct 'On the Performance of Fifteenth-Century Chansons' (1973), the opening essay for the opening issue of *Early Music* (soon to become a leading journal for performance issues), and his more leisurely 'Instruments and Voices in the Fifteenth-Century Chanson' (1976). Each essay offered a slew of possibilities for performance, with ever-changing instrumental groupings at a musician's fingertips.

Into this pleasant iteration of the status quo came two bombshells from Christopher Page, both reprinted here. Chapter 15, 'Machaut's "Pupil" Deschamps on the Performance of Music: Voices or Instruments in the 14th-Century Chanson', looked at a contemporary literary source that called quite specifically for voices to perform chansons and concluded that, indeed, real – not metaphorical – voices were intended. This essay was followed a few years later by 'The Performance of Songs in Late Medieval France: A New Source' (Chapter 16), which drew on another literary selection, this time from the fifteenth century, that led to the same astonishing conclusion.

Page was not the only one pursuing this path; important work by Craig Wright and David Fallows was taking place along these lines at almost exactly the same time. Page's essays had the advantage, though, of being both short and very prominently placed in the widely

---

[22] A similar exploration into the texting of lower voice parts in contemporary secular music was undertaken in Slavin (1991).

[23] Bowers (1995) traces the evolution of these performing forces into the sixteenth century.

circulated *Early Music*, the journal that rapidly took on the appearance of being the house organ for *a cappella* practice.[24] And Page had his own ensemble as well, the highly regarded Gothic Voices, that transformed his scholarly ideas into sound.

Early Music went on to publish not just more of Page's thoughts on the subject but numerous reviews championing non-instrumental performance, as well as supportive essays by other scholars. One of the most important is reprinted here. Lawrence Earp's 'Texting in 15th-Century French Chansons: A Look Ahead from the 14th Century' (Chapter 17) echoed the idea of *a cappella* performance but advocated vocalization rather than texting of lower lines. Gothic Voices ultimately adopted this practice for some repertoire, as did other ensembles.[25]

The question of voices versus instruments has been the most important one to concern the performance of the polyphonic chanson in the last few decades. But it is not the only issue scholars have pursued. The essay by David Fallows given here, 'Embellishment and Urtext in the Fifteenth-Century Song Repertories' (Chapter 18), addresses the assumption of the need for adding ornamentation to a specific repertoire, that of the fifteenth-century chanson, as well as the widespread idea that what survives in manuscript sources provides a blueprint for performance rather than a fixed entity.[26] Working with songs from both earlier and later in the century, transmitted in multiple venues, Fallows argues both that embellishment – which did occur – can detract from a song, and that composers often had a specific conception of the song – an *Urtext*, as it were – that is ill served by additions to it.

Other Matters

Other issues facing performers of medieval music are not genre-specific and are the focus of this closing part. A key topic is musica ficta, both what it means and how it should be applied. Yet again this is an area that has engendered considerable controversy. A classic study, included here, is Margaret Bent's 'Musica Recta and Musica Ficta' (Chapter 19), which draws on both theoretical and practical sources of the fourteenth century to explore the nature of the practice as it was known in the early fifteenth century.[27] Bent's *fons et origo* essay served as a starting point not only for her continued work in the field but for that of many others as well. Her refinements to the original essay and her responses to reactions the work has generated are found in *Counterpoint, Composition, and Musica Ficta* (Bent, 2002).

Another problematic area is the interpretation of proportion signs, which first appear in the very early fifteenth century and are used in both sacred and secular music. Anna Maria Busse Berger's important essay, 'The Origin and Early History of Proportion Signs' (Chapter 20), is significant for its exploration of both theoretical treatises and major musical sources to elucidate the use of proportion signs in the earliest period and especially to demonstrate the

---

[24] Wright's (1981) essay, 'Voices and Instruments in the Art Music of Northern France during the 15th Century', was published in an abridged form; Fallows's (1983) more extended treatment ('Specific Information') had a correspondingly greater impact.

[25] For Page's experiments with this practice, see Page (1992a).

[26] In certain respects the essay is a response to Howard Mayer Brown (1971); see Fallows (Chapter 18, p. 380).

[27] It is rare to find two scholars who agree completely on the application of musica ficta. For some contrasting views, see, for example, the work of Karol Berger and Thomas Brothers.

ways in which this initial use is distinct from the better-known practices described by later writers, specifically Tinctoris and Gaffurius.

The use of instruments, as already indicated, is a major issue affecting almost all medieval music. In addition to the debate over how and where instruments were used, a large bibliography exists on the visual portrayal and construction of many different kinds of instruments. Chapter 21, 'Jerome of Moravia on the *Rubeba* and *Viella*' by Christopher Page, presents rare contemporary information on a different and immensely practical matter: how stringed instruments were tuned. There is wide agreement based on both iconographical and literary evidence that stringed instruments 'were the most important and most widely used, at least for the art music that survives in written form. Jerome of Moravia, writing towards the end of the thirteenth century, is well known for his information – almost unique – on the vielle and rubeba. Page's important essay offers a text and translation to provide more accurate information than previously available; it is basic for any understanding of instrumental performance of the time.[28]

The last contribution takes up a topic that has been of recurring interest in early music performance: the influence of non-Western musical traditions on the performance of medieval music. This influence is sometimes couched as 'Arabian', for various reasons. Muslim presence in Spain was significant from the eighth century until 1492, while the Crusades insured regular cultural interaction between the Middle East and the rest of the West from the late eleventh century on. Instruments depicted in medieval artwork are strikingly similar to some used by traditional musicians today.[29] These and other facts have spurred some performers of medieval music to borrow heavily from non-Western traditions, with scholars examining the implications. The very first issue of the *Basler Jahrbuch für historische Musikpraxis* (1977), for example, was devoted to a symposium on this subject, although performing influences go back to the 1950s and scholarly hypotheses much further. Thomas Binkley, one of the participants in the Basel symposium, was an important figure in this kind of cultural borrowing through his Studio der frühen Musik, though John Haines (2001) has recently demonstrated just how imprecise this borrowing really was. At the same time, the idea of this influence has received considerable resistance from certain sectors of the performing and scholarly world, especially those invested in the vocal purity of the '*a cappella* heresy'. Chapter 22, Shai Burstyn's 'The "Arabian Influence" Thesis Revisited', provides a clear-sighted and thoughtful examination of some of the issues surrounding the idea of 'Arabian' influence on musical style and performance, which continues to be an important factor in today's recreations of medieval music.

---

[28] An important sequel is Page's (1980) 'Fourteenth-Century Instruments and Tunings'.
[29] See, for example, Wishart (1992). Other useful essays are Sachs (1960) and Sawa (1981).

Bibliography

Akioka, Yo (1995), 'Jerome of Moravia's Rules for Performing Chant', *Feris Jyogakuindaigaku Ongakugakubu Kiyo* [Ferris Studies College of Music], **1**, pp. 17–27.

Albarosa, Nino (1983), 'The Pontificio Istituto di Musica Sacra in Rome and the Semiological School of Dom Eugène Cardine', *Journal of the Plainsong and Medieval Music Society*, **6**, pp. 26–33.

Allaire, Gaston G. (1972), *The Theory of Hexachords, Solmization, and the Modal System: A Practical Application*, Musicological Studies and Documents 24, American Institute of Musicology.

Alton, Jeannine and Jeffery, Brian (1976), *Bele buche e bele parleure: A Guide to the Pronunciation of Medieval and Renaissance French for Singers and Others*, London: Tecia.

Anderson, Gordon A. (1968), 'Mode and Change of Mode in Notre Dame Conductus', *Acta musicologica*, **40**, pp. 92–114.

Anderson, Gordon A. (1973a), 'Magister Lambertus and Nine Rhythmic Modes', *Acta musicologica*, **45**, pp. 57–73.

Anderson, Gordon A. (1973b), 'The Rhythm of *cum littera* Sections of Polyphonic Conductus in Mensural Sources', *Journal of the American Musicological Society*, **26**, pp. 288–304.

Anderson, Gordon A. (1975), 'Johannes de Garlandia and the Simultaneous Use of Mixed Rhythmic Modes', *Miscellanea Musicologica: Adelaide Studies in Musicology*, **8**, pp. 11–31.

Anderson, Gordon (1978), 'The Rhythm of the Monophonic Conductus in the Florence Manuscript as Indicated in Parallel Sources in Mensural Notation', *Journal of the American Musicological Society*, **31**, pp. 480–89.

Anderson, Gordon A. (1979), 'Texts and Music in 13th-Century Sacred Song', *Miscellanea musicologica: Adelaide Studies in Musicology*, **10**, pp. 1–27.

Apel, Willi (1948), 'Early History of the Organ', *Speculum*, **23**, pp. 191–216.

Apel, Willi (1949), 'From St. Martial to Notre Dame', *Journal of the American Musicological Society*, **2**, pp. 145–58.

Apel, Willi (1952), 'Communication', *Journal of the American Musicological Society*, **5**, p. 272.

Apel, Willi (1953), *The Notation of Polyphonic Music 900–1600* (5th edn), Medieval Academy of America Publication 38, Cambridge, MA: Medieval Academy of America.

Apel, Willi (1958), *Gregorian Chant*, Bloomington and Indianapolis, IN: Indiana University Press.

Arlettaz, Vincent, Leach, Elizabeth Eva and Naigeon, Alain (2002), *A Short History of the Leading Note: A Contribution to the Study of Musica Ficta*, Vincent Arlettaz.

Arlt, Wulf (1983), 'The "Reconstruction" of Instrumental Music: The Interpretation of the Earliest Practical Sources', in Stanley Boorman (ed.), *Studies in the Performance of Late Mediaeval Music*, Cambridge: Cambridge University Press, pp. 75–100.

Aubrey, Elizabeth (1989), 'References to Music in Old Occitan Literature', *Acta Musicologica*, **61**, pp. 110–49.

Aubrey, Elizabeth (1996), *The Music of the Troubadours*, Bloomington and Indianapolis, IN: Indiana University Press.

Aubry, Pierre (1914/1969), *Trouvères and Troubadours: A Popular Treatise*, trans. Claude Aveling, New York: G. Schirmer, 1914; reprint edition: New York: Cooper Square Publishing, 1969.

Avenary-Loewenstein, H. (1950), 'The Mixture Principle in the Medieval Organ: An Early Evidence', *Musica disciplina*, **4**, pp. 51–57.

Babb, Warren (1978), trans. *Hucbald, Guido, and John on Music: Three Medieval Treatises*, Music Theory Translation Series 3, New Haven, CT and London: Yale University Press.

Bachmann, Werner (1969), *The Origins of Bowing and the Development of Bowed Instruments up to the Thirteenth Century*, trans. Norma Deane, London, New York and Toronto: Oxford University Press.

Bagby, Benjamin (1986), 'Musicology and Make-Believe?', *Early Music*, **14**, pp. 557–58.

Bailey, Terence (ed.) (1979), *Commemoratio brevis de tonis et psalmis modulandis: Introduction, Critical Edition, Translation*, Ottawa Mediaeval Texts and Studies 4, Ottawa: University of Ottawa Press.

Baines, Anthony (1950), 'Fifteenth-Century Instruments in Tinctoris's *De Inventione et Usu Musicae*', *Galpin Society Journal*, **3**, pp. 19–26.

Baines, Francis (1975), 'Introducing the Hurdy-Gurdy', *Early Music*, **3**, pp. 33–37.

Barrett, Sam (2005), 'Performing Medieval Music', *Journal of the Royal Musical Association*, **130**, pp. 119–135.

Barry, Wilson (1985), 'Henri Arnaut de Zwolle's *Clavicordium* and the Origin of the Chekker', *Journal of the American Musical Instrument Society*, **11**, pp. 5–13.

Bedbrook, G.S. (1971), 'The Problem of Instrumental Combination in the Middle Ages', *Revue belge de musicologie*, **25**, pp. 53–67.

Bent, Ian (1970), 'A 12th-Century Extemporizing Technique', *Musical Times*, **111**, pp. 33–37.

Bent, Margaret (1984a), 'Diatonic Ficta', *Early Music History*, **4**, pp. 1–48.

Bent, Margaret (1984b), 'Text Setting in Sacred Music of the Early 15th Century: Evidence and Implications', in Ursula Günther and Ludwig Finscher (eds), *Musik und Text in der Mehrstimmigkeit des 14. und 15. Jahrhunderts: Vorträge des Gastsymposions in der Herzog August Bibliothek Wolfenbüttel 8. bis 12. September 1980*, Göttinger musikwissenschaftliche Arbeiten 10, Kassel, Basel and London: Bärenreiter, pp. 291–326.

Bent, Margaret (1987), 'A Contemporary Perception of Early Fifteenth-Century Style: Bologna Q15 as a Document of Scribal Editorial Initiative', *Musica disciplina*, **41**, pp. 183–201.

Bent, Margaret (1993), 'Reflections on Christopher Page's *Reflections*', *Early Music*, **21**, pp. 625–33.

Bent, Margaret (1994), 'Editing Early Music: The Dilemma of Translation', *Early Music*, **22**, pp. 373–92.

Bent, Margaret (1996), 'The Early Use of the Sign Ø', *Early Music*, **24**, pp. 199–225.

Bent, Margaret (2002), *Counterpoint, Composition, and Musica Ficta*, New York and London: Routledge.

Berger, Anna Maria Busse (1985), 'The Relationship of Perfect and Imperfect Time in Italian Theory of the Renaissance', *Early Music History*, **5**, pp. 1–28.

Berger, Anna Maria Busse (1990), 'The Myth of *Diminutio per Tertiam Partem*', *Journal of Musicology*, **8**, pp. 398–426.

Berger, Anna Maria Busse (1993), *Mensuration and Proportion Signs: Origins and Evolution*, Oxford: Clarendon Press.

Berger, Karol (1981), 'The Hand and the Art of Memory', *Musica disciplina*, **35**, pp. 87–120.

Berger, Karol (1985–86), 'The Expanding Universe of *Musica Ficta* in Theory from 1300 to 1550', *Journal of Musicology*, **4**, pp. 410–30.

Berger, Karol (1987), *Musica Ficta: Theories of Accidental Inflections in Vocal Polyphony from Marchetto da Padova to Gioseffo Zarlino*, Cambridge: Cambridge University Press.

Berger, Karol (1989a), 'The Martyrdom of St. Sebastian: The Function of Accidental Inflections in Dufay's *O beate Sebastiane*', *Early Music*, **17**, pp. 342–57.

Berger, Karol (1989b), 'Musica Ficta', in Howard Mayer Brown and Stanley Sadie (eds), *Performance Practice: Music before 1600*, New York and London: W.W. Norton, pp. 107–25.

[Berry, Mary] Mother Thomas More (1965–66), 'The Performance of Plainsong in the Later Middle Ages and the Sixteenth Century', *Proceedings of the Royal Musical Association*, **92**, pp. 121–34.

[Berry, Mary] Mother Thomas More (1967), 'The Practice of Alternatim: Organ-Playing and Polyphony in the Fifteenth and Sixteenth Centuries, with Special Reference to the Choir of Notre-Dame de Paris', *Journal of Ecclesiastical History*, **18**, pp. 15–32.

Berry, Mary (1979), 'The Restoration of the Chant and Seventy-Five Years of Recording', *Early Music*, **7**, pp. 197–217.

Blachly, Alexander (1995), 'Mensuration and Tempo in 15th-Century Music: Cut Signatures in Theory and Practice', PhD dissertation, Columbia University.

Blades, James (1973), 'Percussion Instruments of the Middle Ages and Renaissance: Their History in Literature and Painting', *Early Music*, **1**, pp. 11–18.

Boorman, Stanley (ed.) (1983), *Studies in the Performance of Late Mediaeval Music*, Cambridge: Cambridge University Press.

Bouterse, Curtis (1979), 'Reconstructing the Medieval Arabic Lute: A Reconsideration of Farmer's "Structure of the Arabic and Persian Lute"', *Galpin Society Journal*, **32**, pp. 2–9.

Bowers, Roger (1980), 'The Performing Pitch of English 15th-Century Church Polyphony', *Early Music*, **8**, pp. 21–28.

Bowers, Roger (1981), 'False Voices: Roger Bowers Replies', *Early Music*, **9**, pp. 73–75.

Bowers, Roger (1995), 'To Chorus from Quartet: The Performing Resource for English Church Polyphony, ca. 1390–1559', in John Morehen (ed.), *English Choral Practice 1400–1650*, Cambridge: Cambridge University Press, pp. 1–47.

Bowers, Roger (1997), 'Key Evidence: Chorus or Quartet? "High Pitch" or "Low"? Just How Was Sacred Polypony Performed in Pre-Reformation England? Roger Bowers Responds to His Critics', *Musical Times*, **138**, pp. 5–10.

Bowles, Edmund A. (1953), 'Instruments at the Court of Burgundy (1363–1467)', *Galpin Society Journal*, **6**, pp. 41–51.

Bowles, Edmund A. (1954), 'Haut and Bas: The Grouping of Musical Instruments in the Middle Ages', *Musica disciplina*, **8**, pp. 115–40.

Bowles, Edmund A. (1957), 'Were Musical Instruments Used in the Liturgical Service during the Middle Ages?', *Galpin Society Journal*, **10**, pp. 40–56.

Bowles, Edmund A. (1958), 'Musical Instruments at the Medieval Banquet', *Revue belge de musicologie*, **12**, pp. 41–51.

Bowles, Edmund A. (1959a), 'Once More "Musical Instruments in the Liturgical Service"', *Galpin Society Journal*, **12**, pp. 89–92.

Bowles, Edmund A. (1959b), 'The Role of Musical Instruments in Medieval Sacred Drama', *Musical Quarterly*, **45**, pp. 67–84.

Bowles, Edmund A. (1961), 'Musical Instruments in Civic Processions during the Middle Ages', *Acta Musicologica*, **33**, pp. 147–61.

Bowles, Edmund A. (1962), 'The Organ in the Medieval Liturgical Service', *Revue belge de musicologie*, **16**, pp. 13–29.

Bowles, Edmund A. (1964), 'Musical Instruments in the Medieval Corpus Christi Procession', *Journal of the American Musicological Society*, **17**, pp. 251–60.

Bowles, Edmund A. (1966), 'On the Origin of the Keyboard Mechanism in the Late Middle Ages', *Technology and Culture*, **7**, pp. 152–62.

Bowles, Edmund A. (1970), 'A Performance History of the Organ in the Middle Ages', *Diapason*, **61**, no. 2, pp. 13–14.

Bowles, Edmund A. (1971), 'Eastern Influences on the Use of Trumpets and Drums during the Middle Ages', *Anuario musical*, **26**, pp. 1–26.

Bowles, Edmund A. (1977), 'Iconography as a Tool for Examining the Loud Consort in the Fifteenth Century', *Journal of the American Musical Instrument Society*, **3**, pp. 100–21.

Bowles, Edmund A. (1983), *Musical Performance in the Late Middle Ages/La Pratique musicale au moyen age*, Minkoff & Lattès.

Brothers, Thomas (1997a), *Chromatic Beauty in the Late Medieval Chanson: An Interpretation of Manuscript Accidentals*, Cambridge: Cambridge University Press.

Brothers, Thomas (1997b), '*Contenance Angloise* and Accidentals in Some Motets by Du Fay', *Plainsong and Medieval Music*, **6**, pp. 21–51.

Brothers, Thomas (1997c), 'Musica Ficta and Harmony in Machaut's Songs', *Journal of Musicology*, **15**, pp. 501–28.
Brown, Howard Mayer (1971), 'Improvised Ornamentation in the Fifteenth-Century Chanson', *Quadrivium*, **12**, pp. 235–58.
Brown, Howard Mayer (1973), 'On the Performance of Fifteenth-Century Chansons', *Early Music*, **1**, pp. 3–10.
Brown, Howard Mayer (1976), 'Instruments and Voices in the Fifteenth-Century Chanson', in John W. Grubbs (ed.), *Current Thought in Musicology*, Symposia in the Arts and Humanities 4, Austin, TX and London: University of Texas Press, pp. 89–137.
Brown, Howard Mayer (1977), 'Fantasia on a Theme by Boccaccio', *Early Music*, **5**, pp. 324–39.
Brown, Howard Mayer (1978), 'Trecento Angels and the Instruments They Play', in Edward Olleson (ed.), *Modern Musical Scholarship*, Stocksfield: Oriel Press, pp. 112–40.
Brown, Howard Mayer (1983), 'The Trecento Harp', in Stanley Boorman (ed.), *Studies in the Performance of Late Mediaeval Music*, Cambridge: Cambridge University Press, pp. 35–73.
Brown, Howard Mayer (1984a, 1985, 1986, 1988), 'Catalogus: A Corpus of Trecento Pictures with Musical Subject Matter', *Imago Musicae*, **1** (1984), pp. 189–243; **2** (1985), pp. 179–281; **3** (1986), pp. 103–87; **5** (1988), pp. 167–241.
Brown, Howard Mayer (1984b), 'St. Augustine, Lady Music, and the Gittern in Fourteenth-Century Italy', *Musica disciplina*, **38**, pp. 25–65.
Brown, Howard Mayer (1987), 'Review of *The Castle of Fair Welcome*', *Early Music*, **15**, pp. 277–79.
Brown, Howard Mayer (1989), 'The Trecento Fiddle and Its Bridges', *Early Music*, **17**, pp. 308–29.
Brown, Howard Mayer and Sadie, Stanley (eds) (1989), *Performance Practice: Music before 1600*, New York and London: W.W. Norton.
Bukofzer, Manfred F. (1950), 'The Beginnings of Choral Polyphony', in *Studies in Medieval & Renaissance Music*, New York: W.W. Norton, pp. 176–89.
Bukofzer, Manfred F. (1954–55), 'Review of Thomas [sic] G. Waite, *The Rhythm of Twelfth-Century Polyphony*.' *Notes*, **12**, pp. 232–36.
Caldwell, John (1966/67), 'The Organ in the Medieval Latin Liturgy, 800–1500', *Proceedings of the Royal Musical Association*, **93**, pp. 11–24.
Caldwell, John (1990), 'Two Polyphonic *Istampite* from the 14th Century', *Early Music*, **18**, pp. 373–80.
Caldwell, John (1992), 'Plainsong and Polyphony 1250–1550', in Thomas Forrest Kelly (ed.), *Plainsong in the Age of Polyphony*, Cambridge Studies in Performance Practice 2, Cambridge: Cambridge University Press, pp. 6–31.
Cardine, Eugène (1982), *Gregorian Semiology*, trans. Robert M. Fowels, Sablé-sur-Sarthe: Abbaye Saint-Pierre de Solesmes.
Cohen, Joel (1990), 'Peirol's Vielle: Instrumental Participation in the Troubadour Repertory', *Historical Performance: The Journal of Early Music America*, **3**, pp. 73–77.
Cosart, Jann (2009), 'Echoes of St. Andrews: Performance Practice Questions in the Chants of W1', in Timothy D. Watkins (ed.), *Performance Practice: Issues and Approaches*, Ann Arbor, MI: Steglein Publishing, pp. 3–14.
Crane, Frederick (1972), *Extant Medieval Musical Instruments: A Provisional Catalogue by Types*, Iowa City, IA: University of Iowa Press.
Crane, Frederick (1979), 'On Performing the *Lo estampies*', *Early Music*, **7**, pp. 25–33.
Crocker, Richard L. (1958), '*Musica Rhythmica* and *Musica Metrica* in Antique and Medieval Theory', *Journal of Music Theory*, **2**, pp. 2–23.
Crocker, Richard A. (1990), 'Rhythm in Early Polyphony', *Current Musicology*, **45–47**, pp. 147–77.
Crocker, Richard (1994), 'Two Recent Editions of Aquitanian Polyphony', *Plainsong and Medieval Music*, **3**, pp. 57–101.

Cross, Lucy (1990), 'Chromatic Alteration and Extrahexachordal Intervals in Fourteenth-Century Polyphonic Repertories', PhD dissertation, Columbia University.

Dalglish, William (1978), 'The Origin of the Hocket', *Journal of the American Musicological Society*, **31**, pp. 3–20.

Davidson, Audrey Ekdahl (2008), *Aspects of Early Music and Performance*, New York: AMS Press.

Davidson, Audrey Ekdahl and Davidson, Clifford (1998), *Performing Medieval Music Drama*, Kalamazoo: Medieval Institute Publications.

Donington, Robert (1958), 'Musical Instruments in the Liturgical Service in the Middle Ages', *Galpin Society Journal*, **11**, pp. 85–87.

Downey, Peter (1984), 'The Renaissance Slide Trumpet: Fact or Fiction?', *Early Music*, **12**, pp. 26–33.

Duffin, Ross W. (1989), 'The *Trompette des Menestrels* in the 15th-Century *Alta Capella*', *Early Music*, **17**, pp. 397–402.

Duffin, Ross W. (1997), 'Backward Bells and Barrel Bells: Some Notes on the Early History of Loud Instruments', *Historic Brass Society Journal*, **9**, pp. 113–29.

Duffin, Ross W. (ed.) (2000), *A Performer's Guide to Medieval Music*, Bloomington and Indianapolis, IN: Indiana University Press.

Dyer, Joseph (1976), 'The Universal Voice', *Early Music*, **4**, pp. 489–91.

Dyer, Joseph (1978), 'Singing with Proper Refinement from *De modo bene cantandi* (1471) by Conrad von Zabern', *Early Music*, **6**, pp. 207–27.

Dyer, Joseph (1980), 'A Thirteenth-Century Choirmaster: The *Scientia Artis Musicae* of Elias Salomon', *Musical Quarterly*, **66**, pp. 83–111.

Dyer, Joseph (1989), 'The Singing of Psalms in the Early-Medieval Office', *Speculum*, **64**, pp. 535–78.

Dyer, Joseph (2000), 'The Voice in the Middle Ages', in John Potter (ed.), *The Cambridge Companion to Singing*, Cambridge: Cambridge University Press, pp. 165–77.

Eberlein, Roland (1992), 'The Faenza Codex: Music for Organ or for Lute Duet?', *Early Music*, **20**, pp. 460–66.

Edwards, Warwick (1996), 'Phrasing in Medieval Song: Perspectives from Traditional Music', *Plainsong and Medieval Music*, **5**, pp. 1–22.

Ellinwood, Leonard (1936), 'Francesco Landini and His Music', *Musical Quarterly*, **22**, pp. 190–216.

Fallows, David (1977), '15th-Century Tablatures for Plucked Instruments: A Summary, a Revision and a Suggestion', *Lute Society Journal*, **19**, pp. 7–33.

Fallows, David (1981–82), 'Medieval Instruments', *Gramophone*, **59**, pp. 862–65.

Fallows, David (1983), 'Specific Information on the Ensembles for Composed Polyphony, 1400–1474', in Stanley Boorman (ed.), *Studies in the Performance of Late Mediaeval Music*, Cambridge: Cambridge University Press, pp. 109–59.

Fallows, David (1996), 'The End of the Ars Subtilior', *Basler Jahrbuch für historische Musikpraxis*, **20**, pp. 21–40.

Fallows, David (1997), 'Two Early Music Revolutions', *Early Music*, **25**, pp. 564–65.

Fallows, David (2005), 'Josquin and Popular Songs', *Basler Jahrbuch für historische Musikpraxis*, **29**, pp. 161–71.

Finlay, Ian F. (1952), 'Musical Instruments in Gotfrid von Strassburg's "Tristan und Isolde"', *Galpin Society Journal*, **5**, pp. 39–43.

Fitzpatrick, Horace (1975), 'The Medieval Recorder', *Early Music*, **3**, pp. 361–64.

Flindell, E. Fred (1967), 'Syllabic Notation and Change of Mode', *Acta musicologica*, **39**, pp. 21–34.

Foster, Genette (1977), 'The Iconology of Musical Instruments and Musical Performance in Thirteenth-Century French Manuscript Illuminations', PhD dissertation, City University of New York.

Fuller, Sarah Ann (1969), 'Aquitainian Polyphony of the Eleventh and Twelfth Centuries', 3 vols, PhD dissertation, University of California at Berkeley.

Fuller, Sarah (1978), 'Discant and the Theory of Fifthing', *Acta musicologica*, **50**, pp. 241–75.

Ghisi, Federico (1966/1978), 'An Angel Concert in a Trecento Sienese Fresco', in Jan LaRue (ed.), *Aspects of Medieval and Renaissance Music: A Birthday Offering to Gustave Reese*, New York: W.W. Norton, 1966, pp. 308–13; reprint edition: New York: Pendragon Press, 1978.

Gillingham, Bryan (1980), 'British Library MS Egerton 945: Further Evidence for a Mensural Interpretation of Sequences', *Music and Letters*, **61**, pp. 50–59.

Godt, Irving (1976), 'Reading Ligatures from their Ground State', *Early Music*, **4**, pp. 44–45.

Godwin, Joscelyn (1977), '"*Mains divers acors*": Some Instrument Collections of the Ars Nova Period', *Early Music*, **5**, pp. 148–59.

Greig, Donald (1995), 'Sight-Reading: Notes on *a cappella* Performance Practice', *Early Music*, **23**, pp. 125–48.

Greig, Donald (2003), 'Ars Subtilior Repertory as Performance Palimpsest', *Early Music*, **31**, pp. 197–209.

Grocheo, Johannes de (1967), *Concerning Music (De Musica)*, trans. Albert Seay, Colorado College Music Press Translations 1, Colorado Spring, CO: Colorado College Music Press.

Gümpel, Karl-Werner (1986–87), 'Gregorian Chant and *Musica ficta*: New Observations from Spanish Theory of the Early Renaissance', *Recerca Musicològica*, **6–7**, pp. 5–27.

Günther, Ursula (1983), 'Fourteenth-Century Music with Texts Revealing Performance Practice', in Stanley Boorman (ed.), *Studies in the Performance of Late Mediaeval Music*, Cambridge: Cambridge University Press, pp. 253–70.

Gushee, Lawrence (1980), 'Two Central Places: Paris and the French Court in the Early Fourteenth Century', in Hellmut Kühn and Peter Nitsche (eds), *Gesellschaft für Musikforschung: Bericht über den internationalen musikwissenschaftlichen Kongress Berlin 1974*, Kassel: Bärenreiter, pp. 135–57.

Haines, John (2001), 'The Arabic Style of Performing Medieval Music', *Early Music*, **29**, pp. 369–78.

Hallmark, Anne (1983), 'Some Evidence for French Influence in Northern Italy, *c*. 1400', in Stanley Boorman (ed.), *Studies in the Performance of Late Mediaeval Music*, Cambridge: Cambridge University Press, pp. 193–225.

Hamm, Charles E. (1964), *A Chronology of the Works of Guillaume Dufay Based on a Study of Mensural Practice*, Princeton, NJ: Princeton University Press.

Harden, [Bettie] Jean (1977), '"Musica ficta" in Machaut', *Early Music*, **5**, pp. 473–77.

Harden, Bettie Jean (1983), 'Sharps, Flats, and Scribes: Musica Ficta in the Machaut Manuscripts', PhD dissertation, Cornell University.

Harrán, Don (1978), 'In Pursuit of Origins: The Earliest Writing on Text Underlay *c*. 1440', *Acta musicologica*, **50**, pp. 217–40.

Harrán, Don (1997), 'How to "Lay" the "Lay": New Thoughts on Text Underlay', *Musica disciplina*, **51**, pp. 231–62.

Harrison, Frank L. (1966/1978), 'Tradition and Innovation in Instrumental Usage 1100–1450', in Jan LaRue (ed.), *Aspects of Medieval and Renaissance Music: A Birthday Offering to Gustave Reese*, New York: W.W. Norton, 1966, pp. 319–35; reprint edition: New York: Pendragon Press, 1978.

Hasselman, Margaret Paine and McGown, David (1983), 'Mimesis and Woodwind Articulation in the Fourteenth Century', in Stanley Boorman (ed.), *Studies in the Performance of Late Mediaeval Music*, Cambridge: Cambridge University Press, pp. 101–07.

Heiman, Lawrence F. (1972), 'The Rhythmic Value of the Final Descending Note after a Punctum in Neums of Codex 239 of the Library of Laon', *Études grégoriennes*, **13**, pp. 151–224.

Heinen, Hubert (1969), '*Minnesang*: Some Metrical Problems', in Stanley N. Werbow (ed.), *Formal Aspects of Medieval German Poetry: A Symposium*, Austin, TX: University of Texas Press, pp. 81–92.

Hibberd, Lloyd (1942), '*Musica Ficta* and Instrumental Music *c*. 1250–*c*. 1350', *Musical Quarterly*, **28**, pp. 216–26.

Hibberd, Lloyd (1946), 'On "Instrumental Style" in Early Melody', *Musical Quarterly*, **32**, pp. 107–30.

Hiley, David (1984), 'The Plica and Liquescence', in *Gordon Athol Anderson (1929–1981): In Memoriam*, Vol. II, Musicological Studies IXL, Henryville, Ottawa and Binningen: Institute of Medieval Music, pp. 379–91.

Hiley, David (1987), 'Musicology and Make-Believe?', *Early Music*, **15**, p. 140.

Hiley, David (1989), 'Chant', in Howard Mayer Brown and Stanley Sadie (eds), *Performance Practice: Music before 1600*, New York and London: W.W. Norton, pp. 37–54.

Hiley, David (1993), *Western Plainchant: A Handbook*, Oxford: Clarendon Press.

Hiley, David (2009), *Gregorian Chant*, Cambridge: Cambridge University Press.

Hirshberg, Jehoash (1980), 'Hexachordal and Modal Structure in Machaut's Polyphonic Chansons', in John Walter Hill (ed.), *Studies in Musicology in Honor of Otto E. Albrecht: A Collection of Essays by His Colleagues and Former Students at the University of Pennsylvania*, Kassel, Basel and London: Bärenreiter, pp. 19–42.

Hoppin, Richard H. (1953), 'Partial Signatures and Musica Ficta in Some Early 15th-Century Sources', *Journal of the American Musicological Society*, **6**, pp. 197–215.

Hoppin, Richard H. (1956), 'Conflicting Signatures Reviewed', *Journal of the American Musicological Society*, **9**, pp. 97–117.

Hughes, Andrew (1965), 'Mensuration and Proportion in Early Fifteenth Century English Music', *Acta musicologica*, **37**, pp. 48–61.

Hughes, Andrew (1966), 'Mensural Polyphony for Choir in 15th-Century England', *Journal of the American Musicological Society*, **19**, pp. 352–69.

Hughes, Andrew (1969a), 'The Choir in Fifteenth-Century English Music: Non-Mensural Polyphony', in Gustave Reese and Robert J. Snow (eds), *Essays in Musicology in Honor of Dragan Plamenac on His 70th Birthday*, Pittsburgh, PA: University of Pittsburgh Press, pp. 127–45.

Hughes, Andrew (1969b), 'Ugolino: The Monochord and Musica Ficta', *Musica disciplina*, **23**, pp. 21–39.

Hughes, Andrew (1972), *Manuscript Accidentals: Ficta in Focus 1350–1450*, Musicological Studies and Documents 27, American Institute of Musicology.

Hughes, Andrew (1974), 'Viella: Facere Non Possumus', in Henrik Glahn, Søren Sørensen and Peter Ryom (eds), *International Musicological Society Report of the Eleventh Congress Copenhagen 1972*, Vol. 2, Copenhagen: Wilhelm Hansen, pp. 453–56.

Huglo, Michel (1992), 'Notated Performance Practices in Parisian Chant Manuscripts of the Thirteenth Century', in Thomas Forrest Kelly (ed.), *Plainsong in the Age of Polyphony*, Cambridge Studies in Performance Practice 2, Cambridge: Cambridge University Press, pp. 32–44.

Igoe, James Thomas (1971), 'Performance Practices in the Polyphonic Mass of the Early Fifteenth Century', PhD dissertation, University of North Carolina at Chapel Hill.

Jeffery, Peter (1984), 'A Four-Part *In seculum* Hocket and a Mensural Sequence in an Unknown Fragment', *Journal of the American Musicological Society*, **37**, pp. 1–48.

Jones, Sterling Scott (1995), *The Lira da Braccio*, Bloomington and Indianapolis, IN: Indiana University Press.

Karp, Theodore (1966), 'Towards a Critical Edition of Notre Dame Organa Dupla', *Musical Quarterly*, **52**, pp. 350–67.

Karp, Theodore (1967), 'St. Martial and Santiago de Compostela: An Analytical Speculation', *Acta musicologica*, **39**, pp. 144–60.

Karp, Theodore (1974), 'Text Underlay and Rhythmic Interpretation of 12th c. Polyphony', in Henrik Glahn, Søren Sørensen and Peter Ryom (eds), *International Musicological Society Report of the Eleventh Congress Copenhagen 1972*, Vol. 2, Copenhagen: Wilhelm Hansen, pp. 482–86.

Karp, Theodore (1992), *The Polyphony of St. Martial and Santiago de Compostela*, 2 vols, Oxford: Clarendon Press; New York: Oxford University Press.

Karp, Theodore (1998), 'Measurability in Medieval Music before 1300', *Orbis musicae*, **12**, pp. 107–39.

Karp, Theodore (1999), 'Evaluating Performances and Editions of Aquitanian Polyphony', *Acta musicologica*, **71**, pp. 19–49.

Kelly, Thomas Forrest (1985), 'Melisma and Prosula: The Performance of Responsory Tropes', in Gabriel Silegi (ed.), *Liturgische Tropen: Referate zweier Colloquien des Corpus Troporum in München (1983) und Canterbury (1984)*, Münchener Beiträge zur Mediävistik und Renaissance-Forschung 36, Munich: Arbeo-Gesellschaft, pp. 163–80.

King, Jonathan (1996), 'Texting in Early Fifteenth-Century Sacred Polyphony', PhD dissertation, Oxford University.

Kinsela, David (1998), 'The Capture of the Chekker', *Galpin Society Journal*, **51**, pp. 64–85.

Knapp, Janet (1979), 'Musical Declamation and Poetic Rhythm in an Early Layer of Notre Dame Conductus', *Journal of the American Musicological Society*, **32**, pp. 383–407.

Knighton, Tess (1992), 'The *A Cappella* Heresy in Spain: An Inquisition into the Performance of the Cancionero Repertory', *Early Music*, **20**, pp. 549–81.

Knighton, Tess and Fallows, David (eds) (1992), *Companion to Medieval and Renaissance Music*, London: J.M. Dent.

Korrick, Leslie (1990), 'Instrumental Music in the Early 16th-Century Mass: New Evidence', *Early Music*, **18**, pp. 359–70.

Kovarik, Edward (1975), 'The Performance of Dufay's Paraphrase Kyries', *Journal of the American Musicological Society*, **28**, pp. 230–44.

Kreitner, Kenneth (1998), 'Bad News, or Not? Thoughts on Renaissance Performance Practice', *Early Music*, **26**, pp. 323–33.

La Rue, Helene (1982), 'The Problem of the Cymbala', *Galpin Society Journal*, **35**, pp. 86–99.

Leech-Wilkinson, Daniel (1993), '*Le Voir Dit* and *La Messe de Nostre Dame*: Aspects of Genre and Style in Late Works of Machaut', *Plainsong and Medieval Music*, **2**, pp. 43–73.

Leech-Wilkinson, Daniel (2002), *The Modern Invention of Medieval Music: Scholarship, Ideology, Performance*, Cambridge: Cambridge University Press.

Leech-Wilkinson, Daniel (2003), 'Articulating Ars Subtilior Song', *Early Music*, **31**, pp. 7–18.

Lefferts, Peter M. (1995), 'Signature-Systems and Tonal Types in the Fourteenth-Century French Chanson', *Plainsong and Medieval Music*, **4**, pp. 117–47.

Levy, Kenneth *et al.* (2001), 'Plainchant', in Stanley Sadie and John Tyrrell (eds), *The New Grove Dictionary of Music and Musicians* (2nd edn), 29 vols, London: Macmillan, vol. 19, pp. 825–86.

Lindley, Mark (1975–76), 'Fifteenth-Century Evidence for Meantone Temperament', *Proceedings of the Royal Musical Association*, **102**, pp. 37–51.

Lindley, Mark (1980), 'Pythagorean Intonation and the Rise of the Triad', *Royal Musical Association Research Chronicle*, **16**, pp. 4–61.

Litterick, Louise (1980), 'Performing Franco-Netherlandish Secular Music of the Late 15th Century: Texted and Untexted Parts in the Sources', *Early Music*, **8**, pp. 474–85.

Lowinsky, Edward E. (1945), 'The Function of Conflicting Signatures in Early Polyphonic Music', *Musical Quarterly*, **31**, pp. 227–60.

Lowinsky, Edward E. (1954), 'Conflicting Views on Conflicting Signatures', *Journal of the American Musicological Society*, **7**, pp. 181–204.

Maddrell, J.E. (1970), '*Mensura* and the Rhythm of Medieval Monodic Song', *Current Musicology*, **10**, pp. 64–69.

Maddrell, J.E. (1971), 'Grocheo and *The Measurability of Medieval Music*: A Reply to Hendrik Vanderwerf', *Current Musicology*, **11**, pp. 89–90.

Marvin, Bob (1983), 'Response to the "Pythagorean Tuning" Article', *The Courant*, **1**, no. 3, pp. 28–29.

McGee, Timothy J. (1982), 'Eastern Influences in Medieval European Dances', in Robert Falck and Timothy Rice (eds), *Cross-Cultural Perspectives on Music*, Toronto, Buffalo and London: University of Toronto Press, pp. 79–100.

McGee, Timothy J. (1985), *Medieval and Renaissance Music: A Performer's Guide*, Toronto, Buffalo and London: University of Toronto Press.

McGee, Timothy J. (1986), 'Instruments and the Faenza Codex', *Early Music*, **14**, pp. 480–490.

McGee, Timothy J. (ed.) (1989), *Medieval Instrumental Dances*, Bloomington and Indianapolis, IN: Indiana University Press.

McGee, Timothy J. (1992), 'Once Again, the Faenza Codex: A Reply to Roland Eberlein', *Early Music*, **20**, pp. 466–68.

McGee, Timothy J. (1992–95), 'Misleading Iconography: The Case of the "Adimari Wedding Cassone"', *Imago Musicae*, **9–12**, pp. 139–57.

McGee, Timothy J. (1993), 'Singing without Text', *Performance Practice Review*, **6**, pp. 1–32.

McGee, Timothy J. (1996), '"Ornamental" Neumes and Early Notation', *Performance Practice Review*, **9**, pp. 39–65.

McGee, Timothy J. (1998), *The Sound of Medieval Song: Ornamentation and Vocal Style according to the Treatises*, Oxford: Clarendon Press.

McGee, Timothy J. (2005), 'Silver or Gold: The Color of Brass Instruments in the Late Middle Ages', *Historic Brass Society Journal*, **17**, pp. 1–6.

McGee, Timothy J. (2009a), *The Ceremonial Musicians of Late Medieval Florence*, Bloomington and Indianapolis, IN: Indiana University Press.

McGee, Timothy J. (ed.) (2009b), *Instruments and Their Music in the Middle Ages*, Farnham and Burlington: Ashgate.

McGee, Timothy J. (ed.) with Rigg, A.G. and Klausner, David N. (1996), *Singing Early Music: The Pronunciation of European Languages in the Late Middle Ages and Renaissance*, Bloomington and Indianapolis, IN: Indiana University Press.

McKinnon, James W. (1968), 'Musical Instruments in Medieval Psalm Commentaries and Psalters', *Journal of the American Musicological Society*, **21**, pp. 3–20.

McKinnon, James W. (1983), 'Fifteenth-Century Northern Book Painting and the *A Cappella* Question: An Essay in Iconographic Method', in Stanley Boorman (ed.), *Studies in the Performance of Late Mediaeval Music*, Cambridge: Cambridge University Press, pp. 1–17.

McKinnon, James W. (1986), 'A Cappella Doctrine Versus a Cappella Practice: A Necessary Distinction', in Marc Honegger, Christian Meyer and Paul Prevost (eds), *La Musique et le rite sacré et profane: Actes du XIIIe Congrès de la Société Internationale de Musicologie Strasbourg, 29 août–3 septembre 1982*, Vol. 1 (2 vols), Strasbourg: Association des Publications près les Universités de Strasbourg, pp. 238–42.

McKinnon, James W. (1995), 'Lector Chant versus Schola Chant: A Question of Historical Plausibility', in Janka Szendrei and David Hiley (eds), *Laborare fratres in unum: Festschrift Laszlo Dobszay zum 60. Geburtstag*, Hildesheim: Weidmann, pp. 201–11.

Moll, Kevin N. (1997), 'Realizing Partial Signatures around 1400: Liebert's Credo as a Test Case', *Performance Practice Review*, **10**, pp. 248–54.

Montagu, Jeremy (1974), 'Early Percussion Techniques', *Early Music*, **2**, pp. 20–24.

Montagu, Jeremy (1975), 'The "Authentic" Sound of Early Music', *Early Music*, **3**, pp. 242–43.

Montagu, Jeremy (1976), *The World of Medieval & Renaissance Musical Instruments*, Newton Abbot, London and Vancouver: David and Charles.

Munrow, David (1973), 'The Art of Courtly Love', *Early Music*, **1**, pp. 194–99.

Munrow, David (1976), *Instruments of the Middle Ages and Renaissance*, London: Oxford University Press.

Murray, Gregory (1957), 'Gregorian Rhythm in the Gregorian Centuries: The Literary Evidence', *Caecilia*, **84**, pp. 177–99.

Murray, Gregory (1963), *Gregorian Chant according to the Manuscripts*, London: L.J. Cary.

Myers, Herbert W. (1989), 'Slide Trumpet Madness: Fact or Fiction?', *Early Music*, **17**, pp. 382–89.

Nadas, John (1981), 'The Structure of MS Panciatichi 26 and the Transmission of Trecento Polyphony', *Journal of the American Musicological Society*, **34**, pp. 393–427.

Newes, Virginia (1984), 'The Relationship of Text to Imitative Techniques in 14th Century Polyphony', in Ursula Günther and Ludwig Finscher (eds), *Musik und Text in der Mehrstimmigkeit des 14. und 15. Jahrhunderts: Vorträge des Gastsymposions in der Herzog August Bibliothek Wolfenbüttel 8. bis 12. September 1980*, Göttinger musikwissenschaftliche Arbeiten 10, Kassel, Basel and London: Bärenreiter, pp. 121–54.

Newes, Virginia (1990), 'Writing, Reading and Memorizing: The Transmission and Resolution of Retrograde Canons from the 14th and Early 15th Centuries', *Early Music*, **18**, pp. 218–34.

Newton, George (1976), 'Singing Early Music', *Early Music*, **4**, p. 229.

Nowacki, Edward (1985–86), 'The Gregorian Office Antiphons and the Comparative Method', *Journal of Musicology*, **4**, pp. 243–75.

Page, Christopher (1974), 'An Aspect of Medieval Fiddle Construction', *Early Music*, **2**, pp. 166–67.

Page, Christopher (1975), 'Christopher Page Replies', *Early Music*, **3**, p. 51.

Page, Christopher (1978), 'Early 15th-Century Instruments in Jean de Gerson's "Tractatus de Canticis"', *Early Music*, **6**, pp. 339–49.

Page, Christopher (1979), 'The Myth of the Chekker', *Early Music*, **7**, pp. 482–89.

Page, Christopher (1980), 'Fourteenth-Century Instruments and Tunings: A Treatise by Jean Vaillant? (Berkeley, MS 744)', *Galpin Society Journal*, **33**, pp. 17–35.

Page, Christopher (1981a), 'False Voices', *Early Music*, **9**, pp. 71–72.

Page, Christopher (1981b), 'The 15th-Century Lute: New and Neglected Sources', *Early Music*, **9**, pp. 11–21.

Page, Christopher (1982), 'German Musicians and Their Instruments: A 14th-Century Account by Konrad of Megenberg', *Early Music*, **10**, pp. 192–200.

Page, Christopher (1982–83), 'The Medieval *Organistrum* and *Symphonia*', *Galpin Society Journal*, **35**, pp. 37–44; **36** (1983), pp. 71–87.

Page, Christopher (1984–85), 'Music and Chivalric Fiction in France, 1150–1300', *Proceedings of the Royal Musical Association*, **111/112**, pp. 1–27.

Page, Christopher (1987), *Voices and Instruments of the Middle Ages: Instrumental Practice and Songs in France 1100–1300*, London and Melbourne: J.M. Dent and Sons.

Page, Christopher (1989a), *The Owl and the Nightingale: Musical Life and Ideas in France 1100–1300*, Berkeley and Los Angeles, CA: University of California Press.

Page, Christopher (1989b), 'Polyphony before 1400', in Howard Mayer Brown and Stanley Sadie (eds), *Performance Practice: Music before 1600*, New York and London: W.W. Norton, pp. 79–104.

Page, Christopher (ed.) (1991), *The Summa Musice: A Thirteenth-Century Manual for Singers*, Cambridge: Cambridge University Press.

Page, Christopher (1992a), 'Going Beyond the Limits: Experiments with Vocalization in the French Chanson, 1340–1440', *Early Music*, **20**, pp. 446–59.

Page, Christopher (1992b), 'A Treatise on Musicians from ?c. 1400: The *Tractatulus de differentiis et gradibus cantorum* by Arnulf de St Ghislain', *Journal of the Royal Musical Association*, **117**, pp. 1–21.

Page, Christopher (1993a), *Discarding Images: Reflections on Music and Culture in Medieval France*, Oxford: Clarendon Press.

Page, Christopher (1993b), 'The English *A Cappella* Renaissance', *Early Music*, **21**, pp. 453–71.

Page, Christopher (1994), 'A Reply to Margaret Bent', *Early Music*, **22**, pp. 127–32.

Page, Christopher (1997a), 'An English Motet of the 14th Century in Performance: Two Contemporary Images', *Early Music*, **25**, pp. 7–32.

Page, Christopher (1997b), *Latin Poetry and Conductus Rhythm in Medieval France*, Royal Musical Association Monographs 8, London: Royal Musical Association.

Page, Christopher (1997c), 'Listening to the Trouvères', *Early Music*, **25**, pp. 638–59.

Page, Christopher (1997d), *Music and Instruments of the Middle Ages: Studies on Texts and Performance*, Aldershot, Great Britain and Brookfield, VT: Variorum.

Page, Christopher (2000), 'Around the Performance of a 13th-Century Motet', *Early Music*, **28**, pp. 343–57.

Parker, Ian (1977), 'The Performance of Troubadour and Trouvère Songs: Some Facts and Conjectures', *Early Music*, **5**, pp. 184–207.

Parrish, Carl (1959), *The Notation of Medieval Music* (corrected edn), New York: W.W. Norton.

Parrot, Andrew (1977), 'Performing Machaut's Mass on Record', *Early Music*, **5**, pp. 492–95.

Parrott, Andrew (1981), 'False Voice: Andrew Parrott Adds', *Early Music*, **9**, p. 72.

Pensom, Roger (1997), 'Performing the Medieval Lyric: A Metrical-Accentual Approach', *Performance Practice Review*, **10**, pp. 212–23.

Pepe, Edward C. (1983), 'Pythagorean Tuning and Its Implications for the Music of the Middle Ages', *The Courant*, **1**, no. 2, pp. 3–16.

Pestell, Richard (1987), 'Medieval Art and the Performance of Medieval Music', *Early Music*, **15**, pp. 56–68.

Phillips, Elizabeth V. and Jackson, John-Paul Christopher (1986), *Performing Medieval and Renaissance Music: An Introductory Guide*, New York: Schirmer; London: Collier Macmillan.

Plamenac, Dragan (1951), 'Keyboard Music of the 14th Century in Codex Faenza 117', *Journal of the American Musicological Society*, **4**, pp. 179–201.

Planchart, Alejandro Enrique (1981a), 'Fifteenth-Century Masses: Notes on Performance and Chronology', *Studi musicali*, **10**, pp. 3–30.

Planchart, Alejandro Enrique (1981b), 'The Relative Speed of *Tempora* in the Period of Dufay', *Royal Musical Association Research Chronicle*, **17**, pp. 33–51.

Planchart, Alejandro E. (1983), 'Parts with Words and without Words: The Evidence for Multiple Texts in Fifteenth-Century Masses', in Stanley Boorman (ed.), *Studies in the Performance of Late Mediaeval Music*, Cambridge: Cambridge University Press, pp. 227–51.

Planchart, Alejandro Enrique (1989), 'Tempo and Proportions', in Howard Mayer Brown and Stanley Sadie (eds), *Performance Practice: Music before 1600*, New York and London: W.W. Norton, pp. 126–44.

Planchart, Alejandro Enrique (2000), 'Organum', in Ross W. Duffin (ed.), *A Performer's Guide to Medieval Music*, Bloomington and Indianapolis, IN: Indiana University Press, pp. 23–51.

Plumley, Yolanda (2003), 'Playing the Citation Game in the Late 14th-Century Chanson', *Early Music*, **31**, pp. 20–39.

Polk, Keith (1969), 'Municipal Wind Music in Flanders in the Late Middle Ages', *Brass and Woodwind Quarterly*, **2**, pp. 1–15.

Polk, Keith (1976), 'Ensemble Performance in Dufay's Time', in Allan W. Atlas (ed.), *Papers Read at the Dufay Quincentenary Conference, Brooklyn College, December 6–7, 1974*, New York: Department of Music, School of Performing Arts, Brooklyn College of the City University of New York, pp. 61–75.

Polk, Keith (1989a), 'The Trombone, the Slide Trumpet and the Ensemble Tradition of the Early Renaissance', *Early Music*, **17**, pp. 389–97.

Polk, Keith (1989b), 'Vedel and Geige–Fiddle and Viol: German String Traditions in the Fifteenth Century', *Journal of the American Musicological Society*, **42**, pp. 504–46.

Polk, Keith (1990), 'Voices and Instruments: Soloists and Ensembles in the 15th Century', *Early Music*, **18**, pp. 179–98.

Polk, Keith (1992), *German Instrumental Music of the Late Middle Ages: Players, Patrons, and Performance Practice*, Cambridge: Cambridge University Press.

Polk, Keith (1994), 'Instrumental Music in the Low Countries in the Fifteenth Century', in Albert Clement and Eric Jas (eds), *From Ciconia to Sweelinck: Donum natalicium Willem Elders*, Chloe Beihefte zum Daphnis 21, Amsterdam and Atlanta: Rodopi, pp. 13–29.

Ramalingam, Vivian S. (1986), 'The *Trumpetum* in Strasbourg M222 C22', in Marc Honegger, Christian Meyer and Paul Prevost (eds), *La Musique et le rite sacré et profane: Actes du XIIIe Congrès de la Société Internationale de Musicologie, Strasbourg, 29 août–3 septembre 1982*, Vol. 2, Strasbourg: Association des Publications près les Universités de Strasbourg, pp. 143–60.

Rastall, Richard (1970–71), 'Minstrelsy, Church and Clergy in Medieval England', *Proceedings of the Royal Musical Association*, 97, pp. 83–98.

Rastall, Richard (1974), 'Some English Consort-Groupings of the Late Middle Ages', *Music and Letters*, 55, pp. 179–202.

Rayburn, John (1964) *Gregorian Chant: A History of the Controversy Concerning Its Rhythm*, New York.

Reaney, Gilbert (1956), 'Voices and Instruments in the Music of Guillaume de Machaut', *Revue belge de musicologie*, 10, pp. 3–17; 93–104.

Reaney, Gilbert (1959), 'A Note on Conductus Rhythm', in Gerald Abraham *et al.* (eds), *Bericht über den siebenten internationalen musikwissenschaftlichen Kongress Köln (1958)*, Kassel: Bärenreiter, pp. 219–21.

Reaney, Gilbert (1966/1978), 'The Performance of Medieval Music', in Jan LaRue (ed.), *Aspects of Medieval and Renaissance Music: A Birthday Offering to Gustave Reese*, New York: W.W. Norton, pp. 704–22; reprint edition: New York: Pendragon Press, 1978.

Reaney, Gilbert (1969), 'Accidentals in Early Fifteenth Century Music', in Jozef Robijns (ed.), *Renaissance-Muziek 1400–1600: Donum natalicium René Bernard Lenaerts*, Musicologica Lovaniensia 1, Leuven: Katholieke Universiteit Seminarie voor Muziekwetenschap, pp. 223–31.

Reaney, Gilbert (1971), 'Accidentals and Fourteenth-Century Counterpoint in England', *Quadrivium*, 12, pp. 195–208.

Reaney, Gilbert (1977), 'The Part Played by Instruments in the Music of Guillaume de Machaut', *Studi musicali*, 6, pp. 3–11.

Reaney, Gilbert (1979), 'Transposition and "Key" Signatures in Late Medieval Music', *Musica disciplina*, 33, pp. 27–41.

Reckow, Fritz (1981), 'Communication', *Journal of the American Musicological Society*, 34, pp. 588–90.

Remnant, Mary (1968), 'The Use of Frets on Rebecs and Mediaeval Fiddles', *Galpin Society Journal*, 21, pp. 146–51.

Remnant, Mary (1968–69), 'Rebec, Fiddle and Crowd in England', *Proceedings of the Royal Musical Association*, 95, pp. 15–28.

Remnant, Mary (1969–70), 'Rebec, Fiddle and Crowd in England: Some Further Observations', *Proceedings of the Royal Musical Association*, 96, pp. 149–50.

Remnant, Mary (1975), 'The Diversity of Medieval Fiddles', *Early Music*, 3, pp. 47–49.

Remnant, Mary (1986), *English Bowed Instruments from Anglo-Saxon to Tudor Times*, Oxford: Clarendon Press.

Renz, Frederick (1977), 'Producing "Le Roman de Fauvel"', *Early Music*, 5, pp. 24–26.

Ripin, Edwin M. (1967), 'The Early Clavichord', *Musical Quarterly*, 53, pp. 518–38.

Ripin, Edwin M. (1974), 'The Norrlanda Organ and the Ghent Altarpiece', in Gustaf Hilleström (ed.), *Festschrift to Ernst Emsheimer on the Occasion of His 70th Birthday, January 15th 1974*, Studia instrumentorum musicae popularis 3, Musikhistoriska museets skrifter 5, Stockholm: Nordiska Musikförlaget, pp. 193–96 and 286–88.

Ripin, Edwin M. (1975), 'Towards an Identification of the Chekker', *Galpin Society Journal*, 28, pp. 11–25.

Roesner, Edward H. (1982), 'Johannes de Garlandia on *Organum in speciali*', *Early Music History*, **2**, pp. 129–60.

Roesner, Edward H. (1990), 'The Emergence of *Musica mensurabilis*', in Eugene K. Wolf and Edward H. Roesner (eds), *Studies in Musical Sources and Style: Essays in Honor of Jan LaRue*, Madison: A-R Editions, pp. 41–74.

Roesner, Edward H. (ed.) (2009), *Ars Antiqua: Organum, Conductus, Motet*, Farnham and Burlington: Ashgate.

Routley, Nicholas (1985), 'A Practical Guide to *Musica Ficta*', *Early Music*, **13**, pp. 59–71.

Sachs, Curt (1960), 'Primitive and Medieval Music: A Parallel', *Journal of the American Musicological Society*, **13**, pp. 43–49.

Sanders, Ernest H. (1962), 'Duple Rhythm and Alternate Third Mode in the 13th Century', *Journal of the American Musicological Society*, **15**, pp. 249–91.

Sanders, Ernest H. (1980a), 'Communication', *Journal of the American Musicological Society*, **33**, pp. 602–07.

Sanders, Ernest H. (1980b), 'Consonance and Rhythm in the Organum of the 12th and 13th Centuries', *Journal of the American Musicological Society*, **33**, pp. 264–86.

Sanders, Ernest H. (1981), 'Communication', *Journal of the American Musicological Society*, **34**, pp. 590–91.

Sandon, Nick (1990), 'Some Thoughts on Making Liturgical Reconstructions', in Gerard Gillen and Harry White (eds), *Musicology in Ireland*, Irish Musical Studies 1, Dublin: Irish Academic Press, pp. 169–80.

Sawa, George D. (1981), 'The Survival of Some Aspects of Medieval Arabic Performance Practice', *Ethnomusicology*, **25**, pp. 73–86.

Schneider, Walter C. (1977–78), 'Percussion Instruments of the Middle Ages', *Percussionist*, **15**, pp. 106–17.

Schroeder, Eunice (1982), 'The Stoke Comes Full Circle: Ø and ₵ in Writings on Music ca. 1450–1540', *Musica disciplina*, **36**, pp. 119–66.

Scott, Ann Besser (1970), 'The Performance of the Old Hall Descant Settings', *Musical Quarterly*, **56**, pp. 14–26.

Seagrave, Barbara Garvey and Thomas, Wesley (1966), *The Songs of the Minnesingers*, Urbana, IL and London: University of Illinois Press.

Seay, Albert (1966/1978), 'The 15th-Century *Coniuncta*: A Preliminary Study', in Jan LaRue (ed.), *Aspects of Medieval and Renaissance Music: A Birthday Offering to Gustave Reese*, New York: W.W. Norton, pp. 723–37; reprint edition: New York: Pendragon Press, 1978.

Seay, Albert (1970), 'The Beginnings of the Coniuncta and Lorenzo Masini's "L'Antefana"', in F. Alberto Gallo (ed.), *L'ars nova italiana del trecento: Secondo Convegno Internazionale 17–22 luglio 1969 sotto il patrocinio della Società Internazionale di Musicologia*, Certaldo: Edizioni Centro di studi sull'ars nova italiana del trecento, pp. 51–65.

Seebass, Tilman (1983), 'The Visualisation of Music through Pictorial Imagery and Notation in Late Mediaeval France', in Stanley Boorman (ed.), *Studies in the Performance of Late Mediaeval Music*, Cambridge: Cambridge University Press, pp. 19–33.

Slavin, Dennis (1991), 'In Support of "Heresy": Manuscript Evidence for the *A Cappella* Performance of Early 15th-Century Songs', *Early Music*, **19**, pp. 178–90.

Smits van Waesberghe, J. (ed.) (1951), *Cymbala (Bells in the Middle Ages)*, Musicological Studies and Documents 1, Rome: American Institute of Musicology.

Smoldon, W.L. (1962a), 'Medieval Church Drama and the Use of Musical Instruments', *Musical Times*, **103**, pp. 836–40.

Smoldon, W.L. (1962b), 'The Music of the Medieval Church Drama', *Musical Quarterly*, **48**, pp. 476–97.

Smoldon, W.L. (1963), 'Medieval Church Drama', *Musical Times*, **104**, p. 342.
Spiess, Lincoln Bunce (1959), 'The Diatonic "Chromaticism" of the *Enchiriadis* Treatises', *Journal of the American Musicological Society*, **12**, pp. 1–6.
Stevens, John (1957–58), 'Music in Mediaeval Drama', *Proceedings of the Royal Musical Association*, **84**, pp. 81–95.
Stevens, John (1986), *Words and Music in the Middle Ages: Song, Narrative, Dance and Drama, 1050–1350*, Cambridge: Cambridge University Press.
Stone, Anne (1996), 'Glimpses of the Unwritten Tradition in Some *Ars subtilior* Works', *Musica disciplina*, **50**, pp. 59–93.
Stone, Anne (2003), 'Self-Reflexive Songs and Their Readers in the Late 14th Century', *Early Music*, **31**, pp. 180–94.
Strohm, Reinhard (1990), *Music in Late Medieval Bruges* (revised edn), Oxford: Clarendon Press; New York: Oxford University Press.
Switten, Margaret L. (1995), *Music and Poetry in the Middle Ages: A Guide to Research on French and Occitan Song, 1100–1400*, Garland Medieval Bibliographies 19, Garland Reference Library in the Humanities 1102, New York: Garland.
Szendrei, Janka (2007), '"'Altius canuntur?": Durandus on the Performance of the *Te deum*', in Terence Bailey and László Dobszay (eds), *Studies in Medieval Chant and Liturgy in Honour of David Hiley*, Musicological Studies 87, Budapest: Institute for Musicology; Ottawa: Institute of Medieval Music, pp. 413–24.
Taylor, Ronald J. (1969), '*Minnesang*—Performance and Interpretation', in Stanley N. Werbow (ed.), *Formal Aspects of Medieval German Poetry: A Symposium*, Austin, TX: University of Texas Press, pp. 9–26.
Thornton, Barbara and Rogers, Nigel (1984), 'The Singer's View', *Early Music*, **12**, pp. 523–25.
Tischler, Hans (1968), 'A Propos a Critical Edition of the Parisian Organa Dupla', *Acta musicologica*, **40**, pp. 28–43.
Tischler, Hans (1969), 'How Were Notre Dame Clausulae Performed?', *Music and Letters*, **50**, pp. 273–77.
Tischler, Hans (1973a), 'Musica Ficta in the Parisian Organa', *Journal of Music Theory*, **17**, pp. 310–18.
Tischler, Hans (1973b), '"Musica Ficta" in the Thirteenth Century', *Music and Letters*, **54**, pp. 38–56.
Tischler, Hans (1982), 'A Propos Meter and Rhythm in the Ars Antiqua', *Journal of Music Theory*, **26**, pp. 313–29.
Tischler, Hans (1983), 'Communication', *Journal of the American Musicological Society*, **36**, pp. 341–344.
Tischler, Hans and Rosenberg, Samuel N. (eds) (1981), *Chanter m'estuet: Songs of the Trouvères*, Bloomington, IN: Indiana University Press.
Toliver, Brooks (1992), 'Improvisation in the Madrigals of the *Rossi Codex*', *Acta musicologica*, **64**, pp. 165–76.
Treitler, Leo (1964), 'The Polyphony of St. Martial', *Journal of the American Musicological Society*, **17**, pp. 29–42.
Treitler, Leo (1968), 'A Reply to Theodore Karp', *Acta musicologica*, **40**, pp. 227–29.
Treitler, Leo (1979), 'Regarding Meter and Rhythm in the *Ars Antiqua*', *Musical Quarterly*, **65**, pp. 524–58.
Treitler, Leo (1980), 'Communication', *Journal of the American Musicological Society*, **33**, pp. 607–11.
Treitler, Leo (1983), 'Regarding "A Propos Meter and Rhythm in the Arts Antiqua"', *Journal of Music Theory*, **27**, pp. 215–22.
Van der Werf, Hendrik (1965), 'The Trouvère Chansons as Creations of a Notationless Musical Culture', *Current Musicology*, **1**, pp. 61–68.

Van der Werf, Hendrik (1970), 'Concerning the Measurability of Medieval Music', *Current Musicology*, **10**, pp. 69–73.
Van der Werf, Hendrik (1972), *The Chansons of the Troubadours and Trouvères*, Utrecht: A Oosthoek's Uitgeversmaatschappij NV.
Van der Werf, Hendrik (1982), 'Review of *Chanter m'estuet: Songs of the Trouvères*, ed. Hans Tischler and Samuel N. Rosenberg', *Journal of the American Musicological Society*, **35**, pp. 539–54.
Van der Werf, Hendrik (1984a), 'Communication', *Journal of the American Musicological Society*, **37**, pp. 206–08.
Van der Werf, Hendrik (1984b), *The Extant Troubadour Melodies: Transcriptions and Essays for Performers and Scholars*, Rochester: the author.
Van Dijk, S.A. (1950), 'Saint Bernard and the *Instituta patrum* of St. Gall', *Musica disciplina*, **4**, pp. 99–109.
Van Dijk, S.J.P. (1952), 'Medieval Terminology and Methods of Psalm Singing', *Musica disciplina*, **6**, pp. 7–26.
Van Dijk, S.J.P. (1963), 'Gregory the Great: Founder of the Urban *Schola Cantorum*', *Ephemerides liturgicae*, **77**, pp. 345–56.
Vollaerts, J.W.A. (1960), *Rhythmic Proportions in Early Medieval Ecclesiastical Chant* (2nd edn), Leiden: E.J. Brill.
Von Ramm, Andrea (1976), 'Singing Early Music', *Early Music*, **4**, pp. 12–15.
Von Ramm, Andrea (1980), 'Style in Early Music Singing', *Early Music*, **8**, pp. 17–20.
Waite, William G. (1952a), 'Communication', *Journal of the American Musicological Society*, **5**, pp. 273–76.
Waite, William G. (1952b), 'Discantus, Copula, Organum', *Journal of the American Musicological Society*, **5**, pp. 77–87.
Waite, William G. (1954), *The Rhythm of Twelfth-Century Polyphony: Its Theory and Practice*, Yale Studies in the History of Music 2, New Haven, CT: Yale University Press.
Weakland, Rembert G. (1961), 'The Rhythmic Modes and Medieval Latin Drama', *Journal of the American Musicological Society*, **14**, pp. 131–46.
Weakland, Rembert G. (1966/1978), 'The Performance of Ambrosian Chant in the 12th Century', in Jan LaRue (ed.), *Aspects of Medieval and Renaissance Music: A Birthday Offering to Gustave Reese*, New York: W.W. Norton, pp. 856–66; reprint edition: New York: Pendragon Press, 1978.
Weber, Jerome F. (1992), 'The Phonograph as Witness to the Performance Practice of Chant', in László Dobszay, Ágnes Papp and Ferenc Sebó (eds), *International Musicological Society Study Group Cantus Planus: Papers Read at the Fourth Meeting, Pécs, Hungary, 3–8 September 1990*, Budapest: Hungarian Academy of Sciences Institute for Musicology, pp. 607–12.
Wegman, Rob C. (1989), 'Concerning Tempo in the English Polyphonic Mass *c.* 1420–70', *Acta musicologica*, **61**, pp. 40–65.
Wegman, Rob C. (1992), 'What Is "Acceleratio Mensurae"?', *Music and Letters*, **73**, pp. 515–24.
Wegman, Rob C. (2000), 'Different Strokes for Different Folks? On Tempo and Diminution in Fifteenth-Century Music', *Journal of the American Musicological Society*, **53**, pp. 461–505.
Welker, Lorenz (1990), 'Some Aspects of the Notation and Performance of German Song around 1400', *Early Music*, **18**, pp. 235–46.
Wellesz, Egon (1963), 'The Interpretation of Plainchant', *Music and Letters*, **44**, pp. 343–49.
White, John Reeves (1969), 'Performing Fourteenth-Century Music', *College Music Symposium*, **9**, pp. 85–90.
Williams, Sarah Jane (1968), 'Vocal Scoring in the Chansons of Machaut', *Journal of the American Musicological Society*, **21**, pp. 251–57.
Wishart, Stevie (1992), 'Echoes of the Past in the Present: Surviving Traditional Instruments and Performance Practices as a Source for Performers of Medieval Secular Monody', in Tess Knighton

and David Fallows (eds), *Companion to Medieval and Renaissance Music*, London: J.M. Dent, pp. 210–22.

Wright, Craig (1979), *Music at the Court of Burgundy 1364–1419: A Documentary History*, Musicological Studies 28, Henryville, Ottawa and Binningen: Institute of Mediaeval Music.

Wright, Craig (1981), 'Voices and Instruments in the Art Music of Northern France during the 15th Century: A Conspectus', in Daniel Heartz and Bonnie Wade (eds), *International Musicological Society Report of the Twelfth Congress, Berkeley 1977*, Kassel, Basel and London: Bärenreiter and the American Musicological Society, pp. 643–49.

Wright, Craig (1989), *Music and Ceremony at Notre Dame of Paris 500–1500*, Cambridge: Cambridge University Press.

Wright, Laurence (1977), 'The Medieval Gittern and Citole: A Case of Mistaken Identity', *Galpin Society Journal*, **30**, pp. 8–42.

Wright, Laurence (1979), 'Sculptures of Medieval Fiddles at Gargilesse', *Galpin Society Journal*, **32**, pp. 66–76.

Yudkin, Jeremy (1983), 'The Rhythm of Organum Purum', *Journal of Musicology*, **2**, pp. 355–76.

Yudkin, Jeremy (1984), 'The Anonymous of St. Emmeram and Anonymous IV on the *Copula*', *Musical Quarterly*, **70**, pp. 1–22.

Part I
Plainchant

[1]

The performance of plainchant
Some preliminary observations of the new era
Lance W. Brunner

In the spring of 1980 I attended a lecture on the problems of producing and performing medieval liturgical drama, given by a very competent director of a university collegium. Although admittedly not a chant specialist, he had successfully directed several performances of liturgical dramas with amateur groups and wanted to share with others his solutions to the problems encountered. The presentation concluded with a stunning performance of excerpts from various dramas. One remark disturbed me, however, because it revealed what seems to be a common misconception. The director said that he had had to reject certain indications of rhythm in a performing edition (presumably distinctions between quavers and crotchets) because he 'could not achieve the smooth-flowing sound that we have all come to associate with chant'. The sound that he was referring to, no doubt, was the one familiar from modern recordings of chant, most of which are either by, or heavily influenced by, the Schola of the Abbey of St Peter in Solesmes. The common misconception is that the Solesmes method is the one 'authentic' way to sing chant.

No area of performance practice, of course, has ignited more controversy than chant, particularly with regard to its rhythm. In the past, however, the fires have usually been safely contained within the scholarly literature. Until recently, recordings of chant continued to flow along undaunted, in the smooth, dignified Solesmes sound 'that we have all come to associate with chant', until the scholarly debate had all but died out. Ewald Jammers, a lifelong champion of an alternative to the Solesmes approach, lamented this triumph of prevailing practice with regard to rhythm in his article 'Gregorianischer Rhythmus: Was ist das?'—the irony in the title reflecting his frustration at the failure of choirs to adopt well-founded alternatives advanced by him and other scholars.[1]

There are now strong indications that the fairly consistent approach to the performance of chant—at least that available on recordings—is finally giving way to the exploration of new possibilities that incorporate the results of recent scholarly research. This was the encouraging assessment advanced by the distinguished chant authority Mary Berry in her impressive 'review' in this journal of the first 75 years of recorded chant performances.[2] Recordings are one of the best barometers of performance practice in chant, and Dr Berry is undoubtedly one of the world's greatest authorities on chant recordings. According to her, we are now entering a new era of performance practice in chant, as the era of 'Old Solesmes' comes to a close.[3] The impetus for the change may well have been the liturgical reforms of the Second Vatican Council, which initially threatened the continuity of chant performance. The temporary break that followed was, in Dr Berry's words, 'something of a blessing in disguise. People have had time to forget the details of a style that might have perpetuated itself for a long time to come'.[4] The opportunity was now at hand to incorporate some of the impressive research that has taken place in the past 25 years or so, of which only minor details had been assimilated 'almost imperceptibly' into the old Solesmes tradition. The new era is heralded by the proliferation of eager performers, both professional and amateur, whose good, new ideas make the time ripe for another Gregorian congress, like the magnificent congress of 1904, associated with Pius X's directive to restore chant melodies according to the earliest manuscripts and traditions.[5]

Dr Berry paints an exhilarating picture of our current situation, and rightly so, but it seems to me that her vision of future trends in performance practice may be too narrowly conceived, for it is still shaped by developments (albeit significant ones) within the Solesmes orbit. The new era she envisages will be based on the research of Dom Eugène Cardine, through whose work 'the whole picture of performance as it is likely to have been at the time of the earliest musical manuscripts is gradually coming into new focus'.[6] In Dr Berry's enthusiastic acceptance of this research I question whether alternatives to what may amount to the 'new Solesmes' method will be considered seriously. She dismisses, for example, the most recent recording by the Schola Antiqua (*Tenth-Century Liturgical Chant*, Nonesuch H-71348) because it takes into account neither Cardine's own research nor his criticism of the approach they adopted.

In my opinion the Schola Antiqua recording is one of the most important developments in recent years in the performance practice of chant and needs to be given serious consideration. Its importance lies not so much in the presentation of new alternatives (many of which have been advanced in scholarly literature), but in their presentation in *performance* rather than on the printed page. Whether or not the research is open to question (which it certainly is) seems less important at the moment than the availability of a fresh approach that will reach beyond a relatively small group of specialists to a wider audience. Such an approach may well prove to be a catalyst for much-needed re-evaluation of long-standing issues. If so, the Schola Antiqua's recording should accelerate our entry into the new era, broaden our constricted vision and make the study of chant all the more immediate and exciting.

On the threshold of this new era, I would like to offer a few preliminary observations on some of the basic practical and aesthetic aspects of the singing of chant. In the past, important problems associated with so-called authentic performance were never clearly defined, which led to unnecessary confusion and controversy. It is unlikely that we shall ever find unequivocal solutions to many of the problems, but we need at least to pose the right questions and consider possible alternatives in order to achieve intelligent performances.

A good way to begin is to consider the decisions one must make in order to bring a performance of chant to life while remaining true to the original intentions and spirit of the music. The following three areas seems to be particularly important because of the range of possibilities involved and the effect that the decisions have on the sound: rhythm, ornamental neumes, and voice production. Issues raised by these three also apply to decisions about such matters as tempo, dynamic level, expression and the place of performance, each of which can have a strong effect on the character of the performance.

Unquestionably the greatest controversy associated with performance practice in chant has been over rhythm. The literature on the subject is so extensive that it cannot be presented here in anything more than a thumb-nail sketch.[7] The controversy has been fuelled by the desire to discover *the* authentic rhythm of chant. To understand why this caused such problems, one needs to know something about the manuscript tradition and the conditions under which the restoration of chant was carried out in this century.

Latin chant has been sung in the celebration of the liturgy over vast areas and for many centuries, and the ways in which it was sung must have varied in different places and periods.[8] Moreover, the manuscript tradition suggests that there was a fundamental change in the approach to rhythm during the 11th century. Many of the earliest manuscripts—dating from the 10th and early 11th centuries—contain rhythmic indications, which began to drop out in later manuscripts. Defining the precise nature of the rhythm in early manuscripts is difficult, but that there was a fundamental change seems clear. To talk about a single authentic rhythmic interpretation in the face of this evidence is misleading; if we are concerned about re-creating performances as they once were (or rather, might have been), then we must acknowledge that there are different approaches that have legitimate claims to authenticity.

The restoration of the chant melodies for use in the liturgy, however, demanded a single solution. The stage was set for controversy in the general guide-lines established by Pius X in his second *motu proprio* (25 April 1904), where he called for restoration to be undertaken 'in accordance with the true text of the most ancient codices, in such a way, however, that due attention be given to the true tradition contained in the codices throughout the centuries, and to the practical usage of contemporary liturgy'.[9] This directive offered a number of possibilities and the Papal Commission established to restore the chant became sharply divided. The Solesmes interests were clearly with the earliest manuscripts, while other members of the commission pressed for modification according to later traditions.[10] In most discussions about chant rhythm, 'authentic' seems to be most frequently equated with that chant preserved in the earliest manuscripts with musical notation. Perhaps confusion in the future can be avoided by making this clear.[11]

Numerous theories have been formulated in response to the debate over chant rhythm. These can be grouped into three approaches: equalist, mensuralist and Solesmes. The equalist approach was officially adopted for the Vatican Edition and was worked out by Dom Joseph Pothier, who headed the Papal Commission for the restoration.[12] Rhythmic flow is determined by the text: accented syllables receive the stress, and for this reason the method is often referred to as 'accentualist'. The free rhythm reflects the oratorical nature of the chant. In melismatic passages the first note of composite neumes receives the stress.

The mensuralist approach actually represents a wide range of theories grouped together because of a common tenet that chant was measured in distinct rhythmic values. Theories range from interpretations of chant in strict 4/4 metre with balanced phrases to free alternation of rhythmic values; from two note values to four or more.[13] Most recent mensuralist interpretations rely on two basic values that stand in the proportion 2:1, that is, with the long value twice that of the short.

What we usually refer to as the Solesmes approach is that based on the principles worked out by Dom André Mocquereau and carried on by his pupil Dom Joseph Gajard.[14] Here the free rhythm and basically equal note values of the equalist interpretation are retained, though certain notes are singled out to be lengthened slightly or doubled. A more fundamental difference between the Solesmes and equalist methods is that in Solesmes the rhythmic organization of the melodies is considered to be independent of textual accent. Pulses are divided into groups of twos and threes, each group beginning with a so-called ictus or impulse, marked in the Solesmes editions, when it is not obvious from other indications, by a vertical stroke (an *episēma*). Rhythmic flow is produced by an alternation between *arsis* (up-beat) and *thesis* (down-beat), which occur on different levels, the two- and three-note groups combining freely to produce larger rhythmic gestures: incises, members, phrases and periods. Since these notions cannot be documented historically, the approach has come under repeated attack from those outside the Solesmes camp and, as Dr Berry suggested, Mocquereau's principles are losing ground now even at Solesmes itself.[15] Nevertheless, because the Solesmes monks have enjoyed a virtual monopoly of performing editions and recordings, their ideas have been the most influential in shaping our conception of rhythm in chant.[16]

New theories have been formulated at Solesmes that will eventually transform the old method and, as mentioned earlier, may well usher in a new era of performance practice in chant. The theories are those of Dom Eugène Cardine, monk of Solesmes and professor of Gregorian palaeography at the Pontifical Institute of Sacred Music in Rome.[17] Cardine's theories are compatible with the old Solesmes method in that the melodies flow smoothly in a series of basically equal notes, but with slight variations in duration, or

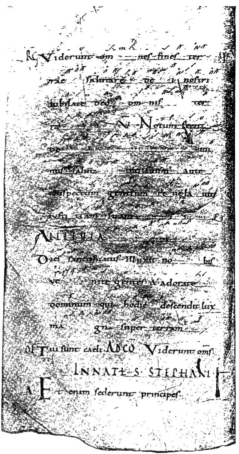

2 St Gall, Stiftsbibliothek, 359, p.40 (before 920)

agogic nuances, in accordance with information provided in the earliest manuscripts. Unlike the older method, however, where the rhythm was marked by a series of two- and three-note groups not necessarily reflected in the manuscripts, Cardine's formulations rely exclusively on palaeography; the 'secrets' of Gregorian rhythm, as he sees it, were always there to be read in the way the melody was captured in the neumatic notation. Cardine regards the notation in the earliest manuscripts as corresponding directly to the hand gestures (cheironomy) of the directors of medieval chant choirs; when interpreted in this way, the early notation reveals important information about the rhythm and expression of the melodies. Consider, for example, the notation of the melisma on the first syllable of 'Dominus' from the verse of the Christmas gradual *Viderunt omnes* in illus.2; it is neither a series of individual symbols, one for each note, nor a continuous unit, but a succession of neumatic groups. Cardine refers to this division or cutting up of the melody into smaller units as 'coupure neumatique' (neumatic caesura) and contends that it was by no means an arbitrary procedure, indeed that the scribes, in the way they formed and separated the neumes (as a director would have shaped phrases with hand gestures during performance), were communicating significant and even very subtle information about how the melody should be articulated.[18] Evidence has been presented that even the simple neumes in syllabic passages appear in different shapes and sizes in a consistent and logical way that may imply subtle rhythmic nuances.[19] What makes Cardine's theories so compelling is that they have been founded on the most extensive and meticulous palaeographical research ever undertaken.

As a result of this intensive research, Cardine has come out strongly against a mensural interpretation of chant rhythm in the earliest manuscripts.[20] He agrees that they contain clear indications of long and short note values but stresses that these were indications for subtle nuances—slight modifications of a basic pulse—and could not possibly represent strict proportional relationships. Mensuralists have not yet, to my knowledge, refuted Cardine's criticism, and recent recordings of mensural interpretations still rely on theories that take no account of the latest research. This research has focused on two categories of evidence that support mensural interpretations: indications in the manuscripts themselves and the testimony of the medieval theorists. To understand the nature of the difficulties with respect to rhythm, we need to look at each category more closely.

The debate over chant rhythm has revolved round a relatively small number of manuscripts from the 10th and early 11th centuries that contain indications of rhythm. Among the most frequently used are the family of manuscripts associated with the Swiss monastery of St Gall and the Gradual Laon 239.[21] Illus.2 provides a good example of the type of information contained in these early manuscripts. Since the notational system at this time did not indicate precise pitches but only general melodic direction, a singer had to know the melody in advance. But the notation is more than a simple memory aid, since it gives subtle performance directions. The two basic neumes used to indicate relationships of individual pitches are the *virga* (originally indicating a higher pitch, and corresponding to the acute accent), and the *punctum* (a lower pitch, derived from the grave accent). Lengthening the duration of the pitch is indicated by simple modification of these neumes: an *episēma* is added to the *virga*, and the *punctum* is replaced by a horizontal stroke (or *tractulus*) (see ex.1). In melismatic sections these simple neumes are usually combined into composite neumes. A *climacus* (a pattern of three descending pitches), for example, can have various combinations of long and short values depending upon how these simple symbols are arranged. Several composite neumes can be found in the gradual *Viderunt omnes* (illus.2) and the possible rhythmic interpretations according to mensuralist theories are shown in ex.2 (L = long, S = short). Numerous examples of other composite neumes, in various forms, can be seen in illus.2.[22] The same information about rhythm is contained in the Gradual Laon 239 (see illus.3), but the notation differs from that of St Gall in some important details; the simple neumes in Laon 239 are shown in ex.3.[23]

In addition to the neumes themselves, the early manuscripts contain rhythmic information in the form of letters, referred to usually as 'litterae significativae' or 'Romanus letters'.[24] The letters are abbreviations for performance directions that embrace pitch and intensity as well as duration. The most common letters referring to duration are *c* (for *cito* or *celeriter*, [sing] quickly), which is used often in illus.2, and *t* (for *tenere* or *trahere*, to hold or draw out), which is used to indicate lengthening of the *virga*—as well as in other contexts—in Laon 239 (see illus.3). The mensuralists contend that the indications of length in both the neumes and the letters point to clearly measured long and short values (that is, proportional values), not subtle nuances. To corroborate this view, most mensuralists have turned to medieval treatises on music.

Medieval theorists often drew analogies between chant and the proportional rhythm of classical quantitative poetry.[25] Berno of Reichenau (d 1048), for example, wrote that just as in poetry a verse is woven together with a certain length of feet, so chant is put together with an appropriate and agreeable joining of short and long tones'.[26] Guido of Arezzo, in Chapter 15 of his *Micrologus*, commented that 'one ought to beat time to a song as though by metrical feet'.[27] Mensuralists have used these and similar passages to

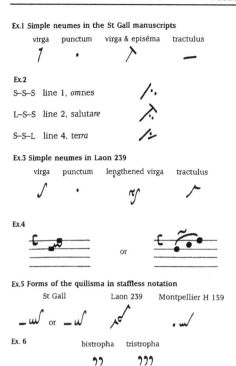

prove that chant flowed in proportional rhythm—a long having twice the duration of a short value—and have claimed therefore that the indications of rhythm in the manuscripts themselves must represent these distinct values.

Interpretation of such seemingly unequivocal passages, however, is fraught with problems. When a medieval theorist drew an analogy to classical poetry, it is difficult to determine whether he was actually describing current practice or simply paying homage to the lost tradition of quantitative verse—trying to salvage terms and concepts from that tradition by applying them in whatever fashion to current musical practice. Theoretical references to possible proportional rhythm involve other problems as well. Richard Crocker has pointed out the danger of translating such familiar-looking terms as *musica, numerus, rhythmica* and *metrica*, since their English cognates, as we know them, have undergone considerable change over the centuries.[28] Crocker also observes that the theorists' tentative and cursory discussion of proportional rhythm suggests only a tenuous connection between such doctrines and the chant.[29] A further warning about the theoretical references to rhythm was issued by Bruno Stäblein, who notes that many of the musical examples cited in treatises are from late accretions to the liturgy (sequences and tropes, for example), and since these represent different categories of chant, one cannot assume that the same rules apply to the earlier Gregorian repertory.[30]

Mensuralists need to respond to these recent indictments of both the theoretical and palaeographical evidence for proportional rhythm. The same theoretical passages have been used to support a wealth of different interpretations, and the mensuralists must demonstrate not only that the theorists can be accepted as evidence for proportional rhythm in chant but that this rhythm was part of the living practice of chant. They must also meet the challenge to proportional rhythm that Cardine has mounted through his intensive study of palaeography.

But the burden of critical re-evaluation does not rest entirely with the mensuralists. Cardine's theories also need objective review by a broad range of scholars for whom the weight of the venerable tradition of Solesmes is not as great as it is for the Benedictines who carry on that tradition. Wider discussion of rhythm in the earliest manuscripts should be easier now, since the *Graduale triplex* has been published.[31] Furthermore, a number of Cardine's ideas need to be clarified and synthesized if the theories are to find acceptance outside the Solesmes orbit. There seems to be considerable latitude, according to Cardine's precepts, in how one translates into sound the subtle nuances and rhythmic impulses implied by the neumes.[32]

A reasonable question at this point is: how can a choir director who is not steeped in the literature on chant rhythm choose from among the tangled web of approaches advanced by scholars, until a consensus is reached, or—as seems more likely—until the various alternatives have been re-evaluated and clearly laid out for practising musicians? One solution would be to avoid the thorniest problems by adopting an equalist approach, which was clearly predominant (though not used exclusively) after about 1100.[33] One can see at a glance, for example, how the numerous indications of rhythm in the earliest manuscripts had all but disappeared in later sources by comparing the gradual *Viderunt omnes* in manuscripts like St Gall 359 or Laon 239 (illus.2 and 3) with the 12th-century manuscript Graz 807 (illus.4). In basing a performance on the later manuscript an 'authentic' interpretation would no

3 Laon, Bibliothèque Municipale, 239, f.10 (c930)

4 Graz, Universitätsbibliothek, 807, f.14v (c1150)

doubt involve an equalist approach. But if the urge to use the earlier manuscripts proves too great (and the temptation is even greater now that the *Graduale triplex* is available), then one must come to terms with those puzzling rhythmic details in the manuscripts.

It seems to me that the most attractive solution, given our current state of knowledge, is that adopted by R. John Blackley in an earlier Schola Antiqua recording (*A Guide to Gregorian Chant*),[34] and also by Pro Cantione Antiqua (*Sacred Monophony*).[35] Neither group settled on a single approach, but both demonstrated important alternatives outlined in the scholarly literature. I do not mean to suggest that we ought to change approaches whimsically with each piece or try out something new in each programme, but rather to emphasize that we do have options which ought to be explored through performance as well as in published research. We are not bound now by official decree to adopt a single approach, as the liturgical reformers during the first part of this century were, but can look at chant as a historical phenomenon, as we do other repertories such as early polyphony. Intelligent performers have a right, perhaps even an obligation, to explore solutions to performance problems and to work with scholars, especially in early music where written evidence is largely absent or perplexingly vague.

These remarks regarding rhythm are just as valid for other areas of performance, particularly the interpretation of those special neumes that are often considered to be ornamental and whose meaning is another controversial aspect of chant.[36] Ornamental neumes occur primarily in the oldest manuscripts and, like indications of rhythm, began to disappear or change character with the development of staff notation during the 11th century. Again, despite the numerous alternatives advanced by scholars, the interpretations of the old Solesmes method have dominated recorded performances and conditioned our conception of ornament in chant. There are two principal types of ornamental neumes, liquescent and repercussive, and there are the following individual neumes: *quilisma, oriscus, salicus, pressus* and *trigon*.[37] The interpretation of these neumes presents a wide range of problems, of which only a few characteristic samples can be discussed here.

The *quilisma* provides an interesting example of the type of interpretative problem associated with ornamental neumes. It occurs as the middle element in a three-note configuration, usually ascending by step through a minor 3rd.[38] In modern chant notation it is indicated by either of the forms shown in ex.4. The early staffless forms vary according to the regional notation; some basic types include those in ex.5. Most have in common a zig-zag pattern that gives the impression of a modern trill or mordent. Scholars have advanced many theories about the execution of the *quilisma*,[39] based on the shape of the neumes themselves, statements by theorists, and the etymology of the term (from the Greek *kylisma*, rolling). Suggestions have included interpretations of the *quilisma* as a trill or mordent, a glissando, a passing-note, and even a type of voice production involving a break in the voice.[40] Despite the variety of theories, until recently this neume has invariably been sung in the Solesmes manner, that is, as a light passing note with the preceding note lengthened slightly. The Schola Antiqua's *Tenth-Century Liturgical Chart* is among the first recordings to interpret the *quilisma* as a trill or mordent. As in the matter of rhythm, until the various theories have been re-evaluated and conclusions clearly formulated, it seems to me that performers should feel free to explore some of the hypotheses on the interpretation of this and many other ornamental neumes.

The most common forms of repercussive neume are the *bistropha* and *tristropha* (ex.6; the *tristropha* occurs in *Viderunt omnes* on '*om*nes' and 'jubila*te*'; see illus.2 lines 1 and 3, the first of which has an *episēma* added to the last element). These neumes occur on a single pitch, usually C or F, and are generally understood to represent the reiteration of the pitch.[41] Even the old Solesmes method acknowledged the original reiterative nature of the repercussive neumes, but, because of the difficulty choirs might encounter in performance, it was suggested that the elements of the neume be joined together and sustained as a single tone of double or triple length. Reiteration is implied both by the separation of the elements within the neumes themselves and by certain references by medieval theorists. The passage cited most often is by Aurelian of Réôme, writing in the middle of the ninth century, in which he admonished the wise singer when singing a *tristropha* to 'make a quick, threefold pulse, like a beating hand'.[42] Reiteration of the notes seems clearly implied, but Aurelian's simile 'like a beating hand' is vague and subject to a wide range of interpretations, as some recent recordings suggest: reiteration ranges from barely perceptible pulses (Choralschola Münsterschwarzach), through gentle but clearly articulated attacks (Pro Cantione Antiqua), to lively glottal stops (Schola Antiqua).[43]

How does one settle on the right interpretation? This question is not, I think, as perplexing as other interpretative problems, because once one has decided to reiterate the individual notes of a repercussive neume, then the aesthetic framework established by the tempo and character of the performance will suggest appropriate solutions to articulation, or at least limit the range of possibilities. A lively performance, like that of the Schola Antiqua, for example, would seem to demand rather crisp reiteration; whereas, in the slow, dignified Solesmes interpretations, a brisk staccato would clearly be out of character. If this assessment is correct, then I think the broader implications for the performance of chant are worth considering.

Aesthetic predispositions have surely influenced research and coloured performances in more ways than most scholars and singers have been willing to admit. Florid ornaments, spirited performance, virtuoso singing—all in evidence in medieval documents, even though their exact nature remains elusive[44]—are outside the aesthetic framework within which the modern restoration of chant was carried out. Moreover, a number of scholars have speculated that early medieval chant was not as securely diatonic as it appears in later manuscripts with staff notation, and that many of the puzzling symbols, especially those associated with ornamental neumes, involved microtonal inflections.[45] Such interpretations, alien to Western musical training and conditioning, could never have been considered seriously by the monastic scholars who helped create and shape the old Solesmes style, a style in which the guiding principle was, as Heinrich Besseler put it, 'to smooth over as much as possible all the rough edges with a soft legato'.[46] Even interpretations according to Cardine's new theories are no doubt heavily influenced by the aesthetic world of Solesmes in which they evolved. When the frame of reference is expanded to include a wider range of possibilities, as in the recording by the Schola Antiqua, bolder interpretations of the ornaments, involving mordents and microtones, are very convincing.[47]

Perhaps the biggest concession to modern tastes made in attempts to achieve authenticity has been the least controversial. It seems to me that it is in the realm of voice production—the quality of sound—more than interpretations of rhythm and ornamental neumes, that our modern performances of chant are set apart from likely medieval ones. There has been relatively little discussion of this aspect of chant owing, no doubt, to lack of evidence, but also because 'correct' voice production is something that is generally agreed upon in any given time, however drastically this aspect of the singing voice may have changed from one generation to the next. As Frank Ll. Harrison has pointed out, in such important aspects of performance of liturgical music as vocal timbre and pronunciation, we have hardly begun to ask the right questions.[48] It is naïve and misleading to boast of modern performances of chant being authentic because of progress in our understanding of rhythm or ornaments without considering the quality of sound. And on these grounds I think it would be wise to abandon the notion of our ever achieving authenticity in performance, since that claim is a constant source of unnecessary controversy. If the quest for authentic interpretations of rhythm

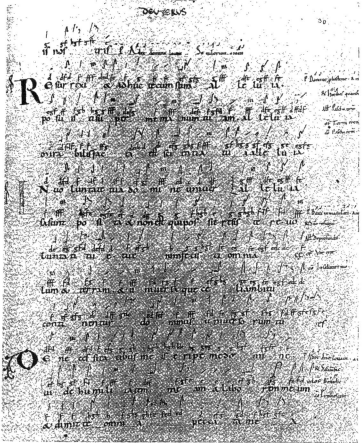

5 Montpellier, Bibliothèque de l'École de Médecine, H 159, f.30 (11th century)

and ornaments is perilous and uncertain, the attempt to discover authentic voice production is hopeless. Voice production and performing style in general are not even hinted at in the notation, and as Michael Morrow has observed with respect to secular music in an earlier article in this journal, we cannot hope to recapture it.[49] This realization is hardly likely to discourage even the most sceptical performers from undertaking 'imaginative reconstructions' of chant, but intelligent performers should take into consideration the two basic approaches to voice production.

The first of these is the one almost invariably (and often unconsciously) adopted, that is, simply our current practice of voice production. Andrea von Ramm has shown that there is a wide range of choices available in singing early music, although this range is seldom explored.[50] In chant, singing that is both appropriate and beautiful is generally based on a sound that is well supported and focused (although more subdued than in later music); clear, open vowels; and a controlled vibrato. It is easy to find historical justification for such characteristics, since throughout the Middle Ages writers on music in various ways exhorted singers to sing beautifully.[51] One of the earliest medieval writers on the subject was Isidore of Seville (d 636), whose description of the perfect voice as being one that was 'high (or bright), sweet and clear' was taken up by others throughout the Middle Ages.[52] Regardless of what was understood to be sweet and clear at that time, we can gear our performances to present-day interpretations of Isidore's dictum, as well as to the more elaborate descriptions of other medieval writers, to produce analogous aesthetic responses at least. The fine coloratura singing on the Schola Antiqua's *Tenth-Century Liturgical Chant* could be justified on such grounds, even if by current standards it is a bit too passionate for use in the service.

The second approach to voice production is to explore alternatives to our modern ideals which may have echoed in the naves of early medieval churches. Such an approach is seldom attempted because it is so highly speculative. There are numerous indications, however, that the Middle Ages knew a wealth of vocal styles (some falling woefully short of Isidore's *vox perfecta*) and also that different ideals were held in different regions.[53] Written accounts of styles of the period are too vague a source from which to attempt to re-create the sound, but speculation as to what that sound may have been like can be based on the range of possibilities suggested by musics from other cultures.

Two fascinating examples that endeavour to re-create a realistic medieval sound ideal in this way were not mentioned in Dr Berry's survey. These are the two chant selections on L'Anthologie Sonore, the first large-scale history of music in sound. The excerpts (*Alleluia. Pascha nostrum* and the gradual *Adiuvabit eam*) were recorded in the 1930s under Guillaume de Van and the general artistic direction of Curt Sachs.[54] The approach to rhythm is clearly mensural and there are bold interpretations of ornamental neumes.[55] But it is the unusual vocal quality that sets these performances apart from other recorded performances—even those of the Schola Antiqua—which explore similar approaches to rhythm and ornament. The de Van–Sachs performances seem to rely on non-Western singers and sound ideals to produce a tight, coarse vocal quality that seems primitive to Western ears. And this must surely have been the intention.

In an article entitled 'Primitive and Medieval Music: a Parallel',[56] Sachs sketches some very basic guidelines about how the study of music of other cultures can be used to deepen our understanding of early medieval music. The parallels he draws in the realms of voice production, melody, intonation and rhythm are fascinating, and although his observations concern secular music, many apply to liturgical music as well. In helping de Van prepare the performances for L'Anthologie Sonore, Sachs must have relied on his remarkable knowledge of world musics in making some of the most basic performance decisions. Our discussions of the wide range of possibilities associated with the performance of chant would be more meaningful now, at the dawn of the new era, if they could include ethnomusicologists.[57] The vigorous, primitive spirit captured in the de Van–Sachs performances is undoubtedly more akin to the fervent religious enthusiasm that charged the singing so passionately denounced by reformers during the Romanesque era than to the lush, highly polished, detached reflections on most modern recordings. But even if the sound on L'Anthologie Sonore is more realistically medieval than that which we have come to associate with chant, would we choose to live with such exotic voice production, so alien to our own ideals of beautiful singing? The answer in most cases would clearly be no.

In making decisions about voice production and other interpretative problems it is of some importance to consider how chant will *function* in a performance. The need for such consideration is greater now, because the context in which chant is performed has broadened in the past few decades, and the implications of this phenomenon have not been widely discussed. The function of chant within the liturgy has always been clear: the chant should be a vehicle to project the sacred texts and enhance devotion. Although performing styles have no doubt changed drastically, along with musical style, since the Middle Ages, during any given period sacred music had to conform to certain norms that were considered appropriate for worship. Pius X's directives in this century were broad enough to allow the restoration of the chant without jeopardizing its primary function. The restoration created a new, living tradition of chant, based not only on what could be salvaged from past traditions but also on a performing style deemed appropriate for contemporary worship.[58]

The growth of interest in early music has created another context for the performance of chant, that is, the concert. Since in this context the function of the chant is no longer liturgical, but rather to reveal an important tradition within our musical heritage, performers have more freedom to explore the many dimensions of that tradition. Performances can be based on individual manuscripts from different periods, and various solutions to interpretative problems and alternative methods of voice production can be tested. Performances designed to reveal chant to large audiences may choose, in effect, to blend historically creative reconstructions of rhythm and ornamentation with 20th-century sound ideals, as in the recordings of the Schola Antiqua. Groups more closely involved with research, however, such as university collegia, have the fewest constraints and might want to try to come as close as possible to medieval sound ideals with the aid of ethnomusicology.

It is this broadening of interest in the performance of chant, perhaps even more than the discoveries of Cardine, that has opened up a new era. Since the Second Vatican Council, chant has no longer been heard in most churches, and hence its performance as a historical phenomenon takes on greater importance. As Dr Berry has suggested, this is indeed an exciting time in the history of performance practice in chant. I also agree that the time is right for a Gregorian congress where a broad spectrum of scholars and performers can come together for constructive discussion about our current situation and future goals. And I wonder if the meeting of the International Musicological Society in Strasbourg in 1982 might not provide an appropriate forum for such discussion.

[1] *Archiv für Musikwissenschaft*, 31 (1974), pp.290–311
[2] M. Berry, 'The restoration of the chant and seventy-five years of recording', *EM* 7/2 (April 1979), pp.197–217
[3] *Ibid*, pp.205–7
[4] *Ibid*, p.207
[5] *Ibid*, p.209
[6] *Ibid*, p.205
[7] For an extensive survey of the literature on rhythm, see J. Rayburn, *Gregorian Chant: a History of the Controversy concerning its Rhythm* (New York, 1964). Gustave Reese's summary of the basic approaches to chant rhythm in the early 20th century in his *Music in the Middle Ages* (New York, 1940) is still quite useful. David Hiley's terse survey of the controversy over rhythm in 'Notation', § III(1), *The New Grove*, 13, pp.351–4, incorporates more recent scholarly positions.
[8] This important point was voiced by Anthony Milner in his review of the Schola Antiqua's three recordings; see *EM* 8/1 (January 1980), pp.113–17.
[9] Cited in R. F. Hayburn, *Papal Legislation on Sacred Music* (Collegeville, Minnesota, 1979), p.256. Hayburn's study presents an impressive range of documentary material with connecting commentary. It is essential reading for anyone concerned with the massive efforts to restore chant that took place during the 19th and early 20th centuries.
[10] See P. Wagner, 'The Attack on the Vatican Edition: a Rejoinder', *Caecilia*, 87 (1960), pp.10–44, or the summary in Rayburn, *op cit*, pp.25–7. For more detailed documentation, see Hayburn, *op cit*, pp.258–65.
[11] Dom Jacques Froger was careful to qualify the word 'authentic' in his research report 'The Critical Edition of the Roman Gradual by the Monks of Solesmes', *Journal of the Plainsong and Mediaeval Music Society*, 1 (1978), pp.81–2.
[12] The 'Vatican Edition', or 'Editio vaticana', is the collective name for the volumes edited by the commission and published by the Vatican Press; the most important volumes include the *Kyriale* (1905), *Graduale* (1908) and *Antiphonale* (1912) (see Hayburn, *op cit*, pp.265–72). For a thoughtful and sympathetic appraisal of Dom Pothier's role in the project, see U. Bomm, 'Von Sinn und Wert der Editio Vaticana', *Musicus–Magister: Festgabe für Theobald Schrems* (Regensburg, 1963), pp.63–75.
[13] Various mensuralist theories are compared in W. Apel, *Gregorian Chant* (Bloomington, Ind., 1958), pp.129–32, and B. Stäblein, 'Thèses équalistes et mensuralistes', *Encyclopédie des musiques sacrées*, ed. J. Porte (Paris, 1969), 2, pp.80–98.
[14] Mocquereau's complex theories reached their final form in *Le nombre musical grégorien*, 2 vols. (Tournai, 1908–27); a summary and clearer explanation is provided in J. Gajard, *La méthode de Solesmes* (Paris, Tournai and Rome, 1956).
[15] Berry, *op cit*, p.207
[16] The Solesmes editions of chant use the same melodies as those in the Vatican Edition, but with rhythmic signs added to clarify the Solesmes method. The history of how the rhythmic signs gained official approval is fascinating; see Rayburn, *op cit*, pp.30–34, or Hayburn, *op cit*, pp.272–85. A critical edition of the melodies by the monks of Solesmes is near completion (see Froger, *op cit*).
[17] Cardine's principal work is 'Sémiologie grégorienne', *Études grégoriennes*, 11 (1970), pp.1–158 (originally published in Italian as a separate monograph, *Semiologia gregoriana* (Rome, 1968)); an English translation by Robert Fowells is now in the press and will be available from the Abbey of Solesmes (72300 Sablé-sur-Sarthe, France). A useful summary of his theories is found in S. Corbin, *Die Neumen*, Paléographie der Musik, i/3 (Cologne, 1977), pp.202–8. Intensive palaeographical research using Cardine's theories as guiding principles has been carried out by his pupils; see Berry, *op cit*, p.216, n.16, and Corbin, *op cit*, p.202. Cardine's recent Festschrift contains a number of articles by his students: see J. B. Göschl, ed., *Ut mens concordet voci: Festschrift Eugène Cardine zum 75. Geburtstag* (St. Ottilien, 1980).
[18] See Cardine, *op cit*, pp.48–55.
[19] See L. F. Heiman, 'The Rhythmic Value of the Final Descending Note after a Punctum in Neums of Codex 239 of the Library of Laon', *Études grégoriennes*, 13 (1972), p.166.
[20] See E. Cardine, 'Le chant grégorien est-il mesuré?', *Études grégoriennes*, 6 (1963), pp.7–38.
[21] J. W. A. Vollaerts, *Rhythmic Proportions in Early Medieval Ecclesiastical Chant* (Leiden, 1958), pp.3–23, contains a good survey of the so-called rhythmic manuscripts. Many of these manuscripts have appeared in facsimile in the important series Paléographie musicale (Solesmes, 1889–).
[22] Cardine, 'Sémiologie grégorienne', p.4, has a detailed table of the various forms of the most common neumes in the St Gall manuscripts. Cardine believes that the normal duration, or 'syllabic beat', is represented by the *virga* and *tractulus*, rather than the *punctum*, and that the *punctum* is a shortening of the basic beat, a *tractulus* with *episēma* a lengthening (*ibid*, p.16).
[23] The notation employed in Laon 239 has been generally referred to as 'Messine' or 'Metz' (after the important Carolingian centre), but in her discussion of the notation, Corbin introduces the term 'Lotharingian', since the notation is found in a much wider range of manuscripts than the term 'Metz' implies (*op cit*, pp.87–94). (In her article 'Neumatic Notations' (*The New Grove*, 13, p.137) the term is translated as 'Lorraine notation'.)
[24] See C. Floros, *Universale Neumenkunde*, 3 vols. (Kassel, 1970), 2, pp.134–69, for a discussion of these letters and a summary of previous research.
[25] The important passages containing references to rhythm are collected in J. G. Schmidt, *Haupttexte der gregorianischen Autoren betreffs Rhythmus* (Düsseldorf, 1921). Schmidt provides Latin texts with German translations; some of the editions he used have been superseded by new critical texts.
[26] Idcirco ut in metro certa pedum dimensione contexitur versus,

ita apta et concordabili brevium [et] longorum sonorum copulatione componitur cantus.' (M. Gerbert, *Scriptores ecclesiastici de musica sacra potissimum*, 3 vols. (St Blasien, 1784), 2, p.77)

[27]'Sicque opus est ut quasi metricis pedibus cantilena plaudatur.' (J. Smits van Waesberghe, ed., *Guidonis Aretini micrologus*, Corpus scriptorum de musica, 4 (Rome, 1955), p.164) For a list of some of the most important literature on this controversial passage see C. V. Palisca, ed., *Hucbald, Guido, and John on Music: Three Medieval Treatises*, trans. W. Babb (New Haven, 1978), p.55, n.39.

[28] See R. Crocker, '*Musica rhythmica* and *musica metrica* in Antique and Medieval Theory', *Journal of Music Theory*, 2 (1958), pp.2–23; in the light of Crocker's remarks, the interpretations of these passages by the devoted mensuralist Gregory Murray in 'Gregorian Rhythm in the Gregorian Centuries: the Literary Evidence', *Caecilia*, 84 (1957), pp.177–99, seem naïve and uncritical.

[29] Crocker, *op cit*, p.21

[30] Stäblein, *op cit*, pp.84ff; Stäblein enumerates other basic problems involved in interpreting the theoretical evidence.

[31] (Solesmes, 1979). The 'Triplex' is a modern edition of the *Graduale* (Solesmes, 1974) in which neumes from Laon 239 and one of several manuscripts from St Gall have been inscribed by Marie-Claire Billecocq and Rupert Fischer. This format, like Cardine's earlier *Graduel neumé* (Solesmes, 1972), is convenient, because it combines the ancient, staffless neumes (with their wealth of performance information) with readable editions (in which pitch was determined from collating later sources). Berry, *op cit*, p.209, includes a facsimile of a page from the 'Triplex'.

[32] There are substantial differences between recordings made by two of Cardine's students: Pater Godehard Joppich (*Münsterschwarzach: Chants on Palm Sunday*, Archiv 2533 320) and the Revd Columba Kelly (*Medieval and Contemporary Liturgical Music*, Pleiades P 150). Joppich's interpretation involves considerable variation in the duration of individual notes, while Kelly's interpretation is essentially equalist, even though his performances are based on the *Liber usualis*.

[33] Chant was occasionally performed mensurally and referred to as 'cantus fractus'; see the literature cited in W. Dalglish, 'The Origin of the Hocket', *JAMS* 31 (1978), p.12, n.35. For a fine example of measured chant performed from a 14th-century manuscript, see Ensemble Vocal Guillaume Dufay, directed by Arsène Bedois, *Officium rhythmicum sancti juvenalis* (Erato STU 71143).

[34] Vanguard VSD 71217

[35] Peters International PLE 114; this is the first of the recordings accompanying W. T. Marrocco and N. Sandon, eds., *Medieval Music*, Oxford Anthology of Music (London, 1977).

[36] Floros gives an extensive survey of earlier research on most of the ornamental neumes (*op cit*, 2, pp.60–122); for a cursory survey in English, see Apel, *op cit*, pp.108–16.

[37] Most books dealing with palaeography have tables showing the ornamental neumes in various regional forms. The most complete is G. M. Suñol, *Introduction à la paléographie musicale grégorienne* (Tournai, 1935; rev. Fr. trans. of *Introduccio a la paleografia musical gregoriana* (Montserrat, 1925)); a more condensed presentation is found in B. Stäblein, *Schriftbild der einstimmigen Musik*, Musikgeschichte in Bildern, iii/4 (Leipzig, 1975), neume table following p.32.

[38] The *quilisma* is occasionally found in other contexts: it may span a major 3rd or a 4th, and in some manuscripts it occurs as a descending pattern. The neume has been described in different ways; Corbin, for example, refers to the middle element as an 'oriscus' (*Die Neumen*, p.190).

[39] W. Wiesli, *Das Quilisma* (Immensee, 1966), pp.3–11, contains the most extensive survey of literature, but see Floros, *op cit*, 2, p.65, n.11, for additions.

[40] The last interpretation was suggested by F. Tack, *Gregorian Chant*, Anthology of Music, 13 (Cologne, 1960), pp.9–10, but the precise meaning of 'throaty nasal "breaking" tone' (*kehlig nasler Umschlagton*) eludes me.

[41] See Mocquereau, *op cit*, 1, pp.336–8, and Apel, *op cit*, pp.106–8. Floros is the only one to my knowledge who sees the repercussive neumes as lengthenings (*op cit*, 2, pp.40–41).

[42] 'Trinum ad instar manus verberantis facias celerum ictum.' (L. Gushee, ed., *Aureliani Reomensis musica disciplina*, Corpus scriptorum de musica, 21 (Rome, 1975), pp.122–3; the term 'trinum' occurs in the apparatus to the printed text, which uses the form 'trina'.)

[43] For Münsterschwarzach see n.32; for Pro Cantione Antiqua see n.35 (reiteration occurs on side 1, bands 4 and 7 only). Schola Antiqua reiterates elements in repercussive neumes in *Tenth-Century Liturgical Chant* and in an earlier recording (*Plainchant and Polyphony from Medieval Germany*, Nonesuch H-71312).

[44] Dalglish cites a number of passages criticizing vocal extravagances in chant during the Romanesque period (*op cit*, pp.4–10).

[45] In Apel's discussion of the early neumes (*op cit*, pp.108–16) the possibility of microtones is suggested frequently. There is strong evidence that microtones are indicated in the manuscript. Montpellier H 159. This manuscript uses a dual system of notation: staffless neumes and pitch letters; in addition to the diatonic pitches (indicated by a continuous sequence of letters, *a* to *p*) special symbols occur that may indicate microtones. In illus.5 a symbol resembling a reversed, lower-case 't' occurs a number of times in the introit *In voluntate* and may well be a note 'between' *e* and *f*. See J. Gmelch, *Die Vierteltonstufen im Messtonale von Montpellier* (Eichstätt, 1911) or F. E. Hansen, *H 159 Montpellier* (Copenhagen, 1974), p.43*.

[46] H. Besseler, *Musik des Mittelalters und der Renaissance* (Potsdam, 1931), p.15

[47] Many of the interpretations advanced by R. John Blackley in the Schola Antiqua's *Tenth-Century Liturgical Chant* involve microtonal inflections (see the supplementary notes that accompany the recording). A clear example is the performance of the *pressus* at the end of the incipit to the Easter *Alleluia, Pascha nostrum*. Compare with the de Van–Sachs interpretation (see n.54 below).

[48] F. Ll. Harrison, 'Music and Cult: the Functions of Music in Social and Religious Systems', *Perspectives in Musicology*, ed. B. S. Brook, E. O. D. Downes and S. Van Solkema (New York, 1972), pp.320–21.

[49] On p.235 of M. Morrow, 'Musical performance and authenticity', *EM* 6/2 (April 1978), pp.233–46

[50] A. von Ramm, 'Singing early music', *EM* 4/1 (January 1976), pp.12–15 (see also correspondence in 4/2 (April 1976), pp.229–31, and especially 4/4 (December 1976), pp.489–91) and 'Style in early music singing', *EM* 8/1 (January 1980), pp.17–20.

[51] F. Müller-Heuser, *Vox humana*, Kölner Beiträge zur Musikforschung, 26 (Regensburg, 1963), especially pp.67–81, cites a number of medieval passages on proper singing; for a fascinating later witness (Conrad von Zabern, 1474) see J. Dyer, 'Singing with proper refinement', *EM* 6/2 (April 1978), pp.207–27.

[52] 'Perfecta autem vox est alta suavis et clara.' (Gerbert, *op cit*, 1, p.22)

[53] Müller-Heuser tries to show that there must have been different standards in the Germanic regions from those south of the Alps (*op cit*, pp.45ff).

[54] Haydn Society AS-1

[55] It is interesting to compare the de Van–Sachs interpretations of the ornamental neumes with those on other recordings. The *bi-* and *tristropha* are unusual in that reiteration is achieved by bending the pitch rather than stopping the sound.

[56] *JAMS* 12 (1960), pp.43–9 (published posthumously)

[57] Even the brief parallels noted in passing by Corbin (*Die Neumen*, pp.196, 209) between present-day Eastern practice and Cardine's rhythmic theories lend another dimension of credibility to those theories. Are there similar parallels with mensural interpretations?

[58] Bomm, *op cit*, outlines how Dom Pothier's work in the restoration of chant relied on both old and new elements to create a new chant practice.

[2]

GIVING VOICE TO GREGORIAN CHANT
OR:
COPING WITH MODERN ORTHODOXIES

by Katarina Livljanić

„Between a stream and its source, which has the purer water?"[1]

These words, attributed to Charlemagne – concerning the decadence of liturgical chant in the Carolingian empire and the necessity of returning to Roman models – come back almost in cycles, during the centuries of what we call Gregorian chant. Uttered by differet personalities, in periods stretched between the 9th and 21st centuries, these words often describe very different realities and witness to a lingering existence of conflicts around that mysterious ideal: the *authenticity* of liturgical chant performance.

Linked to its almost continuous use in liturgy, plainchant doesn't have the privileged (or maybe the unfortunate) fate to be considered only as „medieval music" and does not necessarily obey the esthetic canons of the „early music" world. The almost complete disappearance of Gregorian chant from the liturgy after the Second Vatican Council (1962–65), transformed it into an antiquarian object and opened the door for specialized performers to include it in their historical investigations and concert repertoires. Torn among professional singers, clergymen, musicologists and liturgists, plainchant continuously encourages very different approaches to its performance. Unfortunately, the plurality of performance styles doesn't always reflect a plurality and tolerance of ideas. Often convinced to be bearers of the unique *Truth*, the actors of these „esthetic wars" around Gregorian chant sometimes still secretly cherish an atavistic belief in its „Romanity", or simply in the supremacy of one style above the others.

„*Chant wars*"

Numerous encounters with scholars and performers, and my own position which includes both performance and reasearch in the domain of plainchant, have inspired me to rethink some of those never-ending questions concerning not so much the plainchant itself, but more our view of it. Instead of trying in vain to answer some of the central questions in chant research, I am rather interested in describing modern chant performances as reflected in the mirror of these questions. In the period preceding the Basel conference in November 2002, I was actively involved in the preparation of a research and concert programme „Chant Wars".[2] The work on „Chant Wars" aroused numerous

---

[1] According to John the Deacon, *Vita Gregorii*, in: J. Migne (ed.), *Patrologia latina*, Paris 1892, vol. 75, col. 90–91.

[2] This programme was created in 2003 as a coproduction by the ensembles *Sequentia* (directed by Benjamin Bagby) and *Dialogos* (directed by myself).

questions concerning that first Carolingian „globalization" of liturgical song and its repercussions in the sound universe of chant traditions in 9th century Europe. In the process of choosing the repertoire, reading scholarly literature and listening to various existing chant performances recorded in different periods during the 20th century,[3] it became more and more obvious that the „chant wars" or, to put it less theatrically, conflicts of ideas concerning the genesis and performance of plainchant, were not only a Carolingian, but also at least a 19th and 20th century reality, and that they will probably continue as long as chant performance itself.

The theme of our programme was the legendary 9th century confrontation between the Carolingian cantors and the local musical traditions which they sought to replace by their own repertoires and vocal styles. The use of two separate vocal ensembles made it possible to explore the vocal and performative elements of this confrontation, so that today's listeners could be able to hear the astonishing diversity of chant styles of medieval Europe, at a time when chant traditions were competing for ascendancy in the young empire of Pippin, Charlemagne and their successors.

The imperial reform of the liturgy and its musical structures arrived in the different regions of the Carolingian empire almost as a „cultural revolution", finding in many places an established local liturgy with which it had to contend.[4] In the name of Roman authority, used by Charlemagne in a political goal of unification, many local liturgical and musical traditions were suppressed. Of the local musical traditions which survived this confrontation, each has been preserved in a different way: some survived until our time (Ambrosian chant in Milan); some survived for several centuries before being completely eradicated (Beneventan chant in Southern Italy); and some were merged with layers of other traditions in building the complex, hybrid repertory which we commonly call „Gregorian chant". Texts written in the Carolingian period by such personalities as John the Deacon[5] or Notker of St. Gall[6] often mention differences among these regional traditions. But, do they only refer to the differences between melodies? These are sometimes visible only on our comparative tables in a musicological analysis, but they can remain hidden if we receive them in oral transmission. For Charlemagne's contemporaries, maybe the word *difference* meant rather a diversity in performance styles,

---

[3] See an overview of different performance traditions in J.F. Weber: „The phonograph as witness to performance practice of chant", *Cantus planus* IV, Pécs 1990, 607–614.

[4] It would be impossible to give here an extensive list of publications concerning the Carolingian reform of plainchant. Some of them will be mentioned in the course of this article, accompanying concrete questions, authors and citations. I cite here a more general book about the Carolingian culture with an excellent chapter dedicated to music: Susan K.Rankin, „Carolingian music", in: *Carolingian Culture: Emulation and innovation*, ed. Rosamund McKitterick, Cambridge 1993, 274–316.

[5] John the Deacon, *Vita Gregorii*, in: J. Migne (ed.), *Patrologia latina*, Paris 1892, vol. 75.

[6] *Notkeri Balbuli Gesta Karoli Magni Imperatoris*, ed. H.F. Haefele, *MGH, Scriptorem Rerum Germanicarum, Nova Series*, 12, Berlin 1959.

in the approach to the text articulation? Perhaps they refered to the variable numbers of singers involved in the performance in different regions, or to the pronunciation of Latin? In trying to find concrete vocal solutions to these dilemmas, one notices how delicate is the border between the *same, similar* and *different*, as mentioned by medieval authors. A chant melody can be perceived as *same* from place to place because of its melody, but also because of its text, its liturgical assignment, its sound, the vocal techinque of the performer, or its particular ornamentation style.

In the land of distorting mirrors

Medieval authors and manuscripts are mostly accesible to us through the glasses of modern scholars and through modern performances. However, in the labyrinths of today's chant performance, one immediately notices a number of received ideas concerning medieval liturgical song. Unfortunately, we inherited them from our not-so-distant ancestors. They are hidden behind the obsessive imperative of progressing in historical accuracy, which gives to performances the stamp of approval concerning their „seriousness", regardless of their basic musical or technical qualities (these can sometimes be extremely doubtful and would never be tolerated, for example, if applied to a performance of a string quartet). Chant is rarely considered as a serious vocal art worthy of highest standards of execution, but rather as a musical background, as a lifestyle, or as an object of musicological research. Consequently, chant performance criticism is often limited to recognizing the quantitative facts: how known/unknown is the performed repertory, which is the interpretative school to which the performers belong. More inherently musical parameters, vocal qualities, understanding of text and the fluidity of melodic line, rhetorical structure, presence of vocal mannerisms of various stylistic and geographical provenances, tuning – all these are very often left unconsidered.

Speaking of ancestors and of the generally accepted norms concerning the sound of Gregorian chant, I would like to recall some 19th and 20th century attitudes towards chant performance and their reflections in the present.

*

The world of specialized musicians interested in medieval plainchant performance is relatively small, and yet stylistically very diversified. On the other hand, the number of monastic communities which still practice chant in their daily liturgical life is quite large, and their singing generally serves as a reference for the sound of chant to a large audience, but also to a number of chant scholars and performers.

In a recent publication which includes a chapter about chant performance in the context of reconstructing a medieval, and not a modern liturgical performance, we find the following description:

> A monk once told me that in his monastery, every novice loses his voice within the first few months of singing the Divine Office. Only then does he learn to sing lightly and easily enough that his voice can sustain the extensive singing throughout the

day. This suggests that the choral singing of chant might ideally be with a fairly light voice. Optimizing the head resonance is quite consistent with the slightly forward vowels the French use. The ethos of singing chant presents a challenge to a singer with modern training – it is communal and transcendendent, it does not cultivate individual characteristics but incorporates the voice into a collective sonority and expression. It does not draw attention to itself or even to the specific piece, but rather turns the piece itself to a transcendent purpose. I take this to be the paradigm.[7]

Many centuries earlier, this world of liturgical song we are so desperately trying to reconstruct, is described by Gregory of Tours as he mentions the visit of king Guntram to Orleans on July 4th, 585:

When the meal was more than half-way over, the King ordered me to tell my deacon to sing. This was the man who had chanted the Responsorium at Mass the previous day. While he was singing, Guntram gave me a second commission. I was to be responsible personally for seeing that each of the other bishops present should in turn provide a deacon from his own church to sing before the King. I communicated this order to the bishops. Each of the deacons chosen chanted the Responsorium to the best of his ability, with the King listening.[8]

In the centuries between a testimony provided by Gregory the Great, mentioning in 595 ecclesiastical promotions among the clergy based on the beautiful voices of deacons who were „charming the believers by their singing",[9] and a recent article describing vocal style in Solesmes,[10] a long transformation had taken place in plainchant reception.

One of the key thoughts in this strange confrontation of ideas seem to be expressed by Isidore of Seville (7th century) in his *De ecclesiasticis officiis*. He describes the voice of a *psalmista*, mentioning that it needs to be „appropriate to the holy religion".[11] Among numerous writings about cantors' voices in the

---

[7] William Mahrt, „Chant", in: *Performer's guide to medieval music*, ed. by Ross Duffin, Bloomington 2000, 16–17.
[8] According to *Historiarum libri decem*, ed. B. Krusch and W. Levinson, *MGH, Scriptores rerum merovingicarum*, vol. 1, pars 1, 1962, VIII,3. English edition: Gregory of Tours, *The history of the Franks*, (translated by Lewis Thorpe), London 1974, 435–436.
[9] *Decretum ad clerum in basilica beati Petri apostoli*, Ep. 5, 57, cf. *MGH Epistolae 1*, ed. P. Ewald and L. Hartmann, 2nd ed. 1957, 363.
[10] Cf. Marie-Aude Roux, „A Solesmes, les chantres su silence", *Le Monde*, 26 december 2002. In this article, the author is presenting the organist of Solesmes with the following words: „Musicien et mélomane passionné, le Père Hala possède une basse capable de chanter des airs d'opéra, ou des chœurs russes orthodoxes, pas de se joindre aux voix solesmiennes, réputées pour leur pureté d'intonation et leur vocalisation aiguë. ‚Comme je ne peux pas chanter, je joue de l'orgue', conclut-il".
The cantor in the abbey, Michael Bozell is presented in the following way: „Pas besoin de posséder une belle voix pour être chantre: il y a celles que l'on suit et celles qui font le lien avec les autres – le Père Bozell appartient à la seconde catégorie."
[11] *De ecclesiasticis officiis*, II, 12, in: *Patrologia Latina*, vol. 83, col. 792.

Middle Ages,[12] there is also the 8th century bishop Chrodegang of Metz. In his *Regula canonicorum* he describes the ideal image of a Carolingian cantor: his main duty is not to wither the gift received from god, but to embellish it by humility, sobriety and chastity. According to Chrodegang, the cantor should be distinguished and illustrious thanks to his voice and his art.[13]

But what exactly do these images mean? What did they mean for Isidore, for the Carolingians, for the 19th century monks at Solesmes in the period of chant restoration, and what do words such as *distinguished, illustrious, humility, sobriety* and *chastity* mean for our voices today?

19th century „chant wars"

In the forest of different approaches to chant performance, one of the most influential and omnipresent models was certainly established by the Solesmes Benedictine abbey, reconstituted in 1833 by Dom Prosper Guéranger. But before discussing the issues of performance as formulated in that French Benedictine abbey, it is necessary to make a clear distinction between Solesmes chant research and chant performance. The musicological achievements of the Solesmes monks count among the most important monuments of chant research since the 19th century, and without their publications and scholars the current state of our knowledge about chant would be very different and incomparably weaker.[14] Along with the research, the daily practice of chant in the liturgy was restored in the 19th century.[15]

The decades between the publication of Félix Danjou's *De l'état et de l'avenir du chant ecclésiastique en France* (Paris 1844) and the *Liber gradualis* (Tournai 1883) prepared by Dom Joseph Pothier marked a significant period of chant reform.[16] In the period 1860–65 Guéranger called Dom Jausion from Solesmes to work on the restoration of the chant melodies. Reacting against orchestral masses and romantic oratorios, the 19th-century reformers cultivated a projection on a historical image of an „original" Gregorian chant, coming from the source. Very revealing technical terms were used by liturgical commentators

---

[12] See a compilation of medieval sources in Timothy McGee, *The sound of medieval song. Ornamentation and vocal style according to the treatises*, Oxford 1998. About the role of cantor in medieval monasteries see also M.E. Fassler: „The office of the cantor in early western monastic rules and customaries: a preliminary investigation", *Early Music History* 5 (1985) 29–51.

[13] *Patrologia latina*, vol. 89, col. 1079.

[14] Let me mention here the most essential among Solesmes collections, such as *Paléographie Musicale, Études grégoriennes, Revue du chant grégorien*, along with many other studies published worldwide by current or former monks of Solesmes.

[15] About Solesmes restoration of plainchant in the 19th century, see the book by K. Bergeron: *Decadent Enchantments: the Revival of Gregorian Chant at Solesmes*, Berkeley, 1997.

[16] John A. Emerson/Jane Bellingham/David Hiley, „Plainchant", *The New Grove Dictionary of Music Online* ed. L. Macy (Accessed 25 august 2003), http://www.grovemusic.com. This article offers a useful and concise overview of the plainchant 19th and 20th century reforms.

of that period: „decadent" as opposed to „authentic" chant melodies or chant performance; and „restoration", used to describe efforts to restore plainchant to its place in the liturgy.[17] This enthusiasm for a medieval musical past paralleled an enthusiasm for the restoration of Romanesque and Gothic churches,[18] an idea which coincides with Viollet le Duc's wave of architectural restorations throughout France. His neo-Gothic and neo-Romanesque artworks basically explored the same ideas as the monks of Solesmes in their sound-images. The principles of this modern reinvention of medieval chant could be summed up in this statement by Dom Guéranger: „If in certain cases we are right to believe that we possess a Gregorian melody in its pureness in the case of a particular chant piece, it is because the copies from various distant churches are concordant."[19] The idea of determining and publishing the „archetype", which actually never existed as a written medieval manuscript, was their goal.

In that period of neo-Romanesque churches, of saints' statues with rosy cheeks made of coloured plaster in the workshops around St Sulpice in Paris, a new frame was made for liturgical music. It had to answer the same demands: it had to be sweet, unintruding, hiding any individualism behind the group. The Marian cult and apparitions of the Virgin become extremely popular, feminine congregations were flourishing: this „feminisation" of devotional practices also influenced the sound ideals of 19th century Catholics.[20] The answer to the institution of the village cantor of the *ancien régime*[21] was the new choral sound of a community as in Solesmes.

Turning towards different roots

During the decades of 20th century chant research, scholars specialized in musical paleography and its links to interpretation considered some types of early neumatic notation as rhythmically more precise. They gave a privileged role to the earliest neumes of the Saint Gall and Metz[22] families. Since the same text can reveal different truths to different readers, this knowledge cannot be reduced to a set of tables and recipes for a precise performance of each neume. The discipline known as Gregorian semiology brought a new, enriching perspective to the understanding of the earliest neumes. However, the several performance schools engendered by Gregorian semiology bear witness that

---

[17] See for example: Michel Couturier, *Décadence et restauration de la musique religieuse*, Paris 1862; Anselm Schubiger, *Die Restauration des Kirchengesangs und der Kirchenmusik durch das künftige allgemeine Concilium*, Zürich1869.

[18] Joseph Dyer, „Roman catholic church music", *The New Grove Dictionary of Music Online* ed. L. Macy (Accessed 25 august 2003),http://www.grovemusic.com.

[19] Dom Prosper Guéranger, *Institutions liturgiques*, vol. 1, Paris 1840, 306.

[20] A brief ovierview of this phenomenon is provided in: Patrick Cabanel-Michel Cassan, *Les catholiques français du XVIe au XXe siècle*, Paris 1997, 63–88.

[21] Cf. Jacques Cheyronnaud, „Petite histoire de lutrins", in: *Les voix du plain-chant*, Desclée de Brouwer 2001, 144.

[22] Here I particularly refer to Dom Eugène Cardine's research and his *Semiologia Gregoriana*, Rome 1968.

each of them represents just one possible point of view, an interpretation of an interpretation.[23]

Performances inspired by Dom Eugène Cardine's studies take into account all the subtleties provided by Saint Gall manuscripts with their rich indications for rhythm and neume grouping. Still, besides the importance of careful references to rhythmical nuances in the neumatic script, there are many other levels one may also need to consider when incarnating these signs into sound. There is the text, the rhetorical function of each piece with its profile crystallized over centuries of oral transmission, there is its modal identity, ornamental richness, the architectural space in which it should be performed and understood. All these elements influence decisions about performance. Yet we will never be able to know precisely which was the meaning of terms such as *long* and *short*, *fast* and *slow* for Saint Gall cantors and scribes, how these values relate to each other, and how flexible they were in their symbiosis with the text of a piece. Medieval chant didn't survive only through the mirror of Saint Gall neumes and if we want to perform chant repertory from other sources we shouldn't be trapped by a St. Gall miopia or apply parameters from one notation to another. The ultimate help and guide in the performance of neumes seems to be the text of the song we are singing, the sense of the story we are telling. Only in connection with the text, and with the modal structure of a concrete chant melody, can neumes reveal their inner logic.

This same problem becomes much more complex when we study Roman chant or many other medieval Latin chant repertories of various local European traditions.[24] Their neumatic script doesn't transmit the same types of rhythmical nuances (or rather the same information we tend to consider as precise rythmical nuances) as the neumes from St Gall. Should we then say:

---

[23] It is paradigmatical to compare different chant performances which all take as inspiration E. Cardine's research and believe in their accurate following of the principles of Gregorian semiology. If we listen to chant performances advised by such scholars as Godehard Joppich (ensemble „Singphoniker") and Marie Noël Colette (ensembles „Gilles Binchois", directed by Dominique Vellard, and „Discantus", directed by Brigitte Lesne) in the last decades of the 20th century, we will be astonished by differences in their approach to the rhythm and articulation of chant melodies.
In spite of his highly systematic, grammar-like approach to the interpretation of neumes, E. Cardine himself summarizes in a revealing way this probleme in his late text „Sémiologie et interprétation", in: *Ut mens concordet voci. Festschrift Eugène Cardine*, St Ottilien 1980, 31: „Nous convenons volontiers que les indications fournies par la sémiologie sont élastiques. Le ‚dosage' des valeurs des notes, en plus ou en moins, ne saurait être déterminé avec précision; il apparaît même parfois ‚ad libitum' ... Mais quels que soient les enrichissements de la sémiologie les connaissances acquises en ce domaine ne conduisent pas ‚ipso facto' à une bonne exécution; car elles consistent principalement, et même presque uniquement en *données solfégiques*, qui devront nécessairement être vivifiées par *l'interprétation*."

[24] See in that context the following article: Marie-Noël Colette: „Grégorien et vieux-romain: deux méthodes différentes de collectage de mélodies traditionelles?", in: *Laborare fratres in unum. Festschrift László Dobszay zum 60. Geburtstag*, ed. Janka Szendrei and David Hiley, Hildesheim 1995, 37–52.

„As we do not know how to interprete the rhythm of this type of notation, it is impossible to sing this repertory today"? But, do we really know how to interpret the rhythm of St Gall neumes? It would be very dangerous to apply the presumed knowledge (or the assumptions of interpretation) of one notation to the other types. The sentence one can often hear nowadays concerning chant performance is: „Because of the research done in the field of Gregorian semiology, we can now come closer to knowing how chant was interpreted in 10th century St Gall." But who are „we"? And how many different varieties of „us" can be tolerated?

Leo Treitler gave an excellent insight into this phenomenon in his text: „The politics of reception: Tailoring the present as fulfilment of a desired past".[25] In observing the language used by scholars who studied Gregorian and Old-Roman chant, Treitler notices a strong „Us and the Other" syndrome which applies to Roman chant, putting it in a category of *Otherness* when compared to Gregorian chant. But, since the *Other* actually helps us to define who *We* are, by saying that the *Other* is everything that *We* are not, it is obvious that the idea of the *Other* changes just as the subject speaking about it changes. It reminds me of those kitschy little barometers in shape of a small house: a lady would come out one door to announce sunny weather, a gentleman would come out through another door before the rain. The same problem occurs for those two characters as for our chant research: The two characters will never meet, because the encounter between them would immediately negate their *raison d'être*. From the 19th century image of *Us* as bourgeois urban society, to the late 20th century when *We* became more politically correct and world-music oriented, the sound of plainchant as the source of Western music was shifting just as our image of ourselves was changing; from a soft, choral collective sound towards chant inspired by traditional music, by improvisational techniques, often performed by women's ensembles.

In the later decades of the 20th century, one of the attempts to fill the gap between us and the medieval cantors was the appeal to ethnomusicology and to traditional music.[26] The opening of new perspectives which consider Gregorian chant as a musical corpus in whose (not only) early history oral transmission had an essential role, represented an immense liberation and a

---

[25] Leo Treitler, *With voice and pen, coming to know medieval song and how it was made*, Oxford 2003, 211–229.

[26] An important landmark in the study of medieval plainchant in the perspective of oral tradition was certainly the article by Leo Treitler: „Homer and Gregory: The transmission of epic poetry and plainchant", *Musical Quarterly* 60 (1974), 333–372, recently republished in his book *With voice and pen, coming to know medieval song and how it was made*, Oxford 2003. See also: Peter Jeffery, *Re-envisioning past musical cultures: Ethnomusicology in the study of Gregorian chant*, Chicago Studies in Ethnomusicology, Chicago 1992; Marie-Noël Colette, „Des modes archaïques dans les musiques de tradition orale", *Études grégoriennes* 27 (1999) 165–184.

chance to see aspects of chant composition, transmission and performance in a different light. These scholarly initiatives encouraged a current in chant performance in the 1980's and 90's. As an inspiration for the learning and transmission of chant melodies, these ideas provided significant support to performers. However, values from the world of traditional singers cannot always resonate easily with the modern world of „ready to use" scores, limited rehearsal time and instant access to the music traditions of the whole world. Characterized by processes of slow transmission over long periods of time, these values are often reduced to banal imitations of vocal mannerisms in the performance of certain types of neumes; or they simply give an unusual, vaguely exotic colour to the sound of chant. There is a weak point in this approach to chant: how do we chose *which* traditional singers to take as our models? From *which* country, tradition or type of repertoire?[27] For instance, the fashion of introducing non-Western chant elements into our sound models is a dubious procedure:[28] By including the sounds of such practices, we may unknowingly import modern (e.g. neo-Byzantine, Coptic) characteristics of traditions which have themselves undergone changes, often through contact with other musical cultures. It is an intrusion, just like many other fashionable elements that invade chant performances: costumes, processions, bells, certain types of ornaments, drones, as if deeply in performers' minds there were a latent *horror vacui*, or a fear that this music is, after all, boring to the audience, and that it is absolutely necessary to add something external to it. The existence of these various waves in reconstruction of medieval chant would be *a priori* nothing negative (in context of each particular personal taste) as long as performers would be honest enough to recognize them as a hypothesis of our generation in solving the problem of historical distance between us and the Middle Ages. Instead, sermons about authenticity and, in some cases, superficial research are covering the performers' lack of self-confidence, knowledge and serious study of the repertoire.

---

[27] A deeply inspiring experience in thinking about this problem was my encounter with the traditional singers from Stari Grad and Vrbanj on the Island of Hvar in Croatia. These highly virtuoso traditional singers of Glagolitic tradition come from two neighbouring villages. Their vocal styles (audible on a CD „Za krizem", edited by record comapny *Arcana*, 2002) witness an extremely striking difference, typical also for other villages on the same island. The process of transmission of melodies from father to son demonstrates a very minute accuracy about every detail characteristic for the text articulation, tuning, ornementation. If I were to reconstruct a medieval glagolitic singing from the island of Hvar, which of the villages would I take as a model, if I would dispose for my work only of a written document coming from one main parish church on the island?

[28] In relation to this subject, consult the chapter „A different sense of time. Marcel Pérès on plainchant" in the book by Bernard D. Sherman, *Inside early music. Conversations with performers*, Oxford 1997, 25–42.

The North and the South syndrome

When medieval authors speak about regional differences in matters of liturgical chant performance, they sometimes use very extreme terms.[29] John the Deacon, a 9th century Montecassino monk, expresses from his point of view the eternal North-South problem: „Alpine bodies do not properly make the sweetness of the melody they have adopted resound, since in their voices they make high-sounding noises like thunder. Because the barbarian fierceness, belonging to a drinker's throat, emits rough hard voices when it attempts to produce a soft tone with inflections and repetitions, and does so with a kind of natural roar of the voice, sounding confused, as if you were to throw carts down steps. And so, through bewildering and terrible bawling, it rather disturbs the listeners' minds, which it ought to please [...]."[30]

An eleventh-century witness, Adémar de Chabannes, describes French singers in the following way: „The Franks could not perfectly express the tremulous or the sinuous notes, or the notes that are to be elided or separated, breaking the notes in the throat, with a natural barbaric voice, rather than expressing them."[31]

In our quest for the „authentic" way to perform medieval plainchant, maybe we should actually rather ask ourselves: what do we really want to accomplish when we give voice to plainchant today? Do we really want to make it sound as it had sounded in a medieval liturgy? But then, in which country, and in which century? Do we search to perform it in the manner the theorists wished it to sound? Or in the manner they were criticizing their contemporaries for singing it the way they did?[32] Frankish „drinkers' throats" in the end were some of those who transmitted Gregorian chant over centuries, and they are among our models. So we have at least several, if not thousands, of different vocal images that we could follow, but we cannot know if we would actually *like* one of them particularly if we were miraculously given to hear them. Our

---

[29] See: Susan Rankin, „Ways of telling stories", in: *Essays on medieval music in honor of David G. Hughes*, ed. Graeme M. Boone, Cambridge MA 1995, 371–394; Kenneth Levy, „A new look at the old Roman chant", *Early Music History* 19 (2000) 81–104; vol. 20 (2001) 173–197.

[30] John the Deacon, *Vita Gregorii*, in: J. Migne (ed.), *Patrologia latina*, Paris 1892, vol. 75, col. 90–91. English translation from Susan Rankin, „Ways of telling stories", in: *Essays on medieval music in honor of David G. Hughes*, ed. Graeme M. Boone, Cambridge MA 1995, 372.

[31] *Chronicon*, II, 8, from: Jules Chavanon (ed.), Adémar de Chabannes: *Chronique*, Paris 1897, 81. English translation from James Grier, „Adémar de Chabannes, Carolingian musical practices, and *Nota Romana*", *Journal of the American Musicological Society* 56 (2003) 48.

[32] As an interpolation of a similar problem into a more familiar situation, let me make a banal example: Imagine one of your worst voice students becoming an important factor in transmitting your own vocal style, and then later being criticized by a critic in an influential early music magazine with whom you never got along very well: if that information becomes, centuries later, a source for the reconstruction of your own singing style, what could you imagine as a result?

obsession with historical accuracy, seen in this light, seems self-important and almost ludicrous.[33]

Once, when singing a Gregorian offertory for a small audience of German chant scholars, I received the comment that it was „viel zu mediterran". When I performed the same piece in France, it was perceived as „trop expressif", and in Spain as „muy austero". The belief in a unique, Roman, origin of Gregorian chant, which was put in question in the domain of research during the 20th century – ironically, after the discovery of Old Roman manuscripts[34] – still seems to wait for a serious transformation in the world of performance. We admit the existence of a plurality of local chant traditions in the Middle Ages. We somehow still cannot accept that they can also sound differently, or that they sounded (and still sound) differently to different listeners; and finally, that our visions of them can sound even more differently.

The „central question" about the origin of Gregorian and Roman chant probably will never receive a complete and final answer, simply because there is a lack of information in resolving the dilemma between these two repertoires, similar to: „which came first, the chicken or the egg?" Yet, scholarly studies, using often highly hypothetical methods, are considered as relevant contributions to that question.[35] Recordings of the same repertory can receive the same respect in the scholarly community only when they become archival items, only after decades of their publication, when they start to have the value of a historical document of a performance practice. Curiously, only then do they become „authentic" witnesses of particular performance traditions. The recording made in 1904 of the last Vatican castrato Alessandro Moreschi and the singers of the Sistine Chapel[36] singing a few chant melodies is now considered as a historical curiosity and the object of scholarly analysis. Yet, if the same recording were made some years ago as an attempt at authentic chant reconstruction, it would have probably been considered as ugly, ridiculous and marginal. It is true, there exist a number of performers who „don't care" about the research, and there are also those whose entire working methods repose on the *truth* provided by, usually, one chosen scholar representing a caution of seriousness. However, between these two extremes, there is still a lot of space to explore.

---

[33] A recent book by John Butt, *Playing with history. The historical approach to musical performance*, Cambridge University Press 2002, discusses a similar phenomenon, mostly based on later, baroque and classical music repertoires, in the light of „early music" performance practice.

[34] See a concise synthesis of that process in Michel Huglo, „La recherche en musicologie médiévale au XXe siècle", *Cahiers de civilisation médiévale* 39 (1996) 72–75.

[35] See, among many authors, recently published studies: Philippe Bernard, *Du chant romain au chant grégorien (IVe-XIIIe siècle)*, Paris 1996; James McKinnon: *The Advent project: The later-seventh-century creation of the Roman mass proper*, Berkeley 2000; Kenneth Levy: *Gregorian chant and the Carolingians*. Princeton 1998; Kenneth Levy, „A new look at the Old Roman chant", *Early Music History* 19 (2000) 81–104; 20 (2001) 173–197.

[36] Issued by *Opal* in 1987.

Fashions change: we are flipping through the universe of musical traditions like through a catalogue. Some models become fashionable: music from Corsica, Bulgaria, Ireland, Syria. In a second stage we get used to them, and then they are forgotten. Life-style magazines announce this season a big return of the 80's. In this world of „retro-chic", maybe the next step will be the reconstruction of the 19th century reconstruction of Gregorian chant. Since cycles are becoming shorter and shorter, we may even be able to live to see our own performance credos reflected and reconstructed in the eyes of the next early-music-oriented generation of performers. But, since, our performances are recorded, our successors will have the advantage of achieving a total „second hand authenticity", just like Pierre Menard, a character in a story by J.L. Borges who decides to undertake an entirely useless project, which is to create a minute reconstruction of *Don Quixote*. He decides not to compose *another* Quixote, he wants to write *the* Quixote, not by copying Cervantes's text, but by reconstructing it, word for word:

> It is a revelation to compare the Don Quixote of Pierre Menard with that of Miguel de Cervantes. Cervantes, for example, wrote the following (Part I, chapter IX):
> [...] *truth, whose mother is history, rival of time, depository of deeds, witness of the past, exemplar and adviser to the present, and the future's counselor.*
> [...] Menard, on the other hand, writes:
> [...] *truth, whose mother is history, rival of time, depository of deeds, witness of the past, exemplar and adviser to the present, and the future's counselor.*[37]

Borges, as he talks about „the contrast of styles" in these two books, gives the most brilliant portrait of our attempt to reconstruct an accurate sound of medieval chant: „The archaic style of Menard – who is, in addition, not a native speaker of the language in which he writes – is somehow affected. Not so the style of his precursor, who employs the Spanish of his time with complete naturalness. [...] The Quixote, Menard remarked, was first and foremost a pleasant book; it is now an occasion for patriotic toasts, grammatical arrogance, obscene *de luxe* editions. Fame is a form – perhaps the worst form – of incomprehension".[38]

---

[37] J.L. Borges, „Pierre Menard, author of the Quixote", in: *Collected fictions* (translation by Andrew Hurley) New York 1998, 94.
[38] Ibid.

Part II
Secular Monophony

[3]

RHYTHM, METER, AND MELODIC ORGANIZATION IN MEDIEVAL SONGS

Hans TISCHLER
(Bloomington, Indiana)

More than two thirds of a century have passed since Hugo Riemann, Pierre Aubry, and Jean Beck began to attack the problem of the rhythmic interpretation of the chansons of the troubadours and trouvères and of the minnelieder — as well as each other over it. Yet the discussion has by no means ended. Similarly much ink has been spilled over the melodic organization of these songs without arriving at a generally accepted decision. Several recent publications have once again opened up the discussion of these problems, including that of the concept of poetic meter in medieval poetry — or is it concepts? — and of poetic structure. Four works in particular will serve as points of reference here, viz. Roger Dragonetti's *La technique poétique des trouvères dans la chanson courtoise* ([1]), Paul Sappler's edition of the so-called *Königstein Songbook* ([2]), Hendrik van der Werf's *The Chansons of the Troubadours and Trouvères* ([3]), and Mölk and Wolfzettel's *Répertoire métrique* ... ([4]).

All these books are significant contributions to the literature on their respective subjects. The first is today accepted as the basic treatise on trouvère meter and rhythm; the second makes available the largest 15th-century German songbook, which, moreover, contains the earliest known musical scores for lute, pushing back our knowledge of lute tablatures by about twenty years to the early 1470's, a date that must be the earliest possible one for such tablatures or very close to it ([5]); the third volume reviews the historical and poetic background of the troubadours and trouvères, incidentally involving an important minnesong, and transcribes the various melodies for fifteen poems from numerous sources, discussing both their musical and poetic styles; and the fourth presents all known trouvère poems and French motet texts up to about 1350 in schematic verse and rhyme outlines, ordered by rhyme-scheme similarity ([6]).

The musico-poetic renditions offered in the second and third of these volumes would baffle the modern performer and give the reader a false or

---

[1] Bruges 1960, Rijksuniversiteit Gent.
[2] *Das Königsteiner Liederbuch* (Berlin Ms. germ qu 719 or Mgq 719). Münchener Texte und Untersuchungen zur deutschen Literatur des Mittelalters, vol. 20, 1970.
[3] Oosthoek, Utrecht 1972.
[4] Ulrich Mölk and Friedrich Wolfzettel: *Répertoire métrique de la poésie lyrique française des origines à 1350.* Wilh. Fink, Munich 1972.
[5] Cf. Hans Tischler, «The Earliest Lute Tablature?», *Journal of the Amer. Musicological Soc.*, 27, 1974, pp. 100-103.
[6] Only previously published texts are included, of which a few have been overlooked; but this accounts for 99 % of all extant French texts.

unclear impression of the relationship between music and text, because no rhythm is conveyed by the musical notations. This is so in the four melodies contained in the *Königstein Songbook* because their transcriber was perplexed himself by scribal errors and omissions, and in van der Werf's volume, because meter is consciously rejected by the author as a regulating guide to performance of this repertory. The schematic outlines offered by Mölk and Wolfzettel, on the other hand, lack delineation of structure and insight into stress patterns ([7]).

This paper makes the following basic assumptions : (1) An edition of secular medieval poems and their melodies must convey to the modern performer, reader, and student the probable intent of the poets and musicians who created these works during a time when they constituted part of a living repertory. This can be achieved only through a careful, correlated study of both poems and melodies, resulting hopefully in (a) the elucidation of the syntactic forms, stress patterns, and rhyme schemes of the poems; (b) a transcription of the music into modern note symbols, based on this elucidation; (c) a satisfactory adjustment of the music to the poetry and of the poetry to the music so that they are suitable to one another. (2) A schematic presentation of the poetry should make visible the structure of both poetry and music, the rhyme scheme, and, if possible, also the stress pattern and versification. This task will be greatly helped by a clarification of what syllables are assumed to rhyme and which lines represent quotations (refrains).

In other words, it seems to this writer that the modern editor-scholar must assume the responsibility for interpreting the poetry and the music for the potential user and for guiding him, rather than merely presenting him with a modernized transliteration that will perplex him and let him, the presumably less learned performer or reader, come to his own conclusions. The scholar's advantage is, of course, that he can relate a particular work or series of works to the entire background into which it fits.

For example, the tradition of medieval German song indicates that each text syllable was usually sung to a single melody tone or figure. Exceptions occur occasionally, particularly on penultimate and final verse syllables, less often within a line, but ornaments rarely go beyond three or four tones. Although the *Königstein Songbook*, which dates from the 1470's, is a very late source of medieval songs, works which cannot be designated as minnesongs, their rhythmic approach certainly continues that of the preceding centuries; for German music was very conservative during the Middle Ages. Moreover, the anonymous repertory collected in this volume is only a generation younger than the songs of the last minnesinger, Oswald von Wolkenstein.

([7]) Besides, they involve numerous errors, leaving the peruser puzzled, unenlightened, and merely wondering at the authors' industry.

Illustration 1 shows an attempt at a transcription of one of the four tunes from this book, parallel with the one in Sappler's edition, transcribed by Dr. Kurt Dorfmüller of Munich (S-D : Sappler-Dorfmüller transcription, T : Tischler's).

Our transcription follows the original and arrives at a thoroughly syllabic rendition, in keeping with the tradition. It requires only one small emendation, namely the repetition of a two-note group in verse 3, which the scribe of this early lute tablature may well have overlooked. This transcription further includes bar lines to convey the iambic meter of the poem, and in so doing it arrives at a well rounded tune. The barring seems particularly important for giving the song a musical shape that reflects the versification and for enabling the modern performer to approach the work intelligently.

It will be seen that the transcription of the melody in Sappler's volume assumes a repetition of the first section of the tune, which, though musically and poetically possible, is neither given in the manuscript nor necessary. This assumption further leads to the interpretation of long portions of the tune as melismatic ornaments, which are alien to the style. Thirdly, this interpretation and the rhythm-less transcription give no support to the strict meter of the poem, in fact disturb it.

To return to the assumptions listed above, our transcription gives the performer reader a definite though not necessarily a definitive interpretation, one that does justice to both poem and melody and can be easily used for performance. The a-a-b, c-c-b, d-e-e'-d structure of the poem is paralleled by a well structured melody which cadences very logically and satisfactorily and displays an excellent pattern of antecedent-consequent, antecedent-consequent, antecedent-consequent-echo-like consequent within a through-composed stanza. The beat pattern reflects the obvious iambic meter of the poem, and the rhythm of equally long beats is in keeping with the conservative German tradition, though a 6/8 meter could easily replace the 4/4 here assumed. (No rhythm is indicated in this tablature.) All in all this resolution leads to a satisfactory poetic and musical rendition — as suggested, not necessarily the only possible one — which will undoubtedly gain from the usual expressive freedom employed in any good performance.

The second illustration takes us back several centuries to a poem by perhaps the most eminent minnesinger, Walther von der Vogelweide, one of the few of his that have survived with their melodies. It offers an opportunity to compare a troubadour chanson and a minnesong, since this tune is melodically related to one of Jaufre Rudel's tunes. The two songs are given in parallel transliterations as the first of fifteen transcriptions in van der Werf's volume. But before discussing the two poems and their tunes several problems must be clarified.

The discussion of, or rather dispute over, the rhythm of trouvère melodies has gone on for a long time. The approach has mostly been to decide between two all-or-nothing alternatives, viz. a rendition of all such music in either

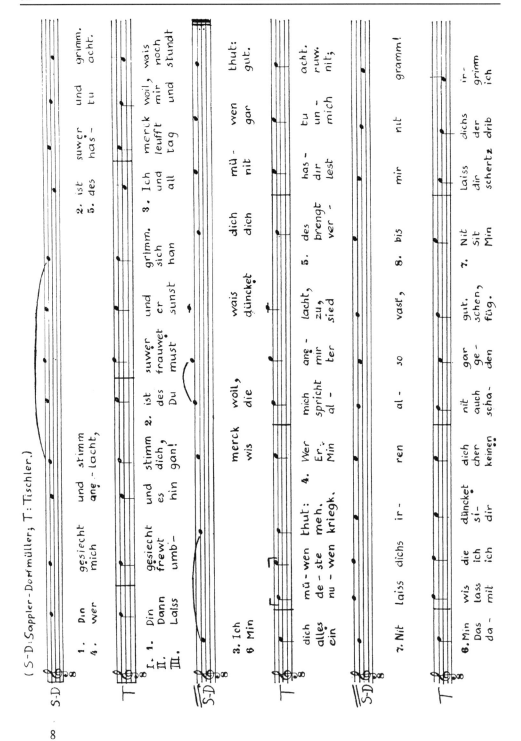

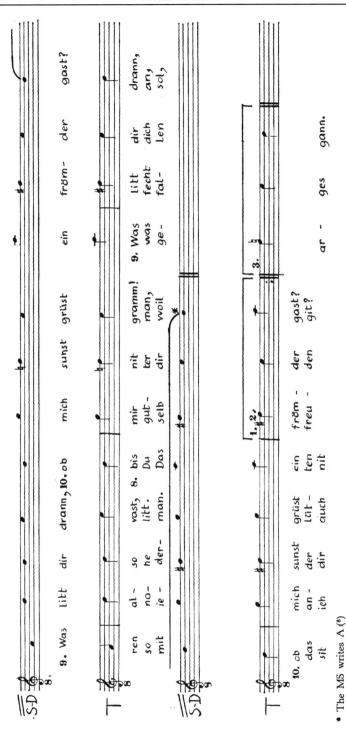

« modal » or free rhythm. The advocates of the former apply in their transcriptions, rigidly or with few irregularities, the patterned 6/8 meters of the Parisian clausulae and motets of the late 12th and early 13th centuries. The other editors render the tunes without bar lines, stresses, or relative note values. To be sure, the melodies of a few troubadour chansons and a number of trouvère songs reappear in motets and conductus or employ music from clausulae, and some are extant in mensural notation. Thus it cannot be denied that some later chansons were, at least at times, sung in metric rhythm. It is true, however, that most troubadour songs, from the late 11th century onward, and many trouvère chansons antedate the rise of modal notation and are written in non-mensural note symbols; modal rhythm may therefore not apply to these earlier songs. It should be remembered, however, that most manuscripts containing the music of these repertories were written in the mid-13th century, a period during which also most major motet sources were written in a notation that did not indicate the rhythm of the melodies, although they were doubtless measured and metrically patterned.

Nevertheless many scholars, including van der Werf, have rejected the application of modal rhythm to any or most troubadour and trouvère tunes, because it appears to be historically unsound to assume that it served all of them ([9]). Once this position is taken and only the two above possibilities are admitted, one is therefore left with a free, unmetric and unmeasured interpretation that lacks any practical, stylistic, or historical guide lines for the performer and analyst as well as any relationship to the text. This concept is called, and recommended as, « declamatory » style by van der Werf. It may be observed that this approach seems to be supported by the widely held view that French — as opposed to German, English, or Latin — poetry was based on counting syllables rather than on any quantitative or qualitative stress patterns.

When weighing this approach, it is well to consider the general tendencies of the period that produced these songs — the Gothic, which is characterized in part by its emphasis on arithmetic. This emphasis is manifest in such relations as that of the circle to its inscribed and circumscribed hexagons in the columns of cathedrals, the proportions of length, width, and height in churches, the numerical relationships in literary structures such as Dante's *Commedia*, the introduction of algebra by Leonardo Fibonacci, the invention of rhythmic, measurable music and musical notation, the cultivation of scholastic-mystic numerology, the cabbalah, alchemy, and astrology, as well as the revival of the ancient verse meters and the invention of new ones such as Alexandre de Bernay's Alexandrine. That a period so occupied with numbers would not reflect this tendency in its lyric and epic poetry by metric rhythm is nearly inconceivable. It must be further added that troubadour

---

([9]) Nevertheless van der Werf gives alternate rhythmic readings for two of his fifteen transcriptions and presents three songs exclusively in rhythmic renderings.

poetry was the product of Western Europe's contacts with the Muslim East and with Moorish Spain in particular, where since the 10th century a new vernacular poetry had risen — a poetry based on equally long lines with rhymes and on a strictly observed theory of meters, a poetry always sung to the accompaniment of instruments, most often that of the lute [10]. Trouvère chanson and minnelied, which sprang in two consecutive steps of direct imitation from troubadour song, must be assumed to share these basic style characteristics, to which belonged rhythmic patterns.

Moreover, the above-mentioned idea that syllable counting precludes the application of metric stress is contrary to the whole context of a culture that stressed architectural rhythm by flying buttresses, produced dance music, hockets, and mensural notation, enjoyed ostinato cantus-firmus patterns, and recited rhymed poetry whose rhyme syllables with very few exceptions demonstrably fall always on metrically strong beats in the music of motets. Indeed, it is a well known fact that the ancient quantitative meters of poetry gave way to qualitative, i. e., stressed meters about the 5th century of our era, and it must be presumed that stress remained fundamental in varying degrees to most Western poetry ever since. If proof of this fact for trouvère lyrics is needed, it is easily found in the feminine verse endings, weak syllables that are not counted by scholars of old French poetry. If it were a matter of mere counting, this procedure would be unthinkable; it can be explained only by assuming that stress was involved; below there will be occasion to refer to anacruses as well. To be sure, the ubiquitous iambs, trochees, and dactyls cannot even be conceived without some kind of agogic, dynamic, or pitch stress or a combination of two or all three of these in languages such as French and English that do not recognize long and short syllables.

As mentioned above, Dragonetti's excellent work has become a standard reference with regard to the versification of trouvère songs. This is what he contributes to the present problem in the key passage in which he analyzes the rhythm and meter of their poetry [11]:

> If the rhythm of a line is something different from its meter, the question is to know whether that rhythm is susceptible to analysis. ... In a regular verse the rhythm is organized with the aid of a rational or proportional time value. ... All rhythm, in fact, implies meter, which is not a simple artifice added to it, but coexists with it because it is an essential condition for the perception of rhythm. ... All rhythmic structure introduces a conflict or combination of two temporal orders, namely between rhythm and a homogeneous beat leading to meter; the former cannot be reduced to equal time divisions because it is a unique creation. The rhythmic structure of a regular verse results from the encounter of these two orders; the style differs according to how the metric squareness reinforces or contradicts the rhythm. Meter thus assumes a structural function which emerges clearly from the analysis of courtly verse where the regulatory action of metric schemes plays a particularly important role.

---

[10] *Cf.* Robert Briffault, *The Troubadours* (translated from the French by the author), Indiana University Press, Bloomington, IN, 1965, p. 31ff.

[11] *Op. cit.*, pp. 500-502; this writer's translation.

True, later in the volume Dragonetti sharply criticizes and rejects the application of modal rhythm to courtly poetry; but his criticism is really directed against the rigid application of modal patterning, practiced by such early scholars as Aubry and Beck, without considering more imaginative possibilities. An interesting argument, illustrated by a dozen examples, is the transcription, by Beck and Aubry respectively, of songs in different modal versions. A dual possibility of interpretation hardly speaks against the application of the rhythmic modes to trouvère poems, of course; indeed, it nicely illustrates a point worth remembering, viz. that the medieval musician might easily perform a piece differently at various times — different in rhythm, in musica ficta (accidentals), in ornamentation, played on an instrument or sung or both, with a different melody to the same poem or with a different text to the same melody. This point is most clearly documented by another song cited by Dragonetti ([12]) which is actually notated by the medieval scribes of two different manuscripts in two different modes, namely in the third mode in the *Chansonnier Cangé* and in the upbeat first mode in the *Chansonnier du Roi* ([13]). And this is a song by Robert de Castel d'Arras who, according to Dragonetti, was active during the third quarter of the 13th century, i.e., during the very time the two manuscripts were copied.

Incidentally, this twofold rhythmic interpretation results, of course, in several metric stresses falling on normally unaccented syllables, a thing that Dragonetti elsewhere calls « massacring the verse. » Apparently, however, the medieval poets felt no great compunction about this crime of giving some naturally weak syllables metric stress and leaving some normally strong ones unstressed; for poetic and prose scanning do not necessarily coincide in any language, whether French, English, or German, not to speak of Latin from which this procedure derives. The ambivalence of stress stands out clearly in 13th-century French motets, all definitely sung in measured rhythm with a strong metric pulse. As is well known, these motets include hundreds of quotations, so-called refrains, from trouvère poetry and *romans*, and all of these confirm not only the appropriate consideration given to feminine endings and anacruses by their metric placement but also the metric treatment of the body of these quoted lines. This source of very pertinent information has been totally neglected hitherto in all discussions of trouvère rhythm.

In general, considering the possibilities of different interpretation and of ambivalent stress or floating accent, it is often difficult to decide which meter was intended. Even the medieval performer had such difficulties, as has just been shown. The problem becomes compounded when the various stanzas of a poem do not exhibit the same stress pattern. In such instances two approaches are helpful for finding the best possible solution: (1) scanning all the stanzas and determining the meter in which the fewest ,,wrong" stresses occur; (2) giving primary evidential weight to the first stanza as the probably most

---
([12]) *Op. cit.*, p. 526.
([13]) Respectively Paris, Bibl. nat. fr. 846 and 844.

carefully considered one, from which the other stanzas may well deviate here and there.

Once the meter, i.e. musically the barring, has been established, the rhythm is the next problem. To be sure, the problem is complex and must be solved individually for each poem. Certainly a trochee, e. g., can be equally well represented by various rhythms, such as |♩. ♩|, |♩ ♪|, |♪ ♩|, and each of these rhythms may be varied by using several shorter notes for either of the two note values, e. g., ˙|♫ ♫| ' |♫ ♫| ' |♫ ♫|

Which of these rhythms may be best applied is a musical question, and it may well be surmised that medieval performers might apply different rhythms to a certain poem at various renderings. Whereas barring, i.e., a basic regularity of stressed and unstressed syllables, seems absolutely necessary for the performer of metric poetry, the choice of rhythm is secondary. It will largely depend on the distribution of the ornaments in the melody, another clue which van der Werf rejects. The reason given is that ornaments do not consistently occur in the same position in various versions of a tune. Here the contemporary motet once more furnishes clear evidence that this circumstance in no way nullifies metric pulse. Indeed, many ornaments were sung on short, unstressed syllables, a fact that van der Werf holds to be contradictory to metric rhythm; and in the multiple versions of many motets the ornaments also freely migrate among strong and weak beats. Yet with the clue to the rhythm furnished in many instances by the patterned tenor (cantus firmus), the overwhelming evidence points to the longer note values of the modal patterns as the carriers of the majority of ornaments. Since this evidence involves many quotations from trouvère songs, its application to the contemporary monophonic repertory in general can be readily accepted.

Although, as has been mentioned, it has hitherto been held that the rhythmic interpretation of trouvère chansons admitted of only two alternatives: either modal rhythm or free declamation, a third possibility does exist. Over twenty years ago Heinrich Husmann showed that at least four trouvère songs share their music with polyphonic conductus [14]. These chansons must therefore be presumed to have been amenable to the same rhythm as the related conductus, and Husmann demonstrated that in both some hexasyllabic verses follow the modified modal rhythm |♩. ♪♩| ♪♩♩.| [15]

One of the four chansons is by the late-12th-century trouvère Blondel de Nesle, and all four seem to have antedated the related conductus, as their typical chanson structures are highly unusual for conductus. This observation

---

[14] Cf. «Zur Rhythmik des Trouvèregesanges», Die Musikforschung 5, 1952, pp. 110-113.

[15] Derived from the second mode: |♪♩ ♪♩| ♪♩ ♪ ♩|..

pushes metric interpretation back into the last decades of the 12th century. There seems to be evidence, however, that polyphonic music of the early 12th century, the so-called St. Martial or Aquitanian repertory, was also sung in measured rhythm ([16]). This may have been a rhythm akin to modal rhythm or perhaps one frequently found in early conductus, viz. one in which all or most syllables have an equal duration, as in the Königstein song cited earlier. Latest research would extend rhythmic interpretation even further back. In a recent paper John Boe showed that a trope of the mid-11th century, which thus antedates William of Aquitain's earliest songs, is notated and was sung in what appears to be a 6/8 meter similar to the first rhythmic mode, expressing the rhythm of an *a-b, a-b, a-b, a* stanza as follows ([17]) :

| ♩. ♩ ♪ | ♩ ♩ 𝄾 | ♩ ♪ ♩ ♪ | ♩. ♩ 𝄾 |.

In the light of what has been said above about Moorish-Spanish poetry this is, indeed, quite possible.

To sum up : The basic fact is that courtly poetry does possess metric structure, and metric structure can be reflected in modern musical notation only by means of bar lines and an intelligible note-value system. Otherwise the meter, which, as Dragonetti firmly states, is an essential structural element of this poetry, is lost in the modern edition. The free rhythm proposed by many scholars in fact mistakes poetry for prose. With some flexibility and some musical sense, metric-rhythmic transcriptions that parallel and support the meter and versification of the troubadour, trouvère, and minnesinger poems can and must be produced, if these are to be brought back to life. A single, pervasive modal approach has to be rejected in favor of at least two possible approaches, viz. either modal solutions with frequent so-called « irregularities » and modal mixtures, such as were taught by Franco of Cologne, or transcriptions in which syllables receive equal length except where lengthy melismas occur; but both types must be barred. The initial time signature, however, may well change in the course of a song, a procedure frequently necessary also in motets.

It should be added that the motets of the last decades of the 13th century prove that meter then declined in poetry, and metric stress disappeared, together with regular line length, as an organizing factor. The poetry of these later motets proceeds in free verse, in lines of greatly differing length, held together by rhymes only, but rhymes without pattern. Considerations of stress, let alone regular stress, are completely absent from that poetry, which is contemporary with the demise of troubadour and trouvère poetry.

([16]) *Cf.* Theodore C. KARP's forthcoming book on the music of St. Martial; also, among others, T. C. KARP, « St. Martial and Santiago de Compostela; an Analytical Speculation, » *Acta musicologica* 39, 1967, pp. 144-160; Bruno STÄBLEIN, « *Modale Rhythmen im Saint-Martial-Repertoire?* », *Festschrift Friedrich Blume*, Bärenreiter-Verlag, Kassel 1963, pp. 340-362.
([17]) *Cf.* « Rhythmical Notation in the Beneventan Gloria Trope *Aureas arces*, » *Musica disciplina* 29 (1975), pp. 5-42.

As stated above, Illustration 2 uses one of the transcriptions offered in van der Werf's book. It connects a chanson by Jaufre Rudel with the famous *Palestine Song* by Walther von der Vogelweide, two tunes that are very similar and partially identical, chiefly in the first half of the melody. But if it is true that Walther adapted Jaufre's melody to his poem, as is claimed by van der Werf, Walther made important changes in it.

With respect to the rhythm of these two songs van der Werf writes as follows ([18]) :

> Scholarly opinion on the meter of the songs ... has varied considerably, so much so that (one scholar gave) a synoptic chart of ten different metrizations ... of the melody preserved with Walther's poem ([19]) ... there are no indications ... of fixed meter in Jaufre Rudel's chanson; ... the way in which the melody is distributed over the text suggest(s) a performance in declamatory rhythm ... This conclusion is in no way contradicted by the fact that Jaufre's melody ... was also used for a German poem. Even though the meter of German lyric poetry of the period ... was based upon a predetermined number of stressed (mark: stressed!) syllables per line, there is no evidence that this poetry was ... performed to a melody in fixed meter.

Not only is this statement contradictory, but the fact is that poetry in Provençal was just as metrically conceived as poetry in German or Latin, i. e., it followed several traditional meters. And the change of meter between the Provençal poem by Jaufre and Walther's German one is highly important here. The former clearly runs in iambic dimeters, as follows :

Lanquan li jorn son lonc en may

m'es belhs dous chans d'auzelhs de lonh,

e quan mi suy partitz de lay

remambra'm d'un' amor de lonh : (etc.)

Walther's poem, on the other hand, proceeds in trochaic dimeters, viz. :

Nu alerst leb' ich mir werde,

sit min sündich auge siht

hie daz lant undt auch die erde

dem man vil der eren giht. (etc.)

That both poems are completely metric cannot be denied. That such poetry can hardly be considered to have been sung or read without reference to the meter is equally certain. And the music fits this assumption very well.

As the above presentation has tried to show, the mere pitch transcription of the melodies is musically and poetically unsatisfactory. Any line of the Rudel

---

([18]) *Op. cit.*, p. 86.
([19]) *Cf.* Burkhard KIPPENBERG, *Der Rhythmus im Minnesang.* C. H. Beck, Munich 1962, p. 226f.

chanson bears this out. Would it be right, e. g., to give each note approximately the same length? This would render verse 2 much longer than verse 1, although both are octosyllabic. On the other hand, should every syllable receive about the same time value? In order to do so one would have to slow up everything inordinately to accommodate the lengthy ornaments that occur at the ends of lines; moreover, the final syllables of most lines would end breathlessly and without a stop, on the last of three, four, five, or even seven notes. This was hardly the composer's intent; a singer has to breathe at line ends, and a pause there seems essential to a good performance. Should this fact not be conveyed to the modern performer by the editor, as it is, e. g., suggested by the small notes added above the verse endings in Illustration 2? Cadential halts at the ends of lines are needed elsewhere as well, e.g., in hymns and chorales, to keep the rhythm from limping and the singer from getting out of breath. They are something like fermatas which inject some not unwelcome rhythmic irregularities.

Any transcription presents problems, to be sure. But just as in editing a medieval poem emendations and added punctuation are taken for granted to render the text intelligible, the musical transcription must be rendered so as to make musical sense to a performer or reader. In both songs it is probably best to give equal length to all syllables except to some at the ends of lines, but the songs must be barred differently. Immediately both assume pleasing musical forms. As conceived by this writer, the bar lines here carry the same psychological implications as in conventional music; the amount of dynamic and agogic emphasis given by the performer to primary and secondary beats is, of course, a matter of taste and training.

Once more returning to the basic assumptions put forward at the beginning of this paper, our interpretation (a) indicates in both songs the poetic and musical stress patterns through the barring, (b) reflects the poetic structure in the musical phrasing, and (c) gives adequate rhythmic expression to the rhymes.

The rhythmic interpretation of medieval monophonic songs greatly influences the interpretation of their melodic organization as well. With regard to this problem the controversy has been as to whether Gregorian modes apply to these repertories or whether other, non-Gregorian modes may be appealed to. Van der Werf adduces two possible non-Gregorian principles, namely those derived from Curt Sachs's analysis of the folksongs of many cultures and formulated in his last, posthumous work, *The Wellsprings of Music* [20]. According to these ideas the chansons are divided into those organized around two focal pitches, usually an interval of a second or third apart, and those that unfold along a so-called structural chain of two to four thirds or two thirds and a fourth.

---

[20] Jaap KUNST, ed., Martinus Nijhoff, The Hague 1962.

To this writer it seems rather unwarranted to apply an analysis of folk-songs to the sophisticated court art of the troubadours and trouvères. After all, the medieval poet-musicians were principally acquainted with Church music, some of it of recent polyphonic workmanship, and with a long tradition of art song enjoyed by courtiers, Churchmen, and students since the times of Charlemagne and the establishment of the Omayyad caliphate in mid-10th-century Spain. Their social standing as feudal lords or guild artisans would effectively prevent them from mingling with the lower classes and singing their songs. Indeed, one of van der Werf's astute remarks points to a kinship between many first lines of trouvère melodies and psalmodic formulas. As a matter of fact, each of the fifteen transcriptions offered by him is clearly organized in one of the Church modes, whereas structural chains of thirds and two-tone schemes can be adduced only with great difficulties and with many exceptions. The latter methods were similarly applied several years ago to the analysis of the melodies of 13th-century motets by Finn Matthiassen [21] and rejected for that repertory as non-productive by the present writer [22].

It is clear that all melodic analyses that do not consider metric stress run into a great obstacle, viz. how to determine the chief pitches. A most striking example of the inherent difficulties of this approach is provided by Illustration 2 above. These are some of the things van der Werf says about the two songs in the introduction to their transcription [23]:

> In its entirety the melody of Jaufre's chanson has a rather ambiguous structure: most lines have F and one line has high C as the most important structural tones; ... although the low C is not very pronounced as structural tone, it serves ... as ending tone of both pedes and of the entire chanson. Thus ... it is difficult to determine whether this melody is a centric one, moving around F, or a standing one with C or perhaps D as basic tone.
>
> It is interesting to compare this rather loose organization with the strong tertial structure in the melody preserved with Walther's poem. The melody ... is based upon the chain D-F-A-C with perhaps C-E-G as a contrasting or secondary chain ... Especially noteworthy are the differences in ending tones ...

Thus the author is at a loss to find the central tones of these two songs, although he recognizes important differences between them. The fact is that Walther reinterpreted the mode of the melody, and this reinterpretation emerges clearly only when the inherent change in metric stress is observed and notationally carried out. Rudel's melody is organized in a clear sixth Gregorian

---

[21] *Cf. The Style of the Early Motet.* Dan Fog, Copenhagen 1966.
[22] *Cf.* the review of Finn MATTHIASSEN's *The Style of the Early Motet, Journal of the Amer. Musicological Soc.* 20, 1967, pp. 489-492.
[23] *Op. cit.*, p. 85.

mode, based on the central *F* with the cofinalis *C*, whereas Walther changed to the first mode with *D* as both central tone and finalis ([24]).

These facts are evident from the first stressed tone in line 1 to the final cadence. In the seven lines of Jaufre's bar form the cadence tones are *D-C*, *D-C*, *G-D-C*, and in Walther's, *C-D*, *C-D*, *A-C-D*. The respective twenty-eight metric stresses are distributed as follows:

in Rudel's chanson: 10*F* — 9*D* — 5*C* — 2*A* — 2*G*; and

in Walther's song: 9*D* — 7*A* — 5*F* — 4*E* — 2*C* — 1*G*.

Thus there are 15 *F*'s and *C*'s as against 11 *D*'s and *A*'s in Jaufre's tune and 16 *D*'s and *A*'s as against 7 *F*'s and *C*'s in Walther's. Moreover, only Rudel's song uses the B_b. Thus these tunes can be easily related to Gregorian modes, whereas their tertial-chain structures are most unclear — in Jaufre's chanson non-existent, in Walther's inconsistent or forced in application.

The analysis of the song given in Illustration 1 has a similarly clear result. Six lines of the poem end on *D*, two on *A*, and two on *E*, and the range of the tune is one octave, a-a^1. The melody therefore employs the second mode, and it is somewhat unexpected to find that the single stanza of music given in the manuscript ends on a^1. The transcription in Sappler's edition changes the *A* to a *D*; but when the three stanzas of the poem are scanned, the *A* appears to be quite appropriate in stanzas 1 and 2, both as reflecting the questions at the ends of these stanzas and as introducing the next stanza. The last stanza, however, does demand a *D* for its conclusion and perhaps an *F* natural as the antepenultimate note to reestablish the prevailing mode. Thus the syntactic meaning here seems to lead to a better emendation of the final note.

Just like the musicologist who does not give the poetic clues their due in the interpretation of the tunes and obtains erroneous or at best ambiguous results, so the linguist fails who neglects the study of the tunes and their notation. The recent comprehensive analysis of the trouvère and early motet-text repertories by Mölk and Wolfzettel is a case in point. In trouvère poems the structure is usually quite clear. Nevertheless there are a good many poems in which the intention of the poet becomes evident only when also the music is considered; the phrasing, indicated by rests, bars at the ends of verses, and the repetitions of melodic segments often give well defined information about the line arrangement, without which wrong conclusions may be drawn.

([24]) Here the Gregorian modes are taken in their later meaning, the one particularly applying to the later hymns and sequences which are contemporary with the secular repertories here concerned — viz. as modal scales organized around two pitches. This concept contrasts with the earlier involvement of traditional melodic formulas in each mode, which applies, e. g., to the psalm tones and the Eastern chants.

A simple example is the anonymous « *Quant li dous tens renouvele:* » [25]

This chanson appears in Mölk's outline as follows :

```
a  b  a  b  b  a  b  a  c   c;
7' 7  7' 7  7  7' 7  7' 4  12
```

but the music shows that (a) there is an inaccuracy in the syllable count of the penultimate line and (b), in fact the last two lines are actually three lines, the last one being sung to a melodic variant of lines 2 and 4. Recalling our basic assumptions, the poetic meter here points to that of the music, whereas the pattern of ornaments suggests the changes of rhythm in the tune in lines 5 and 9; the second change seems to imply the presence of a refrain (quotation) at the end, which, as is characteristic of many refrains, includes an unrhymed line.

As was proposed at the beginning of this paper, a schematic outline should convey to the eye all structural details. To this writer the following way of outlining, using the above poem as an illustration, would seem to be best suited to clarify the poetic and musical structures — syntactical, rhyme-wise, metric-rhythmic, and sectional :

$$a(7_4-) + b(7) \qquad\qquad b(7) - a(7-)$$
$$12 \qquad\qquad1$$
$$a(7-) + b(7) \qquad\qquad b(7) - a(7-) + b(3)$$
$$12 \qquad\qquad1$$
$$\qquad\qquad\qquad\qquad\qquad \frac{x(7) - b(5)}{2^1}$$

---

[25] *Cf.* Hans SPANKE, *G. Raynauds Bibliographie des altfranzösischen Liedes* I, E. J. Brill, Leiden 1955, n° 615. The chanson is extant in Mss. Paris, Bibl. nat. fr. 847, fol. 144-144v, and Paris, Bibl. nat. nouv. acq. fr. 1050, fol. 212v.

Here the letters symbolize the rhymes; the figures in parentheses the numbers of syllables from first to last stress; the subscript figures, the number of stresses (whose pattern is assumed to remain constant unless otherwise indicated, here trochaic); the dashes, feminine endings (or also, ahead of figures, anacruses); the plus sign, the continuous rhythm connecting two lines; the underscoring, a refrain; the figures below letters, recurrent musical phrases (with modifications indicated by subscript or superscript numbers); the lines are arranged in syntactical groups, and a wide space after lines 3-4 or the two-column arrangement of the symbols shows that the poem falls into two stanza-like sections. Whereas (-3) can only mean an iambic dipody, a (4) normally indicates a dactylic line : / ᴗ ᴗ / ; and either line may well conclude with a feminine ending (-3-) or (4-). But (7) may stand for either a trochaic dimeter or a dactylic trimeter : / ᴗ / ᴗ / ᴗ / or / ᴗ ᴗ / ᴗ ᴗ / ; the added subscripts here help to differentiate the two possibilities : (7_4) and (7_3), and unless otherwise indicated, the particular meter will continue in the poem. To be sure, there are many lines that employ irregular stress patterns, such as / ᴗ / ᴗ ᴗ / ᴗ / or / ᴗ / ᴗ / ᴗ ᴗ / (the ancient Glyconic verses), both of which would appear as (8_4); but ᴗ / ᴗ ᴗ / ᴗ ᴗ / would be symbolized by (-7_3).

When it comes to the far more irregularly built texts of motets, the correlated study of music and text becomes even more important ([26]). A short piece may serve as illustration 4 ([27]) :

This is how this poem is presented in Mölk's analysis :

$$a\ b\ a\ b\ a\ a\ a\ a\ a\ c\ a.$$
$$7\ 4\ 7\ 4\ 7\ 7\ 7\ 3\ 3\ 9'\ 3$$

The structure and the versification are quite different, however, viz. :

$\underline{a(7_4) + b(-3)}$	$\underline{a(3) — a(3) + a(3-)}$
	1　　　　　　2
$\underline{a(7)\ + b(-3)}$	$\underline{a(3) — a(3)}$
$\underline{a(7)\ + b(-3)}$	$\underline{x(5) + a(-7)}$
1-2	

The division of Mölk's lines 6 and 7, which actually from lines 6-9, is borne out (1) by the structure of the poem, the first section of which thereby gains consistency of formulation; and (2) by the music, which makes no break

---

([26]) In fact, over 40 % of Mölk's motet-text analyses include serious errors, and many more show mistakes in syllable count — because the related melody was not studied — and other minor flaws.
([27]) The example is here given as it appears in the Ms. Montpellier, Fac. de Méd. H 196, as No 121 (cf. the author's new transcription of this manuscript, forthcoming at A-R Editions, Madison, WI.); with the same text this melody also appears in six other manuscripts, and with other texts in six additional ones, as well as once without text in a three-part clausula (cf. the author's forthcoming Complete Edition of the Earliest Motets, forthcoming at Yale University Press, n° 65).

before line 6, but does make one within it. The new division of the last two lines is proved by the fact that (1) this is a refrain whose last line also recurs elsewhere by itself; and (2) this last line parallels the words « benedicamus Domino » in the Latin text that is set to the same music in other manuscripts ([28]). The « x » stands for an unrhymed line, such unrhymed lines being very frequent in refrains. The dashes in front of syllable counts accomplish a task which theorists of old French verse seem never to consider : just as feminine endings do not change the essential character and length of a line, which depends on the number of stresses rather than that of syllables, i. e.,

---

([28]) Among others in Ms. Florence, Bibl. Med. Laur. pl. 29, 1, fol. 409v-410.

on the number of metric, musical units, so the character and essential length of a line is not changed by an anacrusis. As numerous examples in motets prove, both anacruses and feminine endings may be carried by either short or long note values.

To conclude : The basic assumptions proposed at the beginning of this paper aimed at creating transcriptions of medieval songs that are meaningful to performers and schematic outlines that convey all important analytical information. They have led to fundamental considerations of rhythm and meter of both poetry and music, of mode and accidentals in the music, and of the interdependence of poetry and music. This interdependence and the necessity for a correlated approach cannot be stressed enough. The phrasing of the music often clarifies the versification; the meter of the poetry determines that of the music; the distribution of the ornaments is often a guide to the rhythm; the syntactic meaning of the poetry and the repetition of musical phrases both contribute to the overall structuring of a song and therefore to its performance; the phrasing and the cadence points indicate the melodic mode, have implications for the use of accidentals, and suggest pauses or halts. Above all, neither the poetry nor the music of these repertories can be imagined to have been conceived without meter and metric stress guiding the performance.

This paper is an attempt at encouraging a comprehensive fresh look at the entire repertory of the troubadours, trouvères, minnesingers, and other medieval monophonic songs, leading to editions that would aid in the revival of this charming poetry and music — editions combining linguistic and musicological carefulness with a broad sense of humanistic values, on the one hand, and on the other with a musicianly and poetic approach that would shoulder rather than avoid the responsibility of guiding the generally less learned performer and reader in matters of rhythm, meter, mode, form, and actual pitch, perhaps even of general tempo and dynamics. Such editions would yield insights that are historically and structurally more justifiable than vague appeals to chains of thirds and declamatory rhythm, and would finally render the repertory more widely accessible.

[4]

The "Not-so-precisely Measured" Music of the Middle Ages

Hendrik van der Werf

In the area of performance practice few issues have been debated as fervently and as dogmatically as has rhythm and meter in medieval song. For more than a century researchers have tried to reconstruct the original manner in which these songs were performed and, by the middle of the century, almost every conceivable theory had been broached. In a book published in 1962 Burkhard Kippenberg subjected the existing theories to a thorough scrutiny and came to the conclusion that no logical and decisive evidence had been brought forth for any of them.[1] In addition to the objections voiced by Kippenberg one should mention the monolithic approach as a serious weakness of most research in this area: it has been (and sometimes still is) taken for granted that one type of rhythm governed either all songs in a given language or all songs of the entire medieval period.

Several thousand non-liturgical songs have come down to us. For the majority only the texts have been preserved, but we have both text and melody for well over 2,000 of them, the precise figure depending upon one's own definitions of the terms "non-liturgical," "song," and "Middle

---

1. Burkhard Kippenberg, *Der Rhythmus im Minnesang: eine Kritik der literar- und musikhistorischen Forschung mit einer Übersicht über die musikalischen Quellen* (Munich, 1962).

Ages." It may be regretted that so many of the songs with music have a French text, but this accident of history does have a fortunate aspect in that one genre, often called "trouvère song,"[2] or simply "chanson," has been preserved in such abundance that we can learn much about performance practice from the texts and melodies themselves, from the manner in which they were preserved, and especially from the manner in which a given song varies from one manuscript to another. Although we all would prefer a more direct approach, we have little choice but to take the best known genre as a vantage point from which to study the lesser known repertories. With great caution we can try and determine in what respects the trouvère songs differ from, and in what respects they resemble the other ones. For now, we may restrict our attention to monophonic song in French and Occitan.[3] We must bypass plainchant altogether, and leave other "not-so-precisely-measured" genres for a future occasion.[4]

The Texts

Our study of melodic rhythm must begin with the texts. One of the major principles for versification of troubadour and trouvère songs (and of most subsequent poetry in Romance languages) is the "syllable count." A given line, or verse, normally has a fixed number of syllables in each strophe of a given poem, but there is no fixed position for accented syllables in places other than the rhyme and, in a limited number of poems, the caesura. An occasional line may seem trochaic or dactylic,

---

2. For the sake of this study the term "trouvère" has both the advantage and disadvantage of being vague. Some scholars, especially experts on medieval poetry, have used the term sparingly and usually in the meaning to be proposed here. Others, especially authors of textbooks on the history of music, have used it in reference to all French poet-composers of the twelfth and thirteenth centuries. According to their contents the manuscripts allow a conveniently narrow interpretation of the term. The medieval songs in Old-French have been preserved in a dozen large manuscripts (and in many small and fragmentary collections) dating from the middle of the thirteenth through the beginning of the fourteenth century. They contain a rather wide variety of poems and melodies, but one fairly homogeneous group prevails. The poems in this group are strophic in form and content, and most of them deal with *fin' amor*, nowadays often called "courtly love." Only the first strophe of the poem is provided with a melody. I shall restrict the term "trouvère song" to members of this group.
3. The term "troubadour song" will be used for songs in the Provencal, or Occitan, language.
4. Christopher Page, *Voices and Instruments of the Middle Ages: Instrumental Practice and Songs in France 1100-1300*, (London, 1987) comes to largely the same classification, and considers troubadour and trouvère songs to be in a "high style," the others in "lower styles." With more or less the same results, we can also take attribution as a criterion for categorization because most of the songs that are attributed to a specific author belong to the first group; conversely, many of the songs outside of it are anonymous. Fearing that uninitiated readers may see a value judgment in the terms "high" and "low," I prefer not to use them.

but there is no case in which an entire poem or entire strophe has a regular alternation of accented and unaccented syllables. I may recall here that there is such an alternation in many Latin poems of the same time, including many (not all) Latin motet texts and even some French motets. Traditionally, the syllable count is referred to as the "meter" of the poem. In discussions of melodic meter this could lead to confusion, and one might be tempted to reason that, if there is meter in the poem, there must have been meter in the music. This apodictum is flawed because the term "meter" is used in two meanings. A fixed number of syllables in a poem does not necessarily mean that the melody had a fixed alternation of accented and unaccented or long and short units. Except when the context calls for a general term, and in discussions of "modal rhythm," I will avoid the terms "rhythm" and "meter" in preference for less ambiguous ones, such as "syllable count," "accentuation," and "duration."

Medieval Writings Concerning Measurement

Medieval writings about the poetry of the troubadours and trouvères are devoid of information concerning melodic rhythm. Among the treatises dealing with music, only the one by Johannes de Grocheio contains a few remarks that may pertain to trouvère songs. In order to evaluate his remarks, we must keep in mind the development of the discipline called *musica*.[5] St. Augustine is one of several authors who define *musica* as the "art of measuring" or the "art of measuring well." Some of those who were interested in measuring, including St. Augustine, seem to have found great delight in studying the numbers in those Latin poems that have long and short syllables in a ratio of 2:1. In the fifth chapter (the fifth "book" as medieval people called it) Augustine discusses numerical equalities that we can perceive with our intellect, but not with our senses. In the last chapter the real purpose of Augustine's study emerges when he turns to the harmony found in God. Other learned authors were fascinated with the numbers or ratios found among pitches in the scale. Some transferred these numbers to the universe and organized the heavenly bodies as pitches in an octave. In an almost inscrutable development, the meaning of the term *musica* widened and came to include everything that we now call music. For some time this development went hand in hand with a confusing non-sequitur: since

---

5. For two recent and rather different interpretations of *musica* in reference to duration see van der Werf, *The Emergence of Gregorian Chant: A Comparative Study of Roman, Ambrosian, and Gregorian Chant*, vol. I,1 (published by the author, Rochester, N.Y., 1983), 22-30, and John Stevens, *Words and Music in the Middle Ages: Song, Narrative, Dance and Drama, 1050-1350* (Cambridge, 1986), 413-434.

musica concerns itself with precisely measurable phenomena, everything discussed under the heading *musica* was assumed to be precisely measurable. In the second half of the thirteenth century Franco of Cologne and Johannes de Garlandia discuss in detail measurements in motets, while explicitly stating that plainchant was immeasurable. Johannes de Grocheio disagrees with their latter statement. In his opinion calling "music" immeasurable was contrary to the tradition of *musica*. Circumventing the problem in typical medieval fashion, he concedes that plainchant was "not so precisely measured." Although he is not explicit concerning trouvère songs, Grocheio seems to place them among the "not-so-precisely-measured" genres. Even if I am wrong on the last point, we must reckon with the possibility that not all music of the thirteenth century was precisely measured. Above all, we must be very cautious in taking at face value medieval statements about the measurability of any genre of music.

The Musical Notation

Most musical scribes of troubadour and trouvère songs used the square notation which we know from Gregorian chant and which bears no indications of duration aside from double notes. One of the distinctive features of this notation was its use of simple and compound neumes. In the latter one notational symbol comprises several pitches sung to one syllable. Sometime in the thirteenth century the neumes acquired mensural meaning. Not only the presence or absence of a stem, but also the shape of the compound neume, also called a ligature, determined the duration of its individual pitches. We do not know to what extent the scribes of troubadour and trouvère sources were familiar with this innovation, but it is obvious that non-mensural notation was the norm for the chansons. In a manuscript that almost exclusively contains works by Adam de la Hale mensural notation was used for his rondeaux and motets, all of them polyphonic, while non-mensural notation was used for the chansons and jeux-partis, all of them monophonic. The scribe of the manuscript now known as the *Chansonnier Cangé* demonstrated his familiarity with mensural notation by using it for the major part of a motet for two voices, while his notation of most chansons is decidedly non-mensural.[6] Almost as if to confuse us, he gives the impression of having used some half-hearted form of mensural notation in a limited

---

6. For more details on the semi-mensural notation in the *Chansonnier Cangé* see van der Werf, *The Chansons of the Troubadours and Trouvères a Study of the Melodies and Their Relation to the Poems* (Utrecht, 1972), 36-37 and 139-146. See also the photographic reproduction, transcription, and discussion in Jean B. Beck, *Le Chansonnier Cangé*, 2 vols. (Paris, 1927).

number of chansons by clearly distinguishing between stemmed and unstemmed single notes without giving mensural meaning to his ligatures. Furthermore, the alternation of stemmed and unstemmed single notes varies from completely regular in some melodies to absolutely meaningless in others. This leaves us with the problem of distinguishing between real and make-believe mensuration in this particular manuscript. All in all, the scribal habit of giving chansons in non-mensural notation strengthens the idea that duration in chansons was "not so precisely measured."

Multiple Versions

By a stroke of luck the troubadour and trouvère repertories, especially the latter, present us with a source of information that we have just begun to explore. In many instances a given song has been preserved in more than one manuscript; and some songs occur in up to a dozen sources. The multiple versions are rarely identical. For a long time it was assumed that the extant readings were copied, directly or indirectly, from the author's autograph and that copyists were to be blamed for the many discrepancies. Early in this century another explanation emerged, as literary scholars recognized that initially the songs were disseminated by word of mouth, and that only in the mid thirteenth century was dissemination through writing juxtaposed against a continuing oral tradition. Most importantly, the realization arose that, for both performers and scribes, requirements for faithful transmission were much looser than they are in our print-dominated society. In other words, both the persons involved in the oral tradition and those who preserved songs in written form felt free to vary certain aspects of the texts. Consequently, editors of the poems gave up their attempts at reconstructing the original version of a poem. It is now general practice to select one version as basis for an edition and to list variants from other sources in the critical apparatus.

In retrospect, it is difficult to believe that in the early 1960s I was the first to use differences and similarities among multiple versions as a source of information about musical characteristics, especially the rhythm of troubadour and trouvère melodies. Melodic variants are more numerous (and probably more significant) than textual ones. Moreover, oral transmission can be proven much more convincingly for the music than for the poetry, thanks to the many songs in which the music for the first and the second verse are repeated for the third and the fourth verse (i.e. AB AB X). Almost invariably these first four lines differ less in multiple versions than do the subsequent lines. If there had been a written transmission from poet-composer to extant manuscripts, we could have explained this phenomenon only by assuming that musical scribes turned sleepy and sloppy at the beginning of the fifth verse, but returned to fairly accurate copying when they started the next tune. In an oral tradition, however, a person learning a song from listening to it would hear the A and B melodies twice as often as the X section, and thus retain the former better than the latter. Accepting oral transmission as the normal process does not imply that scribes entered the songs directly into the extant sources either from memory or upon hearing. On the contrary, there are ample indications that they (or someone else) made what we might call "a rough copy" that was used as the model, or exemplar, in the production of a collection in book form. Another feature provides valuable information concerning the scribes. Four of the trouvère sources preserve long groups of songs, often by a single author, in the very same order and with few differences. Clearly, these four scribes had access to the same exemplars, and it is encouraging to learn that they could copy very precisely. Obviously, they made some errors, but it is of more importance to note that they also must have made some deliberate changes.

When evaluating similarities and differences among multiple versions, we must choose between two assumptions. Putting things in black and white, we can assume that the transmitters were connoisseurs who left the essential features of a song intact, or that singers and scribes knew virtually nothing about the subtleties of troubadour and trouvère art, and corrupted both text and music. The texts of the chansons help us solve this riddle in that they suggest that troubadour and trouvère poetry is unlikely to have appealed to the masses. Their dissemination is not likely to have been accomplished by footloose and unsophisticated entertainers who eked out a living as jugglers and storytellers in city streets and town squares. Instead, the poems are rather esoteric and are likely to have been appreciated only by afficionados. It may be argued that these connoisseurs, many of them troubadours or trouvères themselves, were responsible for the transmission. At the beginning of the oral tradition stood the poet-composer himself. Regardless of whether he sang in order to teach his creation to someone else or in order to present it to his peers, the author, as a song's first performer, established the manner of presenting it to an audience. If the transmitters were experts and connoisseurs, they are not likely to have altered any characteristics that were essential to either the genre or the individual song, although they may have varied other features within the boundaries of the poetic and musical customs of the time. In this process the author may also have been the first to vary his song from one presentation to another. If this was the case, the similarities and differences among multiple versions afford us a valuable source of information about the manner in which the songs were actually performed.

The "Approximate" Equality of Individual Notes

The differences between multiple versions make it impossible to reconstruct the original melody in all its details, while the similarities assure us that what the scribes left us must have been closely related to what the poet-composer sang at the "world première" of a given chanson. The multiple versions of many songs agree fairly well on the pitches for a given passage, but differ on how the pitches are to be distributed over the text.[7] Taken all together, such differences inescapably lead to a strong but negative conclusion: they could not have come about if all chansons always had been performed in modal rhythm or in any regular alternation of long-short or accented-unaccented units. Fortunately, the study of similarities and differences also allows a positive conclusion, albeit a vague one: the variants could have come about only if essentially all pitches were of more or less equal importance to the flow and the character of the melody. This gives new meaning to Grocheio's remark that pitches in trouvère songs were "not so precisely measured," i.e. that they were of more or less equal duration, with emphasis on, and great uncertainty about the degree of "more or less." In a performance in which pitches do not have a fixed duration and do not come in a fixed sequence of stress and unstress, any text could be sung as the performer desired. The poet-composer as first performer more or less determined the "not so precisely measured" duration of a pitch, a syllable, and a word.

Although this conclusion is vague, it does solve some problems, e.g., why variants in the choice or order of words can bring about variants in the placement of textual accents. In this type of free rhythm, strophes with different distributions of accents can be performed to the same melody, without injustice to either the text or the music. Even better, in this free rhythm both text and melody can receive proper attention and neither is subservient to the other. This gives meaning, too, to the "double note," i.e., the immediate reiteration of a pitch over a syllable. It seems

---

7. Since my conclusions are based upon the overall situation, I would rather not refer to specific examples and instead suggest the study of many songs in multiple versions. For this purpose see van der Werf, *The Extant Troubadour Melodies: Transcriptions and Essays for Performers and Scholars*, Gerald A. Bond, text editor (published by the author, Rochester, N.Y., 1984) and *Trouvères-Melodien*, Monumenta Monodica Medii Aevi, vols. XI and XII, Bruno Stäblein, general editor (Kassel, 1977-1979).

reasonable that a double note represents a pitch that is longer than the one respresented by a single note.[8] And the duration of a given pitch very likely varied from one performer to another and from one strophe to another. Thus, it should be not surprising that two scribes, notating the same melody, might disagree on whether a given pitch was represented by a double or single note. At the present stage of the research, it is risky to draw conclusions from the fact that double notes occur exclusively as part of a compound neume, i.e., over syllables sung to two or more pitches.

Fluctuation in the duration of pitches must have been so pervasive that even as staunch a believer in *musica* as Grocheio was unable to measure them as precisely as he would have liked. On the other hand, something must have enabled scribes to distinguish between pitches of average and longer than average duration, and to consider most of them average. Probably, the duration of pitches was sufficiently close to equal to create a prevailing, although "not precisely measured" unit of time.

Application to a Specific Chanson

Clearly, the above conclusions pertain to troubadour and trouvère songs, in general. In respect to a specific melody, the search for the original rhythm has a disappointing result, for we are unable to reconstruct precisely how it was performed seven or eight centuries ago. However, two aspects of our general conclusions add up to valuable guidance for today's singer of early music. I am optimistic enough to think that we can come reasonably close to an authentic rendition of troubadour and trouvère songs by applying the general conclusion to a specific chanson. Playing the schoolmaster, I may suggest that performers begin by studying the text (not reciting it without the music). In the next step, sing the entire song (not one strophe at a time) making all single notes fairly equal to one another, and making double notes more or less twice as long as single ones. By concentrating on getting the text across to an audience, one is likely to develop small differences in the duration of individual pitches and, especially, almost continuous but subtly executed fluctuations in tempo. A brief elaboration on the two caveats in the above suggestion may be helpful. Beginning the learning process of a song with reciting the text without music may result in a rendition in which the syllables are of equal duration. For basically syllabic songs, this may not be a serious shortcoming but, for more ornate ones, this type of rhythm may fail to do justice to the melody. If one were to learn

---

8. In existing "precisely-measured" transcriptions such lengthening often conflicts with the meter selected by the editor.

a song a strophe at a time, the first strophe might get fixed so strongly in one's mind that its rhythm gets transferred to subsequent strophes. Needless to say, such uniformity will fail to do justice to the differences of meaning and textual flow in individual strophes.

Perhaps, these theories can be elucidated a bit more with the help of a personal note or two. I am not a trained singer and have virtually no experience in reciting poetry to an audience. I do not give recitals but often sing some chansons to illustrate a lecture. I am convinced that one can do justice to both poem and melody. By trial and error, one can learn how to sing several pitches over a seemingly insignificant syllable, and to sing one pitch and one "not so precisely measured" unit of time for the most important syllable of the sentence. In the process one is likely to develop a great appreciation for what at first may appear a duality in medieval songs: one comes to enjoy singing pitches that have primarily melodic meaning at the same time one is "reciting" a poem. Text and melody may not be wedded as they are in songs by Schubert or Fauré, or in an aria of Mozart, yet they go far beyond the point of coexisting or of merely tolerating one another.

The first time I published the above conclusions I used the terms "declaim" and "declamatory" in an unwise attempt to capture a manifold theory in a single word.[9] Paying more attention to the single term than to the entire theory, some fellow medievalists rejected my conclusions as valid only for syllabic passages. Andrew Hughes wrote that my "theory fails to help with melismatic passages."[10] And as the following excerpt (with a quotation from my book) indicates, my choice of terms seems to have misled John Stevens as well:

> My ... task will be to examine some of the deeply held, if not always deeply questioned, beliefs which are current about words-and-music in medieval song. The assumption that it is the words which substantially determine the rhythm of a song is shared not only by convinced adherents of the 'modal' theory but by its strongest opponents, such as Appel, Monterosso and van der Werf. The practical results they come to are very different; but at root they do have certain beliefs in common.... Van der Werf is more ready to subordinate the melodies to the exigencies of the text: 'the rhythm

---

9. Most notably in van der Werf, "Deklamatorischer Rhythmus in den Chansons der Trouvères," in *Die Musikforschung* 20 (1967): 122-44.
10. Andrew Hughes, *Medieval Music: the Sixth Liberal Art* (Toronto, 1974), 160.

in which one might *declaim* the poem without the music' will shape the musical interpretation.[11]

I apologize to those who were led astray by an isolated term but derive solace from those who understood the total theory. More importantly, I hope that this and other recent discussions of rhythm in chansons rectify whatever wrong impressions I may have given on earlier occasions.[12]

Precisely Measured Melodies

Although they do not seem to be very numerous, there are exceptions to the above generalizations. In fact, it has been known for a long time that there are some trouvère songs in which the pitches are precisely measured. Unfortunately, most studies of them, even the most recent ones, are flawed by preconceived notions. Too often, it is taken for granted that, until the middle of the thirteenth century, modal rhythm was the only form of precise measurement for both monophonic and polyphonic music. In addition, the occurrence of modal rhythm in *some* chansons is still taken as evidence that *all* of them are in modal rhythm.[13] In some other cases the researcher seems preoccupied with the "saving" of modal rhythm for the troubadour and trouvère repertories.[14] What we need is an objective study of all songs that show signs of durational measurement. For the sake of the present discussion we may divide such songs into three groups.

Several of the manuscripts saving primarily chansons contain a separate section with motets.[15] This does not prove much more than that

---

11. Stevens, *Words and Music*, 493-494. I cannot understand how Stevens, p. 502, footnote 28, concludes that I speak "of the concept of 'approximate equality' as applying only to syllabic (i.e. single note) progression."
12. See also van der Werf, *The Extant Troubadour Melodies*, 75-83, and my contribution to the forthcoming *Handbook of the Troubadours*, Ron Akehurst and Judith M. Davis, eds.
13. See my review of *Chanter m'estuet: Songs of the Trouvères*, Samuel N. Rosenberg and Hans Tischler, eds. (Bloomington, 1981) in *Journal of the American Musicological Society* 35 (1982): 539-54. See also Tischler's reaction to my review in the same, 36 (1983): 341-44, and my response in 37 (1984): 206-208. In a review of two of my books in *Journal of the Plainsong and Medieval Music Society* 8 (1985): 59, David Hiley called my evaluation of Tischler's theories "one of the best available descriptions (and refutations) of the idea that modal rhythm provides a key to the interpretation of troubadour songs."
14. This seems to be the case with some of Theodore Karp's publications, e.g. "Three Trouvère Chansons in Mensural Notation" in *Gordon Athol Anderson: in Memoriam* (Henryville, Pa., 1984), 474-94.
15. See especially mss. Paris, B.N. f.fr. 12615 (known as "Chansonnier de Noailles") and Paris B.N. f. fr. 844, published as *Le manuscrit du roi*, 2 vols., Jean B. Beck, ed. (Philadelphia, 1938).

52 Hendrik van der Werf

collectors who were primarily interested in chansons did not necessarily shun motets, and that modal rhythm was not anathema to the connoisseurs of the "not so precisely measured" chansons. Of more interest is the "split personality" behaviour of those pieces that appear as monophonic songs in chansonniers and as motets for two voices in other collections.[16] In the latter, the relation between tenor and upper voice suggests that they were conceived and normally performed in modal rhythm. It does not seem strange that, at least occasionally, certain motets were performed without tenor, but we can only guess at what happened to their modal rhythm in a monophonic rendition. The type of double occurrence discussed here is not the only form in which an extant chanson is related to an extant motet, and a thorough study of all such cases will teach us quite a bit, not only about the compositions involved but also about the differences and similarities among chansons and motets in general.

Some of the more interesting and more elusive exceptions to be mentioned occur exclusively in the Chansonnier Cangé and are anonymous. As discussed above, the scribe of this manuscript occasionally made use of what some have considered an early form of mensural notation, but which I prefer to call a semi-mensural notation, because only the single notes, not the ligatures, appear to express mensuration.[17] As I have shown before, in most instances the rhythm suggested by the semi-mensural notation is flatly contradicted by differences and similarities among multiple versions of the chansons concerned.[18] But in a few cases good reasons exist for accepting that the chansons combine the modal rhythm of motets with features more typical of chansons,[19] one being that no multiple versions can be found that might argue against these songs having been conceived in modal rhythm. But the strongest reason is that these songs resemble motets in the way the modal rhythm fits the melody. Before we can determine the place of such hybrid songs in the poetry and music of the thirteenth century, we need to know more about this particular manuscript.

---

16. See van der Werf, *The Chansons*, example 12, 134-38.
17. The same type of notation is used in the motet collection Paris, B.N. nouv. acq. fr. 13521, published in photographic reproduction by Friedrich Gennrich, *Ein altfranzösischer Mottetenkodex...La Clayette* (Darmstadt, 1958) and by Luther Dittmer, *Paris 13521 & 11411* (Brooklyn, 1958) and in transcription by Gordon A. Anderson, *Motets of the Manuscript La Clayette* (Rome, 1975).
18. *The Chansons*, 36-40.
19. *The Chansons*, 144-47. Some reservation must be made about my following the standard procedure of maintaining one rhythmic mode throughout a composition. In the case of semi-mensural notation it is impossible to determine how strictly the composer adhered to a given rhythmic mode. As I hope to show in the near future, there are several indications that mixing modes was not uncommon.

Someone involved in its compilation seems to have been interested in making it look like a motet collection, and in making its chansons look like motets. The semi-mensural notation is the most striking consequence of this attempt. The order in which the chansons are entered may be another one. This is the only trouvère chansonnier to present the songs in alphabetical order (exclusively according to the first letter of the text), while at least two motet collectors similarly organized their manuscript.[20]

Finally, some chansons contain internal features atypical of their genre compelling us to consider whether they are more precisely measured than is normal. In a chanson by Blondel de Nesle the uniformity in its multiple versions, including the placement of word accents and distribution of pitches over the text, is unusual for the genre. A close examination of these features made me "conclude that *if* this chanson was meant to be performed in one of the rhythmic modes known to us, it probably was performed" in the third mode.[21] None of the rather diverse commentary upon my transcription has brought us any further to a solution of the problems posed by such atypical chansons.[22] I am still not convinced that it was conceived and normally performed in one of the rhythmic modes known to us, but still consider it likely that its pitches were measured more precisely than was usual for chansons.

Recent Performances and Recordings

Until recently, it was customary to perform all troubadour and trouvère songs in strict modal rhythm, in which syllables were the primary durational units in a ratio of either 1:2 or 1:2:3.[23] For syllabic passages, this resulted in an uninspiringly regular alternation of long and short syllables. Judging by recent recordings, performers of early music have completely abandoned this aspect of modal rhythm. For neumatic and especially for very ornate passages, "modal" performance yielded rhythms

---

20. This is the case for ms. Bamberg, Staatl. Bibl., Lit 115, published in photographic reproduction and transcription by Pierre Aubry, *Cent motets du xiiie siècle*, 3 vols. (Paris, 1980), and published in transcription by Gordon A. Anderson, *Compositions of the Bamberg Manuscript* (Stutgart, 1977). It also is the case for several sections of the ms. known as W2, published in photographic reproduction by Luther Dittmer, *Wolfenbüttel 1099 (1206)* (Brooklyn, 1959).

21. See van der Werf, *The Chansons*, 42 and 100-103. See also my remarks concerning chanson R620 by Blondel de Nesle in *Trouvères-Melodien I*, 559 and 26-32.

22. Stevens in *Words and Music*, 448, Charlotte Roederer in *Schirmer History of Music* (New York, 1982), 72-73, and Theodore Karp, "Three Trouvère Chansons in Mensural Notation," in *Gordon Athol Anderson: in Memoriam* (Henryville, Pa., 1984), 491-94.

23. See footnote 13.

which, depending upon one's point of view, were either "fascinating" or "weird"; they often were contrary to the style of motets. In current practice many singers make the duration of individual pitches quite unequal. In ornate passages this interest in unequal lengths is combined with an apparent desire to make the duration of the syllables close to equal. There seems to be no published defense of this practice, so that one cannot help but wonder whether it arose under the influence of the earlier practice wherein the syllable was the controlling factor, and "fascinating" or "weird" rhythms thereby became associated with the troubadours and trouvères.[24] One may also wonder whether the interest in making individual pitches unequal represents an attempt to make secular songs radically different from Gregorian chant. In two respects this desire is without ground. Firstly, our desire for marked differences between religious and secular music is a relatively modern phenomenon which came about slowly well after the Middle Ages, and seems to have gained its greatest impetus during the nineteenth century. In addition, the often quoted pronouncement of Johannes de Grocheio is not the only indication that, throughout the Middle Ages, duration in plainchant was not precisely measured and may not have resembled the equalistic performance advocated by André Mocquereau and his fellow monks of Solesmes.[25]

Dancing Songs

It was for practical, not for ideological reasons, that my publications on non-liturgical music of the Middle Ages have almost exclusively concerned chansons of the troubadours and trouvères. Going beyond those repertories is difficult, almost risky, because of the low number of extant melodies for the other songs. The troubadour sources contain many poems that clearly fall outside of the genre discussed thus far. Alas, only a very few of them are preserved with a melody, and most of these seem to stem from the late thirteenth or early fourteenth centuries. For songs with French texts fate has been more considerate, but still not generous enough to provide us with multiple versions for many of them. Thus, I may be forgiven for making primarily cautionary remarks in the next few paragraphs.

---

24. Stevens's book, *Words and Music*, advocating "isosyllabic" performance of many genres of medieval song was published long after singers went in this direction. For an evaluation of Stevens's theories see my review of his book in the forthcoming issue of *Journal of Musicological Research*.

25. Concerning accentuation and duration in plainchant see van der Werf, *The Emergence of Gregorian Chant: a Comparative Study of Ambrosian, Roman and Gregorian Chant* (published by the author, Rochester, N.Y., 1983), vol. I, 1, 22-42

At first glance, it would appear that pitches in dancing songs were not only precisely measured but also contained regular alternations of stress and unstress. Unfortunately, we do not know enough about medieval dances to either corroborate or contradict this notion. Probably because modal rhythm is associated with ternary meter, medieval dance songs are traditionally transcribed and performed in some kind of "waltz" rhythm, even though we do not know enough about either the dances or the tunes to exclude binary meter from consideration. To make things worse, we even have difficulty identifying dancing songs. Almost the only undeniable cases occur in narratives in which we are told that (certain) people danced to a song, and here the text may be given but the music usually is lacking. Furthermore, such a dancing song is given various labels, such as some form of the words "rondeau" or "carolle," or something like "chanson de carolle," or simply "chanson."[26] As generic terms were used in the Middle Ages, we should be wary of taking for granted that every text said to be a "rondelet" or "carolle" is a dancing song.

About a dozen poems have been preserved, without music, under the heading "estampie," but there is no indication whatsoever that they are dancing songs, or that they were performed to a clearly measured tune.[27] We also have a number of tunes without text called "estampie" that may be dance tunes, but they stem from the fourteenth century. As far as I know, we have only one case in which both text and music have been preserved for a song called "estampie." Moreover, the melody occurs with both a French and an Occitan text; the former is anonymous, the latter is attributed to Raimbaut de Vacqueiras.[28] Nevertheless, we have no clear indication about duration and accentuation in the melody, per se. A confusing factor in the study of the estampie is that it clearly is related to the Latin *sequence*, the German *Leich*, the French *descort* and lyric *lai*, none of which seem to have had anything to do with dancing. Clearly, we need an extensive study not only of the estampies, but also of the various members of the large sequence family. This research must be without preconceived notions; e.g., it must not start with the premise that the Latin sequence is the ancestor of this group.

There is a theory that the rondeau, the virelai, and the ballade either are, or derive from dancing songs. This usually goes together with the

---

26. See also Christopher Page, *Voices and Instruments*, especially 77-87.
27. See also van der Werf, "Estampie," in *New Grove Dictionary of Music and Musicians*, Stanley Sadie, ed.
28. For a brief discussion and complete transcription of both songs see van der Werf, *The Extant Troubadour Melodies*, 291-93.

assumption that their refrains derive from a practice that dance songs were intoned by a soloist, some of whose verses were repeated by the (other) dancers. It is a thankless task to try to disprove a theory that has never been proven. It may suffice to give the most pertinent facts. It should not surprise anyone to learn from the narratives that medieval people did dance, and (occasionally or often?) did so to a song. From some narratives we may also conclude that an alternation between a soloist and others occasionally occurred in dancing songs. Forms of the word "rondeau" occasionally appear as labels for a dancing song. The noun "ballade" seems to be related to the verb *ballare*, meaning "to dance." Some late entries in *Le Manuscrit du Roi*, which in their form resemble the virelai, have the title *danssa*.[29] Beyond that, there is little or nothing to connect all rondeaux, virelais, and ballades to dancing.

Exploring their origin a bit further, I suggest that if the rondeaux, virelais, and ballades of Guillaume de Machaut were descendants of dancing songs, they are at least as far removed from their origin as Beethoven's scherzos are removed from the courtly minuet. From yet a different point of view, we may recall that playing with recurrent thoughts, words, and sentences is a favorite habit among poets in so-called "primitive" as well as "high" cultures, just as playing with recurrent melodic ideas and phrases is popular among composers in notationless cultures. In the fourteenth century these favorite features became stylized and standardized, and this process seems to have been started before the beginning of that century.[30] It is beyond question that the rondeaux (or the *rondets*, as they are called in their sole source) by Guillaume d'Amiens are different from his chansons and from chansons by other trouvères, but no indication has been found that they have anything to do with dancing.[31] Their melodies may have been measured, but there is no reason to consider ternary meter and modal rhythm axiomatic. Since these are the only extant monophonic rondeaux, and since they occur in only one manuscript, we do not have much material for research on duration in their melodies. Despite all this uncertainty, I urge that some systematic and unprejudiced study be made of all the songs that may have had anything to do with dancing, however remote that connection may have been, even though we may never acquire precise knowledge of rhythm or meter in each individual case.

---

29. For further information see van der Werf, "Estampie."
30. For a discussion of the "balete" preserved (without music) in ms. Oxford, Bodleian Library, Douce 308, see van der Werf, *The Chansons*, 153 and 158-59.
31. For an edition of these *rondets* see Friedrich Gennrich, *Rondeaux, Virelais, und Ballades* (Dresden, 1921), 30-38.

Narrative Songs

Some two hundred French poems can be typified as "narrative songs." This does not include large epics, known as "chansons de geste"; it concerns relatively short, more or less strophic songs, most of which were published a century ago by Karl Bartsch under the general labels "romances" and "pastourelles."[32] Several attempts have been made to subdivide this large group into concise and easily recognizable types. Style and content seem to have been the primary criteria for categorization. To some extant the form of the strophe was also considered, but the style and form of the music played no role. Thus, past research has failed to yield reliable information to those interested in reviving these songs in their original rhythm. My own limited research makes me wonder whether a typological study, taking into account all pertinent aspects of text and music, will yield significantly fewer categories than there are narrative songs.

As a group, the narrative songs combine formal aspects of text and music in a manner that links them with both the trouvère song and *chanson de geste*. The former is strophic in the usual meaning, in the latter the counterpart of the strophe is normally called a *laisse*, the length of which may vary widely. The subdivision of the narrative songs under consideration is usually called a strophe even though the individual strophes of a given song may vary somewhat in their number of lines. Five or six strophes is almost standard for trouvère songs, while the number of *laisses* in a *chanson de geste* is unlimited, and the total epic may have a few thousand lines. In the narrative songs the number of strophes ranges from five to ten in most cases, to twenty or thirty in others. In trouvère songs a ten-syllable line has either ten or eleven syllables, depending on whether the rhyme consists of one or two syllables. This curious form of arithmetic is due to the tradition that in French and Occitan poetry the second (unaccented) syllable of a so-called feminine rhyme is not included in the syllable count. In epic poetry and in many narrative songs a ten-syllable line may have ten, eleven, or twelve syllables. The increase in arithmetical problems is due to the fact that, in addition to an unaccented syllable in the rhyme, there may be an unaccented syllable in the *caesura*, that is in the "break" after the fourth or (less often) the sixth syllable. Beyond the frequently occurring AB AB opening, trouvère songs have relatively little repetition of entire melodic lines. In the narrative songs, however, we often find three- or four-fold repetition of the very first phrase, which may well be

---

32. Karl Bartsch, *Altfranzösische Romanzen und Pastourellen* (Leipzig, 1870).

related to a tradition of singing all the lines of a *laisse*, or of an entire *chanson de geste*, to essentially the same melodic phrase.[33] Differences in choice of rhyme schemes among the three genres are important but not of direct relevance to questions of melodic rhythm and meter.

It seems inconceivable that a *chanson de geste* was performed in modal rhythm or in any other alternation of long and short syllables. If "not so precisely measured" duration was useful in any genre, it must have been in epic poetry. Almost every narrative song turns out to have some formal characteristics of both the *chanson de geste* and of the trouvère chanson. Although this does not give incontrovertible evidence for their rhythm, it does justify the speculation that duration in them was "not so precisely measured."[34] Assuming that duration in all troubadour and trouvère songs, in *chansons de geste*, in all romances and pastourelles, and in all of plain chant was "not so precisely measured" does not necessarily mean that it all sounded alike. On the contrary, this rhythmic freedom allows a wide range of differences in expressiveness and rhythm, however subtle the fluctuations may turn out to be. Let us hope that someone will study the entire group of narrative songs, considering each song on its own merits. The purpose of the research should not be to put each song into a category, to deduce the rhythm for one or two in each category, and to decide that all songs in that category had the same type of rhythm or meter. For the present, however, we are left with no alternative but to consider them all as belonging to one category, and assume that duration in a given narrative was "not so precisely measured," unless evidence to the contrary can be found.

Chromatic Alterations

Finally, we must turn to two "technical" aspects of the performance of medieval songs. *Musica ficta*, or in plain English chromatic alterations, may well form the most elusive problem in the performance of medieval music. Although no all-encompassing study of this phenomenon has been undertaken, many strong opinions have been voiced. The troubadour repertory is small enough that a complete survey can be made of the sharp, natural, and flat signs in the four sources involved; at the same time, it is large enough to give meaningful data.[35] For scholars these data are of great significance, but they fail to offer precise

---

33. In a forthcoming publication I hope to explore the ramifications of the theory that in a *chanson de geste* one line of music was repeated for every textual verse.
34. It is unclear to me why Richard H. Hoppin transcribes narrative songs in modal rhythm in his *Medieval Music* (New York, 1978), 292.
35. For these data, see van der Werf, *The Extant Troubadour Melodies*, 38-61.

prescriptions to performers. To begin with, we have no certainty as to how long a given sign of alteration is valid, although some indication exists that it often pertains only to the pitches on the rest of the staff on which it stands. Beyond that, the variants among multiples versions of troubadour and trouvère songs show that changes were made in the diatonic or chromatic nature of some, but by no means many of the melodies; still they neither reveal who made them nor whether chromatic alterations were added or deleted. Medieval performers do not seem to have been as concerned about note-for-note retention of a melody as are present-day musicians. This attitude appears to have affected chromatic alterations as well as other melodic aspects. Scribes contributed to these differences by adding (or omitting) accidentals in accordance with criteria unknown to us. Since all large chansonniers contain at least some chromatic alterations, we can be fairly sure that troubadours and trouvères themselves did not shun them, but we do not know whether a given composer left us exclusively diatonic melodies, whether he altered a pitch frequently, or whether he seldom did so. Thus, when it comes to determining the diatonic or chromatic state of a melody, it is left to the performer to make decisions where the scholar can only plead ignorance.

Instrumental Accompaniment

Instrumental accompaniment is another thorny issue for scholars and performers alike. For a long time, it was widely accepted that the songs of the troubadours and trouvères were always performed to instrumental accompaniment. As many scholars must have done before me, and as especially Christopher Page did after me, I have searched in vain for information about accompaniment. We know that instruments existed in the time of the troubadours and trouvères, and obviously that they were used. It appears that some troubadours and trouvères could play instruments. We also know that the Middle Ages were not unacquainted with the phenomenon of accompanied song. For example, Tristan often accompanied his own singing.[36] But no evidence is present that troubadour and trouvère chansons were accompanied. It is significant that in troubadour and trouvère poems, as well as in the medieval literature concerning them, we find numerous references to singing, but none to accompanying. The mere fact that, occasionally, a musical instrument is mentioned in a poem is no evidence for instrumental

---

36. The fact that both Tristan and Isolde played instruments is a welcome antidote to the myth that in the Middle Ages playing an instruments was considered a base occupation. Tristan and Isolde were highly admired and the story tellers would not have portrayed them as superb instrumentalists, if playing an instrument would have been in conflict with their noble birth.

60 *Hendrik van der Werf*

accompaniment, and even if we could find evidence for accompaniment of a troubadour or a trouvère song on a certain occasion, we would still have no evidence that they were habitually accompanied. In the only extensive study to date of the medieval use of instruments, Page essentially confirmed what I wrote some twenty-five years ago.[37] He went far beyond the troubadour and trouvère repertories so that we now begin to have some information on what genres actually were accompanied. One thing has not changed: we still do not have any manuscript that actually preserves the accompaniment to any song prior to the fourteenth century. Recital and recording situations being as they are, it may be difficult for performers to abandon instrumental accompaniment completely, but I express pleasure at noting that percussion instruments seem to be losing ground in recordings of medieval music.

On more than one occasion I have written that medieval performers of chansons must have sung expressively, but that we do not know just how dramatic their renditions were. We may be able to draw one more conclusion from the nature and the number of variants among multiple versions. As mentioned above, the variants in the melodies are not only more numerous but also more significant than the variants in the poems. Perhaps one can conclude that the similarities and differences among multiple versions suggest that medieval singers concentrated on presenting the poetry but were rather free in their treatment of the music. In this respect we may raise a crude question: are troubadour and trouvère chansons poems that happen to have a melody or are they musical compositions that happen to have a text? We may not want to answer either question with a simple "yes" or "no," but we can safely assume that the poet-composers wanted their texts to be understood. Thus, we may have an objective criterion by which to judge authenticity of present-day performances, and hold that, from a historical point of view, something is seriously wrong when a song is performed in a rhythm and with an accompaniment that obscure the words. For modern performers there is a painful irony in this conclusion. A performer who sings without instrumental accompaniment, who makes the pitches more or less equal, and who gives a perfect rendition of the text, may encounter less audience appreciation than the one who sings in jumpy rhythms, who is accompanied by an ensemble of odd-sounding instruments, and who is dressed in medieval garb.

---

37. Christopher Page, *Voices and Instruments*.

[5]

VOICES AND INSTRUMENTS IN MEDIEVAL FRENCH SECULAR MUSIC: ON THE USE OF LITERARY TEXTS AS EVIDENCE FOR PERFORMANCE PRACTICE

Sylvia Huot

One of the most important questions facing historians and performers of medieval music today is the respective roles of voices and instruments. We do not know exactly which instruments were used for a given repertoire, or in what combinations; and we do not know for sure under what conditions, if any, these instruments (whatever they were) would be combined with the voice.[1] Although considerable literary, archival, and iconographic evidence for medieval performance practice exists, scholars and musicians attempting to codify this material face a task of monumental proportions. The sheer quantity of the material is in itself daunting, and much of it remains unexamined. Moreover, even once a body of material has been assembled, the task of interpreting its lessons is far from easy. Documents are rarely as explicit as we would like them to be; literary and artistic representations of performance often cannot be identified securely with a

---

[*] Preliminary work for this study was supported by a grant from the Exxon Education Foundation for research at the Newberry Library, Chicago. Subsequent work was supported in part by a faculty summer research stipend from the Graduate School, Northern Illinois University. I am extremely grateful for this support. I would also like to thank Mary Springfels of the Newberry Library, Howard Mayer Brown of the University of Chicago, Peter Lefferts of the University of Chicago, and Lawrence Earp of the University of Wisconsin, Madison, for many helpful suggestions during the preparation of this study.

[1] Some studies that address questions of instrumentation and performance practice include the general survey by E. Faral, *Les Jongleurs en France au moyen âge* (Paris, 1910); I.F. Finlay's "Musical Instruments in Gotfrid von Strassburg's "Tristan und Isolde"< *Galpin Society Journal* 5 (March 1952), pp. 39-43; E.A. Bowles, "Instruments at the Court of Burgundy (1363-1467)", *Galpin Society Journal* 6 (July 1953), pp. 41-45; H.M. Brown, "Instruments and Voices in the Fifteenth-Century Chanson", in J.W. Grubbs, et al, eds., *Current Thought in Musicology* (Austin and London, 1976), pp. 89-137; C. Page, "The Performance of Songs in Late Medieval France: A New Source", *Early Music* 10 (1982), pp. 441-50. For a general survey of descriptions of musical performance in Old French literature, see C. Page, "Music and Chivalric Fiction in France, 1150-1300", *Proceedings of the Royal Musical Association* 111/112 (1984-85), pp. 1-27; and Page's *Voices and Instruments of the Middle Ages: Instrumental Practice and Songs in France 1100-1300* (Berkeley and Los Angeles, 1986).

specific repertoire, present ambiguities, and may in any case contain at least as much fancy as fact.

In the present study I have concentrated on descriptions of musical performance in Old and Middle French literature, ranging from the late twelfth to the turn of the fifteenth century: that is, from the time of the trouvères through the first generation of post-Machaut composers. I have not attempted to gather together all descriptions of performance from this period, for that would be a nearly impossible task. My purpose is not to present a history of performance descriptions in medieval French literature, but rather to address the methodological issues that these texts raise. A host of textual, linguistic, and literary problems must be confronted before we can even begin to weigh the evidence of these descriptions. By examining a manageable number of exemplary passages, I hope to establish guidelines for the analysis of literary texts as evidence for performance practice. My approach is twofold. The first part of the study is concerned with philological considerations: the establishment of the text and the resolution of lexical and syntactic problems. The second part examines the content of performance descriptions: the treatment of different repertoires and the literary conventions that influence this treatment. Finally, the examination of the passages included in this study will allow for some preliminary conclusions about the performance of secular music in France during the thirteenth and fourteenth centuries. Owing to the relative scarcity of explicit references to polyphonic performance, these conclusions will be largely about monophony; but certain issues in the performance of polyphony will be addressed as well.

Reading Performance Descriptions, I: Philological Considerations

Before any medieval text can be studied, it must be established. And if a text exists in multiple versions, it is necessary to examine the variant readings before analysis can even begin. The modern critical edition can be misleading: the text it prints does not necessarily correspond to most, or even to any, of the medieval sources. Since my purpose here is not to provide a comprehensive analysis of medieval performance practice as revealed in literary texts, but only to establish the guidelines for such study,

VOICES AND INSTRUMENTS ... 65

I will limit myself to two examples of manuscript variants in performance description. The first passage is taken from Chrétien de Troyes' *Chevalier au Lyon (Yvain)*, composed in the late twelfth century; it appears in seven manuscripts ranging from the early thirteenth century to the turn of the fourteenth century.[2] The subject is Arthur's ceremonial entry into Yvain's newly won castle. All versions agree that Arthur was honored with loud flourishes on horns and buisines and entertained by male acrobats, and all refer as well to an assortment of wind and percussion instruments and to the presence of maidens. The principal variants occur in the three lines that identify these latter instruments and specify the activity of the maidens. Here are the lines as printed in Foerster's edition:

> Contre lui dancent les puceles,
> Sonent flaütes et freteles,
> Timbre, tabletes et tabor.

> The maidens dance towards him; flutes and freteles,
> tambourines, cymbals and tabors play.
> *(Yvain,* vv. 2351-53)

This reading, however, does not actually appear in any manuscript. The variants include the instrumentation, the activity of the maidens, and the relationship of the instrumental music to whatever the maidens are doing. MS *V* is the closest to Foerster's text, differing only in the instrumentation: it reads "trompes" instead of "timbre" in v. 2353. In MSS *G* and *S,* where the instrumentation agrees with Foerster's text, the girls do not dance but simply go out to meet the king, as do, evidently, the musicians:

> Contre lui ivent les puceles, [MS *G:* Encontre 1. vont l.p.]
> Les flahutes et les frestules,
> Timbres, tabletes et tabors. [MS *G:* et tables]

> Towards him went [go] the maidens, the flutes and the

---

[2] I use the sigla adopted by Foerster for the edition of *Yvain:* A = Chantilly, Musée Condé, MS 472; F = Paris, Bibliothèque Nationale fr. 1450; G = B.N. fr. 12560; H = B.N. fr. 794; P = B.N. fr. 1433; S = B.N. fr. 12603; V = Vatican Library Reg. 1725. I am grateful to David Hult of The Johns Hopkins University for his assistance in checking manuscript variants.

freteles, tambourines, [and cymbals] and tabors.
(MS *G*, fol. 15r-15v MS *S*, fol. 95r)

In MS *A*, the girls themselves are the musicians – a possibility perfectly compatible with the reading of MSS *GS* – and the instrumentation is slightly different:

> Contre lui sonnent les puceles
> Et lor timbres et lor vïeles,
> Flahutes, tabletes et tabors.

> The maidens play their timbres, their fiddles,
> flutes, cymbals and tabors towards him [i.e., as a musical welcome].
> (fol. 181v)

The passage in MSS *GSV* conjures up the image of maidens dancing or processing towards the king; in addition, there is ongoing music from wind and percussion, which might or might not be the music to which the girls dance. MS *A*, however, describes a group of female musicians playing for the king. MSS *F* and *H* in turn make it clear that the flute and percussion is the accompaniment for the maidens' procession or dance, without specifying that this takes place as a movement towards (or even anywhere near) the king:

> Et la ou dansent les puceles,
> Sonent flaütes et freiteles,
> Timbres, tabletes et tabor.

> And there where the maidens dance, flutes and freteles,
> tambourines, cymbals and tabors play.
> (MS *F*, fol. 214r)

> La ou descendent les puceles,
> Sonent flaütes et vïeles,
> Tympre, freteles et tabor.

> There where the maidens come down, flutes and fiddles,
> tambourines, freteles and tabors play.
> (MS *H*, fol. 88r)

Finally, MS *P* portrays the flutes and percussion as accompaniment not for dance or movement of any kind, but for song:

> Et la ou chantent les pucheles,
> Sonnent fleütes et freteles,
> Timbres, tabletes et tabours.

> And there where the maidens sing, flutes and freteles,
> tambourines, cymbals and tabors play.
> (fol. 81v)

A single descriptive passage is thus in reality seven descriptions, no two of them quite alike. In the present context, I am not concerned with the issue of what may have been the "original" text or how – and if – we may arrive at it. Rather, I believe that in our search for evidence of medieval performance practice, we must attend to all surviving medieval texts, whether they are the product of a poet or a scribe. Assuming that the scribe in each case was attentive enough not to write anything that did not make sense, how do we account for these discrepancies? There is nothing difficult about the passage, nothing to suggest that scribes were forced to reconstruct, each in his own way, an obscure or corrupt source.[3] Perhaps the answer to this question is that a medieval reader would not have felt that there were any real discrepancies among these seven versions. With the possible exception of "trompes", which could be simply a misreading for "timbres" (sometimes spelled "timpres"), the variations in instrumentation are not enormous: in all cases we have flutes and percussion, and there is nothing odd about finding fiddles in such a context. As for the question of whether the maidens are singing, dancing, or playing instruments, scribes may have been inattentive to this distinction because it would be assumed that maidens would be doing all of these things.

---

[3] The philological problems involved in the study of variant readings for specific passages in the works of Chrétien de Troyes are explored in detail by A. Foulet and K.D. Uitti, "Chrétien's "Laudine": *Yvain*, vv. 2148-55", *Romance Philology* 37 (1983-84), pp. 293-302; K.D. Uitti, "Autant en emporte *li funs:* remarques sur le prologue du *Chevalier de la charrette* de Chrétien de Troyes", *Romania* 105 (1984), pp. 270-91; D.F. Hult, "Lancelot's Two Steps: A Problem in Textual Criticism", *Speculum* 61 (1986), pp. 836-58. For more general discussions of textual criticism and stemmatology, see C. Kleinhenz, ed., *Medieval Manuscripts and Textual Criticism,* Studies in the Romance Languages and Literatures, Symposia 4 (Chapel Hill, 1975).

Certainly it was not uncommon for medieval women to dance to their own singing, often for the pleasure of male spectators.[4] We also know that female musicians could play musical instruments. And as we will see, terms used for performance are not exclusive of other terms: "sonner", for example, does not necessarily exclude singing.

Collectively, the seven versions of the festivities in *Yvain* add up to a scene very much like that of the carol in the first part of the *Roman de la rose* (ca. 1230). The carolers dance to the singing of Lady Happiness *(Rose,* vv. 727-28); flute players and unidentified minstrels are present (vv. 745-46); there are ladies playing cymbals and tambourines who toss their instruments on high and balance them on their finger tips, possibly while executing some sort of dance steps (vv. 751-56); and two maidens do a special dance together for the entertainment of the others (vv. 757-69). Dancing, singing, and playing percussion, in close proximity with flute players and other musicians, are the three interrelated activities engaged in collectively by the ladies in the Garden of Delight. In *Yvain,* the scene that Guillaume de Lorris took nearly fifty lines to describe is evoked in a mere three lines. If each version is slightly different, it is because for a medieval reader the presence of maidens, with a certain type of instrumentation and in a certain context, is sufficient to conjure up a complete picture; the choice of details to be presented is up to the individual scribe.

A note of caution must also be sounded, however: manuscript variants do not invariably provide accurate insights. Sometimes a variant really is an error. The twelfth-century *Roman de Brut,* for example, includes a description of festivities that begins with references to lais being performed on several kinds of instruments, and then continues with a typical catalogue of numerous other instruments, of which I cite here only the first line:

> Lais de vïeles, lais de rotes,
> Lais de harpes, lais de frestels,
> Lires, tympes e chalemels ...

> Lais on fiddles, lais on rotes, lais on harps, lais on fretels; lyres, tympes and shawms.
> *(Brut,* vv. 10548-50)

---

[4] See J. Bédier, "Les Plus Anciennes Danses françaises", *Revue des Deux Mondes* 31 (1906), pp. 398-424.

Most of the manuscripts agree with this reading. In MS Bibliothèque Nationale fr. 1416 (dated 1292), however, we find the variant provided by Arnold in his edition:

> Lais de harpes, lais de rotes,
> Lais de corons, lais de frestels,
> Lais de tympes, de chalemels.

> Lais on harps, lais on rotes, lais on horns, lais on fretels, lais on tympes, on shawms.

Were lais really performed on horns and on tympes? Perhaps so. But in this particular case, I think it is likely that the scribe, having grown accustomed to the repetitive use of "lais" at the beginning of every line and half-line, simply misread "lires" for "lais" in v. 10550, an easy enough mistake to make. A similar inattentiveness might account for the appearance of "corons" in the preceding line; in fact, all manuscripts agree on the reappearance of "coruns" three lines later. Lengthy catalogues of instruments are conventional in medieval narrative poetry, and generally communicate an atmosphere of festive abundance rather than a mimetic account of specific performing ensembles. The scribe might be forgiven for feeling that the precise order in which the instruments were mentioned was not essential, just as a scribe transcribing *Yvain* might not be concerned with the choice of the terms "chanter" or "danser" to describe a group of maidens that he assumed were doing both at once.

Manuscript variants must thus be interpreted with care. We must be alert to outright misreadings, as well as to possible explanations for scribal emendation or inattentiveness to detail. But given the impressionistic nature of most descriptions of musical performance found in medieval literature, the modern scholar needs as much help as possible in reconstructing a complete picture. The judicious comparison of multiple versions is an essential part of the reading of medieval texts, and can help considerably to clarify difficult passages.

Even once we are sure that we have an authentic medieval text, it is not always easy to be sure just what it says. A variety of verbs are used to signify the activity of musical performance, of which the most important are "dire", "chanter", "noter", "sonner", "jouer", and the various terms for playing specific instruments, such as "vïeler" or "harper".[5] In addition, the term "accorder" is commonly used to describe the relationship between the voices and/or instruments in a group performance. Interpreting these terms in a given passage can be difficult for several reasons. Each term can have a range of meanings; usage can be imprecise, as when a musician is said to "play" a song even though he is clearly also singing it; and it can sometimes be difficult, when both singing and playing are described, to determine whether the actions are meant to be simultaneous or sequential.

Precise meaning is most difficult for the first four terms listed above, whose range of meanings in the context of musical performance includes "to speak", "to discourse upon", "to sing", or "to play an instrument". Usually, however, "dire" and "chanter" both imply voice, while "noter" and "sonner" are used for instrumental music. While "chanter" can be used for instrumental music when the instrument is the subject of the verb, this is a figurative use that does not really change the association of "chanter" with voice: the instrument "sings".

Conversely, "sonner" can be used for speech in the phrase "sonner un mot"; but this usage parallels the construction "sonner un instrument", with "sonner" in both cases meaning "to sound".

The distinction between "dire" and "chanter" rests on the association of the former with the spoken word, and the association of the latter with music. The noun forms "dit" and "chant" in particular reflect this distinction: "dit" refers either to a poem without music or to the words of a song, while "chant" refers to music in general, to a song, or even to the tune, as opposed to the words, of a song. I will return below to particular uses of the terms "dit" and "chant". The verbs "dire" and "chanter" are sometimes used in opposition in order to express a distinction between musical and non-musical discourse, as in the mid-thirteenth century *Bestiaire d'amour,* where the narrator refers to the movement from song to prose declamation as that from "canter" to "dire" (p. 10). Often, however, "dire" is used interchangeably with "chanter" to indicate singing. In Jean Renart's early thirteenth-century *Guillaume de Dole,* for example, is the following exchange:

---

[5] Two other lexical studies useful in reading performance descriptions are R. Morgan, "Old French *jogleor* and Kindred Terms", *Romance Philology* 7 (1953-54), pp. 279-325; W. Ulland, *Jouer d'un instrument und die altfranzösischen Bezeichnungen des Instrumentenspiels,* Romanistische Versuche und Vorarbeiten 35 (Bonn, 1970).

VOICES AND INSTRUMENTS ...

> – Dame, fet il, une *chançon*
> car nos *dites*, si ferez bien.
> Ele *chantoit* sor tote rien ...

> "Lady", he says, "do sing us a song, you will do well". She habitually sang about anything at all.
>
> (vv. 1144-46, emphasis mine)

> – Ha, ma tres douce dame, voire,
> *dites* nos en. ...
> Quant el ot sa chançon *chantee* ...

> "Oh, my very sweet lady, truly, sing us some" ... When she had sung her song ...
>
> (vv. 1152-53, 1167, emphasis mine)

Ambiguity arises when "dire" and "chanter" are used in conjunction with musical instruments, in phrases of the form "dire"/"chanter" + preposition + instrument. Are we to understand combined vocal and instrumental or solely instrumental music? In some cases the full context makes it clear that we are meant to understand an activity consisting of singing or chanting the words of a song or tale to instrumental accompaniment:

> Cest vers de bele Marguerite
> ...
> li fet chanter en la vïele:
>   Cele d'Oisseri
>   ne met en oubli ...

> This poem about beautiful Margaret ... he has him sing on the fiddle: She of Oisseri does not forget ...
>
> (*Guillaume de Dole*, vv. 3415, 3418-20)

The citation of the words of the song, as well as the use of the term "vers", which commonly refers to a non-musical poem or to the words of a song, support the interpretation of "chanter en la vïele" as song accompanied by fiddle. A similar case is this reference to the performance of *chanson de geste* in the late twelfth-century *Moniage Guillaume:*

> Hui mais orés canchon de fiere geste,
> Chil jougleour en cantent en vïele.

> Now you will hear a song of bold deeds; these jongleurs sing of it on the fiddle.
> *(Moniage Guillaume,* vv. 2071-72)

"Canter en vïele" here can only imply recitation or chanting with instrumental accompaniment, as one could hardly imagine a purely instrumental rendition of a *chanson de geste.*

The same logic could be applied to Marie de France's statement in *Guigemar* about the Breton lai of Guigemar. The full passage *(Guigemar,* vv. 883-86) appears in two manuscripts:

> De cest cunte k'oï avez
> Fu Guigemar li lais trovez
> Que hum fait en harpe e en rote;
> Bone en est a oïr la note.

> From this tale that you have heard, Guigemar the lai was composed, which people do on harp and on rote; the tune [note] is nice to hear.
> (British Library, Harley 978, mid 13th c.)

The passage is the same in Paris, Bibliothèque Nationale fr. 2168 (Picard, second half of the 13th century), except that v. 885 reads "que hum dist en harpe e en rote". The verb "faire" can mean "to do", "to make", "to compose a poem or a tune", or "to say"; "dire" in Bibl. Nat. fr. 2168 presumably means "to sing" or "to recite". "Note" could mean either the tune to which the tale is sung or, quite possibly, the genre of poetico-musical composition in which the medieval audience would encounter the tale of Guigemar. Although Marie stresses in particular the musical quality of the lai, it is unlikely that she imagines a purely instrumental rendition. In the context of her work, as in Old French literature in general, the Breton lai is important precisely as a sung text recording a particular adventure. In the Prologue appearing in the Harley manuscript, she states that the Breton lais were made "pur remambrance ... des aventures" (in remembrance of the adventures) *(Prologue,* vv. 35-36) and that "Plusurs en ai oï conter" (I have heard many of them recounted) (v. 39). Given the importance of the lai text, both in general and for Marie's project in particular, it would be strange if the reference to the performance of the lai on which her narrative is based was phrased in such a way as to exclude the text. In this case, at least, "faire en harpe/rote" and "dire en harpe/rote" must refer to a process of singing coupled with playing.[6]

In light of these relatively straightforward examples, it is likely that this more ambiguous passage in the prologue of the *Comte d'Anjou* (1316) refers to a combined vocal and instrumental rendition of a variety of pieces:

> Li autre dient en vielles
> Chançons royaus et estempies,
> Dances, noctes, et baleriez,
> En leüst, en psalterion,
> Chascun selonc s'entencion,
> Lais d'amours, descors et balades.

> Others sing on the fiddle chanson royaus and estempies,
> dance tunes, notes and baleries, on the lute, on the psaltery,
> each according to his taste, lais of love, descorts and ballades.
> *(Comte d'Anjou,* vv. 12-17)

The list of pieces included as suitable for rendition on fiddle, lute, or psaltery includes not only various types of dance music, which might be purely instrumental, but also the lai, descort and ballade, poetic forms; and even the chanson royal, a poetic form of which only one musical example – Guillaume de Machaut's *Joie, plaisence et douce nourriture* – is even known today. It may be that the verb "dire" is used in a loose sense that can include either purely instrumental or combined vocal and instrumental rendition. The point of the passage, indeed, is the variety of pieces and of performance techniques: each performer arranges his rendition as he sees fit.

We arrive at a more problematic ambiguity when the instruments linked with "dire" or "chanter" are wind instruments, which one could not possibly play *while* singing. Three possibilities present themselves: (1) a musician plays on his instrument a tune whose words are so well known that they are implied by the mere sound of the melody; (2) a single musician alter-

---

[6] P. Ménard concludes that "les anciens lais bretons étaient à la fois instrumentaux et vocaux", in *Les Lais de Marie de France: Contes d'amour et d'aventure du Moyen Age* (Paris, 1979), p. 55. On the lai more generally, see J. Maillard, *Evolution et esthétique du lai lyrique des origines à la fin du XIVe siècle* (Paris, 1963); and Maillard's "Coutumes musicales au moyen âge d'après le *Tristan* en prose", *Cahiers de Civilisation Médiévale* 2 (1959), pp. 341-53.

nately sings and plays; or (3) a performer sings to the accompaniment of an instrumentalist. It is possible to find less ambiguously worded examples of each of these possibilities.

(1) The purely instrumental rendition of a piece that presumably does have words is implied in certain instances where the verb used is not "dire" or "chanter" but "noter", as in this example from the first half of the thirteenth century:

> En sa main a pris un flagueil
> Molt doucement en flajola
> Et par dedens le flaguel a
> Noté le Lai del Chievrefueil
> Et puis a mis jus le flagueil.

> In his hand he took a flute; he played the flute very sweetly,
> and by means of the flute he played the Lai of the Honeysuckle,
> and then he set down the flute.
> *(Tristan ménestrel, vv. 758-62)*

Tristan here wishes to give a secret message to Iseut by playing the lai that she and he composed together and have never made public. The purely instrumental rendition is entirely appropriate to such a situation, since he does not wish to tell the story expressed by the lai, but only to reveal his identity to Iseut and to remind her of the sentiments it expresses. Since the text specifies that Tristan does not put down the flute until after he has done the lai, it is unlikely that any singing is involved.[7]

(2) The thirteenth-century pastourelle tradition provides several examples in which it is fairly clear that a shepherd or shepherdess alternately sings and plays on flute or pipes:

> Si avoit

---

[7] On the *Lai de Chevrefeuille*, see J. Maillard, "Le "Lai" et la "Note" du Chèvrefeuille", *Musica Disciplina* 13 (1959), pp. 3-13. I would like to add that since the history of musical instruments and their terminology is not central to this essay, and since the translation of medieval terms of musical instruments is often problematic, I have decided to use the general English term "flute" to translate three different Old French words, no doubt designating different types of instruments: "flageol[et]", "fl[ah]ute", and "estives". The reader desiring more specific designation is referred to the Old French passages, none of which are translated without being cited in the original.

VOICES AND INSTRUMENTS ...

> flaiol pipe et baston:
> en haut dist et si notoit
> un novel son,
> en sa pipe refraignoit
> le ver d'une chanson
> puis a dit "amor, amor ..."
>
> Thus she had flute, pipe and [drum?]stick: aloud she sang and
> also played a new song: she played on her pipe the verse of a
> song and then she sang, "Love, love ..."
> (Bartsch, III, no. 51, vv. 3-9)

> S'amie apele au calemel,
> si chante et note "dorenlot!
> eo eo ae ae! oo dorenlot!
> d'amors me doint dex joie."
>
> He calls his girl friend with the shawm; thus he sings
> and plays, "Dorenlot! eo eo ae ae! oo dorenlot! God grant
> me joy in love."
> (Bartsch, III, no. 20, vv. 6-9)

The second example above refers to a performance like that in the preceding example: "Dorenlot! eo eo ..." is an onomatopoeic allusion to instrumental music, which is followed by a sung refrain. A similar performance is evidently intended in the description of the song of Polyphemus in the early fourteenth-century *Ovide moralisé*. The cyclops plays a set of pipes, but he also clearly sings:

> En sa main tint une fleüste
> De cent rosiaus, dont il fleüste.
> ...
> Le chant dou jaiant escoutai
> Et ses paroles bien notai.
>
> In his hand he held a flute of a hundred reeds, which he played.
> ... I listened to the giant's song, and I paid close attention to
> his words.
> (Book 13, vv. 3823-24, 3831-32)

(3) The pastourelle also provides an example in which a singer is accompanied by a bagpipe player:

> Helos nu fu pas muele,
> ains cantoit si a devis
> k'a son cant s'acordoit Guis
> qi leur muse et chalemele
> en la muse au grant bourdon.

> Helos wasn't lax, for he sang so perfectly that Gui,
> who played for them on the bagpipe with the big
> drone, played along with his singing.
> (Bartsch, III, no. 27, vv. 38-42)

A similar kind of performance may be intended in Machaut's description of his patron's singing in the *Fonteinne amoureuse* (ca. 1360):

> Il disoit des dis et des chans
> De lais, de dances et de notes,
> Faites a cornes et a rotes.
>
> He sang the words and tunes of lais, of dance songs
> and of melodies rendered on horns and rotes.
> (vv. 2800-02)

This latter example of singing is not a formal performance, of course; most likely, Machaut's young nobleman – probably meant to represent Jean, duc de Berry – is simply amusing himself and giving free rein to his exuberant spirits by singing along with what would otherwise have been a purely instrumental rendition.

Given that all three types of rendition are possible, then, how are we to interpret statements like the following one in a late twelfth-century epic:

> .i. harpere de l'Trase est de l'roi aprociés.
> De lais dire a flahute estoit bien ensigniés.
> ...
> Devant le tref le roi est li harpere asis
> et commença .i. lai dont il ot mult apris,
> de la harpe à flahute dont il estoit apris.
>
> A harpist from Thrace approached the king. He was very accomplished at
> performing lais on the flute ... The harpist sat at the king's feet and began a
> lai, of which he had learned many, on harp and flute [OR: began a lai, of
> which he had learned many on the harp, on the flute, which he had learned
> how to do].
> (*Alexandre*, p. 73, vv. 9-10, 15-17)

This passage actually raises several questions: exactly which instrument or instruments are being played, and by how many different performers; how, by whom, and indeed whether the text of the lai is being sung. It seems unlikely that the same person would play both harp and flute at the same time. Yet there are no references to other musicians, and the harpist's performance is motivated by his desire to attract Alexander's attention so that he can plead a case with the emperor; this would suggest a solo performance. Enjambement is rare in verse of this type; one would expect the phrase "de la harpe à flahute" to constitute a syntactic unit. The phrase in fact parallels the language used to refer to the playing of pipe and tabor by a single performer in a pastourelle:

> Gui dou tabor au flahutel
> Leur fait ceste estampie.
>
> Gui played this estampie for them on pipe and tabor.
> (Bartsch, III, no. 21, vv. 49-50)

Perhaps, then, the performance in question – an exceptional one, since it gained the musician an audience with the emperor – does involve a combination of flute and harp, with the harp perhaps used to accompany the voice and the flute providing an instrumental prelude or interludes between strophes.

There is, in fact, evidence that some musicians performed lais by alternating vocal and instrumental renditions of each strophe. In a famous passage in the late thirteenth century Anglo-Norman *Horn*,[8] a Breton performs a lai with what is evidently a rather elaborate instrumental prelude:

> Lors prent la harpe a sei. qu'il la ueut atemprer.
> Deus ki dunc lesgardast. cum la sout manier.
> Cum ces cordes tuchoit. cum les fesoit trembler.
> As quantes feiz chanter. as quantes organer.[9]
>
> ...
>
> Quant ses notes ot fait. si la prent a munter.
> E tut par autres tuns. les cordes fait soner.
> Mut se merveillent tuit. quil la sout sibailler.
> E quant il out issi fait. si cummence a noter.
> Le lai dunt orains dis. de Batolf haut e cler.

---

[8] This passage is the main focus of J. Levy, "Musikinstrumente beim Gesang im mittelalterlichen Frankreich, auf Grund altfranzösischer Texte (bis zum 14. Jahrhundert)", *Zeitschrift für Romanische Philologie* 35 (1911), pp. 492-94. It has been discussed in numerous other places as well. Page comments upon the passage and provides references to other discussions of it in *Voices and Instruments*, pp. 4-5 and 92-107.

[9] T. Gérold cites these lines, suggesting that "chanter" means to play the melody of the lai on the harp, while "organer" refers to the addition of "une sorte de contrepoint", in *La Musique au moyen âge*, Classiques Français du Moyen Age (Paris, 1932), p. 375.

MUSICA DISCIPLINA

> Si cum sunt cil bretun. ditiel fait costumier.

> Then he takes up the harp, for he wants to tune it. God! Whoever then watched him [seeing] how he knew how to handle it, how he touched the strings, how he made them vibrate, sometimes he made them sing, other times play a counterpoint ... When he had done his tune, then he takes it up. And he makes the strings sound with all different tones. Everyone marvels that he knows how to manage it like that. And when he had done so, he begins to play the lai that Orains composed about Batolf, loudly and clearly, just as those Bretons are accustomed to doing it.
> (vv. 2830-33, 2836-41)

Although this is evidently an exceptionally skilled performer, the last line makes it clear that he does not actually depart from standard practice. First the musician plays an instrumental prelude; then he does the lai itself. And here, it seems that he first sings words, then repeats the melody on the harp:

> Apres en lestrument. fet les cordes suner.
> Tut issi cum en uoiz. laveit dit tut premier.
>
> Afterwards he made the strings sound in the instrument, just as he had first sung it with his voice.
> *(Horn,* vv. 2842-43)

As we will see in subsequent examples, lais were often described as being performed with simultaneous voice and instrument. But it may be that the musician would still sing a strophe with an instrumental accompaniment, then play that tune again at the end of the strophe. In fact, even a description of a lai being sung without any instruments still calls for antiphonal performance. The *Perceforest* (second quarter of the 14th century) describes an *a capella* performance of the *Lay des jeunes filles* by forty maidens in a pagan temple.[10] The singers are divided into two groups that perform alternate half strophes:[11]

> A ce s'acorderent les pucelles qui estoient en nombre quarante, dont les vingt se mirent en rencg en l'un des lez et les autres vingt a l'autre rencg. Sy commencerent celles du dextre lez a chanter la clause prumiere moult devotement et les autres l'autre clause du lay. Et ainsi le chanterent en la maniere qui s'ensieut tant doulcement que c'estoit droite melodie de les ouÿr.

> The maidens, who were forty in number, agreed to this; twenty of them lined up along one side and the other twenty on the other side. And those on the right side began to sing the first half strophe very devoutly and the others the next half strophe of the lay. And thus they sang it, in the manner that follows, so sweetly that it was a real treat to hear them. [The words of the lay follow.]
> (Bibl. Nat. fr. 109, fol. 288v)

Given this association of the lai with a pattern of alternating vocal and/or instrumental rendition, then there is no reason why a lai could not be sung with wind as well as with string instruments.

Just as the terms "dire" and "chanter" can be used for singing that is actually accompanied by playing, so terms like "sonner" and "jouer" can be used for playing that accompanies song. For this reason, descriptions of instrumental renditions should never be used as evidence for lack of vocal accompaniment unless it is completely clear that such is the case. In the *Perceforest*, for example, the author sometimes states explicitly that a performance includes both voice and instrument, as for example, "Quant

---

[10] The *Perceforest* is largely unedited, and my study of it is based on manuscript consultation. See J. Lods, Le *"Roman de Perceforest": Origines, composition, caractères, valeur et influence,* Société de Publications Romanes et Françaises 32 (Geneva and Lille, 1951); J.H.M. Taylor, ed., *Le Roman de Perceforest: première partie,* Textes Littéraires Français (Geneva, 1979). The lais have been published by J. Lods, ed., *Les Pièces lyriques du "Roman de Perceforest",* Publications Romanes et Françaises 36 (Geneva and Lille, 1953). I discuss an account from the *Perceforest* of the composition and performance of two lais in my *From Song To Book: The Poetics of Writing in Old French Lyric and Lyrical Narrative Poetry* (Ithaca, N.Y., 1987), pp. 297-98; the passage in question is printed as Appendix C, pp. 347-50.

[11] Godefroy defines "clause" as "fin de vers, rime, puis groupe de rimes" (end of a poetic line, rhyme, then group of rhymes). The meaning of "demistrophe" is further borne out by Froissart, who describes the complainte of the *Espinette* as containing "cent clauses desparelles" (v. 2340) (one hundred different *clauses*). The poem contains neither a hundred lines (it has 800) nor a hundred stanzas (it has 500). But it does contain a hundred different rhymes, and each stanza is of the form aaabaaab/bbbabbba. "Clause" most likely refers to a rhyme unit, that is, to the half-stanza unit of the form xxxyxxxy.

la damoiselle eut son lay tres bien joué en la harpe et bien chanté de la bouche" (When the maiden had played her lai very well on the harp and sung it well with her mouth) (Bibl. Nat. fr. 346, fol. 372v). Quite often, however, the author avoids such wordiness – his purpose, after all, is not to provide a manual on performance practice – and simply uses the term "harper" or "jouer" to refer to a performance that must, to judge from the context, include voice as well. In the following passage, for example, the only verb used is "harper", yet the conversation that ensues between minstrel and audience after the performance focuses exclusively on the story told by the lai:

> Lors s'assist ... et prist sa harpe, et commença a harper le dit si hault et si bien que c'estoit une pitié a oÿr. Mais quant il l'eut harpé ... dist l'une des damoiselles au menestrel, "Dy moy, par amours, qui fist ce lay et qui te l'apprist?" – "Dame, dist il, il le m'aprist celluy qui le fist. Et celluy qui le fist est le chevalier a qui le fait est advenu que le lay devise."

> Then he sat down ... and took his harp, and began to play the poem on the harp so loudly and so well that it was a pity to hear. But when he had played it on the harp ... one of the maidens said to the minstrel, "Tell me, for love, who made that lai and who taught it to you?" – "Lady", he said, "he who made it taught it to me. And he who made it is the knight to whom the event described in the lai happened."
> (Bibl. Nat. fr. 346, fol. 236r)

In a subsequent reference back to this passage, the author states that "les pucelles l'avoient trouvé jouant son lay" (the girls had found him playing his lai) (Bibl. Nat. fr. 346, fol. 242v). Yet clearly the minstrel had been singing as well as playing, or the girls could not have known what "the event described in the lai" was.

One can easily gather other examples of passages in which the only form of performance explicitly mentioned is instrumental, yet in which voice is strongly implied. How, for example, could the jongleur in the twelfth-century *Amis et Amile* play a song "about love and friendship" unless he was singing as well as playing:

> Devant li vait un jouglers de Poitiers
> Qui le vielle d'ammors et d'ammistié.

VOICES AND INSTRUMENTS ... 81

> Before him went a jongleur from Poitiers, who played for
> him on the fiddle about love and friendship.
> (vv. 2325-26)

Similarly, the Breton fiddler in the early thirteenth-century *Anseïs de Carthage* tells a story:

> Mais il faisoit un Breton vïeler
> Le lai Guron, coment il dut finer;
> Par fine amor le covint devier.
>
> But he had a Breton play the lai of Guron on the fiddle, how
> he had to die; he had to die from perfect love.
> (vv. 6145-47)

Such examples show that we must not assume too quickly that instrumental performances by minstrels do not include voice.[12] Adenet le Roi, for example, describes a string trio in *Berte aus grans piés* (ca. 1272-74):

> Li uns fu vieleres, on l'apeloit Gautier,
> Et l'autres fu ha[r]peres, s'ot non maistre Garnier;
> L'autres fu leüteres, molt s'en sot bien aidier.
>
> One was a fiddler, he was called Gautier, and the other was a harpist, and his name was Garnier; the third was a lutenist, and he knew how to do well for himself.
> (vv. 294-96)

Might such a band have included singers? The suggestion of vocal accompaniment to a minstrels' band is especially strong, if tantalizingly short of conclusive, in the following passage from Froissart's Chronicles (1350):

---

[12] Page, "Performance of Songs", argues that the dance music provided by minstrels in the fifteenth-century romance *Cleriadus et Meliadice* is purely instrumental and that the "chansons" to which people dance after the minstrels stop playing are purely vocal; he makes a similar assertion with regard to the carol in *Voices and Instruments*, p. 83. While this may be true, it does not mean that minstrels could not have sung chansons with instrumental accompaniment in a different context. The distinction between "danser aux menestrex" and "danser aux chansons" entails two different styles of dance: that appropriate to the ceremonial music provided by professional minstrels and that conducted to the dancers' own singing. It is indeed unlikely that dancers would play instruments, or that loud wind bands would include singers. But these are not the only two kinds of possible performance situations.

> Et faisoit ses menestrelz corner devant lui une danse d'Alemagne, que messire Jehan Chandos, qui là estoit, avoit nouvellement raporté. Et encores par esbatement il faisoit ledit chevalier chanter avoech ses menestrelz, et y prendoit grant plaisance.
>
> And [the King of England] had his minstrels play for him on loud winds a German dance, which Sir John Chandos, who was there, had recently brought back. And then for entertainment he had the said knight sing with his minstrels, and he took great pleasure in it.
>
> *(Chronicles,* IV, p. 91)

Were the minstrels still playing instruments – perhaps a selection of softer winds – when the knight sang with them? The possibility cannot be ruled out.

This last example raises a second interpretive difficulty often encountered in descriptions of musical performance: when a passage includes references to both singing and playing, are these activities simultaneous or sequential? This problem arises in the ubiquitous phrases of the type "And then the minstrels sang and played their instruments". Ambiguity is often no less present even in more elaborately spelled out descriptions, as in this passage from the early thirteenth-century romance *Blancandin:*

> Semonez moi les jugleors
> Et si mandez les harpeors;
> Les harpes ovuec les vïeles
> Orra on bien et les queroles.
> Ne vueil mais qu'il soient en pes,
> Et me diront sonez et les.
>
> Summon me the jongleurs, and also call the harpists; we will well hear the harps with the fiddles, and the carols. I don't want them ever to be still, and they will sing me songs and lais.
>
> (vv. 4263-68)

Evidently the king plans to listen to harp and fiddle ensembles; will the singing of "sonez" and lais take place along with the instrumental music or separately? The contemporary *Bueve de Hantone* tells us that a lai certainly could be sung to the accompaniment of harp and fiddle:

> Lors commencha Josïenne a chanter,
> Notes et lais moult bien a vïeler,
> Li vius Soybaus comencha a harper,
> Bien se commenchent lor son a acorder.

> Then Josienne began to sing, to play notes and lais on the fiddle; old Soybaus began to play the harp; their melodies began to harmonize well.
> (vv. 12087-90)

Thanks to the clarifying statement in v. 12090, we can be reasonably sure that the chain of verbs, chanter – vïeler – harper, represents simultaneous activity. We also know from another contemporary poem, *Gilles de Chyn*, that a "son" could be sung by two minstrels accompanying themselves on fiddles:

> Li vïeleur .i. son d'amour
> A haute vois mout cler cantoient,
> O les vïelez s'acordoient.
>
> The fiddlers sang a love song aloud and very clearly; they sang in tune with the fiddles.
> (vv. 460-62)

Finally, the *Roman de Silence* (second half of the 13th century) provides one unequivocal reference to the use of harp and fiddle to accompany the voice:

> Dont prent sa harpe et sa viiele,
> Si note avoec a sa vois biele.
>
> Then she takes her harp and her fiddle, and she plays on them to [the accompaniment of] her beautiful voice.
> *(Silence*, vv. 3521-22)

Such supporting examples do not, of course, prove that the performance in *Blancandin* is also one involving mixed vocal and instrumental music. But they do show that such performances took place, and there is no reason why the less precise descriptions could not have referred to such practices.

We encounter a similar problem in the prose romance *Paris et Vienne* (ca. 1400). The anonymous author gives us a description of Paris and his friend Edardo serenading Vienne that seems at first glance to be extremely precise, yet upon closer analysis eludes complete resolution.[13] The two young men appear under Vienne's window,

---

[13] On *Paris et Vienne* see Brown, "Instruments and Voices", pp. 102 ff.; Page, "Performance of Songs", p. 445-46.

> faisant oubades de leurs chanssons, quar ilz chantoient souveraynement bien, et puys jouoyent de leur instrumens chanssons mellodyoses, come ceulx qui de celluy mestier estoient les maistres.
>
> serenading her with their songs, for they sang supremely well, and then played on their instruments melodious songs, like those who are masters at this profession.
> *(Paris et Vienne, p. 77)*

At first glance one might easily believe that this passage draws a clear distinction between vocal and instrumental music: Paris and his companion first sang and then played. Such is Christopher Page's reading of the passage: "There is more than a hint of such a separation of vocal and instrumental music in *Paris et Vienne* where the hero and his companion, Edardo, sing and *then* play beneath Vienne's window."[14]

But it must be remembered that the very term "jouer" can be a shorthand way of referring to a performance that does, in fact, include voice as well. Perhaps the passage could be summarized like this: "they serenaded her with chansons, for they were excellent singers; and then they went on to other pieces involving instrumental accompaniment, for they could play beautifully too, like real masters."

In any case, vocal and instrumental music in *Paris et Vienne* are somehow linked. Performance is consistently referred to as "chanter et jouer" or "chanter et sonner". The account begins to sound suspiciously as though the singing and the playing really are two inseparable parts of one and the same activity: "ilz commensserent a chanter et a sonner ... et quant ilz eurent chanté et soné tout a leur plaisir ..." (they began to sing and to play ... and when they had sung and played all they wanted ...) (p. 79). In one source, the terms are reversed, showing at least that the order of singing and playing seemingly specified in the first passage cited above was not inviolable: "ilz commensserent a sonner de leurs instruments et a chanter" (they began to play their instruments and to sing) (cited by Kaltenbacher). The construction "chanter et sonner" closely resembles the wording found elsewhere in texts where the performance surely does involve voice with instrumental accompaniment. In the *Lai de l'Epine* (first half 13th century), for example, we are told:

---

[14] "Performance of Songs", p. 445, emphasis his.

Le lai escouterent d'Aelis
Que uns Ireis sone en sa rote,
Molt doucement le *chante et note*.

They listened to the Lai of Aelis, which an Irishman plays on his rote; very sweetly *he sings and plays* it.
(Epine, vv. 176-78, emphasis mine)

In light of the foregoing, it seems quite plausible to interpret the text as saying that Paris and Edardo began with vocal music and then proceeded to accompany their singing on instruments. This possibility is supported by analogy with other texts in which vocal and instrumental portions of a performance are distinguished. We have seen that the anonymous author of the *Perceforest* sometimes uses the construction "harper + chanter de bouche" (play on the harp + sing with the mouth) to describe the performance of lais. In a similar vein the author of the *Tristan en prose* commonly employs the construction "dit + chant" in reference to the performance of lais, as: "Quant le harpeur a tout son lay finé et de dit et de chant" (when the harpist had finished his whole lay, both words and melody) (Bibl. Nat. fr. 336, fol. 2r).[15] Since it would be very odd to distinguish in this way between the words and the tune to which the voice sings them, I feel that the construction "dit + chant" most likely refers to the coupling of vocal and instrumental music. Voice and instrument are, after all, distinct components of a performance, even if they are simultaneous during most or even all of it. As we have seen, there is some evidence that the performer of a lai would begin with an instrumental prelude. Such a practice is very explicitly described in one instance in the *Tristan en prose:*

Lors comence le lay en tele maniere, mes avant fist l'entree, puis le comença issi: *Aprés ce que je vi victoire.*

---

[15] One version of the *Tristan en prose* has now been edited in its entirety by R. L. Curtis, *Le Roman de Tristan en prose,* I (Munich, 1963); II (Leiden, 1976); III (Woodbridge, Suffolk, and Dover, N.H., 1985). The text exists in other versions, however, and I have based my study on manuscript consultation. See also E. Baumgartner, *"Le Tristan en prose": Essai d'interprétation d'un roman médiéval* (Geneva, 1975); E. Löseth, *Le Roman en prose de Tristan, le roman de Palamède et la compilation de Rusticien de Pise, analyse critique d'après les manuscrits de Paris* (Paris, 1890). On the lais, see J. Lods, "Les parties lyriques du Tristan en prose", *Bulletin Bibliographique de la Société Internationale Arthurienne* 1955, pp. 73-78; J. Maillard, "Lais avec notation dans le Tristan en prose", *Mélanges Rita Lejeune* (Gembloux, 1969), pp. 1347-64. The lais have been published by T. Fotitch and R. Stein, eds., *Les Lais du roman de Tristan en prose,* Münchener Romanistische Arbeiten 38 (Munich, 1974).

> Then she began the lai in such a manner, but first she did the prelude, then she began it thus: *After I saw victory.*
> (Bibl. Nat. fr. 772, fol. 285v)

At another point, though, the narrator stresses (perhaps because it is atypical?) that the harpist begins to sing along with the harp without any instrumental prelude: "Et li harperers comence maintenant le chant et le dit, tot ensemble" (And the harpist now begins the tune and the words, all together) (Bibl. Nat. fr. 12599, fol. 194r). In MS Bibl. Nat. fr. 335, the text reads "le chant et le dit avec" (the tune and the words along with it) (fol. 415v). Still another lai performance is described in terms parallel to those of the *Paris et Vienne* passage: "Et quant il a bien atrempee, il commence son chant et puis son dit" (When he has tuned [the harp] well, he begins his tune and then his words) (Bibl. Nat. fr. 335, 217v). Surely what is at issue here is not an instrumental version of the entire lai followed by a separate vocal rendition, but simply an instrumental opening followed by a rendition with voice and harp. The performance is made up of two kinds of sound, vocal *(dit)* and instrumental *(chant);* but these are essentially simultaneous and closely linked elements. The unity of vocal and instrumental components is stressed in the narrator's closing reference to the performance: "Quant il a parfiné ses vers et harpés au mieulx qu'il scet" (when he has finished his verses and played them on the harp the best he knows how) (Bibl. Nat. fr. 335, fol. 218r). Similarly, the maiden who played the "entree" is said afterwards to have "son lay si bien chanté et noté si doucement" (so well sung and so sweetly played her lai) (Bibl. Nat. fr. 772, fol. 285v). These closing comments cannot be descriptions of a temporal sequence of singing, then playing, for the narrative account of the performance made it quite explicit that the performer first played and then sang.

Again, these supporting examples do not tell us definitely what the author of *Paris et Vienne* intended. But we have seen that the term "jouer" need not exclude voice; that the term "puis" could be used to distinguish not two entirely separate pieces, but simply two moments within one and the same piece; and that a seeming distinction of voice and instrument could be a way of articulating two interacting components of the performance. If this analysis does not arrive at a complete resolution of ambiguous passages, it has at least shown the care with which such passages must be read.

Reading Performance Descriptions, II: Social and Literary Analysis

Once we have decided what a given passage literally says, it remains to analyze the description as a record of performance practice. A number of factors must be taken into account. We need to know not merely whether a given performer was singing, playing, or both, but more precisely what kinds of performers (aristocratic amateurs or minstrels) would be most likely to engage in these activities; what kinds of performances (private or public, spontaneous or formal) a given practice appears in; what kinds of pieces (narrative songs, trouvère songs, dance music, etc.) are associated with a given practice and with a given type of performer; and so on. Finally, it is necessary to consider the narrative function of the performance passage within the frame text, and the extent to which literary conventions, rather than contemporary performance practice, might determine the particular details given by the author.

The categorization of performance descriptions according to the social class of the performer reveals one striking fact: most accounts of instrumental music involve not aristocrats but minstrels, aristocrats disguised as minstrels, and shepherds. Although the various wind and percussion instruments that figure in the pastourelle may correspond somewhat to instruments used in the medieval countryside, the musicians who populate the pastourelle surely reflect aristocratic stereotypes of the amorous, flute-playing rustic rather than actual realities of medieval peasant life. With certain exceptions, however, the behavior of aristocratic protagonists and their minstrels is probably closer to the truth; at the very least, these figures embody the ideals that aristocrats held about themselves and the musicians they employed. It is with these two classes of performer that the following discussion will be concerned.

The aristocratic heroes and heroines of medieval literature sing very frequently, and occasionally play instruments; but they almost never do both at once. The primary exception is the aristocratic penchant for playing lais on the harp. Thomas d'Angleterre, for example, described Iseut's rendition of the lai of Guiron:

> La dame chante dulcement,
> La voiz acorde a l'estrument.

The queen sings sweetly, the voice accords with the instrument.
(Tristan, vv. 843-44)

However, these aristocratic harpers of lais are nearly always set in a distant, Breton past. The most famous aristocratic harpists are Tristan and Iseut, but there are others; one encounters similar figures, for example, in *Horn* and *Galeran de Bretagne*. The narrator of *Horn* even comments on the skill of the Breton lords and ladies for singing and playing lais on the harp, implying that this practice may no longer be current:

A cel tens sorent tuit. harpe bien manier.
Cum plus fu gentilz hom. e plus sout del mester.

At that time everyone knew well how to handle a harp. The more noble a man was, the more he knew of this art.
(Horn, vv. 2824-25)

Whether or not real thirteenth- and fourteenth-century lords and ladies actually learned to accompany themselves on the harp, lords and ladies in thirteenth- and fourteenth-century French literature generally did not unless they belonged to this slightly exotic past. Indeed, there is some evidence that the practice of accompanying one's own singing on an instrument was perceived specifically as an art cultivated by minstrels. In *Aucassin et Nicolette* (ca. 1175-1225), it is not entirely clear whether Nicolette is secretly learning a minstrel's art when she learns to play the fiddle, or taking up an accepted aristocratic pastime. We are told only that "Ele quist une viele, s'aprist a vieler" (she sought out a fiddle, and learned to play it) (38: vv. 13-14) in preparation for her plan to seek Aucassin, disguised as a minstrel. In any case, it is as a minstrel that she sings the tale of Aucassin and Nicolette to the accompaniment of her fiddle. In the slightly later *Roman de la violette* (early 13th century), it is suggested more explicitly that the act of singing and playing simultaneously is proper to the minstrel and not to the aristocrat. The knight Gerart sings love songs on numerous occasions. But when disguised as a minstrel, he must perform a *chanson de geste*. On this occasion he reflects,

Faire m'estuet, quant l'ai empris,
Chou dont je ne sui mie apris:
Chanter et vïeler ensemble.

> Since I have undertaken it, I must do that which I never learned to do: sing and play the fiddle at the same time.
> *(Violette,* vv. 1401-3)

As Christopher Page points out, a slight change in punctuation – easily justified, since the medieval text is not punctuated at all – would change the meaning of the text, suggesting that it was formal public performance rather than instrumental accompaniment to song that Gerart had never learned.[16] The *chanson de geste* itself belongs to the repertoire of the minstrel and not to that of the aristocratic amateur. Still, this is the only one of Gerart's many songs to have instrumental accompaniment. However we punctuate the text, there remains a strong association of simultaneous singing and playing with the profession and repertoire of the minstrel. Aristocrats do sometimes play instruments in contemporary settings, but then there is usually no mention of singing. In the late thirteenth-century *Tournois de Chauvency,* for example, an aristocratic lady plays a fiddle as accompaniment for a masquerade dance staged by two other maidens *(Tournois,* vv. 2547 ff.). Since the author gives the words to so many refrains sung both formally and informally during the festivities, it is probable that the omission of any reference to singing in this instance really does mean that the music was purely instrumental.

Does this mean that aristocrats really never, or hardly ever, did sing and play at the same time? Certainly we would expect an aristocratic amateur to perform in a less virtuosic or professional manner than a trained minstrel or chapel singer; perhaps the combination of voice and instrument was a hallmark of the professional. But what would this mean: that aristocrats performed a repertoire wholly different from that of the minstrels or that they performed a shared or partially shared repertoire without combining voices and instruments? These questions must be answered with extreme caution. I will begin here with a survey of the repertoire associated with aristocratic and professional performers respectively. My remarks, as always, are based entirely on literary sources.

With the exception of the *chansons de toile* sung by ladies and maidens in their chambers, and the lais sung by Breton aristocrats, narrative songs belong to a minstrel/jongleur repertoire. Minstrels also performed lais, as well as *chansons de geste* and unspecified *contes.* And narrative songs seem

---

[16] Page, *Voices and Instruments,* pp. 188-90.

always to be sung or recited to the accompaniment of instruments.[17] The lai in particular could be performed with a wide variety of instrumentation. We have already seen numerous examples of lais played on harps, as well as on fiddles or rotes, and even on flutes. The variety of possible instrumentation is summed up in Wace's *Roman de Brut:*

> Lais de vïeles, lais de rotes,
> Lais de harpes, lais de fresteles.

> Lais on fiddles, lais on rotes, lais
> on harps, lais on freteles.
> *(Brut,* vv. 10548-49)

There was evidently considerable flexibility in the instrumentation that could be used for the ubiquitous lai. To what extent, if any, the different instruments might team up to perform lais as small ensembles is unfortunately impossible to determine from this passage, as is the way that the text of a lai would be handled (if at all) by someone playing it on a wind instrument. But this passage and others like it are nonetheless important reminders of the fluidity of medieval performance practices: we must be careful not to assume that a given text prescribes *the* way that a particular piece would be performed. Even the same lai could be performed with different instrumentation. Gerbert de Montreuil's continuation of *Perceval* (ca. 1230) refers to the performance of a "lai Goron" on *estives* (see *Tristan ménestrel,* p. 526); the early thirteenth-century *Anseïs de Carthage* mentions the performance of a "lai Guron" on fiddle (vv. 6145-46, cited above); and the *Roman de Silence* (ca. 1250) refers to a performance of a series of lais, including a rendition of "Gueron" on harp *(Silence,* v. 2762). Iseut, in the passage cited above, sings the lai of "Guirun" to a harp. These are almost certainly all versions of the same lai.[18] As Maillart states in the Prologue to the *Comte d'Anjou,* cited above, each performer builds up his repertoire and chooses his instrumentation, "chascun selonc s'entencion."

---

[17] Page concludes from his study of *Guillaume de Dole* that instrumental accompaniment is limited to songs of the "Lower Style" and has a "strong link with dance, with narrative and with refrain-form" *(Voices and Instruments,* p. 38).

[18] On the *Lai de Guiron,* see G.E. Brereton, "A Thirteenth-Century List of French Lays and Other Narrative Poems", *Modern Language Review* 45 (1950), pp. 40-45, entry no. 15; and J. Bédier, ed., *Le Roman de Tristan* by Thomas, I, Société des Anciens Textes Français (Paris, 1902), pp. 51, 52-53.

Chansons de geste are usually sung to the fiddle, as in the passages cited above from *Moniage Guillaume* and the *Violette;* one can find other similar examples. But they could also be sung to the hurdy-gurdy:

> On appelle en France cymphonie ung instrument dont les aveugles jouent en chantant les chansons de geste.
>
> In France "cifonie" [hurdy-gurdy] is the term for an instrument that blind people play in singing *chansons de geste.*
> (J. Corbechon, "Propriétés des choses" (dated 1372); cited in Godefroy, s.v. "cifonie")

Obviously, the blind people in question sing for their living, and so can be included in the class of jongleurs. Various stringed instruments are also associated with the performance of other sorts of narratives. In *Claris et Laris* (ca. 1268), for example, an unspecified narrative includes refrains played on the fiddle:[19]

> La escoutoient bonement
> .l. conteor, qui lor contoit
> Une chançon et si notoit
> Ses refrez en un viele.
>
> There they were listening well to a story-teller, who told [narrated] them a song and also played its refrains on a fiddle.
> (vv. 9940-43)

And in a fourteenth-century translation of *Pamphile et Galatée,* the old lady tells the tale of Aristotle's seduction, adding, "Or n'i a villain qui n'en rote" (Now there isn't a peasant who does not play on the rote about it) *(Pamphile,* v. 1783). Again "villain" probably refers to lower-class jongleurs; in any case it certainly excludes aristocrats.

---

[19] It is hard to say exactly what this narrative song with refrains was. Perhaps the "refrains" are simply instrumental interludes between the *laisses* of a *chanson de geste* or the stanzas of a lai. Assuming that they are actual refrains with words, the song could have been a *chanson de toile.* Or it may have been some other sort of sung or chanted narrative with regularly recurring refrains that could be played on a fiddle. There is a hint of such a practice in the *Chastelaine de Saint Gille,* a stanzaic fabliau with a different refrain at the end of each stanza. One of these is introduced: "S'en doi bien dire par réson / Les vers que j'ai tant violé: / J'ai trové le ni de pie ..." (Thus I should well and rightly sing the verses that I have fiddled so often: I found the magpie's nest) (vv. 271-73). Page suggests that the piece in question may have been a rondeau *(Voices and Instruments,* p. 84); but to my mind the verb "conter" implies a narrative song.

The fact that these narrative songs are nearly always specified as being sung to instrumental accompaniment poses no contradiction, then, to our earlier impression that a combined vocal and instrumental performance was the domain of the minstrel. Indeed, this impression is supported in *Guillaume de Dole,* where *chansons de toile* are performed in different situations. When Liënor and her mother sing the songs of Aude and Doon, Bele Aye, and Bele Doe for the entertainment of the emperor's envoy, there is no instrumental accompaniment. At a later point, however, the song of Bele Aiglentine is sung by a man:

> Uns bachelers de Normendie
> chevauchoit la grande chaucie,
> commença cesti a chanter,
> si la fist Jouglet vïeler.
>
> A young man from Normandy was riding along the great path; he began to sing this, and he had Jouglet play it on the fiddle.
> *(Guillaume de Dole,* vv. 2231-34)

The Norman may be an aristocrat, but he is only the singer; the instrumental accompaniment is provided by Jouglet, the emperor's minstrel. All *chanson de toile* performances described in the text are informal; what distinguishes them is the presence of the minstrel in the latter. The passage is a very suggestive indication of the different ways that the *chanson de toile* could be rendered by different types of performers.

Monophonic love songs, such as trouvère and troubadour songs, rondeaux and virelais, and refrains, seem at first glance to belong to an aristocratic repertoire. When such songs appear as lyric insertions in romances, they are virtually always either placed in the mouth of an amorous aristocrat, or sung at the aristocrat's request by his resident minstrel, in celebration of the aristocrat's love affair. They are never accompanied by instruments in any of these instances. But does this mean that such songs really were performed only in spontaneous, purely vocal renditions? Might not the "son d'amour" sung to instrumental accompaniment by the two fiddlers in *Gilles de Chyn* be of the trouvère repertoire?[20] The early thirteenth-century monk Gautier de Coinci, whose songs are closely modelled on trouvère songs in

---

[20] Page cites *Gille de Chyn* and points out that there is no way to tell whether the "son d'amour" is of the High Style or the Lower Style *(Voices and Instruments,* p. 33).

form, language, imagery, and in the incorporation of secular refrains, introduces these songs with references to fiddle and lyre:[21]

> Or veil atant traire ma lire
> Et atemprer veil ma vïele
> Se chanterai de la pucele.
>
> Now I want to get out my lyre and I want to tune my fiddle, thus I will sing of the virgin.
> *(Miracles,* I, Book 1,
> Second Prologue, vv. 56-58)
>
> Ma vïele
> Vïeler vieut un biau son.
>
> My fiddle wants to play a pretty song.
> *(Miracles,* III, Book 2, Ch. 8, vv. 1-2)

Perhaps the "rule" of vocal performance by aristocrats or by their minstrels, in private spontaneous performances, of trouvère songs, is not in fact universal, though it may indeed have been the most common practice. I will return to this point below, in the discussion of literary conventions.

It is extremely difficult to find clear references of any kind to the performance of polyphonic music. One of the few unmistakable references to polyphonic performance is a humorous passage in Gace de la Buigne's *Roman des deduis* (composed 1359-77), in which the baying of a pack of hunting dogs is described as polyphony:

> Les uns vont chantans le motet,
> Les autres font double hoquet.
> Les plus grans chantent la teneur,

---

[21] Page argues that the references to musical instruments in Gautier de Coinci's songs do not reflect possible instrumental accompaniment of such pieces, but are rather imitations of the references to bards in Latin poetry; he also cites the symbolism of musical instruments in Biblical exegesis and in much medieval religious writing *(Voices and Instruments,* pp. 191-93). Yet Page also cites Gautier's version of the Roc-Amadour miracle, in which a minstrel honors the Virgin by singing and accompanying himself on the fiddle *(Ibid.,* pp. 193-94). While Gautier's allusions to fiddle and lyre may indeed carry literary and theological reverberations, and while there is no reason to assume that Gautier himself played either of these instruments, I see no reason why these texts could not be taken as evidence that trouvère songs and their religious imitations and contrafacta were sometimes sung to instrumental accompaniment.

Les autres la contreteneur.
Ceulx qui ont la plus clere gueule
Chantent le tresble sans demeure,
Et les plus petis le quadouble
En faisant la quinte sur double.
Les uns font semithon mineur,
Les autres semithon majeur,
Diapenthé, diapazon,
Les autres dyathesseron.

Some go singing the motet, the others do a double hoquet. The largest sing the tenor, the others the contratenor. Those who have the clearest voice sing the treble without hesitation, and the smallest the fourth part, doing the fifth above the duplum. Some do a minor semitone, the others a major semitone, diapente, diapason, the others diatessaron.
(Deduis, vv. 8081-92)

As the argument is expanded, the dogs are credited with "singing" not only motets and double hoquets, but also rondeaux. Their music is said to be even more beautiful than the *respons* or *alleluye* of the royal chapel.

Though obviously playful, the passage does shed a certain light on the performance of court polyphony. First of all, the plethora of technical terms, together with the comparison to royal chapel musicians, support an identification of polyphony as proper to highly trained, specialized musicians. Secondly, the description refers pretty clearly to a purely vocal rendition of motets or other polyphonic compositions. Not only does the author find no difficulty in conceiving of the mixture of dogs' "voices" as polyphony; but also the definition of polyphony offered in support of the claims being made for dogs' musical abilities stipulates vocal performance:

Et est verité que motés,
Balades ne doubles hoqués
Ne sont rien, bien en sui recors,
Que des chans de divers accors,
Mesurés par proporcions
Pour faire plus gracieux sons,
De pluseurs chantés par mestrie
De doulce et plaisant melodie.

And it is true that motets, balades and double hoquets are nothing, of this I'm sure, other than melodies of different harmonies, measured by proportions so as to make more graceful songs, sung by several through mastery of sweet and pleasant melody.
(Deduis, vv. 10603-10)

It is because "chiens ont vois si flexible" (dogs have such flexible voices) (v. 10632) that they are capable of song. Evidently, the a capella rendition of polyphonic balades, rondeaux, hoquets and motets was sufficiently well established that the author could take it for granted in building his fanciful case for dogs.

Most other allusions to polyphony are much less explicit than the foregoing. One can find references to things that might be polyphonic; the problem is that it is frequently impossible to determine whether the passage refers to a monophonic group performance or to polyphony. Contrasting with the emphasis on the voice in the *Roman des deduis*, for example, are the many descriptions of minstrels playing in ensembles, some of which probably refer to instrumental polyphony. We have seen the trio of fiddle, harp and lute mentioned in *Berte aus grans piés* (vv. 294-96). In the *Roman d'Eledus et Serene* (first half of the 14th century), minstrels play in ensembles, although instruments are not specified:

> Et menestriers de maintes manieres
> Qui de leurs istrumens jouoient,
> Et tous ensemble si s'acordoient.

> And minstrels of all kinds who played their instruments, and thus they harmonized all together.
> *(Eledus et Serene, vv. 4398-4400)*

Finally, there are a few passages – some more explicit than others – that suggest the combination of voices and instruments in polyphony. In the citation above from the *Fonteinne amoureuse*, for example, the duke could be singing to a polyphonic accompaniment of horns and rotes, though we cannot be certain. Similarly, the songs alluded to in *Renart le contrefait* (1319) might be polyphonic pieces with instrumental settings:

> Plus ameroit quatre garchons
> De nuit chanter quatre chanssons
> Avec la trompe et la guisterne.

> He [the average minstrel] would prefer four boys to sing four songs, with trumpet and gittern, at night.
> *(Renart, vv. 36135-37)*

The early thirteenth-century *Durmart le Galois* contains a passage that may be a humorous parody of polyphony. A malevolent knight arrives at court, accompanied by five dwarves:

> Li doi nain vienent flajolant,
> Et li troi vienent tot chantant
> A grosses vois sens point tenir.
> ...
> Les vois ont grosses et bruians,
> Et si n'apointent riens lor chans.
>
> Two of the dwarves came playing flutes, and three came singing in raucous voices without harmonizing at all ... They had raucous and noisy voices, and their respective tunes didn't correspond at all.
> (vv. 10033-35, 10053-54)

This cacophonous "performance" is clearly a violation of good musical taste. Since the narrator stresses that the problem lay in the harshness of the voices and the lack of harmony among parts, we can infer that an ensemble of three singers and two flute players would not be unusual in itself, and that they could be expected to sing or play melodic lines which did harmonize. Still, we do not know whether such a performance would involve actual polyphony or merely a group rendition of a monophonic piece.

The mid-fourteenth century *Voie d'Enfer et de Paradis* includes several descriptions of both angelic and lascivious music. While these tend to be vague, there is one that suggests the rendition by voice and instruments of a polyphonic rondeau: we are told that the angels were

> Jüans de flagols, de fretel,
> D'orghes, harpes, et vïeloient,
> Si glorïeusement cantoient
> Li un, li autre respondoient
> De la Vierge un trés douch rondel.
>
> Playing flutes and fretels, organs, harps, and they were playing the fiddle; thus some were singing gloriously, the others were responding, a very sweet rondeau about the Virgin.
> *(Voie d'Enfer,* vv. 3605-09)

The profusion of voices and instruments, and the sumptuous nature of the performance, raise the very distinct possibility of polyphony.

In a more clearly worded passage in the *Roman de la rose* (1270s), Pygmalion sings motets while accompanying himself on the portative organ:

> Orgues i ra bien maniables,
> a une seule main portables,
> ou il meïsme soufle et touche,
> et chante avec a pleine bouche
> motet ou treble ou teneüre.

> There are organs easily handled, which can be held in a single hand, which he himself pumps and plays, and sings along with a full voice, motet or triplum or tenor.
> *(Rose,* vv. 21007-11)

As the text stands here, it is possible to read it as a monophonic rendition, doubled in voice and organ, of one part of a motet: the motetus part, or the triplum, or the tenor. In fact, the term "motet" is used for monophonic refrains in the contemporary *Renart le nouvel*. However, Langlois in his edition gives the variant reading "motet a treble ou teneüre" [motet with triplum or tenor], which implies that Pygmalion was singing one part of a polyphonic motet and playing the rest on the organ.

In the *Dit de la panthère d'amours* (ca. 1300), voices and instruments combine in the rendition of chansons, motets and conductus. Describing the God of Love's entourage, the narrator lists numerous string, wind, and percussion instruments, and adds:

> Instrumens de toutes manieres
> Y avoit, et a vois plenieres
> Chantoient cil qui les menoient,
> Et qui bien faire le savoient,
> Chançonetes moult cointement,
> Et moult très envoisieement
> Chantoient motés et conduis.

> There was every kind of instrument, and those who were playing them and who knew how to do it well were singing little songs most prettily with full voices, and very very skillfully they were singing motets and conductus.
> *(Panthère,* vv. 165-171)

The profusion of voices and instruments would certainly lend themselves to polyphony, and the repeated emphasis on the skill of the musicians indicates that this is no run-of-the-mill performance.

None of these passages, with the possible exception of that from the *Fonteinne amoureuse*, involve the performance of polyphony by aristocratic amateur musicians. Even in the *Fonteinne*, the aristocrat is of extremely high standing, he is not playing instruments, and the performance is informal. In the other cases, we find "boys", associated with the minstrel class; minstrels; dwarves, parodic figures for the minstrels employed by aristocrats; angels; Pygmalion, a mythological figure of unsurpassed artistic skills who is about to experience a miracle; and the followers of the God of Love, in an allegorical dream vision. Naturally this alone does not prove that aristocratic amateurs never performed polyphony, but it does certainly suggest that, in the thirteenth and fourteenth centuries, polyphony was in a special class. The same can be said for the ability to sing and play an instrument at the same time. If indeed the young men of *Paris et Vienne* were accompanying themselves instrumentally, and especially if they were performing polyphony, this could explain the extreme wonder and admiration expressed by those who heard them "chanter et sonner".

Literary texts, then, make a relatively consistent distinction between narrative songs (performed by professional musicians, with instruments); the Breton lai (performed by past Breton aristocrats and by professionals of all kinds, usually to instrumental accompaniment); monophonic refrains, trouvère or troubadour songs, and *formes fixes* (usually performed by aristocratic amateurs without instruments); and polyphonic motets and *formes fixes* (performed either with or without instruments by minstrels, clerics, and other exceptional or other-worldly figures). How can we determine the extent to which this division corresponds to historical reality? Since my concern here is with literary texts, I will approach the question from the perspective of literary criticism: what role do narrative strategy and literary convention play in determining descriptions of performance? We have already touched on one example of the influence of literary conventions in descriptions of performance in the case of the Breton lai. In fact, when the *Perceforest* describes wandering minstrels who perform quasi-narrative lais on the harp and supplement their song with a narrative account of the adventure that gave rise to the lai, this does not necessarily mean that such was the predominant musical reality in fourteenth-century France. The text is deliberately archaizing, looking back to a sort of pre-history before the Christianization of Britain and imitating the *Tristan en prose*, a text that also looks to the past and, moreover, pre-dates the

Perceforest by about a century. Such texts are no doubt an accurate reflection of the status of the medieval minstrel as source of both news and entertainment. Other details, such as the minstrel's interactions with the aristocratic audience and his or her ability to combine vocal and instrumental performance, may well also reflect fourteenth-century practices; and these texts are in any case invaluable aids in mastering the vocabulary and syntax of Old French performance descriptions. In terms of information about specific poetic and musical genres, however, these accounts undoubtedly tell us less about the performance of lais in fourteenth-century France than about fourteenth-century notions of old-fashioned Breton musical practices.[22]

We must exercise a similar caution in interpreting other literary examples. I have stated, for example, that trouvère and troubadour songs never seem to be sung in formal, public performances. They are usually sung by lovestruck aristocrats, in moments of private meditation on the joys or the sorrows of love. Sometimes, as in a few instances in *Guillaume de Dole*, they are sung by minstrels in a private setting, for the sole benefit of the minstrel's aristocratic patron. Yet we cannot assume that love songs of this type were never performed in formal public presentations. After all, many troubadours and trouvères were minstrels themselves or even tradesmen, who must have encountered the songs in performance situations unlike those recorded in the romances. And one can find allusions to the performance of such songs by minstrels. I have already mentioned the love songs performed by the fiddlers in *Gilles de Chyn*, which may have belonged to the trouvère repertoire. Less ambiguous is the *Castelain de Couci* (late 13th century), where there are occasional references to the Châtelain's songs being performed far and wide, and one explicit statement that his songs were performed by a local minstrel. But these are offhand statements. The songs themselves are inserted into the text in non-performing contexts: the Châtelain composes a song while riding home from a tournament, or on

---

[22] Page similarly concludes that descriptions of harp-playing Bretons probably owe more to literary convention than to contemporary social practices, but also suggests that such conventions may have been powerful enough to influence performance practice at times *(Voices and Instruments,* pp. 102-7). Page's discussion of these texts is most useful, but one of his assertions – that these Breton harpers of lais are always courtly amateurs *(Ibid*, p. 97) – must be modified: both the *Tristan en prose* and the *Perceforest*, to name just two examples, contain numerous descriptions, often quite detailed, of professional minstrels singing lais to the accompaniment of the harp.

his way to or from a meeting with his lady. No medieval writer states that minstrels did not perform love songs or that these songs were not played on instruments. But when these songs are explicitly identified, through lyric insertions, they appear without instruments and usually in the mouth of an aristocrat. When minstrels "sing and play instruments", their repertoire is either the traditional minstrel repertoire of narrative lais and *chansons de geste,* a vague repertoire of "sons", "vers" and "chansonettes" which could include almost anything, or entirely unidentified.

The treatment of trouvère songs, as well as rondeaux, ballades, and other courtly love songs, is as much a function of narrative strategy as of performance practice. These songs are introduced into the narrative for particular reasons, among the most important of which is the desire for greater subjectivity in the development of the amorous hero or heroine. In the later thirteenth and fourteenth centuries, the lyric insertion often fulfills the role of the internal monologue of twelfth-century romance. When love songs are sung in public settings, as is often the case with dance refrains, rondeaux and virelais, lyric insertions may enable a pair of lovers to exchange secret messages in public by singing songs that carry a special meaning for the two of them (and, of course, for the reader). At other times, the refrains allow for general flirtation, as men and ladies alternately sing refrains in a sort of communal dialogue. Sometimes the songs motivate the plot, as when a character hears a song sung by another character, realizes the latter's amorous intentions, and reacts to further or to thwart these intentions. All of these narrative functions of lyric insertions require that the song be sung by the aristocratic protagonist or, at the very least, by a minstrel who speaks for his patron. There is little reason why a medieval romance author would want to focus on the amorous sentiments of a minstrel, and it would serve no narrative purpose to give all the texts of songs performed by minstrels at court festivities. For this reason the professional performances are glossed over fairly rapidly, in sketchy descriptions that evoke a general atmosphere of courtly celebration. And considerable attention is paid to songs, and in particular to the words of songs, that in some cases are hardly even performances at all, any more than the elaborate songs sung by lovers in a Broadway musical can be considered performances – much less reflections of daily life in twentieth-century America – within the context of the play. It is scarcely surprising that musical instruments are not mentioned in these informal "performances". While aristocrats undoubtedly did sing the current popular songs in both public and private, the overwhelming emphasis on this particular type of performance in literary texts should not lead us to believe that it is the only way that these songs were performed.

A similar point can be made with regard to dance music. There can be little doubt that medieval knights and ladies did dance to the accompaniment of their own singing, for there are many accounts of this practice. And at times the author even specifies that this singing is without instrumental accompaniment. In the *Perceforest,* for example, in a scene that probably is based on contemporary practices (there is nothing about it that reflects medieval views of the early Bretons), the assembled company dances for a time to the music of the minstrels. Then, however, the king interrupts the minstrels:

> Car le roy ala dire, "Seigneurs, laissiers ester, car il n'est instrument que de bouche de pucelle." Atant cesserent les menestrelz et le roy dist, "Pucelles doivent commenchier a chanter, car la feste est leur."
>
> For the king said, "Lords, stop, for there is no instrument but the lips of a maiden." At once the minstrels stopped and the king said, "Maidens should begin to sing, for the festivities are theirs."
> (Paris, Bibl. Arsenal 3494, fol. 277r)

In accordance with the king's instructions, two maidens and two knights each sing a "chansonette". Each sings of his or her part in a rather lengthy love debate that the four have been involved in for some time, during which the ladies have never met the men in person. It is in this way that the adventure is revealed to the court and its participants finally allowed to meet face to face.

In the *Prison amoureuse,* Froissart describes a feast at the court of Savoy in 1368, at which the ladies sang to provide music for the carol after the minstrels stopped playing:

> Et quant li menestrel cessoient,
> Les dames pas ne se lassoient,
> Ains caroloient main a main
> Tout le soir jusqu'a l'endemain.
> Et quant chanté li une avoit
> Un virelay, on ne savoit
> Encores s'il avoit fin pris,
> Quant uns aultres estoit repris
> Ou de dame ou de damoiselle.

> And when the minstrels stopped, the ladies didn't grow weary, but they caroled hand in hand all evening until the next day. And when one had sung a virelai, you didn't even know whether or not it was finished yet when another had already been begun by a lady or a maiden.
> *(Prison,* vv. 401-9)

This feast in turn is compared to another, similar carol that Froissart portrays himself as witnessing in the *Prison,* at which ladies again sing virelais after the minstrels cease playing. Froissart is pleased that one of his virelais is sung and well received. But he is shocked when the lady that he loves chooses to sing a virelai in which she rejects the affections of an unwanted admirer, and the following episode is concerned with his meditations on this event, his successful rationalization of her song (it must have been meant for someone other than himself), and the composition of a new song in honor of the occasion.

There is no reason to doubt that dance scenes of this type occured commonly. And in fact the spontaneous, perhaps at times even simultaneous singing of different songs, fragments of songs and refrains by the various dancers could not easily be accompanied by instrumentalists. In the *Perceforest,* indeed, the knights and maidens sing songs that they have composed themselves and which have never been sung before, therefore presumably could not even be known by the minstrels. But should we assume that this was the only way that virelais and other dance tunes could be performed? It is important to remember that the texts cited here are far more specific about the lack of instrumental accompaniment for the songs of the carolers, than about any lack of vocal accompaniment to the instrumental music of the minstrels. In both the *Prison* and the *Perceforest,* there is a clear narrative reason to highlight the songs sung by the participants in the carol, and no reason at all to highlight the songs performed by the nameless musicians. What we see here is not necessarily *the* way, but only one of the ways that dance music could be performed; in particular, it is the way that most lends itself to the use of lyric insertions for narrative development. It may well be for this reason, and not because it was the only method of performance, that it is so commonly featured in romances and *dits.*

Verification of the lack of instrumental accompaniment for caroling ladies can be found in a somewhat unexpected source, the *Contes moralisés* of the fourteenth-century English cleric Nicole Bozon. Bozon, in a passage warning of the dangers of associating with women, draws an analogy between the carol and the hunt. Just as hares flee the sounds of baying hounds and hunting horns, he says, so men should flee the seductive but equally dangerous sounds of caroling maidens:

> quant oyent les chienz questeyer, ce sont les domoiseles qe vont caroler, e lui veneour qe va cornant, e ceo est le tabour qe lour somont a lur peril ...
>
> When they hear the dogs bark, those are the maidens that go caroling; and the hunter who goes sounding his horn, and that is the drum that draws them to their peril.
> *(Contes moralisés,* pp. 27-28)

Bozon has no need to highlight in any special way the songs of the maidens; he simply wants to set up his analogy between a typical carol and a hunt. It is relatively straightforward – and in keeping with what we saw in the *Roman des deduis* – that the "voices" of dogs would be compared to those of the carolers; the hunting horns are the instrumental accompaniment. That the horns should be compared to accompaniment by percussive rather than wind or other melodic instruments strongly suggests that maidens dancing to their own singing really would not be accompanied by anything other than a simple drumbeat. The clerical text confirms the evidence offered by courtly literature as to the activity of aristocratic women; but as to the activity of professional instrumental ensembles, we are still largely in the dark.

The tendency to highlight spontaneous and often informal performances by aristocratic amateurs, and the overriding importance of the words rather than the musical aspects of most songs used in narrative texts, may also help to explain the lack of references to polyphony. Of all the romances and *dits* with lyric insertions, only *Fauvel,* which is atypical in more ways than one, contains polyphonic motets.[23] Although Machaut sometimes uses polyphonic chansons as lyric insertions, only the text is performed within the narrative, and there is never any reference to either vocal or instrumental rendition of the other parts. If the purpose of lyric insertions is to allow

---

[23] On lyric insertions in narrative and dramatic works, see M.V. Coldwell, *"Guillaume de Dole* and Musical Romances with Musical Interpolations", *Musica Disciplina* 35 (1981), pp. 55-86. Coldwell gives Tables of Romances with Musical Interpolations, pp. 71-86. Polyphonic motets appear in the dramatic *Ludus super Anticlaudianus,* the *Fauvel,* and the *Miracles Nostre Dame.* None of these are romances describing the performance at court of secular motets.

the protagonist to assume center stage and express his sentiments, then there really is little reason why an author would insert a two- or three-voiced motet into a narrative, or describe the technical details of a polyphonic performance given by professional musicians.

Conclusions

The foregoing discussion allows for preliminary conclusions, to be augmented or modified in future studies. In terms of methodology, I have outlined textual, semantic, and syntactic considerations that must inform the study of literary sources. The scholar using modern printed editions must ascertain that the text corresponds to a medieval version, and should also check to see if variant readings turn up any new evidence. Individual words must be interpreted with caution; in particular, the statement that a performer plays an instrument need not mean that he or she is not also singing, and vice versa. And the separation of vocal and instrumental music in phrases like "chanter et sonner" or "dit et chant" must likewise be interpreted with care, in order to determine whether the distinction implies a temporal sequence or a logical articulation of simultaneous or interlaced activities. While such decisions can be extremely difficult, careful reading can often make the task easier. Sometimes variant readings may support one or another interpretation, as when Paris and Edardo are said to "chanter et sonner" in one source and to "sonner et chanter" in another: if the order of the activities is unimportant, it could be because they are simultaneous. In other cases, the complete passage may contain more than one account of the same performance, as when the performers of lais in the *Tristan en prose* are first said to play and then to sing, while in the completion of the performance they are said to have sung and then to have played: again, the apparent contradiction is easily resolved if simultaneous vocal and instrumental music is assumed. In still other cases, the context of the performance may clarify its nature, as when a minstrel "plays" a piece and then discusses its words with his audience. Finally, the analysis of a given author's linguistic and stylistic habits can help to determine the precise meaning of difficult passages. For example, the repeated use of the phrase "jouer en la harpe et chanter de la bouche" (play on the harp and sing with the mouth) in the *Perceforest* need not be seen as expressive of a temporal sequence of musical activities, but as a variation on the author's tendency to employ dual modifiers in descriptions: "belle et bonne" (beautiful and good), "chanter si bien et si doucement" (sing so well and so sweetly), "si courroucée et a tel meschief" (so irritated and so upset).

The analysis of literary conventions and narrative strategy helps us to realize that although the performance descriptions that we have probably do not contradict contemporary practices, they should by no means be taken as the total picture. Instead, they afford us a glimpse of medieval performances, with an emphasis on certain kinds of music used in certain contexts that lend themselves to narrative development and characterization. Even within this select set of descriptions, we find considerable variety: monophonic love songs are sung either with or without instrumental accompaniment; lais are played on harp, rote, fiddle, flute; a lai is preceded by an instrumental prelude or it is begun at once in a combined vocal and instrumental rendition; motets are rendered by voice and organ, by an unspecified combination of voices and instruments, or by voices alone; popular songs and dance tunes are performed on fiddle, lute, or psaltery, as the individual performer sees fit. And we see that even a single performance event by a solo musician might include a whole variety of elements. The performance of a Breton lai, for example, can begin with a narrative explanation of the origin of the lai and the story to which it refers, perhaps with dialogue between performer and audience; move on to an elaborate process of tuning the harp; then feature an instrumental prelude to the piece; continue with the rendition in voice and instrument of the lai itself; and end with an instrumental echo of the melody just sung. This lai may in turn remind the minstrel or his audience of another lai featuring the same characters or the same geographic location, which is then duly performed in similar fashion. On the other hand, a lai may be sung quite simply to instrumental accompaniment with no narrative account and no prelude. While certain details of these descriptions of the glorified Breton past may be fanciful, it is likely that the overall flavor of the performance situations they present is a reflection of medieval court life. Not only could practices vary, but even the boundaries of the performance are not strictly defined: verbal or instrumental introduction and song, performer and audience are in a constant and fluid dialogue. No given description, no single source, tells the full story of musical performance in the Middle Ages.

In its broad outlines, the total combined evidence of literary sources is undoubtedly an accurate reflection of medieval musical practices. It is no surprise that long narrative songs, like the *chanson de geste,* belong to the minstrel repertoire: it is logical that it would take a professional to master these long pieces. Similarly, it comes as no surprise that the performance of polyphony is limited to particularly talented and well trained musicians. Nonetheless, it must be remembered that the silences of the literary sources are indeed silences, and not assertions. If minstrels are not described as singing dance tunes, for example, this does not mean that they did not ever do it. The occasional references to combined vocal and instrumental performances, the hints of instrumental ensembles being joined by singers, should be taken seriously and given more weight than their relative infrequency might at first glance imply. As I have shown, this can be explained on purely literary grounds. That such descriptions can be found at all argues that the practice was accepted; it could be alluded to in an offhand manner with no need for elaboration.

It is true that it is very difficult to be sure of the repertoire being performed in a given literary description. Perhaps our various descriptions of vocal and instrumental music refer to purely oral, now lost repertoires. But why posit entire bodies of music for which there is no real evidence? Or perhaps all descriptions of combined vocal and instrumental music refer to monody. Still, if a monophonic ballade or other chanson can be sung to fiddle or psaltery, must we assume that the combination of vocal and instrumental music would necessarily be dropped for a polyphonic piece of the same genre? I do not wish to argue that polyphony was never, or hardly ever, performed in either all vocal or all instrumental renditions; there is certainly evidence for this practice, and such may even have been the most common means of polyphonic performance. But the existence of purely vocal and purely instrumental ensembles still does not rule out other possibilities.

Of course, literary texts are not the only sources for medieval performance practices, and when these literary descriptions are systematically coordinated with iconographic or archival evidence it will be much easier to arrive at an accurate picture of medieval music in general. For example, we have seen that the minstrels in *Gilles de Chyn* sing a love song to the accompaniment of the fiddle, and that the Poitevin jongleur in *Amis et Amile* plays a song on the fiddle about love and friendship. When this evidence is considered in light of the miniatures in chansonniers representing trouvères and troubadours playing the fiddle, and the references in various vidas to a given troubadour's talents as fiddle player, the association of the fiddle with the trouvère and troubadour repertoire is virtually inescapable.[24] And the representation of the trouvère Perrin d'Angecourt holding a portative organ in the early fourteenth-century chansonnier *a* takes on an interesting light in view of Pygmalion's rendition of a love song – in this case a motet – to the accompaniment of a portative organ. A trouvère chanson and a motet belong to two distinct repertoires, of course, and would not necessarily be performed in similar fashion. Nor does the presence of a portative organ in a chansonnier miniature prove that trouvère songs were played on this instrument. Nonetheless, the comparison is intriguing, suggesting at least the possibility that the same combination of voice and instrument might be appropriate in both monophonic and polyphonic repertoires.

Such speculations can only be verified or disproved through the accumulation and accurate interpretation of more evidence than is currently available in print. Clearly the project requires the collaboration of

---

[24] H. van der Werf questions the likelihood of trouvère and troubadour songs being performed instrumentally in *The Chansons of the Troubadours and the Trouvères* (Utrecht, 1972), p. 19. Van der Werf argues that the illustrations in chansonniers do not necessarily illustrate the performance of the songs, pointing out that the miniatures used for aristocratic trouvères – a knight on horseback – surely do not tell us that the aristocratic trouvère typically composed or performed his songs on horseback or to the rhythm of his horse's footsteps. Van der Werf's point is well taken; one must always be careful in the interpretation of iconographic evidence, and the trouvère chanson in any case does not lend itself to elaborate (and certainly not to polyphonic) accompaniment. However, the images of knights on horseback do tell us that the songs were associated with members of the knightly class; the images of musicians similarly tell us that these songs are associated with members of a minstrel class. If the illustrators of the chansonniers felt that images of instrumentalists were appropriate identifiers for the composers and performers of trouvère songs, does this not mean that it was at least possible to associate the trouvère repertoire with instrumental music? In trouvère chansonnier *a* (Vatican Library, Lat. Reg. 1490), for example, considerable care has been taken with the miniatures, to judge from those that have survived. Aristocratic trouvères are pictured with the correct coat of arms. Williames d'Amiens li paignnierres (William of Amiens the painter) is duly represented as a painter, holding a palette and painting a heraldic *blason*. Why, then, should we disregard as mere fancy or meaningless convention the miniatures in the same manuscript that represent Perrin d'Angecourt with a portative organ and Martin le Beguin de Cambrai with bagpipes? While these particular trouvères may never have played these particular instruments, the illuminator of the manuscript evidently felt that these instruments were logical choices for this type of song. Indeed, he may have had some knowledge of the trouvères in question, since he chose the rustic bagpipes for Martin le Beguin, who appears to have been a transient jongleur, and the more prestigious organ for Perrin, who was associated with the high aristocracy, including Charles d'Anjou and Count Gui of Flanders.

specialists in a variety of fields: musicology, literature, linguistics, art history, social history. The material offered here is a contribution to this larger project, and will, I hope, facilitate the discovery of medieval performance practices and aesthetics, and ultimately the re-creation, on the modern stage, of medieval music as it was performed in the Middle Ages.

VOICES AND INSTRUMENTS ... 109

Primary Sources

Alexandre. Lambert li Tors and Alexandre de Bernay, *Romans d'Alexandre.* Ed. H. Michelant. Bibliothek des Literarischen Vereins, 13. Stuttgart, 1846.

Amis et Amile. Ed. P. Dembowski. Classiques Français du Moyen Age. Paris, 1969.

Anseïs de Carthage. Anseïs von Karthago, ed. J. Alton. Bibliothek des Literarischen Vereins, 194. Tübingen, 1892.

Aucassin et Nicolette. Ed. J. Dufournet. Paris, 1973.

Bartsch, K., ed. *Altfranzösische Romanzen und Pastourellen.* Leipzig, 1870.

Berte aus grans piés. Adenet le Roi, *Berte aus grans piés.* Ed. U.T. Holmes, Jr. University of North Carolina Studies in the Romance Languages and Literatures, 6. Chapel Hill, 1946.

Bestiaire d'amours. Richard de Fournival, *Li Bestiaires d'amours di Maistre Richart de Fornival e Li Response du Bestiaire.* Ed. C. Segre. Milan, 1957.

Blancandin. Blancandin et l'Orgueilleuse d'amour. Ed. F.P. Sweetser. Textes Littéraires Français. Geneva and Paris, 1964.

Brut. Wace, *Roman de Brut.* Ed. I. Arnold. Société des Anciens Textes Français. 2 volumes. Paris, 1938-40.

Bueve de Hantone. Der festländische Bueve de Hantone, Fassung III. Ed. A. Stimming. Gesellschaft für Romanische Literatur, 39 and 42. 2 volumes. Dresden, 1914-20.

110   MUSICA DISCIPLINA

Castelain de Couci. Jakemes, *Roman du castelain de Couci et de la dame de Fayel*. Ed. M. Delbouille. Société des Anciens Textes Français. Paris, 1936.

Chastelaine de Saint Gille. *Recueil général des fabliaux*, I. Ed. A. de Montaiglon. Paris, 1872. No. 11.

Chronicles. Jean Froissart, *Chroniques (1346-56)*, IV. Ed. S. Luce. Paris, 1873.

Claris et Laris. *Li Romans de Claris et Laris*. Ed. J. Alton. Bibliothek des Literarischen Vereins, 169. Tübingen, 1884.

Comte d'Anjou. Jean Maillart, *Le Roman du Comte d'Anjou*. Ed. M. Roques. Classiques Français du Moyen Age. Paris, 1931.

Contes moralisés. Nicole Bozon, *Contes moralisés*. Ed L.T. Smith and P. Meyer. Société des Anciens Textes Français. Paris, 1889.

Deduis. Gace de la Buigne, *Roman des deduis*. Ed Å. Blomqvist. Studia Romanica Holmiensia, 3. Stockholm and Paris, 1951.

Durmart le Galois. Ed. E. Stengel. Bibliothek des Literarischen Vereins, 96. Tübingen, 1873.

Eledus et Serene. *Roman d'Eledus et Serene*. Ed. J.R. Reinhard. Austin, 1923.

Epine. "Der Lai de l'Epine." Ed. R. Zenker. *Zeitschrift für Romanische Philologie* 17 (1893), pp. 233-55.

Espinette. Jean Froissart, *L'Espinette amoureuse*. Ed. A. Fourrier. Bibliothèque Française et Romane, sér. B.: Editions Critiques de Textes, 2. Paris, 1972.

Fonteinne amoureuse. Guillaume de Machaut, *Oeuvres*, III. Ed. E. Hoepffner. Société des Anciens Textes Français. Paris, 1921.

VOICES AND INSTRUMENTS ... 111

Galeran de Bretagne. Jean Renart, *Galeran de Bretagne.* Ed. L. Foulet. Classiques Français du Moyen Age. Paris, 1925.

Gilles de Chyn. Gautier de Tournay, *L'Histoire de Gilles de Chyn.* Ed. E.B. Place. Northwestern University Studies in the Humanities, 7. Evanston and Chicago, 1941.

Godefroy, F. *Dictionnaire de l'ancienne langue française et de tous ses dialectes du IXe au XVe siècle.* 10 volumes. Paris, 1880-1902.

Guigemar. Marie de France, *Lais.* Ed. J. Rychner. Classiques Français du Moyen Age. Paris, 1973.

Guillaume de Dole. Jean Renart, *Le Roman de la rose ou de Guillaume de Dole.* Ed. F. Lecoy. Classiques Francais du Moyen Age. Paris, 1970.

Horn. Das anglonormannische Lied vom Wackern Ritter Horn. Ed. R. Brede und E. Stengel. Ausgaben und Abhandlungen aus dem Gebiete der Romanischen Philologie, 8. Marburg, 1883.

Miracles. Gautier de Coinci, *Miracles de Nostre Dame.* Ed. V.F. Koenig. 4 volumes. Geneva and Lille, 1955-70.

Moniage Guillaume. Ed. W. Cloetta. Société des Anciens Textes Français. 2 volumes. Paris, 1906-11.

Ovide moralisé. Ovide moralisé, poème du commencement du quatorzième siècle. Ed. C. de Boer. Verhandelingen der Koninklijke Akademie van Wetenschappen te Amsterdam, Afdeeling Letterkunde, n.s. 15, 21, 30, 37, 43 (Amsterdam, 1915-38).

Pamphile. Jehan Bras-de-Fer de Dammartin-en-Goële, *Pamphile et Galatée.* Ed. J. de Morawski. Paris, 1917.

Panthère. Nicole de Margival, *Le Dit de la panthère d'amours.* Ed. H.A. Todd. Société des Anciens Textes Français. Paris, 1883.

Paris et Vienne. Der altfranzösische Roman Paris et Vienne. Ed. R. Kaltenbacher. Erlangen, 1904.

Perceforest. Le Roman de Perceforest. Consulted in the following manuscripts: Paris, Bibliothèque Nationale fr. 346; Paris, Bibl. Nat. fr. 109; Paris, Bibl. de l'Arsenal 3494.

Prison. Jean Froissart, La Prison amoureuse. Ed. A. Fourrier. Bibliothèque Française et Romane, sér. B: Editions Critiques de Textes, 13. Paris, 1974.

Prologue. Marie de France, Lais. Ed. J. Rychner. Classiques Français du Moyen Age. Paris, 1973.

Renart. Le Roman de Renart le contrefait. Ed. G. Raynaud and H. Lemaître. 2 volumes. Paris, 1914.

Rose. Guillaume de Lorris and Jean de Meun, Le Roman de la rose. Ed. F. Lecoy. 3 volumes. Classiques Français du Moyen Age. Paris, 1973-75.

Silence. Heldris de Cornuälle, Le Roman de Silence. Ed. L. Thorpe. Cambridge, 1972.

Tournois. Jacques Bretel, Les Tournois de Chauvency. Ed. M. Delbouille. Bibliothèque de la Faculté de Philosophie et Lettres de l'Université de Liège, 99. Liège and Paris, 1932.

Tristan. Thomas, Le Roman de Tristan. Ed. J. Bédier. Société des Anciens Textes Français. Paris, 1902-5.

Tristan en prose. Consulted in the following manuscripts: Paris, Bibliothèque Nationale fr. 335; Bibl. Nat. fr. 336; Bibl. Nat. fr. 772; Bibl. Nat. fr. 12599.

Tristan ménestrel. Gerbert de Montreuil. "Tristan Ménestrel: Extrait de la continuation de *Perceval* par Gerbert." Ed. J. Bédier and J.W. Weston. Romania 35 (1906), pp. 497-530.

Violette. Gerbert de Montreuil, *Roman de la violette ou de Gerart de Nevers.* Ed. D.L. Buffum. Société des Anciens Textes Français. Paris, 1928.

Voie d'Enfer. Jehan de la Mote, *La Voie d'Enfer et de Paradis.* Ed. Sister M. A. Pety. Washington, D.C.: 1940.

Yvain. Christian von Troyes, *Sämtliche Werke,* II: *Der Löwenritter.* Ed. W. Foerster. Halle, 1887.

Northern Illinois University

[6]

Johannes de Grocheio on secular music: a corrected text and a new translation

CHRISTOPHER PAGE

It has long been recognized that Johannes de Grocheio's *De musica*[1] is an outstanding source of information about Parisian musical practice *c.* 1300. However, the critical text of the treatise published by Rohloff in 1972 can be improved by returning to the manuscripts,[2] and the pioneering English translation, by Albert Seay, can now be corrected in some important particulars.[3] The purpose of this article is therefore to present a corrected text and a new (annotated) translation of Johannes de Grocheio's remarks about secular music, both monophonic and polyphonic, generally regarded as the most important part of his treatise.[4]

To judge by Grocheio's comments on measured notation, he was writing *c.* 1300; he mentions Franco (whose *Ars cantus mensurabilis* was probably compiled *c.* 1280, according to current opinion), and he refers to the division of the tempus 'into two, into three, and in the same way on up to six'.[5] The text deals with Parisian musical practices, and Grocheio's thoroughness in this regard leaves no doubt that he had sampled the musical life of the capital; his passing references to Aristotelian concepts such as *forma et materia*, and to commentaries upon the *De anima* (among other books), suggest that he had studied in Paris, presumably by attending a

---

[1] I adopt this title since it is the one that Grocheio employs himself; see E. Rohloff, ed., *Die Quellenhandschriften zum Musiktraktat des Johannes de Grocheio* (Leipzig, 1972), p. 171.
[2] Some of Rohloff's interpretations and readings are challenged and discussed in P. A. M. DeWitt, *A New Perspective on Johannes de Grocheio's Ars Musicae*, Ph.D dissertation, University of Michigan (1973). After some years of independent work on French music in the thirteenth century I have returned to this dissertation and found many points of agreement. For further material of interest and importance, see T. J. McGee, 'Medieval Dances: Matching the Repertory with Grocheio's Descriptions', *The Journal of Musicology*, 7 (1989), 498–517, and D. Stockmann, 'Musica Vulgaris bei Johannes de Grocheio', *Beiträge zur Musikwissenschaft*, 25 (1983), 3–56.
[3] A. Seay, trans., *Johannes de Grocheo [sic]: Concerning Music*, 2nd edn (Colorado Springs: Colorado College Music Press, 1974).
[4] This article incorporates and develops the results of research presented in C. Page, *Voices and Instruments of the Middle Ages: Instrumental Practice and Songs in France, 1100–1300* (London, 1987), *passim*, but especially pp. 196–201; idem, *The Owl and the Nightingale: Musical Life and Ideas in France 1100–1300* (London, 1989), *passim*; and idem, *Discarding Images: Reflections on Music and Culture in Medieval France* (Oxford, 1993), Chapter 3, *passim*.
[5] For the text see Rohloff, *Die Quellenhandschriften*, p. 138.

course of lectures.[6] There is no proof that he proceeded to take a degree, however (for this was not an automatic step), and it may be wise to keep an open mind about the note in the Darmstadt manuscript of the text where he is given the title 'magister' and named as a resident teacher at Paris ('regens Parisius');[7] the scribe may have been guessing on the basis of what he had read in the treatise. (It is noteworthy that the word 'Parisius' is added in a later hand.) If modern scholars are agreed that the treatise was written in Paris then it is partly because Paris exerts an extraordinary magnetism in most areas of Ars Antiqua studies; one might well argue that it is a quintessentially *provincial* activity to classify and describe the musical forms and fashions of a capital. Viewed in this light, the *De musica* might have been written in any part of France.

Johannes de Grocheio was almost certainly a Norman by birth. It is conceivable that he took his name from the coastal hamlet of Gruchy some 12 km west of Cherbourg, but a much more tempting hypothesis is that he belonged to the distinguished Norman family of de Grouchy. The de Grouchys are first recorded in the eleventh century (as 'de Groci') and were to become a distinguished minor family in the military history of France.[8] They possessed several fiefs between Rouen and Gournay-en-Bray. The family name derives from the region of Gruchy, near Blainville, about 16 km to the south-west of the de Grouchy lordship of Montérolier (see the Map). In view of the Norman fiefdoms of the de Grouchys it is striking that Normandy is the only provincial region of France that Grocheio mentions in his treatise (see the section below on the *ductia*). It may also be significant that Grocheio, by his own account, explored some important aspects of his treatise in a discourse with a certain Clement, who has recently been identified as a monk of the Benedictine Abbey of Lessay in Normandy.[9] It is possible that Grocheio had some link with this important monastic house, a community of more than thirty monks in his lifetime.[10] It is also possible that Grocheio was a priest, but I have been unable to verify the assertion of Mgr Glorieux that he was definitely a priest 'since we possess some sermons by him'.[11] Those sermons – if they ever existed – are not listed in Schneyer's monumental *Repertorium sermonum*.

---

[6] On this aspect of Grocheio's treatise see DeWitt, *A New Perspective*, passim, and M. Bielitz, 'Materia und forma bei Johannes de Grocheo', *Die Musikforschung*, 38 (1985), 257–77.

[7] See the facsimile in Rohloff, *Die Quellenhandschriften*, p. 107.

[8] On the de Grouchys during the Middle Ages see Le Vicomte de Grouchy and E. Travers, *Etude sur Nicolas de Grouchy* (Paris and Caen, 1878), pp. 4–9; le Marquis de Grouchy, *Mémoires du Maréchal de Grouchy*, 5 vols. (Paris, 1873-4), pp. iv-vii; *Dictionnaire de la Noblesse*, 3rd edn, 9, sv. 'Grouchy'. For the name 'de Groci' in the eleventh century see *Mémoires de la Société des Antiquaires de Normandie*, 4th series, 6 (1961), p. 374 ('Hugo de Groci').

[9] For the identification of Clement's monastery see Page, *The Owl and the Nightingale*, pp. 171–2, and p. 246 note 3. The evidence in question is obliterated in Rohloff's text by his emendation of Grocheio's 'Exaquiensem monachum' (i.e. 'monk of Lessay') to '[exequiarium] monachum' (*Die Quellenhandschriften*, p. 130).

[10] See the references to the community of Lessay in the celebrated *Register* of Odon Rigaud, conveniently accessible in S. M. Brown, trans., *The Register of Eudes of Rouen* (New York and London, 1964), p. 100 (visitation of 1250, thirty-six monks), p. 277 (visitation of 1256, thirty-four monks) and p. 634 (visitation of 1266, thirty-one monks).

[11] P. Glorieux, *La faculté des arts et ses maîtres au XIIIe siècle*, Etudes de philosophie médiévale, 59 (Paris, 1971), sv. Jean de Grouchy.

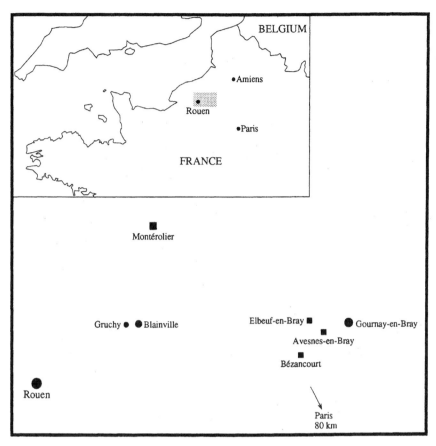

■ de Grouchy fiefs and principal lordships c. 1300
Rouen to Gournay-en-Bray is approximately 30 km

The text given here is derived from the facsimiles of the two manuscript sources of the treatise accompanying Rohloff's edition (a most lavish provision for which the editor and his publishers are to be warmly thanked). Each extract is cued with the appropriate page number in that edition. Rohloff's text has been compared with these manuscripts, producing a significant number of new readings, signalled below. For the sake of consistency, Rohloff's classicizing orthography has been retained. It should be emphasized that what follows is not intended as a comprehensive bibliographical guide to recent research on Grocheio's text and the notes to the translation are therefore generally confined to matters of lexical or interpretative difficulty; the reader is referred to Rohloff's edition for bibliographical material pertaining to the songs and other pieces mentioned by Grocheio.

p. 124 [From the preliminary discussion of how music may be classified.] Alii autem musicam dividunt in planam sive immensurabilem et mensurabilem, per planam sive immensurabilem intellegentes ecclesiasticam, quae secundum Gregorium pluribus tonis determinatur. Per mensurabilem intellegunt illam quae ex diversis sonis simul mensuratis et sonantibus efficitur, sicut in conductibus et motetis. Sed si per immensurabilem intellegant musicam nullo modo mensuratam, immo totaliter ad libitum dictam deficiunt eo quod quaelibet operatio musicae et cuiuslibet artis debet illius artis regulis mensurari. Si autem per immensurabilem non ita praecise mensuratam intellegant, potest, ut videtur, ista divisio remanere. ...Partes autem musicae plures sunt et diversae secundum diversos usus, diversa idiomata vel diversas linguas in civitatibus vel regionibus diversis. Si tamen eam diviserimus secundum quod homines Parisius[12] ea utuntur, et prout ad usum vel convictum civium est necessaria et eius membra, ut oportet, pertractemus, videbitur sufficienter nostra intentio terminari eo quod diebus nostris principia cuiuslibet artis liberalis diligenter Parisiis inquiruntur et usus earum et fere omnium mechanicarum inveniuntur. Dicamus igitur quod musica qua utuntur homines Parisiis potest, ut videtur, ad tria membra generalia reduci. Unum autem membrum dicimus de simplici musica vel civili, quam vulgarem musicam appellamus; aliud autem de musica composita vel regulari vel canonica quam appellant musicam mensuratam. Sed tertium genus est quod ex istis duobus efficitur et ad quod ista duo tamquam ad melius ordinantur quod ecclesiasticam dicitur et ad laudandum creatorem deputatum est.

Others divide music into 'plain' or 'immeasurable' music and 'measurable', understanding 'plain' or 'immeasurable' music to be that of the Church which, following Gregory, has its boundaries set by various modes. By 'measurable' music they understand the music which is made from diverse pitches simultaneously measured and sounding, as in *conducti* and in motets. But if by the term 'immeasurable' they understand music which is in no way measured, but which is entirely performed in an arbitrary fashion, then they are at fault, because every process of music – and of any art – must be calculated according to the rules of that art. If, however, by the term 'immeasurable' they understand music which is not so precisely measured,[13] then it is evident that this division may be allowed to stand.
...There are many elements of music according to diverse usages, diverse dialects and diverse languages in different cities and regions. But if we divide it according to the usage of the Parisians, and if we treat the elements of music, as is fitting, according to how they are necessary for the entertainment and use of [Parisian] citizens, our intention will be seen to be adequately accomplished because in our days the Parisians diligently enquire into the fundamentals of every liberal art and ascertain the practice of them and of virtually every skill. We declare therefore that the music which is employed by the Parisians can be classified, as may be seen, into

---

[12] So both MSS. Rohloff: *Parisiis*
[13] This passage has been much discussed; see H. Van der Werf, 'The "Not-So-Precisely Measured" Music of the Middle Ages', *Performance Practice Review*, 1 (1988), 42–60, and J. Stevens, *Words and Music in the Middle Ages: Song, Narrative, Dance and Drama 1050–1350* (Cambridge, 1986), p. 433 *et passim*.

three general categories. We call one of these monophonic, 'civil' or the lay public's music, and the other comprises composed, regulated or 'canon'[14] music which they call measured music. But there is a third kind which is made from these two and for which these two are structured as if for the better; it is called ecclesiastical music and has been instituted for the praise of the Creator.

p. 128 [From the discussion of the gamut]...alium modum diversitatis invenerunt dicentes unum lineam et aliud spatium, incipientes a Γ ut usque ad d la sol procedentes. Sic itaque apparet quod ponendo signa vel notas in lineis et spatiis omnes concordantias et omnem cantum sufficienter describere potuerunt. Moderni vero propter descriptionem consonantiarum et stantipedum et ductiarum aliud addiderunt, quod *falsam musicam* vocaverunt, quia illa duo signa, scilicet ♭ et ♮ quae in ♭ fa ♮ mi tonum et semitonum designabant, in omnibus aliis faciunt hoc designare ita quod ubi erat semitonus per ♮ illud[15] ad tonum ampliant ut bona concordantia vel consonantia fiat, et similiter ubi tonus inveniebatur illud[16] per ♭ ad semitonum restringunt.

[the Ancients] devised another means of distinguishing [the notes of the gamut], declaring one to be a line and another a space, beginning on gamma *ut* and proceeding as far as d *la sol*. It is therefore apparent that by putting signs or marks upon lines and spaces they were able to notate all intervals, and every melody, in an adequate manner. The Moderns, moreover, in order to produce a notated record of consonances, of *stantipedes* and of *ductiae*,[17] have added another [means of distinguishing the notes of the gamut] which they have called *musica falsa* because they extend the two signs ♭ and ♮, which they use to indicate a tone and semitone step in ♭ fa ♮ mi, to all other [degrees of the gamut] with the same meaning, so that, where there was a semitone, they make it into a tone with ♮, so that there may be good line and good harmony,[18] and in the same way, where there was tone to be found, they compress it into a semitone by means of ♭.

---

[14] The term 'canon' music (*musica canonica*) balances 'civil' music (*musica civilis*), both terms to be understood as in 'canon' and 'civil' law, i.e. as relating to the clergy and to the laity respectively. It is unfortunate that Seay's translation 'composed or regular music by rule' for Grocheio's *musica composita vel regulari vel canonica* misses this distinction (*Concerning Music*, p. 12).

[15] So both MSS. Rohloff: *illum*

[16] So both MSS. Rohloff: *illum*

[17] The passage might also be rendered 'in order to produce a notated record of the consonances of *stantipedes* and of *ductiae*', which narrows the range of purposes for which *musica ficta* was devised in what is perhaps an unacceptable way, and which also, given the meaning Grocheio attaches to *consonantia*, implies polyphonic *stantipedes* and *ductiae*, which seems out of the question in this discussion of monophonic music. On the meaning of the term 'consonantia' in Grocheio's usage see the following note, and for Grocheio's description of the *stantipes* and *ductia* see below.

[18] 'bona concordantia vel consonantia'. Grocheio distinguishes (p. 144) between *concordantia*, when one musical sound relates in a harmonious way to another (*concordantia* therefore relates to line), and *consonantia*, when two or more notes sound simultaneously (*consonantia* therefore relates to harmony). Compare DeWitt, *A New Perspective*, pp. 76f.

p. 130 Dicamus igitur quod formae musicales vel species contentae sub primo membro, quod vulgare dicebamus, ad hoc ordinantur, ut eis mediantibus mitigentur adversitates hominum innatae, quas magis particulavimus in sermone ad Clementem Exaquiensem[19] monachum, et sunt duobus modis, aut enim in voce humana aut in instrumentis artificialibus exercentur. Quae autem in voce humana fiunt duobus modis sunt, aut enim dicimus cantum aut cantilenam. Cantum autem et cantilenam triplici differentia distinguimus. Aut enim [cantum] gestualem aut coronatum aut versiculatum, et cantilenam [aut] rotundam aut stantipedem aut ductiam appellamus.

We say, therefore, that the musical forms or genres that are subsumed by the first category, which we have called the music of the lay public,[20] are ordained for this purpose: that they may soften the sufferings to which all men are born and which I have detailed further in a discourse to Clement, a monk of Lessay.[21] And [these musical forms] are of two kinds, for they are either performed with the human voice or with musical instruments. Those that are made with the human voice are of two kinds: we call them either 'cantus' or 'cantilena'[22] and distinguish three kinds of each. There is a *cantus gestualis, coronatus* and *versiculatus*; there is a *cantilena rotunda, stantipedes* and *ductia*.

p. 130 Cantum vero gestualem dicimus in quo gesta heroum et antiquorum patrum opera recitantur, sicuti vita et martyria sanctorum et proelia et adversitates quas antiqui viri pro fide et veritati passi sunt, sicuti vita beati Stephani protomartyris et historia regis Karoli. Cantus autem iste debet antiquis et civibus laborantibus et mediocribus ministrari dum requiescunt ab opere consueto, ut auditis miseriis et calamitatibus aliorum suas facilius sustineant et quilibet opus suum alacrius aggrediatur. Et ideo iste cantus valet ad conservationem totius civitatis.

---

[19] So MS H; MS D: *exaquiansem*. Rohloff: [*exequiarium*].

[20] There can be no fully satisfactory translation of Grocheio's *vulgare*, here rendered 'of the lay public'. It appears to denote all the laity, from working people to royalty. Seay's translation 'vulgar music' (*Concerning Music*, p. 12) is somewhat unsatisfactory – if etymologically justifiable – given the modern associations of the word 'vulgar'. Compare DeWitt, *A New Perspective*, pp. 122f (an excellent discussion), Stevens, *Words and Music*, p. 431, and Page, *Discarding Images*, Chapter 3, *passim*.

[21] The words 'quas magis particulavimus in sermone ad Clementem Exaquiensem monachum' are consistent with the view that Grocheio discussed these matters with Clement, but it may rather imply a letter or treatise, now lost. The translation offered here ('which I have detailed further in a discourse to Clement, a monk of Lessay') is designed to accommodate both possibilities which are not, of course, mutually exclusive.

[22] Perhaps modelled upon the Old French terms *chanson* and *chansonette*. Grocheio's classification of musical forms has been much discussed and paraphrased; see, for example, DeWitt, *A New Perspective, passim*; F. A. Gallo, *Music of the Middle Ages II* (Cambridge, 1985), pp. 10–13; C. Page, *Voices and Instruments*, pp. 196–201; Stevens, *Words and Music*, pp. 491–5; Stockmann, 'Musica Vulgaris'; H. Wagenaar-Nolthenius, 'Estampie/Stantipes/Stampita', in *L'Ars Nova Italiana del Trecento: 2nd Congress* (Certaldo, 1969), pp. 399–409. A vital essay for the study of French song in Grocheio's lifetime is now L. Earp, 'Lyrics for Reading and Singing in Late Medieval France: The Development of the Dance Lyric from Adam de la Halle to Guillaume de Machaut', in R. A. Baltzer et al., eds., *The Union of Words and Music in Medieval Poetry* (Austin, 1991), pp. 101–31.

We call that kind of *cantus* a *chanson de geste* in which the deeds of heroes and the works of ancient fathers[23] are recounted, such as the life and martyrdom of saints and the battles and adversities which the men of ancient times suffered for the sake of faith and truth, such as the life of St Stephen, the first martyr, and the story of King Charlemagne. This kind of music should be laid on[24] for the elderly, for working citizens and for those of middle station when they rest from their usual toil, so that, having heard the miseries and calamities of others, they may more easily bear their own and so that anyone may undertake his own labour with more alacrity. Therefore this kind of *cantus* has the power to preserve the whole city.[25]

p. 130 Cantus coronatus ab aliquibus simplex conductus dictus est, qui propter eius bonitatem in dictamine et cantu a magistris et studentibus circa sonos coronatur, sicut gallice *Ausi com l'unicorne* vel *Quant li roussignol*, qui etiam a regibus et nobilibus solet componi et etiam coram regibus et principibus terre decantari, ut eorum animos ad audaciam et fortitudinem, magnanimitatem et liberalitatem commoveat, quae omnia faciunt ad bonum regimen. Est enim cantus iste de delectabili materia et ardua, sicut de amicitia et caritate, et ex omnibus longis et perfectis efficitur.

The *cantus coronatus* has been called a 'monophonic conductus' by some; on account of the inherent virtue[26] of its poetry and music it is crowned by masters and students [of the art of songmaking] among pieces,[27] as in the French *Ausi com l'uni-*

---

[23] The 'ancient fathers' are probably not the Fathers of the Church, despite the ubiquity of *Vitae patrum* collections in the Middle Ages; no *chansons de geste* dealing with the lives of Fathers of the Church have survived. Grocheio probably means the ancient fathers of France – such as Charlemagne – whose wars and struggles brought the realm of France into being. See Page, *The Owl and the Nightingale*, pp. 30–33, and idem, 'Le troisième accord pour vièle de Jérôme de Moravie: Jongleurs et "anciens pères de France"', in C. Meyer, ed., *Jérôme de Moravie: un théoricien de la musique dans le milieu intellectuel parisien du XIII siècle* (Paris, 1992), pp. 83–96.

[24] 'should be laid on' translates *debet ministrari*; Grocheio sometimes chooses verbs which imply the politic provision of music for the mitigation of laymen's vices.

[25] It remains uncertain whether *civitas* should be translated 'city' here or taken in the broader sense 'State'. The former conveys Grocheio's interest in the music of a single city, Paris. However, when Grocheio speaks of the way music instils virtue and obedience his conception of the *civitas* is perhaps more expansive. See D. Luscombe, 'City and Politics Before the Coming of the *Politics*: Some Illustrations', in D. Abulafia, M. Franklin and M. Rubin, eds., *Church and City 1000–1500: Essays in Honour of Christopher Brooke* (Cambridge, 1992), pp. 41–55.

[26] The word *bonitas* demands a translation in excess of mere 'excellence', especially in the context of this imagery of crowning. Grocheio is presumably trying to convey a deeper virtue in the *cantus coronatus*, arising from the lofty subject-matter of the poetry, the excellence of its music and the high status of its composers. Grocheio's description of the *cantus coronatus* has been much discussed; for recent accounts see Stevens, *Words and Music*, p. 431, idem, 'Medieval Song' in D. Hiley and R. Crocker, eds., *The Early Middle Ages to 1300*, New Oxford History of Music II, 2nd edn (Oxford, 1990), p. 392, and Page, *Voices and Instruments*, pp. 196–201.

[27] A difficult passage; the sense of 'circa sonos' is not clear. Seay (*Concerning Music*, p. 16) takes it to refer to instrumental accompaniment, as does Rohloff, *Die Quellenhandschriften*, p. 131, but that seems strained. The matter is amply discussed in DeWitt, *A New Perspective*, pp. 133–4. The interpretation offered here is much the same as that of Stevens (*Words and Music*, p. 431). For a very different interpretation see C. Warren, 'Punctus organi and cantus coronatus in the Music of Dufay', in A. Atlas, ed., *Dufay Quincentenary Conference* (Brooklyn, 1976), pp. 128–43.

corne [see Ex. 1] or *Quant li roussignol*. This kind of song is customarily composed by kings and nobles and sung in the presence of kings and princes of the land[28] so that it may move their minds to boldness and fortitude, magnanimity and liberality, all of which things lead to good government. This kind of *cantus* deals with delightful and lofty subject-matter, such as friendship and love, and it is composed entirely from longs – perfect ones at that.[29]

pp. 131–2 Cantus versualis est qui ab aliquibus cantilena dicitur respectu coronati et ab eius bonitate in dictamine et concordantia deficit, sicut gallice *Chanter m'estuet quar ne m'en puis tenir* vel *Au repairier que je fis de Prouvence*. Cantus autem iste debet iuvenibus exhiberi ne in otio totaliter sint reperti. Qui enim refutat laborem et in otio vult vivere ei labor et adversitas est parata. Unde Seneca: Non est viri timere sudorem. Qualiter igitur modi cantus describuntur, sic apparet.

The *cantus versualis* is a species of *cantus* which is called a *cantilena* by some with respect to the [*cantus*] *coronatus* and which lacks the inherent virtue [of the *cantus coronatus*] in poetry and melody, as in the French *Chanter m'estuet quar ne m'en puis tenir*, or *Au repairier que je fis de Prouvence*.[30] This kind of song should be performed for the young lest they be found ever in idleness. He who refuses labour and wishes to live at ease has only travail and adversity in store. Whence Seneca says that 'It is not for a man to fear sweat'.[31] Thus it is plain how the various kinds of *cantus* are to be described.

p. 132 Cantilena vero quaelibet rotunda vel rotundellus a pluribus dicitur eo quod ad modum circuli in se ipsam reflectitur et incipit et terminatur in eodem. Nos autem solum illam rotundam vel rotundellum dicimus cuius partes non habent diversum cantum a cantu responsorii vel refractus. Et longo tractu cantatur velut cantus coronatus, cuiusmodi est gallice *Toute sole passerai le vert boscage*. Et huius-

---

[28] In this passage Grocheio seems determined to present a traditionalist and (by the later thirteenth century) a somewhat archaic image of trouvère monody in the High Style as an aristocratic art, rather than the increasingly urban, mercantile art that it had become with the expansion of the *puis*. In part, Grocheio's comment reflects the prominence of Thibaut, King of Navarre (*d.* 1253) in the later thirteenth-century conception of the trouvères' art. *Ausi com l'unicorne*, which Grocheio cites, is one of his chansons. In the *Chansonnier de l'Arsenal* Thibaut's songs are presented first, preceded by an illumination which shows a fiddler performing before a seated king and queen as courtiers stand nearby. This exactly matches Grocheio's remark that such songs should be performed 'in the presence of kings and princes of the land'. The *Chansonnier de l'Arsenal* continues (again, as some other sources do), to present the works of trouvères whose noble or aristocratic status was well known or assumed, such as Gace Brulé.

[29] The idiomatic translation is required to capture the quality of emphasis in the second conjunction: 'et ex omnibus longis *et* perfectis efficitur'. For discussions of this passage see J. Knapp, 'Musical Declamation and Poetic Rhythm in an Early Layer of Notre Dame Conductus', *Journal of the American Musicological Society*, 32 (1979), pp. 406–7, and Stevens, *Words and Music*, pp. 431–2, with bibliography there cited.

[30] On the distinction between the *cantus coronatus* and the *cantus versualis* see Stevens, 'Medieval Song', pp. 412 and 420, and Page, *Voices and Instruments*, pp. 199–200.

[31] *Epistulae Morales*, XXXI.

Ex. 1

modi cantilena versus occidentem, puta in Normannia, solet decantari a puellis et iuvenibus in festis et magnis conviviis ad eorum decorationem.

There are indeed many who call any *cantilena* a 'rotunda' or 'rotundellus' because it turns back on itself in the manner of a circle, beginning and ending in the same way [i.e. with a refrain].[32] However, I only call the kind of song a 'rotunda' or 'rotundellus' whose parts have the same music as the music of the response or refrain.[33] When it is sung it is drawn out in an expansive way like the *cantus coronatus*. The French song *Toute sole passerai le vert boscage* is of this kind. This kind of song is customarily sung towards the West – in Normandy, for example – by girls and by young men as an adornment to holiday celebrations and to great banquets.[34]

p. 132 Cantilena quae dicitur *stantipes* est illa in qua est diversitas in partibus et refractu tam in consonantia dictaminis quam in cantu, sicut gallice *A l'entrant d'amors* vel *Certes mie ne cuidoie*. Haec autem facit animos iuvenum et puellarum propter sui difficultatem circa hanc stare et eos a prava cogitatione divertit.

In the kind of *cantilena* which is called 'stantipes' there is a diversity – both in the rhymes of the poem and in the music – that distinguishes the verses from the refrain, as in the French song *A l'entrant d'amors* or *Certes mie ne cuidoie*. On account of its difficulty, this [distinction] makes the minds of young men and of girls dwell upon this [kind of *cantilena*][35] and leads them away from depraved thoughts.

p. 132 Ductia vero est cantilena levis et velox in ascensu et descensu quae in choreis a iuvenibus et puellis decantatur, sicut gallice *Chi encor querez amoretes*. Haec enim ducit corda puellarum et iuvenum et a vanitate removet et contra passionem quae dicitur 'amor hereos'[36] valere dicitur.

The *ductia* is a kind of *cantilena* that is light and rapid in its ascents and descents and which is sung in caroles[37] by young men and girls, like the French song *Chi encor querez amoretes*. This [kind of cantilena] directs the sentiments[38] of girls and

---

[32] As it is a distinguishing feature of *cantilene* that they begin and end with a refrain it would appear that some musicians called them all *rotunda* or *rotundellus*, since this term denoted the rondeau (see next note), beginning and ending with a refrain.

[33] Indicating that Grocheio's *rotunda* or *rotundellus* is a rondeau, no doubt of standard fourteenth-century structure, already cultivated at this date by his Parisian contemporary Jean de l'Escurel.

[34] On this reference to Grocheio's homeland see above.

[35] 'dwell upon this [kind of *cantilena*]' renders Grocheio's idiom *circa hanc stare*, an etymologizing phrase (compare *stare*, present participle *stans*, accusative *stantem*, and *stantipes*). Grocheio employs this idiom again in his later remarks about the *stantipes*.

[36] So both MSS. Rohloff: *amor vel* ερoσ

[37] Seay (*Concerning Music*, p. 17) translates 'sung in chorus', but this is an error; the translation 'in caroles' is in accordance with standard usage in thirteenth-century Latin. Grocheio is referring to company dances performed in a ring or in a line. See Stevens, *Words and Music*, pp. 162–71; Page, *Voices and Instruments*, pp. 77–84; idem, *The Owl and the Nightingale*, pp. 110–33.

[38] 'directs the sentiments' (*ducit corda*); once again, Grocheio is etymologizing the name of a genre (*ductia*), or at least assaying a point of Latin style, by establishing the pairing *ductia/ducere*.

young men and draws them away from vain thoughts, and is said to have power against that passion which is called 'erotic love'.[39]

p. 133 Est etiam alius modus cantilenarum, quem *cantum insertum* vel *cantilenam entatam*[40] vocant, qui ad modum cantilenarum incipit et earum fine clauditur vel finitur, sicut gallice *Je m'endormi el sentier.*

There is also another kind of *cantilena* which they [i.e. the Parisians] call 'ornamented song' or 'grafted song'.[41] It begins in the manner of *cantilene* and ends or comes to a close in their fashion, as in the French song *Je m'endormi el sentier.*

p. 132 Sic igitur apparet descriptio istorum tam cantuum quam cantilenarum. Partes autem eorum multipliciter dicuntur, ut versus, refractorium vel responsorium et additamenta. Versus autem in cantu gestuali [est] qui ex pluribus versiculis efficitur et in eadem[42] consonantia dictaminis cadunt; In aliquo tamen cantu clauditur per versiculum [both MSS: versum] ab aliis consonantia discordantem, sicut in gesta quae dicitur de Girardo de Viana. Numerus autem versuum in cantu gestuali non est determinatus sed secundum copiam materiae et voluntatem compositoris ampliatur. Idem etiam cantus debet in omnibus versiculis [both MSS: versibus] reiterari.

---

[39] Unaccountably, Rohloff abolishes the readings of both manuscripts at this point and emends *amor hereos* to *amor vel eros*, breaking into Greek characters for the last word. There is no doubt about the correctness of the MS readings, however, for Grocheio's term *amor (h)ereos* (or simply *(h)ereos*) is found in numerous medical textbooks of the thirteenth and fourteenth centuries. Compare B. Lawn, ed., *The Prose Salernitan Questions*, Auctores Britannici Medii Aevi, V (London, 1979), p. 280: 'in passione que hereos dicitur'. These questions, by an anonymous English author, date from *c.* 1200. The phraseology of the passage quoted is very similar to Grocheio's and may therefore stand close to a source consulted by him. Grocheio had certainly read some material by the celebrated physician Galen, whom he mentions (Rohloff, *Die Quellenhandschriften*, p. 144).

[40] So both MSS. Rohloff: *entratam*

[41] 'Grafted' translates *entatam*, which is clearly the reading of both manuscripts. Rohloff's emendation to *entratam* is not necessary; there is no difficulty in regarding *entatam* as a Latinized form of the Old French past participle *enté* (from *enter*, 'to graft'), a term whose use in musical contexts during the thirteenth century is well established. See Godefroy, *Dictionnaire de l'ancienne langue française*, sv. *enter*; Tobler-Lommatzsch, *Altfranzösisches Wörterbuch*, sv. *enter*. The term has long been used in modern scholarship to denote motet texts that begin and end with quotations of the music and/or the words of pre-existing songs. Grocheio is presumably referring to a kind of song that begins and ends with a quotation, perhaps both musical and poetic, from a pre-existing song, and therefore to one manifestation of the phenomenon known to literary scholars and musicologists as the *refrain*. This is consistent with his statement that the *cantilena entata* begins and ends in the fashion of a *cantilena*, that is to say it begins and ends with a refrain or with something that, in registral terms, could be one. The song cited by Grocheio as an example of this form appears not to have survived. There may be little reason to perpetuate the musicological convention of limiting the thirteenth-century term *motet enté* to denote the texts of motets with refrain insertions split between the beginning and end of a text; as is well known, the meaning of the term *motet* was quite broad in Old French, and in Old French usage a *motet enté* may have been any song, whether monophonic or polyphonic, that contained *refrain* citations.

[42] So both MSS. Rohloff: *ex pluribus versiculis efficitur.* [*Versiculi*] *in eadem.*

Thus the description of these things, both of the varieties of *cantus* and of *cantilena*, is plain. Their parts are referred to in many ways, as verse, refrain or response, and the supplements.[43] The verse in a *chanson de geste* is that which is constituted from many versicles[44] which fall together with the same accord of verbal sound;[45] in some *chansons de geste* the verse ends with a versicle which does not accord in verbal sound with the others, as in the *geste* which is called 'Concerning Girard de Vienne'.[46] The number of verses in a *chanson de geste* is not fixed and may be extended according to the abundance of the raw material and the wish of the one whom makes the song. The same melody must be repeated in every versicle.

pp. 132-4 Versus vero in cantu coronato est qui ex pluribus punctis et concordantiis ad se invicem harmoniam facientibus efficitur. Numerus vero versuum in cantu coronato ratione septem concordantiarum determinatus est ad septem. Tot enim versus debent totam sententiam materiae, nec plus nec minus, continere.

The verse in a *cantus coronatus* is composed from numerous verbal constructions[47] and harmonious members producing a mutual accord. By analogy with the seven concords the number of verses in a *cantus coronatus* has been set at seven. This number of verses – no more and no less – must encompass all the subject-matter.

p. 134 Versus vero in cantu versiculari illi de cantu coronato, secundum quod potest, assimilatur. Numerus vero versuum in tali cantu non est determinatus, sed in aliquibus plus, in aliquibus minus, secundum copiam materiae et voluntatem compositoris ampliatur.

The verse in a *cantus versicularis* is made as similar to that of a *cantus coronatus* as is possible. The number of verses in such a *cantus* is not fixed, but is extended more in some, less in others, according to the wealth of the raw material and the wish of the poet.

---

[43] Rendering *additamenta* and denoting all the material of a refrain form which is not the refrain as fully constituted as both its text and music.

[44] Since this passage provides the only surviving description of the way *chansons de geste* were performed it is alarming that both manuscripts agree in transmitting a text that appears to confuse the crucial terms *versus* (laisse) and *versiculus* (line). The confusion has rarely been given its proper weight in discussions of Grocheio's evidence. Compare Stevens, *Words and Music*, pp. 233, 236 and 241; *idem*, 'Medieval Song', pp. 408–10.

[45] Literally 'in the same consonance of poetry'. Many of the surviving *chansons de geste* are constructed from assonating laisses. Some later examples, under the influence of romance, are in monorhymed laisses. Grocheio, writing c. 1300, may be thinking of both.

[46] Seay's translation (*Concerning Music*, p. 18) 'in the chanson de geste which is said to be by Girarde de Viana' is wide of the mark. Grocheio is referring to the *chanson de geste* of *Girart de Vienne*, composed, perhaps between 1205 and 1225, by Bertrand de Bar-sur-Aube. For this identification, with an extract from the text of the epic (which exactly corresponds to Grocheio's description of it), see Page, *The Owl and the Nightingale*, pp. 72–3.

[47] At first sight Grocheio's Latin ('ex pluribus punctis') suggests that he is referring to musical phrases, but throughout this section Grocheio's comments seem to relate exclusively to the poetic forms of the genres described. My translation assumes that he is referring to the pointed (i.e. punctuated) constructions of the sense. If Grocheio is using the term 'versus' to mean stanza here, then seven seems a large number.

p. 134 Responsorium vero est quo omnis cantilena incipit et terminatur. Additamenta vero differunt in rotundello, ductia et stantipede. In rotundello vero consonant et concordant in dictamine cum responsorio. In ductia vero et stantipede differunt quaedam et alia consonant et concordant. In ductia etiam et stantipede responsorium cum additamentis versus appellatur quorum numerus non est determinatus sed secundum voluntatem compositoris et copiam sententiae augmentatur.

The refrain is the part with which every *cantilena* begins and ends. The supplements differ in a *rotundellus*, *ductia* and *stantipes*. In the *rotundellus* [i.e. the rondeau] they rhyme and agree in their metrical form with the refrain. In the *ductia* and *stantipes* some supplements differ [from the refrain] and others rhyme and agree in their metrical form. Also, in the *ductia* and *stantipes* the refrain with the supplements is called the verse and the number of verses is not fixed but may be augmented according to the wish of the poet and the scope of the subject-matter.[48]

p. 134 Haec itaque sunt partes cantus et cantilenae diversae. De modo igitur componendi cantum et cantilenam nunc dicamus. Modus autem componendi haec generaliter est unus, quemadmodum in natura, primo enim dictamina loco materiae praeparantur, postea vero cantus unicuique dictamini proportionalis loco formae introducitur. Dico autem *unicuique proportionalis* quia alium cantum habet cantus gestualis et coronatus et versiculatus ut eorum descriptiones aliae sunt, quemadmodum superius dicebatur.

These are therefore the elements of the various kinds of *cantus* and *cantilena*. Let us therefore now discuss the manner of composing a *cantus* and a *cantilena*. There is generally one way of composing these things, as in nature,[49] for in the first place the poems are prepared beforehand, serving as the raw material, and then a correctly designed melody is introduced into each poem, serving as the form. I say 'correctly designed into each [poem]', because the *cantus gestualis*, *coronatus* and *versiculatus* all have their own kinds of melody just as their descriptions are different, as has been said above.

pp. 134–6 De formis igitur musicalibus quae in voce humana exercentur haec dicta sint. De instrumentalibus vero nunc prosequamur. Instrumenta vero a quibusdam

---

[48] This is a difficult passage because Grocheio is using musical terms for aspects of poetic form. It would appear that the verb 'consono' (or as a noun, sometimes reinforced as 'consonantia dictaminis') denotes rhyming, while 'concordo' (sometimes reinforced as 'concordant in dictamine') denotes identity of metrical form.

[49] Grocheio's point is that the composition of these song forms is analogous to creation in the natural world. He makes this plain by using the terms *materia* and *forma*, an ultimately Aristotelian distinction. Cf. *De anima*, II:1 'Matter is identical with potentiality, form with actuality'. Grocheio is therefore regarding the poems of these musical forms as *materia* – as matter with the potentiality to become a certain kind of song – while the music is the *forma*, transforming the raw material into a form by creating the set of musical repeats and changes that define the musical form of the genre in question. See M. Bielitz, '*Materia* und *forma* bei Johannes de Grocheo', and DeWitt, *A New Perspective*, pp. 51f.

dividuntur divisione soni artificialis in eis generati, dicunt enim sonum in instrumentis fieri afflatu, puta in tubis, calamis, fistulis et organis, vel percussione puta in chordis, tympanis, cymbalis et campanis. Sed si haec omnia subtiliter considerentur, inveniuntur a percussione fieri cum omnis sonus percutiendo causetur prout in sermonibus de anima comprobatum est. Nos autem hic non intendimus[50] instrumentorum compositionem vel divisionem nisi propter diversitatem formarum musicalium quae in eis generantur. Inter quae instrumenta cum chordis principatum obtinent, cuiusmodi sunt psalterium, cithara, lyra, quitarra sarracenica et viella. In eis enim [est] subtilior et melior soni discretio[51] propter abbreviationem et elongationem chordarum. Et adhuc inter omnia instrumenta chordosa visa a nobis viella videtur praevalere. Quemadmodum enim anima intellectiva alias formas naturales in se virtualiter includit et ut tetragonum trigonum et maior numerus minorem, ita viella in se virtualiter alia continet instrumenta. Licet enim aliqua instrumenta suo sono magis moveant animos hominum – puta in festis, hastiludiis et torneamentis tympanum et tuba – in viella tamen omnes formae musicales subtilius discernuntur et ideo de his tantummodo nunc dicatur.

These things have been said concerning the musical forms which are performed with the human voice. We now turn to consider instrumental forms. Instruments are classified by some according to the different kind of manufactured sound that is generated by them, for they declare that sound is produced in musical instruments by the breath, as in *tube, calami, fistule* and *organa*, or by beating, as in strings, *tympana, cymbala* and *campana*.[52] But if all these things are given careful consideration then all these sounds are found to be made by beating since every sound is produced by striking, as has been proved in the discourses concerning the soul.[53] Here, however, we do not intend to encompass the construction or classification of musical instruments unless it relates to the diversity of the musical forms that are executed with them. Among which instruments the strings hold pride of place; of this kind are the *psalterium*, the *cithara*, the *lyra*, the *quitarra sarracenica* and the *viella*.[54]

---

[50] So both MSS. Rohloff: *intendimus [notificare]*

[51] So MS H (f. 4v). MS D (f. 61v): *soni descriptio*

[52] These instrument-names cannot all be identified with certainty. *Tube* will be trumpets, while *fistula* may denote flutes and/or duct flutes. *Calami* presumably denotes wind instruments with reeds. *Organa* may safely be interpreted as organs. *Tympana* are probably frame drums of various kinds, while *cymbala* may be identified with cymbals or small bells (but perhaps not with rows of chime bells). There seems no reason to doubt that *campana* are large, tower bells or other signalling bells.

[53] The reference is to Aristotle's *De anima*, II:8, or possibly to a commentary upon it, perhaps by Grocheio himself.

[54] *Psalterium* may be safely associated with psalteries, generally of pig-snout shape in Grocheio's time and strung with metallic materials. *Cithara* is generally (but by no means exclusively) associated with forms of the Germanic word *harp(e)* in medieval word lists and translations, generally denoting a pillar harp c. 1300. The *lyra* may possibly be the lute, while the *quitarra sarracenica* is perhaps to be associated with either the gittern or the citole, although this is very uncertain. The *viella* is undoubtedly the fiddle. For the evidence on which these identifications are based see P. Bec., *Vièles ou Violes* (Paris, 1992), *passim*; Page, *Voices and Instruments*, pp. 139–50; L. Wright, 'The Medieval Gittern and Citole: A Case of Mistaken Identity', *Galpin Society Journal*, 30 (1977), 8–42 and C. Young, 'Zur Klassifikation und ikonographischen Interpretation mittelalterlicher Zupfinstrumente', *Basler Jahrbuch für Historische Musikpraxis*, 8 (1984), 67–103.

With these instruments there is a more exact and a better means of distinguishing[55] any melody on account of the shortening and lengthening of the strings. Furthermore, the *viella* evidently prevails over all the musical instruments known to us, for just as the scope of the intellective soul includes other natural forms within itself, and as the square includes the triangle and the greater number includes the lesser, so the scope of the *viella* includes all other instruments within itself.[56] Even if there are some instruments whose sound has greater power to move the souls of men – as the *tympanum* and *tuba* do in feasts, hastiludes[57] and tournaments – on the *viella* all musical forms can be discerned more exactly, and therefore it only remains to speak of those musical forms.[58]

p. 136 Bonus autem artifex in viella omnem cantum et cantilenam et omnem formam musicalem generaliter introducit. Illa tamen quae coram divitibus in festis et ludis fiunt communiter ad tria generaliter reducuntur, puta cantum coronatum, ductiam et stantipedem. Sed de cantu coronato prius dictum est, de ductia igitur et stantipede nunc [est] dicendum. Est autem ductia sonus illiteratus cum decenti percussione mensuratus. Dico autem *illiteratus* quia licet in voce humana fieri possit et per figuras repraesentari non tamen per litteras scribi potest quia littera et dictamine caret. Sed *cum recta percussione* eo quod ictus eam mensurant et motum facientis et excitant animum hominis ad ornate movendum secundum artem quam ballare vocant, et eius motum mensurant in ductiis et choreis.

A good player of the *viella* generally performs every *cantus* and *cantilena*, and all achieved musical design.[59] The genres which are usually performed before mag-

---

[55] Or possibly, following the reading of MS D, 'a better account'.
[56] The concept of an instrument which includes the scope of all others within itself is a familiar one in medieval music theory; compare John 'of Affligem' on the *musa* which, he says, *omnium [instrumentorum] vim atque modum in se continet* (J. Smits van Waesberghe, ed., *Johannis...De Musica*, Corpus Scriptorum de Musica 1 (American Institute of Musicology, 1950), p. 54). Grocheio's comments upon the *viella*, however, reveal a higher level of abstraction than those of Johannes two centuries earlier and reflect Grocheio's reading of Aristotle's *De anima*, II:3 'The types of soul resemble the series of figures. For, both in figures and in things animate, the earlier form exists potentially in the later, as, for instance, the triangle exists potentially in the quadrilateral and the nutritive soul exists potentially in the sensate soul'. The intellective soul is the highest function of the soul, standing above sensate soul (characterized by sense perception, more or less complex depending upon the species of creature at issue), and nutritive soul (characterized by the basic functions of nutrition and reproduction). This analogy between the status of the *viella* and intellective soul therefore implies the highest possible standing for the *viella* as an instrument that can encompass what every other instrument can do but which adds qualities that Grocheio compares to the distinctively human faculties of intellection and abstraction. In the context of thirteenth-century theology – much preoccupied with the nature of the soul – this analogy is less strained than it may now appear.
[57] On the distinction between hastiludes and tournaments, which is often difficult to establish, see J. Vale, *Edward III and Chivalry* (Woodbridge, 1982), pp. 57ff.
[58] Grocheio thus signals his intention to speak only of *viella* repertory. It remains unknown whether other instruments performed the musical forms he now goes on to describe, or whether other instruments were associated with specific repertoire in the same way as the *viella*.
[59] The construction is *bonus artifex in viella...formam introducit*, which might be translated 'a good player creates *forma* upon the *viella*...'. This seems a rather cumbersome and gratuitously cerebral way for Grocheio to express his meaning, but the sense seems clear none the less. The verb *introduco* here has

nates in festivities and sportive gatherings[60] can generally be reduced to three, that is to say the *cantus coronatus*, the *ductia* and the *stantipes*. However, since we have already given an account of the *cantus coronatus*, we must now therefore speak of the *ductia* and the *stantipes*. The *ductia* is a melody without words, measured with an appropriate beat. I say 'without words' because even though it can be performed by the human voice and expressed in musical notation, it cannot be written down with letters because it lacks a text and a poem. But it has 'a correct beat' because beats measure the *ductia*[61] and the movement of one who dances it, and [these beats] excite people to move in an elaborate fashion according to the art which they call 'dancing', and they measure the movement [of this art] in *ductiae* and in caroles.

p. 136 Stantipes vero est sonus illiteratus habens difficilem concordantiarum discretionem per puncta determinatus. Dico autem *habens difficilem* etc. propter enim eius difficultatem facit animum facientis circa eam stare et etiam animum advertentis et multoties animos divitum a prava cogitatione divertit. Dico etiam *per puncta determinatus* eo quod percussione quae est in ductia caret et solum punctorum distinctione cognoscitur.

The *stantipes* is a textless melody having a difficult structure of agreements and distinguished by its sections.[62] I say 'having a difficult [structure of agreements]', for, on account of its difficulty, it causes the mind of anyone who performs it – and of anyone who listens – to dwell upon it[63] and it often diverts the minds of the powerful from perverse reflection. I say 'distinguished by its sections', because it lacks the beat of the *ductia* and is only recognized by the distinction of its sections.

---

nothing to do with the performance of 'introductory' preludes upon the fiddle; *introduco* + accusative + *in* + ablative is Grocheio's idiom for referring to the creation of *forma* in its Aristotelian sense of actual, accomplished form rather than mere raw material (*materia*). For a parallel passage in Grocheio's treatise compare Rohloff, *Die Quellenhandschriften*, p. 114. Grocheio's point is that with the *viella* a good player can play every *cantus* and *cantilena* and can shape every kind of achieved musical design. For contrasting proposals about the interpretation of Grocheio's evidence see H. M. Brown, 'Instruments', in H. M. Brown and S. Sadie, eds., *Performance Practice*, 2 vols. (London, 1989), 1, pp. 18–23; D. Fallows, 'Secular Polyphony in the Fifteenth Century', *ibid*, p. 206; L. Gushee, 'Two Central Places: Paris and the French Court in the Early Fourteenth Century', in *Bericht über den Internationalen Musikwissenschaftlichen Kongress Berlin 1974*, ed. H. Kuhn and P. Nitsche (Kassel, etc., 1980), p. 143.

[60] The appropriate translation for 'ludi' is not easy to establish; it may encompass tournaments.

[61] 'correct beat' renders *recta percussione*. The noun *ictus* is not a common one in either the plainchant theory or the polyphonic theory of the Middle Ages, but its appearance in this context can be explained in terms of the choreography of *caroles*. There is abundant evidence that *caroles* were sometimes danced with clapping of the hands and stamping of the feet; Grocheio is here presenting such accentuation as a characteristic feature of melodies designed for the *carole*. See Page, *The Owl and the Nightingale*, p. 115.

[62] There is no adequate English equivalent of Grocheio's *puncta*, denoting a complex musical phrase capable of forming one unit of an estampie and of bearing an open or closed ending.

[63] On the etymologizing explanation *circa eam stare* see above. For commentary upon this passage see L Hibberd, '*Estampie* and *Stantipes*', *Speculum*, 19 (1944), 222–49; K. Vellekoop, 'Die Estampie: ihre Besetzung und Funktion', *Basler Jahrbuch für Historische Musikpraxis*, 8 (1983), 51–65, and H. Wagenaar-Nolthenius, 'Estampie/Stantipes/Stampita', in *L'Ars Nova Italiana del Trecento: 2nd Congress* (Certaldo, 1969), pp. 399–409.

p. 136 Partes autem ductiae et stantipedis puncta communiter dicuntur. Punctus autem est ordinata aggregatio concordantiarum harmoniam facientium ascendendo et descendendo, duas habens partes in principio similes, in fine differentes, quae *clausum* et *apertum* communiter appellantur. Dico autem *duas habens partes* etc. ad similitudinem duarum linearum quarum una sit maior alia. Maior enim minorem claudit et est fine differens a minori. Numerum vero punctorum in ductia ad numerum trium consonantiarum perfectarum attendentes ad tria posuerunt. Sunt tamen aliquae *notae* vocatae quattuor punctorum quae ad ductiam vel stantipedem imperfectam reduci possunt. Sunt etiam aliquae ductiae quattuor habentes puncta puta ductia 'Pierron'. Numerum vero punctorum in stantipede quidam ad sex posuerunt ad rationes vocum inspicientes. Alii tamen de novo inspicientes forte ad numerum septem concordantiarum vel naturali inclinatione ducti, puta Tassinus, numerum ad septem augmentant. Huiusmodi autem stantipedes [sunt] 'res cum septem cordis' vel difficiles 'res Tassini'.

The elements of the *ductia* and *stantipes* are commonly called *puncta*. A *punctus* is a structured collection of agreements producing euphony as they rise and fall, having two parts, similar at the beginning, different at the end, which are commonly called 'open' and 'closed'. I say 'having two parts etc.' by analogy with two lines, one of which is longer than the other. The greater includes the lesser and differs from the lesser at its end. [Musicians] have set the number of *puncta* in a *ductia* at three, giving consideration to the three perfect consonances. There are some [*ductiae*], however, with four *puncta*, called *notae*, which can be assimilated to an imperfect *ductia* or *stantipes*. There are also some *ductiae* having four puncta, such as the *ductia* 'Pierron'.[64] Some [musicians] have set the number of *puncta* in a *stantipes* at six by analogy with the hexachord. Others, however, such as Tassin, considering the matter afresh, have enlarged the number of *puncta* to seven [see Ex. 2] perhaps by analogy with the seven concords or because they were led by natural inclination to do so. *Stantipedes* of this kind are 'the piece with seven strings' or the difficult 'pieces of Tassin'.[65]

pp. 136–8 Componere ductiam et stantipedem est sonum per puncta et rectas percussiones in ductia et stantipede determinare. Quemadmodum enim materia naturalis per formam naturalem determinatur ita sonus determinatus[66] per puncta et per formam artificialem ei ab artifice attributam. Quid igitur sit ductia et stantipes, et quae earum partes et quae earum compositio, sic sit dictum. In quo propositum

---

[64] It remains uncertain whether this is a reference to a *ductia* called Pierron or *by* Pierron. It may be both.

[65] There is a severe textual difficulty in the last sentence of the Latin. The manuscripts are unanimous in their readings for the whole sentence, save that only MS H has the *sunt*, added by a later hand and placed here in square brackets. Rohloff emends the received text in two places, reading 'Huiusmodi autem stantipedes sunt res cum septem *concordantiis, ut* difficiles res Tassini' (my italics). It is not certain that these emendations are required; 'res cum septem cordis' is presumably the title of an estampie (or if *res* is construed as a plural, as a series of estampies), analogous to 'res Tassini'.

[66] So both MSS. Rohloff: *determinatur*

Ex. 2

de simplici seu vulgari musica terminatur. De musica igitur composita et regulari sermonem perquiramus.

To compose a *ductia* and *stantipes* is to shape musical sound into the *puncta* and correct pulses for a *ductia* and *stantipes*. Just as raw material in nature is given identity by natural form, so musical sound [is given identity] through *puncta* and through the man-made design that the composer gives to it. Thus we have given an account of the *ductia* and the *stantipes*, their parts and their composition. This discussion of monophonic or the music of the lay public now comes to a close. Let us turn our discussion to constructed[67] and regulated music.

p. 138 Quidam autem per experientiam attendentes ad consonantias tam perfectas quam imperfectas cantum ex duobus compositum invenerunt, quem *quintum* et *discantum* seu *duplum organum* appellaverunt, et de hoc plures regulas invenerunt, ut apparet eorum tractatus aspicienti. Si tamen aliquis praedictas consonantias sufficienter cognoverit ex modicis regulis poterit talem cantum et eius partes et eius compositionem cognoscere, sunt enim aliqui qui ex industria naturali et per usum talem cantum cognoscunt et componere sciunt. Sed alii, ad tres consonantias perfectas attendentes, cantum ex tribus compositum uniformi mensura regulatum invenerunt, quem *cantum praecise mensuratum* vocaverunt, et isto cantu moderni Parisiis utuntur quem antiqui pluribus modis diviserunt; nos vero secundum usum modernorum in tres generaliter dividimus, puta *motetos, organum* et cantum abscisum quem *hoquetos* vocant.

Some musicians, moreover, studying both perfect and imperfect consonances through experience of them, devised a kind of music composed in two parts, which they have called 'quintus' and 'discantus' or 'organum duplum', and they have devised many rules pertaining to this, as will be apparent to anyone who looks into a treatise of theirs.[68] However, if anyone is sufficiently familiar with the aforementioned consonances he will be able to have a thorough knowledge of such music, its component parts and its composition, from a few rules, for there are some who are proficient in this music and who know how to compose it through experience and innate diligence. Others, however, pondering upon the three perfect consonances, devised a form of music composed in a threefold way,[69] regulated according to a uniform measure, which they called 'precisely measured music', and it is this kind of music which the Moderns in Paris employ. The Ancients divided it in numerous ways; we, following the usage of the Moderns, generally distinguish three kinds, that is to say motets, organum and a 'cut' music that they call 'hockets'.

[67] 'constructed' renders Grocheio's *composita*, which cannot mean simply 'composed' because this would not distinguish polyphony from monophonic forms. The key sense here is surely that of 'assembled, put together', having reference to the scrupulous calibration of polyphonic parts in terms of intervals and duration.

[68] On this passage see K.-J. Sachs, 'Die Contrapunctus-Lehre im 14. und 15. Jh.', in *Die Mittelalterliche Lehre von der Mehrstimmigkeit*, ed. H. H. Eggebrecht (Darmstadt, 1984), pp. 161–256, especially pp. 169–70.

[69] 'in a threefold way', rendering *ex tribus*, a reference to the perfection; cf. Rohloff, *Die Quellenhandschriften*, p. 140: 'Est enim perfectio mensura ex tribus temporibus constans. ...Ista autem mensura moderni utuntur et hac totum summ cantum et cantando et figurando mensurant'.

36   *Christopher Page*

[An account of the rhythmic modes follows, Grocheio expressing his preference for the standard division into six. The symbols of mensural notation are discussed and Grocheio emphasizes the variability of their meaning for different singers. He now begins his account of polyphonic genres.]

p. 144 Motetus vero est cantus ex pluribus compositus, habens plura dictamina vel multimodam discretionem syllabarum, utrobique harmonialiter consonans. Dico autem *ex pluribus compositus* eo quod ibi sunt tres cantus vel quattuor, *plura* autem *dictamina* quia quilibet debet habere discretionem syllabarum, tenore excepto qui in aliquibus habet dictamen et in aliquibus non. Sed dico *utrobique harmonialiter consonans* eo quod quilibet debet cum alio consonare secundum aliquam perfectarum cononantiarum, puta secundum diatessaron vel diapente vel diapason de quibus superius diximus cum de principiis tractabamus. Cantus autem iste non debet coram vulgaribus propinari eo quod eius subtilitatem non advertunt[70] nec in eius auditu delectantur sed coram litteratis et illis qui subtilitates artium sunt quaerentes. Et solet in eorum festis decantari ad eorum decorationem, quemadmodum cantilena quae dicitur rotundellus in festis vulgarium laicorum.

The motet is a music assembled from numerous elements, having numerous poetic texts or a multifarious structure of syllables, according together at every point. I say 'assembled from numerous elements' because in a motet there are three or four parts; [I say] having 'numerous poetic texts' because each [part] must have its structure of syllables save the tenor, which in some [motets] has a poetic text and in some does not. I say 'according together at every point' because each [part] must harmonize with the other according to one of the perfect consonances, that is to say a fourth, fifth or octave, which we discussed above when we treated the fundamentals. This kind of music should not be set before a lay public[71] because they are not alert to its refinement nor are they delighted by hearing it, but [it should only be performed] before the clergy[72] and those who look for the refinements of skills. It is the custom for the motet to be sung in their holiday festivities to adorn them, just as the *cantilena* which is called 'rotundellus' [is customarily sung] in the festivities of the lay public.[73]

p. 144 Organum vero, prout hic sumitur, est cantus ex pluribus harmonice com-

---

[70] So both MSS. Rohloff: *animadvertunt*
[71] This passage has given rise to much misunderstanding. Seay's translation 'the vulgar' (*Concerning Music*, p. 26) has been highly influential but is most ill-judged, since Grocheio is contrasting the *laity* with the *clergy* at this point. See the next note and, for a full discussion of this point, Page, *Discarding Images*, Chapter 3, *passim*, and compare Stevens, *Words and Music*, p. 431 and note 50.
[72] Grocheio's term *litterati* has been translated in many ways by modern scholars ('the literati', 'men of letters', 'exclusive social circles'); see, for example, DeWitt, *A New Perspective*, p. 177. Virtually all of these authors seek to convey what they take to have been the elite audience for the motet; there can be little doubt that Grocheio is using the word *litterati* in its traditional sense of 'the clergy'.
[73] Grocheio is alluding to his own phraseology at this point. See his account of the *rotundellus* above.

positus unum tantum habens dictamen vel discretionem syllabarum. Dico autem *tantum habens unum dictamen* eo quod omnes cantus fundantur super unam discretionem syllabarum. Cantus autem iste dupliciter variatur. Est enim quidam qui supra cantum determinatum, puta ecclesiasticum, fundatur, qui ecclesiis[74] vel locis sanctis decantatur ad dei laudem et reverentiam summitatis, et cantus iste appropriato nomine *organum* appellatur. Alius autem fundatur supra cantum cum eo compositum qui solet in conviviis et festis coram litteratis et divitibus decantari, et ex his nomen trahens appropriato nomine *conductus* appellatur. Communiter tamen loquentes totum hoc *organum* dicunt et sic communis est eis descriptio supradicta.

Organum, as it is interpreted here, is a music harmoniously assembled from numerous elements, having only one poem or structure of syllables. I say 'having only one poem' because all the parts are founded upon one structure of syllables. This music is of two kinds. There is one kind which is founded upon a modal melody,[75] that is to say an ecclesiastical one, which is sung in churches or in holy places[76] to the praise of God and for the worship of the Most High, and this is appropriately named *organum*. Another is founded upon a melody composed with it and which is customarily sung at meals and festivities before clergy and magnates, and taking its name from them it is called by the appropriate name *conductus*.[77] All of this is commonly called *organum* and thus the above description relates generally to them all.

pp. 144–6 Hoquetus est cantus abscisus ex duobus vel pluribus compositus. Dico autem *ex pluribus compositus* quia licet abscisio vel truncatio sit sufficiens inter duos, possunt tamen esse plures ut cum truncatione consonantia sit perfecta. Cantus autem iste cholericis et iuvenibus appetibilis est propter sui mobilitatem et velocitatem, simile enim sibi simile quaerit et in suo simili delectatur.[78] Partes autem istorum plures sunt puta *tenor, motetus, triplum, quadruplum* et in hoquetis *primus, secundus* et ultimo eorum *duplum*. Tenor autem est illa pars supra quam omnes aliae fundantur quemadmodum partes domus vel aedificii super suum fundamentum et eas regulat et eis dat quantitatem quemadmodum ossa partibus aliis. Motetus vero est cantus ille qui supra tenorem immediate ordinatur et in diapente ut plurimum incipit et in eadem proportione[79] qua incipit continuatur vel diapa-

---

[74] Rohloff: [in] *ecclesiis*
[75] For the use of *determinare* to indicate definition according to (plainchant) mode see Grocheio's remarks in the first Latin passage given above (Rohloff, *Die Quellenhandschriften*, p. 124).
[76] The phrase 'holy places' is often used in medieval Latin to denote the immediate environs of any ecclesiastical building. Grocheio may be referring to the use of organum in processions.
[77] Grocheio is presumably judging *conductus* to be an appropriate name for a genre performed where the learned and powerful are gathered together because *conductus* can be etymologized as 'brought or drawn together'. See B. Gillingham, 'A New Etiology and Etymology for the Conductus', *Musical Quarterly*, 75 (1991), 59–73, especially pp. 61–2.
[78] Compare Walther, *Sprichwörter*, 7418, 11012, 15304 etc.
[79] Rohloff: *proportione* [in] *qua incipit*

son[80] ascendit, et in hoquetis ab aliquibus dicitur *magistrans*, ut in hoqueto qui dicitur *Ego mundus*.[81] Triplum vero est cantus ille qui supra tenorem in diapason proportione incipere debet et in eadem proportione ut plurimum continuari. Dico autem *ut plurimum* quia aliquoties in tenore[82] vel diapente descendit propter euphoniam, quemadmodum motetus aliquando in diapason ascendit. Quadruplum vero est cantus qui aliquibus additur propter consonantiam perficiendam. Dico autem *aliquibus* etc., quia in aliquibus sunt tantum tres et ibi sufficiunt cum perfecta consonantia ex tribus causetur. In aliquibus vero quartus additur ut dum unus trium pausat vel ornate[83] ascendit, vel duo adinvicem se truncant, quartus consonantiam servet.

The hocket is a 'cut' song composed from two or more parts. I say 'composed from more parts' because even though the cutting away or truncation can be adequate between two parts, it is possible for there to be more so that the harmony may be complete with the truncation. This music appeals to the choleric and to the young on account of its motion and speed, for like seeks like and delights in it. The elements of these [genres] are many, including the tenor, motetus, triplum and quadruplum, and in hockets the prime, the second and – the last of them – the duplum.[84] The tenor is the part upon which all the others are founded, as the parts of a house or edifice [rest] upon a foundation, and it regulates them and gives substance, as bones do, to the other parts. The motetus is the part which is placed immediately above the tenor, and as often as possible it begins a fifth above the tenor and continues in the same proportion as it began, or ascends to the octave; in hockets, some call this part the *magistrans*, as in the hocket which is called *Ego mundus*. The triplum is the part which should begin above the tenor in the proportion of an octave and which should be continued in the same proportion as often as possible. I say 'as often as possible', because it sometimes descends into the range of the tenor, or descends a fifth, for the sake of euphony, just as the motetus sometimes ascends to the octave. The quadruplum is the part which is added in some pieces to complete the harmony. I say 'to some' etc., because in some pieces there are only three parts and they suffice, since complete music can be established with three parts. In some pieces, indeed, a fourth voice is added, so that while one of the three voices pauses or ascends in an ornate fashion, or two together have rests, the fourth may preserve the harmony.

p. 146 Primus vero in hoquetis est[85] qui primo truncare incipit, sed secundus qui

---

[80] Rohloff: *vel* [*in*] *diapason ascendit*
[81] So both MSS. Rohloff: *Echo montis*
[82] So both MSS. Rohloff: *motetum*
[83] So both MSS. Rohloff: *ordinatim*
[84] Grocheio's phraseology seems designed to exclude the possibility of four-part hockets. For an account of a four-part hocket see P. Jeffery, 'A Four-Part *In seculum* Hocket and a Mensural Sequence in an Unknown Fragment', *Journal of the American Musicological Society*, 37 (1984), 1–48.
[85] So both MSS. Rohloff: *hoquetis est* [*cantus*]

secundo post primum truncat. Duplum vero est[86] qui cum tenore[87] minutam facit abscisionem et cum eo aliquoties in diapente consonat et aliquando in diapason proportione, ad quod multum iuvat bona discretio decantantis. Volens autem ista componere primo debet tenorem ordinare vel componere et ei modum et mensuram dare. Pars enim principalior debet formari primo, quoniam ea mediante postea formantur aliae, quemadmodum Natura in generatione animalium primo format membra principalia, puta cor, hepar, cerebrum, et illis mediantibus alia post formantur. Dico autem *ordinare*, quoniam in motellis et organo tenor ex cantu antiquo est et prius composito, sed ab artifice per modum et rectam mensuram amplius determinatur. Et dico *componere*, quoniam in conductibus tenor totaliter fit[88] et secundum voluntatem artificis modificatur et durat.

The 'prime' voice in hockets is the one which begins to have rests first, and the second is the one that begins to have rests after it. The duplum is the part which has minute rests with the tenor and which harmonizes with it sometimes at the fifth and sometimes at the octave, an effect which relies greatly upon the good accuracy of the performer. Anyone who wishes to compose these kinds of music should first lay out or compose the tenor and assign it both [rhythmic] mode and measure. The principal part must be formed first for it is with its help that the others are formed, just as Nature, when she forms animals, first makes the principal members such as the heart, the liver, the brain; with the help of these others are formed afterwards. I say 'lay out' because in motets and organum the tenor is derived from an old melody and is pre-composed, but it is given further definition with mode and correct measure by the composer. I say 'compose', because in *conducti* the tenor is created entire; it is modified, and its extent is set, according to the wish of the composer.

pp. 146–8 Tenore autem composito vel ordinato debet supra eum motetum componere vel ordinare qui ut plurimum cum tenore in diapente proportione resonat et propter sui harmoniam aliquoties ascendit vel descendit. Sed ulterius debet istis triplum superaddi quod cum tenore ut plurimum debet in diapason proportione resonare et propter sui harmoniam potest in locis mediis sistere vel usque ad diapente aliquoties descendere. Et quamquam ex istis tribus consonantia perficiatur potest tamen eis aliquoties decenter addi quadruplum quod cum alii cantus descendent vel ascendent ordinate vel abscisionem facient vel pausabunt consonantiam resonabit. In componendo vero organum modorum alternationem quam plurimum faciunt sed in compondendo motellos et alia modorum unitatem magis servant. Et cum in motellis plura sint dictamina, si unum syllabis vel dictionibus aliud excedat potes eum per appositionem brevium et semibrevium alteri coaequare. Volens autem hoquetum ex duobus, puta primo et secundo, componere,

---

[86] So both MSS. Rohloff: *Duplum vero est [cantus]*
[87] So both MSS. Rohloff: *qui [supra] tenorem*
[88] So both MSS. Rohloff: *totaliter [de novo] fit*

debet cantum vel cantilenam supra quod fit hoquetus partiri et unicuique partem distribuere. Et potest aliquantulum rectus cantus exire cum decenti additione nisi quod eius mensuram observet. Sic enim unus iacet super alium ad modum tegularum et cooperturae domus et sic continua abscisio fiet. Volens ultimo duplum componere debet minutam abscisionem supra tenorem facere et aliquoties consonare.

Once the tenor has been composed or laid out, the motetus must be composed or laid out upon it, sounding with the tenor in the interval of a fifth as often as possible; for the sake of euphony it sometimes ascends or descends. The triplum must be further added to these, and it should sound with the tenor as often as possible in the proportion of an octave, and for the sake of euphony it may stand in medial positions or sometimes descend to the fifth. And even though complete harmony can be made from these three parts, a quadruplum may sometimes be fittingly added to them so that, when the other parts descend or ascend in an ordered fashion, or have a momentary rest or pause, [the quadruplum] will produce consonance. In composing organum [duplum, composers] produce as much variation of [rhythmic] mode as possible, but in composing motets and other genres they chiefly preserve unity [of mode]. And since there are several poems in motets, if one exceeds the other in syllables or words you can make it equal the other by the juxtaposition of breves and semibreves. He who wishes to compose a hocket in two parts, that is to say with a *primus* and *secundus*, must divide the *cantus* or *cantilena* upon which the hocket is to be made and distribute it among the two parts. And the true melody may proceed with a degree of appropriate ornamentation, unless it must keep to the measure of the original tune.[89] Thus, one part lies upon the other in the manner of tiles[90] and the covering of a house and thus continuous hocketing may be accomplished. He who wishes to add a duplum to this must make a minute 'cutting' upon the tenor and make it accord somewhat.

[Grocheio now introduces his section on plainchant, from which the following excerpts are taken, the selection being restricted to those that confirm or elucidate matters relating to secular forms.]

p. 160 Cantus autem iste [i.e. antiphona] post psalmos decantatur et aliquoties neupma additur puta post psalmos evangelistas. Est autem neupma quasi cauda vel exitus sequens antiphonam quamadmodum in viella post cantum coronatum vel stantipedem exitus quem *modum* viellatores appellant.

This kind of chant [i.e. an antiphon] is sung after the psalms, and sometimes a

---

[89] This passage, a difficult one, presumably means that when a melody is split up between different voices to make a hocket, it can be ornamented and added to in various ways, unless it is important for some reason that the hocketed version of the melody should last exactly the same amount of time as the original.
[90] Rohloff's emendation of *regularum* (in both MSS) to *tegularum* ('of tiles') can surely be accepted and is accordingly followed here.

neuma is added – as after the evangelistic psalms. A *neuma* is a kind of tail or postlude following the antiphon, comparable to the postlude which is performed on the *viella* after the *cantus coronatus*, or *stantipes*, which fiddlers call a *modus*.

p. 162 Isti autem cantus [i.e. *Gloria in excelsis deo* et *Kyrie eleison*] cantantur tractim et ex longis et perfectis ad modum cantus coronati ut corda audientium ad devote orandum promoveantur et ad devote audiendum orationem quam immediate dicit sacerdos vel ad hoc ordinatus.

These chants [i.e. *Gloria in excelsis deo* and *Kyrie eleison*] are sung slowly and from perfect longs in the manner of a *cantus coronatus*, so that the hearts of those who listen may be moved to devout prayer and to devoutly hear the prayer which the priest, or the one deputed to the task, says immediately afterwards.

p. 164 Responsorium autem et alleluia decantantur ad modum stantipedis vel cantus coronati, ut devotionem et humilitatem in cordibus auditorum imponant. Sed sequentia cantatur ad modum ductiae. ...Offertorium...cantatur ad modum ductiae vel cantus coronati ut corda fidelium excitet ad devote offerendum.

The responsory and alleluia are sung in the manner of a *stantipes* or of a *cantus coronatus* so that they may bring devotion and humility to the hearts of those who hear them. The sequence, however, is sung in the manner of a *ductia*. ...The offertory...is sung in the manner of a *ductia* or of a *cantus coronatus* so that it may inspire the hearts of the faithful to make their offerings devoutly.

Part III
Polyphony to 1300

[7]

The performance of Parisian organum

EDWARD ROESNER

The brilliant cycle of organum created over several decades by Leonin, Perotin, and their fellow composers at the Cathedral of Notre Dame and other Parisian churches 'for the enhancement of the Divine Service', as the English writer Anonymous IV puts it, circulated throughout 13th-century Europe.[1] Great *libri organi* containing the Paris repertory appeared in religious institutions from Scotland and the English Chapel Royal to as far east as Poland, and a substantial body of theoretical literature arose to explain and teach the style. The repertory led an 'active' existence, being added to by *organistae* from both Paris and elsewhere, and, in the case of the large body of two-voice organa (*organa dupla*), undergoing seemingly continuous recomposition throughout its history. It was regarded—and still is today—as a virtuoso art, a tour de force for composer and performer alike. Small wonder, then, that an elaborate and highly refined performance practice grew up around the organa, developing directly from the style of the music and, in turn, moulding the nature of the idiom in no small way. It is primarily for this reason that the theorists of the *ars antiqua*, struggling to come to grips with the organum style, provide a fair amount of information on its performance. Although it must be pieced together from many sources, none of the writers having intended to write a performance manual as would a later Quantz or Couperin, the tradition that emerges is a richer and more detailed one than can be reconstructed for perhaps any other kind of medieval polyphony. It is a tradition that can directly influence our understanding of Parisian organum and that will, I suspect, remove much of the aura of forbidding esotericism that too often has caused modern performances of this genre to be somewhat less than successful.

First a note on the performing forces called for in Parisian organum. The conclusion seems inescapable that this genre, like most polyphony from the *ars antiqua*, was intended for voices alone and for soloists. Organa are for the most part settings of the solo parts only of the responsorial chant that follows Scripture readings in Mass and Office—graduals, alleluias and great responsories. As such they are part of a liturgical tradition of virtuoso cantorial singing that goes back to the early days of Christianity, and before.[2] The continuation of this soloistic tradition is confirmed by the small size of surviving manuscripts, cantor's books or display copies of them, which precludes use by more than a handful of performers. (Indeed these sources provide no music for the choral portions of the chant at all; this must be obtained from a gradual or antiphonary.) Equally significant, the notation can often suggest two or more equally 'correct' rhythmic interpretations, even to musicians intimately familiar with the style.[3] This is particularly true of *organum purum* (sections of two-voice organum in which the duplum voice moves in long, florid melismas over sustained notes in the tenor), but is less often a problem in *discantus* sections (where both duplum and tenor move rhythmically), or *organum triplum* and *quadruplum*, in all of which the necessity for co-ordination between the moving parts restrains both the rhythmic freedom of the duplum and, as a consequence, the vagueness of its notation. Although modern performers may find it expedient to support the long-held tenors in *organum purum* with an organ, I know of no evidence that an organ existed at Notre Dame in the 12th or 13th centuries,[4] or that such an instrument was ever used to accompany responsorial chant in the medieval

Miniature from the 13th-century 'Notre Dame' manuscript, Florence, plut. 29.1, f.99r. (A detail from f.65r is shown on p. 176)

service. (The organ did participate in the liturgy at many institutions, of course, being used most commonly with the singing of the *Te Deum* and other hymns, and the sequence at Mass, i.e. with choral chants.)[5] The use of bells, hurdy-gurdy, or other instruments on either the tenor or one of the upper parts, while attractive to some modern audiences, is completely foreign to this music and results in little more than a parody of the style cultivated by the medieval *organistae*.[6]

'Solo' does not necessarily imply that every part was sung by only one man, however. An edict of 1198 by the Bishop of Paris, Eude de Sully, mentions the singing of responsories by four subdeacons in the same sentence in which it alludes to performance of the Vespers responsory and Benedicamus 'in triplo vel quadruplo vel organo'.[7] The use of four singers for monophonic as well as four-part performance of responsorial chant suggests that several singers could also have taken part in the presentation of *organum duplum*.[8] Although the upper voice would of necessity have been taken by one singer only, the other performers could have joined forces on the tenor. There can be no doubt that the tenor in *organum purum* is to be held out, despite its notation as simple longs. Anonymous IV alludes to the variable duration of longs in organum tenors,[9] and the scribe of Wolfenbüttel 628 often repeats a tenor note at the beginning of a new stave if it is carried over from the preceding one. Several singers, breathing alternately, would greatly reduce the strain of singing such a tenor. But the tenor was not meant to be brought forth as a mere drone. In the recently discovered Aberdeen fragment, the one duplum melisma of major proportions is supported by a tenor note written out three times, while readings of the same music in other sources present the pitch only once.[10] The tenor notes in Aberdeen are aligned with pauses in the duplum melisma. And in the *organa tripla* preserved in the Montpellier codex, strokes indicating either a rest or a *suspiratio* (breathing place) appear several times in the tenor, far from the nearest written note and, like the repeated note in Aberdeen, aligned with phrase endings in the upper voices. They presumably indicate points at which the singer could catch his breath, and should undoubtedly be followed by a resumption of the preceding pitch.[11] The evidence in these two sources suggests a broader practice, one that permits the individual tenor singer to pause for breath as often as he wishes, but in concert with the duplum or another upper part. (I take the indications in Montpellier and Aberdeen to be mere suggestions for interpretation, perhaps taken over from exemplars that were 'edited' performance copies, rather than signs that the singer is obliged to follow.) As a result the tenor singer, whose burden is less oppressive than might at first appear, contributes subtly to the articulation of the musical fabric.

The music of the Parisian tradition is organized primarily around consonant sonorities, dissonance appearing primarily in unaccented positions. The one major exception to this is the penultimate sonority in a phrase or section, where strong-beat dissonance is not only tolerated but even sought after.[12] Within this consonant framework, however, the extended melismas in *organum purum* clearly occupied a rather special position, since the likelihood of long notes in the duplum forming dissonances with the tenor is obviously very great. To quote Anonymous IV: 'Sometimes there are a great many longs on account of the flavour (*color*) or beauty of the melody, whether concords or not'.[13] In *organum*

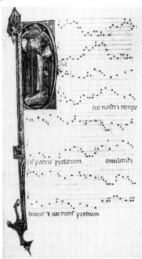

Presul nostri *a 2 (Wolfenbuttel 1099 Helmst. f.92r)*

purum long, consonant, stable notes in the duplum are most essential at key structural points in the music, where the sustained tenor changes pitch. But long, dissonant notes elsewhere in the duplum line, although an integral part of the organum idiom, did not necessarily pass by without receiving special treatment in performance. Franco of Cologne recommends that the singer 'let the tenor be silent or feign concord'.[14] Anonymous II, a writer heavily reliant on Franco, prescribes the same procedure when a stressed dissonance occurs in *discantus*, and Anonymous IV says something similar regarding *organum triplum*.[15] While 'let the tenor be silent' is clear enough, what Franco had in mind by 'feign concord' is equivocal. It seems highly unlikely that he meant the singer actually to change pitch, but he may have thought in terms of a descrescendo or, conceivably, the opposite: holding the note *as though* it were consonant by singing it forthrightly, even emphasizing the dissonance by crescendoing somewhat on it. This last possibility finds support in the suggestion by Walter Odington, another follower of Franco, that the singer 'let the tenor be held *tremulo*, even in the event of a discord'.[16] *Tremulo* is a word with many connotations, to be sure, but all of them imply some form of expressive performance. (We shall encounter it again in the discussion to follow, and I will return to Odington's remark on p. 183.) Thus, although Odington does not mention the other alternative, that the tenor fall silent, all four writers are agreed on the essential point: the tenor singer must deliver his seemingly static line in a flexible and expressive manner, responding to what is happening in the other voices. This conclusion, which is in keeping with my suggestion regarding the introduction of tenor rests, is yet another argument against the use of an organ on the tenor line.

Despite the importance of the tenor, it is obviously the upper voices that draw most attention to themselves. As florid as the added voice in *organum duplum* may be, it appears to have been subjected to still greater embellishment in performance, and nowhere more so than in the already richly ornamental *organum purum* sections. Anonymous IV states that 'two notes on the same pitch, whether consonant [with the tenor] or not, are rendered as a *longa florata*'[17] (literally, a 'long bedecked with flowers', or even a 'fragrant long'). Franco agrees, noting that when several notes on the same pitch occur in succession, only the first is articulated and all together are sung *in floratura*.[18] Anonymous IV, again, recommends that the first, consonant tenor-duplum sonority in a piece be rendered as a *duplex longa florata*[19]—that is, held out, and executed with a flourish. It may be the excessive use of such embellishments that Anonymous IV had in mind when, in one of his frequent historical asides, he recalls that Robertus de Sabilone, one of Perotin's successors and an important teacher of the Paris style, 'caused the singing of the melodic line to stand out too extravagantly'.[20]

What form did these embellishments take? Our most specific information comes from the Dominican pedagogue Jerome of Moravia. In a chapter on *organum triplum* added to the text of Garlandia's treatise on the Parisian style (included in Jerome's compilation of writings about music) Jerome mentions an ornamental device that he calls *florificatio vocis* ('embellishment of the pitch').[21] He says only that it should be performed conjunctly rather than disjunctly, and he offers the following example:

Ex. 1

This example is reminiscent of figures that occur with some frequency in Wolfenbüttel 628, and also in the Worcester Fragments and some other manuscripts. (See, for example, the beginnings of major sections in illus. 2 and 3 and, in illus. 3, the end of the second duplum stave.) Without doubt Jerome's example is also related to the devices mentioned by Franco and Anonymous IV. It is anything but clear, however, leaving us in the dark as to exactly what is being illustrated—the ornamentation of a single note, F, or of two notes, F and E in alternation—and offering no explanation as to just how the repeated notes are to be performed. Fortunately, Jerome provides clues to the nature of the *florificatio vocis* elsewhere in his treatise, in a chapter on the rendition of plainchant, from which it appears that he intended the repeated-note figure to connote some form of trill. (It is not an attempted graphic representation of some medieval ancestor of the early Baroque *trillo*.) Jerome's remarks on the ornamentation of plainchant[22] bear consideration here, since, although they are intended specifically for monophony, the author briefly mentions the subject of organum, noting that singers often mix it with the chant. (After all, the organum singer and the solo chant-singer are likely to have been one and the same person.) Moreover his comments agree in general with the little we have gleaned so far from Franco and Anonymous IV.

Ornamentation, as applied by Jerome to plainchant, is only to be used on long notes (in chant, for Jerome, these include the penultimate and final notes of a phrase, some *plicae*,[23] many initial notes and a few others). Although Jerome supplies no examples of the ornaments, as he has done for the *florificatio vocis*, his descriptions of them are relatively explicit. A long note may be introduced by a *reverberatio*, a short, rapid, appoggiatura-like ornament that approaches the main note from below, usually from a semitone or whole tone, but occasionally from some other interval. The *reverberatio*, moreover, serves as an obligatory preparation for another ornament, the *flos harmonicus*. This 'musical flower' consists of a slow oscillation (*vibratio*) between the main note and an ornamental tone introduced a half or whole step above it, depending on the mode. The plicated long is sung with a *flos* in which the oscillation gains in speed (Jerome mentions only *vibratio* at the half step, but it seems unlikely that this ornament was only performed at that interval). The concluding note of a phrase is to be sung as a *nota procellaris* ('agitated note'), in which the main note oscillates slowly with an ornamental one that appears to lie a half step away, and that has 'the definite appearance of movement, but without interrupting the sound or the pitch'.[24] Is Jerome attempting to describe vibrato?

However rigidly the academic Jerome may have codified his ornaments, he himself admits that his French contemporaries used them with considerable flexibility, avoiding the *nota procellaris* altogether and declaring 'everyone using it to have quavery voices' (*voces tremulae*).[25] We ought not to view them, then, as highly stylized ornamental formulas—in the manner of many ornaments used in the French Baroque, for example. They are rather

177

suggestions of the *kinds* and flavours of extemporary flourishes appropriate to 13th-century solo singers performing either plainchant or polyphonic settings of it. The practice of adding a *flos* to the first note of a phrase is reminiscent of Anonymous IV's suggestions for treating opening sonorities, and the *reverberatio* that introduces the *flos* may help to explain the written-in 'appoggiaturas' at the beginning of many sections of *organum purum* (and, less often, *discantus*). Anonymous IV describes a method for singing these figures that is very different from Jerome's *reverberatio*, however.[26] Since his views are ignored by most modern editors and performers, I quote them here in full:

> In *organum purum* the longs and breves are recognized in many a way and manner. One technique is this: every initial note—whether or not it be consonant in one of the above-mentioned concords—is either a *longa parva*, a *longa tarda*, or a *media*, whatever the ligature [in which it appears], whether it be of two [notes] or of three, etc. But the difference will be as follows: if it be consonant, the tenor will sound or be held over, but if it is not consonant the tenor will be silent or quiet. . . . Also, there is a certain *duplex longa florata*. This is placed at the beginning—*in nomine sanctissimi Alpha*—and is called 'the beginning before the beginning', and is always consonant. Moreover, there are some who put two or three [notes] in the place of one; the first may be either consonant or dissonant, however, and [, if dissonant,] it always begins shortly before the tenor and the tenor begins with the second one, if it is consonant, or with the third. And [then] this third note is elongated, as described above, and ornamented. And some may place three or four in ligature before the start of the tenor; if the last one is consonant the tenor will begin with it, and if it is dissonant the entrance will be with the first concord to follow.

The sense of this passage seems clear: if the first note of the duplum at the start of a piece or internal section in *organum purum* is not consonant with the tenor, the entrance of the tenor should be delayed until the duplum reaches a note that will be suitably concordant with it. This first consonant sonority is to be sung as a *duplex longa florata*, and the value of any preceding note or notes in the duplum is subject to considerable variation in performance ('poor long' probably indicates one shorter than usual, 'late long', one longer than usual, 'medium', one of normal length). In numerous written-out opening appoggiaturas the ex-tempore elongation of the first duplum note is graphically suggested in the notation. And in many of the local works added to the Parisian repertory in Wolfenbüttel 628 (organa by insular composers, copied from books that may have indicated nuances of performance more fully than the books from which the Notre-Dame works were drawn), the ornamental character of the *duplex longa florata* and its dissonant preparation are clearly shown in the notation. These graphic hints may be seen in illus. 1, 2, and 3, the first from the Parisian repertory of the Wolfenbüttel manuscript, the others from its local works, organa of English or Scottish origin. They are transcribed here in ex. 2a-c, with a rhythmic interpretation that holds to the spirit of Anonymous IV's recommendations while following the suggestions in the *Discantus positio vulgaris* for reading elongated ligatures.[27] (— indicates a note of indefinite but usually extended length, ° a very short note, ⁓ a *flos*, ⌢ notes that should be sung together in one flourish, and * a place

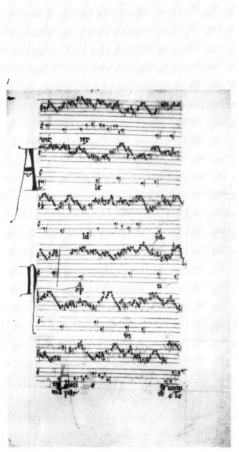
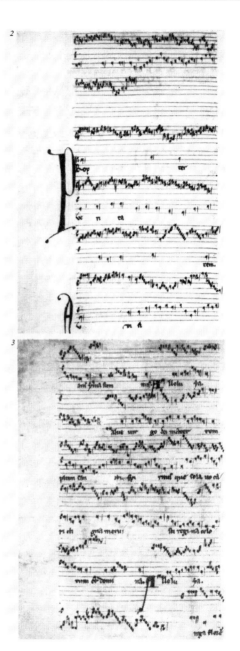

1. A folio from the Parisian repertory in the Wolfenbüttel manuscript (Wolfenbüttel 628, f.42r)
2. Organa of English or Scottish origin (Wolfenbüttel 628, f.23v)
3. Wolfenbüttel 628, f.197v

where the tenor might 'be silent or feign concord'.)

Ex. 2. Wolfenbüttel 628
a Alleluia, Nativitas (opening), cf. illus. 1

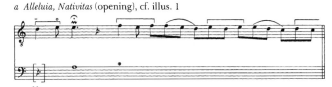

b Propter veritatem (opening), cf. illus. 2

c Alleluia, Salve virgo (opening), cf. illus. 3

In all examples brackets indicate ligatures, slurs indicate *coniuncturae* (chains of rhomb-shaped notes preceded by a square note or a ligature), and a slash through a note stem indicates the unwritten note in a *plica*.

Note that the duplum, by starting before the tenor, is allowed to establish the pitch—a sensible practice, in view of the generally wider range and much greater difficulty of the upper part. Such formulas, which function both as intonations and as opening flourishes, appear in some copies of an organum, but not in others. Compare, for example, illus. 1 with the Florence copy of the same music in illus. 4. In the latter, *both* the alleluia and its verse, not just the verse, open with an appoggiatura. The modern duplum singer should feel at liberty to add such a formula to the beginning of an *organum purum* section, especially if it opens the work, if it is not already present in the music. What he is not free to do—unless he chooses to regard Anonymous IV's recommendations as idiosyncratic or of only local, non-Parisian origin—is to begin with a stressed dissonance, either sustained or quickly resolved. (Viewed in this light, many of Waite's transcriptions should be emended in performance.)

Other passages in the upper voice might also be sung *in floratura*. In the penultimate sonority the duplum is often written as a repeated-note figure, with the second note drawn as a *plica*,[28] that undoubtedly corresponds to the theorists' *longa florata*. (See, for example, the duplum figures preceding '-le-' and '-ya-' in illus. 1 and 4.) This figure is frequently found in other positions as well (in illus. 3 it appears in an opening flourish), and probably should always be given some form of embellishment by the performer. So

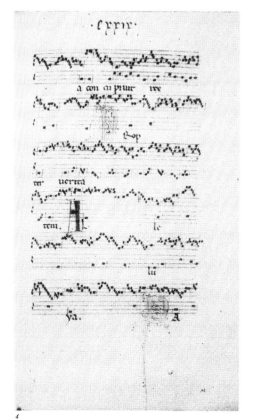
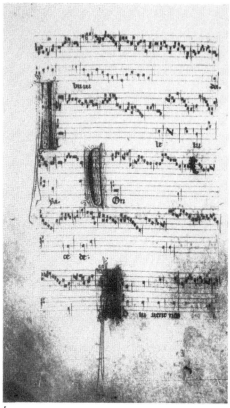

4. *The opening of* Alleluia, Nativitas *in the Florence copy, f.129r (compare with the Wolfenbuttel manuscript in illus. 1)*
5. *Berlin, f.1v, showing the scribe's attention to rhythmic details*

also should another form of duplum 'penultimate', one in which both the dissonance and its resolution fall over the final tenor note, most often at a change of syllable. (See illus. 1 and 4, at '–le–' and '–ti–'.) This figure is consistently notated to suggest long-long in the Berlin fragment, a source in which the scribe is at pains to clarify many details of the rhythm, and in other sources as well on occasion.[29] This may be seen in illus. 5, above '–le–' and above '–ya–', the latter an example of a penultimate and its resolution followed by a second, more elaborate flourish leading to yet another cadence. Both passages are transcribed in ex. 3 (p. 182). If two such 'penultimates' occur in succession, one over the second-last tenor note and the other over the final note, the duplum singer will have to shape his *flores* so that one leads naturally into the other, or else choose which, if either, figure he wishes to embellish.

181

Ex. 3. *Alleluia, Nativitas* (conclusion) after Berlin, cf. illus. 5

[I assume that the flat at the beginning of the duplum in the MS applies only to the *organum purum* clausula on 'Alle–'. Note that the following duplum stave has no flat.]

One other ornamental device in *organum purum* needs mention here, the long descending chain of rhomb-shaped *currentes* ('running notes') that is often found near a cadential point and that is likely to span an octave or more. Anonymous IV discusses the performance of such figures immediately after mentioning the *longa florata*, and uses as an example an eleven-note descending flourish from the two-voice *Viderunt omnes*:[30]

[These notes] have a style different from others: whether consonant or not they descend as evenly and quickly as possible. If the first note be a *currens*, then its preparation is the one before it, the one before that, or the third before, etc. In the descending passage cited here the preparation is not the one before [the first *currens*], but the second one before, and it is long, and the one before, despite the fact that it ascends, is regarded as a *currens*. Thus there are twelve *currentes* and not eleven, and the second one before is long, sounding at the concord of the fifth. It would be long even if it were not consonant, however, but the tenor would be silent, because every note before [the start of the flourish], or the second or third before, must be long to facilitate the descent.

A glance at the passage mentioned by Anonymous IV will clarify these somewhat laboured remarks (ex. 4). The flourish, performed rapidly and evenly, should be preceded by a sustained preparatory note, probably to allow the singer time to ready himself for the coming cadenza. It is worth noting that according to Anonymous IV the flourish may begin before the chain of *currentes* proper, a nuance of performance that cannot be divined from the notation.

Ex. 4. *Currentes* flourish from *Viderunt omnes* after Wolfenbüttel 628 f.25r

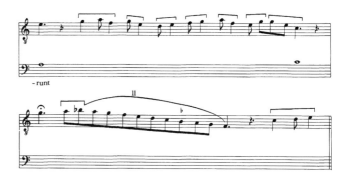

Although Anonymous IV does not say so, I assume that the last note of the figure should fall on the beat and be a long. One final point: Odington's allusion to *tremulo* in the tenor, mentioned earlier, was made specifically in connection with rapid descending passages in the duplum, suggesting that the tenor singer might enhance the flourish by embellishing his own part in an appropriate manner.

Singing *in floratura* has obvious implications for the tempo at which organum should be performed. Although the St Emmeram Anonymous, among others, refers to a quick pace in *organum purum*, such remarks tend to be concerned with the profusion of rapid notes in this highly florid style, not with the tempo per se.[31] The unit of measure in the 13th century was the *tempus*, defined by Anonymous IV as 'a duration that is neither the smallest nor the largest, but that can be produced in a moderately short space of time, so that it can be divided into two, three, or four more notes by the human voice in rapid motion'.[32] The *tempus* falls on the breve, and the long of three breves ordinarily carries the beat. The result is precisely the kind of moderate tempo needed for the addition of embellishments and other refinements in performance. (Jerome observes that the breve of one *tempus* can be divided into three *instantiae*. The *instantia*, he notes, had at one time been regarded as the *tempus*,[33] a hint that the tempo of plainchant had slowed down by the second half of the 13th century, possibly owing to attempts, like Jerome's, to adapt the chant to a system of measured rhythm.)

This moderate pace may not have been kept throughout an entire work, however. Franco describes a style that he calls *copula*, which appears to use a sustained-note texture, and in which the duplum melisma is sung much more rapidly than usual.[34] Regarding an example that appears to be in the second rhythmic mode, Franco notes that 'it differs in performance from the second mode, since the second [mode] is brought forth in normal breves and imperfect longs, while that *copula* is performed quickly, as though in semibreves and breves through to the end'. Another example, written all in breves, is said to require a rapid delivery, probably with the breves being treated as semibreves. It may be that this cryptic passage refers to the stereotyped duplum formulas, sung over sustained tenor notes, that often appear at the end of a *discantus* clausula or sections of *organum purum*. If so, passages like this one from the end of *Concede* as preserved in the Berlin fragment (ex. 5; see also illus. 5) ought to be performed much more quickly than the music that precedes them. Such a technique, if it is indeed what Franco had in mind, would be yet another performance device for embellishing a structural point in the composition.

Ex. 5. *Concede* (conclusion) after Berlin, cf. illus. 5

The rather flexible treatment of rhythm that we have noticed from time to time is, in fact, a major feature of organum performance. The author of the *Discantus positio vulgaris* observes that a rest in *discantus*—he mentions the motet specifically—could be held 'at pleasure' when it appears simultaneously in all voices.[35] Anonymous IV writes that rests in *organum purum* may be treated 'with considerable freedom, according to what seems better to the *cantor* or *operator*, and this with regard to the smallest, larger, and medium-sized ones (but *duplex* [*longa* rests] are seldom found in *organum purum*)'.[36] Ad libitum treatment of rests by the performer can do much to alleviate the seeming abruptness of a shift from the patterns of one rhythmic mode to those of another, and can contribute significantly to the sense of rhythmic plasticity that is one of the most striking features of *organum purum*. (However, it is a device that should be used sparingly in *discantus*, to avoid disrupting the steady forward motion of the tenor that is one of the most important elements of this style.)

The flexible rhythmic character of *organum purum* often appears to have only a slight relationship with the patterns of rhythmic modes taught by theorists of the 13th century. The sustained tenor notes permit the duplum to flow in wide-ranging, often rhapsodic and seemingly improvisatory lines, with a profusion of decorative writing and, going hand-in-hand with it, a rhythmic movement that is often rapid and highly varied. The rhythmic modes, in comparison, often appear to be little more than theoretical constructs, formalized reductions of the living rhythmic language to its most basic components. (In somewhat the same way, a metre, organizing the music into regular 'measures' with consistently recurring patterns of strong and weak beats, is a theoretical reduction of the richly varied rhythmic elements in the works of Mozart or Brahms.) *Organum purum* is conceived in 'modal rhythm', but the 'modes' that are formulated by the theorists to describe this rhythm are skeleton outlines.

To one of these writers, the St Emmeram Anonymous, the disparity between practice and theory in *organum purum* is great enough for him to conclude that the sustained-note style 'abandons strict mode and the proper arrangement of the figures', producing a music 'out of which irregularity rebounds'.[37]

This 'irregularity'—absence of the *mensura recta* ('correct measure') provided by the strict repetition of a modal pattern—has an analogue of sorts in another kind of 'irregularity', one that could be cultivated by the performer, for the duplum singer was free to treat durations of individual note-values with considerable latitude. Anonymous IV, a true child of the Age of Scholasticism, codifies this freedom in a set of seven 'irregular modes', a systematic formalization of the ad-libitum ('voluntarii') alterations in performance of the values suggested by the notation.[38] His treatment is at once telegraphic and verbose. But it is nevertheless worth examining here in some detail because it is the only extended discussion of the rhythmic liberties available to the performer at a time when most theorists were striving to provide exact measurements for all note values. (Indeed, this 'system' is the only known attempt from before the 16th century to consider this aspect of performance.)

The first six irregular modes are indistinguishable in writing from the six rhythmic modes taught by Garlandia and other theorists, differing from them only in the way in which they are performed. The first mode (long-breve-long etc, ♩ ♫) is to be performed thus: *longa duplex* (a note held longer than a normal long)—semibreve or minim (i.e. a very short note)—*longa debita* ('owing long', perhaps a synonym for, or scribal corruption of, *longa duplex*). The result would be ♩ ♫ , not unlike the *notes inégales* of the French Baroque. The second mode (breve-long-breve etc, ♫ ♪) reverses this pattern: *brevis parva* ('meagre breve') or minim—*longa duplex* or *nimia longa* ('overlong long') etc, thus ♪ ♩ ♪

Anonymous IV describes a few different possibilities for the irregular treatment of the third mode (long-breve-breve-long etc, ♩ ♫ ♩). The pattern begins with a *nimia* followed by two *longae tardae* ('late longs', i.e. sung *tenuto*) and a *mediocris* (a 'medium' note, probably a normal long). If the singer wishes, he may change from this irregular pattern to a different one. Thus he might sing the breve-breve-long pattern as two *nimiae breves* ('overlong breves') and a *mediocris* or a *nimia longa*. Or he might execute the pattern first with its normal values and then as two *festinantes* ('hurried notes') followed by either a *mediocris* or a *nimia*. Whatever the exact forms of the irregular third mode may be—they are far from clear—there can be no doubt that they involve a rhythmic delivery of extraordinary flexibility. Unlike the first and second irregular modes, an irregular reading of the third mode would appear to disregard the underlying beat. At the outset of the pattern the 'overlong long', held beyond its normal value of three *tempora*, removes the rhythm from coordination with the beat, and many of the notes that follow increase the lack of coordination still further.

The fourth mode (breve-breve-long etc, ♫ ♩) can be altered in ways similar to the third. The fifth, which moves entirely in longs (♩ ♩ ♩ ♩), uses all *longae mediae* (normal longs) except for the first and penultimate notes of the pattern, which are *nimia*: ♩ ♩ ♩ ♩ ♩. In the sixth mode, all in breves (♫♫ , notated as a single four-note ligature followed by a chain of three-note ones), the penultimate note of each ligature is *nimia* while all the rest are normal, i.e. 𝅘𝅥𝅮𝅘𝅥𝅮𝅘𝅥𝅮𝅘𝅥𝅮𝅘𝅥𝅮𝅘𝅥𝅮𝅘𝅥𝅮. In the fourth, fifth, and sixth irregular modes, then, the rhythmic flow is again disassociated from the underlying pulse.

Finally, Anonymous IV describes a *seventh* irregular mode, 'the noblest and worthiest [of all], freer and more pleasing [than the others]. This mode is a mixed, common mode, and it is made up of all the two-note ligatures mentioned above, and of all the three-note and four-note ones, etc.' This 'mode' is without doubt an attempt by the theorist to embrace within his system those rhythmic elements that, to borrow the words of the St Emmeram Anonymous, 'abandon strict mode and the proper arrangement of the figures'—i.e. the many passages in which no one rhythmic pattern appears without variation throughout a phrase.

Nowhere does Anonymous IV imply that irregular delivery should be used throughout a passage of *organum purum*; to do so would surely be to invite bizarre results. These 'modes' must be viewed, like the conventional rhythmic modes on which they are modelled, as theoretical abstractions, systematic presentations of durational relationships that might be introduced only sparingly in performance. One phrase might be performed normally, the following one with some 'irregularities'. The irregular modes would appear to be particularly well suited to passages involving sequential repetition or variation, commonly featured in many organum melismas. A single ligature, perhaps, or even a single note might be rendered irregularly. As an example of the first irregular mode, Anonymous IV cites a passage from Perotin's *Alleluia, Posui adiutorium*, music that appears in the Montpellier manuscript notated in a way that corresponds graphically to the alterations in duration mentioned by the theorist.[39] Significantly, I believe, it is only the very beginning of the phrase that is notated irregularly. (See ex. 6; I would treat the first two notes after the opening flourish in ex. 2a in a similar manner.)

Ex. 6—from Perotin: *Alleluia, Posui adiutorium*, after Montpellier f.17r

- le -

Elsewhere in a composition an irregular mode can be used to produce—or to 'explain', using the rhythmic vocabulary of the *ars antiqua*—a cadential *ritardando* or a lingering on a melodic peak. Used with restraint, this tradition of rhythmic flexibility can breathe life and meaning into music that we too often hear as abstruse, or even as somewhat aimless and mechanical.

The opening section from the responsary *Cornelius centurio* may be included here to illustrate many of the points mentioned in the preceding pages (ex. 7).

Ex. 7. *Cornelius centurio* (opening), after Florence f.73v-74r

In the opening phrase the scribe has written the second-last duplum note as a *duplex longa*, suggesting that this line is to be sung in the manner of the irregular fifth mode. The music of this phrase is a standard cliché for the beginning of many organa, but is usually notated without such graphic indications for performance.

Anonymous IV has been our principal witness to the highly developed performance tradition of Parisian organum. Although we cannot be certain that some of the techniques described by this English writer are not simply local ones, most are corroborated by other theorists, or by the *libri organi* themselves. Thus 'irregular' rhythmic performance is attested to both by elongated notes in some manuscripts and, in the vaguest of language, by a German writer, the St Emmeram Anonymous.[40] Although my method of juxtaposing information drawn from sources of differing backgrounds may seem dangerously eclectic, reminiscent of writers on baroque performance who lump together Caccini and Quantz, I feel that this approach is justified owing to the relative paucity of information, the consistency of most of it, and its general character which reveals little evidence of local or personal performance practices. Even Jerome's *flores* and Anonymous IV's irregular patterns are not so much fixed *agréments* or stylized formulas as hints of the *kinds* of things a performer might do with this music. I have concentrated on organum, but many of the practices outlined here can be applied to other kinds of Parisian polyphony if suitable adjustments are made for different textures and manners of declamation, and for the effect these have on harmonic usage and melodic and rhythmic style. Many conducti begin with a *duplex longa florata*, and Jerome mentions the monophonic conductus in the same phrase as the *florificatio vocis*. For the music of the Parisian *liber organi*—whether organum, conductus, or the motet in its early forms—is all conceived in essentially the same language, just as a Haydn Mass and symphony share a common style. The Parisian organum style, like that of the Gothic cathedral, took Europe by storm. Performed as its creators intended, it is not difficult to see why.

Edward H. Roesner teaches at New York University. He is preparing for publication a number of organa dupla *and the complete repertory of three- and four-part* organa, *and will present a lecture on filiation, chronology and style in the* organa dupla *at the conference on medieval and renaissance music at King's College, Cambridge, in August 1979.*

[1] See the remarks of Anonymous IV, our principal historical witness to the creation and dissemination of the Parisian repertory, in the edition of Fritz Reckow, *Der Musiktraktat des Anonymus 4*, 2 vols (Beihefte zum Archiv für Musikwissenschaft, 4 and 5, Wiesbaden, 1967), 1, pp. 46, 50f and passim. The two-part organa in Wolfenbüttel, Herzog-August-Bibliothek, MS 628 Helmst. are edited in William G. Waite, *The Rhythm of Twelfth-Century Polyphony* (New Haven, 1954), and all the three- and four-voice organa are transcribed in Heinrich Husmann ed., *Die drei- und vierstimmigen Notre-Dame-Organa* (Publikationen älterer Musik, 11, Leipzig, 1940). Hans Tischler has announced a complete edition of all the two-voice organa, to be published by A–R Editions. Performers using these or other editions should also consult the MS sources, nearly all of which have been published in facsimile. The most important for organum are: Florence, Bibl. Medicea Laurenziana, plut 29.1, facsimile in Luther A. Dittmer, *Firenze, Biblioteca Mediceo-Laurenziana, pluteo 29.1*, 2 vols (Publications of Mediaeval Musical Manuscripts, 10 and 11, Brooklyn, n.d.); Wolfenbüttel 628 Helmst., facsimile in J. H. Baxter, *An Old St Andrews Music Book* (St Andrews University Publications, 30, London, 1931); Wolfenbüttel 1099 Helmst., facsimile in Dittmer, *Wolfenbüttel 1099* (Publications of Mediaeval Musical Manuscripts, 2, Brooklyn, 1960). The standard guide to these MSS is Friedrich Ludwig, *Repertorium organorum recentioris et motetorum vetustissimi stili*, vol 1, part 1 (Halle, 1910).
[2] For a 13th-century view of the nature of responsorial chant see Guillelmus Duranti, *Rationale divinorum officiorum* (various editions), Lib. 4, 19f and 5,2, summarized and analysed in Herbert Douteil, *Studien zur Durantis 'Rationale divinorum officiorum' als kirchenmusikalischer Quelle* (Kölner Beiträge zur Musikforschung, 52, Regensburg, 1969), pp. 82-113 and 242-50.
[3] See the revealing comments of Anonymous IV in Reckow, op cit, 1, pp. 49f and 51.
[4] See Jean Perrot, *L'Orgue de ses origines hellénestiques à la fin du XIIIe siècle* (Paris, 1965), pp. 300 and 302; cf. Craig Wright, 'Performance Practices at the Cathedral of Cambrai 1475-1550', *Musical Quarterly*, 64 (1978), pp. 324f.
[5] See Frank Ll. Harrison, *Music in Medieval Britain*, 2nd edition (London, 1963), pp. 202-8. References made during a discussion of organum to an 'instrumentum' by Anonymous IV (e.g. Reckow, 1, pp. 56 and 86) or to an 'instrumentum artificiale' by the St Emmeram Anonymous—Heinrich Sowa ed., *Ein anonymer glossierter Mensuraltraktat 1279* (Kassel, 1930), pp. 128f—are, as a careful reading will show, made for the purpose of analogy or as scholastic asides sparked by the word 'organum'. For the different connotations of this 'verbum aequivocum', see Reckow, 'Organum-Begriff und frühe Mehrstimmigkeit', *Forum musicologicum*, 1 (1975), pp. 31-167, and idem 'Organum', *Handwörterbuch der musikalischen Terminologie* (Wiesbaden, 1971).
[6] On the use of bells in the service see Richard Rastall, 'Minstrelsy, Church, and Clergy in Medieval England', *Proceedings of the Royal Musical Association*, 97 (1970/1), pp. 93-8, and Duranti, as discussed in Douteil, op cit, pp. 31-8. Regarding the hurdy-gurdy and similar instruments compare the unconvincing arguments in Marianne Bröcker, *Die Drehleier*, 2 vols (Düsseldorf, 1973), 1, pp. 259-81.
[7] Printed in Jacques Handschin, 'Zur Geschichte von Notre Dame', *Acta musicologica*, 4 (1932), p. 6 (cf. pp. 7-10).
[8] The use of more than one singer to a part in *discantus* is mentioned by Jacques de Liège writing in the 1320s, in his *Speculum musicae* (Roger Bragard ed., 7 vols, Corpus scriptorum de musica, 3, American Institute of Musicology, 1955-73, 7, p. 8) and, perhaps, in the *Summa* attributed by Gerbert to Jean de Muris—Martin Gerbert ed.,

Scriptores ecclesiastici de musica, 3 vols (St Blasien, 1784), 3, p. 240.

[9] Reckow, *Anon 4*, 1, p. 44.

[10] Aberdeen, University Library MS 2379/1, discovered by Geoffrey Chew, who describes it and provides a facsimile in 'A *Magnus Liber Organi* Fragment at Aberdeen', *Journal of the American Musicological Society*, 31 (1978), pp. 326-43. I am grateful to Professor Chew for sharing his work with me prior to its publication.

[11] See, for example, the facsimile of Montpellier, f.16v, in Yvonne Rokseth ed., *Polyphonies du XIIIe siècle*, 4 vols (Paris, 1935-9), vol 1. This solution was first proposed in Heinrich Husmann, *Die dreistimmigen Organa der Notre-Dame-Schule* (Leipzig, 1935), pp. 46f, and is adopted in Mme Rokseth's Montpellier edition, but not in Husman's *Die drei- und vierstimmigen Notre-Dame-Organa*.

[12] See, for example, Reckow, *Anon 4*, 1, pp. 80, 86, and 88f.

[13] Reckow, *Anon 4*, 1, p. 88. On the intimate relationship between consonance and long notes in *organum purum* see Johannes de Garlandia, in Erich Reimer ed., *Johannes de Garlandia: De mensurabili musica*, 2 vols (Beihefte zum Archiv für Musikwissenschaft, 10 and 11, Wiesbaden, 1972), 1, p. 89, and the gloss of this passage by Anonymous IV, in Reckow, 1, pp. 86f.

[14] Franco of Cologne, *Ars cantus mensurabilis*, ed. Gilbert Reaney and André Gilles (Corpus scriptorum de musica, 18, American Institute of Musicology, 1974), pp. 80f; quoted here from the translation in Oliver Strunk, *Source Readings in Music History* (New York, 1950), p. 158.

[15] Anonymous II, Edmonde de Coussemaker ed., *Scriptorum de musica medii aevi*, 4 vols (Paris, 1864-76), 1, p. 312; Anonymous IV, Reckow, 1, p. 83.

[16] Walter Odington, *Summa de speculatione musicae*, ed. Frederick F. Hammond (Corpus scriptorum de musica, 14, American Institute of Musicology, 1970), p. 141.

[17] Reckow, *Anon 4*, 1, p. 87.

[18] Franco, loc cit, p. 81.

[19] Reckow, *Anon 4*, 1, p. 88.

[20] ibid, p. 50.

[21] Reimer, op cit, 1, p. 95.

[22] Simon M. Cserba ed., *Hieronymus de Moravia O.P., Tractatus de musica* (Freiburger Studien zur Musikwissenschaft, 2, Regensburg, 1935), pp. 183-8.

[23] The *plica* is a note with stems on *both* sides of the note head and is meant to be sung as two pitches, the first one specified by the position of the note head, the second one unspecified, but lying above or below the first note, depending on the direction of the stems.

[24] Cserba, op cit, p. 185.

[25] ibid, p. 187.

[26] Reckow, *Anon 4*, 1, pp. 86 and 88.

[27] Cserba, p. 190.

[28] In addition to Jerome's suggestion that it be sung with a *flos*, evidence pointing to the ornamental character of the *plica* includes the variable pitch of the unwritten note (see Lambertus, in Coussemaker, 1, p. 273), its appearance in some copies of a work but not others (it is totally absent from the Aberdeen fragment), and the novel, if vaguely described style of vocal production that some writers recommend for it (see Lambertus, loc cit, and *Ars musicae mensurabilis secundum Franconem*, ed. Gilbert Reaney and André Gilles (Corpus scriptorum de musica, 15, American Institute of Musicology, 1971), p. 45.

[29] Berlin-Dahlem, Staatsbibliothek der Stiftung Preussischer Kulturbesitz, lat. 4° 523; facsimile in Kurt von Fischer, 'Neue Quellen zur Musik des 13., 14., und 15. Jahrhunderts', *Acta musicologica*, 36 (1964), pl. 1-3. It must be admitted that opinions are divided regarding the rhythmic interpretation of such figures, their alignment with the tenor, and even where the syllable change takes place in the duplum. Theodore Karp argues against the necessity of changing syllables at the beginning of a ligature in 'Text Underlay and Rhythmic Interpretation in 12th C. Polyphony', *International Musicological Society: Report of the 11th Congress, Copenhagen, 1972*, 2 vols (Copenhagen, 1974), 2, pp. 482-6. The theory that such figures should be read long-long whether or not the notation expressly indicates it finds some support—although vague—in a passage in Anonymous IV; see Reckow, 1, pp. 79f. Again, Waite's transcriptions should be emended where necessary.

[30] Reckow, *Anon 4*, 1, pp. 87f.

[31] Sowa, op cit, p. 130. A fast pace, involving the use of numerous short values, was widely associated with instrumental music and with hockets; see Reckow, *Anon 4*, 1, p. 39, and Ernst Rohloff ed., *Die Quellenhandschriften zum Musiktraktat des Johannes de Grocheio* (Leipzig, 1967), p. 146.

[32] Reckow, *Anon 4*, 1, p. 23.

[33] Cserba, p. 180.

[34] Franco, loc cit, pp. 75-7. See the interpretation of this passage in Reckow, *Die Copula* (Wiesbaden, 1972), pp. 28-45.

[35] Cserba, p. 193.

[36] Reckow, *Anon 4*, 1, p. 85.

[37] Sowa, pp. 130 and 127. The relations between the rhythmic modes and *organum purum* continue to be a topic of controversy, one that I plan to pursue in a forthcoming study and in the revised edition of *Music in the Middle Ages* by the late Gustave Reese and myself (to be finished in 1979). Cf. the discussions in Waite, op cit; Reckow, *Anon 4*, 2; and Theodore Karp, 'Towards a Critical Edition of Notre Dame Organa Dupla', *Musical Quarterly*, 52 (1966), pp. 350-67.

[38] Reckow, *Anon 4*, 1, pp. 84f.

[39] ibid, p. 84. Cf. the facsimile of Montpellier, f.17r, in Rokseth, 1.

[40] Sowa, p. 53.

[8]
FRANCO OF COLOGNE ON THE RHYTHM OF ORGANUM PURUM*

CHARLES M. ATKINSON

Thanks in part to a fine translation by Oliver Strunk,[1] the *Ars cantus mensurabilis* of Franco of Cologne is a treatise we all think we know. It is perhaps for this reason that Franco's treatise has been all but ignored in most of the recent discussions of the rhythm of Notre Dame organum.[2] The one noteworthy exception to this is Fritz Reckow's discussion of organum purum in his dissertation on Anonymous IV and in his various articles on organum and related topics in the *Handwörterbuch der musikalischen Terminologie*, in the Schrade *Gedenkschrift*, and elsewhere.[3] But for Reckow, and presum-

---

*This article is the revised version of a paper delivered at the Annual Meeting of the American Musicological Society, Baltimore, November 1988, and which was presented to Janet Knapp in an unpublished *Festgabe* on the occasion of her retirement from Vassar College.

[1] O. Strunk, *Source Readings in Music History* (New York, 1950), pp. 139–59.
[2] The interest of scholars has been focused more upon the ideas of Johannes de Garlandia, Anonymous IV and the St Emmeram Anonymous, among the Notre Dame theorists of the mid- to late thirteenth century, or upon the de la Fage Anonymous or the Vatican Organum Treatise in the earlier part of the century. See, for example, E. Roesner's discussion of 'Johannes de Garlandia on *organum in speciali*', *Early Music History*, 2 (1982), pp. 129–60, and his 'The Performance of Parisian Organum', *Early Music*, 7 (1979), pp. 174–89. (Roesner's discussion of Franco's term *floratura* will be reviewed later in this study.) See also E. H. Sanders, 'Consonance and Rhythm in the Organum of the 12th and 13th Centuries', *Journal of the American Musicological Society*, 33 (1980), pp. 264–86; J. Yudkin, 'The Rhythm of Organum Purum', *The Journal of Musicology*, 2 (1983), 355–76; idem, 'Notre Dame Theory: A Study of Terminology, including a New Translation of the Music Treatise of Anonymous IV' (Ph.D. dissertation, Stanford University, 1982); S. Fuller, 'Theoretical Foundations of Early Organum Theory', *Acta Musicologica*, 53 (1981), pp. 52–84; and S. Immel, 'The Vatican Organum Treatise Re-examined', *Abstracts of Papers Read at the Fiftieth Annual Meeting of the American Musicological Society* (Philadelphia, 1984), p. 18. For a more complete listing and assessment of recent scholarship on organum, see Yudkin's 'Notre Dame Theory', in particular his Introduction and Chapter 1 (pp. 1–48).
[3] F. Reckow, *Der Musiktraktat des Anonymus 4*, Beihefte zum Archiv für Musikwissenschaft 4 and 5 (Wiesbaden, 1967); 'Proprietas und perfectio: Zur Geschichte des Rhythmus, seiner Aufzeichnung und Terminologie im 13. Jahrhundert', *Acta Musicologica*, 39 (1967), pp. 115–43; 'Organum', *Handwörterbuch der musikalischen Terminologie* (Wiesbaden, 1971);

ably for most other scholars as well, Franco's description of organum is strongly coloured by his theories of mensuration, appearing to place even organum purum under the heading of 'mensurable music'.[4] This in turn seems to distance Franco from the earliest layer of organum composition at Notre Dame, rendering his ideas of little value in arriving at an interpretation of the rhythmic character of this music.[5]

The seeming neglect of Franco as a source of information about the rhythm of organum purum is thus in part a logical consequence of the very innovations for which his treatise is justifiably famous. As I hope to demonstrate, however, whatever neglect the treatise has been subject to vis-à-vis organum is not justifiable. The *Ars cantus mensurabilis* is in fact a treatise that can still offer us fresh perspectives not just on mensural notation, but also on the rhythm of organum purum – perspectives that heretofore may have been concealed from view under a veneer of translation.

The key to uncovering these perspectives is, I believe, the terminology Franco uses to describe the music with which he is dealing. Trying to gain access to the character of Notre Dame

---

Die Copula: Über einige Zusammenhänge zwischen Setzweise, Formbildung, Rhythmus und Vortragsstil in der Mehrstimmigkeit von Notre Dame, Akademie der Wissenschaften und der Literatur zu Mainz: Abhandlungen der geistes- und sozialwissenschaftlichen Klasse, Jg. 1972, Nr. 13 (Wiesbaden, 1972); 'Das Organum', *Gattungen der Musik in Einzeldarstellungen: Gedenkschrift Leo Schrade*, 1. Folge, ed. W. Arlt, E. Lichtenhahn and H. Oesch (Bern, 1973), pp. 434–96; 'Organum', sections 1–5, *The New Grove Dictionary of Music and Musicians*, ed. S. Sadie, 20 vols. (London, 1980), XIII, pp. 796–803.

[4] See the discussion of this issue below, pp. 6–10. In his article 'Organum' for the *Handwörterbuch*, Reckow shows Franco as placing organum under the genus 'musica mensurabilis', stating: 'Bei Franco spielt der rhythmische Charakter bei der Mehrstimmigkeits-Klassifikation gar keine Rolle mehr, da für ihn alle Mehrstimmigkeit (von den Tenor-Haltetönen abgesehen) als rhythmisch-proportional gemessen gilt' (*op. cit.*, pp. 9–10). In *Der Musiktraktat des Anonymus 4*, II, pp. 40–5, Reckow hypothesises that Franco must already have been dealing with manuscript settings of organum purum in which the upper voice was written in modal, or perhaps even mensural notation: '[Franco's] Regelung setzt die Anwendung eines vom Zusammenklang zunächst völlig unabhängigen Rhythmisierungsverfahrens im Duplum voraus, und dieses Verfahren kann nur die modalrhythmische Lesung der Melismen sein, eventuell bereits nach mensuraler Umschrift' (*op. cit.*, p. 40).

[5] Franco's remarks on organum purum – a type of music that formed an important part of Leonin's *Magnus liber* – seem to form a sharp contrast with those of other thirteenth-century theorists. Whereas writers such as Johannes de Garlandia emphasise consonance or dissonance with the given tenor as the determinant of long and short note values in organum purum, Franco's stating that in organum purum 'Whatever is written as a *longa simplex* is long; as a breve, short; as a semibreve, still shorter', and 'Whatever is long requires concord with respect to the tenor,' does indeed seem to suggest that he was dealing with a later version of this type of music, just as Reckow hypothesised.

Franco of Cologne on the rhythm of organum purum

organum through the door of Franco's treatise brings us into the broader arena of terminological history and the relationships of terms to the concepts they describe. This is, of course, an area in which pioneering work has been done by Fritz Reckow, and which has been explored more recently by Edward Roesner and Jeremy Yudkin.[6] In approaching this topic I have therefore tried to follow the dictates of Franco himself: 'not hesitating to interpolate things well said by others or to eradicate and avert [their] errors and, if we have discovered something new, to uphold and prove it with good reasons'.[7]

Although he reserves his principal discussion of organum for the end of his work, two of the areas Franco touches upon in the first chapter lay important groundwork for the last one.[8] The first of these is his definition of mensurable music and *mensura*:

Excerpt 1. Franco, *Ars cantus mensurabilis*, chapter I
(1) Mensurabilis musica est cantus longis brevibusque temporibus mensuratus. (2) Gratia huius diffinitionis, videndum est quid sit mensura et quid tempus. (3) Mensura est habitudo quantitativa longitudinem et brevitatem cuiuslibet cantus mensurabilis manifestans. (4) Mensurabilis dico, quia in plana musica non attenditur talis mensura. (CSM 18, pp. 24–5)

In Franco's words, 'Mensurable music is *cantus* that is measured in long and short *tempora*' (or 'units of time'). He contrasts this with plainchant, in which, as he says, 'this kind of measure is not attendant' (sentence 4). Taking care to define his terms precisely, in the best Scholastic tradition, he goes on to define *mensura*, saying that 'Measure is a quantitative attribute making manifest the length and brevity of any mensurable melody' (sentence 3) or, using the version of the sentence as it appears in Jerome of Moravia's copy of Franco, 'Measure is an attribute showing the quantity, the length and brevity, of any mensurable *cantus*'.[9]

---

[6] See the works cited in nn. 2 and 3 above.
[7] 'Proponimus igitur ipsam mensurabilem musicam sub compendio declarare; bene dictaque aliorum non recusabimus interponere, erroresque destruere et fugare; et si quid novi a nobis inventum fuerit, bonis rationibus sustinere et probare'; *Franconis de Colonia Ars cantus mensvrabilis*, ed. G. Reaney and A. Gilles, Corpus Scriptorum de Musica [hereafter CSM] 18 ([Rome], 1974), p. 24. All translations are mine unless otherwise indicated.
[8] The division and numbering of chapters is that given in CSM 18.
[9] Jerome's version reads: 'Mensura est habitudo quantitatem, longitudinem et brevitatem cujuslibet cantus mensurabilis manifestans'. For the complete text see *Hieronymus de Moravia O.P.: Tractatus de musica*, ed. S. Cserba O.P., Freiburger Studien zur Musikwissenschaft 2 (Regensburg, 1935).

Charles M. Atkinson

Franco's use of the terms 'quantitative' or 'quantity' in this passage is, I think, important. These are terms not found in the parallel passages in Johannes de Garlandia or Anonymous IV,[10] and to my mind signal the striving for order, specificity and precision characteristic both of Franco's treatise and of Scholasticism in general.[11]

A second aspect of Franco's first chapter is pivotal both within the treatise and for the topic with which we are concerned:

Excerpt 2. Franco, *Ars cantus mensurabilis*, chapter I
(7) Dividitur autem mensurabilis musica in mensurabilem simpliciter et partim. (8) Mensurabilis simpliciter est discantus, eo quod in omni parte sua tempore mensuratur. (9) Partim mensurabilis dicitur organum pro tanto quod non in qualibet parte sua mensuratur. (10) Et sciendum quod organum dupliciter sumitur, proprie et communiter. (11) Est enim organum proprie sumptum organum duplum, quod purum organum appellatur. (CSM 18, p. 25)

Franco first subdivides mensurable music into two categories, namely, that which is wholly measurable and that which is only

[10] For the parallel passages in Johannes de Garlandia see Reimer, *Johannes de Garlandia*, Beihefte zum Archiv für Musikwissenschaft 10 (Wiesbaden, 1972), p. 35, lines 1–3 (*musica mensurabilis*), and p. 36, sent. 5–8, and p. 37, sent. 16–20 (*mensura*); for Anon. IV, see Reckow, *Der Musiktraktat des Anonymus 4*, I, p. 22, lines 3–6 (*mensura*). In Anon. IV, see also p. 76, lines 12–35, and p. 77, lines 1–6. Somewhat surprising, given his dependence upon Johannes de Garlandia for certain aspects of his theory, is the fact that the St Emmeram Anonymous also uses the word 'quantitas' to distinguish between non-mensurable and mensurable music: 'Et nota, quod inmensurabilis est illa, ubi non sunt longe uel breues uel aliqua *quantitas* temporum sub certo numero distributa. Mensurabilis est illa, in qua sua *quantitas* temporum reperitur', H. Sowa, ed., *Ein anonymer glossierter Mensuraltraktat 1279*, Königsberger Studien zur Musikwissenschaft 9 (Kassel, 1930), p. 5 (my italics).

[11] In his famous essay on *Gothic Architecture and Scholasticism* (Cleveland and New York, 1957) E. Panofsky pointed to the importance of the Scholastic *summa* as a conceptual model that could operate in architecture just as in the various types of philosophical, scientific and theological writings that were its primary manifestation. Its principal attributes were: (1) totality (sufficient enumeration), (2) arrangement according to a system of homologous parts and parts of parts (sufficient articulation), (3) distinctness and deductive cogency (sufficient interrelation) (see Panofsky, p. 31). In the *summa*, as in other Scholastic writing, the commanding ideal was a mode of expression that would make the orderliness and logic of the author's thought palpably explicit and clear. Although I would not go so far as to characterise Franco's *Ars cantus mensurabilis* as a 'summa' in the sense of Aquinas's *Summa theologica*, Franco himself refers to his work as a 'compendium', and it does exhibit a number of traits (e.g. its striving to be comprehensive, the logical, hierarchical arrangement of its parts, the clarity and specificity of its treatment) that place it squarely in the Scholastic tradition as Panofsky and others have characterised it. (The classic treatment of Scholasticism is of course M. Grabmann's *Geschichte der scholastischen Methode*, 2 vols. [Freiburg, 1909–11; repr. 1957], and the subject is treated in almost any work on medieval intellectual history. Two recent treatments are those of M. De Wulf, *An Introduction to Scholastic Philosophy*, trans. P. Coffey [New York, 1956] and J. Pieper, *Scholasticism* [London, 1960].)

Franco of Cologne on the rhythm of organum purum

partly so. The former (*simpliciter*) is discant, Franco says in sentence 8, 'because it is measured by time in its every part'; 'partly mensurable', on the other hand, 'is [that] called organum, in so far as it is that which is not measured in its every part'. This sentence is important – important enough for Franco to return to it later on in his discussion. We shall do the same.

Yet another matter that should be mentioned here is a comment Franco makes about the formal relationship of discant to organum. At the very close of his chapter XI, 'On Discant and its Species', Franco makes the following statement: 'Be it observed also that in discant, as well as in tripla etc., the equivalence in the perfections of longs, breves, and semibreves ought always to be borne in mind, so that there may be as many perfections in the discant, triplum, etc., as there are in the tenor, or conversely, counting both actual sounds and their omissions as far as the *penultimate*, where such measure is not attendant, *there being rather a point of organum in that place*'.[12]

Let us now turn to Franco's last chapter to see what that organum should be like:

Excerpt 3. Franco, *Ars cantus mensurabilis*, chapter XIV (beginning) (1) Organum proprie sumptum est cantus non in omni parte sua mensuratus. (2) Sciendum quod purum organum haberi non potest, nisi supra tenorem ubi sola nota est in unisono, ita quod, quando tenor accipit plures notas simul, statim est discantus, ut hic:

(CSM 18, p. 80)

Franco begins his treatment by recalling two sentences from the first chapter of his work.[13] His first sentence is 'Organum, taken in itself, is *cantus* not measured in its every part,' which in the earlier chapter was followed almost immediately by the statement that 'organum taken in itself is organum duplum, which is called organum purum'. He now goes on to describe the chief identifying feature of organum

---
[12] 'Notandum quod tam in discantu quam in triplicibus etc. inspicienda est aequipollentia in perfectionibus longarum, brevium et semibrevium, ita quod tot perfectiones in tenore habeantur quot in discantu vel in triplo etc., vel e converso, computando tam voces rectas quam obmissas usque ad *penultimam*, ubi non attenditur talis mensura, *sed magis est organicus ibi punctus*' (CSM 18, p. 75; my italics).
[13] The relevant sentences in chapter I are sentences 9 and 11. See Excerpt 2 above.

purum within a two-voice texture (Excerpt 3, sentence 2): 'Be it known that there can be no organum purum except over a tenor where there is a single note on a single pitch [i.e. a sustained note], for when the tenor takes several notes together, discant begins at once'.[14]

There are, of course, distant echoes of both the St Emmeram Anonymous and Johannes de Garlandia in the last sentence above. But it is in the second section of Franco's treatment of organum purum that one finds the closest ties with Johannes de Garlandia. At the same time, this section demonstrates a fundamental shift from Johannes's views:

Excerpt 4. Franco's 'Rules of Consonance'
(3) Ipsius organi longae et breves tribus regulis cognoscuntur. (4) Prima est: quicquid notatur in longa simplici nota longum est, et in brevi breve, et in semibrevi semibreve. (5) Secunda regula est: quicquid est longum indiget concordantia respectu tenoris; sed si in discordantia venerit, tenor taceat vel se in concordantiam fingat, ut hic patet:

[Iu - - - dea et Iherusalem]

(6) Tertia regula est: quicquid accipitur immediate ante pausationem quae finis punctorum dicitur, est longum, quia omnis penultima longa est. (CSM 18, pp. 80–1)

Here, Franco presents his three 'rules of consonance', which follow

---

[14] Cf. the description of organum purum (=*organum speciale*) in the St Emmeram Anonymous's discussion of the four-note ligature with perfection and with opposite propriety: 'Ipsa figura quaternaria figurata per oppositum et perfecta semper in dispositione *organi specialis* nascitur sibi esse; id est quociensconque in cantu aliquo ordinatur, *supra burdonem tenoris* edificari cernitur a natura et sub dispositione organi specialis.' ('This quaternary figure, written *per oppositum* and perfect, always arises in the disposition of *organum speciale*; that is, whenever it is disposed in some melody [*cantus*] it is perceived to be erected *over a burdo of the tenor* by the nature and under the disposition of *organum speciale*'.) Sowa, ed., *Ein anonymer glossierter Mensuraltraktat*, p. 53, lines 2–6; my italics.) Franco's use of the phrase *in unisono* in this passage has a direct parallel in the treatise of Johannes de Garlandia. In his discussion of organum *cum alio*, Johannes states: 'eius aequipollentia tantum se tenet *in unisono* usque ad finem alicuius puncti, ut secum convenit secundum aliquam concordantiam' ('its equivalence is maintained *in unisono* [i.e. over a single pitch sustained in the tenor] as far as the end of a section, so that it might come together with it in some consonance'; Reimer, *Johannes de Garlandia*, I, pp. 88–9; my italics.) See also the discussion below, pp. 15–16.

Franco of Cologne on the rhythm of organum purum

Johannes de Garlandia's rules of consonance in number if not in content. (Johannes's rules appear in Excerpt 5.)

Excerpt 5. Johannes de Garlandia's 'Rules of Consonance'
(11) Longae et breves in organo tali modo dinoscuntur, scilicet per [concordantiam], per figuram, per paenultimam. (12) Unde regula: omne id, quod accidit in aliquo secundum virtutem [concordantiarum], dicitur longum. (13) Alia regula: quidquid figuratur longum secundum organa ante pausationem vel loco [concordantiae] dicitur longum. (14) Alia regula: quidquid accipitur ante longam pausationem vel ante perfectam concordantiam dicitur esse longum. (Reimer, *Johannes de Garlandia*, I, p. 89)

Both begin in a similar fashion, Johannes stating that the longs and breves in organum are distinguished by consonance, by *figura* (or note shape) and 'by the penultima'; Franco simply says that the longs and breves of organum purum can be understood by three rules. At this point, however, the two authors begin to diverge.

Johannes de Garlandia's first rule (sentence 12 in Excerpt 5) states: 'All that which falls anywhere [lit. 'somewhere'] in accord with the *virtus* of the consonances is said to be long.'[15] In other words, whatever creates a consonance should be long. Franco turns this rule on its head, as it were, stating (sentence 4 of Excerpt 4): 'Whatever is notated as a *longa simplex* note is long; [whatever is notated] as a breve is short; as a semibreve, even shorter.' This is actually closer to Johannes's second rule (sentence 13 in Excerpt 5): 'According to the precepts of organa, whatever is notated as a long before a rest, that is, in the position of a consonance, is said to be long.'[16]

[15] On the translation of the phrase 'omne id quod accidit' in this passage and the significance it holds for the interpretation of Johannes's ideas, see E. Sanders, 'Consonance and Rhythm in the Organum of the 12th and 13th Centuries', *Journal of the American Musicological Society*, 33 (1980), pp. 269–71, and the Communications of Professors Reckow and Sanders, *ibid.*, 34 (1981), pp. 588–91. On Johannes's 'rules of consonance' themselves, see W. Apel, 'From St. Martial to Notre Dame', *Journal of the American Musicological Society*, 2 (1949), pp. 145–58, and W. Waite, 'Discantus, Copula, Organum', *Journal of the American Musicological Society*, 5 (1952), pp. 77–87, and *The Rhythm of Twelfth-Century Polyphony* (New Haven and London, 1954), pp. 120–2. Both of these authors based their discussion on Coussemaker's edition (E. de Coussemaker, ed., *Scriptorum de musica medii aevi nova series* [hereafter *CS*], I, pp. 97–117 and 175–82). F. Reckow (*Der Musiktraktat des Anonymus 4*, II, pp. 35–9, 45) arrived at a new interpretation of Garlandia in part through a series of astute text-critical observations. He demonstrated clearly that the text in Coussemaker was faulty, and that a new edition was needed. For treatments based on the new edition by Reimer (*Johannes de Garlandia*, I–II) see Sanders, 'Consonance and Rhythm', pp. 267–74, Roesner, 'Johannes de Garlandia', pp. 153–6, and Yudkin, 'The Rhythm of Organum Purum'.

[16] As both Reckow and Roesner point out, Garlandia's second and third rules are 'codicils' to the first, addressing specific instances in which the general rule does not apply. The import

Important here is that for Franco in this first rule, the rhythmically significant note-shape takes precedence over all else, presumably including consonance, as a determinant of length. Such a rule is quite in keeping with the innovative character of Franco's treatise, which perhaps for the first time defines precise mensural values and proportionate relationships for individual notes as well as for ligatures.[17] Indeed it may be these newly mensurated notes, the *notae simplices*, to which Franco is referring in this passage. His phrase is 'quicquid notatur in longa *simplici* nota'.[18] Whether the whole sentence is meant to refer to individual notes or to longs, breves, and semibreves in ligatures, it makes clear that it is note-shape, and not harmonic context, that dictates length.

This principle is reinforced further in Franco's second rule (sentence 5 in Excerpt 4): 'Whatever is long requires concord with respect to the tenor; but if it is in discord, the tenor should be silent or should form itself into a concord [*in concordantiam fingat*], as evident here.'

[Iu - - - dea et Iherusalem]

This rule has been discussed by Edward Roesner in his article 'The Performance of Parisian Organum' in the 1979 volume of *Early Music*. After quoting Strunk's translation, that if a long should occur as a discord, the singer should 'let the tenor remain silent or feign concord', Roesner states that 'what Franco had in mind by "feign concord" is equivocal. It seems highly unlikely that he meant the singer to change pitch'.[19] But as both the Latin 'se in concordantiam

---

of the second rule, in Roesner's words, is that 'the modal pattern takes precedence over the first rule at the ends of phrases' (Roesner, 'Johannes de Garlandia', p. 154). In Franco, the 'rule of the *figura*' has become the first one, and presumably applies anywhere in the course of the duplum melody.

[17] On this point see A. Hughes, 'Franco of Cologne', *The New Grove Dictionary*, vi, pp. 794–7, and W. Apel, *The Notation of Polyphonic Music 900–1600*, 5th edn (Cambridge, MA, 1953), pp. 310–15. On the relationship of Franco's treatise to others in the thirteenth and early fourteenth centuries see W. Arlt and M. Haas, 'Pariser modale Mehrstimmigkeit in einem Fragment der Basler Universitätsbibliothek', *Forum Musicologicum*, Basler Studien zur Musikgeschichte 1 (Bern, 1975), pp. 231–41.

[18] The example illustrating these rules, however, is written in modal, not mensural, notation in all manuscripts of the treatise except Paris, Bibliothèque Nationale, MS fonds lat. 16663. Cf. Reckow, *Der Musiktraktat des Anonymus 4*, ii, p. 40 n. 9, and Cserba, ed., *Hieronymus de Moravia*, p. 258.

[19] Roesner, 'The Performance of Parisian Organum', p. 176.

Franco of Cologne on the rhythm of organum purum

fingat' and the musical example following this sentence show, it is precisely a change of pitch in the tenor that Franco does intend. As Reckow had pointed out in his dissertation, no extant version of *Iudea et Iherusalem* exhibits the *E* that is the second tenor note in Franco's example.[20] The reason it is there must be to show how the tenor can 'form itself into a consonance' – in this case an octave – under the successive *e*'s in the duplum, which according to either a modal or a Franconian reading would sound for three *tempora*.[21]

Taken together, the two rules just discussed demonstrate how far Franco has moved away from Johannes de Garlandia in extending the sphere of influence of mensuration. Whereas in Johannes's work the notes of the upper voice of a section of organum were to be lengthened or shortened according to whether they were consonant or dissonant with the underlying tenor, Franco places the rhythmic component first, and then says that if the resultant interval under a long of the duplum happens to be a dissonance, then it is the tenor – not the duplum – that should make the adjustment.

Moving on to the third of Franco's rules (sentence 6 in Excerpt 4), we finally come back to territory shared by both Franco and Johannes. The latter had stated (sentence 14 of Excerpt 5): 'Whatever is taken before a long rest or before a perfect consonance is said to be long.' Franco, using wording that duplicates that of Johannes in large measure, says that 'Whatever is taken immediately before the rest which is called a *finis punctorum* is long, because every penultimate is long.'

---

[20] Reckow, *Der Musiktraktat des Anonymus 4*, II, p. 41 n. 9.

[21] As pointed out in n. 18 above, the example is written in modal notation in all manuscripts of the treatise except Paris, BN, fonds lat. 16663. Cf. the notation of *Iudea et Iherusalem* in Wolfenbüttel, Herzog August Bibliothek, MS 628 Helmst. (W₁), fol. 13, and Florence, Biblioteca Medicea-Laurenziana, MS Plut. 29.1, fol. 65, both readily available in C. Parrish, *The Notation of Medieval Music* (New York, 1959), plates xxviia and xxviib. The version in W₁ is particularly striking, since it begins with what looks like a Franconian *ternaria* without propriety and with perfection, but is in fact a *longa simplex* followed by a *binaria*.

Although the sources for the *Magnus liber* show that singers were not willing to go so far as to follow Franco's suggestion of changing the notes of the plainchant in order to create a consonance with a newly composed duplum, there is nonetheless some evidence in practical sources to show that the successive *e*'s in the duplum of the first phrase of *Iudea et Iherusalem* did indeed create a problematic dissonance with the *F* in the tenor. Reckow (*Der Musiktraktat des Anonymus 4*, II, p. 41 n. 9) found that in a setting of *Benedicamus domino* on fol. 24ᵛ of the Las Huelgas manuscript – one with the same opening phrase as *Iudea et Iherusalem* – the last *binaria* of the phrase (with the pitches *e–c*) had been changed to a *ternaria* with the pitches *f–d–c*, followed by a *longa simplex* on *c*. Thus, instead of having an *e* of three *tempora* against the *F* in the tenor, the Las Huelgas setting forces the *e* of the penultimate ligature to sound for only one *tempus*.

As suggested earlier, Franco's three 'rules of consonance' give such weight to precise rhythmic denotation that one is virtually forced to assume that Franco is dealing with a duplum that is already 'rhythmisch streng festgelegt', as Fritz Reckow put it. This would in turn suggest, as it did for Reckow, that the 'part' referred to in Franco's definition of organum purum as a '*cantus* not measured in its every part' was the tenor.[22] This certainly seems logical, especially in as much as writers such as Anonymous VII and the St Emmeram Anonymous use the term *pars* in reference to a 'voice part', and beyond that in specific reference to the tenor.[23] It may be worth pointing out, however, that neither Johannes de Garlandia nor Franco himself in other parts of his treatise uses the term unequivocally in that way. Thus, before we simply accept Reckow's view and declare the case closed, let us see if Franco himself has anything further to say about the matter by turning our attention to the last sentence in his treatment – a sentence that to my mind is the most interesting and difficult of all.

The last sentence of Franco's treatment of organum purum reads as follows:

Excerpt 6. Franco, *Ars cantus mensurabilis*, chapter XIV, sentence 7
Item notandum, quod quotienscumque in organo puro plures figurae simul in unisono evenerint, sola prima debet percuti, reliquae vero omnes in floratura teneantur, ut hic.

(CSM 18, pp. 81–2)

[22] In Reckow's words: 'Infolgedessen [the statement quoted in n. 4 of the present article] kann sich die Einschränkung, daß das Organum purum ein *cantus non in omni parte sua mensuratus* sei . . ., nicht auf "Teile" (Abschnitte) der Oberstimmen-Melismen – diese sind nach Franco insgesamt rhythmisch streng festgelegt –, sondern nur auf die Tenor- "Stimme" und ihre Haltetöne selbst beziehen; denn diese allein sind (wenn auch nur der Schreibweise nach, nämlich als einfache *longae*) in ihrem Wert für Franco noch nicht exakt "gemessen".' (*Der Musiktraktat des Anonymus 4*, II, p. 41).

[23] Anon. VII: 'tenor est fundamentum motelli et dignior pars' (*CS* I, p. 379b); St Emmeram Anonymous: 'tenor . . . eo quod sit dignior pars' (Sowa, ed., *Ein anonymer glossierter Mensuraltraktat*, p. 92, lines 19f); Johannes de Grocheio: 'Tenor autem est illa pars, supra quam . . .' (E. Rohloff, *Der Musiktraktat des Johannes de Grocheo*, Media Latinitas Musica 2 [Leipzig, 1943], p. 57, line 12); Pseudo-Johannes de Muris: 'dum . . . pars una multum ascendit, reliqua vero multum descendit . . .' (*CS* III, p. 240b). These are cited after Reckow, *Der Musiktraktat des Anonymus 4*, II, p. 41 n. 11.

Franco of Cologne on the rhythm of organum purum

Strunk translates: 'Be it also observed that in organum purum, whenever several similar figures occur in unison, only the first is to be sounded; let all the rest observe the florid style' (Strunk, *Source Readings*, p. 159). He then transcribes the example as follows:

What is one to make of this? As a rendering of the Latin text, Strunk's translation is perfectly adequate. There is only one trouble with it: as far as I can determine, it makes somewhere from little to no sense.

In his article on 'The Performance of Parisian Organum' mentioned above, Edward Roesner places Franco's sentence in apposition to a statement by Anonymous IV dealing with the *longa florata*. In Roesner's words: 'Anonymous IV states that "two notes on the same pitch, whether consonant [with the tenor] or not, are rendered as a *longa florata*" (literally, a "long bedecked with flowers", or even a "fragrant long"). Franco agrees, noting that when several notes on the same pitch occur in succession, only the first is articulated and all together are sung *in floratura*.'[24]

Leaving aside for the time being the question of the relationship of the two passages – indeed, whether they have anything at all to do with each other – one can at least state that Roesner's paraphrase does no particular violence to the Latin. But again one has questions about what the passage should be taken to mean. Roesner cites Franco to make the point that the upper voice of organum purum was performed in a florid style – in a style, moreover, that was not just inherently florid, but one that 'appears to have been subjected to still greater embellishment in performance'.[25] In support of this view, Roesner follows his paraphrase of the problematic sentence in Franco with another passage in Anonymous IV, linked to the first two by the appearance of the word *florata*. Quoting Roesner again: 'Anonymous IV ... recommends that the first, consonant tenor–duplum sonority in a piece be rendered as a *duplex longa florata* – that

---

[24] Roesner, 'The Performance of Parisian Organum', p. 176.   [25] *Ibid.*

is, held out, and executed with a flourish.'[26] Roesner then goes on to portray the outlines of what such embellished, 'floratura' performance might be like, drawing upon the supplement to the treatise of Johannes de Garlandia – presumably attributable to Jerome of Moravia[27] – and Jerome's own treatise on plainchant.

Roesner first discusses the *florificatio vocis* that appears in the section on *colores* in the supplement to Johannes de Garlandia,[28] explaining it by reference to Jerome's *flos harmonicus*, a slow *vibratio* or oscillation between the principal note and an ornamental note a semitone or whole tone above it.[29] Other ornaments Jerome mentions are the *reverberatio*, 'a short, rapid, appoggiatura-like ornament that approaches the main note from below',[30] and the *nota procellaris* ('agitated note'), 'in which the main note oscillates slowly with an ornamental one that appears to lie a half step away, and that has "the definite appearance of movement, but without interrupting the sound or the pitch"'.[31]

Roesner goes on to discuss in rich detail the possibilities for embellishment of organum purum, all presumably capable of being subsumed under Franco's term 'floratura'. Indeed, Roesner says of the *florificatio vocis* that 'Without doubt Jerome's example is also related to the devices mentioned by Franco and Anonymous IV'.[32]

Roesner may well be right, but I must admit to some doubts, at

[26] *Ibid.* [27] I shall refer to the author of this supplement as 'Pseudo-Garlandia'.
[28] Reimer, *Johannes de Garlandia*, I, p. 95.
[29] For Jerome's discussion of the *flos harmonicus*, see Cserba, *Hieronymus de Moravia*, pp. 183–8. It is clear from Jerome's description of the *flos harmonicus* that it is indeed performed as Roesner ('The Performance of Parisian Organum', p. 177) states. What is not so clear is its connection with Pseudo-Garlandia's *florificatio vocis*. Roesner is convinced that the connection is close, and that the *florificatio vocis* 'is not an attempted graphic representation of some medieval ancestor of the early Baroque *trillo*' (p. 177). From his study of the term and concept of *color* in the thirteenth and fourteenth centuries, R. Voogt ('Repetition and Structure in the Three- and Four-Part Conductus of the Notre Dame School' [Ph.D. dissertation, The Ohio State University, 1982], pp. 23–67, esp. pp. 34–48) is equally convinced that the *florificatio vocis* is in fact what Roesner says it is not – namely, a series of repetitions of a single pitch, which in performance would probably sound rather like the Baroque *trillo*. Voogt feels that the model for Pseudo-Garlandia's *florificatio vocis* may have been the repercussive neumes of plainchant, examples of which also appear in the Aquitanian versus (cf. Voogt, 'Repetition and Structure', p. 40, and S. Fuller, 'Aquitanian Polyphony of the Eleventh and Twelfth Centuries' [Ph.D. dissertation, University of California at Berkeley, 1969], III, nos. 20–4).
[30] Roesner, 'The Performance of Parisian Organum', p. 177. For Jerome's description of the *reverberatio* see Cserba, *Hieronymus de Moravia*, pp. 183–7.
[31] 'Nota procellaris in cantu fieri debet cum apparentia quidem motus absque tamen soni vel vocis interruptione' (Cserba, *Hieronymus de Moravia*, p. 185); translation from Roesner, 'The Performance of Parisian Organum', p. 177.
[32] Roesner, 'The Performance of Parisian Organum', p. 177.

Franco of Cologne on the rhythm of organum purum

least vis-à-vis Franco. I am not at all sure that Franco's statement should be related to the types of embellishment Roesner discusses, nor am I sure that it should be placed in apposition to the statements by Anonymous IV on the *longa florata*. Why? To gain an answer, let us return to Franco's statement (Excerpt 6) and analyse it more closely with reference to the interpretations already suggested, and then see if there might not be available to us any alternative interpretative possibilities.

Franco states that whenever, in organum purum, several 'figurae' occur together 'in unisono', only the first ought to be 'percuti'; all of the remainder should be taken 'in floratura'.

Our first question here, I think, should be 'What is a *figura*?' The author of the *Discantus positio vulgaris*[33] does not use the term at all, preferring instead the term *nota*.[34] Johannes de Garlandia begins the second chapter of his work by saying: 'Sequitur de repraesentatione figurarum sive notularum, videlicet quomodo per huiusmodi figuras denotetur longitudo vel brevitas. Unde figura est repraesentatio soni secundum suum modum.' (Reimer, *Johannes de Garlandia*, I, p. 44; 'The following concerns the representation of the *figurae* or *notae*, that is, in what fashion length or brevity may be denoted by means of such figures. Whence, *figura* is the representation of sound according to its mode.')

In Jerome's version of John's treatise the corresponding version of the passage reads: '*Figura*, as it is taken here, is a sign denoting a sound – or sounds – in length and brevity according to its tempus.'[35] Finally, Franco himself had defined *figura* in the following manner at the beginning of his fourth chapter: 'Figura est repraesentatio vocis in aliquo modorum ordinatae, per quod patet quod figurae signifi-

---

[33] Cserba, *Hieronymus de Moravia*, pp. 189–94, and *CS* I, pp. 94b–97; translated by Janet Knapp in 'Two XIII-Century Treatises on Modal Rhythm and the Discant', *Journal of Music Theory*, 6 (1962), pp. 200–16.

[34] The word *nota* had, since Antiquity, carried the meaning of a 'graphic sign', 'mark' or 'character', and was used from late Antiquity (cf. Boethius, *De institutione musica*, bk IV, ch. 3) through the Middle Ages (cf. Jacques de Liège, *Speculum musicae*, bk VI, ch. 72) as the standard designation for the graphic signs representing music. For further discussion and bibliography see M. Huglo, 'Les noms des neumes et leur origine', *Études Grégoriennes*, 1 (1954), pp. 53–67; A.-M. Bautier-Régnier, 'A propos du sens de *neuma* et de *nota* en latin médiéval', *Revue Belge de Musicologie*, 18 (1964), pp. 1–9; B. Stäblein, *Schriftbild der einstimmigen Musik*, Musikgeschichte in Bildern, III: Musik des Mittelalters und der Renaissance, Lfg 4 (Leipzig, 1975), pp. 6–8, 19, 26, 30, and S. Corbin, *Die Neumen*, Paläographie der Musik, I/3 (Cologne, 1977), pp. 3.1–3.5.

[35] 'Figura, ut hic accipitur, est signum denotans sonum vel sonos secundum suum tempus longitudinis atque brevitatis' (Cserba, *Hieronymus de Moravia*, p. 197).

care debent modos, et non e converso.' (CSM 18, p. 29; '*Figura* is a representation of pitch disposed in some one of the modes, through which it is evident that figures ought to signify modes, and not the converse.') The term *figura* is one that for Franco seems to have the significance of a graphic notational sign conveying a fixed rhythmic value or values.[36]

[36] Franco and Johannes de Garlandia are not alone among thirteenth-century theorists in using the term *figura* in this way. Cf. the St Emmeram Anonymous: 'Cum ergo figura sit causa et principium omnis cantus, que et sub certa diminutione temporis seu temporum mensurata compositioni huius artis fons esse dicitur et origo' (Sowa, *Ein anonymer glossierter Mensuraltraktat*, p. 13, lines 9–12). What is unusual about this is that *figura* should have been used at all as a designation for a notational sign. As mentioned in n. 34, the standard medieval designation for the graphic signs used to represent music was *nota*, not *figura*. The most common use of the term *figura* in earlier treatises on music is to indicate a diagram (e.g. Aribo, *De musica* [c. 1070], ed. J. Smits van Waesberghe, CSM 2 [Rome, 1951], pp. 1–5; the *Quaestiones in musica* [c. 1120] attributed to Rudolf of St Trond [1070–1138], ed. R. Steglich, *Publikationen der Internationalen Musik-Gesellschaft*, Beihefte, II/10 [Leipzig, 1911], p. 18), although it is sometimes used to designate pitches, particularly in conjunction with the measurement of the monochord (e.g. Pseudo-Odo, *Dialogus in musica*, ed. M. Gerbert, *Scriptores Ecclesiastici de Musica*, I [St Blasien, 1784]; repr. Milan, 1931], p. 253b; Guido, *Micrologus*, CSM 4 [1955], pp. 91–5; Wilhelm of Hirsau, *Musica*, ed. D. Harbinson, CSM 23 [1975], p. 74). As far as I have been able to determine, the earliest use of *figura* as a term designating practical notational signs seems to be in the thirteenth century, in treatises dealing with mensurable music. Although it is sometimes equated with *nota*, as in both Anon. VII and Anon. IV (cf. Reckow, *Der Musiktraktat des Anonymus 4*, I, pp. 40–1), *figura* – especially when used by itself – carries with it the connotation of a precise, measurable value. This usage must derive from its long tradition as a technical term in mathematics. (Cf. Bede's *De temporum ratione*, ed. C. W. Jones, *Bedae opera de temporibus* [Cambridge, MA, 1943], p. 181, lines 76–82, or the various mathematical works either by or attributed to Gerbert of Aurillac [later Pope Silvester II], ed. N. Bubnov, *Gerberti . . . Opera mathematica (972–1003)* [Berlin, 1899], *passim* [see Index].) Its association with mathematics may likewise have had something to do with use of *figura* in the theory of metrics, although the term already had a connection with poetry via rhetoric. (See, for example, the poem on metrical theory attributed to Walahfrid Strabo, ed. J. Huemer, *Neues Archiv der Gesellschaft für ältere deutsche Geschichtskunde*, 10 [1885], pp. 166–9, where *figura* seems to be synonymous with 'verse'. On rhetorical figures, see L. Arbusow, *Colores rhetorici* [Göttingen, 1948], E. Faral, *Les arts poétiques du XII*ᵉ *et du XIII*ᵉ *siècle* [Paris, 1924], and J. Murphy, *Rhetoric in the Middle Ages* [Berkeley, 1974].) It is worth noting here that the author of the *Summa musicae* (c. 1300), attributed to Johannes de Muris, comments that 'nota idem operatur in cantu, quod figura in metro', and goes on to say that 'Est enim intentio actoris in cantu & actoris in metro una in genere, scilicet ut vox cum materia dictaminis sui (concordet)' (Gerbert, *Scriptores*, III, p. 234b).

A terminological study of *figura* is still lacking; when done, it should provide fascinating insights into the relationships between music and its sister *artes* in the Middle Ages. M. Appel's *Terminologie in den mittelalterlichen Musiktraktaten* (Berlin, 1935), p. 9, and H. P. Gysin's *Studien zum Vokabular der Musiktheorie im Mittelalter* (Amsterdam, 1958), pp. 98–9, 104, are useful starting-points. I offer the above references – whose list is by no means complete – as a small additional contribution to such a study. I should here like to thank Dr Theresia Payr of the *Mittellateinisches Wörterbuch* and Dr Michael Bernhard of the *Lexicon musicum latinum* (both in Munich), and Dr Christoph von Blumröder of the *Handwörterbuch der musikalischen Terminologie* (Freiburg im Breisgau), for permission to work in their respective archives during the summers of 1982 and 1986 in preparation for this essay.

Franco of Cologne on the rhythm of organum purum

The next problematic phrase in Franco's sentence 7 (see Excerpt 6) is 'in unisono'. This could mean 'at the same pitch level' as it does in *Discantus positio vulgaris*: 'A ligature is the binding together of several successive notes – something which cannot be effected with notes of the same pitch' (*in unisono*).[37] If one applies this meaning to sentence 7 in Franco, the phrase would seem to refer to the iterations of the pitch *f* – four times altogether – in the musical example that follows this sentence.[38] Such a view is reinforced by the version of this example that appears in the manuscript Paris, Bibliothèque Nationale, fonds lat. 16663, the one containing Jerome of Moravia's compilation.[39] In that manuscript only the duplum is given, not the tenor, suggesting that it is primarily the duplum with which Franco is concerned here.

But there is yet another possible meaning for the phrase 'in unisono', one that is suggested by Johannes de Garlandia and even by Franco himself. The ninth sentence of Johannes's treatment of organum *in speciali*, in the section devoted to organum *cum alio*, contains the phrase *in unisono*: 'Et eius aequipollentia tantum se tenet *in unisono* usque ad finem alicuius puncti, ut secum convenit secundum aliquam concordantiam.' ('And its equivalence is maintained *in unisono* as far as the end of a section, so that it can come together with it in some consonance.')[40] All modern authors I know of have taken the phrase 'in unisono' here to be a reference to the sustained, single pitch in the tenor.[41] Franco, too, had used the phrase in a similar fashion in the second sentence of the present chapter (cf. Excerpt 3 above): 'Sciendum quod purum organum haberi non potest, nisi supra tenorem ubi sola nota est *in unisono* . . .' ('One should know that organum purum cannot obtain except over a tenor where there is a single note on a single pitch [*in unisono*]'.) Taking the phrase 'in unisono' to be a reference to a sustained pitch in the tenor, one might translate the first clause of Franco's now-familiar sentence 7 (Excerpt 6) as 'whenever several figures come

---

[37] 'Ligatura est plurium notarum invicem conjunctarum ligatio, quae quidem *in unisono* fieri non debet' (Cserba, *Hieronymus de Moravia*, p. 190; my italics). The translation is by Janet Knapp ('Two XIII-Century Treatises', p. 203).
[38] This interpretation is advanced by both Voogt ('Repetition and Structure', pp. 40–3) and Roesner ('The Performance of Parisian Organum', p. 176) in their respective interpretations of the passage in question here.
[39] See Cserba, *Hieronymus de Moravia*, p. 259.
[40] Cf. n. 14 above.
[41] See, for example, the works cited in n. 15 above.

together over a single pitch in the tenor'. Still, this interpretation is not one that I wish to push too far – at least, not yet.

This brings us to the final clause in the sentence (Excerpt 6) and to the last and most difficult pair of words of all: *percuti* and *floratura*. The clause reads as follows: 'sola prima debet percuti, reliquae vero omnes in floratura teneantur'.[42] As we saw earlier, Strunk translates this phrase 'only the first is to be sounded; let all the rest observe the florid style'.[43] Roesner's version is 'when several notes on the same pitch occur in succession, only the first is articulated and all together are sung in floratura'.[44] I should like to suggest that there is yet another way to read this passage.

Both *percuti* and *floratura* are words that are quite rare in writings on music, not only in the twelfth and thirteenth centuries, but virtually throughout the Middle Ages. Of the two, 'percuti', the passive infinitive of the verb *percutio* (to strike), and its nominative form, *percussio*, are the more common, being used in Boethius, Cassiodorus, Isidore and other writers to refer to either the striking or plucking of the strings of an instrument, or to the vibrations created by such striking.[45]

At the same time, though, there is another usage of these terms that has a venerable tradition of its own that starts in Antiquity and continues through the thirteenth century and beyond. Although it is most closely connected with the arts of grammar and rhetoric, this usage is at the same time intrinsically linked to music. I am referring here to the tradition of demarcating or 'beating' the temporal units of metric poetry, described not just via the words *percutio* or *percussio*, but also with the terms *ictus* and *plausus*.[46]

The fundamental principle of *percussio* is described well by the fourth-century grammarian Marius Victorinus: 'est autem *percussio* cuiuslibet metri in pedes divisio'[47] ('*Percussio* is the division of any

---

[42] CSM 18, pp. 81–2.
[43] Strunk, *Source Readings*, p. 159.
[44] Roesner, 'The Performance of Parisian Organum', p. 176.
[45] Cf. Boethius, *De institutione musica libri quinque*, ed. G. Friedlein (Leipzig, 1867), I, 3, p. 189, lines 15–19, 22–3, and I, 31, p. 222, lines 6–12; Cassiodorus, *Institutiones*, ed. R. A. B. Mynors (Oxford, 1937), II, 5, sections 6 and 7, also in Gerbert, *Scriptores*, I, pp. 16–17; Isidore, *Etymologiarum sive Originum libri xx*, ed. W. M. Lindsay, 2 vols. (Oxford, 1911), bk III, section 22, also in Gerbert, *Scriptores*, I, pp. 23–4.
[46] For a treatment of these terms in Antiquity, see R. Wagner, 'Der Berliner Notenpapyrus, nebst Untersuchungen zur rhythmischen Notierung und Theorie', *Philologus*, 77 (1921), pp. 256–310, esp. pp. 301–7.
[47] '*Percutitur* vero versus anapaestus praecipue per dipodian, interdum et per singulos pedes.

Franco of Cologne on the rhythm of organum purum

metre into feet'). Perhaps the earliest evidence for *percussio* as a *terminus technicus* is found in Cicero, *De oratore*: 'Among the variety of metres, the frequent use of the iambus and the tribrach is forbidden to the orator by Aristotle, the master of your school, Catulus. They nonetheless invade our oratory and conversational style by natural affinity; but the *percussiones* of their rhythms are (strongly) marked, and their feet are short.'[48] Quintilian's *Institutio oratoria* provides a number of instances. In book 9, for example, in urging the orator not to employ verse, such as iambic trimeter, in prose, he says: 'One can refer to [this verse] as either trimetrum or senarium, since it has six feet and three *percussiones*.'[49]

That these *percussiones* were actually beaten, and that their beating could at times be rather noisy, is suggested by a passage in Rufinus's commentary on the metres of Terence. Bassus says to Nero: 'Moreover the iambic: Whenever it assumes feet of the dactylic genus, the iambic appears to end unless you should dispose it by means of the *percussio* so that whenever you stamp your foot [*pedem supplodes*], you strike an iamb; therefore those places of the *percussio* do not receive anything other than the iamb and a tribrach equal to it, or they will have exhibited another species of metre.'[50]

The examples I have just cited are only a few among a great many that could be adduced to document the use of *percussio* in Antiquity. For the Middle Ages, however, the *locus classicus* for both the theory and practice of *percutio*, as well as *ictus* and *plausus*, is Augustine.[51] His

---

est autem *percussio* cuiuslibet metri in pedes divisio.' Marius Victorinus, *Artis grammaticae libri III*, in H. Keil, *Grammatici latini*, 8 vols. (Leipzig, 1855–80), VI, p. 75, lines 26–9 (my italics).

[48] 'Nam cum sint numeri plures, iambum et trochaeum frequentem segregat ab oratore Aristoteles, Catule, vester; qui natura tamen incurrunt ipsi in orationem sermonemque nostrum, sed sunt insignes *percussiones* eorum numerorum e minuti pedes.' Cicero, *De oratore*, ed. and trans. H. H. Rackham (Cambridge, MA, 1942), III, 182–3, pp. 144–5 (my italics; the translation is a modified version of Rackham's). See also *De oratore*, III, 185–6, and *Orator*, ed. and trans. H. M. Hubbell (London, 1952), 198–9.

[49] 'Trimetrum et senarium promisce dicere licet, sex enim pedes, tres *percussiones* habet.' Quintilian, *Institutio oratoria*, ed. and trans. H. E. Butler (London, 1953), IX, 4, 75, pp. 548–9 (my italics). See also *Institutio oratoria* IX, 4, 51–2, and XI, 3, 108–9.

[50] 'Iambicus autem, cum pedes etiam dactylici generis adsumat, desinit iambicus videri, nisi *percussione* ita moderaveris, ut, cum pedem supplodes, iambum ferias; ideoque illa loca *percussionis* non recipiunt alium quam iambum et ei parem tribrachyn, aut alterius exhibuerint metri speciem.' Rufinus, *Commentarium in metra Terentiana*, in Keil, *Grammatici latini*, VI, p. 555, lines 23–7 (my italics).

[51] Edition and French translation by G. Finaert and F.-J. Thonnard, *De musica libri sex*, Oeuvres de Saint Augustin, 1ʳᵉ série: Opuscules, VII: *Dialogues philosophiques*, IV: *La musique* (Bruges, 1947); English translation by R. C. Taliaferro in *Writings of Saint Augustine*, II, Fathers of the Church 4 (New York, 1947).

De musica abounds in references to these terms.[52] For our purposes two will have to suffice.

In book II, chapter 13, the master says that he will run through several poetic feet 'with the accompanying *plausus*' so that the disciple may see whether there is any flaw. He tells the student: 'Fix your ears on the sound and your eyes on the beat [*plausus*]. For the hand beating time is not to be heard but seen, and note must be taken of the amount of time given to the arsis and to the thesis.'[53] After this has been done, the student says: 'I certainly wonder how those feet with a division in a ratio of one to two could have been beaten [*percutio*] to this time.'[54]

In book IV, chapter 1, the following dialogue takes place between master and student: M. 'What quantity must the rest be when it is repeated? D. One tempus, the length of one short syllable [*brevis*]. M. Come now, beat [*percute*] this meter, not with the voice, but with the hand. D. I have. M. Then beat the anapest in the same way.'[55]

As mentioned, many more examples of the use of *percutio* and *plausus* in Augustine could be cited. For our purposes, though, it is necessary to ask whether any of this might have been known to Franco in the mid- to late thirteenth century. The answer, I believe, must be 'Yes'. Evidence for this comes from several aspects of Franco's treatise itself – such as his justification for the perfect long of three tempora[56] – and from at least two authors intimately involved

---

[52] Since there is no *Index verborum* for the edition, I provide a list of these references here, listed by book, chapter, and section: *Percutio*: I, I, 1; II, XI, 20; II, XIII, 24; IV, I, 1; IV, VII, 8; VI, V, 11; VI, VIII, 20. *Percussio*: II, XI, 20; II, XI, 21; IV, II, 2; IV, XIV, 24; VI, X, 25. *Plaudo*: I, V, 10; I, XIII, 27; II, X, 18; II, XIII, 24; II, XIII, 25; II, XIV, 26; III, IV, 9; III, VII, 15; III, VII, 16; IV, II, 2; IV, XI, 12; IV, XVI, 30; IV, XVI, 33; V, XI, 24; VI, I, 1; VI, X, 27; *Plausus*: I, VI, 11; I, XIII, 27; II, XI, 20; II, XIII, 24; II, XIII, 25; II, XIV, 26; III, III, 5; III, III, 6; III, IV, 7; III, IV, 8; III, IV, 9; III, IV, 10; III, V, 11; III, V, 12; III, VII, 15; III, VIII, 18; IV, I, 1; IV, II, 2; IV, VII, 8; IV, XVII, 35; V, XI, 24; VI, X, 27; VI, XIV, 47. *Ictus*: I, IV, 9.

[53] 'Intende ergo et aurem in sonum, et in *plausum* oculos: non enim audiri, sed videri opus est plaudentem manum, et animadverti acriter quanta temporis mora in levatione, quanta in positione sit.' Augustine, *De musica*, II, XIII, 24; Taliaferro translation, p. 233.

[54] 'Vehementer admiror quomodo eo *percuti* potuerint illi pedes, quorum divisio simpli et dupli ratione constat.' *Ibid*.; my italics.

[55] 'M. Quantum ergo silendum est, dum repetitur? D. Unum tempus, quod est unius brevis syllabae spatium. M. Age, jam *percute* hoc metrum, non voce, sed *plausu*. D. Feci. M. *Percute* etiam hoc modo anapaestum. D. Et hoc feci.' Augustine, *De musica*, IV, I, 1; Taliaferro, p. 260.

[56] Franco defines the perfect long as follows: '(6) Longa perfecta prima dicitur et principalis. (7) Nam in ea omnes aliae includuntur, ad eam etiam omnes aliae reducuntur. (8) *Perfecta dicitur eo quod tribus temporibus mensuratur*' (CSM 18, p. 29; my italics). His justification for this new concept of the long is: 'Est enim ternarius numerus inter numeros perfectissimus pro eo quod a summa trinitate, quae vera est et pura perfectio, nomen sumpsit' (CSM

Franco of Cologne on the rhythm of organum purum

with mid-thirteenth-century Parisian intellectual life with whom Franco may have had contact: Roger Bacon and John of Garland.[57]

In his *Opus majus* and *Opus tertium*, both apparently completed in 1267,[58] Bacon exhorts his colleagues to the study of the liberal arts with the aim of 'reforming the teaching of Christian wisdom', as Etienne Gilson puts it.[59] As one might expect of Bacon, his primary focus is upon the mathematical arts, including music. But whereas Boethius is his prime authority for arithmetic, his chief witness for music is not Boethius, but rather Augustine.[60] Accordingly, Bacon spends much of his time discussing metrics, drawing a large portion of his discussion in the *Opus tertium* directly from Augustine, specifically from the second book. At the end of this section, just before turning to a defence of mathematics in general, he states that

18, pp. 29–30; my italics). I would posit that the source of this justification was Augustine. Cf. Augustine's statement on the perfection of the number three in I, XII, 20 of *De musica*: 'Quare in *ternario numero* quamdam esse *perfectionem* vides, quia totus est: habet enim principium, medium et finem' (Finaert and Thonnard, p. 70; my italics).

[57] On Bacon, see A. B. Emden, 'Bacon', *A Biographical Register of the University of Oxford to A.D. 1500*, I (Oxford, 1957), pp. 87–8. The principal source of biographical material for Emden's article is S. C. Easton, *Roger Bacon and his Search for a Universal Science* (New York, 1952). See also J. S. Brewer, ed., *Fr. Rogeri Bacon opera quaedam hactenus inedita*, Rerum Britannicarum Medii Aevi Scriptores (Rolls Series) 15 (London, 1859; repr. Frankfurt, 1964), Preface, and R. B. Burke, trans., *The Opus majus of Roger Bacon* (New York, 1928; repr. 1962), Introduction. For the place of Bacon's work within the intellectual life of the thirteenth century, see P. Kibre, 'The *Quadrivium* in the Thirteenth Century Universities', *Arts libéraux et philosophie au moyen âge: Actes du quatrième congrès international de philosophie médiévale*, 1967 (Montreal, 1969), pp. 175–91, and L. Ellinwood, 'Ars musica', *Speculum*, 20 (1945), pp. 290–9. The starting-point for any study of John of Garland must be L. J. Paetow, *The Morale Scolarium of John of Garland, with an Introduction to his Life and Works*, Memoirs of the University of California, IV/2 (Berkeley, 1927). See also Paetow's *The Arts Course at Medieval Universities, with Special Reference to Grammar and Rhetoric*, The University of Illinois: The University Studies, III/7 (Urbana-Champaign, 1910), and T. Lawler, *The Parisiana Poetria of John of Garland*, Yale Studies in the History of English 182 (New Haven, 1974), Introduction.

[58] *Opus majus*, ed. J. H. Bridges, *The 'Opus majus' of Roger Bacon* (London, 1900; repr. Frankfurt, 1964); *Opus tertium*, ed. Brewer, *Fr. Rogeri Bacon opera quaedam hactenus inedita*, pp. 1–310. According to Easton, *Roger Bacon*, p. 153, the two works were composed in the same year. Bacon's own remarks in the *Opus tertium* (e.g. 'Nam secundum quod exposui in Opere Majori...', Brewer, *Opus tertium*, p. 228) make it clear that the *Opus majus* was the earlier of the two works.

[59] E. Gilson, *History of Christian Philosophy in the Middle Ages* (New York, 1955), p. 294. This remark was made specifically with regard to the *Opus majus*, but certainly pertains to its companion work as well. On the relationship of these two works to each other and to Bacon's *Opus minus*, see Easton, *Roger Bacon*, pp. 144–66.

[60] Cf. Waite, *The Rhythm of Twelfth-Century Polyphony*, p. 36. The fact that Boethius plays such an important role in Bacon's discussion of arithmetic, but a distinctly secondary role in his discussion of music, is not mentioned by Waite, but it further buttresses his own case for the influence of Augustine on the development of the system of the rhythmic modes (*ibid.*, pp. 29–39).

motions of various kinds – gesticulation, exultation, leaping, clapping, singing, and all the movements of the body – are an important component of music. He continues: 'This indeed is a necessary part of music, just as Augustine teaches in the second book of his *Musica*, saying that *plausus* is necessary, because delight is necessary not only for the hearing but for the eye' – a direct reference to book II, chapter 13 quoted above.[61]

That the theory and practice of *percutio* were known not just to students of theology, but to poets and musicians as well, is suggested finally by the use of the term in a work by John of Garland – a man himself mentioned favourably by Roger Bacon in 1272,[62] and one whose putative connections with music are well known.[63] In his *Parisiana poetria de arte prosaica, metrica, et rithmica*, written in the first half of the thirteenth century, John provides a rather full discussion of poetic metres in his chapters on *Rithmica*.[64] As the following excerpt will show, this discussion makes extensive use of the concept of *percussio*, beginning with discussion of the simplest type of rhythmic poetry, the iambic dimeter:

A simpliciori igitur erit inchoandum, scilicet a rithmo qui constat ex duabus *percussionibus*, quia, cum rithmus imitetur metrum in aliquo, illud metrum quod est breuius constat ex duabus *percussionibus*, sicut iambicum dimetrum, quod constat ex duobus metris, et metrum ex duabus *percussionibus* ... Rithmus dispondaicus continet quattuor *percussiones*, que sunt ex quattuor dictionibus uel partibus earundem dictionum. (Lawler, *Parisiana poetria*, p. 160; my italics.)

[61] 'Illa enim est pars necessaria musicae, sicut *Augustinus docet secundo Musicae*, dicens quod *plausus* necessarius est, quia non solum est delectatio auditus necessaria, sed visus.' Bacon, *Opus tertium*, cap. LXIV, ed. Brewer, *Opus tertium*, pp. 267–8 (my italics). Cf. the passage quoted from Augustine, II, XIII, 24, cited in n. 53 above.
[62] Cf. Paetow, *Morale scolarium*, pp. 95–6. See also Lawler, *Parisiana poetria*, p. xi.
[63] Among the many works attempting to answer this question, see in particular A. Machabey, 'Jean de Garlande, compositeur', *Revue Musicale*, no. 221 (1953), pp. 20–2; W. Waite, 'Johannes de Garlandia: Poet and Musician', *Speculum*, 35 (1960), pp. 179–95; R. A. Rasch, *Iohannes de Garlandia en de ontwikkeling van de voor-Franconische notatie*, Musicological Studies 20 (Brooklyn, 1969), and most recently Reimer, *Johannes de Garlandia*, I, pp. 1–17. Reimer feels that John of Garland the poet and Johannes de Garlandia the author of *De mensurabili musica* are not the same person.
[64] Ed. Lawler, *Parisiana poetria*. For a study of the relationship of John's *Parisiana poetria* to the contemporanous Parisian sequence and, in turn, to the theory and practice of rhythm in the late twelfth and thirteenth centuries, see M. Fassler, 'The Role of the Parisian Sequence in the Evolution of Notre-Dame Polyphony', *Speculum*, 62 (1987), pp. 345–74. Like the present author, Fassler underscores the importance of the beat or *ictus*, which John of Garland describes with the term *percussio* (see in particular pp. 358–61 of Fassler's study).

Franco of Cologne on the rhythm of organum purum

('We should begin with what is simplest, namely with a rhymed poem whose line consists of two stresses, for rhymed poetry imitates quantitative poetry in various ways, and the shortest quantitative measure consists of two stresses; iambic dimeter, for instance, has two measures, and each measure has two stresses ... A dispondaic couplet has four stresses, whether in four separate words or as parts of the same words.' *Ibid.*, p. 161)

Clearly, the concept of *percussio* as a rhythmic beat or stress was current in mid-thirteenth-century Paris. That it had also penetrated into musical theory by the late thirteenth century is demonstrated by its use in the music treatise of Johannes de Grocheio. In his description of the ductia, we find the following words: 'A ductia is an untexted musical piece [*sonus*] measured with an appropriate beat [*percussio*]. I say ... "with a proper beat" because strokes [*ictus*] measure it and the motion of the person performing it, and they impel one's spirit to ornate movement according to the art that they call dancing, and they measure its motion in *ductiae* and *choreii*.'[65] Later he makes the statement: 'To compose a ductia or stantipes is to demarcate the piece via puncta and proper *percussiones* [beats].'[66]

I believe that we have now heard enough testimony to suggest a new reading for *percuti* in Franco's seventh sentence. But what to make of *floratura*? This word is so rare that there is only one witness to it in the entire card file of the *Mittellateinisches Wörterbuch* in Munich, not to mention any other of the medieval Latin dictionaries or glossaries I have consulted.[67] That single reference is the one found

---

[65] 'Est autem ductia sonus illitteratus, cum decenti percussione mensuratus. Dico ... *cum recta percussione*, eo quod ictus eam mensurant et motum facientis et excitant animum hominis ad ornate movendum secundum artem, quam ballare vocant, et eius motum mensurant in ductiis et choreiis.' Johannes de Grocheio, [*De musica*], ed. E. Rohloff, *Der Musiktraktat des Johannes de Grocheo*, Media Latinitas Musica 2 (Leipzig, 1943), p. 52, lines 38–44, and Rohloff, ed., *Die Quellenhandschriften zum Musiktraktat des Johannes de Grocheio* (Leipzig, n.d.), p. 136, lines 13–20.

[66] 'Componere ductiam et stantipedem est sonum per puncta et rectas *percussiones* in ductia et stantipede determinare.' Rohloff, *Der Musiktraktat*, p. 53, lines 23–4; *Die Quellenhandschriften*, p. 136, lines 147–8.

[67] The lexica and glossaries consulted include the following: F. Arnaldi, *Latinitatis italicae medii aevi ... lexicon imperfectum* (Brussels, 1939); A. Bartal, *Glossarium mediae et infimae latinitatis regni hungariae* (Leipzig, 1901; repr. Hildesheim, 1970); J. H. Baxter and C. Johnson, *Medieval Latin Word List from British and Irish Sources* (Oxford, 1934); A. Blaise, *Lexicon latinitatis medii aevi*, Corpus Christianorum, Continuatio Medievalis (Turnhout, 1975); A. Castro, *Glosarios latino-españoles de la edad media* (Madrid, 1936); L. Diefenbach, *Glossarium latino-germanicum mediae et infimae aetatis* (Frankfurt, 1857); C. Du Cange, *Glossarium mediae et infimae latinitatis* (Niort, 1883–7; repr. Graz, 1954); A. Forcellini, *Totius latinitatis lexicon* (Padua, 1864–98); *Glossarium mediae latinitatis sueciae* (Stockholm, 1968); R. E. Latham, *Revised Medieval Latin Word List from British and Irish Sources* (Oxford, 1965); *Lexicon mediae et infimae latinitatis polonorum* (Wrocław, Warsaw, Kraków and Gdańsk,

Charles M. Atkinson

in Franco. There is, however, at least one other appearance of the word that may finally solve the puzzle of *percuti* and *floratura*.

In the seventh book of his *Speculum musicae*, Jacques de Liège, a great admirer and ardent glossator of Franco's treatise, makes the following statement in his chapter 'Quid sit cantus mensurabilis':

> Haec et alia multa ars requirit mensurabilis . . . et propterea cantus hic dicitur quia in eo distinctae voces simul sub aliqua temporis morula certa vel incerta proferuntur. Dico autem 'incerta' propter organum duplum quod ubique non est certa temporis mensura mensuratum ut, in *floraturis*, in penultimis ubi supra vocem unam tenoris in discantu multae sonantur voces.[68]

'The art of mensurable [music] requires these and many other things . . . and for that reason [this type of] cantus is discussed at this point, because in it diverse pitches are performed under some determinate or indeterminate sustaining of the time. I say "indeterminate", moreover, on account of organum duplum, which is not measured everywhere in a fixed measure of time, as for example in *floraturae* on penultimates [notes or syllables] where many pitches are sounded in the discant over one pitch of the tenor' (my italics).

Jacques's use and description of *floratura* forges a direct terminological and conceptual link with Franco. The problematic final

---

1975); W.-H. Maigne d'Arnis, *Lexicon manuale ad scriptores mediae et infimae latinitatis* (Paris, 1866); J. F. Niermeyer, *Mediae latinitatis lexicon minus* (Leiden, 1976); A. Souter, *A Glossary of Later Latin to 600 A.D.* (Oxford, 1949); *Thesavrvs lingvae latinae* (Leipzig, 1940–).

[68] Jacques de Liège, *Speculum musicae*, ed. R. Bragard, *Jacobi Leodiensis Specvlvm mvsicae*, CSM 3 (1973), bk vii, cap. ii, pp. 7–8. The edition reads 'fioraturis' instead of 'floraturis'. For the passage in question, however, both of the manuscripts containing it (Florence, Biblioteca Medicea-Laurenziana, Plut. 29.16, fol. 122ᵛ, and Paris, Bibliothèque Nationale, fonds lat. 7207, fol. 275ᵛ) have 'floraturis', with 'l', not 'i', in the first syllable. I wish to thank Dr Anna Lenzuni, of the Biblioteca Medicea-Laurenziana, and Dr François Avril, of the Bibliothèque Nationale, for their assistance in confirming these readings.

I should also like to thank Professor Peter Lefferts for informing me (in a letter of 30 November 1988) of two further references to *floritura/floratura*. The first is in maxim 11 of rubric xiii of Robertus de Handlo's *Regule*, in which Handlo gives examples of the types of music exhibiting the fifth of Franco's rhythmic modes, consisting of breves and semibreves (I quote from the draft text of Professor Lefferts's forthcoming edition of the treatise): 'Ab hoc siquidem modo proveniunt hoketi omnes, rundelli, ballade, coree, cantifractus, estampete, floriture, . . .' (cf. *CS* i, p. 402b). The second reference occurs in both versions of the *quartum principale* of the *Quatuor principalia* (*CS* iii, p. 354b=*CS* iv, p. 278a): 'Discantus enim sic dividitur . . . alius est copulatus qui dicitur copula, id est floritura.' As Lefferts points out, this passage is a gloss on Franco's initial mention of *copula* as a type of discant in chapter 2 of the *Ars cantus mensurabilis* (CSM 18, p. 26). As both of these references would suggest, the relationship between *copula* and *floritura* is one that deserves a thoroughgoing treatment. (I should note here that the *quartum principale*, glossing the first sentence of Franco's chapter on organum purum, says 'organum proprie sumptum mensuram non retinet' [*CS* iii, p. 363b=*CS* iv, p. 297a], but does not mention *floratura* in this context; indeed, it does not treat of sentence 7 of the chapter at all.)

22

Franco of Cologne on the rhythm of organum purum

sentence (sentence 7, Excerpt 6 above) of Franco's discussion of organum purum can now be read as follows: 'It should be noted that whenever in organum purum several *figurae* come together over a single pitch [in the tenor], only the first should be beaten in fixed rhythm; all the rest should be taken in *floratura* [that is, performed in a rhythmically free fashion].'

The formal picture one gets from this passage in Franco and its parallel in Jacques de Liège is one in which a section of organum begins over a penultimate in the tenor with the duplum in fixed rhythm, the rhythm of discant, but which ends in non-fixed rhythm. It is thus reminiscent of a passage in the de la Fage Anonymous, in which the author states that if one wants to make discant more beautiful and elegant, one can place a section of organum at the end, 'on either the ultimate or penultimate syllable of the text'.[69] This is of course a technique found rather frequently in the polyphony of both St Martial and Notre Dame. It is also a technique documented by Franco himself. In chapter XI of his work, as mentioned earlier, Franco had stated that discant should continue in its measured rhythm 'as far as the *penultimate*, where such measure is not attendant, there being rather a *point of organum in that place*'.[70]

Following Franco's and Jacques's descriptions, then, one would progress from a section of discant to a section of organum on the penultimate note or syllable in the tenor. The performer would then be expected to take the first ligature of the duplum in the organum section in measured rhythm; the remainder would then be in unmeasured rhythm. (I would posit that it may have been this division into measured and unmeasured parts that Franco alludes to when he says that 'organum is a kind of music not measured in its every part'.)[71]

---

[69] 'Sed si forte in fine clausulae in *ultima* aut in *penultima dictionis sillaba*, ut discantus pulchrior et facetior habeatur et ab auscultantibus libentius audiatur, aliquos *organi modulos* volueris admiscere licet facere.' A. Seay, ed., 'An Anonymous Treatise from St. Martial', *Annales Musicologiques*, 5 (1957), pp. 7–42; passage quoted from p. 33 (my italics).

[70] CSM 10, p. 75 (my italics), cf. n. 12 above.

[71] Cf. n. 22 above. There is yet a further interpretation of Franco's statement that should at least be mentioned here as a hypothesis. As discussed earlier in this paper, some parts of organum purum seem in Franco's view to involve a duplum whose notation is rhythmically fixed – 'rhythmisch streng festgelegt', in Reckow's words. It may be no accident that the musical example manifesting this conception is the opening section or 'pars' of *Iudea et Iherusalem*, which in both the practical sources and the manuscripts of Franco's treatise is written in a clear first-mode pattern. It was this example and the 'rules of consonance' connected with it that led Reckow to hypothesise that Franco might have been working

In addition to their witness to certain structural features of organum, Franco's remarks also tell us something important about the performance of this genre. Specifically, they allow us to confirm for at least some parts of organum purum a performance style that is relatively free and unfettered from a rhythmic point of view.[72] The de la Fage Anonymous had described this style as being 'joined with its cantus not note against note, but with an unlimited multiplicity and a kind of wondrous flexibility'. 'It ought to begin', he says, 'with one of the consonances or together with the chant, and from there, in a modulating or frolicking fashion, as it seems appropriate and as the organisator wishes, it ought to ascend above or descend below and finally place a terminus at the octave or together with the chant.'[73] Later on, the same author says that the ascent and descent, 'in a modulating or frolicking fashion', should take place 'cito' (quickly).[74] Johannes de Garlandia's remarks about the rhythmic freedom of organum *in speciali* are well known, thanks to Professor Roesner's work, as are the views of the author of the *Discantus positio vulgaris* (thanks to Professor Knapp). The *Discantus positio* states that

   with settings of organum written in modal notation or perhaps even rewritten in mensural notation. Evidence that would support this view has been offered by Roesner, who points out ('Johannes de Garlandia on *organum in speciali*', p. 159 n. 85) that in the manuscript Berlin, Staatsbibliothek der Stiftung Preussischer Kulturbesitz, lat. 4° 523, material notated in *modus non rectus* in other sources has been re-notated mensurally. Reckow's hypothesis thus seems quite plausible. Under such circumstances it could well be that the one 'part' of organum purum still being performed in its original manner in Franco's time was that 'on penultimates', which – even if notated in *figurae* suggesting fixed rhythmic values – was to be performed in a rhythmically free fashion.

[72] With this point in mind, one contemplating an edition of this music would be well advised to read the remarks by F. Zaminer, *Der vatikanische Organum-Traktat (Ottob. lat. 3025): Organum-Praxis der frühen Notre Dame-Schule und ihrer Vorstufen*, Münchner Veröffentlichungen zur Musikgeschichte 2 (Tutzing, 1959), pp. 99–100, and H. H. Eggebrecht, 'Organum purum', *Musikalische Edition im Wandel des historischen Bewußtseins*, ed. T. Georgiades (Kassel, 1971), pp. 93–112, esp. pp. 110–12. See also J. Yudkin, 'The Rhythm of Organum Purum', especially pp. 374–6.

[73] 'Organum autem non aequalitate punctorum sed infinita multiplicitate ac mira quadam flexibilitate cantui suo concordat in aliqua, ut dictum est, consonantiarum, aut cum cantu debet incipere et inde modulando vel lasciviendo, prout oportuerit et organizator voluerit, vel ascendere superius vel inferius descendere, tandem vero in diapason aut cum cantu terminum ponere' (Seay, 'An Anonymous Treatise', p. 35, sent. 11). On the treatise itself, and specifically on this passage and its significance, see H. H. Eggebrecht, 'Die Mehrstimmigkeitslehre von ihren Anfängen bis zum 12. Jahrhundert', *Die mittelalterliche Lehre von der Mehrstimmigkeit*, Geschichte der Musiktheorie 5 (Darmstadt, 1984), pp. 9–87, esp. pp. 59–66. Eggebrecht points out that the edition by Seay needs to be revised to incorporate readings from Barcelona, Biblioteca Central, MS 883, and Parma, Biblioteca Palatina, MS parm. 1158. My translation is a modified version of that by E. Sanders ('Consonance and Rhythm', p. 265).

[74] Seay, 'An Anonymous Treatise', p. 35, sent. 13.

Franco of Cologne on the rhythm of organum purum

ligatures of more than four notes 'are not, as it were, subject to rule, but are executed at pleasure [*ad placitum*]. These are associated particularly with the organum and the conductus.'[75] Finally, the phrase applied to organum by the *Discantus positio* is echoed by the author of a supplement to Robert Kilwardby's *De ortu scientiarum*, written shortly before 1250.[76]

The anonymous author of this work provides stylistic descriptions of discant, of cantilena 'quam Gallici "motez" vocant', of conductus, and finally of the type of music 'qui proprie "organum" appellatur, quod solum a duobus diversis poterit modulari'. Of this genre 'which is properly called organum', he goes on to say that 'while the lower voice is held in a rather long and protracted fashion, the upper voice scampers about *ad placitum*' ('dum inferior vox longius protrahendo tenetur, superior *ad placitum* discurrit' – my italics).[77]

As the testimony of the 'Kilwardby Anonymous' and other authors makes clear, a free style of performance – 'ad placitum' – was held to be a central feature of organum purum in the thirteenth century. By taking a fresh look at Franco and the terms he uses to describe organum purum we may now be able to say that despite his attempt to bring as much polyphonic music as possible under rational, mensural control – an understandable Scholastic position[78] – Franco is not quite the 'compleat mensuralist' that he has been thought to be. Instead, even he is forced to admit that parts of organum purum must be performed in a rhythmically free fashion –

---

[75] 'Quodsi plures quam quatuor fuerint, tunc quasi regulis non subjacent, sed *ad placitum* proferuntur. Quae etiam ad organum et conductum pertinent singulariter' (Cserba, *Hieronymus de Moravia*, p. 190; my italics). Translation by Janet Knapp ('Two XIII-Century Treatises', p. 203).

[76] On Kilwardby, who taught in Paris c. 1240, see pp. xi–xvii of the Introduction to the edition of *De ortu scientiarum* by A. G. Judy O.P., Auctores Britannici Medii Aevi 4 (Oxford and Toronto, 1976) and M. Haas, 'Studien zur mittelalterlichen Musiklehre I: Eine Übersicht über die Musiklehre im Kontext der Philosophie des 13. und frühen 14. Jahrhunderts', *Forum Musicologicum*, 3 (Winterthur, 1982), pp. 323–456, esp. pp. 403–8. According to Judy (*op. cit.*, pp. xvii–xxxi), the supplement is contained in the manuscripts Munich, Bayerische Staatsbibliothek, clm 28186, fols. 258r–259^v; Florence, Biblioteca Medicea Laurenziana, Plut. XXVII, dext., cod. 9, fol. 143^v–145^r; and Kraków, Biblioteka Jagiellońska 754, fols. 42, 43^v, 44^r. It has been discussed briefly by F. Reckow on p. 283 of his '"Ratio potest esse, quia . . .": Über die Nachdenklichkeit mittelalterlicher Musiktheorie', *Die Musikforschung*, 37 (1984), pp. 281–8. I am very grateful to Professor Reckow for information about the treatise and the forthcoming edition of its text.

[77] The quotations are from the draft text of the edition of the 'Kilwardby Anonymous' now being prepared by Dr Ulrike Hascher-Burger. I am most grateful to Dr Hascher-Burger for allowing me to quote from her text before its publication.

[78] Cf. n. 11 of this study.

in *floratura*. He thus takes a logical place within the tradition of thirteenth-century writing about music, and our picture of both that music and its theory is richer and more consistent than ever before.

The Ohio State University

[9]

THE *COPULA* ACCORDING TO JOHANNES DE GARLANDIA

JEREMY YUDKIN

There are some fundamental questions about the music of Notre Dame, the answers to which have remained elusive. In past research the emphasis has been on transcription of the music, relying in difficult passages on solutions which are said to be "musically convincing" or "reasonable" – judgements which, though they may be sound in themselves, are not necessarily based on historical criteria.

This rush to transcribe has a tendency to obscure some of the underlying problems rather than to clarify them. A similar situation has obtained with the theorists. Inaccurate texts, and careless translations, have hindered many otherwise useful investigations.

In the past ten or fifteen years some critical editions have replaced the inadequate texts provided for us over a hundred years ago by Coussemaker. It appears therefore to be an appropriate time to return to a careful and thorough analysis of the treatises, which can provide us with some insights unobtainable through any other means.

This article will restrict itself to consideration of a single treatise, and a single concept in that treatise. Of the three species of music as Johannes de Garlandia described them *(discantus, copula et organum)*, the *copula* is certainly the least understood. Garlandia was writing at a time nearest to the early compositions in the *Magnus Liber* and his definition therefore deserves the closest possible attention.

The *copula*-theory of the later writers, such as the Anonymous of St. Emmeram and Anonymous IV, was directly influenced by that of Garlandia; and these treatises, which provide important confirmation of the conclusions reached here, will be considered in detail on another occasion.

Johannes de Garlandia's discussion of *copula* appears towards the end of his treatise and is given here in full:

> Dicto de discantu dicendum est de copula, quae multum valet ad discantum, quia discantus numquam perfecte scitur nisi mediante copula. Unde copula dicitur esse id, quod est inter discantum et organum. Alio modo dicitur copula: copula est id, quod profertur recto modo aequipollente unisono. Alio modo dicitur: copula est id, ubicumque fit mul-

titudo punctorum. Punctus, ut hic sumitur, est, ubicumque fit multitudo tractuum. Et ista pars dividitur in duo aequalia. Unde prima pars dicitur antecedens, secunda vero consequens, et utraque pars continet multitudinem tractuum. Unde tractus fit, ubicumque fit multitudo specierum univoce, ut unisoni aut toni secundum numerum ordinatum ordine debito. Et haec sufficiant ad <copulam>.[1]

The most thorough analysis of this passage to date is certainly that of Fritz Reckow.[2] William Waite's views[3] are vitiated from the outset by his conviction that modal rhythm is to be applied to *organum purum,* thus obscuring the first distinction between *organum* and *copula* — that *organum* "profertur secundum aliquem modum . . . non rectum"[4], and *copula* "profertur recto modo."[5]

Reckow traces the word *copula* from its grammatical antecedents in late Antiquity to its use as a poetical term in the late twelfth century, before investigating its appearances in music theory. In so doing, he touches upon what proves to be the key to a proper understanding of the Garlandia passage:

---

[1] Erich Reimer, *Johannes de Garlandia: De Mensurabili Musica.* Beihefte zum Archiv für Musikwissenschaft, X (Wiesbaden: Franz Steiner, 1972) (hereafter cited as Reimer 1), p. 88: XII, 1–9.

[2] His views are to be found in the *Handwörterbuch der musikalischen Terminologie* (Wiesbaden: Franz Steiner, 1971-), entry "Copula," p. 4, and in fuller form in Fritz Reckow, *Die Copula: Über einige Zusammenhänge zwischen Setzweise, Formbildung, - Rhythmus und Vortragstil in der Mehrstimmigkeit von Notre-Dame,* Akademie der Wissenschaften und der Literatur, Abhandlungen der Geistes- und Sozialwissenschaftlichen Klasse 1972, no. 13 (Wiesbaden: Franz Steiner, 1972), pp. 12–28.

[3] William Waite, *The Rhythm of Twelfth-Century Polyphony* (New Haven: Yale University Press, 1954) pp. 115–119; idem, "Discantus, Copula, Organum," *JAMS* V, 2 (Summer 1952): pp. 77–87; idem, "Johannes de Garlandia. Poet and Musician," *Speculum* XXXV, 1960, pp. 179–195.

[4] Reimer 1, p. 88–89: XIII, 4. The elliptical nature of his sentence in its complete form ("Organum per se dicitur id esse, quidquid profertur secundum aliquem modum non rectum, sed non rectum") led Coussemaker to emend the "sed" to an "aut," thus fatally obscuring the sense for many later readers. Reckow's discussion and emendation of this passage (*Der Musiktraktat des Anonymus 4.* Beihefte zum Archiv für Musikwissenschaft, V. (Wiesbaden: Franz Steiner, 1967), pp. 35–37) are sensible but unnecessary, as Reimer shows in the volume of commentary that accompanies his critical edition (*Johannes de Garlandia: De Mensurabili Musica.* Beihefte zum Archiv für Musikwissenschaft, XI (Wiesbaden: Franz Steiner, 1972) (hereafter cited as Reimer 2)), pp. 37–38.

[5] Reimer 1, p. 88: XII, 3.

THE *COPULA*

> Als sprachphilosophischer Terminus für das Verbum als 'Verbindung' von Subiectum und Praedicatum ist copula seit der Frühscholastik bezeugt. Abaelards *Dialectica* (nach 1125) dürfte eine der ersten Quellen für diesen Sprachgebrauch sein.[6]

However, he does not pursue this line of thought any further, or apply it to the Garlandia passage in particular.

The primary influence on the language of Garlandia's discussion of the *copula* is that of medieval Logic.[7] Its terminology saturates this passage, as does also the terminology of Grammar, which was an essential component of dialectical investigation. The Scholastics placed Logic at the center of their philosophical concerns. Peter of Spain, who taught at the University of Paris until about 1245[8], and possibly contemporaneously with Johannes de Garlandia,[9] wrote:

> Dialectica est ars artium, scientia scientiarum, ad omnium methodorum principia viam habens. Sola enim dialectica probabiliter disputat de principiis omnium aliarum scientiarum. Et ideo in acquisitione omnium aliarum scientiarum dialectica dicitur esse prior.[10]

And in the same way that in the fourth and third centuries B.C. the interests of Aristotle's followers had turned away from the Logical quest for truth to the grammatical construction of a proposition, so too, in the Middle Ages, Grammar was pressed into the service of Logic.

In the *Commentum super Priscianum* of Petrus Heliae (mid-twelfth century) Grammar and Logic are linked as one, and this symbiosis reaches its most developed form in the concept of the "modi significandi" of Martin of Dacia and others — the connecting of that which

---

[6] Reckow, *Handwörterbuch*, "Copula," p. 2.

[7] For an example of a different use of dialectics as a frame of reference in music theory, see Hans Eggebrecht and Frieder Zaminer, *Ad Organum Faciendum* (Mainz: B. Schott's Söhne, 1970), p. 49 and pp. 83–89.

[8] See Joseph Mullally, *The Summulae Logicales of Peter of Spain* (Notre Dame, Indiana, 1945) p. xviii. The *Summulae* was enormously important as a Logic textbook in the thirteenth century, both because of its nature as a summary of typical currents in medieval Logical thought, and because of the fame its author later acquired as Pope John XXI.

[9] See Reimer 1, pp. 12–17.

[10] Petrus Hispanus, *Summulae Logicales*, Tractatus I. Quoted by Mullally, *Summulae*, p. xxi, fn. 1.

is thought to that which is designated by words. This theory is discussed most fully in a work of John of Dacia (fl. 1280), entitled, significantly, *Grammatica Speculativa*.[11]

The words that are used in their Grammatical or Logical sense in the Garlandia passage, or are influenced by the terminology of Logic or Grammar are the following: *Copula, valet, aequipollente, multitudo, aequalia, antecedens, consequens, specierum, univoce*. Each of these will be analyzed in turn.

Copula appears with three distinct branches of meaning in Logical thought. Firstly it is used to describe the verb "to be" in a categorical proposition[12]:

> Propositionum alia categorica, alia hypothetica. Categorica est illa, quae habet subiectum et praedicatum sicut partes principales, sive ut "homo currit"; in hac enim propositione "homo" est subiectum, "currit" vero praedicatum et quod coniungit unum cum alio dicitur esse "copula", quod patet in resolvendo sic: "homo currit" — "homo est currens". Hoc nomen quod dico "homo" est subiectum et "currens" praedicatum et hoc verbum "est" copulat unum cum altero.[13]

This is the primary meaning of "copula" in the terminology of medieval Logic, and this in itself would be sufficient to explain the infusion of Logical terms into the rest of Garlandia's description. However there are further resonances to the word.

A copulative proposition was said to be one in which two categorical propositions were joined by the conjunction "et":

---

[11] See James J. Murphy, *Rhetoric in the Middle Ages: A History of Rhetorical Theory from St. Augustine to the Renaissance* (Berkely: University of California Press, 1974), p. 155. A clear and concise précis of the *modi significandi* is given in Anton Dumitriu, *History of Logic* (Tunbridge Wells: Abacus Press, 1977) II, pp. 139–141.

[12] Aristotle had already replaced all the verbs in judgments with the single statement ἐστί or οὐκ ἔστι

[13] *Petri Hispani Summulae Logicales*, ed. I. M. Bochenski (Freiburg: Marietti, 1947), 1.07 (p. 3). The word is first established in this sense by Abelard, as Reckow has already pointed out. See S. Heinimann, "Zur Geschichte der grammatischen Terminologie im Mittelalter," *Zeitschrift für Romanische Philologie*, LXXIX (1963): p. 24.

> Propositionum hypotheticarum alia est conditionalis, alia copulativa, alia disiunctiva. . . . . . . Copulativa est, in qua coniunguntur duae categoricae per hanc coniunctionem "et", ut "Socrates currit et Plato disputat."[14]

And finally, "copulatio" is the characterization of a noun by an adjective. This usage appears in Boethius and Abelard,[15] and is succinctly stated by Petrus Hispanus:

> Copulatio est acceptio termini adiectivi pro aliquo.[16]

Given the strength and multiplicity of the Logical connotations to the word *copula*, it is therefore not surprising that Johannes de Garlandia, who may have taught in the Parisian arts faculty himself,[17] should make such extensive use of Logical and Grammatical terms when describing the musical *copula*.

The remainder of these terms may be elucidated as follows:

Valet was used to denote the appropriateness or validity of an argument, as in "Valet consequentia" (the argument is sound).[18]

Aequipollentia was an important term in Logic, referring to the equivalency of certain propositions. Petrus Hispanus explains *aequipollentia* at length:

> Sequitur de aequipollentiis. *Aequipollentia* est quaedam convertibilitas propositionum, quae provenit ex ordinatione huius adverbi "non" positi ex parte ante ad contradictorias, ex parte post ad contrarias, ex parte ante et post ad subalternas cum signis universalibus et particularibus. Duplex est aequipollentia: simplex et composita. *Simplex* est in ipsis verbis, ut "risibile" convertitur cum "homine" et haec appellatur "de simplici inhaerentia", de qua non est dicendum. *Composita* est, de qua dantur tales regulae.
> Prima talis est: si alicui signo tam universali, quam particulari praeponatur negatio, aequipollet suo contradictorio. Unde istae aequipollent:

---

[14] Bochenski, 1.22 (pp. 7–8). This usage may also be found in the *Summa Logicae* of William Ockham:
Opposita contradictoria copulativae est una disiunctiva composita ex contradictoriis partium copulativae.
(Quoted in Philotheus Boehner, *Medieval Logic* (Manchester University Press, 1952), p. 67.)

[15] See Mullally, *Summulae*, p. xlv.

[16] Bochenski, 6.03 (p. 58).

[17] See Reimer 1, p. 16.

[18] See William and Martha Kneale, *The Development of Logic* (Oxford: The Clarendon Press, 1962), p. 277.

> "non omnis homo currit" − "quidam homo non currit", "non nullus homo currit" − "quidam homo currit" et e converso. Secunda regula talis est: si alicui signo universali postponatur negatio, aequipollet suo contrario, ut "omnis homo non currit" − "nullus homo currit" et e converso. Tertia regula talis est: si alicui signo universali et particulari praeponatur et postponatur negatio, aequipollet suo subalterno, ut "non omnis homo non currit" − "quidam homo currit", "non nullus homo non currit" − "quidam homo non currit".
> Ex illis regulis sequitur alia regula talis: si duo signa universalia negativa ponuntur in eadem locutione, ita quod unum sit in subiecto, reliquum in praedicato, primum aequipollet suo contrario, reliquum suo contradictorio. Unde istae aequipollent: "nihil est nihil" huic "quodlibet est aliquid" per secundam regulam; "quodlibet non" et "nihil" aequipollent, quia sicut "omnis non" et "nullus" aequipollent per secundam regulam, ita "quodlibet non" et "nullus"; sed per primam regulam "non nullus" et "aliquid" aequipollent. Unde ista "nihil est nihil" aequipollet huic: "quodlibet est aliquid", quoniam "non nihil" et "aliquid" aequipollent. Similiter haec "nullus homo est nullum animal" et "omnis homo est aliquod animal" vel sic: "neuter est neuter" − "uter est aliquis".[19]

Multitudo is a word that, apart from its meaning as a large quantity, had been established since Classical times simply as a grammatical term for the plural:

> Quod alia vocabula singularia sint solum ut cicer, alia multitudinis solum ut scalae ......[20]

This meaning is retained in the fourth-century grammarians:

> ... in multitudine, hoc est plurali numero.[21]

By the time of the Scholastic philosophers this basic grammatical sense was still sufficiently strong that the word could take on the additional conceptual overtones of plurality or diversity:

> Ut longitudo per lineam, multitudo per numerum......[22]

---

[19] Bochenski, 1.24−1.26 (pp. 8−9).
[20] Varro, *De Lingua Latina* (ed. Kent Harvard University Press, 1938) II, p. 486. (New York: American Book Company, 1907).
[21] Keil, *Grammatici Latini* I (Leipzig: Teubner, 1864) p. 64, 16B.
[22] Abelard, *Glossae ad categorias*, p. 168, 11, quoted in *Novum Glossarium Mediae Latinitatis* (Copenhagen: Munksgaard, 1957-), s.v. "multitudo."

THE *COPULA*

> ..... eademque sola proprie ac vere simplex essentia divina, uti nec partium nec accidentium seu quarumlibet formarum ulla est diversitas sive variatio vel multitudo.[23]

Aequus does not necessarily mean equal in length or size. It also means equal in quality or type. This usage is found in the fourth-century grammarian Dositheus:

> Sunt aequalia nomina (participiis), quae nominativo casu participiis similia videntur ut 'cultus', 'passus', 'visus' . . . .[24]

and commonly in Priscian, whose *Institutiones Grammaticae* (c. 500 A. D.) was one of the primary authorities for the teaching of grammar in the Middle Ages:

> Omnia verba perfectam habentia declinationem et aequalem vel in 'o' desinunt vel in 'or'.[25]

> Omnia verba, quae aequali regula declinantur. . . . . .[26]

> . . . . . in omnibus aequalibus verbis.[27]

Boethius, an author of great influence in medieval Logic, uses the word in this way in his commentary on Aristotle's ΠΕΡΙ ΕΡΜΗΝΕΙΑΣ:

> Rursus aequale est (subiectum praedicato), cum sic dicimus 'homo risibilis est'. 'Homo' subiectum est, 'risibile' praedicatum, sed homo atque risibile aequalia sunt . . . . .[28]

> Enuntiatio vero est in qua veritas et falsitas inveniri potest. Qua in re et adfirmatio et negatio aequales sunt. Aequaliter enim et adfirmatio et negatio veritate et falsitate participant.[29]

Antecedens, consequens. These terms were already associated with Logical reasoning in Classical times:

---

[23] Petrus Lombardus, *Sententiarum Libri IV*, I, 8, 3, p. 61, quoted in *Novum Glossarium*.

[24] *Ars grammatica* in Keil, *Grammatici Latini* VII, p. 408, 15.

[25] Keil II, p. 373, 12.

[26] Keil II, p. 442, 29.

[27] Keil II, p. 457, 7.

[28] *Anicii Manlii Severini Boetii Commentarii in Librum Aristotelis* ΠΕΡΙ ΕΡΜΗΝΕΙΑΣ, ed. Meiser (Leipzig: Teubner, 1877) I, p. 91, 15.

[29] Meiser II, p. 18, 12.

MUSICA DISCIPLINA

> Deinceps est locus dialecticorum proprius ex consequentibus et antecendentibus . . . . . , nam coniuncta . . . . . non semper eveniunt, consequentia autem semper.[30]

And they were adopted by the Scholastic Logicians:

> Sequitur de propositione hypothetica. Propositio hypothetica est illa, quae habet duas categoricas sub se principales partes sui, ut "si homo currit, homo movetur" . . . . . (Propositio) conditionalis est illa, in qua coniuguntur duae categoricae per hanc coniunctionem "si", ut "si homo currit, homo movetur;" et illa categorica, cui immediate coniungitur haec coniunctio "si" dicitur "antecedens", alia vera "consequens".[31]

(It should be noticed at this point that though the antecedent and consequent may be described as equal, they are not identical in length.)

In the theory of consequences, which was developed particularly by the Scholastics, the terms *antecedens* and *consequens* are of central importance. Duns Scotus defines the *consequentia* as follows:

> Consequentia est propositio hypothetica composita ex antecedente et consequente mediante coniunctione conditionali vel rationali, quae denotat, quod impossibile est ipsis, sc. antecedente et consequente simul formatis, quod antecedens sit verum et consequens falsum.[32]

The *consequentia* can apply to a piece of reasoning with more than one premise, in which case the *antecedens* can refer to several propositions and the *consequens* to a single conclusion:

> . . . in consequentia syllogistica, videlicet in syllogismo, antecedens non habet oppositum, quia antecedens syllogisticum est propositiones plures inconiunctae . . . . .[33]

Species is a word that is used for classification in many disciplines, though it has an important place in Logic. Boethius uses *species* as a

---

[30] Cicero, *Topica*, 53 (ed. Hubbell, Harvard University Press, 1949) p. 420

[31] Bochenski, 1.22 (pp. 7–8).

[32] Duns Scotus, *Quaestiones in Universam Logicam*, quoted in Dumitriu, *History of Logic* II, p. 153.

[33] Walter Burleigh, *De Puritate Artis Logicae Tractatus Longior*, ed. Boehner (St. Bonaventure, N.Y., 1955). Quoted in Kneale, *The Development of Logic*, p. 278.

THE *COPULA*

translation of Aristotle's το εἶδος[34] (that which is seen; form, shape; kind) and the word appears *passim* in Petrus Hispanus in discussions of type and class.[35]

Univoce, however, is specifically a Logical term that refers to the use of a word that has only one, uniform, unambiguous meaning:

> Praedicari autem univoce est praedicari secundum unum nomen et rationem unam sumptam secundum illud nomen, ut homo secundum idem nomen praedicatur de Socrate et Platone, ut Socrates est homo, Plato est homo; et ratio eius secundum illud nomen est una, ut animal rationale mortale . . . . .[36]

This is contrasted with the term *aequivoce* which refers to the use of a word that has several different meanings:

> Praedicari autem aequivoce est praedicari nomine uno et diversis rationibus sumptis secundum illud nomen, ut "canis" nomine uno praedicatur de latrabili et marina belua et coelesti sidere. Ratio autem secundum illud nomen non est eadem de omnibus, sed alia et alia.[37]

It can be seen, therefore, that there are many terms in Garlandia's description of the *copula* which derive from specialized terminology. Of these perhaps the most important for our ability to understand the passage in musical terms are *multitudo, aequalia, antecedens* and *consequens*. To summarize, *multitudo* means "a number," "more than one." *Aequalia* means "parts that are parallel or equivalent (but not necessarily equal in length)." *Antecedens* and *consequens* mean "antecedent" and "consequent" but again they are not required to be of exactly equal length.

The passage can therefore be translated literally as follows, leaving the specifically musical terminology in the original Latin for the moment:

> Having discussed *discantus*, we must now discuss *copula*, which is very important for *discantus*, because *discantus* is never perfectly known

---

[34] Meiser II, p. 447, 6.

[35] See Bochenski, index, p. 137, and especially 2.07.

[36] Bochenski, 2.20 (p. 21). The term can also be found in Boethius: "Omne enim genus univoce de speciebus propriis praedicatur." (Meiser II, p. 119, 16).

[37] Bochenski, 2.21 (p. 22). Anonymous IV in his treatise refers to *organum* as a "verbum aequivocum." (Reckow, *Der Musiktraktat des Anonymus 4*, I, p. 70, 26).

without the help of *copula*. Whence *copula* is said to be that which is between *discantus* and *organum*. *Copula* is described in another way: *copula* is that which is performed in a *rectus* mode with an equivalent *unisonus*. It is described in another way: *copula* is that, wherever there occurs a number of *puncti*. *Punctus*, as used here, is wherever there is a number of *tractus*. And that part (i. e. the *copula*) is divided into two parallel parts. Whence the first part is called the antecedent, but the second the consequent, and each part contains a number of *tractus*. Whence a *tractus* occurs, wherever there occurs a number of *species* in a uniform manner, for example *unisoni* or *toni*, according to an arranged number in a fixed order. And that is enough (to describe) <the *copula*>.

Let us now proceed to an examination of the specifically musical terms in this passage.

The first musical term encountered (apart from the names of the musical styles) is *unisonus* in the third sentence. Here *unisonus* is used to describe the held tenor-tone which stays on a single pitch. It is this sentence which amplifies the preceding description of *copula* as being "inter discantum et organum." The *rectus modus* is the attribute of discant, the held tenor-tone the attribute of *organum*. "Aequipollente unisono" therefore means "with the tenor-tone being equivalent," i.e. "with the tenor-tone being held for the length of time that corresponds to the time taken by the upper part." This meaning becomes entirely clear in the following chapter of the treatise in the description of *organum*:

Et eius aequipollentia . . . . . se tenet in unisono . . . . .[38]

The next two terms, *punctus* and *tractus*, are crucial. Reckow argues that *punctus* means ligature,[39] and that *tractus* are the "Verbindungsstriche in den Ligaturen."[40] Despite his arguments, it seems clear that neither of these interpretations can be sustained.

---

[38] Reimer 1, p. 89: XIII, 9.

[39] Reckow, *Die Copula*, pp. 13–14.

[40] Ibid. p. 16. Reimer had the same view: "Die auf die Definition folgenden Sätze 4 und 5 grenzen die Copula vom Discantus ab, indem sie in wörtlicher Anlehnung an die Definition der *Figura ligata* feststellen, dass bei der Copula – im Unterschied zum Discantus – einem einzigen Tenorton eine Vielzahl von Noten der Oberstimme ('multitudo punctorum') und somit eine Vielzahl von Tractus (Satz 5), die die einzelnen Puncti zu Ligaturen verbinden, gegenübertritt." (Reimer 2, p. 36).

THE *COPULA* 77

In the first place, Garlandia would not have described a *copula* as "id, ubicumque fit multitudo punctorum" (that where there occurs a number of *ligatures*) since such a description does not distinguish the *copula* from any other part of the music. It would then be no different from *organum* or *discantus.*

Secondly, Garlandia has, up to this point in the treatise, used *punctus* only in the sense of a single note. In the chapter immediately following the passage on the *copula, punctus* is used in the sense of a section within a piece:

> Organum autem <cum alio> dicitur, quidquid profertur per <aliquam> rectam mensuram, ut dictum est superius. Et eius aequipollentia tantum se tenet in unisono usque ad finem alicuius puncti, ut secum convenit secundum aliquam concordantiam.[41]

The phrase "ut hic sumitur" in the *copula* passage shows that Garlandia is abandoning the previous meaning of the word (a single note) for a new meaning. And this new meaning (a section) is maintained, with no explanation now necessary, in the following chapter.[42]

Finally, if Garlandia had wanted to describe the *copula* as a species of music that contains a number of ligatures (which, as mentioned above, is not very likely), he could have used a term he had already defined earlier in the treatise:

> Figura ligata est, ubicumque fit multitudo punctorum simul iunctorum per suos tractus.[43]

---

[41] Reimer 1, p. 89: XIII, 8-9.

[42] Klaus-Jürgen Sachs argued for this interpretation in his *Der Contrapunctus im 14. and 15. Jahrhundert* (Ph. D. dissertation, Freiburg, 1967). Reckow dismisses his suggestions (*Die Copula*, p. 14, fn. 1) by means of a quotation from the Anonymous of St. Emmeram, where *punctus* is said to represent a "pluralitas." However this treatise is about forty years later than Garlandia's, and "pluralitas" does not necessarily imply a ligature. In the revised edition of his work (published as Vol. XIII of the Beihefte zum Archiv für Musikwissenschaft, 1974) Sachs changed his views and agreed with Reckow: "... im fraglichen Satz bedeutet *punctus* nicht 'Abschnitt' ......, sondern 'Notengruppe' (Ligatur)." (p. 14). Neither Reckow nor Sachs appears to have noticed the clearly defined new usage of *punctus* in Garlandia's next chapter. But for the establishment of this usage among later thirteenth-century authors, see Sachs (Beihefte XIII), pp. 11-16. Anonymous IV uses *punctus* synonymously with *clausula* (see *Handwörterbuch,* entry "punctus," p. 10).

[43] Reimer 1, p. 45: II, 8. Here *punctus* is clearly used in the sense of a single note.

The word *tractus* is certainly used in Garlandia's treatise to mean the line connecting notes in a ligature, as can be seen from the above quotation. However, there is another completely different meaning also:

> Sequitur de figuris pausationum. Unde figura pausationis est signum vel tractus significans dimissionem soni factam in debita quantitate. Pausationum vel tractuum quaedam dicitur recta brevis, quaedam longa, quaedam finis punctorum, quaedam divisio modorum, quaedam divisio sillabarum, quaedam suspiratio.[44]

These are the small vertical lines that divide off groups of notes from one another, and they can be found in all the manuscripts. It seems clear that it is in this sense that Garlandia uses the word *tractus* in the *copula* passage. For, again, if *punctus* means section, Garlandia would not have written: "A *punctus* (section), as used here, is wherever there occurs a number of lines that connect notes in a ligature."

These two sentences can therefore be interpreted as follows:

> Copula est id, ubicumque fit multitudo punctorum. Punctus, ut hic sumitur, est, ubicumque fit multitudo tractuum.
>
> "A *copula* is that, wherever there occurs a number of *puncti* (sections). A *punctus* (section), as used here, is wherever there occurs a number of *tractus* (lines of division marking off groups of notes)."

There remains only the problem of the penultimate sentence of the passage — the sentence, it turns out, which provides the major clue for an understanding of the *copula:*

> Unde tractus fit, ubicumque fit multitudo specierum univoce, ut unisoni aut toni secundum numerum ordinatum ordine debito.

The word *species* is used in Garlandia for the classification of modes, ligatures and types of discant, but especially for the classification of intervals:

---

[44] Reimer 1, p. 66: VIII, 1–3. The term 'finis punctorum' in this quotation must mean 'the end of the notes' since 'punctorum' is plural, and a single *tractus* cannot denote the end of more than one section. Cf. Sachs (Beihefte XIII) pp. 13–15. This would be in keeping with the suggestion that Garlandia is using a new meaning for *punctus* in the *copula* passage and thereafter.

THE *COPULA*

> . . . . . sunt duae species, scilicet ditonus et semiditonus.[45]
> . . . . . duae sunt species, scilicet diapente et diatesseron.[46]
> . . . . . sex sunt species concordantiae . . . . .[47]
> Iste species dissonantiae sunt septem . . . . .[48]
>
> etc.

The phrase "ut unisoni aut toni" confirms this meaning here.

The words "secundum numerum ordinatum ordine debito" can also be explained by parallel usages within the treatise. In the discussion on discant, Garlandia writes:

> Et sciendum est, quod a parte primi tria sunt consideranda, scilicet sonus, ordinatio et modus. . . . . . ordinatio sumitur pro numero punctorum ante pausationem . . . . .[49]

The word *ordo* is used in Garlandia either in the sense of the arrangement of modal quantities[50] or simply in the non-technical sense of "order":

> Sciendum est ergo, quod ipsius organi generaliter accepti tres sunt species, scilicet discantus, copula et organum, de quibus dicendum est per ordinem.[51]

The adjective "debitus" suggests that it is this normal sense that is intended here.

The sentence can therefore be translated as follows:

> Whence a *tractus* (line of division) occurs, wherever there occurs a number of intervals in a uniform manner, for example unisons or whole steps, according to an arranged number in a fixed order.

Again there is confirmation of the interpretation of *tractus* as 'line of division,' for it would make no sense (*pace* Reckow) to have a 'line connecting notes to a ligature' described in this way. Also the sentence begins with the words "tractus fit" — "a tractus occurs," not

---

[45] Reimer 1, p. 68: IX, 8.
[46] Reimer 1, p. 69: IX, 10.
[47] Reimer 1, p. 69: IX, 12.
[48] Reimer 1, p. 72: IX, 34.
[49] Reimer 1, p. 75: XI, 7.
[50] See Reimer 1, p. 77: XI, 20 ff.
[51] Reimer 1, p. 35: I, 3.

"tractus est" — "a tractus is", as had the descriptions of the *copula* ("Copula est id . . . . .") and the *punctus* ("Punctus, ut hic sumitur, est . . . . .").

One further point: the addition of a comma to Reimer's text after the words "ut unisoni aut toni" ("ubicumque fit multitudo specierum univoce, ut unisoni aut toni, secundum . . . . .") would serve to clarify the point that *unisoni* and *toni* are *examples* of intervals, not requirements ("ut" means "for example," not "namely"), that they are mentioned to elucidate "specierum," and also that the phrase "secundum numerum ordinatum ordine debito" qualifies "multitudo specierum univoce," and not "unisoni aut toni."[52]

With this investigation into the terminology of the *copula* passage completed, an interpretation of Garlandia's description is made possible.

The following are the features of *copula:*
1. It is between discant and *organum.*
2. It is performed in modal rhythm over a held tenor-tone.
3. It contains a number of sections.
4. A section contains a number of groups of notes separated by division lines..
5. The *copula* is divided into two parallel (but not necessarily equal) parts.
6. The first part is called the antecedent, the second the consequent, and each part contains a number of groups of notes separated by division lines.
7. A division line occurs wherever there are a number of intervals uniformly in an arranged number and in a fixed order.

Feature 1 may be interpreted either stylistically or factually. As mentioned before, the *copula* may be shown to be "inter discantum et organum" stylistically because of Feature 2: it has the modal rhythm of discant and the held tenor-tone of *organum.* But it can be demonstrated that in fact the *copula* is not found at the beginning of any of the pieces in the *Magnus Liber* (the majority of which start with

---

[52] Reckow's musical example and discussion of this sentence *(Die Copula,* pp. 17–19) suggest that he has misunderstood this. Significantly, his reprinting of the text omits even the first comma.

THE *COPULA*

organum), and may therefore be said to be factually "inter discantum et organum" as well.[53]

Feature 2 shows why the musical *copula* is the analogue of the *copula* in Logic. It is the *link* between *organum*, with its held tenor, and discant, with its modal rhythm.

Features 3–6 may be schematized as follows:

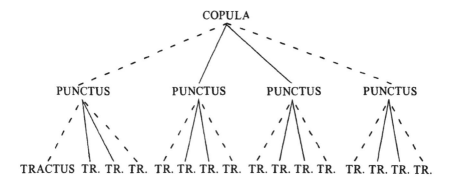

prima pars *(antecedens)*   secunda pars *(consequens)*

The *copula* contains a number (two or more, but otherwise undefined) of *puncti* (sections). A *punctus* contains a number of *tractus* (lines marking off note-groups). The *copula* is divided into two parallel parts, and each part contains a number of *tractus*.

It is Feature 7 that provides the finest details of the definition and the key to the ultimate understanding of the *copula*.

"A number of intervals uniformly in an arranged number and in a fixed order" can only be a description of a technique of musical writing found frequently in the music of Notre Dame: the technique of melodic sequence. The intervals appear in an arranged number and in a fixed order each time, and, though they may be on a different pitch level, they are uniform and convey the same sense ("univoce") each time.

It is these sequences that are set off by *tractus* and form the smallest, but the most distinctive, unit of the *copula*.

---

[53] Cf. Reckow, *Handwörterbuch*, "Copula," p. 4.

MUSICA DISCIPLINA

All the features of the *copula* as described by Garlandia may be seen in *Judea et Jerusalem,* the opening piece of the *Magnus Liber.* Beginning on the second syllable of the ⅴ '(Con-) stan- (tes)' at the end of the third accolade on folio 65 of the Florence manuscript[54] is a short phrase that is set off from the previous passage by its skip of a fifth, that falls squarely into the first mode, that is immediately sequenced, and that is marked off by a *tractus*. This phrase opens the *copula,* which continues through to the end of the setting of (esto-) te (beginning of the fifth accolade) and is rounded off by a brief phrase in sixth mode. The next (discant) section is introduced by a change of clef and range, which also serve to mark the end of the *copula*.

[54] Firenze, Biblioteca Laurenziana, Pluteo 29, 1. The piece may also be found in W_1 (Wolfenbüttel, Herzog-August-Bibliothek, codex 628 Helmstadiensis) on folio 17, and in W_2 (Wolfenbüttel, Herzog-August-Bibliothek, codex 1099 Helmstadiensis) on folio 47.

THE *COPULA* 83

In the facsimile above, the sequences are marked by letters. There are two statements of A, followed by three statements of B. Then follows a short discant setting ('esto-'). A returns in varied form (A') and is repeated with a changed final note. B is stated once more and the *copula* ends with the sixth-mode phrase that is not unrelated to B.

The *copula* appears after an organal setting ('Con-') and before a discant setting ('Videbitis')- it is therefore "inter discantum et organum."

It has a number of sections (a section may be said to be each series of sequences: A+A, B+B+B, etc.) — "multitudo punctorum."

Each section contains a number of *tractus* — "multitudo tractuum."

The *copula* is divided into two parallel or equivalent parts: A+A+B+B+B is parallel or equivalent to A' + A' + B — "ista pars dividitur in duo aequalia."

Each part contains a number of *tractus* — "multitudinem tractuum."

And each *tractus* occurs after a phrase that has the same number of intervals uniformly each time, and in the same order — "multitudo specierum univoce . . . . . secundum numerum ordinatum ordine debito."

This kind of sequential writing occurs frequently in the *Magnus Liber*. Often the passage consists only of one or two sequences of a phrase, in which case not all the levels of Garlandia's description of the *copula* may obtain. In the case of the *copula,* either all the levels of sectionalization do not always appear, or these levels may be conflated. In the following example:[55]

the *copula* contains the units A+A+B. In this case, the first *punctus* is made up of A+A and forms the *prima pars*, the second *punctus* (B) is not subdivided and is in itself the *secunda pars.*

[55] Florence, folio 82, acc. 1.

The most important facts about the *copula* according to Johannes de Garlandia have thus been established. It is characterized by modal rhythm over a held tenore-tone, by sectionalization, and by melodic sequence.

Thus all three species of music in the Notre Dame repertoire, as described by Johannes de Garlandia, and not just *discantus* and *organum,* can be recognized in their original notation and distinguished from one another.

Stanford University

[10]

Conductus and Modal Rhythm

By ERNEST H. SANDERS

IT HAS BEEN MORE THAN EIGHTY YEARS since Friedrich Ludwig (1872–1930), arguably the greatest of the seminal figures in twentieth-century musicology, began to publish his studies of medieval music. His single-handed occupation of the field, his absolute sovereignty over the entire repertoire and all issues of scholarly significance arising from it, and his enormous, inescapably determinative influence on the thinking of his successors, most of whom had studied with him, explain the epithet *der Grosse* he was given on at least one occasion.[1] Almost his entire professional energies were devoted to the music of the twelfth and, particularly, the thirteenth centuries, as well as to the polyphony of the fourteenth century, which he began to explore in depth in the 1920s. His stringent devotion to the facts and to conclusions supported by them was a trait singled out by several commentators.[2]

Ludwig's insistence on scholarly rigor, however, cannot be said to account completely for his *Modaltheorie*, which appeared to posit the applicability of modal rhythm to all music of the Notre Dame period—except organal style—and of the pre-Garlandian (or pre-Franconian) thirteenth century, including particularly the musical settings of poetry. Much of the pre-Garlandian ligature notation in thirteenth-century sources of melismatic polyphonic compositions of the first half of that century (clausulae, organa for more than two voices) and of melismatic portions of certain genres, such as the *caudae* of conducti,[3] signifies modal rhythms, and the appropriateness of the modal system cannot be disputed in this context. Its validity for

---

[1] Hans Spanke dedicated his "St. Martial-Studien: Ein Beitrag zur frühromanischen Metrik," *Zeitschrift für französische Sprache und Literatur*, LIV (1931), 282–317, 385–422, "Dem Andenken Friedrich Ludwigs, des Grossen, Unvergesslichen." For a summary of Ludwig's stature, see David Hiley's brief article in *The New Grove Dictionary*, XI, 307–308.

[2] See the obituaries listed in Hiley, "Ludwig," p. 308.

[3] The numerous quotations from thirteenth-century treatises given below show that for medieval writers *conductus* was a noun of the second declension; see also Fritz Reckow, "Conductus," *Handwörterbuch der musikalischen Terminologie*, ed. Hans Heinrich Eggebrecht (Wiesbaden, 1973).

syllabic music, notated until the mid-thirteenth century with undifferentiated and rhythmically insignificant note symbols, is more problematic. Those symbols (*virgae*), traditionally associated in the Middle Ages with *musica non mensurata* (Gregorian chant) and, in the Notre Dame period, with *musica ultra mensuram* (Gregorian chant tenors in both organal and discant portions of Leoninian organa), were used in the first half of the thirteenth century for all syllabic music, including the newly invented genre of the motet, all of whose ingredients were precisely and modally measured. Thus, the same symbol came to designate indeterminate as well as exactly and proportionately determined durational events. While the vernacular monophonic repertoires that were so notated have, in the twentieth century, been subject to the imposition of more than one rhythmic system,[4] most scholars who saw justification in attaching precise values to the ambiguous notation of all syllabic music, including applicable portions of conducti, have favored the *Modaltheorie* because it seemed persuasive to assign to the *virgae* durational values in a manner similar or identical to the procedures required in motets. Many musicologists trained in Germany in the first half of the twentieth century took for granted the applicability, in principle, of modal rhythm to these repertoires. So have their students and, all in all, the students of such German-trained musicologists in this country as Curt Sachs, Willi Apel, Manfred Bukofzer, and, especially, Leo Schrade. To Ludwig's musicological children and grandchildren must be added the name of one prominent indirect descendant, that of the recently and prematurely deceased powerhouse of medieval musical scholarship Gordon A. Anderson, in whose work on the conductus the *Modaltheorie* figures prominently.[5]

Chiefly what gave rise to Ludwig's *Modaltheorie* was the apparent analogy between modal patterns and certain basic metrical schemes of poetry, which could be seen to have some degree of applicability in the motet repertoire of the first half of the thirteenth century. Although this observation seems, by and large, to have led to the doctrine that musical rhythm must be deduced from poetic meter, it

---

[4] See Burkhard Kippenberg, *Der Rhythmus im Minnesang: Eine Kritik der literar- und musikhistorischen Forschung mit einer Übersicht über die Musikalischen Quellen*, Münchener Texte und Untersuchungen zur deutschen Literatur des Mittelalters, 3 (Munich, 1962).

[5] "Mode and Change of Mode in Notre-Dame Conductus," *Acta musicologica*, XL (1968), 92–114; "The Rhythm of *cum littera* Sections of Polyphonic Conductus in Mensural Sources," this JOURNAL, XXVI (1973), 288–304; "The Rhythm of the Monophonic Conductus in the Florence Manuscript As Indicated in Parallel Sources in Mensural Notation," this JOURNAL, XXXI (1978), 480–89.

was the latter theory (rather than the *Modaltheorie*) that Ludwig articulated first.[6] His view of modal rhythm (only the first three modes) as a corollary of poetic meter appears for the first time in his letter to Pierre Aubry of 13 April 1907.[7] Ludwig restated it some three years later, not without conceding that "the application of modal rhythm to the older chansons rests on analogies (*Analogieschlüssen*)" and on "the manifest parallelism of the rhythm (*Rhythmik*) in motets and chansons."[8] He also formulated it in his *Repertorium*, where, in addition, he specifically claimed priority for "also [i.e., in addition to the motet repertoire] solving, in principle, the question of the transcription of large portions of the French monophonic repertoire of the twelfth and thirteenth centuries in the manner of 'modal interpretation.' . . ."[9]

Two other circumstances that came to be cited in support of the *Modaltheorie* were (1) the existence of Notre Dame music other than motets in mensural sources, i.e., notated with specific rhythmic symbols,[10] and (2) the melodic identity, in certain conducti, of some syllabic portions with *caudae* written in modal ligature notation.[11]

In his published writings, Ludwig was cautious about the validity of modal rhythm in Minnelieder and in conducti. In fact, he publicly addressed that problem in the former repertoire only when it con-

---

[6] Friedrich Ludwig, "Studien über die Geschichte der mehrstimmigen Musik im Mittelalter, II, Die 50 Beispiele Coussemaker's aus der Handschrift von Montpellier," *Sammelbände der Internationalen Musik-Gesellschaft*, V (1904), 184; *idem*, "Die Aufgaben der Forschung auf dem Gebiete der mittelalterlichen Musikgeschichte," *Beilage zur [Münchener] Allgemeinen Zeitung*, nos. 13 and 14 (1906), 99 (where Hugo Riemann is credited with the first articulation of this "correct principle") and 107.

[7] Published in Jacques Chailley's "Quel est l'auteur de la 'théorie modale' dite de Beck-Aubry?" *Archiv für Musikwissenschaft*, X (1953), 213–22; in a passage on p. 220, Ludwig specifically mentions the role played by poetic meter in the recognition of modal rhythm in motets and, therefore (p. 221), in the monophonic settings of poetry "in the vernacular languages," as well as in Latin poetry (p. 216).

[8] "Zur 'modalen Interpretation' von Melodien des 12. und 13. Jahrhunderts," *Zeitschrift der Internationalen Musikgesellschaft*, XI (1910), 379–82, specifically p. 380.

[9] *Repertorium organorum recentioris et motetorum vetustissimi stili*, I, *Catalogue raisonné der Quellen* (Halle, 1910), 54–56: "Für die prinzipielle Lösung der Frage der Übertragung auch grosser Partien des französischen 1st. Repertoires des 12. und 13. Jahrhunderts im Sinn der 'modalen Interpretation' . . ." (p. 56).

[10] The earliest mention of this fact in this context occurs in Ludwig's "Die Aufgaben," pp. 107–108. See also Heinrich Husmann, "Zur Grundlegung der musikalischen Rhythmik des mittellateinischen Liedes," *Archiv für Musikwissenschaft*, IX (1952), 3–26.

[11] The first to exploit this feature was Manfred F. Bukofzer in his "Rhythm and Meter in the Notre-Dame Conductus," *Bulletin of the American Musicological Society*, XI–XII–XIII (1948), 63–65, an abstract of a paper read in 1946. But the priority of its observation was Jacques Handschin's; see his "Zur Frage der Conductus-Rhythmik," *Acta musicologica*, XXIV (1952), 113. See also Husmann, "Zur Grundlegung."

fronted him in the context of the survey he had undertaken to write for Guido Adler's *Handbuch der Musikgeschichte*.[12] His approach to the rhythmic interpretation of Minnelieder was noncommittal.[13] While, for stated or implicit reasons, he presented the syllabic portions of his examples of monophonic conducti in modal rhythm,[14] he chose not to deal with the problem in his brief discussion of polyphonic conducti,[15] in contrast to some of his successors.[16]

*   *   *

A careful examination of the issue of rhythm in the syllabic portions of conducti and, in particular, of the applicability of modal rhythm must begin by consulting the professionals of the time, so as to extract from their writings the relevant passages concerning the conductus,[17] and to establish in this connection just "quid sit modus," as Johannes de Garlandia put it,[18] and what it is not.

---

[12] 1st ed. (Frankfurt, 1924); 2nd ed. (Berlin, 1930).
[13] *Ibid.*, p. 204 (2nd ed.); cf. Kippenberg, *Der Rhythmus im Minnesang*, p. 135.
[14] Adler, *Handbuch*, pp. 184–87.
[15] *Ibid.*, pp. 221–24.
[16] For instance, Heinrich Husmann, "Zur Rhythmik des Trouvèregesanges," *Die Musikforschung*, V (1952), 111: "Die modale Rhythmik beherrscht . . . die Kompositionsgattungen des Organums, der Motette und des mittellateinischen Liedes." ("Modal rhythm governs . . . the compositional genres of organum, motet, and medieval Latin song.") A footnote explains that "Lied soll also gleichbedeutend mit Konduktus sein." ("Song is meant to be equivalent to conductus.") Leo Schrade, "Political Compositions in French Music of the 12th and 13th Centuries: The Coronation of French Kings," *Annales musicologiques*, I (1953), 33–34, put the matter more apodictically than anyone. That all conducti "are subject to modal rhythm," he asserted, "can no longer be doubted." And he continued that "it is also absolutely certain that the modal rhythm pertains to both the melismatic and syllabic passages, whereby conductus must be included that consist of nothing but syllabic composition. . . . All evidence points to the modal rhythm as valid for all types and parts of conductus. . . . This principle is as much alive in conductus of the second half of the 12th century as it is in those of the 13th century. . . ." Two years later, however, he wrote, more cautiously, that the puzzle of conductus rhythm required abstention "from being too categorical. . . ." ("Unknown Motets in a Recovered Thirteenth-Century Manuscript," *Speculum: A Journal of Mediaeval Studies*, XXX [1955], 406, n. 23.) Most recently, Hans Tischler emphatically asserted, as the first of ten theses, that "Conductus müssen innerhalb des Systems der rhythmischen Modi übertragen werden." ("Conductus must be transcribed within the system of the rhythmic modes.") ("Versmass und musikalischer Rhythmus in Notre-Dame-Conductus," *Archiv für Musikwissenschaft*, XXXVII [1980], 303.)
[17] For a comprehensive treatment of the subject, see Fritz Reckow, "Conductus," specifically pp. 6–8.
[18] Erich Reimer, ed., *Johannes de Garlandia: De mensurabili musica, Kritische Edition mit Kommentar und Interpretation der Notationslehre*, I, *Quellenuntersuchungen und Edition*, Beihefte zum Archiv für Musikwissenschaft, 10 (Wiesbaden, 1972), 36.

CONDUCTUS AND MODAL RHYTHM 443

Garlandia mentions the conductus in only two suggestive sentences. The first occurs near the beginning of the second chapter, which deals with the notational representation of durational values, or, as he puts it more precisely, of "longitudo vel brevitas." "Et sciendum quod huiusmodi figura aliquando ponitur sine littera et aliquando cum littera; sine littera ut in caudis et in conductis, cum littera ut in motellis." ("And one needs to know that a note symbol of that sort is sometimes given without text and sometimes with text; without text as in *caudae* and in conducti, with text as in motets.")[19] Near the end of the short third chapter, in which he presents a general introduction to the rhythmic meaning of ligatures with and without propriety and perfection, Garlandia states, "Et totum hoc intelligitur in conductis vel motellis, quando sumitur sine littera vel cum littera, si proprio modo figurantur." ("And all this [i.e., all general aspects of ligature notation] is seen in conducti or motets, inasmuch as it is applied without text or with text, if they are properly notated.")[20] In the first of these two statements, the motet is solely and specifically associated with notation *cum littera*. The second can well be understood in the same way, unless one were to assume that the term "motellus" meant for Garlandia not only a texted part but also its melismatic model (the upper voice of a clausula); his citation of a motetus voice in ligature notation and his labeling of that passage as "In discantu Lonc tans a"[21] proves, however, that this would be an incorrect assumption. Understandably, modern commentators have restricted Garlandia's association of the conductus with notation *sine littera* to its melismatic *caudae*.[22] It is not impossible, however, to understand the first passage literally as applying to the syllabic

---

[19] *Ibid.*, p. 44.

[20] *Ibid.*, p. 51. Both passages are cited in accordance with MS Brugge, Stadsbibliotheek, 528. The chapters generally regarded as inauthentic are here left out of account. In any case, the conductus is there mentioned only in connection with ornamentation, including voice exchange.

[21] The clausula presumably quoted by Garlandia (Reimer, *Garlandia*, p. 41) failed to be included in the clausula and discant repertoire preserved in the extant Notre Dame sources. In view of its advanced style, which allows it to be dated near 1240 (see Yvonne Rokseth, *Polyphonies du XIIIe siècle: Le Manuscrit H 196 de la Faculté de Médecine de Montpellier*, IV, Etude et commentaires [Paris, 1939], 140), it may not yet have been available to the scribe of MS *F* (Florence, Biblioteca Medicea-Laurenziana, Pluteus 29.1).

[22] E.g., Erich Reimer, ed., *Johannes de Garlandia: De mensurabili musica, Kritische Edition mit Kommentar und Interpretation der Notationslehre*, II, *Kommentar und Interpretation der Notationslehre*, Beihefte zum Archiv für Musikwissenschaft, 11 (Wiesbaden, 1972), 14 and 51, n. 30.

portions as well, to the extent that they (particularly the upper voices) are not performed like motets.[23]

The older part of the *Discantus positio vulgaris*,[24] whose contents must have originated in the first quarter of the thirteenth century, mentions the conductus only in conjunction with ligatures containing more than four notes, which are beyond the pale of measured music: "Quasi regulis non subjacent, sed ad placitum proferuntur; quae etiam ad organum et conductum pertinent singulariter." ("They are not really subject to rules but are performed ad libitum; and they are particularly applicable to organum and conductus.")[25]

The second part of the treatise, which may date from the 1270s, defines certain polyphonic genres; although seemingly more specific, it is not much more informative with respect to the conductus. "Conductus autem est super unum metrum multiplex consonans cantus, qui etiam secundarias recipit consonantias." ("The conductus, on the other hand, is a vocal polyphonic setting *super unum metrum*, which also admits secondary consonances.")[26] The crucial and troublingly ambiguous term here is "metrum."[27] The *Novum glossarium mediae latinitatis* lists the following secondary meanings: "mètre poétique [i.e., quantitative meter]; vers, poésie; pièce de vers, poème; mesure de capacité." The main definition is given as "mesure poétique en général"; in fact, in its most general sense, *metrum* is an assimilated Greek synonym for *mensura*. And *mensura* is defined as follows: "mesure, grandeur ou quantité finie susceptible d'évaluation . . . ; mesure du temps, durée; mesure, rythme." Now, in his definition of the motet, with its modal rhythm, as polyphony containing divers (simultaneous) texts, the author of the treatise uses the expression "diversus in prosis multiplex consonans cantus." The term "prosa" also appears in his definitions of discant and of organum, consistent

---

[23] In quite a few cases such an interpretation would lead to the sort of transcription made plausible, at least for some conducti, by Gilbert Reaney's "A Note on Conductus Rhythm," *Bericht über den siebenten internationalen musikwissenschaftlichen Kongress Köln 1958*, ed. Gerald Abraham et al. (Kassel, 1959), pp. 219–21. See, in this connection, the references to the practice of reduction, p. 449 and n. 52 below.

[24] See Ernest H. Sanders, "Consonance and Rhythm in the Organum of the 12th and 13th Centuries," this JOURNAL, XXXIII (1980), 266, n. 2.

[25] Simon M. Cserba, ed., *Hieronymus de Moravia, O.P. Tractatus de musica*, Freiburger Studien zur Musikwissenschaft, ser. 2, (Regensburg, 1935), p. 190; Edmond de Coussemaker, *Scriptorum de musica medii aevi: Novam seriem a Gerbertina alteram*, I (Paris, 1864; repr. Hildesheim, 1963), 95.

[26] Cserba, ed., *Hieronymus de Moravia*, p. 193; Coussemaker, *Scriptorum*, p. 96.

[27] See Jacques Handschin's discussion in "Notizen über die Notre-Dame-Conductus," *Bericht über den I. musikwissenschaftlichen Kongress der deutschen Musikgesellschaft in Leipzig* (Leipzig, 1926), p. 209.

CONDUCTUS AND MODAL RHYTHM 445

with the two meanings of *prosa* as prose and rhymed nonquantitative poetry. It seems likely, therefore, that the words "super unum metrum" here are to be understood not as "one poem" but as synonymous with "super unam mensuram," i.e., "using one single unit of poetic [and musical] measurement," which, in contrast to the motet, must therefore be isochronous.

In spite of his garrulity, Anonymous IV provides very little information specifically on the conductus in his treatise (*ca.* 1275). Two passages relate that Perotinus composed conducti for three voices, as well as for two and one, and that three volumes, respectively, contained conducti for three voices with *caudae*, conducti for two voices with *caudae*, and conducti for four, three, and two voices without *caudae*.[28] Elsewhere he observes that, in contrast to discant, whose Gregorian tenors are notated on four-line staves, all voices of conducti are customarily notated on five-line staves.[29] In another passage he comments that *organum* is an equivocal term because some people apply it indiscriminately, including "improperly," to conducti, and that the organum called "universal" by the old practitioners (i.e., note-against-note counterpoint) embraced everything except, of course, monophonic conducti.[30] The reference to "conducti lagi" remains obscure and quite possibly a scribal error.[31]

In a passage recalling, yet differing significantly from, one of the two quoted sentences in Garlandia's treatise,[32] Lambertus (1278 or a couple of years earlier), in discussing note symbols, observes that "hujusmodi figure aliquando ponuntur cum littera, aliquando sine. Cum littera vero, ut in motellis et similibus, sine littera, ut in neumatibus conductorum et similia."[33] Since the conductus differs fundamentally from the motet, it seems unlikely that Lambertus's intention was to include the syllabic portions of conducti in the expression "in motellis et similibus." He may be referring to hockets, which are indeed similar to motets. What is new, however, is his restriction of melismatic (*sine littera*) notation specifically to the *caudae*

---

[29] Fritz Reckow, ed., *Der Musiktraktat des Anonymus 4*, I, *Edition*, Beihefte zum Archiv für Musikwissenschaft, 4 (Wiesbaden, 1967), 46, 82.

[29] *Ibid.*, p. 60: "Sed nota, quod organistae utuntur in libris suis quinque regulis, sed in tenoribus discantuum quatuor tantum, quia semper tenor solebat sumi ex cantu ecclesiastico notato quatuor regulis etc. Sunt quidam alii . . . [qui] faciunt semper quinque, sive procedunt per modum discantus sive non, ut patet inter conductos. . . ."

[30] *Ibid.*, pp. 70–71. I read *universale* for *universales* on p. 71, line 2.

[31] *Ibid.*, pp. 82 and 94, n. 42.

[32] See p. 443 above.

[33] Coussemaker, *Scriptorum*, p. 269.

("neumata") of conducti. Whether this represents a clarification or a reinterpretation of Garlandia's statement remains a moot question.

The two passages pertaining to the conductus in the treatise of Lambertus's respondent, the so-called St.-Emmeram Anonymous, will be discussed later.[34]

Franco (*ca.* 1280) is the first writer to describe conductus as a species of discant: "Cum littera et sine fit discantus in conductis. . . ." The only other mention of conductus occurs in the well-known observation that in such pieces both the tenor and the polyphonic superstructure must be invented by the composer.[35]

Walter Odington (*ca.* 1300) defines conductus as "quasi plures cantus decori conducti" ("several suitable melodies brought together, as it were"), in contrast to the rondellus, in which several (three) people sing the phrase ingredients of one melody, but at different times.[36] Thus, "conducti sunt compositi ex pluribus canticis decoris cognitis vel inventis et in diversis modis ac punctis iteratis in eodem tono vel in diversis. . . ." ("Conducti are composed of a number of suitable melodies, known or invented, and in various modes and with phrases repeated at the same pitch [in the same mode] or others. . . .")[37]

Odington's contemporary Johannes de Grocheio is the last writer who needs to be considered. After giving conductus and motet as types of polyphony, i.e., mensural music, Grocheio twice paraphrases Franco's observation that in conducti the tenor is newly composed.[38] His only other mention of the term is in a paragraph on

---

[34] Heinrich Sowa, *Ein anonymer glossierter Mensuraltraktat 1279* (Kassel, 1930). See pp. 448–49 below.

[35] Franco of Cologne, *Ars cantus mensurabilis*, ed. Gilbert Reaney and André Gilles, Corpus scriptorum de musica, 18 ([Rome,] 1974), pp. 69, 73–74.

[36] Both genres are called species of discant. This inclusive view of discant is specifically Franconian. Those authors of the first half of the fourteenth century who continue to present it all derived it from Franco. In England all discant treatises of the fourteenth and fifteenth centuries considered discant as elaboration of a cantus planus. See Ernest H. Sanders, "Cantilena and Discant in 14th-Century England," *Musica disciplina*, XIX (1965), 31, n. 74.

[37] Walter Odington, *Summa de speculatione musicae*, ed. Frederick F. Hammond, Corpus scriptorum de musica, 14 ([Rome,] 1970), pp. 139–40, 142; Coussemaker, *Scriptorum*, pp. 245, 247.

[38] Ernst Rohloff, ed., *Der Musiktraktat des Johannes de Grocheo, nach den Quellen neu herausgegeben mit Übersetzung ins Deutsche und Revisionsbericht*, Media latinitas musica, 2 (Leipzig, 1943), pp. 47, 56, 57; idem, ed., *Die Quellenhandschriften zum Musiktraktat des Johannes de Grocheio: Im Faksimile herausgegeben nebst Übertragung des Textes und Übersetzung ins Deutsche, dazu Bericht, Literaturschau, Tabellen und Indices* (Leipzig, 1972), pp. 124, 144, 146.

the *cantus coronatus*, which "ab aliquibus simplex conductus dictus est." Such a song, he says, "ex omnibus longis et perfectis efficitur,"[39] a statement reminiscent of the expression "unum metrum" in the *Discantus positio vulgaris*.[40]

Before a summary of the evidence presented so far, a brief survey of those passages not already cited that deal with the concepts of *sine littera* and *cum littera* is essential. Apart from the two passages quoted earlier,[41] Garlandia addresses the matter of presence or absence of text only once, in the sixth chapter: "Item omnis figura simplex sumitur secundum suum nomen, si sit cum littera vel sine littera."[42] ("Further, the meaning of every single note is taken according to its particular nature as a symbol [its cachet], regardless of whether it has text.")[43] Garlandia, in effect, states that a *virga*, a *punctus*, and a diamond are long, breve, and semibreve, respectively, and that therefore the durational value of notes is no longer, in the modal way, derived from their contextual position.

Anonymous IV adds nothing further. He reports that notes without text are ligated as much as possible, that "cum litera quandoque sic, quandoque non," i.e., depending on the number of notes allotted to each syllable, that in music *cum littera* the duration of single notes is unambiguous if they are well written, i.e., according to Garlandian precepts, and that therefore, i.e., if the rules of propriety and perfection are observed, "maxima pars dubitationis librorum antiquorum solvitur, et hoc supra literam vel sine litera. . . ." ("Most of the uncertainty of the old books is resolved, both in syllabic and in melismatic polyphony. . . .")[44]

The treatise by Lambertus largely restates information given by his predecessors.

> Unde figura est representatio soni secundum suum modum, et secundum equipollentiam sui equipollentis; sed hujusmodi figure aliquando ponuntur cum littera, aliquando sine. Cum littera vero, ut in motellis et similibus; sine littera, ut in neumatibus conductorum et similia. Inter

---

[39] Rohloff, ed., *Der Musiktraktat*, p. 50; and *idem*, ed., *Die Quellenhandschriften*, p. 130. On the *cantus coronatus*, see Hendrik van der Werf, "Cantus coronatus," especially Exkurs 2, *Handwörterbuch der musikalischen Terminologie*, ed. Hans Heinrich Eggebrecht (Wiesbaden, 1983), pp. 7–8.

[40] See pp. 444–45 above.

[41] See p. 443 above.

[42] Reimer, *Garlandia*, I, 63.

[43] For the applicable meanings of *nomen*, see *Novum glossarium mediae latinitatis ab anno DCCC usque ad annum MCC*, [VII], ed. Franz Blatt ([Copenhagen], 1967), cols. 1330–44.

[44] Reckow, *Der Musiktraktat des Anonymus 4*, I, 45, 48, 53.

enim figuras que sunt cum littera, vel sine, talis datur differentia: quoniam ille que sunt sine littera, debent prout possunt amplius ad invicem ligari. Sed hujus proprietas aliquando omittitur propter litteram his figuris associatam.[45]

("Hence, a note symbol represents a pitch with respect to its extent and to its agreement with its equivalent [part]. But such symbols are set down sometimes with text and sometimes without; with text, as in motets and similar things, without text, as in *caudae* of conducti and similar things. The difference between note symbols with text and those without is that those without must be ligated as much as possible; but this characteristic notational procedure is sometimes not observed because of text associated with these note symbols.")

Subsequently he maintains repeatedly that ligatures have unequivocal meanings, whether text is associated with them or not.[46] Like the similar statement of Anonymous IV, this represents a significant break with pre-Garlandian notational concepts.

Lambertus's view of ligatures also crops up repeatedly in examples given by the St.-Emmeram Anonymous.[47] In other ways, too, the latter's treatise is often derivative, despite its frequently fanciful language. For instance, the quoted excerpt from Lambertus's treatise appears with little change.[48] One of the two passages dealing with the conductus reports the practice of some scribes and musicians to write perfect binary ligatures at points in motets and texted portions of conducti where properly they should have been imperfect. Although this is incorrect, the author fails to disapprove the practice because it is sanctioned by tradition and because the descending imperfect ligature looks awkward and unsightly.[49] The second passage[50] represents an interesting adaptation of formulations by Garlandia and Anonymous IV:[51]

---

[45] Coussemaker, *Scriptorum*, p. 269.
[46] *Ibid.*, pp. 273–75.
[47] Sowa, *Ein anonymer*, pp. 60–61, 80, 85.
[48] *Ibid.*, p. 14.
[49] *Ibid.*, p. 59. One can imagine the following conversation: "A binaria imperfecta is a ternaria perfecta (e.g., ▞) from which the last note has been separated. A descending binaria imperfecta is therefore written like this: ▞ ." "But that looks like a binaria perfecta. How can one tell the difference?" "The context should make it clear." "But that's just the sort of approach we want to get away from. I propose that it be written as an incomplete porrectus: ▚ ." "Oh, but what an unnatural, illegitimate, and ugly note symbol!"
[50] *Ibid.*, p. 72.
[51] See Reimer, *Garlandia*, I, 63 and nn. 7 and 9.

CONDUCTUS AND MODAL RHYTHM 449

Omnis figura simplex, et hoc propter litteram vel aliquam aliam superhabundantiam, quemadmodum in motellis et conductis cum littera et similibus, decet reduci ad figuram compositam in toto vel in parte secundum perfectiones modorum vel imperfectiones. Et hoc est quia modus sive maneries per figuram compositam et nonquam per simplicem cognoscitur et etiam compilatur. . . .[52]

("Because of text or some other addition, as in motets and in conductus [passages] with text and in similar cases, every single note is properly reduced to [i.e., taken as] a constituent of a ligature in full or in part, in accordance with the perfections and imperfections of the modes. And this is because mode [or manner] is recognized and, in fact, written by means of the ligature and never by means of the single note. . . .")

A summary of the cited passages, taken together with a synopsis of the various accounts of the system of rhythmic modes given by thirteenth-century writers,[53] leads to the recognition of several major stages and aspects of the epochal rise and evolution of measured music.

1. Before the codification of the modal system about 1210,[54] there existed a system of melismatic notation in which binary, ternary, and quaternary ligatures for the first time conveyed rhythmic meaning. The earliest writer to summarize the few necessary rules governing this premodal notation was the author of the older part of the *Discantus positio vulgaris*, in a passage just preceding his mention of the

---

[52] See n. 23 above. This notion of "reduction," elaborately described by Anonymous IV (Reckow, ed., *Der Musiktraktat des Anonymus 4*, I, 48–49, 51), was first reported by Garlandia (Reimer, *Garlandia*, I, 63: "Item omnis figura non ligata debet reduci ad figuram compositam per aequipollentiam"). The anonymous author adds an important qualification, however: "Et ratione diversitatis sillabarum secundum aliquos quilibet punctus absolutus dicitur, prout non reducitur ad figuram ligatam" (Reckow, ed., *Der Musiktraktat des Anonymus 4*, I, 48). ("But according to some [presumably the older musicians] any single note, because of the separateness of the syllables, is called an independent note, inasmuch as it is not combined with any ligature.") Such a note could not have a value of less than a ternary long.

[53] See Wolf Frobenius, "Modus (Rhythmuslehre)," *Handwörterbuch der musikalischen Terminologie*, ed. Hans Heinrich Eggebrecht (Wiesbaden, 1974).

[54] See Ernest H. Sanders, "The Question of Perotin's Oeuvre and Dates," *Festschrift Walter Wiora zum 30. Dezember 1966*, ed. Ludwig Finscher and Christoph-Hellmut Mahling (Kassel, 1967), p. 243 ff.; and idem, "Style and Technique in Datable Polyphonic Notre-Dame Conductus," *Gordon Athol Anderson (1929–1981) In Memoriam, von seinen Studenten, Freunden und Kollegen*, Musicological Studies, 39 (Henryville, Pa., 1984), p. 510. The arguments presented in the former article in 1967 evidently have not been challenged or disproved. Nonetheless, the view that the six rhythmic modes were standardized "by Perotin in Paris during the last two decades of the twelfth century" (Hans Tischler, ed., *The Montpellier Codex*, I, *Critical Commentary*, Fascicles 1 and 2, Recent Researches in the Music of the Middle Ages and Early Renaissance, 2–3 [Madison, 1978], xxxii) continues to be offered without any

conductus.[55] Anonymous IV confirms him and links the practice with Perotinus and Leoninus (or Leo),[56] allowing us to date its rise as far back as the beginning of the last quarter of the twelfth century: "Istae regulae utuntur in pluribus libris antiquorum, et hoc a tempore et in suo tempore Perotini Magni . . . et similiter a tempore Leonis pro parte, quoniam duae ligatae tunc temporis pro brevi longa ponebantur, et tres ligatae . . . pro longa brevi longa etc." And, he remarks elsewhere, the old composers "paucis modis utebantur iuxta diversitates ordinum supradictorum. . . ."[57] ("They use those rules [those rules are used?] in a good many books of the older generation, i.e., in and from the time of Perotinus Magnus . . . and similarly from the time of Leo, for his part [to some extent?] because at that time two ligated notes stood for a breve and a long, and three . . . for a long, a breve, and a long, etc. . . . [The old composers] used few durations beyond the various above-mentioned arrangements.")

2. The rhythmic modes were also originally and fundamentally a system of melismatic notation that codified the ligature notation of the growing variety of rhythmic patterns. This can be concluded from the circumstances cited by Reimer[58] and from the fact that all of Garlandia's examples of modal notation are given in ligatures (e.g., "tertius modus sumitur ita per figuram, scilicet prima longa et tres ligatae et tres et tres et tres. . . ."),[59] including even the motetus voice cited on page 443 above. Likewise Anonymous IV explains modal notation as a system of ligatures.[60] Particularly conclusive is the

---

countervailing arguments in support of it. There is no practical or theoretical evidence showing the existence or need of a rhythmic modal taxonomy before some time in the first decade of the thirteenth century, when, evidently, the second mode came into being. At that time, or some time thereafter, the familiar motion in breves came to be called sixth mode, and the pattern *si 3li* began to receive the rhythmic interpretation known as third mode, in contrast to the premodal way it used to be performed, which persisted for some time as a less and less acceptable alternative, an "alternate third mode," as it were. See the two references cited at the end of n. 57 below.

[55] See p. 444 above.

[56] See Reckow, ed., *Der Musiktraktat des Anonymus 4*, I, 98.

[57] Ibid., pp. 46, 32. The resulting style is briefly described in the *Discantus positio vulgaris*; see Ernest H. Sanders, "Duple Rhythm and Alternate Third Mode in the 13th Century," this JOURNAL, XV (1962), 282-83; and *idem*, "Consonance and Rhythm," pp. 266-67 and 276, n. 36.

[58] *Garlandia*, II, 52, 53.

[59] *Ibid.*, I, 54.

[60] Reckow, ed., *Der Musiktraktat des Anonymus 4*, I, 22 ff., 43-44.

CONDUCTUS AND MODAL RHYTHM

above-mentioned concept of reduction, as well as the statement of the St.-Emmeram Anonymous that mode is conceived, written, and recognized by means of ligatures and never by means of single notes. The rhythmic modes originated as a conceptual system of configurational notation.

3. Musical rhythm was, thus, primary, and poetic verses were invented, in a manner reminiscent of the prosa, so as to have a sufficient number of syllables, to be adapted to each note of the upper voice(s) of preexisting melismatic discant polyphony (motet).

4. In view of Garlandia's cautionary remark quoted earlier, the assignment of specific durational significance to single notes (*longa, duplex longa, brevis*, and *semibrevis*) must have been a novelty when he wrote his treatise (presumably in the 1250s).[61] Two decades later, Anonymous IV still finds it noteworthy to observe that "the duration of single notes is unambiguous if they are well written."[62] It is not long, therefore, before implicit or explicit evidence begins to appear that thinking in terms of individual ingredients replaces what might be called molecular or catenary concepts (patterned phrases). This is most plainly stated by, of all people, the St.-Emmeram Anonymous, in spite of his insistence on the old order. He justifies the sequence of his topics (single notes, ligatures, semibreves, modes, etc.) with the remark that any explanation of a complex system must begin with the smallest element.[63] Correspondingly, Dietricus writes his examples of

---

[61] Cf. Reimer, *Garlandia*, II, 53. Neither W_1 nor F, both written in the 1240s (except for the addenda to the latter), contains differentiated single notes. Although W_1 is usually dated into the last quarter of the thirteenth century—most recently by Hans Tischler, "The Evolution of the *Magnus liber organi*," *The Musical Quarterly*, LXX (1984), 168—the most reliable, reasonable, and authentic date established by Julian Brown, Sonia Patterson, and David Hiley, "Further Observations on W_1," *Journal of the Plainsong & Mediaeval Music Society*, IV (1981), 53–80, should no longer be disregarded.

[62] See p. 447 above. Hence, his well-known remark that in his day one could learn in one hour what used to take seven (Reckow, ed., *Der Musiktraktat des Anonymus 4*, I, 50).

[63] Sowa, *Ein anonymer*, p. 73. His ambivalence is strikingly highlighted by the fact that this statement follows his strict description of modes as a ligature notation (see p. 448 above) and is, in turn, followed some pages later by the remark that "quia figura composita in hac arte dignior est et generalior quam sit simplex—nam simplices, ut supra patuit, sunt ad compositas reducende, tamquam pars ad totum—ideo patet ordo" ("because in this practice ligatures clearly rank higher and are more general than single notes—for single notes, as was explained above, have to be reduced to ligatures, as a part to the whole—therefore the arrangement is obvious").

the modes with single notes,[64] and Lambertus gives first syllabic and then melismatic examples for eight of his nine modes.[65] Finally, both Franco and Odington relegate the ligature notation of the modes[66] to a chapter that comes well after their definition.[67]

5. The modal system is specifically applicable to motets and their melismatic models (clausulae, discant sections in organa).[68]

6. It has been claimed that the conductus, like the motet, was consistently regarded by thirteenth-century musicians as a species of discant and that, therefore, both were "among the genres governed by the rhythmic modes."[69] But the subsumption of the conductus under the heading of discant, in fact, applies only to Franco and some of the many writers he influenced.[70] That it was not Garlandia's view is borne out by the fact that all but two of his examples of modal notation, other than those he invented for Chapter 11, are taken from Gregorian chant; the two exceptions—examples of imperfect modes—are *dupla*: one being part of a conductus *cauda*, the other part of a *motetus* but also written *sine littera*.[71] The only genres he refers to in his chapter on discant are organum (i.e., portions in discant style) and motet.[72] In the inauthentic fifteenth chapter, "discantus" is specifical-

---

[64] Hans Müller, *Eine Abhandlung über Mensuralmusik in der Karlsruher Handschrift St. Peter pergamen. 29a*, Mittheilungen aus der Grossherzoglich Badischen Hof- und Landesbibliothek und Münzsammlung, 6 (Leipzig, 1886), p. 5. Characteristically, they are not given as conventional modal phrases but as feet, i.e., as units of imperfect modes (e.g., not LBLBL | but LBLB).

[65] Coussemaker, *Scriptorum*, pp. 279–81. His ninth mode (groups of three semibreves) cannot be ligated.

[66] *Ibid.*, p. 238; Franco of Cologne, *Ars cantus mensurabilis*, ed. Reaney and Gilles, Corpus scriptorum de musica, 18, pp. 26 ff.

[67] Coussemaker, *Scriptorum*, pp. 244–45; Franco of Cologne, *Ars cantus mensurabilis*, ed. Reaney and Gilles, Corpus scriptorum de musica, 18, pp. 60 ff.

[68] Regarding this statement and some of the foregoing conclusions, also see Ernest H. Sanders, "Continuity in English Music," communication in *Music & Letters*, XLVII (1966), 188–89. For the traditional concept of the *modi motellorum* or *mothetorum*, see Frobenius, "Modus (Rhythmuslehre)," p. 3.

[69] Janet Knapp, "Conductus," *The New Grove Dictionary*, IV, 653.

[70] See p. 446 above and n. 35. The author of the later part of the *Discantus positio vulgaris* may or may not be understood to regard conductus as a kind of discant, depending on whether his use of the word *alius* is translated as either "something else" (i.e., "different from [discant]") or "another" (i.e., "another [kind of discant]"). The latter translation is probably preferable. But in any case, the designation of conductus as a kind of discant seems not to have occurred before the 1270s. The older part of the treatise sets organum and conductus apart from discantus. See p. 444 above.

[71] See p. 443 above.

[72] See Reimer, *Garlandia*, I, 76.

ly juxtaposed with "cantus planus."[73] More revealing are the first two sentences of the copula chapter: "Dicto de discantu dicendum est de copula, quae multum valet ad discantum, quia discantus numquam perfecte scitur nisi mediante copula. Unde copula dicitur esse id, quod est inter discantum et organum."[74] That Anonymous IV also regarded discant as the polyphony resulting from the addition of a countermelody (*discantus*) to a preexistent melody (*cantus planus, cantus ecclesiasticus*) is demonstrated by the passage quoted previously.[75]

7. Notwithstanding the possibility that six of the meters of ancient poetry may have been the models for Garlandia's modal taxonomy,[76] no medieval writer links poetry with the modes, not even Odington, whose elaborately systematic juxtaposition of quantitative poetic meters with perfect and imperfect modes serves only abstract didactic purposes.[77] He merely says, in effect, that the various rhythmic patterns of these modes are parallel to certain poetic meters, most of which are, in fact, not represented in the poetry of the time. There is, then, no evidence in the treatises that poetic meter served as cue for musical rhythm, modal or otherwise.

Although no medieval authors, with the exception of the St.-Emmeram Anonymous (1279), specifically associate the syllabic portions of conducti with the modal system, their silence (except for the significant expression "super unum metrum" in the second part of the *Discantus positio vulgaris*) does not, by itself, disprove its applicability. Our knowledge of whether and to what extent modal rhythm governed such passages depends, therefore, on two factors: (1) the degree to which the notation in the sources provides incontrovertible proof one way or another and (2) our insight into medieval concepts of versification.

In evaluating the notational evidence, one must keep in mind, first of all, that the datable specimens of conducti show the species to have flourished for at least three quarters of a century.[78] Moreover, the

---

[73] *Ibid.*, p. 95.
[74] *Ibid.*, p. 88. For a complete translation of this chapter, see Sanders, "Consonance and Rhythm," p. 283.
[75] See n. 29 above.
[76] See Sanders, "Consonance and Rhythm," p. 279, n. 46.
[77] Coussemaker, *Scriptorum*, p. 238; Odington, *Summa de speculatione musicae*, ed. Hammond, Corpus scriptorum de musica, 14, p. 131.
[78] See Sanders, "Style and Technique," pp. 505 ff.

preservation of some of them in either of two particular sources of the early fourteenth century shows that the conductus repertoire of the "Notre Dame School" was still alive nearly a century and a half after its earliest known specimens were written. The former period may be compared with the time span between, say, Haydn's Op. 17 and Schumann's Op. 41 or between 1826, the year in which Schubert completed his last symphony, and 1895 (?), the time when Mahler undertook to edit and arrange it.[79] One cannot talk, therefore, about "the rhythm" of "the conductus," especially as momentous changes in the concept of rhythm and its notation occurred in the first half of the thirteenth century.[80] The rhythms of the full modal system cannot be applied to compositions written earlier than those with which the system was first associated, i.e., before the first decade of the thirteenth century was well along. Moreover, the versions of Notre Dame conducti in such mensural sources as *Heid, Sab, Da, Fauv,* and *Hu*[81] must be viewed with at least the same degree of caution regarding their reliability as, for instance, Czerny's version of *The Well-Tempered Clavier*. In fact, no mensurally notated source of a Notre Dame conductus can be automatically regarded as dependable evidence for its original rhythms (and, at times, melodies). To the example of fourteenth-century perversion of a thirteenth-century conductus (*Crucifigat omnes*) given in a recent article,[82] can be added a plethora of further instances of inconsistencies and distortions.[83]

---

[79] Peter Andraschke, "Die Retuschen Gustav Mahlers an der 7. Symphonie von Franz Schubert," *Archiv für Musikwissenschaft*, XXXII (1975), 107–108.

[80] One might as well equate the harmony of *Fidelio* and *Parsifal*. Handschin had more than once called for consideration of the chronological *Schichtung* of the repertoire, e.g., "Conductus-Spicilegien," *Archiv für Musikwissenschaft*, IX (1952), 107–13.

[81] Heidelberg, Universitätsbibliothek, 2588; Rome, Convento di Santa Sabina, Biblioteca della Curia Generalizia dei Domenicani, XIV L 3; Darmstadt, Hessische Landes- und Hochschulbibliothek, 347; Paris, Bibliothèque Nationale, Fonds français, 146; Burgos, Monasterio de Las Huelgas.

[82] Sanders, "Style and Technique," pp. 517–18. *Crucifigat omnes* represents a foolproof case, since it is a texted version of the final *cauda* of another conductus.

[83] Manifest misunderstanding or—less likely—disregard of pre-Garlandian models occurs, for instance, in *Columbe simplicitas* ("fel horret malicie turturis"), *Quod promisit* ("munda caro"), *Parit preter morem* ("retinens verum dei decorem," "deitatis sue deus honorem," and "qui struit non destruit"), *Flos de spina procreatur* ("stillant montes colles fluunt"), *Nulli beneficium* ("te pastorem"), *O varium fortune* ("lubricum"), *Clavus pungens* (several passages), etc. The one motet in *Sab* exhibits meticulous mensural notation. But to the extent (if any) that the conducti in that source may be said to be mensurally notated, they certainly do not show modal rhythm. All kinds of

CONDUCTUS AND MODAL RHYTHM

There are only three syllabic conducti that require modal reading, namely those pieces that are newly texted versions of *caudae* of other conducti.[84] For compositions containing syllabic portions melodically identical with melismas, the rhythmic identity of the former passages to the latter has been advocated as self-evident.[85] Undeniably this is a persuasive argument, yet, even in these cases, a degree of caution is advisable.[86] Augmentation or diminution occurs not only in the tenors of two remarkable "St.-Victor" clausulae (nos. 25 and 35) as well as of Perotinus's *Alleluia V Nativitas (Juda)* but in the conductus *Soli nitorem*, where there is melodic identity between one syllabic passage and two rhythmically different *caudae* (first mode and ternary longs). There is no evidence in the notation of this piece in the pre-Garlandian manuscript *F* that the scribe of *Hu*, the other source preserving this composition, was (or was not) correct in choosing the first mode for the syllabic passage.

But, quite apart from the often enormous problems attendant upon insistence on modal transcriptions of many syllabic conducti or portions of conducti, both Continental and English sources provide concrete evidence that the assumption of modal rhythm for such music is often unjustifiable. *Qui servare puberem*, an early conductus motet of the repertoire, is one of six that appear without tenor, i.e., as conducti, in W_1, which is the only Notre Dame manuscript to transmit no motets. A comparison of three versions of the endings of the first and last phrases ("Qui servare puberem / vagam claudere" and, particularly, "novo gaudet veterem / amicum pellere") shows clearly that the scribe of W_1 or his predecessor, evidently unaware of or unfriendly to the original nature of this piece as a motet, assigned it nonmodal rhythms, even though the rhythms of all three voices of the motet were originally modal (see Figs. 1–3). The notation of

---

adjustments to the modal system are necessary to call the rhythms of any of these conducti modal—and Husmann is often inclined to make them. See "Ein Faszikel Notre-Dame-Kompositionen auf Texte des Pariser Kanzlers Philipp in einer Dominikanerhandschrift (Rom, Santa Sabina XIV L 3)," *Archiv für Musikwissenschaft*, XXIV (1967), 1–23.

[84] In addition to *Crucifigat omnes* they are *Bulla fulminante* and *Minor natu filius*. *Anima iugi*, somewhat loosely referred to as a newly texted version of the *cauda* of another conductus in Sanders, "Style and Technique," p. 505, is actually a unique case of the conversion of the three successive stanzas of a monophonic conductus into a double motet on a separately texted tenor (see Schrade, "Unknown Motets," pp. 404–12). It is hard to believe that this composition was not conceived *à double emploi* from the outset.

[85] See n. 11 above.

[86] Cf. Handschin, "Zur Frage der Conductus-Rhythmik," pp. 113–30.

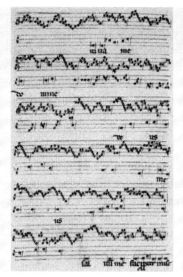

Figure 1. Florence, Biblioteca Medicea-Laurenziana, Pluteus 29.1, fol. 101ᵛ

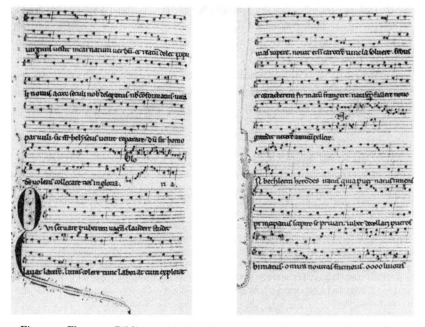

Figure 2. Florence, Biblioteca Medicea-Laurenziana, Pluteus 29.1, fols. 381ᵛ–82

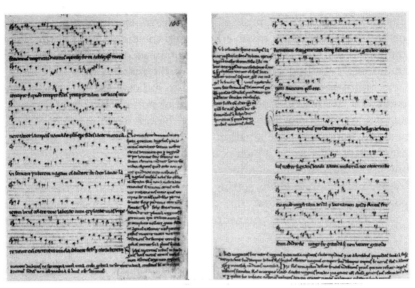

Figure 3. Wolfenbüttel, Herzog-August-Bibliothek, 677, fols. 115 (106)–115ᵛ (106ᵛ)

the endings of the first and third phrases (see Ex. 1)—especially the double *virgae*, with or without *plicae*—and the setting of the penultimate syllable in the upper voice exclude the possibility of modal rhythm. The discant section and its motet version, however, begin

Example 1
W₁, fol. 115ʳ⁻ᵛ (106ʳ⁻ᵛ)

and end as shown in Example 2. Thus, the transmutation in W_1 of the motet into a conductus involved not only the elimination of the tenor but interpretation of the syllabic notation in accordance with the older traditions prevailing prior to the rise of the motet.

A number of English sources seem to indicate that the traditional nonmodal rhythm of conducti, like that of polyphonic chant settings, maintained itself for quite some time before yielding to the more modern "motetish" declamation involving breves as well as longs. Manuscript GB-Cjec 1, which contains several Notre Dame conducti, one apparently insular conductus, as well as one complete and one fragmentary troped chant setting, uses *virga* notation for the syllabic portions of the conducti (as do most other English sources of conducti), but English mensural notation[87] for the troped chant

Example 2
(a) F, fol. 101ᵛ
(b) F, fols. 381ᵛ–82ʳ

---

[87] See Sanders, "Duple Rhythm," pp. 263 ff.

Ex. 2, cont.

settings, the upper voices of which behave like the upper voices of motets. In the English conductus repertoire, the rise of the fast modern declamation can be traced, because of the appearance of rondellus sections with text, in some of the more elaborate compositions, probably written in the third quarter of the century. The most striking example is the conductus *Flos regalis* (see Fig. 4).[88] Not only does it show rondellus sections to have originated as special types of *caudae*, but it also consistently differentiates between the slow, presumably traditional *virga* notation and rhythm of ordinary passages *cum littera* and the English mensural notation of the texted phrases of the rondelli.

Ultimately the more modern declamation came to be preferred for the syllabic portions of English conducti as well. A particularly intriguing case is that of *In te concipitur*, one of four conductus settings in manuscript *GB-Ob 257*.[89] In contrast to the other three, it is written

---

[88] Transcribed in *Polyphonic Music of the Fourteenth Century*, XIV, *English Music of the Thirteenth and Early Fourteenth Centuries*, ed. Ernest H. Sanders (Monaco, 1979), 46; commentary on p. 240. For three similar compositions, see pp. 53–60.
[89] Transcribed *ibid.*, pp. 189–90, 188, 191, 192.

Figure 4. Oxford, Bodleian Library, Corpus Christi College 489, no. 22, fol. 1

in English mensural notation, perhaps still something of a novelty for polyphony *cum littera*. A differently remarkable case is *Equitas in curia*,[90] a conductus written in parts, quite possibly because its advanced declamation and the concomitant English mensural notation made it appear to the scribe like a motet. Other English conducti exhibiting the new advanced declamation and its notation, in part or throughout, are *Quem trina polluit* and *In excelsis gloria*, respectively.[91]

That neither accentuation nor versification determined the musical rhythm of a good many polyphonic conducti is proved by numerous compositions preserved in the Notre Dame sources. The prosody is

[90] Transcribed *ibid.*, pp. 195–97.

[91] Transcribed *ibid.*, pp. 61–63, 66–68. The sources are relevant because (1) there is quite a bit of evidence that Continental and English musicians knew and appropriated each other's repertoire, (2) the notations are similar, and (3) at the time of the appearance of Johannes de Garlandia's notation, English specimens reveal notational details of significance for both conductus traditions.

often irregular, indicating that for purposes of delivery, including, probably, spoken delivery, the syllables of poetry were regarded as neutrally equivalent and therefore subject to basically isochronous setting. This would account for the convention of syllabic treatment[92] of traditional meters apparently prevalent until at least some time in the thirteenth century.[93] Since the regular or irregular stress patterns formed by the words in nonquantitative (and, for that matter, in quantitative) versification were—and are—on the whole not bound to systematic quantification, there was, therefore, no regular prosodic scheme with which neumatic or melismatic ornamentation could interfere; hence, the latter could be applied in conducti wherever the composer saw the purely musical need for it.

The conductus *Deduc Syon* ends with the following quatrain:

scelus hoc ulciscere
veni iudex gentium
cathedras vendentium
columbas evertere.

Such heptasyllabic verses would seem tailor-made for first-mode delivery of their musical setting, as it appears in the Notre Dame sources, even though the pattern of the beginnings of the last two lines disturbs the expected trochaic regularity. As often happens, however, a *cauda* separates the penultimate from the final syllable, which, as in most cases, is allotted to the last note (see the syllable stroke preceding that note in both voices in Figure 5; the text scribe of *F* erroneously omitted the syllable at that point, as is shown by all concordances). If the entire syllabic passage had been intended to be sung in first mode, with each phrase containing four beats, the last two notes preceding the *cauda* would have had to be ligated, as both are allotted to the penultimate syllable. Since they are, in fact, written as single notes (*sine littera*), they must be read as longs. There is probability verging on certainty, therefore, that all four phrases consist of eight beats and that the notes for each syllable are equivalent to one ternary long. A fair number of such cases can be cited, which are particularly persuasive when the final word is proparoxytonic.

---

[92] See Heinrich Husmann, "Das Prinzip der Silbenzählung im Lied des zentralen Mittelalters," *Die Musikforschung*, VI (1953), 8–20.

[93] It surely was this view of syllables and words as neutral raw material (within a poetic frame) that allowed them to be shaped in motets, regardless of accent or syntax. There was, of course, bound to be a considerable congruence between the rhythmic pattern of the first mode and the most common accent patterns of Latin. But this is no more than a congruence (cf. Sanders, "The Medieval Motet," *Gattungen der Musik in*

Figure 6 presents a passage from *Austro terris*. For the phrase "potens datur carceri," the characteristic lengthening of the penultimate syllable vitiates any attempt at modal reading to accord with the apparently trochaic poetry. The musical setting of "ab erroris via flexus/ patris redit in amplexus" divides this distich into five phrases of eight, four, four, six, and eight beats, blithely separating in the process the last word of the first verse from its remainder—a fine example of medieval *laceramento della poesia* (Ex. 3). In a second excerpt

Example 3
F, fol. 300ʳ

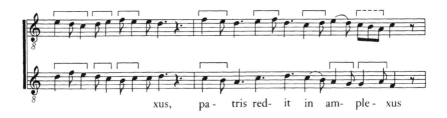

from the same conductus, the composer, rather than separating the last word from its verse, has united the first word of the third verse with the entire second verse. Again, as in *Deduc Syon*, the last syllable of the final word of the stanza is delayed for the sake of a long intervening *cauda* (Fig. 7). Here—and in many of the more elaborate

---

Einzeldarstellungen: Gedenkschrift Leo Schrade, ed. Wulf Arlt, Ernst Lichtenhahn, and Hans Oesch [Bern, 1973], p. 511). Although more frequent in motets of the late thirteenth century, disregard of accentuation—as well as irregular versification—are endemic in the motet from its beginning. It is not surprising that Hugo Riemann's perceptive observation of this feature was roundly criticized by Ludwig; see Hugo Riemann, "Die Beck-Aubry'sche 'modale Interpretation' der Troubadourmelodien," *Sammelbände der Internationalen Musikgesellschaft*, XI (1909–10), 583; and Friedrich Ludwig, "Zur 'modalen Interpretation' von Melodien des 12. und 13. Jahrhunderts," *Zeitschrift der Internationalen Musikgesellschaft*, XI (1910), 379 ff.

Figure 7. Florence, Biblioteca Medicea-Laurenziana, Pluteus 29.1, fol. 299ᵛ

Figure 6. Florence, Biblioteca Medicea-Laurenziana, Pluteus 29.1, fol. 300

Figure 5. Florence, Biblioteca Medicea-Laurenziana, Pluteus 29.1, fol. 337

conducti—one finds that, as in some of the works of the visual arts of the time, the ornamental impulse all but obscures the substance being ornamented, as if a bucket of music had been poured out over the words. The procedure in the conductus *cum caudis* is comparable to manuscript illumination with its growing profusion of elaborate historiated initials.[94] All the music of a conductus decorates the words of the text, in conducti *cum caudis* often with such wonderfully indiscriminate luxuriance that the *cauda* seems to be wagging the dog.

Figure 8 presents a different case of the irrelevance of regular versification to the musical setting of the poetry. The verse scheme of the quoted passage from *O felix Bituria* (presumably written in 1209)[95] is entirely straightforward:

> Mundus hic a crimine
> vixit et in mundo
> honores a limine
> salutavit mundo
> corde vixit munere
> mundus in profundo
> non submersus remige
> Christo fuit fundo
> tibi preces inclite
> pro me funde Christo
> ut sub recto tramite
> cursu curram isto.

It seems, however, that the particularly artful display of the technique of enjambment caused the composer to articulate the text as prose, perhaps to clarify the syntax.

> Mundus hic a crimine vixit
> et in mundo, honores a limine salutavit;
> mundo corde vixit, munere mundus;
> in profundo non submersus remige Christo fuit;
> fundo tibi preces, inclite;
> pro me funde Christo,
> ut sub recto tramite cursu curram isto.
>
> (This man has lived free from crime
> and in this world has paid scant regard to honors;

---

[94] For the entirely different role and function of poetry in the motet, see Sanders, "The Medieval Motet," p. 528.

[95] See Sanders, "Style and Technique," p. 510.

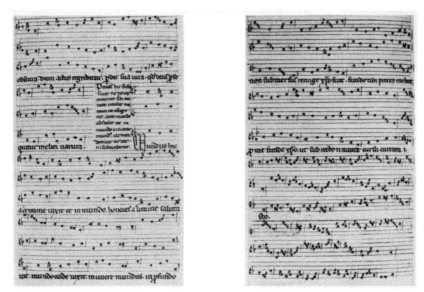

Figure 8. Florence, Biblioteca Medicea-Laurenziana, Pluteus 29.1, fol. 210[r-v]

he has lived with a pure heart, clean in office,
and, with Christ as oarsman, he was not submerged in the depths;
I pour out my prayers to you, famous man,
pour them out for me to Christ,
so that I may run that course along the right path.)

Instances of the composers' unconcern with verse schemes and accentuations abound in the repertoire. The evidence of theory and practice militates against modal reading of such passages, whether they appear in pre-Garlandian manuscripts or, more or less faultily, in mensural sources. Clearly, the convention of syllabic approach to traditional meters[96] must have been strong and persistent enough to

---

[96] For its genesis, see Dag Norberg, *Introduction à l'étude de la versification latine médiévale*, Studia latina Stockholmiensia, 5 (Stockholm, 1958), especially pp. 124 ff., 186; Paul Klopsch, *Einführung in die mittellateinische Verslehre* (Darmstadt, 1972), especially pp. 12–13, 19. Particularly significant is Ewald Jammers's "Der Vers der Trobadors und Trouveres und die deutschen Kontrafakten," *Medium aevum vivum: Festschrift für Walther Bulst*, ed. Hans Robert Jauss and Dieter Schaller (Heidelberg, 1960), pp. 147–60. On pp. 148 ff., he deals insightfully with syllabic versification, referring to psalmody as its preliminary state, raised in effect to a heightened poetic level by rhyme with unvarying accent and by numerically regulated syllable content of the verses.

make this treatment of poetry by medieval musicians seem natural. While the introduction of the measured breve in syllabic notation made musical reinforcement of accentual delivery of poetry more feasible and attractive, the many instances of disregard of prosodic proprieties in the polyphony of the thirteenth and fourteenth centuries show that only in the fifteenth and sixteenth centuries was this attitude replaced gradually by increasing word consciousness and the growth of metrical music.[97]

* * *

Two questions remain to be examined briefly. To what extent and how can the ambiguous pre-Garlandian notation of conducti be interpreted, and what, in the face of the evidence and in view of the often awkward and unmusical results, caused the *Modaltheorie* to hold such largely unchallenged sway?

As it happens, two of the three syllabic conducti made from preexistent *caudae* can be dated (1219 and 1223).[98] That this technique could have followed the rise of the Latin motet[99] by about ten years seems quite plausible. Only with the motet did a reliable musical yardstick become available for the measurement and rigid modal

---

[97] Modal rhythm is not metrical rhythm; see Ernest H. Sanders, communication, this JOURNAL, XXXIII (1980), 607; as well as Sanders, "The Medieval Motet," nn. 127 and 128. Much of the Latin cantilena polyphony composed in England in the first half of the fourteenth century is exceptional in its metrical regularity. In a recent article by Ritva Jonsson and Leo Treitler, "Medieval Music and Language: A Reconsideration of the Relationship," *Studies in the History of Music*, I, *Music and Language* (New York, 1983), 1-23, the authors take exception to the commonly held view that only in the course of the fifteenth century did composers begin to be concerned with the prosodic and semantic values of text. It is clear, however, that all the musicologists (Brown, Blume, Sanders, and Hoppin) singled out for this view (pp. 2-3) made their comments in the context of the singularly important field of polyphonic composition, while Jonsson's and Treitler's article deals with the music-language relationship in early Latin monophony. It is hard to understand how, for instance, a comparison of fundamental features of "music" composed in and after the fifteenth century as against "music" composed earlier—in the communication cited at the beginning of this note—could be seen to pertain to anything other than polyphony, the more so as that communication responded to an article concerned only with medieval polyphonic music. But I wonder, especially in view of the common practice of adaptation, whether even Latin monophony (including chants and tropes) is always capable of the sort of carefully shaped analytical demonstration given in Jonsson's and Treitler's article.

[98] See Sanders, "Style and Technique," pp. 516-17.

[99] See *idem*, "The Question," p. 248.

CONDUCTUS AND MODAL RHYTHM

patterning of poetry that was not based on systematic arrangements of stressed and unstressed syllables but displayed rhyme, with identical accentuation, and number of syllables as the sole fixed elements of versification. "The evidence is quite strong that prior to . . . approximately the second decade of the thirteenth century and probably for some time thereafter most syllables in polyphonic genres other than the motet had the durational value of one perfect long, some more, none less."[100] (This can also serve as a useful guideline for much non-Gregorian monophony.) In that notation, two or more successive ligatures over one syllable should normally be viewed as *sine littera*. Some, at least, of the purely syllabic conducti, on the other hand, might well be suspected of being derived from preexisting melismatic material; even if such suspicions cannot be confirmed, modal reading may be appropriate, although the incidence of modes other than the first and perhaps third (or alternate third) is likely to be quite small.[101] It is such cases, doubtless becoming more common in the third quarter of the century, to which the above-quoted (p. 449) passage in the treatise by the St.-Emmeram Anonymous would seem to be particularly applicable.

---

[100] *Polyphonic Music of the Fourteenth Century*, XIV, xiv; also Sanders, "The Medieval Motet," p. 530, n. 127. Cf. the important remark of Anonymous IV quoted in n. 52 above. Both the theoretical and the practical evidence seem to indicate that the tradition in which the *virgae* were read *absolute* was succeeded by the practice of *reductio*; the latter was, in turn, clarified and ultimately superseded by the use of different symbols for single notes of different duration instituted by Johannes de Garlandia. But the notation of the conducti in the "St.-Victor" manuscript (Paris, B.N., lat. 15139) leaves little doubt that the traditional slow declamation of conductus texts was the rule (with few exceptions) throughout the first half of the thirteenth century.

[101] Janet Knapp has recognized the necessity for alternatives to the application of modal rhythm to syllabic portions of conducti. The cases she discusses in "Musical Declamation and Poetic Rhythm in an Early Layer of Notre Dame Conductus," this JOURNAL, XXXII (1979), 386–405, she transcribes isochronously, calling the rhythms those of the fifth mode. The frequent designation by scholars of such declamation as fifth mode is inappropriate, however, since the latter is basically a tenor mode, as Handschin had pointed out on pp. 114–15 and 130 of his 1952 article (see n. 11 above). Less useful is the recurrent use by some modern musicologists of the fourth mode as a rhythmic template to fit the versification of certain conductus poems; Ludwig had excluded it from his modal canon (see p. 440 above). The fourth mode is a purely theoretical construct balancing the third, so as to allow the modal system to be presented as consisting of three pairs of modes. Dietricus observes sensibly and correctly that "tertius [modus constat] ex una longa et sequentibus duabus brevibus. . . . Quartus modus posset esse e converso ex duabus brevibus et sequenti longa, sed non est in usu" (Müller, *Eine Abhandlung*, p. 5). ("The [pattern of the] third mode is made up of one long followed by two breves. . . . The fourth mode, conversely, could exhibit the sequence of two breves and a subsequent long, but it is not in use.")

The *Modaltheorie* was applied first and foremost to the troubadour[102] and trouvère repertoires. Its staunchest proponent, Friedrich Gennrich, was also particularly prominent in proclaiming its validity for the Minnelieder. With respect to the latter, it was laid to rest by Kippenberg[103] and, with regard to the former, by Kippenberg and Hendrik van der Werf.[104] Its hold on medieval musicology has been extraordinary from the beginning, causing not only a series of heated controversies about its authorship that lasted for decades but even a death by duel and an emigration.[105] It is clear that modal rhythm spread from discant (i.e., discant passages in organa, clausulae, and motets) to gain some influence on the rhythmic facture of specimens of other repertoires; the limits of this influence remain to be explored and, if possible, to be more precisely determined.[106] But the excessive claims established and extended for the *Modaltheorie* can only be adduced to a Cartesian penchant for order and system, anachronistically incompatible with the pre-Franconian evidence and in distressing conflict with the superb scholarly standards of its author.[107] It is

---

[102] Not by Husmann, however, who saw the prevalence of modal rhythm only beginning in troubadour songs after 1180; see Husmann, "Das Prinzip."

[103] His book, an exhaustive investigation of the problems of rhythm in vernacular song of the Middle Ages, is a model of intelligent and rigorous scholarship. It clears the air with impeccable impartiality. Only once does the author allow the impression of passion to break through, when he characterizes—understandably enough—a particularly excessive aspect of Gennrich's "Modaldogma" as monstrous (pp. 23–24). For the relevant articles by Gennrich, see Kippenberg's bibliography.

[104] Hendrik van der Werf, *The Chansons of the Troubadours and Trouvères* (Utrecht, 1972), pp. 35–45. There is, of course, no reason to assume that monophony was governed by a rhythmic system; also see Kippenberg, *Der Rhythmus im Minnesang*, pp. 63, 100. Also see the conclusions presented by John Stevens, "The Manuscript Presentation and Notation of Adam de la Halle's Courtly Chansons," *Source Materials and the Interpretation of Music: A Memorial Volume to Thurston Dart*, ed. Ian Bent (London, 1981), pp. 52–53.

[105] For historical surveys of this eighty-year-old issue, see Heinrich Husmann, "Das System der modalen Rhythmik," *Archiv für Musikwissenschaft*, XI (1954), 2 ff.; Chailley's article cited in n. 7 above; and, most authoritatively, Friedrich Gennrich, "Wer ist der Initiator der Modaltheorie?" *Miscelánea en homenaje a Monseñor Higinio Anglés* (Barcelona, 1958–61), pp. 315–30. Actually, Aubry died of a wound he received in training for his duel with Jean Beck.

[106] For those purposes Bryan Gillingham's recently published *The Polyphonic Sequences in Codex Wolfenbuettel 677*, Musicological Studies, 35 (Henryville, Pa., 1982), should be left out of account.

[107] This is still apparent in the conclusion Husmann reached with a seeming tinge of regret in the course of the last of his series of articles concerning rhythm in music of the twelfth and thirteenth centuries ("Das System," p. 31): "Man wird sich also damit

essential to recognize that each musical and notational style—except for electronic music—carries within it its own particular levels of determinacy and indeterminacy. The inability of past medieval musicological scholarship to recognize the persistence of elements of indeterminacy in much of the music of the early High Gothic serves as an eloquent warning against freighting historiography with-misleading preconceptions.[108]

Columbia University

---

abfinden müssen, dass es Konduktus gibt, die eine Rhythmik besitzen, deren Unregelmässigkeit die Grenzen des der Modalnotation Darstellbaren überschreitet." ("Thus, one will have to come to terms with the fact that there are conductus possessing rhythms that transcend the limits of what modal notation could represent [sic].") Cf. Kippenberg, *Der Rhythmus im Minnesang*, pp. 61, 64; William Beare, *Latin Verse and European Song: A Study in Accent and Rhythm* (London, 1957), pp. 102, 287 ff. The latter put it that "most Germans . . . cannot accept the idea that there may be a form of verse which is quite free from alternating rhythm" (p. 102)—a statement that, happily, has been rendered invalid by the work of such men as Jammers and Kippenberg, followed by a degree of reorientation on the part of Husmann ("Deklamation und Akzent in der Vertonung mittellateinischer Dichtung," *Archiv für Musikwissenschaft*, XIX/XX [1962/63], 1–8).

[108] My special thanks go to Mr. Stanley Weiss, without whose helpful intercessions this article could not have been completed.

[11]

The performance of Ars Antiqua motets
Christopher Page

This article is dedicated to the memory of Professor Frank Harrison, a scholar whose delight in the sound of medieval music was an inspiration to all who knew him.

1 A young cleric (perhaps a student at the University of Paris) offers money to a girl who, to judge by the frame-drum (? or tambourine) in her hand, is off to dance in a carole. From a 13th-century Bible moralisée produced in Paris (London, British Library MS Harley 1526, f.31r).

Sequitur bene psallite ei   id est non vane leticie lascivie sicut illi qui cantant mundo in motetis, cantilenis et choreis . . .[1]

Praise the Lord well . . . not with vainglorious and wanton pleasure like those who sing for the world in motets, lyrics and dance-songs.

The author of these words, the early 14th-century and renowned theologian Pierre de Palude, suggests an association between the motet and the sprightly dances (or *caroles*) that were performed in streets and churchyards by young men and women. He clearly despises the 'wanton pleasure' that motets provide, and the implication is that they share the joyful and primaveral colours always worn by secular music in the Middle Ages.

The treatise *De Musica* by de Palude's contemporary, Johannes de Grocheio, presents an altogether different picture.[2] When Pierre speaks of the motet he opens a window that lets in the sound of dance music; Johannes de Grocheio, in contrast, closes a door that shuts the motet into all the solid and professional chambers of Parisian life. Such music should not be performed for the laity, he declares, because it only baffles them; let these pieces be sung for the *litterati*—in other words for the theologians, the Masters of Arts, the prosperous lawyers and the successful physicians who thrived on the banks of the Seine.[3]

The paradox of the 13th-century motet is that it is both playful and learned at the same time. Though Pierre de Palude and Johannes de Grocheio disagree, it is clear that each represents part of the truth; surveying the repertory as a whole, each fulfils a helpful role as guide. Pierre was right to speak of motets and dance songs in the same breath, for some Ars Antiqua motets incorporate scraps of dance songs (see ex.1). These quotations give many motets a light and informal air, confirming the impression that the genre's social background lies, in part, with the amorous interplay between Parisian students and the local girls with their ring-dances. Even in 'learned' pieces the freshness of dance music is rarely far away (see ex.2).

Ex.1 A dance-song, or rondet de carole, whose words are preserved in the early 13th-century romance of Guillaume de Dole by Jean Renart, and whose music can be reconstructed from a 'quotation' in a two-part motet. From F. Gennrich, Rondeaux, Virelais und Balladen (Dresden, 1921), i, p.10

Ex.2 Triplum, bars 1–8, of Ut celesti possimus/Cum sit natus hodie/Hec dies as it appears in the Bamberg MS. From Anderson, CMM, lxviii, no.21

On the other hand, Johannes de Grocheio was well-advised to emphasize the learned appeal of a genre in which two, sometimes three, songs are performed at the same time, their texts and melodies colliding together in a way that seems to obliterate the very lightness and charm that has been admired (ex.3). And while the upper parts possess a melodiousness that may have an instant appeal for the modern listener, the tenor parts do their best to sound like a three-inch tape-loop. With unyielding determination they repeat their rhythmic (and often melodic) material, thus effacing the very qualities which most modern performers and listeners regard as the essence of medieval chant: an expressive melodiousness and a freedom from any mensural organization.

Above all, it is in the texture of these pieces that the force of Johannes de Grocheio's words about the learned character of the motet may be sensed. The harmony is intellectual—or at least highly controlled—in a way that may seem to be at odds with the gracious and appealing melodies from which the vertical sonorities are made. With a strictness of method that rivals the scholastic philosophy of the 13th century, virtually every perfection in a motet (represented by a dotted crotchet in ex.3) opens with a perfect consonance. This was usually an open 5th or octave, but it could also include the $^8_4$ chord (the first sonority of bar 5 in ex.3) which even medieval theorists regarded as less *jocundus* than the $^8_5$. The harmonic structure of an Ars Antiqua motet is therefore subject to a rigorous counting process, and for 13th-century musicians this was part of the mystique of measured music; in their eyes *mensurabilis* was to *musica* as *sapiens* is now to *homo*, implying a new departure in evolution with reason emerging triumphant after untold ages in which men had been governed by instinct alone.

Poised between the serious and the playful—between 'earnest and game', to borrow a phrase from Chaucer—the 13th-century motet offers much to modern performers and listeners, and by collating several hints in contemporary treatises with the results of practical experiment it becomes possible to reconstruct, at least in part, the manner of their performance. Needless to say, this cannot be a wholly objective enquiry, and what follows is based upon my own experience with professional British singers, most of whom received their training in the choir of some cathedral or collegiate establishment in England.

What kinds of voices were used for motets in the 13th century? I believe that the existence of something like the counter-tenor voice must be granted at the outset. In his *Scientia artis musice* of 1274, the French theorist

Ex.3 Encontre le tans/Quant fuellent/In ordorem, from Thomas, Robin and Marion motets, ii

Elias of Salomon describes a form of improvized organum in which four associates double a chant at the 5th, octave and 12th,[4] and when a plainsong with a range of seven or eight notes is performed in this way the lowest and highest sounding notes in the organum will lie some two octaves and a 5th apart. This is a very generous compass (sufficing for most of Dufay's music, for example) and it may be concluded that some 13th-century churches could muster singers with a compass of 20 notes between them. If Elias intends that one or more of the singers should be boys, he does not say so;[5] nor does he say whether the chant should be transposed downwards from its customary range to make the parallelism possible. The most plausible interpretation of his directions would seem to be that the lowest part in this organum was sung in something approximating to a bass voice while the upper part was sung by some kind of high tenor who could move into falsetto.

However, the mere existence of such voices does not prove that they were used in composed polyphonic music where the total compass used before 1300 never attains 20 notes and is often restricted to ten or even less. Elias is describing a technique which the Parisian *discantores* who performed motets would have regarded as rudimentary; it is possible that different standards of performance were involved in the two repertoires.[6] It may be added that the sound of Elias's organum would have been so thick—especially in a resonant acoustic—and so full of interlocking harmonics, that the singer on the top of the texture would not necessarily have been required to possess a voice good enough to be exposed in motets.

A survey of the compass used in motets, taken together with the evidence of certain literary sources, makes it possible to assemble a rather more definite

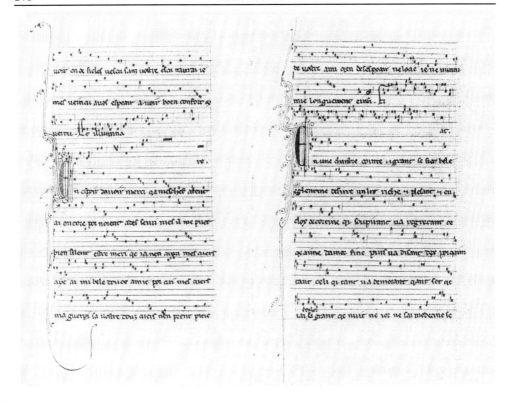

2 This and illus.3 and 4 show pieces from the earliest layer of Ars Antiqua vernacular motets, as found in the tenth fascicle of W2. They have been chosen to show how systematically the first motet composers raided the contemporary monophonic tradition for poetic styles. On this opening are the two part motets En espoir d'avoir merci/Fiat and En une chanbre cointe et grant/Et gaudebit. The first is a brisk and informal version of the high-style love language of the trouvères, ubiquitous in the motet repertory. The second attempts the manner of a chanson de toile (literally 'a song to sing while spinning cloth', a minor but fascinating genre in the monophonic song repertory). W₂, f.232v and 233r.

picture of the voice types used in this repertory. For example, many of the motets in the Bamberg manuscript (probably dating from c.1285) exploit a range of around eleven notes from top to bottom,[7] while some individual voice parts also employ this compass.[8] It would therefore seem that 13th-century motets were conceived to exploit the resources of two, three or four equal voices; one singer, in other words, could normally perform any part in a motet—tenor, duplum, triplum or quadruplum—without undue difficulty. The result would have been a well-blended sound with each part distinguished by its text rather than by its colour.

This conclusion needs some modification, perhaps, for practical experience suggests that it will often be wise to place the tenor part with a singer who is at his best about a 3rd lower than his colleagues. If this means that the tenor line always falls to the same person so much the better, for there is no greater asset to performers of this music than a singer who has accepted the initially thankless task of confining himself to tenors so that he can master their idioms and styles.

If motets were performed by identical (or by nearly identical) voices then a cherished assumption about medieval music may be called into question. It is often claimed that Gothic polyphony is essentially linear in character and that modern performers must therefore make each melodic line stand out, perhaps with the aid of contrasting instrumental timbres: a fiddle for the tenor, a harp for the duplum, and so on.[9] We shall return to the question of instrumental participation; for the moment let us concede the linear character of the motet, a genre where each line above the tenor has a well-wrought melody and its own text. That said, however, the evidence of voice ranges suggests that blend, and not contrast, is the guiding colour principle of the Ars Antiqua motet. This is quintessentially music for singers, designed to exploit the sounds of Latin and Old French as put into song by voices of very similar type singing in very much the same kind of way. Experience suggests that the contrasts between the voices of any motet become both more subtle and, strange though it may seem, more apparent when the piece is essentially monochromatic. I would therefore tentatively propose that Ars Antiqua motets, whether sacred or secular, preserved much of the sound world originally associated with the liturgical *clausulae* from which they were ultimately derived.

The question of performing pitch is a delicate one since it is generally accepted that there was no absolute pitch standard in the Middle Ages (none, that is, with more than a strictly local influence, since the members of individual religious communities may have followed a note provided by a bell or by an organ, if they possessed one). The musical sources suggest a certain amount of movement in performing pitch, for while 'transposition' cannot exist without reference to a standard pitch, it may be significant that some motets survive in variant versions a 5th apart (although the question remains open as to whether there may be some purely notational reason for these shifts).[10]

Even allowing for this movement, however, it may be possible to define the pitch range most commonly employed for motets in the 13th century (at least when they were sung by men). Long ago Yvonne Rokseth drew attention to the number of literary sources from the 13th century in which singers are praised for the *haut* or *alta* quality of their voices, and concluded that the favoured pitch of 13th-century polyphony was 'as high as possible'.[11] Does this mean that motets should be performed by women or falsettists at the top of their range? Almost certainly not. Let us look again at Old French *haut* and its Latin parent *alta*. It is now well-known (although it was perhaps not altogether clear to Rokseth) that these two terms meant both 'high-pitched' and 'loud' during the Gothic period.[12] This high/loud ambiguity is convincingly demonstrated by a hitherto unnoticed text of c1340, a sermon by Armand de Belvezér containing a brief discussion of a figure of speech current among singers:

consuevit dici quando aliquis frater habens vocem sic altam sic pulchram quod eo cantante non est in ecclesia angulus quem non faciat resonare.[13]

when a brother has a voice so *alta* and so beautiful it is customary to say that when he sings there is not a corner of the church which he cannot make resound.

Here it seems that an *alta* voice is a loud one that sets every corner of a church echoing with sound, and yet in another passage from the same source the word *alta* clearly means 'high-pitched':

Est autem sciendum quod aliquis dicitur habere vocem altam qui pre aliis cantat altius .v. punctis . . .[14]

It should be noted that any man is said to have an *alta* voice who sings five notes higher than his fellows . . .

There is nothing surprising about the convergence of the two meanings 'high-pitched' and 'loud' upon a single word, for if a singer wanders high then he will be loud unless, in deference to contemporary taste or to musical context, he 'covers' the sound in order to become less conspicuous or to soften the contrast between the lower and the higher regions of his voice. Nor is there anything surprising about the praise which medieval writers lavish upon loud and high voices, for modern experience shows that audiences admire them still; hence the present popularity of sopranos and tenors as opposed to contraltos, baritones and basses. In the Middle Ages, as now, singers who could soar above the common run, and who could even rise above their professional colleagues, won lavish praise.

In the 13th century the standard for judging whether a man had an *alta* voice was probably set by choral plainchant, the music likely to have established a sense of what most male singers could achieve in terms of range, and therefore to have defined what was 'high'. The entire plainchant repertory lies, for the greater part, within the compass of about a 9th; for most men who can sing reasonably well (but who have not received a special training designed to increase their range upwards) its optimum position may be tentatively placed in the region of $C-d'$. As we have seen, Armand de Belvezér records that *alta* singers could sing a 5th above the common run, suggesting that the 'high' male singers of the 13th century were high tenors with a total compass of about $C-a'$ but mostly working in the upper octave of this range. These 13 notes are sufficient for most of the Ars Antiqua motets that have been preserved.

Both the theorists and the musical sources confirm

that a ritardando was often employed in the penultimate measure of a motet. The theorists usually referred to this device as *organicus punctus*,[15] a term that likens it to the musical effect of two-part organum where, at least in the earlier 13th century, an upper voice executed an elaborate but (it may now be supposed) rhythmically free melody over the sustained and unmeasured notes of the tenor.[16] The musical

Ex.4 Conclusion of Pucelete bele/Je langui/Domino, from the Montpellier codex, f.193v. The penultimate note of the triplum, marked with a fermata in the transcription, is written as a longa in the manuscript and clearly indicates a ritardando. The penultimate bars of the motetus part are also 'stretched'. In performance the semiquavers in parallel 4ths at the start of the penultimate bar should obviously lock together, and therefore the time should be strict at this point. As so often in this repertory, it is best to begin the ritardando late, on the second beat of the penultimate perfection or possibly even further forward (as signalled for the top part by the original notation).

sources also reveal the ritardandi that performers used in the penultimate bars of motets, for there are many instances where the rules of mensural notation break down as the scribes introduced long note values where they do not belong. These can neither be performed nor transcribed strictly; they are clearly designed to indicate a ritardando (see ex.4).[17]

The theorists also mention the device of an internal ritardando, however, and these pauses can be of considerable help in shaping a piece. They are described in the later layer (?1270s) of the anonymous treatise known since Coussemaker as the *Discantus positio vulgaris*; the author discusses the ways in which the modal patterns of motetus parts accord with the modal patterns of tenors thus:

Et primo de primo modo. Cujus quidem tenor aliquando concordat cum motheto in notis, sicut hic: Virgo decus castitatis [ex.5], *et tunc semper nota longa de motheto notae longae correspondet de tenore et brevis brevi et e converso. Pausa vero utriusque valet unam brevem, nisi simul pauset uterque cum tripla, et tunc pausae cantus ecclesiastici tenentur ad placitum*[18]

Firstly, concerning mode 1. The tenor can concord somewhat with the motetus in notes, as in *Virgo decus castitatis*, and then a long note in the motetus will correspond to a long note of the tenor, and a breve to a breve, and vice versa. The pause of each [the motetus and the tenor] is worth one breve unless both of them pause with the triplum, and then let plainchant pauses be held for as long as may be pleasing.

The writer is referring to pieces with passages in which both the tenor and the motetus lock together in mode 1 rhythms, producing extended passages of note-against-note writing (see ex.5). He then says, quite correctly,

Ex.5 Res nova mirabilis/Virgo decus castitatis/Alleluya, from Anderson, op cit, no.95 (triplum omitted)

that when such parts rest the pause will be worth one breve (a quaver after the customary reduction of note values in the earlier motet repertory by a factor of 16):

However, he goes on to say that when there is a third part,[19] then the places where all three parts—tenor, motetus and triplum—phrase together are to be marked not by a measured pause of a breve, but by an unmeasured pause *ad placitum* such as would be employed in plainchant (*cantus ecclesiasticus*).

How were these internal pauses executed? The anonymous *Compendium musicae mensurabilis artis antiquae* (c1300) offers the advice that when the three parts of a motet phrase together, the penultimate notes before the general pause should be unmeasured:

quando [inveniuntur] tres cantus insimul concordantes, facientes insimul suas pausas, tunc debent in tenore et in moteto et in triplo fieri duo tractus ad significandum quod penultime note inmensurabiles fieri debent . . .[20]

when three parts [are found] concording with one another and making their pauses together, then two strokes should be made in the tenor, motetus and triplum to signify that the penultimate notes are to be sung in an unmeasured way . . .

The writer even gives an extract from a double motet showing how this notational device should be employed. Unfortunately it is incomplete, as is the only independent source of the piece, which lacks the tenor part.[21] By collating the two sources, however, it is possible to arrive at a plausible reconstruction of what was intended (ex.6).

Ex.6 Quomodo fiet/O stupor/tenor, reconstructed from Compendium musicae mensurabilis artis antiquae (c1300) and D-Mbs lat.5539, ff.76v–78r.

In practice, this device of an internal pause will often make good musical sense. A constant overlap of musical and poetic phrases is the essence of motet style, so when all the parts phrase together something is clearly called for in performance. These concerted pauses form an admirable check against the tendency of the brisker motets to rollick and become relentless.

Ex.3 shows how composers sometimes took these internal pauses for granted and disposed the musical material around them in a strategic fashion. In bar 7, for example, the general pause coincides with the end of an unusual sequential figure in the duplum. The triplum also changes character at this point; after the crowded movement of the first six bars it thins to a series of longs, which by bar 10 have developed into the smooth trochaic figures that form the bulk of the triplum material throughout the piece. The general pause in bar 37 has comparable significance; in bar 34 the composer signals that something is approaching by changing the rhythmic mode in the upper voices from mode 1 to mode 3; after the general pause in bar 37 the triplum immediately returns to mode 1 while the duplum retains mode 3 until bar 48, creating a new counterplay of rhythms. It is almost always worthwhile to register these changes of mode in performance; they will stand a good deal of emphasis. Modes 2 and 3, when they make *brief* appearances like these, and especially when they are momentarily set against mode 1, may sometimes be emphasized by detaching the quavers in a forceful way, though this would be impractical for pieces cast entirely in these two modes.

Perhaps the most perplexing performance problem of all concerns what is to be done with the wordless tenor parts. Here the answer must vary according to the texture of the motet. In general, the individual tenor notes in an Ars Antiqua motet behave like momentary pedal points. In a passage like the one shown in ex.7, the first sonority of each perfection is invariably a perfect consonance with the tenor forming the root. Next, the upper parts move towards the consonance that will open the next perfection, but the tenor remains stranded at the point where it began. This feeling of a perfect consonance which sounds and then dissolves during the course of the bar is highly characteristic of the Ars Antiqua motet; it accounts for the momentary pedal-like effect of almost every perfection in our example. In pieces where the tenor moves in this way it will usually be wise to choose a sustained sound for the tenor part. In most cases the ideal solution will be to vocalize the tenor, perhaps using as a cue any syllable (or syllables) of plainchant text that may accompany it.[22] This style

Ex.7 Par une matinee/Mellis stilla/Domino, bars 1–10, from Thomas, Robin and Marion motets, i

of performance has hardly ever been adopted by early music ensembles so far, but it should never be forgotten that the motet emerged from a tradition of liturgical and therefore of exclusively vocal polyphony;[23] the one thing that is certain about these motet tenors is that 13th-century musicians would have considered them idiomatic for singing.

Mark Everist has recently drawn attention to an intriguing piece of evidence that bears upon this problem.[24] In the manuscript *GB-Lbm* Cotton Vespasian A.XVIII the motet *Amor veint tout/Au tens d'esté/Et gaudebit* appears with the chant text *Et gaudebit* stretched under the tenor part. There is nothing striking about that, of course, for motet tenors were often written down in this way. Here, however, it seems that the scribe had some definite plan in mind, for the tenor melody appears twice, with the syllable *gau*- placed exactly at the point where the repetition begins, while -*bit* is placed at the end (see ex.8). None of these details corresponds to the original Gregorian underlay, so it may be that the scribe intended the performer to change his syllable at a point that would emphasize the structure of the piece, introducing a change of vowel colour at the crucial moment. Might this have been a common practice? Experiment shows that if vocalization is used to supply the lack of a chant cue then the crucial factor in success or failure is usually the vowel that has been chosen. The vowel *o* (as in southern English 'pot') can become somewhat ominous in a resonant acoustic, seeming very dark and very large, while *i* (as in southern English 'feet') can produce a much brighter and (paradoxical though this may seem) less intrusive colour; being a high front vowel it lends itself very well to precise, meticulous articulation. It is ideal for ex.3.

A major performance problem is created by the brevity (sometimes extreme) of these motets. The obvious solution is to perform three-part pieces once through as a duplum/tenor duet and then again with the triplum. This is not entirely satisfactory, however, for in some cases it cannot be done without turning the performance into two distinct renditions, each with its own tempo and movement, because there are many duplum parts in the motet repertory which must be sung with more pace when they are to be exposed than when they participate in a three-voice texture.[25] Furthermore there are many two-part motets (which cannot be treated in this 'layered' fashion) that are irredeemably short, and in performance it is probably best to accept that these pieces were as brief as they

Ex.8 The tenor of Amor veint tout/Au tens d'esté/Et gaudebit as it appears in GB-Lbm Cotton Vespasian A. XVIII, f.164v–165r, from Everist, op cit

look on the page. Another worry is that the passage often cited as evidence of such 'layered' performance, from the *Speculum Musicae* of Jacques de Liège, proves to be referring to something quite different—the practice of performing a motet voice entirely alone, as a free-standing song.[26] Perhaps this provides the best guide. A plausible solution may be that the duplum and triplum were sometimes performed as solo songs without the tenor, each with its own pace and character, and that the performers then joined forces to create the motet, each adjusting the pace of his line as seemed necessary.

What were the customary performing forces? The evidence that can be brought to bear upon this question is unfortunately very slim indeed. It seems to be universally agreed that most medieval polyphony was intended for soloists, although specific information

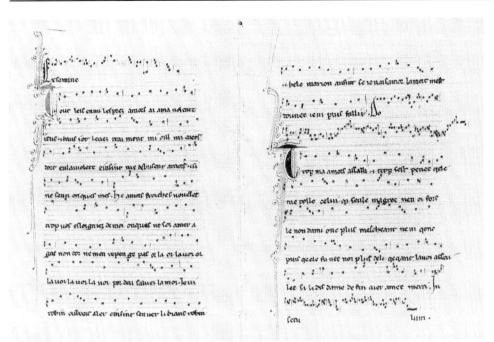

3 The two-part motets Tout leis enmi les prez/Do [minus] and Trop m'a amors asalli/In seculum. The first begins with a quotation (both verbal and musical) from the dance-song, or rondet de carole, shown in the text as ex.1. W$_2$, f.247v and 248.

about the Ars Antiqua motet is lacking.[27] Instrumental participation (in addition, that is, to instrumental performance of the textless tenor parts) is a possibility, but there is no firm evidence for this practice and no obvious reason why it should be recommended.[28]

The more subjective areas of performance practice where modern singers have only their own musical instincts to guide them may now be considered. To a large extent, I believe, the things that may profitably be asked of singers performing Ars Antiqua motets are much the same as those required in any accurate ensemble singing.

Something is often to be gained by pitching these motets in a way that lifts the singers on the upper parts away from the comfortable range where they can coast or croon. When the music is lifted above this range the relatively higher pitch brings many things under closer control because the vocal cords are vibrating more quickly and because the singers, recognizing that danger is only about a tone away, begin to work hard in a fashion that is always beneficial to this music (and perhaps to any music; modern critics generally seem to admire performers who introduce an element of risk into their performances). Few motets last more than two minutes, even at the most lugubrious speeds, and they therefore ask both singers and listeners to make a concentrated effort. If they are sung in a forthright manner (that is to say with a good supply of wind and a great deal of busy vowel and consonant formation towards the front of the mouth) then it becomes possible to approach the crispness of diction, fullness of tone and scrupulous intonation that these pieces surely demand. It seems probable that the 'high' and 'loud' singers of the 13th century were praised for their ability to perform in this way.

In music as densely texted as this, and so dependent for its success upon a burst of energy, the manner of articulation is of cardinal importance. The motet emerged as a form when words were added to pre-existing sections of melismatic polyphony,[29] and it succeeds very well in performance when the two elements in this history—melisma and text—are allowed to co-exist. This can be achieved by singing the lines in a legato fashion and by allowing the words to look after the articulation. Many singers will instinctively attempt to 'enliven' chains of mode 1 rhythms, for example, by imposing a kind of automatic articulation, 'coming away' during the course of the longer notes and almost turning

into ♩ ♪ | ♩ ♪ | ♩ ⁊ |
♪ ⁊ ♪ | ♪ ⁊ ♪ | ♩ ⁊ |

which soon tires the ear. It will usually make good musical sense to maintain full tone and volume through the course of every long note value in a 13th-century motet; if the words are clearly pronounced then they will establish an appropriate manner of articulation.

A correct historical pronunciation of every text is therefore a great asset in the performance of this music.[30] Old French possessed many consonants that have softened a little down the centuries, or that have faded away altogether, and these crisp sounds help to project the principal features of medieval motet style in performance. Most notable amongst these are a texture in which two (or three) assertive and clearly articulated songs seem to compete for mastery, and a crowded sound picture in which the piece appears to be on the point of bursting the taut intellectual constraints that bind it together.

The importance of historical pronunciation to the shaping of phrases is considerable. In a line like the following, for example,   ♩. | ♩. | ♩. | ♪· |
En   a - mours

the listener should hear not only the final *s* of *amours* but also the rolled *r* immediately before it; both sounds must be rapidly produced at almost the last possible moment. In this way the word *amours* points the end of the melodic phrase in a most decisive manner. When lines ending in consonants follow one another in rapid succession (as when lines rhyme on *-er* verbs), the effect on melodic phrasing can be very marked indeed.

Two further points can contribute substantially to a successful performance of these pieces. The first relates to the shape of each note. When singing Ars Antiqua motets (and, perhaps, any medieval music) it is important that each note should start firmly with as much—or nearly as much—tone as it is ever to possess. A firm beginning counts for a great deal, and notes which are blown up like a balloon during their duration seem out of place in this repertory.

The second point concerns tuning. It is plain that singers of the 13th-century attached great importance to accuracy in this respect. The music treatises of the period devote considerable space to the mathematical basis of intervals, confirming the impression that medieval singers regarded polyphony as an advanced method of producing musical beauty by means of meticulous measurement. It is necessary only to glance at Ars Antiqua motets, with their abundance of perfect intervals, to realize that high standards must have been aimed for. Unless the intervals of octave, 4th and 5th are placed with precision (and with far more than is required to place 3rds and 6ths, whether major or minor) a 13th-century motet will tend to sound feeble and needlessly dissonant. The supreme goal is therefore accuracy, together with the strong, straight tone without vibrato that allows the ear to savour the purity of the perfect intervals and to detect the distinctive buzz that they possess when true.

What of the imperfect intervals, the 3rds and 6ths? Here it is almost always profitable (at least in French pieces—English music of this period is altogether different) to steer towards the Pythagorean tuning whose principles are expounded time and again in medieval treatises on music. The technical details of this tuning can be found in many places;[31] the immediate practical consequences for the modern performer are straightforward and easily summarized. All perfect intervals are pure. All notes with a semitone step above them need to be raised (in other words E, A and B natural should, in most circumstances, be noticeably high). Major 3rds and 6ths should be appreciably wider than in equal temperament, giving a sense of strain to cadences where a major 6th widens to an octave or a major 3rd moves outwards to a 5th. Finally, all tone steps may be allowed to expand a little; it is never required in the Ars Antiqua motet that a tone step be narrowed.

This brings us to what is perhaps one of the most delicate questions about the performance of these pieces: the question of tempo. Some 14th-century theorists distinguish between 'fast', 'medium' and 'slow' manners of execution,[32] but this is of no more practical help to the modern singer of medieval music than the doctrine of 'high', 'middle' and 'low' styles in rhetoric is a help to readers of Chaucer's poetry. Indeed the comments of the theorists, most of whom are discussing 14th-century notational practices when they broach this subject, reduce to little more than a codification of what would be expected, namely that the fewer note values a piece contains, the faster it goes. Crudely speaking, this means that a piece made

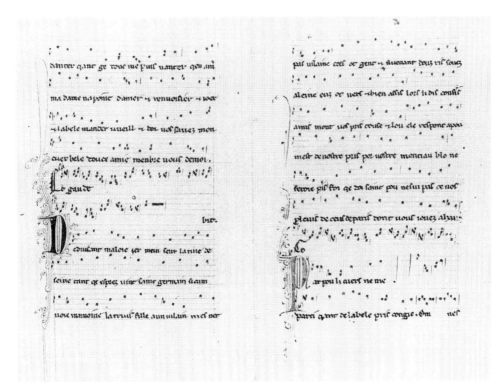

4 The two-part motet Deduisant m'aloie/Go. This is an ingenious adaptation of the genre of the pastourelle (where a man, often a knight, meets a shepherdess or comes upon rustics as they sing or indulge in other country pleasures). Here the encounter takes place outside the walls of Paris in the suburb of St Germain (prez . . saint germain in the second line of the motet). W$_2$, f.251v and 252.

up exclusively (in modern transcription) of crotchets and quavers can go appreciably faster than one where the quavers are frequently (or even occasionally) broken into pairs of semiquavers.

Where the theorists fail, modern performers must use their own musical judgement. The principal objective is to overcome the consequences of the triple time which dominates Ars Antiqua polyphony. To some extent, perhaps, this is not an historical problem, for it may be imagined that 13th-century performers were not troubled by the relentless ternaries of the motet; when did they ever sing as many motets in sequence as today's musicians are required to do in one concert? Whatever the answer may be, the art of handling rhythm in 13th-century motets is a subtle one that must be acquired. I do not believe that the problem is one of speed. No doubt many modern singers are liable to sing these pieces too fast—especially when they have learned their parts well and have become confident—and it will be wise to correct this tendency as soon as it makes itself apparent. Nonetheless, the speed of music has no necessary connection with its iterative qualities in performance; a fast piece in triple time need not be more emphatically 'in three' than a slow waltz where each beat is felt individually.

I prefer to suggest that the triple-time problem in 13th-century polyphony is essentially one of stability. The prime danger in this music is that modern singers, confronted by a motet transcribed with the customary bar lines, will start to compress the second beat of the bar and then lunge—very slightly, but nonetheless fatally—towards the beginning of the next bar. It becomes especially serious with the use of the very common rhythmic figure

which seems ideally designed to cause trouble. Many singers will tend to 'come away' from the crotchet a little (probably around the start of the second beat); they will then come back and hammer the notes of the triplet figure in the hope of making them distinct. In doing so they will rush on to the next crotchet. If this occurs, the advice should always be to begin the long note with as much tone and conviction as it is ever to possess, to keep this tone and conviction absolutely steady throughout the note, and then to toss the triplets away as lightly as possible—to treat them as ornaments, in other words, which they are, rather than as tune, which they are not. The secret of success is rhythmic accuracy of a scrupulous kind. It must also be remembered that in this, as in all medieval music, perfect consonances accent themselves; there is no need to accent the start of a bar.

Two further considerations prove useful in shaping a performance. The first relates to the balance of the voices. As suggested above, medieval motet style exploits the excitement that can be created when the listener feels that the two or three upper parts are strenuously competing for attention. The triplum is generally rather more active than the duplum in the Ars Antiqua repertory (see ex.9), but this does not mean that in a double motet, for example, the busier part should be the more assertive one in performance. In ex.9 the singer of the duplum will do well to sing as if the triplum were not there; in practical terms this means giving long notes (minims in this example) full tone and commitment throughout their written value, without 'coming away'.

A second consideration relates to harmonic colouring. The composers of Ars Antiqua motets were remarkably strict in their adherence to the theorists' rule that every perfection should begin with a perfect consonance. Accordingly, it will often make musical sense to emphasize the places where this rule is broken. Ex.10 shows an extract from a double motet where the appearance of a *refrain* (a pre-existing piece of text and/or music)[33] in the triplum, coinciding with one complete statement of the tenor, is introduced by an uncharacteristic 6–5 movement at the beginning of bar 17 (uncharacteristic, that is, for the start of a

Ex.9 Conclusion of Par une matinee/Mellis stilla/Domino, from Thomas, Robin and Marion motets, i

Ex.10 Extract from Je m'en vois/Tels a mout/Omnes, from Anderson, op cit, no.90

perfection). There are also two stark (but in performance surprisingly gracious) dissonances at the opening of the second perfection in bar 19 and of the first perfection in bar 20.

Whatever tempo is chosen, the basic pulse should be absolutely strict. Medieval singers regarded polyphony as an art of accurate measurement and the terms which they associated with musical excellence include *recta* (correct), *integralis* (whole), and (perhaps most frequently of all) *regularis* (disciplined).[34] One theorist of the mid-14th century, for example, records that the tenor parts of motets are best performed 'in a whole and secure fashion'.[35]

Ornamentation was probably a major factor governing the choice of tempo. 'Let anyone who wishes to indulge in practical music beware that he does not exult too much in his voice', warns Johannes de Muris,[36] though there can be no doubt that his words often went unheeded by singers determined to show off their skill. References to liturgical singing in the writings of outraged churchmen suggest that polyphony was performed with Romanesque exuberance and Gothic flamboyance in the 12th and 13th centuries; even when allowances have been made for the exaggerated language of these moralists, the impression remains that polyphony, whether sacred or secular, was declaimed by singers determined to enjoy the experience and to make an impression. According to the late 13th-century writer Elias of Salomon, the task of keeping control over their exuberance fell to the *rector*,[37] who was required to correct any colleague who ornamented his part excessively by whispering a reproach into his ear. Elias is discussing improvised polyphony, but even motets, which look so busy with their chafing texts, were sometimes ornamented. An anonymous (possibly English) theorist of the 14th century makes this clear:

Sciendum secundum curiam romanam et francigenos et omnes musicales cantores quod tenor, qui discantum tenet, integre et solide pronunciari debet in mensura, ne supra discantantes dissonantiam incurrant; et hoc ratio exigit nam super instabile fundamentum stabile edificium construi non potest, sic nec instabilem tenorem vix sine dissonantia discantus pronunciari potest. In motetis quippe et rundallis ac etiam in aliis cantilenis tenor prout figuratur pronunciari debet, tamen non est contradicendum tenorem pronuncianti, et pulcras ascenciones et descenciones facienti, quando sentit se discantu non impedire, sed pocius comendandum.[38]

It should be known that according to the singers of the Roman curia, according to the French and according to all musical singers, the tenor, which holds the polyphony together, must be performed in a whole and secure fashion in strict measure, lest those who are singing the upper parts fall into discord. And this principle imposes itself in many things, for just as a stable building cannot be constructed upon a shaky foundation, neither can polyphony be sung over a shaky tenor without discord. Certainly, in motets, rondelli and also in other kinds of music the tenor must be sung just as it is written; however there should be no reproach for the singer of the tenor who makes beautiful ascents and descents when he senses that he is not becoming entangled in the polyphony; he should rather be congratulated.

Here it seems that the performer of the tenor may be allowed to make 'beautiful ascents and descents' if he can do it well enough not to become entangled in the upper parts and produce cacophony. If this was acceptable in the performance of a tenor, the *fundamentum totius cantus*, it is likely that singers of duplum, triplum and quadruplum voices would also have been free to decorate their lines. The melodic variants found in the motet repertory, readily available for study in several collected editions, may give some clue to the character of this ornamentation (see ex.11).

Ex.11 Au cuer ai un mal/Ja ne m'en departirai/Jolietement, duplum. Upper stave from Bamberg MS (Anderson, op cit, no.53, lower stave from GB-Ob Douce 139, f.179v (as ed. M. Everist, Five Anglo-Norman Motets (1986), p.10). To facilitate comparison I have halved the note-values of Anderson's edition.

The Ars Antiqua motet seems to come into its own when it has one singer on each part—a singer with a strong, straight tone who is able to go directly to the centre of the note and who, in return for complete freedom from instrumental doubling, can tune intervals in a tactical way, now wide, now narrow, according to the demands of the texture. The beauty of this music— and perhaps of all medieval music—surely lies in the opportunity it gives us to savour clear and fresh sounds being combined with perfect accuracy, and without any thickening from vibrato or any other source that might overscore the lines that make up this delightful geometry.

I am most grateful to David Fallows, Daniel Leech-Wilkinson, Mark Everist, Jeremy Summerly and Shane Fletcher for their comments upon an earlier draft of this article.

Christopher Page is senior research fellow in music at Sidney Sussex College, Cambridge, and director of the ensemble Gothic Voices.

[1]*F-T* MS 144, vol.1, f.305r Pierre de Palude, *In psalmos*.

The bulk of the 13th-century motet repertory is available in the following editions: H. Tischler, *The earliest motets a complete comparative edition*, 3 vols, (Yale Univ. Press, 1982); idem, *The Montpellier codex*, 4 vols, (Madison, 1978 and 1985); G. Anderson, *Compositions of the Bamberg manuscript*, Corpus mensurabilis musicae [CMM], lxxv (1977); idem, *The motets of the manuscript La Clayette*, CMM, lxviii (1975); idem, *The Las Huelgas manuscript*, CMM, lxxix (1982). The motets of the Montpellier codex, the major 13th-century collection, are also available in Y. Rokseth, *Polyphonies du XIIIe siècle*, 4 vols, (Paris, 1935–48). A recent performing edition that may be highly recommended to male singers (for all the pieces either lie in—or have been transposed to fit—the range of tenors and baritones) is W. Thomas, *Robin and Marion motets*, 2 vols, Antico edn, AE 22 and 25 (1985 and 1987). A third volume is in preparation.

On the performance of motets, see E. H. Roesner's introductions to two reprints of L. Schrade, *Polyphonic Music of the Fourteenth Century: Le Roman de Fauvel* (Monaco, 1956/R1984), v–vii; and *The Works of Philippe de Vitry* (Monaco, 1956/R1984), v–vi; H. Tischler, *The style and evolution of the earliest motets (to c1270)*, 4 vols, Musicological Studies and Documents, xl (Henryville, 1985), i, p.207ff; idem, *op cit*, *The Montpellier codex*, i, pp.xxxi–xxxiii; Rokseth, *op cit*, *Polyphonies*, iv, p.41f; Thomas, *op cit*, *Robin and Marion motets* (introductory sections to both volumes); P. Jeffery, 'A Four-Part *In Seculum* Hocket and a Mensural Sequence in an Unknown Fragment', *JAMS*, xxxvii (1984), pp.1–48; and C. Page, 'The performance of medieval polyphony', in H. M. Brown and S. Sadie, eds, *Handbook of Performance Practice* (in the press).

[2]Text in E. Rohloff, ed., *Die Quellenhandschriften zum Musiktraktat des Johannes de Grocheio* (Leipzig, 1972); for comments on the motet, see p 144. Eng. trans. (to be employed with considerable caution), by A. Seay, *Johannes de Grocheo [sic] Concerning Music* (Colorado Springs, 2/1973), esp. p.26

[3]For this identification of those whom Johannes de Grocheio means by the litterati (to which he adds 'illis, qui subtilitates artium sunt quaerentes' (those who are investigating the finer points of the arts)) see, for example, the sermon which the 13th-century Dominican, Humbert of Romans, writing in Paris, addressed *Ad omnes litteratos* in *Sermones Beati Umberti Burgundi* (Venice, 1603), 2 vols, sermon lvi: 'ut patet in Medicis, et Advocatis, et Magistris in liberalibus artibus, et in similibus'.

[4]See M. Gerbert, *Scriptores* (St Blasien, 1784/R1963), iii, p.57ff, and also J. Dyer, 'A thirteenth-century choirmaster: the *Scientia Artis Musicae* of Elias Salomon', *MQ*, lxvi (1980), pp.83–111.

[5]It is possible that the upper level of such organum was sometimes performed by boys in the 13th century; in the absence of any explicit testimony, however, it is probably safest to assume that the singers envisaged by Elias were adult males.

[6]Compare, for example, the practice of 'fifthing', a technique for singing in parallel 5ths with contrary motion at the beginnings and ends of phrases; this was regarded as a preparatory stage in the training of a true *discantor*. See S. Fuller, 'Discant and the theory of fifthing', *Acta Musicologica*, l (1978), pp.241–75.

[7]For examples with a total compass of eleven notes, see Anderson, *op cit*, CMM, lxxxv, nos 3, 8, 9, 11, 18, 22, 23, 28, 36, etc. Ranges of a 10th (nos 4, 7, 12, 13, etc) and a 12th (nos 2, 10, 16, 17, 24, 26, 27, etc) are also fairly common. The compass of a 14th in no.48 is unusual. The average total compass of the motets in the Bamberg anthology is 11 5 notes. For a discussion of the ranges in the Montpellier motets, see Tischler, *op cit*, *Montpellier codex*, i, p.xxxiii.

[8]For some eleven-note voice-parts, see Bamberg nos 16 (both triplum and duplum), 18 (triplum, where the total compass of the piece is an 11th), 22 (duplum, again where the whole piece spans but an 11th), 30 (duplum), 38 (duplum), 47 (duplum), etc.

[9]See, for example, Tischler, *op cit*, *Montpellier codex*, i, p.xxxii, where reference is made to the 'distinct rhythm, phrasing, text, and timbre of the several lines of music' in motets. See also G. Reaney, 'Voices and Instruments in the Music of Guillaume de Machaut', *Revue Belge de Musicologie*, x (1956), pp.3–17 and pp.93–104. I have already questioned this view in 'The performance of songs in late medieval France: a new source', *EM*, x/4 (Oct. 1982), pp.441–50. Cf D. Leech-Wilkinson, 'Machaut's *Rose, lis* and the problems of early music analysis', *Music Analysis*, iii/1 (1984), pp.25–6, fn.13.

[10]The notational explanation may perhaps be that scribes wished to avoid certain accidentals wherever possible. A piece requiring F♯ in the triplum, for example, and possessing no other accidental, would become free of all such markings if written out 'in C'.

[11]Rokseth, *op cit*, *Polyphonies*, iv, pp.46–8

[12]The point is well made in E. Bowles, 'Haut and Bas: the Grouping of Musical Instruments in the Middle Ages', *Musica Disciplina*, viii (1954), pp.115–40.

[13]F. *Armandi de Bellovisu . . Sermones plane divini assumptis ex solo Psalterio Davidico Thematis*, (Lyons, 1525), f.75v

[14]*Ibid*, f.156. The passage continues: 'sed altiorem si .x. altissimam autem si .xv. hoc enim nunquam visum fuit'. Thus a singer was said to have a 'higher' voice if he could sing ten notes above the common run, and 'highest' if he could sing fifteen, 'but this is unheard of'. Whether this represents genuine usage, or merely Armandus's determination to pursue the issue of 'high' voices through the comparative and superlative stages of the adjective *alta*, is difficult to determine. As far as 'highest' voices are concerned, Armandus is clearly propelled by passion for neatness at this point since he acknowledges, in effect, that the term can never be used, for such voices are 'unheard of'.

[15]Anonymous 1 in C.-E.-H. de Coussemaker, *Scriptorum de musica*, iii, p.362. The device of the final ritardando was probably carried over from plainchant; for the technique of drawing out a chant 'slightly near the end', see C. Palisca, *Hucbald, Guido and John on Music* (New Haven, 1979), p.139

[16]This is still a matter of controversy; for recent literature see Page, *op cit*, 'The performance of medieval polyphony'.

[17]Needless to say, these ritardandi must be carefully controlled, and should hardly ever begin earlier than the second beat of the penultimate bar.

[18]S. M. Cserba, ed., *Hieronymus de Moravia O. P Tractatus de Musica*, (Regensburg, 1935), p.193

[19]His term is *tripla* ('cum tripla'), where *triplo* would have been the expected form. It is possible that the author, having seen the neuter plural *tripla* in other writings, construed the form as a feminine nominative singular. I am otherwise unable to explain *cum tripla*, but have no doubt that a third part is meant.

[20]F. A. Gallo, ed., *Compendium musicae mensurabilis artis antiquae*, Corpus Scriptorum de Musica [CSM], xv (1971), p.71. As Gallo points out, (p.65), the 'content of the work refers to the moment of transition from the Franconian teaching to the notation of the fourteenth century'.

[21]*D-Mbs* 5539. See G. Reaney, *Manuscripts of Polyphonic Music (cl320–1400)* (München-Duisburg, 1969), p.78

[22]This question is discussed in Jeffery, *op cit*.

[23]The unconvincing arguments that have been advanced in favour of instrumental participation in the Notre Dame clausula repertory have been finally exploded by E. Roesner, 'The performance of Parisian organum', *EM*, vii/2 (Apr.1979), pp.174–189.

[24]M. Everist, ed., *Five Anglo-Norman Motets* (Antico Edition, 1986), AE 24

[25]An example is provided by the motet *Quant vient/Ne sai que/Amons [Johannes]*, in both the Bamberg and Montpellier manuscripts. The most recent edition is in Thomas, *op cit*, *Robin and Marion motets*, i, pp 13–15. The duplum and tenor survive as a two-part work in some sources (the *Roman de Fauvel*, for example, where the duplum bears the text *Veritas arpie*), and the duplum, which has only two note values, seems to demand a brisk tempo if it is to be exposed in a layered performance of perhaps dotted minim = 100. The duplum, a much more active line, requires a tempo in the region of

dotted minim = 48. In order to make the motet work in performance as a three-part composition it is necessary to take the tempo from the triplum, and for the duplum singer to perform his line in a way that will feel very slow to him.

[26] Rokseth, op cit, Polyphonies, iv, p.221. See also R. Bragard, ed., Jacobi Leodiensis Speculum Musicae, CSM, iii/7, (1955–73) p.9.

[27] For a more detailed account of instrumental practice in Ars Antiqua music, see Page, op cit, 'The performance of medieval polyphony'. It has been suggested (for example, by Tischler, op cit, The Montpellier Codex, i, p.xxxiv), that the instruments sometimes named in motets are a guide to the instrumentation of these pieces. The striking feature of Tischler's comprehensive listing of references in the Montpellier corpus is that the most popular instruments of 13th-century culture, the harp and fiddle, are missing. The case of the motet In seculum viellatons remains as puzzling as ever.

[28] The often-cited passage from the Roman de la Rose in which Pygmalion plays the portative organ and sings Motet ou treble ou teneüre, probably refers to the performance of motet voices as isolated monophonic songs. For the text, see E. Langlois, ed., Le Roman de la Rose (Paris, 1914–24), line 21041. On the portative organ, see Page, op cit, 'The performance of medieval polyphony'. See also L. Gushee, 'Two Central Places: Paris and the French Court in the Early Fourteenth Century', in H. Kühn and P. Nitsche, eds, Bericht uber den Internationalen Musikwissenschaftlichen Kongress Berlin 1974 (Kassel etc, 1980), p.143.

[29] The earliest motets and their source clausulae can now be examined in bulk in the complete and comparative edition by Tischler, op cit, The earliest motets.

[30] The standard guide is J. Alton and B. Jeffery, Bele Buche e Bele Parleure, a guide to the pronunciation of medieval and renaissance French for singers and others (London, 1976). The usefulness of this volume is immeasurably increased by the accompanying cassette.

[31] For a clear exposition of the Pythagorean system and its mathematics see J. Backhus, The Acoustical Foundations of Music, (London, 1970), p.116f. See also Page, op cit, 'The performance of medieval polyphony'. The subject of tuning in medieval music has principally been investigated in terms of keyboard temperaments, with a marked emphasis upon the 15th century; see, for example, M. Lindley, 'Fifteenth-century evidence for meantone temperament', PRMA, cii, (1975–6), pp.37–51, and idem, 'Pythagorean Intonation and the Rise of the Triad', RMA Research Chronicle, xvi (1980), pp.4–61.

[32] Roesner, op cit, pp.vi–vii.

[33] The standard guide to the refrain material is still N. Van den Boogaard, Rondeaux et refrains du XIIe siècle au début du XIVe (Paris, 1969).

[34] See, for example, the Ars discantus secundum Johannem de Muris in Coussemaker, op cit, Scriptores, iii, p.110.

[35] Ibid, p.362

[36] Ibid, p.60

[37] Dyer, op cit

[38] As the manuscript GB-Lbm Cotton Tiberius B.IX was severely damaged in the fire of 1731, I have followed the early 18th-century copy (GB-Lbm Add. MS 4909, f.54r), checking this, where possible, against the original (f.213v). There seems no reason to believe that the 18th-century transcript is unreliable. Indeed it is more reliable than the text which Coussemaker printed in his Scriptores, iii. The same material also appears in the Quatuor principalia musica (op cit, iv, p.295).

Part IV
Mass and Motet after 1300

[12]

Representations of the Mass in Medieval and Renaissance Art

By JAMES W. MC KINNON

IT IS A USEFUL SIMPLIFICATION to view the historiography of the *a cappella* question in three stages: a nineteenth-century *a cappella* ideal, a sweeping twentieth-century reaction, and a recently emerging, highly-qualified *a cappella* hypothesis.

The nineteenth-century position, as advocated by figures like E. T. A. Hoffmann, Anton Thibaut, and the Caecilians, certainly was an ideal; whatever its historical underpinnings it was characterized by an aura of romantic religiosity which would guarantee the opposition of twentieth-century musicologists. But the twentieth-century reaction when it first came with scholars like Riemann and Leichtentritt was not so sweeping as suggested above, nor was it much characterized by anti-romantic animus. Riemann's aims were essentially moderate: his primary concern was to show through stylistic evidence that genres such as the *Trecento* song, the Burgundian *chanson*, and the *frottola* were composed for a combination of voices and instruments. He had comparatively little to say on the issue of instruments in church as such and actually helped to establish the concept of an *a cappella* style of late-fifteenth-century vocal homogeneity.[1] Leichtentritt, who introduced iconographic evidence into the question, emphasized the overwhelming presence of instruments in musical artistic representation, but nevertheless expressed the little-noticed qualification that those few illustrations which showed singers alone were from the ecclesiastical sphere.[2] It was only with Schering that a frontal assault on the vocal character of church music was launched;[3] but his views were found to be exaggerated, not only by *a cappella* advocates like Kroyer, but by the musicological community at large.[4]

[1] Hugo Riemann, *Handbuch der Musikgeschichte*, II, 1 (Leipzig, 1907), pp. 32-57, 271-2, 351-8.

[2] Hugo Leichtentritt, "Was lehren uns die Bildwerke des 14.-17. Jahrhunderts über die Instrumentalmusik ihrer Zeit?", *Sammelbände der Internationalen Musikgesellschaft*, VII (1905-6), pp. 317, 348.

[3] Arnold Schering, *Die Niederlandische Orgelmesse im Zeitalter Josquins* (Leipzig, 1912); and *Aufführungspraxis alter Musik* (Leipzig, 1931).

[4] For Theodor Kroyer's reaction see especially "Das A-cappella-Ideal," *Acta Musicologica*, VI (1934), pp. 152-69. For an early example of a generally sympathetic critic who found Schering's views exaggerated see Hugo Leichtentritt, "Einige Bemerkungen über Verwendung der Instrumente im Zeitalter Josquins," *Zeitschrift der Internationalen Musikgesellschaft*, XIV (1912-13), pp. 359-65.

Yet the period after World War II saw a view nearly as extreme as Schering's established in the secondary literature—for example, in virtually all of the most respected American text books.[5] The *a cappella* ideal was seen as a romantic myth, and church music, with the singular exception of the papal chapel, was presumed to have been performed by whatever combination of voices and instruments happened to have been available. The ease with which the view has been accepted is an historiographic curiosity, supported as it is by casual references to pictorial representations, to scattered literary allusions, and to the absence of text underlay, rather than by specific studies on the subject. Its most serious consequence is that avowedly authentic performances of sacred polyphonic music, especially in Germany and the United States, have come to employ a kaleidoscopic profusion of musical instruments.

But in the most recent years there are signs of a reaction to the established twentieth-century position. Whatever the climate of opinion among musicologists in general, those undertaking special studies in performing practice seem increasingly inclined toward a view closer to that of the nineteenth than to that of the twentieth century.[6] They avoid, needless to say, the religiosity of the romantic view or any other sort of absolute position, but they conclude, principally from archival study, that an *a cappella* practice did in fact predominate, at least for the particular region or period in which they specialize. If I may venture a tentative and oversimplified hypothesis which synthesizes their findings: the music of the medieval and Renaissance Church was generally performed by voices alone until well into the sixteenth century; apart from the widespread *alternatim* usage of organ versets, the employment of instruments was occasional rather than normal.

The full exploration of this hypothesis is clearly beyond the scope of the present essay, which sets for itself the comparatively modest aim of bringing some order to the iconographic aspect of the question. This, in itself, is a twofold task: a negative one now largely complete, and a positive one only at a beginning. The negative task is to demonstrate that the iconographic evidence generally cited in support of instrumental usage is unacceptable; the positive task is to study works of art actually depicting liturgical scenes. The latter is the proper subject of this paper, but it can be understood adequately only after a brief recapitulation of the negative phase.

In turning to this recapitulation we must recall that those who invoked iconographic evidence against the *a cappella* ideal did not cite specific representations of instruments being played in liturgical settings; rather they made general reference to a great quantity of instrumental depiction in religious art

---

[5] There seems little point in listing references to such familiar works, but it might be useful to cite a less obvious example: Manfred Bukofzer, "On the Performance of Renaissance Music," *MTNA Proceedings*, Series 36 (1941), pp. 225–35.

[6] These authors will be cited and discussed in the concluding remarks to this essay.

which, presumably, had some relationship to liturgical performance.[7] Now, however, the musicologist who has kept pace with the musical iconographic developments of the past decade would acknowledge that this seemingly undifferentiated mass must be categorized into a group of conventional iconographic themes which have little or no relationship with liturgical performance. Two biblical sources account for the overwhelming majority: the Apocalypse[8] and the Psalter.[9]

The Apocalypse displays two major musical themes: the seven angel trumpeters who illustrate chapters seven and eight; and the twenty-four elders, each holding aloft a cithara in one hand and a bowl of incense in the other, who illustrate chapters four and five. Scholars have not been much tempted to describe these heavenly musicians of the Apocalypse as participants in the earthly liturgy, but it has been a different matter with the more variegated performers of the Psalter. Arnold Schering, for example, described groups like that in Figure 1a as medieval quartets;[10] today, of course, we recognize them to be David and the four Levites, Ethan, Heman, Asaph, and Idithun, whom, according to 1 Chronicles xv and xxv, he placed in charge of priestly music. They form the standard frontispiece to the Biblical Psalter of the earlier Middle Ages, where they illustrate not a specific psalm, but a type of prologue to the Psalter, which tells of David's authorship of the psalms and his organization of Levitical music.[11]

The more lavishly illustrated Biblical Psalters illustrate every psalm, so that we may encounter instrumentalists for every one of the approximately fifteen that mention instruments: Psalm 150, for example, with its invocation to praise the Lord on every manner of instrument, has particularly notable illumination (Fig. 1b). On the other hand, the much more common liturgical Psalter of the thirteenth through fifteenth centuries usually illustrates only eight psalms: those initiating matins for each day of the week and Sunday vespers. Musical iconography fares well in this distribution, however, with three out of the eight having musical illustrations: Psalm 1, *Beatus vir*, with David holding his harp; Psalm 80, *Exultate deo*, with David playing bells; and Psalm 97, *Cantate domino canticum novum*, with singing clerics. These singing clerics form an exception to the rule of liturgical irrelevance; inspired by the phrase "new song," they are meant to represent the liturgy of the New

---

[7] See, especially, Schering, *Aufführungspraxis*, p. 11.

[8] See Reinhold Hammerstein, *Die Musik der Engel* (Bern, 1962).

[9] See Tilman Seebass, *Musikdarstellung und Psalterillustration im früheren Mittelalter*, 2 vols. (Bern, 1973), and Hugo Steger, *David rex et propheta* (Nürnberg, 1961); and for the later liturgical Psalter see Günter Haseloff, *Die Psalterillustration im 13. Jahrhundert* (Kiel, 1938).

[10] Schering, *Aufführungspraxis*, p. 11.

[11] See James W. McKinnon, "Musical Instruments in Medieval Psalm Commentaries and Psalters," this JOURNAL, XXI (1968), p. 14.

Figure 1. (a) Psalter-Hymnary, 11th c. France, Paris, Bibliothèque Nationale, MS lat. 11550, f. 7ᵛ; (b) *Psalter of Blessed Elizabeth*, 13th c. Germany, Cividale del Friuli, Museo Archeologico Nationale, MS 137; (c) *Stuttgart Psalter*, early 9th c. France, Stuttgart, Landesbibliothek (bibl. fol. 23), f. 152.

Testament in contrast to the prevailingly Old Testament character of Psalter musical illustration.[12]

This survey is necessarily over-simplified: it fails to mention, for example, the themes derived from the Apocalypse such as the Renaissance scenes of Christ in Glory with their choirs of angel instrumentalists, or the wonderfully profuse instrumental drolleries peopling the margins of every manner of fourteenth- and fifteenth-century manuscript. It does not attempt to explain the anachronistic reliance of medieval artists upon contemporary motifs when illustrating Old Testament themes, and it only hints at the positive iconographic riches of the late medieval liturgical Psalter that await discovery. Yet one hopes that the central point is clear: the vast majority of medieval musical iconography is biblical illustration, not depiction of medieval liturgy. The point is best summarized perhaps in the *reductio ad absurdum* occasioned by the *Stuttgart Psalter's* illustration of Psalm 136, *Super flumina Babylonis* (Fig. 1c). Does it depict liturgical performing practice or does it illustrate the psalm, which tells us of the captive Israelites sitting by the rivers of Babylon weeping and exclaiming, "in salicibus ... suspendimus organa nostra" (on the willow trees we hung our pipe organs)?

In turning from the negative to the positive phase of the evidence, the question arises: why only now are scholars beginning to concentrate on actual liturgical scenes when examples like Philip the Good at mass (Fig. 4c) and the Christmas Mass of the *Très riches heures* (Fig. 6c) have been appearing in reproductions for years?[13] There is, first of all, the general circumstance that musical iconography is a new field, only now beginning to gain a degree of control over the more basic issues. Then there is the very nature of the negative argument: it diverted attention from these illustrations because the whole point of it was to demonstrate the general irrelevance of musical illustration to liturgical practice. And finally there is the quantitative element; it is only natural that scholars would seek first to establish some order among the tens of thousands of angel musicians, elders, and Psalter instrumentalists while maintaining the vague notion that these few mass scenes are isolated examples rather than representatives of established iconographic types. However, once one focuses upon them it becomes clear that there does exist a substantial body of medieval and Renaissance liturgical representation, even if it is slight in comparison to the great mass of biblical illustration. It is, in fact, substantial enough to warrant a division between mass and office, and the concentration in this study upon the former.

---

[12] For the iconography of Psalm 97 see Mc Kinnon, "*Canticum novum* in the Isabella Book," to appear in *Medievalia*, II (1976).

[13] I am not alone in undertaking the systematic study of liturgical representations; priority in the effort belongs to Edmund Bowles, who will publish a rich selection of fifteenth-century examples in his forthcoming volume in the *Musikgeschichte in Bildern* series. Dr. Bowles has been exceedingly generous in sharing his material.

In pursuing this survey of mass scenes there will be little explicit reference to the *a cappella* question; the reader will note simply that instruments do not appear in the illustrations. Instead, discussion will center upon a number of subsidiary issues having to do chiefly with the methodology of interpreting liturgical representations.

Possibly the earliest extant representation of a sung mass appears on a Carolingian book cover (Fig. 2a), now divided, with the left panel at Cambridge and the right at Frankfurt am Main.[14] The left panel, according to Goldschmidt's convincing interpretation, depicts the teaching of the *cantus romanus* among the Franks. Toward the top there is a group of deacons and below them the large figure of a bishop, wearing a chasuble with the *pallium*, the symbol of delegated papal authority. He holds open a book with the significant text, *Ad te levavi*, the introit for the First Sunday of Advent, and as such the opening chant of the *temporale* of the mass; gathered about him is a group of priests, identifiable by their chasubles, who appear to look toward him and to sing. On the right panel we see a similar group of deacons and the bishop, now celebrating mass at an altar with chalice, bread, and a book open to the text *Te igitur*, the first words of the Canon of the Mass; below him is the group of singing priests. Perhaps the most striking feature of the two panels is the explicitness of the inscribed liturgical texts, alerting the scholar to the possibility of similar liturgical detail in subsequent representation.

Such expectations are fulfilled in the eleventh through thirteenth centuries, in the *Exultet* rolls of southern Italy.[15] The *Exultet* is a chant of special solemnity sung by the deacon toward the beginning of the pre-mass ceremonies of Holy Saturday; during its singing the deacon pauses to fix five grains of incense in the paschal candle and to light it with the newly blessed fire, actions which are separately pictured on several rolls. The most striking characteristic of the *Exultet* roll is that its text and accompanying Beneventan neumes appear to be upside down in relationship to the illustrations. Actually, from the deacon's point of view the text is upright and the illustrations are upside down, so that they will appear upright to the assemblage as the roll is allowed to fall over the front of the lectern. We see this in the opening illustration of a

---

[14] See Adolph Goldschmidt, *Die Elfenbeinskulpturen aus der Zeit der Karolingischen und Sächsischen Kaiser*, I (Berlin, 1914), pp. 61-2. The inscriptions are clearly legible in Goldschmidt.

[15] There is a substantial literature on *Exultet* rolls. The late Myrtilla Avery reproduced all the known extant rolls in *The Exultet Rolls of South Italy*, II (Princeton, 1936), but failed to complete the volume of commentary. There are three manuscripts from Bari and three from Troia reproduced in color along with extensive commentary in Gugliemo Cavallo, *Rotoli di Exultet dell' Italia meridionale* ... (Bari, 1973). Reinhold Hammerstein's "*Tuba intonet salutaris*: Die Musik auf den süditalienischen Exultet-Rollen," *Acta Musicologica*, XXXI (1959), pp. 109-29, discusses the musical iconography of the rolls, with the curious exception of the liturgical scenes.

Figure 2. (a) Ivory book cover, 9-10th c. France, Cambridge, Fitzwilliam Museum and Frankfurt am Main, Stadtbibliothek, No. 20; (b) Exultet roll, 11th c. S. Italy, London, British Library, Add. 30337, illustration No. 1; (c) Orgagna, altarpiece, Christ and Saints, 1354-57, Florence, Strozzi Chapel, Santa Maria Novella

twelfth-century roll now in the possession of the British Library (Fig. 2b);[16] we also see two groups of clergy, the one on the right including a bishop with *pallium*, and, presumably, one or both groups including the chorus. An interesting feature of this and most other rolls is what appears to be members of the faithful, pictured in this case as minute figures at the foot of the lectern. Accustomed as we are to think of the enclosed northern Gothic choir, the inclusion of laity in a liturgical scene is noteworthy. There are a number of possible explanations for it: for one, the general openness of Italian churches, where the architectural choir is formed only by waist-high *cancelli;* for another, the wish to picture those for whom the roll's illustrations were intended. But the telling explanation from a properly iconographic point of view[17] is that the people illustrate the words occurring in the first section of the *Exultet:* "et magnis populorum vocibus haec aula resultet". In any case the existence of some twenty rolls affords us at the very least a glimpse of south Italian liturgical groupings from the eleventh to the thirteenth centuries.

We have something more than a glimpse in a miniature executed at Bologna in about 1320 (Fig. 3b), which illustrates the Corpus Christi Office, appearing after the antiphons and before the chapter of first vespers. It is an early example of an integral mass scene, showing a priest in red chasuble at an altar on which lies a host; three clerics, identifiable by their tonsures, and an unexplained hooded figure kneel behind him, while four tonsured clerical choristers sing from an open book upon a lectern. The absence of a chalice on the altar is a curiosity, due perhaps to a lapse of the less than superbly skilled illuminator. The appearance of a mass scene as illustration for an office might seem to be a similar lapse, but has solid iconographic grounds in this case: the feast of Corpus Christi was established in the thirteenth century to honor the eucharist, and the celebration of mass is an altogether appropriate theme for the illumination of its office.

The lower left-hand panel of Orcagna's altarpiece in the Strozzi Chapel of Santa Maria Novella, Florence (1354–7) shows a larger group of singers than is customary in contemporary manuscript illumination (Fig. 2c). We see St. Thomas Aquinas, identifiable by his halo as well as by his appearance on the central panel, saying mass, assisted by two Dominican friars and an acolyte, while several friars sing at a lectern. The smallish figures at the front of this last group might be meant to portray boys studying at the Dominican priory

---

[16] There is a facsimile and discussion of this roll in J. P. Gilson, *An Exultet Roll Illuminated in the XIth Century at the Abbey of Monte Cassino* (London, 1929); for a more recent discussion see Peter Baldass, "Die Miniaturen zweier Exultet-Rollen (London, Add. 30337; Vat. Barb. Lat. 592)," *Scriptorium,* VII (1954), pp. 75–88, 205–19.

[17] My position on what constitutes "a properly iconographic point of view" is expressed in "Musical Iconography: A Definition," *RIdIM/RCMI Newsletter,* II/2 (1977), pp. 15–18.

Figure 3. (a) Decretals of Gregory IX, c. 1360 School of Nocolò da Bologna, New York, Pierpont Morgan Library, MS 716, fourth of four leaves; (b) Breviary, Ravenna use, c. 1320 Bologna, New York, Morgan 373, f. 303^v; (c) Missal, c. 1395 London, London, B.L., Add. 29704, f. 6^v

as aspirants to the Order; the tonsure was generally administered in the Middle Ages to such pre-clerical youths long before their ordination.[18]

Both the Orcagna panel and the Bolognese miniature lack an architectural setting, the former by choice and the latter because it predates the development of that fundamentally important stylistic resource. It is supplied, however, in a miniature from a Bolognese manuscript of c. 1360, illustrating Book III of Gregory IX's Decretals, where the clergy are reminded of their obligation to say mass for the people (Fig. 3a).[19] The setting is not the naturalistic architectural interior which was to develop around the turn of the century, but the intermediate type Panofsky calls the "doll house", consisting of a toy-like building open on one side.[20] The mass scene within has considerably more detail than any we have seen up to this point. The priest is bowing over the uncovered host prior to elevating it; this we can tell from the lighted torch, which acolytes hold only during the Canon of the Mass, and from the kneeling posture of people and choir. It follows that the portion of the mass the choir sings is the Sanctus.

We turn now to the north for our final pre-fifteenth-century illustration:[21] an historiated initial from a late-fourteenth-century missal prepared for the Carmelite community of Whitefriars, London, which shows Carmelite monks at Holy Saturday Mass (Fig. 3c).[22] The D is the initial of the collect for that day, *Deus, qui hanc sacratissimam noctem;* the choir, of course, does not sing the collect, which is recited by the officiating priest, and therefore these monks might be thought to sing the immediately preceding Gloria, a musical high point of the Holy Saturday Mass traditionally accompanied by the ringing of bells (note the bell-ringer to the left). Why the artist placed the illustration in

---

[18] See William H. W. Fanning, "Tonsure," *The Catholic Encyclopedia,* XIV (New York, 1913), p. 779.

[19] Mr. William Voelkle, Associate Curator of Medieval and Renaissance Manuscripts at the Pierpont Morgan Library, New York, identified the manuscript for me from an unattributed reproduction. The *Decretales* of Pope Gregory IX (1227–41) was an attempt to reconcile the differences among earlier collections of papal rulings and to establish an authorized text of them along with standard glosses. Book III is on the duties of the clergy, prominent among which is the celebration of mass for the faithful.

[20] Erwin Panofsky, *Early Netherlandish Painting* (Cambridge, Mass., 1953; repr. New York, 1971), I, p. 30.

[21] Mass scenes which definitely include singers are sufficiently rare before 1400 to warrant mention of examples not discussed in the text up to this point. The following are in the author's collection at present: (1) several panels of a Carolingian ivory book cover, Paris, Louvre, Moliner Catalogue, no. 15—see Goldschmidt, Taf. 144b; (2) the introductory illustration to an early-fourteenth-century Italian Durandus, *Rationale divinorum officiorum,* London, British Library, Add. 31032 (1), f. 1; (3) a *bas-de-page* in the mid-fourteenth-century *Carew-Poyntz Hours,* Cambridge, Fitzwilliam Museum, MS 48, f. 180; and (4) several illustrations of the "Liège type" of Psalm 97, including New York, Pierpont Morgan, MS 440, f. 87v and Oxford, Bodleian Library, Douce 131, f. 81v—for discussion see Mc Kinnon, "*Canticum novum.*" Citation is omitted here of the substantial number of mass scenes from the period which do not include singers.

[22] See Margaret Richert, *The Reconstructed Carmelite Missal* (London, 1952), p. 99.

the unusual position of the collect initial can be explained by two circumstances: that the Gloria is a common chant and as such does not find place here in the *temporale* of a missal; and that the mass for Holy Saturday has no introit, so that the collect is the first proper section to appear in the manuscript. As our first northern example since Carolingian times, it displays the northern architectural characteristic of the lateral choir stall as opposed to the more open choir area of the Italian examples. The explicit pictorial reference to bells at Holy Saturday Mass seems to indicate a further step in the specific representation of liturgical detail.

In reviewing the six scenes so far discussed we may observe one final detail: the four fourteenth-century illustrations show the choir singing from a book while the two earlier ones show it singing without a book. This might simply be a matter of stylistic limitation, but on the other hand it does correspond with the earlier medieval practice of singing from memory not only chant melodies, but also substantial portions of liturgical texts.

The area of greatest interest for our subject is the manuscript illumination of fifteenth-century northern Europe, this taken broadly enough to include at one chronological pole the progressive artists associated with Paris in the late fourteenth century, and at the other the last masters of Flemish book illumination working in Ghent and Bruges during the early sixteenth.

It is an area at first bewildering by the sheer quantity of extant illumination; how is one to conduct an orderly search for representations of the mass? Proper iconographic method suggests a systematic inspection of the same place within the same genres of book where mass scenes were found previously. However, sound as this principle might be in the abstract, its practical application is limited. For example, possibly the most valuable illustration we have seen up to this point was that for the Bolognese Decretals of Gregory IX (Fig. 3a), but this genre of manuscript is quite rare in fifteenth-century manuscript illumination. And then the appropriately familiar picture of Philip the Good at mass (Fig. 4c) represents an extremely rare, possibly unique, case: Jean Miélot's French translation of a commentary on the *Pater noster*. There is not quite so wide a discrepancy with our general principle when one considers missals, one of which is the source of the Carmelite Holy Saturday Gloria (Fig. 3c). For one thing, missals, while certainly not the most common type of fifteenth-century illuminated manuscript, are considerably more plentiful than Decretals of Gregory IX or Miélot's *Pater noster* commentary. And for another, while the typical missal illumination is a devotional scene illustrating an introit initial, say the risen Christ for the *Resurrexi* of Easter, there are conventional locations where one often finds a liturgical scene. Among introit initials the best possibilities are the *Cibavit eos* of Corpus Christi and the *Terribilis es* of the common for the dedication of a church, but the most promising locus of all is the *Te igitur* page, which appears in the short Ordinary section of a missal. These words, with which the Canon of the Mass begins, appear typically on a *recto* page, while on the facing *verso* there is a full-page painting of the crucifixion. This crucifixion scene is the artistic high point of a missal, indeed one of the most important in the entire history of book painting; and by a kind of aesthetic contamination the *Te igitur* page benefits from the special attention of the artist. Various iconographic themes are appropriate to it, but none, perhaps, more than the Elevation of the Mass; its depiction can range in elaboration from that of a fourteenth-century *Ordo missae* of Niccolò da Bologna showing only celebrant and two singers before a Sanctus page (Fig. 4a), to the heavily-populated scene in the early-fifteenth-century Bolognese *Missal of Pope John XXIII* (Fig. 4b).

The personal taste of Philip the Good, Duke of Burgundy (1419–67), plays a part of some significance in this question of genre. He commissioned books of every sort for his magnificent library, but showed a special preference for *historia* in the broad medieval sense, that is, biblical and classical history, romances, contemporary chronicles, and hagiographic works, mostly in translation, which he had read to him regularly each day.[23] Not unexpectedly events involving the mass occur with some frequency in medieval narrative resulting in a goodly number of mass illustrations; especially notable are those in Jean Tavernier's two volumes of grisaille miniatures for the *Miracles de la glorieuse Vierge Marie*, translated by the industrious Jean Miélot. Pictured here (Fig. 4d) is the eleventh miracle of volume II, in which a kneeling cleric confesses his fault before his colleagues at mass in the Church of St. Michael.

To summarize the part that the principle of genre plays in all of this, it is fundamental even if not reducible to a simple pragmatic formula. Suffice it to say that, while often enough it does serve as a guide to discovery, it functions more importantly after the fact. It makes intelligible what was found by an accident of the eye, and serves as an organizational and interpretative principle every bit as valid as that involved in, say, eighteenth- and nineteenth-century musical genres like symphony and quartet.

Up to this point there has been no mention of that genre with the most obvious relevance to our subject, the Book of Hours. As is well known, it was not a book used in the performance of the liturgy, but rather a prayer book of the wealthy laity. The contents vary from book to book, but virtually all are constructed around an essential core consisting of a calendar, the Hours of the Virgin Mary (whence the book takes its name), the penitential psalms, the

---

[23] "Philippe de Bourgongne a dès longtemps accoustumé de journellement faire devant lui lire les anciennes histoires," wrote David Aubert, one of Philip's favorite historians, in the preface to a chronicle of about 1462, quoted in Camille Gaspar and Frédéric Lyna, *Philippe le Bon et ses Beaux Livres* (Brussels, 1944). For an overview of Philip's library see this volume and especially the catalogue prepared by Georges Dogaer and Marguerite Debae for the 500th anniversary of his death, *La Libraire de Philippe le Bon* (Brussels, 1967).

REPRESENTATIONS OF THE MASS 33

Figure 4. (a) *Ordo missae*, 14th c. Nicolò da Bologna, New York, Morgan 800, f. 40; (b) *Missal of Pope John XXIII*, early 15th c. Bologna, Oxford, Bodleian Library, Astor A. 5, f.130; (c) Commentary on the Pater noster, trans. by Jean Miélot, third quarter of 15th c. Tavernier?, Brussels, Bibliothèque Royale, MS 9092, f. 9; (d) *Miracles de la glorieuse Vierge Marie*, trans. by Jean Miélot, third quarter of 15th c. Tavernier, Oxford, Bod., Douce 374, f. 10ᵛ

litany, the suffrages, and the Office of the Dead.[24] Unfortunately masses are rarely included, an understandable omission if one takes into account the historical circumstance that the Book of Hours is derived from the office rather than the mass.[25] When masses are included, they appear as the proper texts for a selection of important feasts and frequently employed commons. Generally the introit is illustrated with some devotional scene, precisely in the manner of the missal, but in exceptional instances a liturgical scene appears. This results in a small minority of a small minority, but the overall quantity of *Horae* is so great that we have a substantial number of such mass scenes. Among them are some of exceptional value like the Christmas Mass of the Limbourg brothers' *Très riches heures* (Fig. 6c) and a charming depiction of the Mass of the Virgin Mary, or the *Missa Salve* as it was called at the time, by the Boucicaut Master, complete with lay patrons within the chapel choir accompanied by their dog (Fig. 5a).

But the central source for fifteenth-century mass representation is the Office of the Dead section of *Horae*. Unlike other portions of the *Horae* which are devoted to liturgies celebrating particular saints or events in the life of Christ, the Office of the Dead does not readily suggest a standard iconographic theme. Occasionally the legend of the three quick and the three dead is depicted, more often as a *bas-de-page* than as a principal miniature, while towards the end of the fifteenth century Job might be portrayed,[26] but there exists no single theme of compelling relevance. The liturgical scene seems an obvious enough choice to fill this iconographic vacuum, and, accordingly, artists in the vast majority of cases favor us with one, very often choosing the celebration of the funeral mass even though the text of the *Requiem* appears only exceptionally. We thus find ourselves facing several hundred extant fifteenth-century representations of the *Requiem* Mass. It is a prospect at first daunting, but one which offers the unique opportunity to observe the stylistic development of a particular liturgical scene.

One can distinguish three stages of increasing naturalism in its depiction during the late fourteenth and early fifteenth centuries, a period which must be considered the golden age of Book of Hours production, a time when book painting was possibly the most progressive artistic force in Europe.[27] There is

---

[24] For general information on the Book of Hours, see the introduction to Victor Leroquais's standard *Les Livres d'heures manuscrits de la Bibliothèque Nationale*, 3 vols. and Supplement (Paris, 1927–43).

[25] The classic study on the liturgical sources of *Horae*, upon which Leroquais himself relies heavily, is Edmund Bishop, "On the Origin of the Prymer," *Liturgica Historica* (Oxford, 1918), pp. 211–37.

[26] For an example of each, see, respectively: Oxford, Bodleian Library, Douce 93, f. 57v–58; New York, Morgan Library, MS 618, f. 68v.

[27] Thanks to the monumental work of Millard Meiss which occupied his last 30 years we now have an authoritative guide to the period. It appears in three studies under the general title *French Painting in the Time of Jean de Berry: The Late Fourteenth Century and the*

REPRESENTATIONS OF THE MASS 35

Figure 5. (a) Hours, early 15th c. Boucicaut workshop, Paris, B.N., lat. 1161, f. 192; (b) Hours, late 14th c. Pseudo-Jacquemart, Paris, B.N., lat. 18014, f. 134^v; (c) Hours, early 15th c. Boucicaut follower, Paris, B.N., nouv. acq. lat. 3107, f. 237; (d) Hours, early 15th c. Egerton Workshop, London, B.L., Egerton 1070, f. 54^v

first the typical late-fourteenth-century type as seen in this miniature of Pseudo-Jacquemart (Fig. 5b): it consists of a small group of singers and sometimes mourners bunched closely together with celebrating priest and catafalque. There is no attempt at an architectural setting except for what Panofsky calls the "interior by implication",[28] which is indicated usually by a patterned background and a tilting floor. It lags behind our earlier fourteenth-century Italian examples. The second stage is not represented by a single conventional type, but rather comprises a variety of attempts to achieve a more complete architectural interior, illustrated here with an example by a follower of the Boucicaut Master (Fig. 5c), and another from the Egerton workshop, picturing the Office of the Dead rather than the mass, incidentally, as we can determine by the absence of a celebrating priest at the altar (Fig. 5d). They represent a dramatic advance over the first stage, even if their ambitious efforts suffer from the most obvious violations of perspective and proportion.

Finally, the third stage is achieved only in a handful of early-fifteenth-century miniatures: the liturgical scenes of the Limbourg brothers' *Très riches heures*, and those of the Boucicaut Master's little Book of Hours in the British Library, painted about 1415–17.[29] Perhaps the most outstanding single example is the *Requiem* scene from the latter book (Fig. 6a): the mass is celebrated within the enclosed choir of a chapel with the choir screen surmounted by a lectern which is clearly visible on the left; present are the priest, a boy acolyte, two groups of clerics, and two groups of mourners. It is an extraordinary picture for its time. Needless to say, it does not display geometric linear perspective which the Italians themselves would not discover until the next decade and which the outstanding northerners would choose to ignore for much of the century.[30] More to the point, a close examination will reveal a number of disproportionate elements: the figures are slightly beyond scale, the presbytery unduly cramped, and the ceiling not really so high as it ought to be. But these are quibbles, invoking a photographic rather than an artistic standard; the miniature displays what is possibly the most successful attempt in its time to create the illusion of a large architectural interior. Accordingly it convinces one that an integral contemporary funeral mass is depicted; there should be serious doubt only on the number of human figures represented in each group—a certain license with matters of quantity seems to be an essential element in the Boucicaut Master's striving for a naturalistic impression.

Patronage of the Duke, 2 vols. (London, 1967); *The Boucicaut Master* (London, 1968); and *The Limbourgs and Their Contemporaries*, 2 vols. (New York, 1974). Needless to say, the present study is heavily dependent upon them.

[28] *Early Netherlandish Painting*, I, p. 19.

[29] Meiss, *The Boucicaut Master*, pp. 25, 92.

[30] On perspective I follow especially Samuel Edgerton Jr., *The Renaissance Rediscovery of Linear Perspective* (New York, 1975).

Figure 6. (a) Hours, 1415–17 Boucicaut Master, London, B.L., Add. 16997, f. 119ᵛ; (b) Hours, 1415–17 Boucicaut Master and Workshop, London, B.L., Add. 16997, f. 145; (c) *Très riches heures*, c. 1413–16 Limbourg Brothers, Chantilly, Musée Condé, MS 65, f. 158; (d) Drawing, 17th c., Paris, B.N., Cabinet des Estampes

His success in painting an architectural interior prompts the music historian to ask whether this miniature shows not just a realistic, but a real building. Unfortunately we have little to guide us other than the negative indication that the two other chapel interiors of this manuscript show divergent details, as we see here in the Elevation of the Mass illustrating the Thursday office of the blessed sacrament (Fig. 6b).[31] Evidently the Boucicaut Master portrays generalized interiors, probably similar to those he observed in Paris. This latter picture, however, raises several incidental points of considerable importance. It is probably the earliest extant depiction of choirboys within a northern chapel organization; they are choirboys certainly, not acolytes, because of their position near the lectern. The figures vested in copes appear to be cantors; that cantors or *rectores chori* wore copes, and that they sang at a lectern rather than from the choir stalls, are liturgical details cited by numerous ecclesiastical documents,[32] giving credence to the realism of the scene. Finally, the number of singers is less than we should expect: from four to six choirboys, for example, is the typical early-fifteenth-century complement, not two;[33] but where would the Boucicaut Master have put them without creating a crowded visual effect?

To return to the question of a real versus a merely realistic chapel interior, Millard Meiss argues convincingly that the chapel depicted in the Christmas Mass scene of the *Très riches heures* (Fig. 6c) is inspired by Jean de Berry's *Sainte Chapelle* at Bourges.[34] Completed in 1405, this was built adjoining the duke's palace to house his splendid collection of relics and to serve as his final resting place. It consisted of a nave with six bays, and a sixteenth-century description tells us that large statues of the apostles and evangelists stood on each pier; in the miniature we see three bays separated from the remainder of the nave by a choir screen, with statues on each pier. We know from the famous calendar scenes of this book that the Limbourg brothers made a practice of depicting the buildings of Jean de Berry's many residences; we know also that, unlike the Boucicaut Master who operated independently in Paris, they spent many years in residence at Bourges. There is thus some likelihood that this scene, painted between 1413 and 1416, is inspired by Christmas Mass at Bourges between 1405 and 1412, the date when the duke fled to Paris. Noteworthy among the details are the organ surmounting the choir screen and the figure behind the curtain just to the left of the choir: the

---

[31] I am indebted to my colleague Jeremy Noble for identifying the liturgical context of this illustration. There is a third liturgical scene, the Office of the Dead, on f. 171v.

[32] See, for example, the rubrics for Sunday matins at Hereford: "Deinde rectores chori in capis in medio chori simul incipiant Invitatorium," *The Hereford Breviary*, Walter H. Frere and Langton E. G. Brown, eds., Henry Bradshaw Society, Vol. XXVI (London, 1904), I, p. 95.

[33] Occasionally as many as twelve, but most often four, five, or six; see Otto F. Becker, *The Maîstrise in Northern France and Burgundy during the Fifteenth Century*, Ph. D. dissertation (George Peabody College for Teachers, Nashville, Tenn., 1967), pp. 28-55.

[34] Meiss, *French Painting*, pp. 38-9; Meiss, *Limbourgs*, pp. 208-9.

latter probably represents Jean himself, who, as we know from a contemporary description, "maintained in his house many chaplains who day and night sang the praises of God and celebrated mass, and ... took care to compliment them whenever the service lasted longer or was more elaborate than usual."[35] Unfortunately the chapel at Bourges, the exterior of which can be seen in this seventeenth-century drawing (Fig. 6d), was abandoned to the weather following a dispute in the following century between its clergy and the cathedral chapter; today it no longer stands.

In the 1420s the focus of northern artistic development shifts from manuscript illumination to panel painting with Campin and the van Eycks. Yet Book of Hours production continued unabated throughout the century, indeed increased to a flood after the Hundred Years' War. What was there to prevent the advances made in panel painting from spilling over into book painting? At first it seems wholly reasonable to expect a fourth stage of the liturgical scene to develop: one which would utilize the virtuosic ability of the Flemish artist to depict both soaring gothic interiors and the most minute details. One visualizes this scene not in a modest chapel, but in some great church, say the cathedral at Cambrai, with the full choral and ecclesiastical establishment filling the choir and presbytery during the performance of Dufay's *Requiem*.

Unfortunately, however, there is little likelihood that such a scene does or ever did exist. For one thing the typical liturgical scene in Books of Hours from the 1430s to the 1460s is distinctly disappointing: seldom is one encountered which remotely approaches those of the Boucicaut Master's London book in scope and technique, let alone originality. Apparently, there were scores of inferior craftsmen reproducing the less ambitiously conceived patterns from the early fifteenth century, what we have called the second stage. There was, however, a dramatic change for the better in the work of the Master of Mary of Burgundy, who flourished from about 1465 to 1485. He was a genuine creator, while his artistic progeny, such as the *Hortulus animae* master and the masters of the Bening and Horebout workshops, were craftsmen of the first order. Together they can be said to constitute a silver age of *Horae*, flourishing in Ghent and Bruges during the late fifteenth and early sixteenth centuries.[36]

One's hope for the fourth stage mass scene is renewed in viewing the marvelous page from the Master of Mary of Burgundy's Vienna book, in which an imaginary window opens into a magnificent gothic choir with the Virgin and Child in the foreground (Fig. 7a). Closer examination, however,

---

[35] *Chronique du religieux de Saint-Denys, contenant le règne de Charles VI, de 1380 à 1422*, ed. M. L. Bellaguet, Vol. VI (Paris, 1852), p. 32; quoted in Meiss, *French Painting*, p. 39.

[36] For an overview of the period I rely upon Otto Pächt, *The Master of Mary of Burgundy* (London, 1948).

reveals various artistic liberties belying the picture's overall impression of great realism. The most notable of these, and a clever stroke indeed on the part of the Master, is the moving of the altar from its normal position at the east end of the choir into the foreground; here it forms a visually plausible backdrop for the figures, permitting them to be drawn larger than scale without jarring our sense of naturalism. The picture illustrates well the artistic problem which makes the ultimate northern liturgical scene virtually unattainable; there is a fundamental clash between two of the painter's most cherished goals: the rendering of soaring gothic interiors and the depiction of naturalistic human groupings. Our hypothetical fourth stage would require figures so tiny as to violate the latter and more essential of these goals.

How then do the better illuminators of the period portray liturgical scenes? Many of them skirt the problem by picturing outdoor funeral processions or burial scenes, but the Master of Mary of Burgundy creates a characteristically ingenious solution (Fig. 7b). He removes the funeral mass from the choir and places it at an altar on the edge of the transept; there he paints a small group at close range with the high walls of what appears to be the south transept in the far background. An early-sixteenth-century Flemish master follows suit in an attractive depiction of the *Missa Salve* (Fig. 7c). However satisfying aesthetically this solution is, it offers little of evidentiary value to the music historian, since it is so obviously appropriate to a private rather than to a choral mass. When the artists of the period turn to the choral mass they are apparently unwilling to depict a large contemporary complement of say twenty to thirty singers.[37] In some cases they resort to a scene not unlike our third stage (Fig. 7d): here we see an early-sixteenth-century depiction of the Elevation set in a chapel with a raised choir over a crypt and with a group of laymen kneeling in the foreground. It displays the authentic touch of vesting the cantors in copes and placing them at a lectern, but it shows only three or at most four additional singers in the stalls. A device which enables the artist to picture an appreciable number of singers while maintaining a reasonable scale for the human figure is employed in a miniature painted in the style of Jean Colombe, c. 1471 (Fig. 8a); it shows only one side of the choir, facilitating the depiction of a more authentic two-tiered choir stall.[38] But this device, employed here by a French rather than a Flemish artist incidentally, is used very rarely, as late-fifteenth- and early-sixteenth-century illuminators favor a central view and the corollary single-level choir stall. The artistic license involved is clear from a final illustration of the Office of the

---

[37] As, for example, at Cambrai with its approximately 12 chaplain choristers who sang chant, approximately 15 *petits vicaires* who sang both chant and polyphony, and 6 to 8 choirboys who did likewise; see Craig Wright, "Dufay at Cambrai: Discoveries and Revisions," this JOURNAL, XXVIII (1975), pp. 195-6.

[38] There is a notable early employment of the device in the striking series of scenes of religious orders in choir, added in about 1421 by the Master of St. Jerome to the *Psalterium ad usum regis Henrici VI*, London, British Library, Cot. Domit. A. XVII.

REPRESENTATIONS OF THE MASS 41

Figure 7. (a) Hours, c. 1480 Master of Mary of Burgundy, Vienna, Österreichische National-bibliothek, Codex 1857, f. 14ᵛ; (b) Hours, c. 1490–95 Master of Mary of Burgundy, Madrid, Biblioteca Nacional, MS E. XIV Tesoro (Vit. 25-5), f. 238; (c) Hours, c. 1525 attributed to Simon Bening, Oxford, Bod. Astor A. 25, f. 176; (d) Hours (excerpts from), c. 1492 Flemish, London, B.L., Add. 25698, No. 2 of 11 leaves (retouched by a Mrs. Wing after fire damage; see Otto King, *Fakes* (London, 1948), p. 87).

Dead (Fig. 8b). At first glance its finely-wrought figures and expertly-drawn stalls give the impression of great realism, but the suspicions aroused by a single-level stall are confirmed by inspecting the architectural background. It shows the apse of a large cathedral-sized church: the backs of the choir stalls should, of course, abut the columns ringing the choir area, but they do not, so that there exists the blatant contradiction of a tiny choir filling the broad expanse of a great chancel.

Examples can be multiplied, but we have seen most of the more common formats, and all demonstrate the illuminator sacrificing quantitative reality to the artistic need for human figures to dominate his foreground. The hypothetical fourth stage, which would subordinate human figures to the architectural background of a cathedral choir, is unattainable, and indeed, further reflection on the architectural realities reveals the limitations of the third stage. It can accurately portray only a very small chapel. An important fifteenth-century chapel, it should be noted—chapel in the sense of an independent court or university chapel, not a subsidiary chapel within a large church—must accommodate a comparable assemblage to the choir of an important cathedral. Indeed architecturally and functionally a gothic chapel should be conceived of not as a small church, but as the choir area of a large church, removed from its surrounding aisles, transepts, extended nave, and surmounting towers. Its height will be considerably less because its vaulting lacks the extra support given by the structural systems which form the aisles; its length is adjustable, depending upon function, frequently with a less extended presbytery than the cathedral and only a token nave outside its choir screen to serve as a vestibule; but its width and thus the area of the choir stalls is comparable to that of a large cathedral. To take a very obvious example, the interior width of the Paris *Sainte Chapelle* is 9.5 meters, while that of Notre Dame cathedral's choir is 12.5 meters. The width of Jean de Berry's *Sainte Chapelle* at Bourges, judging from pictorial evidence and from comparison with the duke's existing Sainte Chapelle at Riom, was at least comparable.[39] Thus what we suspected of the Boucicaut Master's chapels is probably true also of that pictured in the Limbourg brothers' Christmas Mass scene (Fig. 6c): they achieved much greater realism than the typical contemporary, but seem nevertheless to have contracted the dimensions of the chapel and very probably to have rendered a two-tiered or even three-tiered choir stall into a single-level one.

All this may be disappointing to the investigator of musical performing practice, but it ought not to be. For one thing there is something faintly Philistine about the attitude of an historian who loses interest in a related discipline the moment it ceases to supply the most precise data for the problem

---

[39] Meiss (*French Painting*, p. 38) refers to the chapel at Bourges as "similar to its model in Paris but larger"; I have no more precise information than this. For a photograph of the Riom interior, see Meiss, pl. 426.

Figure 8. (a) Hours, c. 1571 Bourges, Jean Colombe?, New York, Morgan 677, f. 261ᵛ; (b) Prayer Book, early 16th c. Flemish, London, B.L. Egerton 2125, f. 117ᵛ; (c) Pedro González Beruguete, The Virgin Mary Appearing to Bernardine Monks during Mass, one of a series painted at the Convent of San Tome, Avila, 1482-93; (d) Engraved title page by Master of Monogram F.I., *Secundus liber tres missas continet*, published by Pierre Attaingnant, Paris, 1532

engaging him at the moment. This consideration aside, however, it must be emphasized that it is only in matters of number and dimension that the fifteenth-century artist chooses to ignore reality; and what he does not tell us about quantity may be gleaned from pay records and similar archival documents which are becoming increasingly known to us through the recent work of a number of scholars, to be discussed in my concluding remarks. In the meantime the artist furnishes us with a wealth of authentic detail; for after all the dominating force in fifteenth-century art, both northern and southern, is the pursuit of realism. Thus we have mass scenes with properly vested priest, deacon, and subdeacon, engaged at a properly set altar in some clearly identifiable moment during the mass; singers are depicted in stalls on either side of the choir, while cantors, vested in copes, and occasionally choirboys, stand at lecterns in the middle of the choir. According to circumstances, additional clergy may inhabit the presbytery, acolytes hold torches, and the ruling prince kneel beneath a canopy. One revealing detail is that laity are regularly pictured in chapels, but not within cathedral choirs. Finally, most scenes look toward the altar and hence seldom present a direct view of the choir screen; but on several occasions when they do, a positive organ surmounts the screen.[40] Most if not all of these points we can derive from scattered literary and archival references, but their consistent appearance in manuscript illumination gives the historian both the confidence that comes with confirming evidence and a readily assimilable composite view not otherwise available.

The sixteenth century furnishes something of an epilogue to our subject, giving a sense of resolution to the keen interpretative problems of fifteenth-century manuscript illumination. There are two main reasons for this. The first is that sixteenth-century art is less conventional; we are dealing now not with dozens of similar illustrations at the expected place within the same type of book, but rather with a great variety of genres and media requiring a variety of new solutions. The second is that sixteenth-century art, dominated by Italian influence, is not subject to the Netherlandish tendency to place liturgical scenes within impressive gothic interiors. The overall result is a lesser quantity of mass depiction, but a greater diversity of types, which display a new freedom in the way human figures are grouped and willingness to portray them in considerably greater quantity.

The first example from what must be a miscellaneous sampling is a late-

---

[40] There is, of course, the Christmas Mass of the *Très riches heures* (Fig. 6c). Church organs are most frequently depicted in Annunciation scenes, which are usually set within a church interior. Most notable in this respect are those of the Bedford Master, London, British Library, Add. 18850, f. 32, and his workshop; see Meiss, *The De Lévis Hours and the Bedford Workshop* (New Haven, 1972).

fifteenth-century Spanish panel by the elder Berruguete (Fig. 8c). It shows the Virgin Mary appearing to Bernardine monks at the *Asperges* procession which precedes the Sunday conventual mass; on the right a devil struggles with a tardy monk, trying to prevent his attendance.

In a familiar woodcut, executed about 1518 by the Master of Petrarch, the emperor Maximilian I is portrayed hearing mass at Augsburg (Fig. 9a). There is an organist in the left middle ground, generally believed to Hofhaimer, and in the right foreground a chorus of six boys and a comparable group of men, the outermost members cut off, possibly, by the edge of the picture. While there is no reason to suppose that the artist portrays a precisely accurate number of singers, he does, unlike his fifteenth-century counterpart, show a number in substantial correspondence with the emperor's *chapelle*.[41] Liturgically, the lighted candles held by acolytes, Maximilian's kneeling posture, the placement of the missal and the position of the priest's hands indicate that the Canon of the Mass is in progress and that the Sanctus is being sung. Even more specifically, the monstrance above the altar indicates that it is mass on the feast of Corpus Christi, a circumstance which prompts a final reflection on the high expectations raised earlier in this study over the depiction of liturgical minutiae. There is without doubt a consistent display of striking liturgical detail in medieval and Renaissance mass scenes, but on the other hand this detail appears within the context of a limited repertory of liturgical situations, such as the Elevation, the Sanctus, and the feast of Corpus Christi. That we find ourselves categorizing this famous sixteenth-century woodcut according to such a repertory may seem to gainsay what we have claimed for sixteenth-century art's freedom from convention. A distinction should be made here: the art of the High Renaissance frequently portrays conventional medieval and early Renaissance themes, but in an unconventional manner; the new diversity of media and freedom in the portrayal of human groupings does indeed give the historian reason to speak of an increased realism.

This is borne out in another frequently reproduced portrayal of a great Renaissance monarch at mass: Francis I, in an engraving by the Master of the Monogram F.I., which appears as the title page to a collection of masses published by Attaignant in 1532 (Fig. 8d). Again we have the conventional theme of the Elevation, even if with the added touch of authenticity that the choir book shows the text *O salutaris hostia,* a eucharistic hymn sung during the Elevation at Paris since 1512.[42] But what is distinctly sixteenth-century in character is the number of participants pictured: in addition to Francis I beneath the canopy on the upper left and Queen Eleanor on the right, there

---

[41] See Louise Cuyler, *The Emperor Maximilian I and Music* (London, 1973), p. 56.

[42] See Walter Salmen, *Musikleben im 16. Jahrhundert. Musikgeschichte in Bildern,* III, 9 (Leipzig, 1976), p. 184.

are members of the royal family, cardinals and bishops identifiable by their arms, lesser clergy, choir, courtiers, warriors, and faithful mastiff.

The next example is an exception among sixteenth-century mass scenes (Fig. 9b). Appearing in the mid-sixteenth-century *Prayer Book of Archduchess Magdalena*, it is not only conventional in theme, but appears to be patterned after the woodcut of Maximilian I (Fig. 9a) down to the smallest detail. It reminds us how the obsolescent medium of manuscript illumination in the hands of a lesser artist can revert to a fifteenth-century mode of conventionality.[43]

More representative of sixteenth-century art, and demonstrating that even manuscript illumination can share in its diversity of presentation, is the famous miniature painted by Hans Muelich for the large choirbook of 1570 which contains Orlando di Lasso's *Penitential Psalms* (Fig. 9c). Lasso is generally presumed to be pictured to the left of the lectern as he directs a large choir of approximately thirty men and boys who sing, one presumes again, in the Bavarian ducal chapel of St. Lawrence. If the artist had a specific liturgical occasion in mind, it must have been the mass. One concludes this from the corner of the altar in the lower left and the deacon and subdeacon vested in dalmatic and tunicle; virtually any other liturgical occasion would require one of them to hold an incensorium. There could hardly be a more telling contrast between this illustration with its *a cappella* singing and the equally familiar illustration from the succeeding folio of the same manuscript, in which the ducal chapel participates in a vocal and instrumental chamber concert.

Finally there is this striking engraving by Philippe Gall for the *Encomium musices* of Johannes Stradanus, dating from some time between 1589 and 1598 (Fig. 9d). It shows a mass with a bishop as celebrant; liturgical indications mentioned several times above suggest that the Sanctus or an Elevation motet is in progress, performed by two groups of singers and instrumentalists, one before and one behind the altar. Arguments can be made against the evidentiary value of the picture. The *Encomium musices* as a whole smacks of biblical and classical allegory; Michel Brenet claims that the instrumentalists are not facing the choir books and therefore do not participate in polyphonic music but merely join in psalmody at the unison.[44] However,

---

[43] At the risk of complicating the line of thought presented here, I must point out that this is a "Mass of St. Gregory" scene; this is clear from the figure to the left of the altar holding the papal tiara and from the image of Christ pointing to his wounds. Several minor artists of the 16th century expanded the type common in fifteenth-century manuscript illumination to include a choir. Two other notable examples are by an anonymous student of Lucas Cranach the Elder, Aschaffenburg, Schlossgalerie, reproduced in Ernst Brochhagen, *Galerie Aschaffenburg. Katalog* (Munich, 1964), pl. 4; and by a Lower Saxon, possibly Braunschweiger artist, c. 1506, Braunschweig Gemaldegalerie no. 33, reproduced in Eduard Flechsig, *Verzeichnis der Gemaldesammlung im Landes-Museum zu Braunschweig* (Braunschweig, 1922).

[44] Brenet, "Notes sur l'introduction des instruments dans les églises de France," Riemann-Festschrift (Leipzig, 1909), pp. 282-3.

REPRESENTATIONS OF THE MASS 47

Figure 9. (a) Woodcut by Master of Petrarch, c. 1518, Vienna, Albertina, Inv. N. 1949/416; (b) *Prayer Book of Archduccess Magdalena*, c. 1555 Austria, Vienna, O. N. Ms. 1880, f. 149; (c) Choirbook, miniatures by Hans Muelich c. 1570, Munich Bayerische Staatsbibliothek, Mus. Ms. A. II, f. 186; (d) *Ecomium musices* by Johannes Stradanus, engraving No. 17 by Philippe Galle, between 1589-98, Brussels, Cabinet des Estampes

the interpretative framework set forth in this essay suggests that the picture be taken by and large at face value. It may have allegorical intent and the engraver may employ a sort of artistic hyperbole, but the essential visual elements are probably drawn from contemporary life. What is most significant is that the singers and instrumentalists gather together before the same choir book, rather than appear in separate locations; this suggests that they perform simultaneously, a genuine breakdown of *a cappella* practice, rather than antiphonally or at different times during the service. In any case, the engraving is one of the earliest extant portrayals of instruments at mass, and its appearance in the last years of the sixteenth century nicely accommodates the new *a cappella* hypothesis described in our introductory remarks.[45]

What precisely is the contribution of these mass scenes to the *a cappella* question? It is that they present us for the first time with a readily accessible panoramic view of medieval and Renaissance liturgical performance. A single illustration from a particular time and place means little, but a century-by-century progression of Italian churches, English monasteries, and French and German court chapels, appearing on altar panels, in illuminated manuscripts and engravings, should make it easier for the music historian to accept the proper starting point for a fruitful consideration of the *a cappella* question— that liturgical performance without instruments was the norm. Certainly there were scattered exceptions throughout the Middle Ages and early Renaissance, and, in the course of the sixteenth century, a systematic country-by-country increase in the liturgical use of instruments. But in the absence of a clear and visible context there has been a tendency to elevate the exceptions to the norm; it is easy to forget that there were literally millions of sung masses celebrated throughout the Middle Ages and the Renaissance, and to conclude too much from the appearance of, say, a *trompetta* part in an early-fifteenth-century mass or from splendid occasions like the frequently cited wedding of Costanzo Sforza and Camilla of Aragon at Pesaro in 1475.[46] The iconographic evidence offers a massive and immediate corrective to this tendency by

---

[45] The only other unequivocal example with which I am familiar is that showing a group of singers with one wind player, on the prefatory page of a tenor part book, *Liber Primus Missarum Quinque Vocum*, printed by Tilman Susato (Antwerp, 1546), reproduced in Salmen, *Musikleben*, p. 182. An illustration by Muelich from Vol. I of Lasso's *Penitential Psalms*, Munich, Bayerische Staatsbibliothek, Mus. MS A. I, f. 204, is described as "*Mehrchörige Kirchenmusik*" in *Musik in Bayern*, Robert Munster and Hans Schmid, eds., (Tützing, 1972), plate 2. However, the hats, beards, and garb of the singers, the exotic appearance of the instruments, the lack of any recognizable liturgical configuration among the participants, as well as the lack of any resemblance to Muelich's later illustration of the Bavarian ducal chapel, gives more the impression of a 16th-century conception of Old Testament Temple worship.

[46] For the documentation of this and the similar event at Torgau in 1500 see Otto Kinkeldey, *Orgel und Klavier in der Musik des 16. Jahrhunderts* (Leipzig, 1910), pp. 165-6, 192.

providing a context in which to view the exceptions; at a glance the historian sees artists over five centuries portraying the sung mass without instruments.

Actually a similar picture is available from other evidence, chiefly archival, but only after the process of synthesizing a large number of regional studies. Among these, the one that comes closest to a comprehensive view is Frank Harrison's *Music in Medieval Britain;* that splendid model of modern archival and liturgical research shows us in closest detail an English church music using no instruments other than the organ up until the Reformation.[47] Peter le Huray continues with the post-Reformation situation in England, concluding that "there is no reason to suppose that cornetts, sackbutts or any other kinds of wind or stringed instruments were used in church before about 1575."[48] By far the earliest of the archivists to turn their attention to the *a cappella* question was Michel Brenet. In her contribution to the Riemann *Festschrift* (1909), "Notes sur l'introduction des instruments dans les églises de France," she cites virtually every known instrumental reference of French provenance, concluding: "Ces mélanges de voix et d'instruments, cependant, restaient exceptionels."[49] As one who knew the French royal archives intimately, she had the context in which to place the exceptions.[50]

A number of archival studies do not address the issue explicitly, but present a broad picture of a predominantly vocal liturgy with a sharp separation between the singers of a court *chapelle* and the instrumentalist *ménestrels*. Most notable among these are the studies on the Burgundian court by Jeanne Marix and G. van Doorslaer;[51] the latter narrates Philip the Fair's extraordinary tour of 1501–3 during which *chapelle* and *ménestrels* collaborated at mass on more than one occasion, events, it should be noted, already taken into account by Brenet. Recently Marie-Thérèse Bouquet published a similar study of the Savoy *cappella* from 1450 to 1500.[52] An intriguing exception here is the occasional appearance of a single trumpet player in the lists of the *cappella* itself,[53] suggesting his performance of the *trompetta* part in a mass, or more obviously the tenor part in an isorhythmic motet.

[47] F. Ll. Harrison, *Music in Medieval Britain* (London, 1958; 2nd ed., 1963); see especially p. xiv.

[48] *Music and the Reformation in England 1549–1660* (Oxford, 1967), pp. 125–6.

[49] p. 282.

[50] She was, of course, the author of *Les Musiciens de la Sainte-Chapelle du Palais* (Paris, 1910).

[51] Jeanne Marix, *Histoire de la musique et des musiciens de la cour de Bourgogne sous le règne de Philippe le Bon (1420–1467)* (Strassbourg, 1939); G. Van Doorslaer, "La chapelle musicale de Philippe le Beau," *Revue Belge d'Archéologie et d'Histoire de l'Art*, IV (1934), pp. 21–57. Philip the Fair's tour is described on pp. 50–2 of the latter.

[52] Bouquet, "La cappella musicale dei Duchi di Savoia dal 1450 al 1500," *Revista Italiana di Musicologia*, III (1968), pp. 233–85.

[53] Bouquet, p. 236. Jeremy Noble provides more precise information from his personal inspection of the Savoy archives. The trumpet player, Stepanus Forrier by name, appears on the pay lists from their inception in 1449 until 1455. The fact that he was not replaced along with the fact that his annual salary was only 50 florins as opposed to 100–125 for singers and organist suggests a limited role for him within the *cappella*.

Cathedral and church archives have been studied recently by Craig Wright for Cambrai[54] and Frank D'Accone for Florence and other northern Italian cities in the fifteenth and earlier sixteenth centuries.[55] Instruments other than the organ appear rarely in the Italian churches and never in Cambrai cathedral; indeed an organ did not even exist at that great northern musical establishment. A scholar who approaches the subject from a completely different direction is Keith Polk, who specializes in fifteenth-century northern wind ensembles; he sees them figuring only exceptionally in church music.[56]

On the other hand, Lewis Lockwood maintains that the strictly *a cappella* ecclesiastical music of Ruffo's and Borromeo's Milan is exceptional for later sixteenth-century Italy,[57] a position supported by an impressive number of instrumental references in two earlier essays by Denis Arnold.[58] Meanwhile in sixteenth-century Spain we witness a wholesale incursion of instrumental music into all the outstanding cathedral music organizations. Robert Stevenson demonstrates this with overwhelming documentation, showing, among other things, how instrumentalists progress from supernumeraries in the early sixteenth century, hired on very special occasions, to salaried ensembles, playing a wide spectrum of greater and lesser feast days.[59] Indeed, as he points out, Marguerite of Valois, referring in her memoirs to a mass she attended at Madrid in 1577, called it *"une messe a la facon d'Espagne, avec musique, violons, et cornets,"*[60] an anecdote, incidentally, which did not escape the attention of Brenet.

The composite picture emerging from these studies is, as suggested above, one of scattered exceptions in the fifteenth century, and in the sixteenth an

---

[54] Wright, "Performance Practices and Pedagogy at the Cathedral of Cambrai, 1475–1550," a paper presented at the national meeting of the A.M.S., November, 1976, Washington, D.C., to be published soon in an expanded version, a typescript of which Professor Wright kindly allowed me to read. He is at this time extending his study beyond Cambrai to other major northern ecclesiastical centers.

[55] See especially his most recent of several studies in this area where he addresses himself for the first time to the *a cappella* question: "The Performance of Sacred Music in Italy during Josquin's Time, c. 1475–1525," *Josquin des Prez*, Edward E. Lowinsky, ed. (New York, 1976), pp. 614–18. Professor D'Accone kindly allowed me to read the article in typescript.

[56] Polk, *Flemish Wind Bands in the Late Middle Ages. A Study of Improvisatory Instrumental Practices* (Ph.D. diss., Berkeley, 1968), pp. 72–3; and "Ensemble Performance in Dufay's Time," *Dufay Quincentenary Conference*, Allan W. Atlas, ed. (Brooklyn, N.Y., 1976), p. 66.

[57] Lockwood, *The Counter-Reformation and the Masses of Vincenzo Ruffo* (Venice, 1970), pp. 115–16.

[58] Arnold, "Instruments in Church," *Monthly Musical Record*, LXXXV (1955), pp. 32–8; and "Brass Instruments in Italian Church Music of the Sixteenth and Early Seventeenth Centuries," *Brass Quarterly*, I (1957), pp. 81–92.

[59] Stevenson, *Spanish Cathedral Music in the Golden Age* (Berkeley, 1961), *passim*, but especially pp. 32, 139, 144, 148–68, 245, 298.

[60] Stevenson, p. 341.

increasing employment of instruments which varies widely from region to region. The process is well under way in Spain by the second quarter of the century; in Italy, to a somewhat lesser extent, by the second half; in England, to a still lesser extent, by the last quarter; and in France not until after the close of the century. This broad picture nicely complements that provided by the iconographic evidence, the one fortifying the impression created by the other.

However, as accurate as it might be on the simple issue of the presence or absence of instruments, it remains a superficial impression, one that only stands as a prerequisite to the remarkably precise knowledge of ecclesiastical performing practice that archival and liturgical study, aided by architectural history, can now provide, and indeed in some instances already has. The ideal is first to determine, within the framework of the entire church year and the daily course of offices and masses, which texts are sung in chant, which set in polyphony, which employ improvised polyphony, and which are claimed by the organ. We must further distinguish among the kinds of institutions, such as monastery, cathedral, collegiate church, court chapel, and university chapel; and the categories and quantities of singers attached to them, such as canons, choral vicars, choirboys, and chapel members. And finally we must study the actual buildings, seeking to determine the original placement of stalls, organ, screen, lecterns, and chapels; and to determine where the various liturgical items were performed. Within this context, then, we may integrate the manuscript and stylistic studies which have rightfully occupied the burden of our profession's interest through the years.

It is perhaps an impossible ideal to accomplish perfectly, but one which can be carried out remarkably well for some establishments favored by the accidents of documentary and architectural survival. Indeed Frank Harrison has succeeded almost too well in this respect; one gathers the impression that he has presented such a wealth of new information in so succinct a manner that our discipline is uncommonly slow to digest it. Possibly Craig Wright's more self-contained study of Cambrai will have greater immediate impact; we see there with superb clarity, for example, the performance circumstances of Dufay's late Masses. Of even greater potential interest to our subject, perhaps, is sixteenth-century Spain; whereas Harrison and Wright show us an *a cappella* liturgy, Stevenson shows us that the evidence exists to study the precise manner whereby instruments enter into the liturgy. What is needed is a further refinement of Stevenson's work along the lines suggested above. There are sufficient preliminary indications to justify the initial hypothesis that Spanish instrumental usage conformed roughly to what Harrison has taught us about fourteenth- and fifteenth-century English organ usage: that is, that the instruments, rather than mix regularly with the voices in polyphonic music, more often played independent pieces at set places in the service, substituted for the choir in the performance of certain well-known texts, and alternated with them in the performance of others.[61]

There are any number of other questions to be studied in a similar manner, for example, that of the fourteenth- and earlier fifteenth-century tenor *cantus firmus* and that of those instances of masses celebrated in connection with royal weddings and similar splendid occasions. At the very least we can expect more educated speculation on them than has prevailed up to now.

All of this might appear to take us well beyond the sphere of iconographic evidence. Yet we have seen that in those instances where the sort of study we are suggesting has been completed successfully, any number of details received striking corroboration in the artistic representations. But, perhaps more important, the approach through iconographic evidence shows at a glance that *a cappella* ecclesiastical performance was the norm, while disposing of the unhelpful notion that any and all instruments participated in liturgical music in a totally *ad hoc* manner. In thus enunciating a norm and not an absolute, it welcomes the discovery of more exceptions, insisting only on their responsible interpretation. It serves, therefore, not only to bring a degree of unifying viewpoint to a badly fragmented question, but to encourage further performing practice study of historical precision and musical sensitivity.

State University of New York at Buffalo

This essay derives from a paper which evolved over a goodly number of presentations, most notably one given at the Fourth International Conference on Musical Iconography, 24 April 1976, City University of New York; see *RIdIM/RCMI* Newsletter, II/1 (1976), pp. 4–5. The present version differs from that chiefly in the area of fifteenth-century manuscript illumination as a result of study during the summer of 1976 in the collections of the Pierpont Morgan Library, New York; the British Library, London; and the Bodleian Library, Oxford. Professors Jeremy Noble and Howard M. Brown have read it in typescript and made numerous helpful suggestions. I am most grateful to the libraries concerned for making available the illustrations reproduced here.

---

[61] For example, their separate locations, p. 139; separate books, p. 148; instrumentalists playing a *marche* while singers move to the lectern, p. 164; instrumentalists playing verses, p. 164.

[13]

The performing ensemble for English church polyphony, *c*. 1320 – *c*. 1390

ROGER BOWERS

In any attempt at reconstructing an artistically acceptable performance of a piece of mediaeval or renaissance music, almost the first factor which has to be resolved is the identification of the nature and exact constitution of a performing ensemble appropriate to the execution of the music. The necessity for this procedure arises from the well-known circumstance that this important information is almost never vouchsafed by the sources themselves; and certainly the manuscripts which preserve English polyphony of the fourteenth century emulate their continental counterparts exactly in this respect, inasmuch as not a single one bears on the face of the record any indication, overt or even indirect, of the nature of the medium (or media) by which either the copyist or the original composer envisaged the music being performed.

The very fact that such an omission could be made at all is itself highly informative. It seems to be compatible only with the proposition that, in the particular circumstances of the time, no such instructions were either considered or ever found to be necessary. This implication, in turn, appears to indicate the operation of one or the other of only two possible alternative circumstances. On the one hand, it may indicate that the ability to perform polyphonic music was so diverse and widespread, and that the potential performing media were consequently so various, fluid and unpredictable, that composers wrote music, and scribes copied it, without having in mind any particular ensemble – vocal, instrumental or mixed. Such circumstances would render it inappropriate, indeed inapposite, even to attempt to identify on the face of the manuscript any particular performing medium, optimum or (even) merely suggested.[1] Alternatively, the universal absence of ensemble identification may indicate that every example of the performing medium available to execute any given piece of music was so formalised and stereotyped in its

---

1 This line of enquiry is developed in detail by Howard Mayer Brown in 'On the performance of fifteenth-century chansons', *Early Music*, i (1973), pp. 3-10, and in 'Instruments and voices in the fifteenth-century chanson', *Current thought in musicology*, ed. John W. Grubbs (Austin, Texas, 1976), pp. 89-137. Professor Brown's investigations concern only secular music, and he does not consider the extent to which his conclusions might be considered applicable also to the performance of other repertoires, such as the sacred music under consideration here.

membership, and so narrow and circumscribed in its resources, that there was in practice only one way in which that piece of music could ever be scored. In this case, no useful purpose could be served by writing into the manuscript the identification of the expected performing medium; in the complete absence of any scope for choice or flexibility, the demands made by the music itself resolved all potential ambiguities.

Under the first alternative, therefore, identification of the medium was omitted since no specific manner of performance was ever envisaged; rather, there was some sort of disciplined free-for-all, bound (if bound at all) only by broad conventions which were so well known that, again, they did not need to be indicated. Under the second alternative, identification was omitted because the music was tailored to fit a single performance potential, one that was of so limited a nature that the allocation of the individual lines was immediately self-evident upon inspection of the source, and was immune from misunderstanding or derangement.

It does not seem possible that any position between these two can be considered tenable. For, generally speaking, it was not the contemporary practice to omit information and instructions of a practical nature from manuscript sources of performing material when the insertion of such information was clearly necessary to pre-empt some ambiguity or imprecision that was unacceptable. Manuscripts of plays, for instance, did not fail to identify the speaker of each set of lines. Further, in cases in which there existed certain levels of ambiguity or imprecision that were both acceptable and welcomed, and more extreme levels that were not, it was not usual to fail to append instructions delimiting the options that were open. Service-books, for example, were lavishly rubricated with instructions of every kind, leaving almost nothing to chance and not a great deal even to custom; and, in particular, where alternatives were permissible they were clearly described. Evidently, the performance of polyphonic music from its manuscript sources was characterised by circumstances quite different from those obtaining in these two examples – by circumstances, that is, under which the omission of performance instructions gave rise to none of those degrees of imprecision or undefined scope for alternatives from which contemporaries normally recoiled. While argument simply by analogy can never, of course, be wholly convincing, yet these considerations do seem to render very unlikely the possibility that the absence of performing instructions from the manuscripts of polyphonic music can be compatible with any merely modest degree of variability or flexibility in the way in which contemporaries scored it for performance. Had there really been scope for the sort of limited flexibility generally propounded by present-day scholars, it seems certain that at least some indication of its nature and extent would have been expressed in a written instruction. The universal absence of such instructions argues only for either total fixity or total freedom.

English church polyphony, c. 1320 – c. 1390

In respect of any single repertoire, these two hypotheses are, of course, mutually exclusive; it is clear that, for every repertoire, confirmation of one and elimination of the other depends on the establishment of one crucial piece of information. In order to resolve the problem of reconstructing the performing medium (or possible media) appropriate to any given piece of music, it is necessary to discover – as part of the initial stock of data to be established before any attempt to draw valid conclusions can even be begun – precisely *who* originally performed the piece, and *what resources* were available to them. This will establish the broad constitution of the group (or groups) concerned. Thereafter, in order to identify the most appropriate manner for the several lines of music to have been distributed among the members of the ensemble, it is necessary to establish the nature of the demands made on the performer by each line, and to match these with the potential offered by each member of the group. These analyses should, when they are possible, establish exactly which performer (or performers) performed which line of the music.

In respect of the whole body of fourteenth-century European music, there are three principal bodies of evidence which can be used as sources of this specific information: archival and kindred documents; contemporary pictorial and literary representations of performing groups in action; and the music itself. Traditionally, the first of these fields has been little exploited,[2] and so – rather oddly – has the third:[3] reliance on the second – the iconographical study – has been almost total. This is potentially unfortunate, since this body of evidence is well known as being extremely difficult to interpret reliably and accurately, and, if used by itself without corroboration, can produce results which at best can never be considered truly trustworthy.[4] In the context of the present discussion, pictorial material represents essentially a secondary source of evidence,

---

2 Numerous archival studies of particular churches and household chapels have appeared; however, as studies of single institutions, they cannot yield principles of general application. Frank Ll. Harrison, *Music in medieval Britain* (2nd edn, London, 1963), chapters 1 ('The institutions and their choirs', pp. 1-45) and 4 ('The institutions and the cultivation of polyphony from 1400 to the Reformation', pp. 156-219), remains without emulators as a more comprehensive investigation of the institutions of a whole region.

3 Ann Besser Scott, 'The performance of the Old Hall descant settings', *The Musical Quarterly*, lvi (1970), pp. 14-26, seems to be the sole attempt yet made, for English music of this period, to deduce aspects of performance practice from the notes themselves; however, the conclusions presented there appear to be negated by the present study.

4 I wish to stress that this observation applies solely to the context of the particular subject matter in hand – that of identifying precisely the nature of the ensembles which performed mediaeval music. For other purposes – such as determining the nature and technological evolution of instruments, their playing position and so on – informed and careful use of the pictorial evidence is of much greater validity. In this context, it is important to recognise, and to observe, the essential distinction between things and situations, between artefacts and the manners of their use. When all other circumstances seem favourable, then depictions of artefacts such as musical instruments may be accorded some cautious validity – indeed, for most of the mediaeval period there is commonly no other source of information. However, in even the most apparently realistic, plausible and credible settings, the manners and situations in which beings (either human or celestial) were depicted as combining to make use of artefacts such as musical instruments is so likely to have been determined not by observation but rather by some now remote

best used to corroborate conclusions already drawn from the primary, documentary, sources; and whenever conclusions conflict, it is those drawn from iconographical analysis that should normally be set aside, as stemming from the less suitable type of source.

The present paper is offered as a study not of the whole European repertoire but rather of a small and manageable section of it, and of the nature of the forces available to perform it during the period in which it remained in use. In eschewing the use of pictorial evidence, I shall attempt to reach conclusions solely through investigation of the two normally neglected types of source – archival documents and the music itself – the two bodies of evidence which, from the very start, had as their overt purpose the business of recording what happened in a purely objective way.

It is practical to begin with analyses of the vocal scoring of the music – the overall compass, the compass of each constituent voice and the disposition of the several voices within the polyphonic whole. For the greater part of the fourteenth century, as this paper will demonstrate, there can be discerned a consistent tradition of vocal scoring in the repertoire of English church polyphony, based on the stratification of unequal voices. At the beginning of the century, this prevailing 'terraced' scoring was already known, but was still co-existing with the final manifestations of the practice of 'voice-exchange' (in which the character of the vocal scoring was predetermined by the obligatory equality of the voices participating in the exchange of musical phrases). At the very end of the century, renewed contact with music of French origin, especially the polyphonic secular chanson, caused a decisive shift away from 'terraced' scoring in favour of a pattern involving the equality of the two lower voices. It is to the music of the central sector of the century, datable roughly (in our currently very imperfect grasp of its chronology) to *c.* 1320-*c.* 1390, that this study will be restricted.

During this period, the composition of church polyphony in England observed three principal forms: the motet,[5] and the two superficially similar

        and alien set of conventions responding to covert patterns of allegory and symbol, that no valid conclusions can be drawn from examination of them – at least in the absence of corroboration from one of the other bodies of evidence discussed above. See, in this context, Emanuel Winternitz's articles 'The knowledge of musical instruments as an aid to the art historian', *Musical instruments and their symbolism in Western art* (2nd edn, London, 1979), pp. 43-56, and 'On angel concerts in the 15th century: a critical approach to realism and symbolism in sacred painting', reprinted in *Musical instruments and their symbolism*, pp. 137-49. The interpretation of evidence elicited from contemporary literary works, whether overtly fictional or ostensibly factual, is equally fraught with pitfalls of a similar nature.

5 Ed. Frank Ll. Harrison, *Motets of English provenance*, Polyphonic Music of the Fourteenth Century, xv (Monaco, 1980). The editor's particular definition of a motet (for which see Harrison and Roger Wibberley's *Manuscripts of fourteenth century English polyphony: facsimiles*, Early English Church Music, xxvi, London, 1981, pp. xvi-xviii) may not be universally acceptable (*cf.* Peter Lefferts, 'The motet in England in the 14th century', *Current Musicology*, xxviii, 1979, pp. 65, 74 n. 25), but, for present purposes, it does offer the benefit of excluding

English church polyphony, c. 1320 – c. 1390

forms to which modern scholarship has given the names of cantilena and descant – the former being entirely free-composed, the latter distinguished by its incorporating a pre-existent cantus firmus drawn from plainsong.[6] The motets were invariably written out in *cantus collateralis*; cantilena and descant pieces were written out in score or pseudo-score. For convenience, the whole body of music in these latter forms will be referred to here as the 'score repertoire'.

It may be convenient first to discuss two general points concerning the following analyses. First, although it is not difficult to perceive pervasive principles behind the several patterns of vocal scoring adopted for the various compositional forms, it sometimes happens that one voice may take slight liberties with the range and tessitura apparently most appropriate to it in its context, by indulging in performing occasional notes a semitone or tone outside its predicated range. Such slight elasticity is only to be expected, and does not compromise the validity of the general principles.

Secondly, it is necessary to distinguish between 'texted' and 'untexted' lines of music. It is widely accepted that all the lines of works in the score repertoire are to be taken as texted, even though it was normal to write the (single) text under the lowest voice alone: all the parts were thus to be sung, to words, by the human voice. In the motet repertoire, however, some parts are completely untexted, or have only one or a few incipits, or have a text which (by virtue of its non-ecclesiastical nature) could not have been pronounced in a church service. It cannot be assumed that such a line was necessarily instrumental. In any great church at this period, polyphony was an occasional event, performed by a handful of skilled soloists whose principal work and whose qualifications, experience and training lay overwhelmingly in the field of plainsong. Such singers were well used to the phenomenon of the line of music without words; melismas of twenty to thirty notes or more were common in the gradual and antiphoner, while, in the sequence and prose, the service-books sometimes directed that the music of whole stanzas be sung without words and to a single vowel sound.[7] No performer of church polyphony need ever have been at all discomfited by the prospect of vocalising to an untexted line of music. As a

a number of pieces from the earlier part of the century which exhibit some motet-like features (such as polytextuality) but which are rendered irrelevant to the present study by virtue of their exploiting the technique of 'voice-exchange'.

6   Ernest Sanders, 'Cantilena and discant in 14th-century England', *Musica disciplina*, xix (1965), pp. 7-52; a complete edition of the music, prepared by Ernest Sanders, Frank Ll. Harrison and Peter Lefferts, will appear in Polyphonic Music of the Fourteenth Century, xvi and xvii.

7   Examples are quoted in Harrison, *Music in medieval Britain*, pp. 68-70; Mother Thomas More, 'The practice of alternatim: some problems of terminology', *Journal of Ecclesiastical History*, xviii (1967), p. 16; Mother Thomas More, 'The performance of plainsong in the later middle ages and the sixteenth century', *Proceedings of the Royal Musical Association*, xcii (1965-6), p. 124; and Denis Stevens' discussion of *Epiphaniam domino* (the sequence for High Mass on the feast of the Epiphany) on the sleeve of the record *The Worcester Fragments*, Nonesuch H-71308 (New York, 1975).

result, the mere absence of text reveals nothing about the manner of performance; the line could have been either vocalised or performed on an instrument, and only further examination will disclose which was the more likely in any specific instance.

For present purposes, it will be convenient to discuss the score repertoire – cantilena and descant – as one group, and the motets as another. This division is not artificial, even though the two groups do have a number of relevant features in common – for instance, no item in either is scored for more than four voices (and the great majority employ three), and both observe the same maximum overall compass of two octaves and a second (sixteen notes). However, as will become clear, the respective arrangements of the three or four constituent voices within that overall compass are so distinctive for each repertoire that it makes good sense to consider them separately.

Data have been drawn from fourteen of the principal manuscripts which include descant and cantilena pieces,[8] yielding seventy-eight individual compositions – a fair proportion of the total surviving repertoire. Of these, five are for two voices and two for four voices: the remaining seventy-one are all for the standard texture of three voices. Only one has an overall compass exceeding sixteen notes,[9] and only four a compass of fewer than thirteen. There are thirteen pieces which reach a total of sixteen notes: however, in every case but one of these,[10] the prevailing compass is actually fifteen notes, extended to sixteen by a single instance of a rogue note, usually in the highest voice. As a result, in seventy-two of the seventy-eight pieces, the overall compass of the score repertoire is restricted to a narrow range of between thirteen and fifteen notes.

In the case of the top and middle voices, the individual parts normally have a compass of a seventh, an octave or a ninth. The wider compass of a tenth or an eleventh is found very infrequently. The span of the lowest voice is commonly a little wider, rarely less than an octave; ninths and tenths are common, and elevenths occasional. Each of these three voices normally operates in a range of its own, with only a limited amount of voice-crossing. Throughout this repertoire, therefore, the standard, working, maximum overall compass can be taken to have been two octaves, and the compasses of the individual voices a ninth for the top and middle, and a tenth for the lowest.

Further analysis reveals that the distribution of these three voices within the overall span is far from random or arbitrary: rather, the vocal scoring of almost

---

8 Cambridge, Corpus Christi College, MS 65; Cambridge, Gonville and Caius College, MSS 334/727 and 512/543; Cambridge, University Library, MS Kk.i.6; Durham, Library of the Dean and Chapter, MSS A.III.11 and C.I.8; Leeds, Public Library, MS Vyner 6120; London, British Library, MSS Arundel 14, Cotton Titus D xxiv, Sloane 1210, Add. 24199 and Add. 40725; New York, Pierpont Morgan Library, MS 978; and Norwich, Norfolk and Norwich Record Office, MS Flitcham 299.

9 There are single instances each of e'' and d'' in the top voice of the second setting of the Kyrie in MS Flitcham 299, which extend its prevailing compass of fifteen notes to seventeen.

10 The exception is [*Gaude*] *virgo immaculata* in Pierpont Morgan MS 978, f. 1*v*.

every piece adheres to a single common ground-plan, with no more than the slightest degree of elasticity. Only three of the seventy-one three-voice pieces fail to adhere to the relative disposition of voices shown in Figure 1a. (In this and subsequent figures, a seven-line clefless stave shows the normal overall compass of fifteen notes, without specifying the notated pitches, while the optional extension to a sixteenth note is represented by the leger line above the stave.) The three voices are disposed in 'terraced' fashion through the two-octave range; there is only the slightest degree of flexibility in their differentials, insofar as two slightly different alignments of the middle voice in relation to the outer ones can be observed. Normally, the two lower voices lie fairly close together, usually about a third apart, while the top lies significantly higher, about a fifth above the middle voice: this configuration is represented by voices I–IIb–III of Figure 1a. In some twenty cases, however, the range of the middle voice lies one step higher, more nearly bisecting the other two: voices I–IIa–III. The difference between these two patterns seems too slight to have been significant; examples of both are commonly found together in the same manuscript, and, indeed, the combined compass of the middle parts of both configurations could be realised by a single voice able to span no more than a tenth.

This distribution of the three voices is virtually uniform for the three-part repertoire, and the vocal scoring of all five of the two-part pieces shows that they also drew their two voices from among the standard three. The three three-part pieces which deviate from this pattern are all examples in which two voices occupy the same range, thus departing from the normal 'terraced' pattern.[11] These will be set aside from consideration for the moment, alongside the two four-part pieces.

To summarise, analysis of the music of the repertoire of descant and cantilena reveals that a performing ensemble needed to be able to deploy voices of three (and no more than three) adjacent timbres. Of these three, the middle lay somewhat closer to the bottom than to the top in an overall range that spanned two octaves (optionally, although not often, extended upwards by one note in the top voice). This standard disposition of the three voices is shown in Figure 1b.

---

11 These are the Sanctus in Pierpont Morgan MS 978, f. 6*v*, and Kyries 1 and 2 in MS Flitcham 299, f. 1*r*. For the two four-part motets see below, n. 27 and p. 172 (with n. 28).

168   Roger Bowers

In respect of the motet repertoire, data have been drawn from a total of thirty-three compositions which, whether originally of English or of continental provenance, appear through the circumstance of their preservation in insular manuscripts to have belonged within the mainstream tradition of performance in England. These include twenty-nine pieces published by Harrison in the complete corpus of English fourteenth-century motets,[12] supplemented by one continental composition not included in that edition (*Domine quis habitabit/ De veri cordis adipe/Concupisco*) and by the three items contained in the recently discovered 'Bradfer–Lawrence Fragment'.[13] This repertoire likewise displays a significantly restricted number of patterns of scoring and vocal layout. All the pieces are for three or four voices. In only one does the overall compass fall below twelve notes;[14] while the normal extreme range is sixteen notes, only exceptionally does it exceed fifteen.[15]

12 *Motets of English provenance*. This edition contains thirty-six motets, but whole voices have been lost from two (Nos. 8 and 17), rendering them unusable for the analysis presented here. Two others (Nos. 11 and 20), although probably written in the early fourteenth century, employ elements of the earlier, thirteenth-century technique of voice-exchange. All four voices in these pieces, whether texted or not, have much the same degree of rhythmic agility, while the exchange of musical phrases between pairs of voices requires that each pair, upper and lower, have the same range and tessitura. Thus, these pieces represent a tradition of composition and vocal scoring that is earlier than that of the main fourteenth-century phase of development which forms the subject of this study. One other motet printed in this edition is excluded here (No. 36), as almost certainly post-dating the terminal date of *c*. 1390 (see Harrison, *Ibid.*, p. xii).

Of the remaining motets several, although appearing in manuscripts of insular origin, are certainly or very probably not themselves originally of English provenance; this applies especially to certain motets of French provenance in Oxford, Bodleian Library, MS e mus.7, pp. 529-36, and Oxford, New College, MS 362. (In this context, see Lefferts, 'The motet in England', pp. 60-6, and Margaret Bent, 'The transmission of English music 1300-1500: some aspects of repertory and presentation', *Studien zur Tradition in der Musik: Kurt von Fischer zum 60. Geburtstag*, ed. Hans Heinrich Eggebrecht and Max Lütolf, Munich, 1973, p. 66.) For the present discussion, the rational course is to include all those items, whether of English or continental origin, which appear in manuscripts evidently compiled for use within the main stream of the English performing tradition. I have therefore included all the items in these two manuscripts, among them the motet *Domine quis habitabit* (MS e mus.7, No. 16), which was omitted from Harrison's edition because it had appeared in his *Motets of French provenance*, Polyphonic Music of the Fourteenth Century, v (Monaco, 1968), No. 16a.

I have excluded all items from Durham, Library of the Dean and Chapter, MS C.I.20, ff. 336*-339. These fly-leaves do not appear to come from the same (certainly English) manuscript as do the front leaves (ff. 1-4); they seem to display no English features at all but, rather, to present an aspect consistent with the view that they are from a source of French origin, preserving an exclusively French repertoire, fortuitously preserved in England. All eight of the complete motets preserved there are excluded (including Nos. 34-5 of Harrison's edition), as probably never having belonged within any tradition of performance in England.

13 Cambridge, Fitzwilliam Museum, MS 47-1980. See my contribution in 'New sources of English thirteenth- and fourteenth-century polyphony', compiled by Peter M. Lefferts and Margaret Bent, *Early Music History*, ii (1982), pp. 281-94. The three motets on this isolated bifolium will henceforth be referred to as BL1-3.

14 Harrison, No. 15, discussed further below.

15 There are five such instances: in Harrison, Nos. 14 and 31, the basic compass is fifteen notes, extended in each case to sixteen by a single rogue d'' in the triplum; in Harrison, Nos. 16 and 19, each statement of the tenor extends a basic compass of thirteen notes downwards to a total of sixteen (in No. 16 the range of f-d'' is extended down to c, while in No. 19 the range of c-a' is expanded by single excursions to A and G). The top voice of BL2 (*Iesu redemptor/Iesu labentes/ Iesu redemptor omnium*) reaches a single d'', thereby extending the overall compass to seventeen notes.

As regards the character of the individual voices, the motet repertoire introduces a phenomenon not found in the descant and cantilena pieces, namely, that of a line of music that is effectively untexted. For present purposes, these parts without words can be separated into two categories. Some, despite the absence of text, adopt the same or a very similar degree of movement and rhythmic agility as the texted voices; such parts may be either completely undistinguishable from them (Harrison, Nos. 6 and 7 are examples), or may move at basically the same speed as the texted voices, avoiding use only of their smallest note-values (e.g. the tenors of Harrison, Nos. 1, 4, 5, 30 and 32). Others, about half the total number, use notes of much longer duration than those in the texted voices. In terms of the demands made on the performers, the untexted voices in the former category are closely akin to the upper texted voices. Generally, any texted voice in a motet, and any untexted voice in the same rhythmic style as one with text, occupies a range of between an octave and a tenth – occasionally reaching an eleventh, and very rarely any further; the slow-moving untexted voices are distinct from both, only utilising a range of between a fourth and a ninth. For the purposes of these analyses, then, the working compass of any texted or equivalent voice can be taken as a tenth, and that of a slow-moving untexted voice as a ninth.

On first acquaintance, the disposition of voices in the motets seems rather less prone to stereotyping than that of the score repertoire, for in the motets there is certainly no one single disposition to which all adhere. Nevertheless, analysis shows that the seven or so prevailing patterns are all permutations drawn from a very limited reservoir of resources.

Among the twenty-seven three-part motets, one pattern is common to no fewer than fifteen. This layout comprises two high voices – both texted and sharing the same (or virtually the same) range and tessitura – supported by a normally untexted cantus firmus pitched substantially lower. In eight of nine kindred works,[16] the bottom voice (though untexted) is written in a rhythmic style undistinguishable for practical purposes from that of the texted voices. Indeed, in the last of these nine cases, all three voices carry text: the tenor is rhythmically undifferentiated from the upper voices, while to it is underlaid in black ink two lines of secular French poetry which express a sentiment so bland that they could well have been pronounced in church without giving offence – thereby a tri-textual motet is created.[17] The vocal scoring and distribution associated with these motets is shown in Figure 2a, as layout B. This is also the pattern followed by the three items of the score repertoire that do not follow the

---

16 These are Nos. 2, 5, 7, 21, 27 and 32 in Harrison's edition, and BL1 and BL3.
17 Harrison, No. 23. Indeed, the words of the tenor could well have been understood to express human devotion to the Virgin Mary. Musically, the result of these procedures in this motet has more in common with the score repertoire than with the motets proper.

'terraced' pattern.[18] In the six motets remaining from this group of fifteen,[19] the tenor of the motet is untexted, disposed in long note-values and generally fragmented by the frequent interpolation of rests. The vocal scoring associated with these pieces is shown as layout C in Figure 2b.[20]

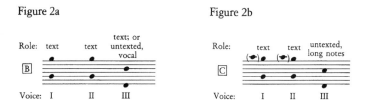

Figure 2a   Figure 2b

A second motet layout, one apparently cultivated almost exclusively in England,[21] places a narrow-ranged untexted voice, the tenor, in the middle of the texture. The two outer voices, both texted, lie at the extremes of the overall thirteen- to fifteen-note compass. The tenor – sometimes marked 'medius cantus' and always moving in long notes, untexted and fragmented by rests – shares the highest pitch of the lowest voice, although (being of a narrower range) it does not descend so low. There are six instances of this distribution,[22] shown as layout D in Figure 3.

Figure 3

Of the remaining three-part motets, four others[23] also contain two texted voices of different pitches, sustained by an untexted tenor: in these instances, the tenor is so pitched that its lowest note approximates that of the lower texted

---

18 See above, n. 11.
19 These are Nos. 12, 16, 24, 26, 28 and 29 in Harrison's edition. In No. 29, the tenor – a slow-moving line in long notes – carries a crude, secular French text; it is, however, inscribed in red ink, apparently indicating that it was entered for identification purposes only and was not to be sung. See Harrison's commentary to this piece, p. 164, and also that to No. 20, p. 162.
20 As reconstructed by the editor, Harrison, No. 8 also observes this layout.
21 Harrison's edition, p. xii.
22 These are Nos. 3, 10, 13, 14, 30 and 31 in Harrison's edition. In no instance does the range of the tenor exceed an octave. No. 14 is a little unusual, in that it employs unusually wide ranges for both top and bottom voices. These may readily be seen to observe prevailing pitches of, respectively, $a\text{-}c''$ and $c\text{-}e'$ – as a result of which the 'medius cantus' must be regarded as extending a third higher than usual, $c'\text{-}g'$.
23 Harrison, Nos. 4 and 22, *Domine quis habitabit* and the three-part version of Harrison, No. 33: this last is found in Cambridge, Gonville and Caius College, MS 512/543, ff. 256v-257r, where it lacks the triplum of the four-part version preserved in Durham, Library of the Dean and Chapter, MS C.I.20, ff. 3v-4r.

English church polyphony, c. 1320 – c. 1390

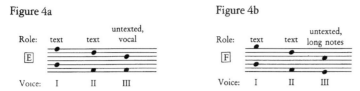

voice, although it again has a narrower range. The distribution of the voices of these four pieces is shown in Figure 4a and b: layout E represents the one piece[24] of a homogeneous texture, and layout F the other three, with long-note tenors.

Three three-part pieces remain for consideration. Of these, one (Harrison, No. 19) has three fully-texted voices, and another (BL2) has two texted voices and a tenor consisting of a complete hymn tune with a verbal incipit; the phrases of the tune are not broken up by rests, and the words of one stanza could be underlaid without difficulty. In both motets, the voices are 'terraced' in pitch: indeed, they use virtually the same arrangement of voices as cantilena and descant pieces (Figure 1b), suggesting that they were given a fully vocal performance as tri-textual motets, by the same forces as those used for the score repertoire.[25]

Of the motets for four voices, six[26] come within the terms of the present study. In all, the texture is capped by two high voices, both texted and sharing the same range and tessitura; in all, at least one other voice either carries a text or is written with a rhythmic character matching that of the texted voices. In other words, no motet ever has more than one voice that is both written in long note-values and restricted in compass. In two motets (Nos. 1 and 6), all the voices, whether texted or not, have a similar rhythmic nature; the vocal scoring associated with these pieces of homogeneous texture is shown as layout G in Figure 5a.[27] In three other motets (Nos. 9, 18 and 33), the tenor is written in long notes: the vocal scoring adopted in these cases is shown as layout H in Figure 5b.

24 Harrison, No. 4. The vocal ranges given in the edition need correction: they are, for the duplum, $f\text{-}a'$ and, for the tenor, $f\text{-}f'$. The tenor has a French-language incipit, but no further text.
25 Both pieces have overall compasses marginally wider than the standard two octaves, accommodated by requiring the lowest voice to extend one pitch lower than usual.
26 Harrison, Nos. 1, 6, 9, 15, 18 and 33.
27 As completed by Harrison, No. 17 also observes this layout. It is also followed by one of the two four-voice cantilena settings, the response *Deo gracias*, found in Pierpont Morgan MS 978, f. 6v.

172   Roger Bowers

One three-part and one four-part motet remaining to be considered stand outside these schemes. Motet No. 15 has three texted upper voices, sharing the same range (g-a'), and an untexted tenor in long notes, pitched only a little lower (f-d'): thus the whole motet employs an overall compass of only a tenth (f-a'). This layout appears to be unique among English compositions, and cannot be accommodated to any of the contemporary schemes of vocal scoring. The three-voice motet No. 25, with a homogeneous texture, employs a full two-octave compass, with two low voices descending to the lowest available pitch. Likewise, the four-voice setting, laid out in score, of *Alleluia* ℣ *Nativitas*[28] uses two equal low voices (with two equal high voices) in its two-octave compass. This employment of two equal low voices at the bottom of a full fifteen-note compass places both these pieces outside the prevailing patterns of vocal scoring. Thus, together with motet No. 15, they will have to be regarded as exceptions to the patterns which can be discerned in the remaining 108 pieces: the following discussion will proceed without further reference to them.

The number of vocal layouts adopted in the rest of the motet repertoire thus reaches seven. However, when the constituent elements of these seven are aligned and compared, all may be seen to have been selecting from a maximum of five individual performing resources. These certainly included four singers, whose skills extended both to singing texted lines and, in the case of the two lower voices, also to vocalising the untexted lines; of these four voices, two were of high pitch, one medium and one low. In addition, however, there appears to be some scope for considering the inclusion of one other performing resource, low-pitched and with a range of a tenth or so, that was able to execute such untexted lines as were disposed in long notes. There is, of course, no feature of these long-note tenors that could not have been vocalised by one of the lower voices. However, their appearance on the manuscript page is so distinct from that of tenors in motets of homogeneous texture, and their individual compasses are commonly so much narrower, that, at least for the moment, the possibility should be kept open that some different mode of performance was envisaged or intended for these parts. The facts that no more than four of these elements were ever used at once, and that the characteristic role of this putative fifth element was non-verbal and technically undemanding, both suggest strongly that this last element, if it existed, would not have been a fifth singer but rather an instrument which, when required and appropriate, one performer played instead of singing. Discussion of the likelihood of the existence of a separate, fifth performing element can therefore best await a more detailed consideration of the nature of what can be shown to have been the only instrument

---

28   Found in Cambridge, Corpus Christi, MS 65, f. 135r. The vocal scoring of this piece conforms to the thirteenth-century tradition exemplified by voice-exchange pieces, rather than to fourteenth-century patterns.

available.[29] Pending this discussion, these five elements — the four certain, and the fifth, putative element — with their respective roles and relative pitches, may be displayed as in Figure 6.

Figure 6. Performance elements employed in English fourteenth-century motets

Meanwhile, it can also be seen that the performing resources required by the vocal scoring of the motet repertoire contain within them, as voices 1, 3 and 4, media of performance which meet exactly the demands made on its performers by the vocal scoring of the score repertoire (see Figure 1b). Therefore any performing ensemble able to tackle the motet repertoire could, by definition, perform any item in the score repertoire also. Indeed, there thus emerges from these analyses the remarkable circumstance that every combination of performing resources demanded by English church polyphony of the period c. 1320 – c. 1390 consists of a permutation drawn from a maximum of only five individual elements – of which, moreover, no more than four were ever used at the same time. The several combinations actually demanded by the music may therefore be arranged as in Table 1. It will be noted that use of the performing resource here numbered 5 – the putative instrumental medium – is nowhere obligatory; if its existence be discounted, then the pairs of layouts joined by brackets can be amalgamated, further reducing the total number.

Table 1. *Construction of ensembles from the available performance elements*

Category	Layout	I	II	III	IV
Cantilena and Descant	A	1	3	4	
⌈ Motet	B	1	2	4	
⌊ Motet	C	1	2	4 or 5	
Motet	D	1	3 or 5	4	
⌈ Motet	E	1	3	4	
⌊ Motet	F	1	3	4 or 5	
⌈ Motet	G	1	2	3	4
⌊ Motet	H	1	2	3	4 or 5

---

29 This was the church organ. See below, pp. 180-4.

Analysis of the music has thus led to a clear conclusion. The vocal scoring of the repertoire considered here is by no means random or arbitrary. Rather, it transpires that there existed for the small groups of singers of polyphony found in the major English churches and household chapels of this period a single, recognised and standard pattern of membership, one for which the entire repertoire of church music was composed. This optimum standard ensemble may be seen to have consisted of just four singers, comprising two high voices of identical pitch and character and two lower voices covering respectively the upper and lower tenths of a total compass of a twelfth. Further, such a group may also have had access to an instrument capable of a range of at least a tenth: if so, then for any piece in which this instrument was used, there was always at least one singer not involved in rendering a vocal line, and thus free to play it.

It may perhaps be added at this point that the degree of standardisation that has been discerned in the vocal scoring of this music is much more readily evident and detectable in the original manuscripts than it is in modern editions. The regrettable modern practice of representing (or, rather, misrepresenting) the original clef by some direct analogue from modern notation results in the presentation of the music at any one of a wide variety of pitches, high in the treble range, low in the bass, or anywhere in between. In fact, the clefs used in the original notation did not then, and cannot now, serve to identify the pitch and timbre of the participating voices. It still needs to be emphasised that, in all vocal polyphony of this period, the clef conveyed to the singer no more than did the clef in plainsong: it told him precisely where, in his usual performing compass of the tenth or so displayed on his particular stave, he should place the semitone intervals of the diatonic scale – and that was all it told him.[30] Not until the late fifteenth century at the earliest did the clef even begin to assume any aspect of its modern role of conveying to the performer the exact sounding

---

30 It is still possible to encounter modern observations on the intended pitch of performance for parts of this repertoire which presume that the fourteenth-century clef can be considered to have had exactly the same role, function and effect as the modern clef: for example, Harrison, *Motets of English provenance*, p. xv, says 'The singers were probably adult males, since the highest voice does not go above d'', except in no.25, where it goes to f'', suggesting the use of boys' voices.' Quite apart from the evident anachronism of such an approach, there are more immediate grounds for believing that view to be impossible to sustain. The 'highest' written note in music of this period is f'' (*Motets of English provenance*, No. 25, and Durham, MS A.III.11, f. 11v: Kyrie *Cuthberte*) and the 'lowest' is F (e.g. London, British Library, Sloane MS 1210, No. 1) - a total apparent compass of three octaves. The fact that such pitches are entirely illusory may be deduced from the fact that, although such extremes do occur and may perfectly well be found even in the same manuscript (e.g. the F just cited and an e'' in the same manuscript, No. 14), they never occur in the same work. It must be asked why, if there really were available some voices able to sing up to f'' and others capable of reaching down to F, they were never used together. Rather, it must be deduced that the choice of a clef and clef-configuration were determined not by consideration of the intended sounding pitch or by any other exterior consideration, but by a desire to achieve the twin objectives of containing the vocal range within the five-line stave while expressing the music in only the simplest (or without any) hexachord transpositions. A wish to preserve the original clef used in the service-book may also have been a factor in the case of some cantus firmi of liturgical origin.

pitch of the music that it preceded. Fourteenth-century polyphony no more has a notationally prescribed pitch than does any piece of plainsong; an appropriate performing pitch and vocal scoring, therefore, can now be established only by discovering the identity of the original performers and by aligning the demands made by the music with the resources that those performers can be shown to have been able to offer. Indeed, the misrepresentation of the original clef by a modern analogue helps to obscure completely a fundamental feature of the composition and construction of the music in this repertoire – its strict adherence to constraints of vocal scoring imposed on the composer by the limitations inherent in what was for him a traditional, standard and obligatory performing medium. All that the original performers needed to know in order to dispose themselves appropriately to perform any given piece could quickly be discerned by the briefest glance at the layout of the music on the written page, and at the relative disposition of the pitches of the several voices.

The results gained so far have been drawn solely from a study of the music; this information is, of course, very incomplete as a body of data from which to attempt a reconstruction of the original performing ensemble. These analyses have disclosed the possible availability and use of an instrument – but they have not helped to identify it; they have also revealed the number of voices comprising an ensemble and their pitches relative to each other – but their timbre and actual sounding pitches remain unknown. The music itself cannot yield this additional information. Happily, it is possible to turn to archival material – not only to confirm the results already laid out, but also to supplement them, both by identifying the nature and timbre of the human voices involved, and by establishing the identity of the only instrument that could have been at their disposal.

The performance of fourteenth-century church polyphony was undertaken by the most musically literate members of the choirs of the major churches and of the various royal and aristocratic household chapels, of which, at any given moment, there were probably never more than thirty-five or forty where written polyphony was performed. These choirs included those of the major secular churches (the nine secular cathedrals and a handful of collegiate churches), a declining number of monasteries (principally Benedictine and Augustinian), the sovereign's Chapel Royal, and an increasing number of private chapels maintained within their households by the most senior churchmen and aristocracy.[31]

The full membership of these choirs was in many instances very numerous, including (in the case of the non-monastic institutions) boys as well as men;

---

31 For some account of many of these institutions, see Harrison, *Music in medieval Britain*, chapters 1 ('The institutions and their choirs', pp. 1-45) and 3 ('The polyphony of the liturgy from 1100 to 1400', pp. 104-55).

but it is now well accepted that, throughout the fourteenth century, the performance of polyphony was committed only to soloists;[32] and, although there are only few surviving archival references dealing explicitly with these singers, yet such references do help to identify them, to enumerate them and to disclose the resources – vocal and instrumental – available in institutions for the performance of polyphony.

At the cathedral church of Lincoln, for instance, the body of thirty-six to forty vicars choral included a specific sub-group, called the Cantores Sancte Marie. It is known that, in the early fifteenth century, they were four in number, and that their duties included the performance of daily Lady Mass with polyphony;[33] and their history, and that of the polyphonic performance of the Lady Mass, can be traced back at least to 1368/9 and probably some way further beyond that.[34]

32 Manfred Bukofzer, 'The beginnings of choral polyphony', *Studies in medieval and renaissance music* (New York, 1950), pp. 176-89. Andrew Hughes, in 'The choir in fifteenth-century English music: non-mensural polyphony', *Essays in musicology in honor of Dragan Plamenac on his 70th birthday*, ed. Gustave Reese and Robert J. Snow (Pittsburgh, 1969), pp. 139-42, suggests that pieces in descant and cantilena style might commonly have been performed by a small chorus. However, the evidence he offers applies in the first instance only to music of the middle of the fifteenth century, and its extension backwards to the fourteenth is proposed only on the basis of analogy: in the absence of any firm evidence, this is difficult to accept.

33 This group of singers was certainly already in existence by 1404: 'Admissio domini J[ohannis] Grymesby in socium altaris beate Marie. Item xxi° die mensis Junii Anno domini supradicto [1404] Decanus et Capitulum Capitulariter admiserunt dominum J[ohannem] Grymesby vicarium in Socium et participem reddituum et proventuum deputatorum cantoribus misse beate marie in ecclesia lincolniensi memorata' (Acts of Chapter: Lincoln, Archives of the Dean and Chapter, MS A.2.29, f. 9r). On 23 February 1432 the 'Cantores ad missam cotidianam de sancta Maria vocatam Salve sancta parens in ecclesia lincolniensi celebratam', numbering four altogether (William Stevenot, William ffaucus, John Hamond and William Jaye), appeared before the President and Chapter to demand payment of 2s. which they claimed to be due to them from the chaplains of the chantry of Henry Lexington, late Bishop of Lincoln; evidently these four singers constituted a recognised and fully defined sub-group within the body of vicars choral, since they enjoyed in their capacity as 'Cantores ad missam cotidianam de sancta Maria' an independent endowment (managed by one of their number as *prepositus*: f. 98r), and in evidence were able to present 'Rotulos suos [i.e., account rolls] Rentales et alias suas evidencias' (*Ibid.*, MS A.2.32, f. 59v). On 6 November 1434, in a further episode in the same dispute, reference was made to these four singers as 'Cantores misse beate marie in capella eiusdem hora prima cotidie organice decantate' ('sung in polyphony': *Ibid.*, f. 97v). On 18 December 1434, the Chapter required that wax and candles be supplied for the Lady Chapel by Richard Ingoldsby, canon resident, in his capacity as (administrative) 'supervisor sive magister altaris beate marie et capelle eiusdem ubi canitur missa de eadem cotidie organice' (*Ibid.*, f. 99r). References in the same vein to this daily Lady Mass sung in polyphony occur *Ibid.*, ff. 104v, 114r (1435, 1436).

34 This is revealed by the informative manner in which the record of a set of payments, made since the beginning of the century and recorded in an entry of fixed wording, was updated and expanded in that year. Account of the Clerk of the Common 1368/9: Lincoln, Archives of the Dean and Chapter, MS Bj.2.6/11, f. 8v:

[*Obitus mortuorum*] . . . Item idem J[ohannes de Braunscepath] computator solvit in communis unius capellani < dicti in agendis *interlined* > xj pauperum clericorum et < duorum *lined out* > vicariorum ministrancium < et cantancium organum *interlined* > ad missam beate marie hora prima < videlicet per septimanam vij d *interlined*> per totum annum videlicet per Lij septimanas xvj li viij d.

The meaning of the original wording was: '[Account of revenues arising from the deaths of canons]: [Expenses include:] Further, the same John Brancepeth, accountant, has paid: as the

English church polyphony, c. 1320 – c. 1390

That this instance of the promotion of four particular singers to perform polyphony was not an isolated case is suggested by a passage in a Lollard tract of c. 1380; this passage condemns exactly this manner of incorporating polyphony into the conduct of the plainsong service in explicit terms as apparently a common and well-known feature of the conduct of the liturgy in the greater churches of the time. In the course of an extensive diatribe condemning the diversion of the church's resources away from the preaching of the gospel in favour of such pernicious practices as (among others) the cultivation of polyphonic music, the author demanded rhetorically to know:

> where is more disceit in feiþ, hope and charite? for whanne þer ben fourty or fyfty in a queer þre or foure proude and lecherous lorellis schullen knacke[35] þe most devout servyce þat noman schal here þe sentence, and alle oþere schullen be doumbe and loken on hem as foolis.[36]

Great caution must of course be exercised, in using a source of this nature, before building too grand an argument on the merely incidental quotation of a number: precise arithmetical exactitude is hardly to be expected in what is, after all, a committed polemical work of censorious indignation. Indeed, the author is anonymous, so that his credentials for writing such a passage remain impossible to establish. Nonetheless, the whole tract does appear to be free of any features which could give grounds for doubting the veracity of the writer's observation of the contemporary practices he condemns. Indeed, the Lollard polemicists evidently believed sufficiently firmly in the strength of their case for there to be no need for them to risk damaging their credibility by reinforcing their accusations with imaginary evidence, too insubstantial to bear scrutiny. It may be accepted, therefore, that the commitment of the performance of polyphony in church to a group of 'þre or foure' singers was a practice sufficiently

---

commons of one chaplain; and of eleven Poor Clerks; and of two vicars ministering at the Mass of St Mary [celebrated] at the first hour [of the day], throughout the whole year, for fifty-two weeks – £16 0s. 8d.' This records three wholly unrelated payments for commons, drawn on a single source of income: for one of the chantry chaplains (the chaplain of the Chantry *In Agendis*, i.e., the 'Works' Chantry); for the whole body of eleven *pauperes clerici* ('Poor Clerks', i.e., the youths who served the Masses celebrated at the chantry altars); and for two vicars who ministered at the daily Lady Mass. The wording in which this payment was recorded had been fixed since at least the time of the earliest surviving account, that for 1290/1 (MS Bj.5/13 (18), m. 1*r*). However, at some time between 1290 and 1368/9 the introduction of polyphonic music at the Lady Mass had begun to require the attendance of more than two vicars; consequently, when the wording of this whole section was updated and clarified in 1368/9, the number 'two' was struck out, leaving the number of vicars unstated, and the qualification 'ministering *and singing polyphony*' was inserted.

35 The terms 'knack' and 'knacking', used to denote the performance of polyphonic music, occur frequently in these Wycliffite tracts; in the edition cited in n. 36 below see, for example, pp. 76–7, 91 ('wiþ knackynge of newe song, as orgen or deschant and motetis'), 169 and 191-2.

36   Of feyned contemplatif lif, of song, of þe ordynal of salisbury, and of bodely almes and worldly bysynesse of prestis; hou bi þes foure þe fend lettiþ hem fro prechynge of þe gospel.

The English works of Wyclif hitherto unprinted, ed. F. D. Matthew, Early English Text Society, old ser., lxxiv (1880), p. 192.

widespread at the time for the educated readership for which such tracts were prepared to be able to recognise readily the point that the writer was trying to make.[37]

One further, and much more explicit reference, derives from about the middle of the century. Between 1344 and 1351, John, Lord Mowbray and certain associates founded at Epworth on the Isle of Axholme, Lincolnshire, a small chantry college staffed by a warden, two priests and four adult clerks. The foundation ordinance, confirmed in 1351, required that the four clerks be able to undertake the performance of polyphony; and probably because it was unusual for such ambitious music to be required of the personnel of so small a college, the exact performing qualifications and abilities required of the polyphonists were spelled out in some detail, apparently for the guidance of the warden, upon whom fell the responsibility for their appointment. The founders directed that, of the four singers, 'unus tenorem, et alius medium, et ceteri duo cantum tertium sciant canere competenter.'[38]

This directive is of enormous value. The group can be seen to have been required to consist of four adult singers, comprising two high voices, one middle and one 'tenor' or foundation voice. This conformation, of course, coincides exactly with the specification of the particular performing ensemble that has already been revealed, by analysis of the music, as being the optimum ensemble, for which all church polyphony of the period was written. That is to say, the requirements which the founders of the Epworth chantry chose to spell out in detail added up (in all probability) to what was simply the standard contemporary conformation for any ensemble of singers of polyphony, one which – in the less unusual context of, for instance, the foundation statutes of a major collegiate church – could be and normally was left unspecified.

Some conclusions concerning the timbre and pitch of the voices of these four singers can be tentatively proposed. As has been observed above, they might be called upon to achieve an overall compass of sixteen notes, although two octaves was more commonly the working maximum. Archival sources show clearly that boys' voices were not involved in the performance of written polyphony at this date; the duties of the boys' instructors, as laid down in statutes,

---

37 The complex and severe difficulties involved in using literary evidence of this (or any) sort to substantiate modern historical or musicological argument render necessary this attempt to assess (rather than take for granted) the credibility of both the writer, in the light of his premises and purpose, and of the particular passage, in the light of its immediate and its general context.

38 'Let one know adequately how to sing the tenor, and another the medius (mean, *medius cantus*) and the other two the treble' (Lincoln, The Castle, Lincolnshire Archives Office, Archives of the Dean and Chapter, MS D.ii 51/3(4)): calendared in Charles Foster and Alexander Hamilton Thompson, 'The chantry certificates for Lincoln and Lincolnshire', *Associated Architectural Societies' Reports and Papers*, xxxvi (1921), pp. 246-53.

The terms 'tertius cantus', 'triplex', 'trebyll' and other similar terms had no association with the boy's unbroken voice at this period; the terms merely denoted the highest part required to create threefold (the strict meaning of 'triplex') harmony.

contracts and acts of chapter, did not begin to include teaching the singing of composed polyphony until the beginning of the second half of the fifteenth century.[39] Therefore, the fourteenth-century performing ensemble for polyphony consisted only of adult male voices.[40] Modern taste and tradition divides the naturally occurring timbres of such voices into three basic types – bass, tenor and alto. It would not, of course, be safe to assume that fourteenth-century throats produced, or that fourteenth-century ears perceived, the several vocal timbres in precisely the same way as do their modern counterparts. Nevertheless, the consistent layering, and the standardised spacing of the voices used in this repertoire, certainly suggest that a stratification of vocal timbres into self-contained, discrete categories was perceived, and indeed exploited in the process of composition. To avoid possible anachronisms, reference will be made to these voices in what appears to have been the contemporary terms: working upwards, tenor, medius and tertius. Relating these names to the prevailing configuration of voices revealed by the preceding analysis of the music produces the disposition shown below in Figure 7a.

Between them, the three timbres of modern male adult voices can realise an overall working range of some twenty notes, around F-c'' in terms of modern pitch ($a' = 440$). The fifteen- or sixteen-note compass of fourteenth-century music did not, therefore, employ the whole range realisable by men's voices, and thus it becomes important to identify those pitches which were not used. This question cannot be resolved with complete conviction, but three admittedly very inferential lines of argument do all point to one single conclusion.

(1) Fourteenth-century polyphony did not emerge from a vacuum: it grew from traditions developed since the middle of the previous century, when the greater English churches first began to enhance their religious services with composed polyphony on a regular basis and in a systematic way. The performing medium had grown organically with the music. Until about the 1270s, virtually all music, whether in two parts or three, was constrained within an overall compass of a ninth, a tenth or (at most) an eleventh. Thereafter the compass widened, and, by 1300 or so, the expansion to two octaves had been accomplished, at least in progressive circles if not yet generally.[41] The

39 See Roger Bowers, 'Choral institutions within the English church: their constitution and development, 1340-1500' (Ph.D. dissertation, University of East Anglia, 1975), pp. 6008-20, 6066-75.

40 It has recently been suggested that the circumstances surrounding the survival of at least one item of fourteenth-century church polyphony (the motet *Zelo tui langueo/Reor nescia/*[Tenor]) 'leave no doubt' that it was to be sung by women's voices: see Harrison and Wibberley, *Manuscripts of fourteenth century English polyphony*, pp. xiii-xv. For some consideration of this improbable contention, see Appendix.

41 Editions of a broad cross-section of the surviving music are available in Ernest Sanders' *English music of the thirteenth and early fourteenth centuries*, Polyphonic Music of the Fourteenth Century, xiv (Monaco, 1979). For examples of pieces written by *c.* 1300 and using an overall compass of fourteen notes, see Nos. 44, 52, 53, 55, 61, 62, 70 and 80, and Nos. 12 and 27 of the Appendix; and for pieces using two octaves, see No. 66 and Appendix No. 13.

manner in which this expansion was achieved constitutes a lengthy study on its own; here, it must suffice to say that the extension of range appears to have been entirely upwards. If it be accepted that the earliest generations of singers of polyphony placed its overall compass of a tenth or so at much the same pitch as that at which they sang plainsong, and if it be accepted further that plainsong was usually sung at a pitch that was found to lie comfortably at about the middle of the normal vocal range, then the polyphony of the earlier period, up to *c.* 1270, was performed by singers of something like modern tenor and baritone ranges, and the subsequent extension of its compass to two octaves was achieved by adding voices of something like the modern alto range.

(2) There are no contemporary archival references to singers using a bass timbre of voice; but there do exist references to singers using what seems to have been the alto timbre. These consist mostly of twelfth- and thirteenth-century prohibitions of its use, contained in the statutes of new and austere religious orders.[42] For accurate interpretation, each citation needs a lengthy discussion within its full and proper context, a procedure too extensive to be undertaken here.[43] However, it can be said that the technique of singing with the alto timbre does certainly seem to have been known in the high middle ages; and in the secular churches, and among the longer-established religious orders, there were no prohibitions of its use.

(3) Towards the end of the fourteenth century, English composers began to adopt certain compositional procedures derived from the French polyphonic chanson. This involved a slight modification of the pitch (and the timbre) of the middle voice (the medius), lowering it to the same range as that of the lowest voice – thereby substituting the tenor/contratenor relationship for the old one of tenor/medius. The three resulting voices subsequently became the core of the five-part vocal texture of the second half of the fifteenth century; in this context, they can be shown to have been sung by one alto and two tenor voices, singing at, or never far from, the modern pitch range of *c-c"*.[44]

None of these lines of enquiry is very substantial in itself; however, taken

---

42 For example, the Gilbertine canons and the Cistercian monks; see W. Dugdale, *Monasticon Anglicanum*, new edn by J. Caley, H. Ellis and B. Bandinel (London, 1817-30), vi, part 2, p. xlii* (intercalated between pp. 945 and 946), and *Statuta capitulorum generalium ordinis Cisterciensis*, ed. J. M. Canivez, Bibliothèque de la Revue d'histoire ecclésiastique, ix-xiv (Louvain, 1933-41), i, p. 30. Further apparent references to falsetto singing in the writings of Aelred, Abbot of Rievaulx, and of John de Sarisberia, Bishop of Chartres, require more extensive consideration in their total contexts than is possible here. At this early period, such use of the alto timbre must have been confined to the performance of unwritten, improvised polyphony, if used in polyphony at all.

43 Taken out of context, even apparently straightforward references such as these appear to be can be shown to be subject to various contradictory interpretations: see Roger Bowers, 'The performing pitch of English fifteenth-century church polyphony', *Early Music*, viii (1980), p. 22; Christopher Page, 'False voices', *Early Music*, ix (1981), p. 71, with Bowers' reply on p. 73. In all circumstances, the glib quotation of choice plums of information, extracted from their sources without consideration of context, is likely to produce misinterpretation and confusion.

44 Bowers, 'The performing pitch', pp. 21-8.

together, they have the merit of mutual agreement, and add up to a case which, at least, deserves consideration. It suggests that, of the pitches actually realisable by adult male voices, it was the bass range which was not used in the fourteenth century, and that the voices used to cover the basic two-octave compass consisted of altos and the next adjacent timbres downwards. If the highest working note of the alto be taken as c'' (in modern terms), then there emerge rough sounding pitches for the fourteenth-century vocal timbres as shown in Figure 7b: tertius, medius and tenor turn out to have been akin, respectively, to the modern alto, tenor and baritone.

Figure 7. Identification of vocal pitches and timbres

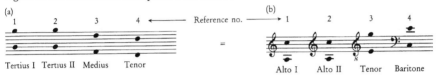

If the singers had recourse at any time to an instrument, then archival sources reveal that there was only one instrument that it could have been. Twenty-five years ago, Frank Harrison observed that there is no evidence to suggest that any instrument other than the organ was normally played in church;[45] and, after duplicating Harrison's research and conducting a great deal more besides, I can confirm such a finding absolutely and without reservation.

There are frequent references in the archives of the greater churches to the construction, maintenance and use of one organ, or even two;[46] but there is not the slightest or even the most oblique reference to the use of any other instrument in church under any circumstances, let alone during the conduct of the services.[47] However, the actual nature of the church organs of this period is extremely obscure. From the terse and laconic archival accounts of their construction and repair, it is quite impossible even to visualise in detail the sort or sorts of instrument then in use, or any part of their mechanism. Very few

---

45 Harrison, *Music in medieval Britain*, p. xiv.
46 For collections of appropriate references, see Harrison, *Music in medieval Britain,* pp. 202-14, and Cecil Clutton and Austin Niland, *The British organ* (London, 1963), pp. 46-7. I have not yet encountered any reference to the existence of an organ among the equipment of any fourteenth-century royal, aristocratic or episcopal household chapel - the peripatetic nature of which would, of course, have rendered the adoption of any organ other than the very smallest decidedly inconvenient. This omission would tend to suggest that organ participation was not obligatory for the performance of any of the church music, monophonic or polyphonic, that was cultivated by these choirs; nevertheless, in the present imperfect state of knowledge, it would be premature to attempt to draw conclusions from evidence that is essentially negative in character.
47 Richard Rastall, 'Minstrelsy, church and clergy in medieval England', *Proceedings of the Royal Musical Association*, xcvii (1970-1), pp. 87-8, lists a few scattered instances in which one or a few players of instruments, otherwise unconnected with the church, did perform privately within the buildings of certain greater churches, on occasions when the king or a member of the royal family was making an oblation at a (usually somewhat remote) altar; but he gives no instances in which any instrumentalist performed during a service.

pictorial representations of the instrument have yet been found in sources of English origin from the late thirteenth or fourteenth centuries,[48] and no conclusions can be derived even from these until it can be established whether the artists were representing instruments they had actually seen, or were merely copying other pictorial sources, possibly ultimately of a non-English origin. In construction and character, therefore, the organ remains the element of greatest obscurity among such musical resources as were available at the greater English fourteenth-century churches.

Consideration of the function and location of the organ, however, does render very unlikely the possibility that it can have contributed in any way to the performances of composed polyphony. Certainly, it is clear that the organ cannot have participated in the performance of the score repertoire. In the greater churches, the organ in the choir appears normally to have stood on an elevated platform at some distance from the singers – on the pulpitum in the secular churches,[49] and on a raised gallery behind one set of choir stalls in the monastic churches.[50] The practice of installing a second, smaller instrument in the Lady Chapel did not begin to emerge until the 1370s or 1380s, and did not become general until the early years of the next century.[51] Meanwhile, the identity of the verbal texts chosen for setting in cantilena and descant styles shows that virtually the whole of the score repertoire was written for execution either at High Mass or Office on the floor of the choir, or at Lady Mass and the Marian antiphon sung in the Lady Chapel. Given the manner in which all the

---

48 The best known are those in the Peterborough Psalter (Brussels, Bibliothèque Royale, MS 9961, f. 66r) of c. 1315 (reproduced, among other places, in Harrison, *Music in medieval Britain*, Pl. 16) and the Belvoir Psalter of c. 1270 (reproduced in William L. Sumner, *The organ*, 3rd edn, London, 1962, Pl. 2).

49 Harrison, *Music in medieval Britain*, p. 207.

50 In secular churches, the choir stalls normally stood in the westernmost bays of the presbytery; in monastic churches, under the crossing. This phenomenon explains the different locations adopted for the organ in the two types of church. The criteria would appear to have been the need for an elevated position in a location from which the instrument could speak to all parts of the building, coupled with reasonable proximity to the choir, whence the player could reach the instrument without too long a walk from his normal place.

51 The earliest known references to the existence of a separate Lady Chapel organ are: Norwich Cathedral in 1379/80 (Precentor 1379/80, *Expense*: Norwich, Archives of the Dean and Chapter, A/c NR 880); Ely Cathedral in 1381/2 (an extract by James Bentham, c. 1750, from A/c Custos Capelle Beate Marie 1381/2, now no longer extant: Cambridge, University Library, Add. MS 2957, f. 57r); Abbey of St Benet at Hulme in 1395 (A/c Custos altaris Beate Marie 1395, *Expense*: Archives of the Bishop of Norwich, Norfolk and Norwich Record Office, unnumbered roll in box Dioc. Arch. EST/13); Worcester Cathedral in 1417/18 (Custos Capelle 1417/8, *Minute*: Worcester, Archives of the Dean and Chapter, A/c C269); Durham Cathedral in 1440/1 (Durham, Archives of the Dean and Chapter, A/c Cellarer 1440/1, *Stipendia*); Canterbury Cathedral in 1456/7 (Canterbury, Archives of the Dean and Chapter, A/c Prior 15, *Expense forinsece*); etc. In most cases, these are accounts for the repair of an instrument already in use, which may be presumed to have been acquired and installed at least a year or two earlier. It should be added that in almost all the above cases, and especially for the cathedrals of Norwich, Ely, Worcester and Durham, there survives abundant material of earlier dates in which it seems virtually certain that mentions of (or at least incidental allusions to) the existence of a Lady Chapel organ would have arisen had such an instrument been in existence at any earlier time.

constituent voices of any piece of music (whether in two, three or four parts) were always written together in a single manuscript, it is clear that the performers must all have been grouped around the book in a single location. If any group of singers were to have been accompanied by an organ, the instrument would have had to be immediately adjacent to them. However, neither location at which the score repertoire was performed was at all close to an organ; no organ participation could have been contemplated therefore, but rather, only execution by unaccompanied voices.[52]

If the organ was used at all in the repertoire of composed polyphony, therefore, its use was necessarily confined to the motets, for the execution of the slow-moving, untexted tenors. The verbal texts of the motets show them to have been items extrinsic to the proper liturgy, and the physical location in church from which they were performed is far from self-evident. It is conceivable, and has been suggested,[53] that motets were performed in choir, on appropriate feast-days, during otherwise flat or unoccupied moments in the course of the celebration of Mass or the Office. If this were so, then it is remotely possible that the polyphonists gathered to perform them from the organ-loft, where any rhythmically active untexted line could be vocalised and any slow-moving untexted tenor executed on the organ.

Yet the weight of the evidence seems to lie strongly against the employment of the organ in the performance of the polyphonic vocal repertoire, even in this limited respect. The mere absence of text, or movement in long note-values, does not necessarily indicate instrumental performance: the slow-moving untexted tenors contain no features that could not have been vocalised by one or the other of the two lower singing voices. It is probably significant that the prevailing combinations of the five apparent performing resources shown in Table 1 above include no permutation (such as 1, 2, 4 and 5 in the terms of the Table) that would render unavoidable the adoption of No. 5, the putative instrumental resource. Even more revealing is consideration of the historical role of the organ in church. Although the available information is very sketchy, it seems clear that when, in the tenth century, the organ originally achieved inclusion among the appurtenances of worship in church, it did so not as an instrument of music, but as a creator of noise – a generator of joyful sound, to

---

52 This factor was not taken into account in Scott, 'The performance of the Old Hall descant settings', and does unfortunately negate an important aspect of her conclusions. If the composers of these settings conspicuously avoided the low B♭, they are more likely to have done so because the note was absent from the gamut than because it was absent from the contemporary organ. In any event, there was, of course, no actual connection between any written note bearing a particular letter and the sound of any particular pitch.

53 Harrison, *Music in medieval Britain*, pp. 126-8, 207-9; Harrison, *Motets of French provenance*, pp. xv-xvii; Harrison, *Motets of English provenance*, pp. x, xv. It should be added that all the evidence suggesting that motets might be performed in secular contexts, outside church, is to be found only in continental sources: the extension of this suggestion to English music receives no support from surviving evidence of insular origin.

be activated on feast-days and used in a manner and spirit exactly analogous to that of peals and clashes of bells.[54] True control over the amount and the pitch of the noise produced may well not have been possible until the invention of the finger-pressure keyboard, apparently in the latter part of the thirteenth century.[55] Yet motet tenors disposed in long notes antedate this development by several decades, suggesting strongly that they originated as a vocal phenomenon, and at a time prior to that at which the organ was even capable of executing them. Indeed, the greatest likelihood is that the several roles of the organ and voices in church remained wholly separate and distinct throughout the mediaeval and early and mid renaissance periods, and that the use of the organ actually to accompany voices was an innovation of the later sixteenth century. Thus the mediaeval repertoire of sacred composed polyphony is best understood as a purely and exclusively vocal phenomenon.

It is possible, therefore, to draw the following conclusions. English fourteenth-century church polyphony appears to have been composed for performance by the resources available within small ensembles constituted according to a single standard plan. This plan predicated a membership of just four singers, comprising voices which corresponded roughly (in modern terms) to two altos, one tenor and one baritone; this ensemble performed its repertoire entirely *a cappella*. This standard constitution represented, of course, an optimum – from which particular circumstances may sometimes have caused particular institutions to diverge to some extent, especially if their resources were not adequate to supply the full requirement. In particular, given the clear dichotomy of function between the score repertoire and the motets, it is conceivable that some institutions might have chosen to eschew altogether the performance of motets (the great majority of which require two high voices), and to sing only three-part items in score: such a decision would allow their performing groups to consist of only three singers, one of each timbre. If the perceptible decline in the incidence of motets after *c*. 1350 reflects a genuine trend, rather than merely an illusion created by the loss of the appropriate manuscripts, then groups of this sort may have been growing increasingly common during the second half of the century.

Many scholars and performers have grown accustomed to the proposition that mediaeval and early renaissance music was normally conceived without any specific performing ensemble in mind, and was performed by anyone who had a will to do so with such resources as happened to be available; such

---

54 The various fragments of information which, when assessed and aligned, seem to yield this conclusion will be discussed in a future paper on 'The church organ in England, 960-1400'.

55 Peter Williams, *A new history of the organ* (London, 1980), p. 43. The evidence is pictorial, and therefore to be treated with circumspection. As Dr Williams observes of this period, 'it can never be known whether such treatises and iconography conveyed anything more practical than a corpus of knowledge passed along a literate stratum [of society] far removed from the world of illiterate craftsmen' (p. 45; see also p. 47).

English church polyphony, c. 1320 – c. 1390 185

musicians may find themselves disconcerted, perhaps even repelled, by a proposal that is undoubtedly somewhat inflexible and narrowly circumscribed. It may seem intrinsically improbable that some thirty-five or forty major ecclesiastical institutions, of various orders and types and from a wide geographical spread, should all have performed the polyphonic repertoire in very much the same way and with identical resources. But, in reality, such a proposal is in complete accord with the nature of the environment and the circumstances in which this music was performed, and with the character of those who performed it. In fourteenth-century circumstances, nobody *needed* church polyphony; the plainsong liturgy was entirely self-sufficient, and composed polyphony was grafted onto it as a voluntary offering to God made by a few suitably informed enthusiasts, who pursued it largely as an unsolicited hobby.[56] As members of ecclesiastical communities, their whole musical world was one of restraint and ordered regularity, characterised by the strictness of their obligatory adherence to the ceremony and ritual dictated by the Ordinal and Customary, and to the music prescribed by the authorised service-books. This was not an atmosphere likely to stimulate, or even suggest spontaneity, divergence or casual (or even calculated) experiment; rather, it was much more likely to engender a positive appreciation of the stability resulting from conservatism and from an unthinking compliance with established practices and customs.[57] The concept of some thirty-five to forty groups all constituted in accordance with a single ground-plan is not really in any manner improbable or inappropriate to the prevailing circumstances.

In some respects, this paper has done little more than present detailed and reasoned support for conclusions already reached intuitively by earlier scholars, or confirmation of the results of their research.[58] If the paper has any value beyond that, perhaps it lies in its wider implications for the rest of the fourteenth- and fifteenth-century repertoire, continental as well as English. Especially, it may lie in the paths which are suggested here for the conduct of

---

56 This evaluation applies to the manner in which composed polyphony was cultivated in monastic and collegiate churches. By *c.* 1390, the terminal date for the present study, it is possible that in certain household chapel choirs the performance of polyphony was already beginning to be cultivated less as a gratuitous hobby than as an obligatory part of the duties of at least some of the singers, as a means of advertising the glory of the patron as well as that of God. However, if this were so, the new evaluation of the role of polyphony that this development implies was not yet widespread.

57 Additionally, if the polyphonists of one institution wished to adopt pieces from the repertoires of other churches – and the number of concordances suggests that this happened not infrequently – there was necessarily little alternative but to constitute their own group in precisely the same manner as did all their neighbours.

58 For example, Harrison has already said: 'Though the actual pitch was partly a matter of convenience, it is clear that the range of polyphony until the second half of the fifteenth century corresponded to that of the tenor and countertenor voices of today' (*Music in medieval Britain*, p. 311).

future research into the reconstruction of the specific nature of the various performing ensembles, each appropriate to the many other repertoires of mediaeval and early and mid renaissance polyphony. Close analysis of the scoring of the music, not of individual pieces but of whole repertoires, coupled with documentary investigation of the forces available for its performance – these seem to have much to offer such an enquiry.

Eventually the whole matter, in all repertoires whether sacred or secular, revolves around resolution of the issue with which I began this paper: that of the contemporary practice of omitting from the sources instructions specifying some expected or envisaged performing medium, and of constructing a valid and defensible interpretation of this phenomenon. For one small (and possibly idiosyncratic) repertoire, that issue is now resolved. It is clear that the small groups of enthusiasts who performed English church polyphony of the fourteenth century formed themselves into ensembles which were very little less fixed and stereotyped in their constitution than is the modern string quartet. The initial question of this paper can be answered, in respect of this repertoire, therefore, by saying that the absence of ensemble identification in the manuscripts was the consequence not of the first alternative proposed at the start of the paper – a prevailing fluidity and indeterminacy in the performing medium – but, rather, of the second – the inability of a stereotyped and highly circumscribed and limited medium to offer more than one manner of performance for any given piece of music. This is a reflection of the way in which composers tailored the music to fit precisely the resources that the performing medium could offer.

To how many other repertoires does the same conclusion apply? The absence of ensemble identification is not unique to the English ecclesiastical repertoire; it is ubiquitous throughout European music well into the sixteenth century. Immediately the question arises as to how far the common phenomenon had a common cause. Can it be the case that most, or perhaps all, mediaeval and early to mid renaissance repertoires were likewise composed for performance by small, largely uniform, narrowly based groups of non-amateur performers, groups with constitutions as fixed and traditionally determined, and with resources as limited, as those of the English fourteenth-century polyphonists?[59] This question cannot, of course, be resolved until research into the

---

59 Preliminary work on the analysis of the vocal scoring of several continental repertoires of secular music reveals that their composers, no less than the English, observed strictly circumscribed patterns of scoring. In view of the total absence of documentary research establishing the identity of the original performers and the extent of their available resources, it is not yet possible to follow up the implications of these findings, except to state that it is not easy to reconcile them with the idea that secular music was conceived without particular performing resources in mind. At present, therefore, the appropriate parameters of performance resources for the continental secular repertoires of the fourteenth and fifteenth centuries remain unknown: they may, in fact, have been considerably narrower than is at present conventionally supposed.

English church polyphony, c. 1320 – c. 1390 187

appropriate sources, musical and documentary, begins to yield the necessary information. Yet it does need to be asked, not least because the example provided by English church polyphony of the fourteenth century indicates that an affirmative answer is certainly possible.[60]

60 This paper represents a somewhat rewritten and abbreviated version of the initial draft prepared for presentation at the Conference. I am very grateful to Dr David Fallows for reading that first draft, and for making many constructive observations which have much informed and assisted the process of revision; for the opinions and conclusions expressed here, however, I am solely responsible.

Appendix

In Professor Frank Ll. Harrison's recent discussion of the provenance of certain manuscripts of English fourteenth-century music, it is asserted that York, Minster Library, MS xvi N 3, which is one of the two surviving sources of the motet *Zelo tui langueo/Reor nescia*/[Tenor], and also has a further page of monophonic music, originated at the Gilbertine nunnery of the Holy Cross and St Mary at Shouldham, Norfolk; and, further, that the use of feminine forms and word-endings in the texts of the triplum and duplum suggest that they were conceived as conveying the thoughts and reflections of women. Taken together, Harrison suggests, these circumstances 'leave no doubt that it [the motet] was sung by Shouldham nuns . . . Though a nun could not celebrate Mass, communities of women could perform the other liturgical parts of the Mass, and the offices. The present instance establishes their singing of a motet'.[1] This introduction of the possibility that the performance of polyphony could be undertaken by women's voices is clearly incompatible with any of the conclusions reached in my paper above, and warrants careful examination.

In fact, these assertions are suspect on several grounds. The attribution of the manuscript to Shouldham Priory is attested by no unequivocal inscription or recognisable library mark; rather, it is reached by deduction, which on examination turns out to be faulty. The music is written on a blank leaf (f. 10v) at the end of the list of chapter-headings which precedes the main text of a late thirteenth-century devotional poem, Pierre of Peckham's *La lumiere as lais*. Together the list and the text occupy ff. 5-222; they are preceded by an incomplete liturgical Calendar (ff. 1-4), and followed by another literary item, *Les dictes de Caton* (ff. 223-234).[2] In seeking items of evidence wherewith to

---

[1] Frank Ll. Harrison and Roger Wibberley, eds., *Manuscripts of fourteenth century English polyphony: facsimiles*, Early English Church Music, xxvi (London, 1981), pp. xiii-xv and Plates 36-7, 213-14. In Harrison's transcription of the colophon (p. xiv), *novel lyu* (= *lieu*) should be read for *novel lyn*. The motet *Zelo tui langueo* is transcribed in Frank Ll. Harrison, ed., *Motets of English provenance*, Polyphonic Music of the Fourteenth Century, xv (Monaco, 1980), No. 14.

[2] For further description of this manuscript and discussion of the music, see Peter Lefferts' contribution on York, Minister Library, MS XVI. N. 3, in 'New sources of English thirteenth- and fourteenth-century polyphony', compiled by Lefferts and Margaret Bent, *Early Music History*, ii (1982), pp. 358-61.

English church polyphony, c. 1320 – c. 1390

determine whether or not the manuscript of the *Lumiere* was holograph, M. Dominica Legge examined the Calendar, and, with some assistance from liturgical experts, concluded that its particular constellation of saints and feasts could plausibly be considered appropriate only to one institution, Shouldham Priory. She then determined that all three layers of the manuscript were in the same hand, or, at the very least, written by scribes who all 'belonged to the same school', the manuscript being the product of a single professional scriptorium; and she concluded that the manuscript, and the totality of its contents, was written for and derived from Shouldham Priory.[3] Harrison has accepted this attribution – not only for the original layers, but also for the later musical accretions. Lefferts, however, has noted Neil Ker's significant silence on the subject of the manuscript's provenance.[4]

In fact, this line of reasoning fails to survive close scrutiny. Though very far from certain, it may indeed be true that the Calendar originated at Shouldham. However, the provenance of the Calendar is of no relevance to the provenance of the two pages of music, since both the latter occur as additions on blank leaves in the second layer, the *Lumiere as lais* and its list of chapter-headings,[5] and there is no reason to believe that the Calendar and the poem were ever located together until long after the musical additions were made. A Calendar was an item of practical liturgical use; it might properly precede a Book of Hours, or certain types of service-book, but it could never have been usefully appended to a literary manuscript during the period of its practical working life. Further, *pace* Dominica Legge, the Calendar and the *Lumiere* (with its list of chapter-headings) are perfectly clearly not in the same hand. That of the *Lumiere* is skilled and professional; that of the Calendar is uneven and amateurish. Indeed, comparison of the adjacent pages of each (ff. 4v, 5r) shows that they are not even of the same period; the hand of the *Lumiere* is of the late thirteenth century, while that of the Calendar appears to be not earlier than the middle of the fourteenth. The dimensions of both layers are now the same, but the *Lumiere* has been trimmed at top and right, while the Calendar may not have been trimmed at all. There is no contemporary continuous foliation or system of signatures extending through both layers;[6] and though both contain

---

3 M. Dominica Legge, 'Pierre of Peckham and his "Lumiere as Lais"', *The Modern Language Review*, xxiv (1929), pp. 37-47, 153-71; and, more especially, Legge, '"La Lumiere as Lais" – a postscript', *Ibid.*, xlvi (1951), pp. 191-5.
4 Lefferts, 'New sources', p. 359.
5 Lefferts ('New sources', p. 359) describes the collation of the gathering on which the surviving voices of *Zelo tui langueo* occur as 'three nested bifolia', but this requires correction. The list of chapter-headings (ff. 5r-10r) occupies six folios of a gathering originally of eight, of which the last two have been cut away. The music leaf (f. 10v) was thus originally followed by two folios now missing; the first recto, no doubt, contained the lost voices of the two motets now incomplete on f. 10v, while further music was possibly inscribed on the succeeding leaves. The collation of the first two gatherings is as follows: 1^6 (1 and 6 wanting) 2^8 (7 and 8 wanting).
6 The original signatures and catch-words (at the foot of the verso of the last folio in each group of six bifolia) enumerate the gatherings only from the beginning of the poem proper, excluding both the Calendar and the list of chapter-headings.

line-drawings in their respective margins, those on the Calendar (ff. 2r, 3r) are executed in a hand so much cruder than that which has illustrated the poem (f. 11r) that there can be no suspicion that the two can have been identical.

Clearly, therefore, there are no good grounds for believing that the present association of the Calendar and the manuscript of the poem is anything other than purely fortuitous. A liturgical Calendar had no business to be attached to a literary work, and it seems most likely that it became associated with the poem only after being discarded at the Reformation and rescued for use as fly-leaves.[7] The present binding bears the legend 'York Minster', and is relatively modern; it appears to be mostly of early nineteenth-century date, though the spine is yet more recent.[8] The manuscript reached York Minster in 1737, from the collection of Marmaduke Fothergill (1652-1731).[9] Fothergill's press-mark F. 8. 173 appears on f. 1r, the opening leaf of the Calendar; the absence of separate Fothergill press-marks for the subsequent sections of the manuscript indicates that its three distinct layers either were joined by him for the purpose of binding or were already associated by the time he acquired them. The earlier history of its component parts is not now known, and cannot be determined. Certainly, the provenance of this copy of the *Lumiere as lais*, and its location at the time the music additions were made, cannot now be established, and must be considered unknown. No attribution to a nunnery, whether Shouldham Priory or any other, can be sustained.

At this point, it may be noted that even if it had been possible to confirm the attribution to Shouldham, this circumstance still would not have predicated performance by women's voices of the motets contained in this source. For, *pace* both Legge and Harrison, Shouldham Priory was not, in fact, a nunnery. In common with all the major Gilbertine monasteries, it was a double house under a prior; alongside the body of nuns, a group of canons, numbering at various dates from six to nine, formed an integral and senior part of the monastery community.[10] The performance of the liturgy was not conducted only by women, therefore; there was no shortage of male voices, who could have performed polyphony at services in the church when required – if ever.

However, the particular use of the feminine forms of one pronoun and one substantive adjective in the texts of *Zelo tui langueo/Reor nescia* still remains

---

7   F. 1r is rubbed and dirty, and was evidently on the outside of something at least at some time in its career. Since this leaf deals with the month of March, its use as a cover clearly postdated its use as a Calendar, following the loss of its outer bifolium.
8   It was presumably at one or other of these operations that the edges of the leaves, trimmed to uniform size, underwent the gilding now evident through all three layers.
9   For some notice of Fothergill, see F. Drake, *Eboracum: or the history and antiquities of the city of York* (London, 1736), pp. 379-80.
10 J. C. Cox, 'Shouldham Priory', *Victoria county history of Norfolk*, ed. W. Page (London, 1902-6), ii, pp. 412-14; D. Knowles and R.N. Hadcock, *Medieval religious houses: England and Wales* (2nd edn, London, 1971), pp. 194, 196.

for consideration, since this phenomenon by itself might be considered to suggest performance by women's voices. First, however, the true extent of the incidence of this feature must be examined. It may be noted that Harrison's discussion of the triplum text, *Zelo tui langueo*, draws attention to the occurrence of only a single instance of an apparently feminine form, the pronoun *que* in the penultimate line. However, he transcribes and translates the corrupt version of the text transmitted by British Library, MS Sloane 1210, f. 142*v*, and also confuses its metrical and grammatical structure, jumbling together phrases which belong to separate sentences. In the superior York version, the final pair of lines reads:

> ergo david cara filia   que laudum preconia
> tibi condecent apte [di] ci   ob tot beneficia.

A literal translation runs: 'Therefore, dear daughter of David [i.e., St Mary], these proclamations of praise are fitting to be said duly to you, on account of [your] so many beneficent deeds'; *que* is not the feminine plural but the neuter plural form of the relative pronoun *qui*, agreeing with *preconia*. Harrison's translation, in which the corrupt reading *que . . . condocent* is adopted, and rendered 'may these women, who are instructing together . . . ', cannot be sustained. In fact, the text of the triplum is perfectly straightforward and standard in its mode of expression.[11]

Nevertheless, the single example of a feminine word-formation occurring in the duplum (*Reor nescia* . . . : 'An ignorant woman, I consider . . . ') certainly appears to be genuine. Even so, no contention that this phenomenon necessarily predicates performance by a woman's voice can be entertained. To take a parallel case, a similar use of feminine forms occurs in the top part of the fifteenth-century English motet *Cantemus domino, socie*/[*Cantemus*]/[Contratenor]/*Gaudent in celis*, found in London, British Library, MS Egerton 3307, ff. 75*v*-77*r*;[12] and in this instance, the reason for the use of such a device can be exactly established, and it turns out to be totally unrelated to concern for the manner of performance envisaged for the motet. The texts of the triplum and tenor have no liturgical connection; their association together, and subsequent simultaneous incorporation into a single piece of music, derive instead from the way in which both were transmitted in very close proximity in a well-known literary source – the several versions and editions of Osbern's 'Life of St Dunstan'. Osbern's narrative of two miraculous visions revealed to the saint describes the singing of the antiphon *Gaudent in celis* by a group of maidens, and also of the fifth-century hymn of Caelius Sedulius *Cantemus socii, Domino cantemus honorem*; however, in the story, the latter is addressed by two

---

11 The transcription, and the translation by Peter Lefferts, in Harrison, *Motets of English provenance*, p. 184, is decently close to accuracy; however, the text is quite clearly in honour of the Virgin Mary, not of the Holy Cross, as stated there.
12 Transcribed in Gwyn McPeek, *Egerton 3307* (London, 1963), pp. 96-101.

precantatrices to a chorus of virgins, thus necessitating the adoption of feminine word-forms in the text, beginning *Cantemus domino, socie*.[13] The motet was presumably composed to honour the feast of St Dunstan, and it was directly from this literary source that it drew both its tenor and its text – including, of course, the local modifications to the latter. In fact, none of the institutions so far suggested as the provenance of Egerton 3307 (the Chapel Royal, the royal free chapel of St George, Windsor, and – very improbably – Meaux Abbey, Yorkshire[14]) included women among its membership, and there can be little doubt that this text, its feminine word-forms notwithstanding, was sung by male voices. If this is true of *Cantemus domino, socie*, similar circumstances could apply equally well in the case of *Zelo tui langueo*.

Indeed, the commitment to males of the task of voicing the thoughts and speech of female characters was common enough in the context of the performance of the liturgy and its accretions. The representation of the Three Marys in Eastertide liturgical (and other) drama by boys or men is an obvious example. In the case of *Reor nescia*, the thoughts and sentiments expressed are in no respect pre-eminently appropriate only to a fourteenth-century nun; rather, they appear to be intended to be those of Eve, complementing the reflections on the fate of Adam expressed later in the duplum and also in the triplum. There appear to be no reasons why, in an ecclesiastical context, such sentiments could not be expressed by a male voice.

Critical scrutiny and consideration, therefore, show that there is nothing in either the music, the texts or the provenance of the pieces preserved in York, Minster Library, MS xvi N 3, which requires that they be performed by women's voices, or even raises the possibility that women ever undertook to participate in the performance of written church polyphony. The discovery of this source in no way necessitates revision of the axiom adopted throughout the paper above, that the performance of such polyphony was executed by male voices only.

13 R. L. Greene, 'Two medieval musical manuscripts: Egerton 3307 and some University of Chicago fragments', *Journal of the American Musicological Society*, vii (1954), pp. 10-12.
14 For these various claims, see Greene, 'Two medieval musical manuscripts', pp. 1-27; B. Schofield, 'A newly-discovered manuscript of the English Chapel Royal', *The Musical Quarterly*, xxxii (1946), pp. 514-15; McPeek, *Egerton 3307*, pp. 7-14. Despite its early date (*c.* 1440?) it seems probable that the highest voice of the four (which sometimes divides into two independent parts) was composed for performance by boys; for although there is no bassus part beneath the tenor and contratenor, the overall compass of the motet still extends to eighteen notes, and the two parts above tenor and contratenor are for voices of quite different pitches and characters, apparently alto and treble.

[14]

Text Underlay in Early Fifteenth-Century Musical Manuscripts

GILBERT REANEY
University of California, Los Angeles

ONE of the most striking features of musical manuscripts written after 1400 is the gradual increase in compositions which have a text or partial text in their lower voices. At first, this is particularly true of Latin texts, and a glance at Volume IV (*Fragmenta Missarum*) of the complete Dufay edition will show how important this development has become by the mid-fifteenth century. In the fourteenth century, motets, Mass movements, and polyphonic songs nearly always have no text in the tenor and contratenor parts. The reason is not immediately obvious. Traditionally, the historian has assumed that these lower parts—which don't look very vocal, particularly in some of the polyphonic songs—were intended for instruments. He may be right, but let us consider why tenors and contratenors have no text. Those compositions from the fourteenth century that do have a text usually involve polytextual writing. An example is Machaut's *De triste cuer—Certes, je di—Quant vrais amans*, Ballade 29 in the editions of both Ludwig and Schrade. Could the reason for the omission of a text in lower parts be that it was identical with the upper voice, and hence could be easily inserted? Parchment was expensive in the Middle Ages, and every little space was used. If a previous copyist had left a space, a later one would enter a new composition there. Examples of this are legion, and include the added secular compositions in Codex Bologna, Biblioteca del Conservatorio G. B. Martini, Q.15 (BL). Notation, too, was a means of conserving space, and ligatures rather than single notes were used wherever possible.

Needless to say, I am not trying to suggest that instruments did not perform the lower parts of late medieval polyphonic music. On the other hand, we do tend to assume that all textless parts are not vocal, when perhaps we should add the upper voice text to the lower parts. This situation becomes particularly clear in early fifteenth-century music, where a piece may appear in one source with a text in the tenor and in another without it. Moreover, the process is continued, though less frequently, in the contratenor. For instance, a two-part composition which has text in both parts in MSS. BL and O (Oxford, Bodleian Library, Canonici misc. 213) has a textless tenor in Codex Pz (Paris, Bibliothèque Nationale, nouv. acq. fr., 4917). This is the Rondeau refrain by Briquet, *Ma seul amour*, published in my *Early Fifteenth-Century Music*, Volume II (1959), p. 13. Yet this piece also has clearly instrumental interludes in both parts at the end of each half of the composition.

A particularly interesting piece from the same point of view is Grossin's *Imera dat hodierno*, No. 15 in *Early Fifteenth-Century Music*, Volume III (1966), and also published in the *Denkmäler der Tonkunst in Österreich*, Jahrgang VII (1900), p. 209. It occurs in no less than six sources, though in one of these only the tenor part is given. It might be expected that a work as thoroughly homophonic as this one would have the text in all three parts, but not one manuscript gives such a version. However, both BL and BU (Bologna, Biblioteca Universitaria, 2216) have the text in the tenor as well as in the *cantus*, whereas Em (Munich, Staatsbibliothek, Mus. 3232a) is so exceptional as to have the text in the contratenor but not in the tenor. Since this source is a little peripheral, it is possible that the copyist intended to place the text in the tenor and put it in the contratenor by accident—that is, he may have mistaken the contratenor for the tenor, quite an easy error to make, since the two voices are much alike. It would seem, however, that all three voices should have had the text—an assumption already made by the editors of the *Denkmäler* volume, although O and Tr have the text only in the *cantus*, and the notation of the textless lower voices often makes use of ligatures and frequently replaces groups of three unison eighth-notes with dotted quarters. The presence of many text cues in the contratenor of BL supports the use of text in all voices. Of course, it may be alleged, though I believe there is no foundation for such an assumption, that the application of text to lower parts is a peculiarly Italian custom; and it does seem true that Italian scribes were fond of indicating the presence of text in lower parts. But we should not forget that it is partly a matter of chance that we have so many Italian manuscripts from the first half of the fifteenth century.

It does at any rate seem clear that the Italian MSS. BL and BU show us the way performers applied text to voices that were often notated without a text. A good example is Reson's *Salve regina*, published in my *Early Fifteenth-Century Music*, Volume II, p. 111. The tenor given in the transcription is the textless version of BL, but the tenor of BU with the full text appears in the Critical Notes on page lv. The process of applying a text to a textless voice, although it may involve musical variants, is usually simple. A dotted half-note in 6/8 may be split into two dotted quarters to accommodate two syllables. Often, however, it is clear that in order to preserve the trochaic rhythms, a dotted quarter-note is divided into a quarter plus an eighth, and a dotted half-note may be unequally divided into a dotted quarter-note tied to a normal quarter and followed by an eighth-note. Usually, the division into smaller values produces unisons, but in a comparison with the original an occasional second or third may be expected to appear.

The presence in BL and other sources of many partial texts in tenors and contratenors is perhaps even more interesting. I find that I cannot follow Professor Besseler's opinion, that text incipits indicate instrumental performance (Dufay edition, Volume II, p. xv). Surely these incipits are more likely to indicate what the voice should be singing, as compared with the *cantus*, even though the complete text is not given. I am convinced that the use of partially complete texts confirms a vocal performance, though I am inclined to agree with Professor Besseler that instruments may often have been used as well. Perhaps I shall be accused here of lack of consistency—a doubtful virtue anyhow—since in my edition of Cesaris' *A l'aventure va Gauvain*, published in *Early Fifteenth-Century Music*, Volume I, p. 21, I included a line of text in the tenor and contratenor, which are otherwise textless. Now it is curious that such snatches of text do appear in the lower parts of polyphonic songs, usually in connection with imitation, as in *A l'aventure*. On the face of it, there would seem to be little necessity for indicating this text-line in tenor and contratenor, since the *cantus* has the same notes. However, the use of imitation tends to displace the text, so that, if voices do sing the full text in tenor and contratenor, the *cantus* will be differently placed when there is imitation. Otherwise, all voices presumably are to sing the same words at the same time. And I must say that I have never felt drawn toward the theory that an instrumentalist might suddenly start to sing and as suddenly stop again—a possibility for the player of a stringed but hardly of a wind instrument! I should like to think, therefore, either that this piece was performed by three voices, with the tenor and contratenor arranging the text much as I proposed in the Reson *Salve regina*, or that the same two parts were performed on instruments. It may be that the *cantus* too had an instrumental doubling, since there seems to be a textless prelude and postlude to the work.

A composition that seems clearly to confirm the idea that a tenor or contratenor may be fully vocal, even when only a partial text occurs in the manuscript, is the *Patrem Scabroso* by Zacar (BL, folios 68v–71). Presumably this work should be attributed to Antonio Zachara, rather than to Zacharias since it is evidently a parody work based on one of the composer's polyphonic songs, probably a lost ballata. It is of course another matter to decide whether Zachara wrote the Mass movement as well as the song on which it is based. It may be that the name Zacar in the BL codex simply refers to the composer of the original song, and that a different composer wrote a parody Mass on it. Still, so long as we have no further information on this matter, we probably must continue to regard Zachara as the composer of both the original and the parody. But to return to the question of the text underlay: it is striking that the contratenor of the *Patrem* has the complete text on two pages, whereas the third or middle page lacks it almost entirely. Surely this lack can be explained only by the scribe's casual attitude to the text: he didn't want the bother of writing it on the middle page.

Turning now to Besseler's *Fragmenta Missarum*, Volume IV of the Dufay edition, we find partially complete texts in a striking number of Mass movements. The Credo on page 25 is again from BL. The tenor text is fairly complete up to the "Crucifixus." A

TEXT UNDERLAY IN EARLY MANUSCRIPTS / 249

glance at the manuscript confirms our immediate suspicion. The "Crucifixus" begins on the following double page. Again the copyist didn't want the bother of writing more text. And we can probably assume that the omission of the word "omnipotentem" after "Patrem" was due to being crowded out by the preceding word "Tenor." Moreover, the missing words "Et in unum dominum" could easily be accommodated in bar 20 by splitting the preceding long into a dotted half-note plus six eighths in unison with it.

Up to now this article has been concerned with underlaying texts that are missing or partly missing from the manuscripts. In the upper parts, the text is usually present, but unfortunately it is never placed exactly as it should be: in other words, even very accurate manuscripts do not place all the syllables exactly under the notes to which they must be sung. Leaving out of consideration sources in which the text underlay is very casual, such as Em and the Trent codices, it is possible to say that syllabic passages in which there are as many notes as syllables are in general correctly underlaid. Those few exceptions in which the alignment is *not* good are in themselves no problem. A different matter, however, is the long melisma ending a section of music. Generally the copyist has simply placed the final syllable approximately under the last note of the section. Where BL, as often happens, places this syllable beneath the penultimate note, it seems reasonable to apply it to the final note; but for some pieces such a procedure is almost impossible, and the position of the text and ligatures suggests rather that the final syllable should be sung to the penultimate note. This is often true of sections employing long notes, such as the passages at "miserere nobis" and "Iesu Christe" in Grossin's *Et in terra*, No. 9 in *Early Fifteenth-Century Music*, Volume III (also in *Denkmäler der Tonkunst in Österreich*, Volume 61, p. 7). More commonly the copyist did not bother to align the syllables under an extended final series of notes. He would arrange the preceding syllables correctly; but, when he saw there were too many notes for the final word or words, he merely wrote down the word, assuming that the performer would make the correct alignment. This surely does not mean, as we in the mid-twentieth century are too prone to believe, that there was a prescribed way of making the alignment. It is much more likely that the performers lined up final notes and syllables in whatever way suited them best, though it seems clear that where the syllables fall on main beats, they were intended to do so. Often enough, a group can be divided so that each syllable falls on the first note of a bar. The most difficult type of underlay consists of a moderately large group of notes with rather fewer syllables; and I cannot see how rules could be given for such an underlay. However, it is possible to find at times some *point de repère* in the tenor text—when there is one—since the tenor usually consists of slower notes than the upper parts and is thus more simply underlaid.

For the modern editor textual underlaying in the polyphonic Kyrie is particularly difficult. In the manuscripts the word "Kyrie" or "Christe" usually appears at the very beginning, and the word "[e]leyson" at the end, of the principal musical sections. Perhaps we are only making the situation more difficult for ourselves than it really is. We would like to see various words beneath most of the notes, when all that we have is a word at the beginning and one at the end, with a huge gap in between. Like other editors, I have sometimes tried to introduce the triple invocation Kyrie—Kyrie—Kyrie, Christe—Christe—Christe, Kyrie—Kyrie—Kyrie into fourteenth- and early fifteenth-century works. But the truth seems to be that we are well provided for already. We hate to acknowledge that medieval composers and performers, not to mention their audiences, did not mind the multiple musical repetitions often indicated in the manuscripts. Machaut's Mass clearly indicates triple statements of the first Kyrie and of the Christe, just as these repetitions occur in the plainsong he used. Similarly, many of Dufay's Kyries are marked plainly with signs that show the correct repetition, usually three statements. To be sure, there are passages like the "Kyrie cum iubilo," No. 14 of the modern edition, which alternate plainsong with polyphony. In such passages, repetition of the polyphony does not occur in the Kyrie sections, because the triple invocation consists of plainsong—polyphony—plainsong. In the Christe, however, where a similar procedure would have avoided repetition, the polyphony begins and the plainsong follows, so that we have polyphony—plainsong—polyphony. The composer again did not wish to avoid repetition, and still he got his triple invocations. The question seems to be: why introduce further invocations and syllable arrangements into the texts? They are not necessary, and the text form "Kyrie

TEXT UNDERLAY IN EARLY MANUSCRIPTS / 251

leison" clearly indicates that early polyphonic Kyries were mainly vocalized to the vowel *e*.

The correct positioning of texts in late medieval compositions, and the problem of how to employ voices and instruments, are questions that still need much study. An examination of textual planning as it occurs in individual manuscripts can help to clear up some difficulties. At all events, it is to be hoped that the few points I have brought up will be of use and stimulate further thought. Textless or partially textless works may form a useful point of departure.

Part V
The Polyphonic Chanson

Machaut's 'Pupil' Deschamps on the Performance of Music

Voices or instruments in the 14th-century chanson

CHRISTOPHER PAGE

1 *Deschamps presents his* Livret de la fragilité d'humaine nature *to Charles VI, from the dedicatory copy sent to the king in 1383. Paris, Bib. nat., f.fr. 20028, f.4v.*

The modern performer of Machaut's music is encouraged to believe by almost all authorities that the untexted tenor and contratenor lines of the polyphonic chansons were rendered instrumentally.[1] Recordings and concert performances show that this view commands complete acceptance.

The 'authenticity' of the instruments generally used in modern performances of Machaut's music is a subject that invites comment,[2] but more important is the general question of how far these performances correspond to medieval practice. It is not the purpose of this article to survey all the evidence bearing upon this question, but to give text and translation of some hitherto little-noticed remarks on the subject by Machaut's 'pupil', Eustache Deschamps (*Art de Dictier et de Fere Chançons*, 1392).[3]

Deschamps, a Champenois like Guillaume de Machaut and Philippe de Vitry, was born *c* 1346. The author of the *Règles de la Seconde Rhétorique* states that he was Machaut's nephew (*nepveux de maistre Guillaume de Machault*),[4] and though we have no proof of this, it is clear that the two poets were on intimate terms. In a poem sent to Péronne d'Armentières (inspiratrice of Machaut's *Voir Dit*) Deschamps claims that Machaut 'brought me up and did me many kindnesses',[5] and in the second of his two ballades on the death of the older poet, Deschamps refers to him as 'very sweet master'.[6] Machaut settled into the relatively peaceful life of a canon in the 1340s[7] and would thus have been in a position to educate the young Deschamps. It is pleasing, if fanciful, to suppose that some of the references to music lessons in Deschamps's poetry derive ultimately from his early experiences as Machaut's pupil at Rheims:[8]

Aprenez le fa et le mi,
Bien vous monstreray l'escripture
Tant que vous n'arez jamais cure
D'autre art sçavoir, fors de compter
Une, deux, les temps mesurer
Et fleureter plus que le cours.[9]

Deschamps was undoubtedly familiar with his master's music, just as he knew his literary works. Strictly speaking, there is no solid evidence in the poems (and there is no external evidence) that Deschamps was a musician with performing skills, but we may assume that he was at least a keen and discriminating listener.[10]

In the *Art de Dictier* Deschamps is primarily concerned with poetic forms and other aspects of *réthorique*, the *science de parler-droictement*. The treatise opens with an account of the seven liberal arts, which he studied at the University of Orleans.[11]

In the section on music Deschamps distinguishes between *musique artificiele* (music of voices and instruments) and *musique naturele* (poetry and verse).[12] Contrasting the two forms of music, he states that both are pleasant to hear alone. Poems that are without a musical setting may be recited or read, and music 'may be sung with the voice in an artistic way without words (*par art, sanz parole*)'. The explicitness of *par art* strongly suggests that Deschamps is thinking of polyphonic chansons (rather than simple monodies such as Machaut's *virelais* which do not appear outside of the composer's own manuscripts and were clearly of limited appeal).[13] The artistic music which is sung but which is *sanz parole* must surely be the generally textless tenors and contratenors of these pieces, which are almost invariably performed instrumentally today?

Deschamps proceeds to make a fuller allusion to the vocalisation of these parts, though his statements present difficulties and must be read with circumspection. Continuing the comparison between the two forms of music, he states that the texts of chansons may be recited before one who is ill, or in the presence of lords and ladies in privacy, where music does not always have a place. This is puzzling, for there is abundant evidence to show that the music of voices and instruments was considered therapeutic[14] (a view to which Deschamps subscribes in the opening lines of his chapter on music), and that the music of small instrumental ensembles was considered an appropriate entertainment for intimate aristocratic gatherings.[15] Even if we accept the theory proposed by some scholars that Deschamps, not a musician, is deliberately underestimating the artistic value and social acceptability of music in the *Art de Dictier*,[16] it must seem unlikely that he would make statements in a manual of this kind bearing no relation to the experience of his readers. It is possible that Deschamps's remarks have reference only to the court of the unknown noble for whom he composed the treatise,[17] but this cannot be confirmed. Taken as they stand, they imply that Deschamps understood the music of chansons to be a special artistic genre not to be rendered in the same informal circumstances as the poems.

Deschamps gives two reasons for this state of affairs. Primarily, there is the *haulteur* of this music. This may be interpreted in three ways: as a reference to the music's courtly and noble character; to its high pitch;

Guillaume de Machaut

2 *The medicinal effects of music. The text accompanying the illustration in the MS begins:* Organare cantum vel sonare. Natura est quaedam raucha et cantus violentus. *('To play a song with instruments. By nature it is somewhat harsh and the singing violent'),* Tacuinum Sanitatis, Österreichische Nationalbibliothek Codex Vindobonensis series nova 2644. *f.103v. Italian, late 14th century.*

or to its loudness.[18] The first and second interpretations are not indefensible, but neither makes very convincing sense of Deschamps's passage as a whole. Music that is courtly and noble in character would not thereby be excluded from performance in private circumstances, nor necessarily from performance in the sick-room. Music of predominantly high pitch might be somewhat incongenial to a *malade*, but why should *seigneurs et dames* have any aversion to it? A reference to the loudness of the music seems the most plausible interpretation. Unfortunately it is not clear whether Deschamps is making the relatively trivial point that the singing voice may make more noise than the reading voice, or whether he intends a specific reference to a cultivated stylistic feature of artistic singing (cf. illusn. 2).[19]

Deschamps's second reason for the inappropriateness of music to the private chamber and the sick-room is that it requires *'three voices for the tenors and*

Guillaume de Machaut

contratenors . . . to perform the said music perfectly with two or three people'.

A reference to the vocal performance of tenors and contratenors by a 14th-century writer who had undoubtedly heard Machaut's music performed is a valuable document of performance practice. Before we accept Deschamps' testimony we must reassure ourselves that 'three voices' is a just translation of the crucial words *triplicité des voix*.

Certainly this rendering creates a difficulty. How can 'two or three people' render a composition with 'three voices'? The problem would be solved by translating *triplicité des voix* as 'three parts'. Two people can render three parts if one of them both sings and plays an instrument. However, *voix* in the transferred sense 'part of a musical composition' is not recorded in Old French,[20] nor is *vox* used in this way in the Latin musical treatises of the period.[21] This translation is therefore untenable.

A second conceivable translation of *voix* would be 'pitches' or 'notes' both vocally and instrumentally produced (cf. Deschamps' reference to *instrumens des voix*). This is certainly in keeping with the theorists' use of *vox* when they are not referring exclusively to the human voice.[22] However, 'three notes' or 'three pitches' does not make good sense in the full context of Deschamps' passage. One might argue that 'three pitches' is a reference to the registers of *cantus, tenor* and *contratenor*, but in actual fact the latter two parts generally operate within much the same range in the 14th-century chanson. A further objection to this translation is that we must explain why such a straightforward matter of musical architectonics as the different registers of polyphonic parts should render chansons unfit for private performance before aristocrats and convalescents.

The most satisfactory translation for *triplicité des voix*, and the one that strains the sense of Deschamps' passage least, is 'three voices', and we are therefore left with an explicit reference to the vocalization of the generally textless tenors and contratenors of chansons, accompanied by a statement that this must be done for the 'perfection' of the music.

A final ambiguity remains. Can Deschamps' reference to *triplicité des voix* for tenor and contratenor parts be taken to indicate that these lines were sung three to a part? This interpretation does not strain the text, but it is an unlikely one.

Pictorial sources and the internal stylistic evidence of the music itself suggest that the individual lines of

3 *The medicinal effects of vocal music. The text accompanying the illustration in the MS begins:* Cantus. Natura concordari voces ystrumentorum sonis, quorum non sunt usus *('Singing. Its nature consists in making voices harmonize with the sounds of instruments which, however, are not used'). MS as illusn. 2, fol. 103r*

14th-century chansons were sung by soloists occasionally doubled by instruments.[23] Many of Machaut's finely delineated tenor and contratenor parts would be unduly thickened and blurred by 'choral' performance (some modern scholars have taken objection to instrumental doubling for this reason).[24] Deschamps's *triplicité des voix pour les teneurs et contreteneurs* surely implies just three vocal parts like *triplicibus* ('in three [parts]') in the *Quatuor Principalia Musica*,[25] and *cum tribus [scilicet cum tenore carmine et contratenore]* ('with three [that is with tenor and contratenor]') in the anonymous 14th-century treatise *Ars Discantus*?[26]

What then of Deschamps's puzzling reference to the performance of three-part vocal polyphony by 'two or three people'? Deschamps's prose is not a model of clarity, and the syntax of the passage in question is tortuous. In this particular case we cannot avoid forming the impression that the sentence is at least elliptical, if not actually careless in expression. The point Deschamps wishes to make is that the performance of music involves more than the *homme seul* that suffices for the recitation of verse. He notes that the number may be increased from one to include two or three performers, but introduces this thought with a reference to the standard chanson arrangement of his day (cantus, tenor and contratenor) that is only consonant with a group of three performers. The two parts of the sentence are not fully congruent, but the overall implication is not obscured.

Deschamps' references to the vocal performance of tenors and contratenors, problematic though they are, are by no means unsupported. Gace de la Buigne, in his poem *Le Roman des Deduis* (written 1359-77) presents a debate between *Amour de Chiens* and *Amour d'Oyseaulx* in which the spokesman for the hunting dogs describes a pack in full cry in terms of part-singing:[27]

Les plus grans chantent la teneur,
Les autres la contreteneur,
Ceulx qui ont la plus clere gueule
Chantent le tresble sans demeure,
Et les plus petis le quadouble
En faisant la quinte sur double.

The relation of such a reference to actual musical practice may seem somewhat oblique, but it is the essence of this literary genre that animals do as humans do. Birds 'deschant',[28] and in contemporary Gothic art animal musicians play instruments demonstrably drawn from the real world. There is no reason to doubt that Gace de la Buigne's passage derives from his experience of music in performance and reflects actual practice.

The hypothesis that the tenors and contratenors of Machaut's polyphonic chansons were generally performed instrumentally in the 14th-century has strong practical appeal. At this present stage of the early music 'revival', crumhorns, viols, sackbuts and other (anachronistic) instruments that can supply these lines at written pitch are readily available, whereas singers willing (and able) to vocalize them are not. Certainly there is no reason to suppose that the apparently entirely vocal performance envisaged by Deschamps was the *only* way in which Machaut's chansons were performed,[29] but his reference should inspire far more experiment with this method of performance. This would please the growing number of musicologists who believe that the question of instrumental participation in various forms of medieval music needs to be re-examined.[30]

It is true that some 14th-century tenor and contratenor lines are by no means easy to sing effectively (ex. 1, for instance), but singers should be discouraged from assuming that it is possible to make absolute judgements about what is 'vocal' or 'unvocal'.[31] As Lloyd Hibberd has written in a penetrating analysis of the proposition that certain things in music 'are especially suitable and idiomatic for instruments and awkward or even impossible for voices':[32]

'... the argument that short melodic fragments are "unvocal" *per se*, rests largely on a question of taste. Such parts do not often, it is true, seem very expressive to modern ears, in vocal music, but earlier epochs may have felt quite otherwise about them ... As regards "awkward" leaps, rapidity of movement, continuous activity, short melodic fragments, melodic sequences and coloratura passages—the exclusive "instrumentalness" of all these becomes increasingly dubious on closer examination.'

Ex. 1; Section of the contratenor added in five of a total of eleven sources to Machaut's Ballade 18, *De petit po*, one of the most widely diffused of his works. In the five Machaut manuscripts this part does not appear.[33] Quoted here from the edition of Leo Schrade, *Polyphonic Music of the Fourteenth Century*, vols. II and III (Monaco, 1956).

The text
The text given here is that published by Gaston Raynaud in the seventh volume of the *Oeuvres complètes*. It is reproduced by kind permission of the *Société des Anciens Textes Français*.

The translation
The translation aims to be literal without distorting English idiom. In order that it may read clearly and fluently, Deschamps's long and involved sentences have been generally split into smaller units and punctuated accordingly.

Guillaume de Machaut

The frequency with which Deschamps uses certain technical terms in a variety of contexts is somewhat confusing. The following translations are used here:

Chant, chans: Apparently music in general (both vocal and instrumental music in the first paragraph). It is rendered 'melody' here, as this word may be put into the plural when the context requires (unlike 'music').

Chant de la musique artificiele: 'Music', Deschamps explains the terms 'natural' music and 'artificial' music in the text.

Chant musicant: 'Music', this usage is related to the above.

Chansons natureles: 'Poems'. Deschamps explains the terminology in the text.

The translations of other musical terms (e.g. *deschanter, doubler*) are explained in the notes.

All instrument names have been left in their original forms. Little would be gained by substituting 'gittern' for *guiterne*, etc.

Extracts from *L'Art de Dictier* of Eustache Deschamps (completed 25 November 1392).

Text
De Musique

Musique est la derreniere science ainsis comme la medicine des .VII. ars; car quant le couraige et l'esperit des creatures ententives aux autres ars dessus declairez sont lassez et ennuyez de leurs labours, musique, par la douçour de sa science et la melodie de sa voix, leur chante par ses .VI. notes tierçoyées,[34] quintes et doublées,[35] ses chans delectables et plaisans, lesquelz elle fait aucunefoiz en orgues et chalumeaux par souflement de bouche et touchement de doiz; autrefoiz en harpe, en rebebe, en vielle, en douçaine, en sons de tabours, en fleuthes et autres instrumens musicans, tant que par sa melodie delectable les cuers et esperis de ceuls qui auxdiz ars, par pensée, ymaginaison et labours de bras estoient traveilliez, pesans et ennuiez, sont medicinez et recreez, et plus habiles après a estudier et labourer aux autres .VI. ars dessus nommez.

Et est a sçavoir que nous avons deux musiques, dont l'une est *artificiele* et l'autre est *naturele*.

L'*artificiele* est celle dont dessus est faicte mencion; et est appellée artificiele de son art, car par ses .VI. notes, qui sont appellées *us, ré, my, fa, sol, la*, l'en puet aprandre[36] a chanter, acorder, doubler, quintoier,[37] tierçoier, tenir,[38] deschanter,[39] par figure de notes, par clefs et par lignes, le plus rude homme du monde, ou au moins tant faire, que, supposé ore qu'il n'eust pas la voix habile pour chanter ou bien acorder, sçaroit il et pourroit congnoistre les accors ou discors avecques tout l'art d'icelle science, par laquelle et les notes dessus dictes l'en acorde et donne l'en son divers aux aciers, aux fers, aux boys et aux metaulx, par diverses infusions interposées d'estain, de plomb, d'arain et de cuivre, si comme il puet apparoir es sons des cloches mises en divers orloges, lesqueles par le touchement des marteaulx donnent sons acordables selon lesdictes .VI. notes, proferans les sequences et autres choses des chans de saincte Eglise. Et ainsi puet estre entendu des autres instrumens des voix comme rebebes, guiternes, vielles et psalterions, par la diversité des tailles, la nature des cordes et le touchement des doiz, et des fleutes et haulx instrumens semblables,[40] avecques le vent de la bouche qui baillié leur est.

Et aussi ces deux musiques sont si consonans l'une avecques l'autre, que chascune puet bien estre appellée musique, pour la douceur tant du chant comme des paroles qui toutes sont prononcées et pointoyées par douçour de voix et ouverture de bouche; et est de ces deux ainsis comme un mariage en conjunction de science, par les chans qui sont plus anobliz et mieulx seans par la parole et faconde des diz qu'elle ne seroit seule de soy. Et semblablement les chançons natureles sont delectables et embellies par la melodie et les teneurs, trebles et contreteneurs du chant de la musique artificiele. Et neantmoins est chascune de ces deux plaisant a oïr par soy; et se puet l'une chanter par voix et par art, sanz parole; et aussis les diz des chançons se puent souventefoiz recorder en pluseurs lieux ou ilz sont moult vouluntiers ois, ou le chant de la musique artificiele n'aroit pas tousjours lieu, comme entre seigneurs et dames estans a leur privé et secretement, ou la musique naturele se puet dire et recorder par un homme seul, de bouche, ou lire aucun livre de ces choses plaisans devant un malade, et autres cas semblables ou le chant musicant n'aroit point lieu pour la haulteur d'icellui, et la triplicité des voix pour les teneurs et contreteneurs necessaires a ycellui chant proferer par deux ou trois personnes pour la perfection dudit chant.

Translation
Concerning Music

Music is the final, and the medicinal science of the seven arts; for when the heart and spirit of those

Guillaume de Machaut

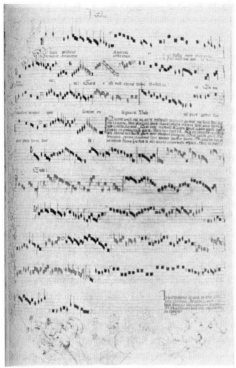

4 *Chantilly, Musée Condé MS 564 (olim 1047), f.37. 3-part Ballade* Le Sault perilleux *by Jean Galiot (red notation obscured in photograph). Monks sing in the lower border. Are they singing plainchant or Galiot's Ballade?*

applied to the other arts treated above are wearied and vexed with their labours, Music, by the sweetness of her science and the melodiousness of her voice, sings them her delectable and pleasant melodies with her six notes in thirds, fifths, and octaves. These she performs sometimes with *orgues* and *chalumeaux* by blowing with the mouth and touching with the fingers; otherwise with the *harpe, rebebe, vielle, douçaine,* with noise of *tabours,* with *fleuthes,* and other musical instruments, so much so that by her delectable melody the hearts and minds of those who were fatigued, weighed down, and troubled with the said arts by thought, imagination or labour are revived and restored. Thus they are afterwards more able to study and labour with the other six arts named above.

It must be understood that we have two kinds of music: one is *artificial* and the other is *natural*.

Artificial music is that which is mentioned above. It is called *artificial* as an art for by its six notes, which are called *us, ré, my, fa, sol, la,* one may teach the most uncultivated man in the world to sing, make harmony and an octave, fifth and third, make a tenor, and descant by the form of notes, by clefs and by staves. Or at least one may do so much, supposing now he did not have a voice suitable for singing or making harmony well, that he would know and be able to recognize accords and discords with all the art of this science by which, and by the notes mentioned above, one tunes and gives diverse sound to steels, irons, woods and metals, by various additives of tin, lead, bronze, and copper, as may be evident in the sounds of bells enclosed in various clocks. These, by the touch of hammers, give harmonious sounds according to the said six notes, uttering sequences and other things of the melodies of Holy Church. This harmony may be heard on other musical instruments such as *rebebes, guiternes, vielles,* and *psalterions* by the variety of their size, the nature of the strings and the action of the fingers. Also on *fleutes* and on similar loud instruments,[40] with the breath that is introduced into them.

Also these two musics are so consonant with one another that each may well be called 'music', as much for the sweetness of both the melody and of the words which are all pronounced and articulated by the pleasantness of the voice and opening of the mouth. It is with these two as a marriage, that is, a conjunction of science, through the melodies which are more ennobled and are more seemly with the words and the fluency of the texts than they [lit. *it*] would be alone. Similarly, poems are made more delightful and embellished by the melody and the tenors, trebles and contratenors of music. However, each of these two [i.e., music and poetry] is pleasant to hear by itself. One may be sung with the voice in an artistic way without words; also the texts of chansons may often be recited in many places where they are very willingly heard, and where their music would not always be appropriate as among lords and ladies remaining in private, where poetry may be recited by a single person, or where some book of these pleasant things may be read before one who is ill. There are other similar cases where music would have no place because of its loudness, and because of the three voices for the tenors and contratenors that are necessary to perform the said music perfectly with two or three people.

489

Guillaume de Machaut

Abbreviations

CS E. de Coussemaker. *Scriptorum de Musica Medii Aevi Nova Series*, 4 vols., Paris, 1864-76.
GS Martin Gerbert, *Scriptores Ecclesiastici de Musica*, 3 vols., Typis San-Blasianis, 1784.
PL J. P. Migne, *Patrologiae cursus Completus: Series Latina*, 221 vols., Paris, 1844-64.

Notes

[1] See, for example, G. Reese, *Music in the Middle Ages*, London, 1941, p. 383; P. H. Lang, *Music in Western Civilisation*, London, 1942, p. 153; Gilbert Reaney, 'Ars Nova in France', in *New Oxford History of Music, III, Ars Nova and the Renaissance, 1300-1540*, ed. Dom A. Hughes and G. Abraham, London, 1960, p. 25; W. Smoldon, *A History of Music*, London, 1965, p. 76; D. J. Grout, *A History of Western Music*, revised ed., London, 1973, p. 124. This view is often argued on the basis of the purely hypothetical notion that the tenors of 13th-century motets were performed upon instruments.

[2] See, for example, Jeremy Montagu, 'The "Authentic" sound of early music', *Early Music*, 3 (1975), 3, pp. 242-243.

[3] Text in *Oeuvres complètes d'Eustache Deschamps*, ed. Le Marquis de Queux de Saint-Hilaire and Gaston Raynaud, Société des Anciens Textes Français, pubs. 9, Paris, 1878-1903, VII, pp. 266-92. The work is mentioned briefly in Gilbert Reaney, 'Voices and Instruments in the music of Guillaume de Machaut', *Revue Belge de Musicologie*, X (1956), fasc. 1-2, p. 3 (note 2) and p. 8.

[4] *Oeuvres*, XI, p. 11, n. 4.

[5] Ballade 447 (*Oeuvres*, III, p. 259-60) "*Machaut... Qui m'a nourry et fait mantes douçours*". In this poem, written after Machaut's death, Deschamps asks to be Péronne's *loyal ami* for *l'onneur* of Machaut.

[6] *Oeuvres*, 1, p. 245.

[7] A. Machabey, *Guillaume de Machault*, Paris, 1955, 1, p. 34f.

[8] Cf. Nan Cooke Carpenter, *Music in the Medieval and Renaissance Universities*, University of Oklahoma Press, 1958 (reprinted Da Capo Press, New York, 1972), p. 75.

[9] Ballade 1169 (*Oeuvres*, VI, p. 113).

[10] Concerning a possible reference by Deschamps to composition of his own music see the *Oeuvres*, XI, p. 156. Nigel Wilkins ('The post-Machaut Generation of Poet-Musicians', *Nottingham Mediaeval Studies*, XII (1968), p. 83) states that 'Deschamps... was not a musician...' For discussion of the view that Deschamps, unlike previous poets, was unable to compose music, and that he wrote the *Art de Dictier* in an attempt to have 'spoken verse accorded the same recognition as the best known poetry before him' see Glending Olson, 'Deschamps' *Art de Dictier* and Chaucer's Literary Environment', *Speculum*, XLVIII (1973), 4, pp. 714-723; Kenneth Varty, 'Deschamps' *Art de Dictier*', *French Studies*, XIX (1965), pp. 164-68; I. S. Laurie, 'Deschamps and the Lyric as Natural Music', *Modern Language Review*, LIX (1964), pp. 561-70.

[11] For the view that this account concentrates more on the practical application of the seven arts than former treatments, see R. Dragonetti, '"La Poesie... ceste musique naturele": Essai d'exégèse d'un passage de l'*Art de Dictier* d'Eustache Deschamps', *Fin du Moyen Age et Renaissance; Mélanges de philologie française offerts à Robert Guiette*, Anvers, 1961, p. 53. For a discussion of music and the liberal arts at the University of Orléans in the Middle Ages with special reference to Deschamps and the *Art de Dictier* see Nan Cooke Carpenter, op cit, pp. 69-76.

[12] The inclusion of poetry under the heading of *Musica* may be found in the *Poetria* of Johannes de Garlandia (text and translation in T. Lawler, *The 'Parisiana Poetria' of John of Garland*, Yale University Press, 1974, ch. I, lines 54-5, and 7, lines 469-70), and to some extent in the *De Musica* of Boethius (PL, LXIII, col. 1196). In the musical theorists the terms *naturalis* and *artificalis* are used in a variety of ways. See, for example, the writings of Regino of Prüm (GS, I, p. 236), Aribo Scholasticus (GS, II, p. 225), John of Affligem (GS, II, p. 232), Marchettus de Padua (GS, IV, pp. 68 and 152), Adam of Fulda (GS, IV, p. 333) and the treatises *Summa Musicae* (GS, IV, p. 199), and *Ars Discantus* (CS, III, p. 103). The author of the *Quatuor Principalia Musica* distinguishes between 'natural' and 'artificial' instruments of practical music. The 'natural' instruments are the lungs and teeth, etc., and the 'artificial' are '*organa, viella, cithara, cistolla, psalterium et cetera*' (CS, IV, p. 205).

[13] Gilbert Reaney, 'Machaut's Influence on Late Medieval Music', *The Monthly Music Record*, 88 (1958), p. 51.

[14] For an elaborate account of the medicinal and therapeutic qualities of music see Tinctoris's treatises *Complexus Effectuum Musices* (CS, IV, p. 191f) and *Complexus Viginti Effectuum Nobilis Artis Musices* (ibid 195f) (both versions of the same work). See also plates 2 and 3.

[15] See, for example, the quotations from 14th-century and 15th-century texts gathered in E. A. Bowles, 'Musical Instruments at the Medieval Banquet', *Revue Belge de Musicologie*, 12 (1958), p. 41-51.

[16] See note 10.

[17] Raynaud (*Oeuvres*, XI, p. 155) suggests that the work was composed for the Duke of Burgundy.

[18] See Tobler-Lommatzsch, *Altfranzösisches Wörterbuch* (Berlin, 1925; Wiesbaden, 1954-), 4 (1960), *haut*.

[19] For references to voices as *haut* see Tobler-Lommatzsch, *op. cit.*, 4, *haut*. For related references in Latin see Yvonne Rokseth, *Polyphonies du XIIIe siècle; le manuscrit H 196 de la Faculté de Médecine de Montpellier*, Paris, 4 vols., 1935-39, vol. IV, p. 220f.

[20] See W. v. Wartburg, *Französisches Etymologisches Wörterbuch*, Basel, vol. 14, 1961, p. 638, where the earliest recorded use of *vox* in this sense is dated 1765. The transferred meaning is not given in Antoine Furetière's *Dictionnaire Universel* (3 vols., The Hague and Rotterdam, 1690 (reprinted by Slatkine Reprints, Geneva, 1970) *voix*), although the author lists several specialized musical senses of the word. Ralph de Gorog (*Lexique Français Moderne—Ancien Français*, University of Georgia Press, 1973, p. 328) gives *parçon* as the Old French equivalent of Modern French *partie* in the musical sense (see F. Godefroy, *Dictionnaire de l'Ancienne Langue Française* (Paris, 1880-1902), 5 (1888), *parçon*).

[21] The primary transferred sense of *vox* in the musical theorists is 'note' or 'pitch'; see, for example, Marchettus of Padua, *Lucidarium* (GS, IV, p. 85); *Summa Musicae* (GS, IV, p. 201), *Ars Discantus* (CS, III, p. 110), Johannis Veruli de Anagnia, *Liber de Musica* (CS, III, p. 131), Prosdocimus de Beldemandis, *Tractatus de Contrapuncto* (CS, III, p. 194) and Anon., *Quatuor Principalia Musica* (CS, IV, p. 226). When discussing counterpoint, the theorists either refer to parts by their names (*tenor, contratenor, discantus*, etc.), use the term *pars*, or employ *cum* followed by a numerical adjective with implied noun, e.g. *cum tribus* ('with three [parts]'). See the discussions of part-writing in the *Ars Discantus* (CS, III, p. 93), and in the *Tractatus de Cantus Mensurabilis* of Aegidius de Murino (CS, III, p. 124f).

[22] See previous note.

[23] See Reaney, op cit, pp. 5 and 94.

[24] See Joscelyn Godwin, 'Mains Divers Acors', *Early Music*, 5 (1977), 2, p. 159.

[25] *Quatuor Principalia Musica* (CS, IV, p. 295).

[26] CS, III, p. 93.

[27] Gace de la Bugne *Le Roman des Dedus*, Ed. Åke Blomqvist, Studia Romanica Holmiensia, III, Karlshamn, 1951, line 8083f.

[28] Godefroy, op cit, 2 (1882), *deschanter*.

[29] There is, for example, an explicit reference to the performance of *teneur* and *contreteneur* on the *psalterium* in the *Pratique du Psalterium Mystique* of Jean de Gerson (d 1429), see Mgr. Glorieux, ed., *Jean de Gerson Oeuvres Complètes*, 10 vols. in 11, Tournai, 1960-73, 7(1), p. 421.

[30] See, for example, with regard to the music of the troubadours, H. van der Werf, *The Chansons of the troubadours and trouvères: A study of the melodies and their relation to the poems*, Utrecht, 1972, and on the

textless parts of the Old Hall manuscript, Margaret Bent's note to the music supplement of *Early Music*, January 1974; 'Vocalization is a likely solution, and one to which modern singers of early music may have to grow more accustomed.'

[31] Cf. Reaney, op cit, p. 8: 'Although certain tenors and contratenors may have been performed vocally, the great majority of those employed in Machaut's polyphonic songs are undoubtedly instrumental. They look so unvocal with their passagework and leaps that we can hardly apply to them Deschamps' important statement that three voices are necessary when a song is properly performed with tenors and contratenors by two or three people.'

[32] Lloyd Hibberd, 'On "Instrumental Style" in Early Melody', *Musical Quarterly*, 32 (1946), pp. 107-130.

[33] See Sarah Jane Williams, 'Vocal Scoring in the Chansons of Machaut', *Journal of the American Musicological Society*, 21 (1968), 3, p. 252.

[34] Deschamps apparently puns on the musical meaning of this word in his Ballade 300 (see the Oeuvres, II, p. 161).

[35] The translation 'in octaves' for *doublées* is supported by (1), the earliest French vernacular musical treatise *Quiconques veut deschanter* (MS 13c) where *doubles* is defined as the *Witisme* ('eighth') note above unison (quoted here from the facsimile of the original MS in *The Music in the St. Victor Manuscript Paris lat. 15139*, Introduction and facsimiles by Ethel Thurston, Toronto, 1959, p. 21 fol. 269); (2), the French vernacular treatise of Anonymous XIII (end of 13c) in CS, III, p. 497: *Qui veult faire bon deschant il doilt commenchier et finir par acort parfait, c'est à scavoir par unisson, quinte ou double*. . . . (3), by Gace de la Buigne's reference (*Le Roman des Deduis*, in Blomqvist, *op. cit.*, lines 8087-8088) to the *quadouble* part being sung '*la quinte sur double*', i.e., a fifth above the octave above the tenor.

[36] Deschamps is presumably thinking of the rules for composing polyphonic music such as are given in the *Ars Discantus* (CS, III, p. 93), in the *Tractatus Cantus Mensurabilis* of Aegidius de Murino (CS, III, p. 124f), and in the *Tractatus de Musica Figurata et de Contrapuncto* (CS, IV, 446f).

[37] The verb *quintoier* simply means 'to sound a fifth', but it appears in several Old French texts where its actual technical meaning is far from clear (see, for example, Gautier de Coinci, *Les Miracles de la Sainte Vierge*, ed. A. E. Poquet, Paris, 1862, col. 320, line 262). If Deschamps is referring to the rules for composing polyphonic music in this passage (see previous note) then all the verbs he uses derived from the names of intervals must denote the process of putting parts together as described in the treatises (cf. for example, CS, IV, p. 448-9).

[38] Apparently only in Deschamps (see Tobler-Lommatzsch, *op. cit.* (Zweite Lieferung des X bandes, Wiesbaden, 1974) *tenir*, col. 218). My translation is based upon the assumption that Deschamps is referring to composition. However, all the verbs used here may also imply aspects of performance, and one might therefore translate 'perform a tenor'. For a treatise on the composition of motet tenors see Aegidius de Murino, *Tractatus Cantus Mensurabilis* (CS, III, p. 124f).

[39] The *discantus* was the top line in a chanson (also called *superius, cantus, treble*). Again, Deschamps may be referring to performance, or to the composition of a part above a tenor (see Godefroy, op cit, 2 (1883), *Deschant, Deschanter*, and Tobler Lommatzsch, 2 (n.d.), *deschant, deschanter*). The word is used somewhat loosely in vernacular texts, and it is difficult to know how precise in reference Deschamps wishes to be.

[40] Deschamps appears to be implicitly distinguishing the stringed (*bas*) instruments from the winds, predominantly loud (*haulx*). However, the explicit mention of *fleutes* as representative of the *haulx* instruments is puzzling (see E. A. Bowles, ' "Haut et Bas": the grouping of musical instruments in the Middle Ages', *Musica Disciplina*, 8 (1954), pp. 120-1, 126-7).

Acknowledgements

I am most grateful to David Fallows of the University of Manchester and Professor Elizabeth Salter of the Centre for Medieval Studies, University of York, who read the first draft of this article and made many valuable suggestions. I would also like to thank Stephen Minta of the Department of English and Related Literature at York, who examined my translation and use of Old French materials.

Nature *presents her daughters* Sens, Retorique *and* Musique *to Machaut. Bibl. natl., f.fr. 9221 f. 1r. By courtesy of Scottish Academic Press*

[16]

The performance of songs in late medieval France
A new source
Christopher Page

1 King Philipus of Britain in his hall; illustration from *Cleriadus et Meliadice* (British Library, Royal 20 C.ii, f.1r)

We have reached a critical stage in our understanding of the role of instruments in medieval music, both sacred and secular. Few scholars and performers in the English-speaking world now believe that instruments generally participated in liturgical music,[1] and lately some deeply entrenched views concerning the use of instruments in the secular repertories have come under scrutiny.[2] We have already reached a position where we cannot tacitly assume significant instrumental involvement in monophonic courtly songs, motets or polyphonic chansons.

Yet the study of performance practice is concerned with far more than questions of procedure—questions of what should be done; a change in performance conventions can influence the entire emotional and intellectual structure of our reaction to a particular repertory. Ultimately—and this is what raises the study of performance practice to a position of the first importance—such a change can affect the aesthetic and subjective feelings that are largely responsible for our 'sense of the past'. Consider the hints which Marix offered to performers more than 40 years ago: 'It will be best to choose instruments of contrasting sonority [for the textless tenor and contratenor parts] so as to distinguish the frequent crossing of these lines and, by contrast of timbre, to fill the emptiness of unisons'.[3]

Such counsel has inspired countless performances and has prompted some impressionistic—but compelling—analogies between the bright, uncompromising sounds of medieval instruments (as we are accustomed to imagine them) and the brilliant colours of contemporary painting, the pungent spices of medieval cookery.[4] Many seem convinced that the differentiation of timbre produced by these 'broken' instrumental groupings embodies a truth about late medieval music; 14th- and 15th-century chansons are often imagined in terms of boldly individualized lines collaborating in a polyphony which is extrovert and almost heraldic in colour, which is candid, even naïve, in its directness of address to the listener. Yet this is much more than a conception of a repertory; it is an interpretation, in miniature, of late medieval culture in France and Burgundy. We see how easily it accords with one of the most persuasive accounts of that subject ever written, Huizinga's *The Waning of the Middle Ages*: 'To the world when it was half a thousand years younger, the outlines of all things seemed more clearly marked than to us . . . All experience had yet to the minds of men the directness and absoluteness of the pleasure and pain of child-life'.[5]

If this is an accurate summary of the influence of instruments—and of Huizinga—upon our thinking about this music then there are various comments by medieval theorists which must give us pause. 'Voices are more perfect than instruments', wrote Jacques de Liège during the years of Guillaume de Machaut's boyhood, 'and Art imitates Nature: there is no small musicality in voices which instruments can never match.'[6] Instruments have been considered inferior to voices during most periods of Western music but the idea was more than a commonplace, a theoretical nicety, during the Middle Ages. The surviving musical manuscripts endorse the remarks of Jacques de Liège. Almost all the secular music which they contain can be classified as song; somewhere, and invariably in the most important place, it has words. To compose in the Middle Ages was to exploit what singers did best; to succeed was to create something that singers could control and dominate.

When we attempt to pursue these medieval priorities and establish rules to govern our performances we meet a major difficulty. This is not, as is often assumed, created by scarcity of sources; the problem is rather that the number of potentially valuable sources is legion and we do not know where we may most safely invest time and energy. Important—indeed crucial—references can turn up almost anywhere in the spectacular amount of literary and documentary material waiting to be sifted. With our present state of method and research we are at the mercy of chance finds for our understanding of performance practice, so it is inevitable that the picture we assemble from them can scarcely be regarded as more than a damaged mosaic. Here are some new fragments of the whole, gathered from a 15th-century French romance, Cleriadus et Meliadice, which has not been published in modern times.[7] They call much accepted thinking into question.

Cleriadus et Meliadice is a cluttered tale written to celebrate extremes of valour, sentiment and ceremonial. It caters for an insatiable appetite for adventure with many stock episodes of medieval romance: the crusade against the Saracens; the royal maiden disinherited by trickery, saved from murder, and forced to live in poverty until recognized by her lover; the young knight who triumphs over all his rivals, in battle and tournament, to win the heroine. Yet the author provides for a limitless interest in courts and courtesy (it is no surprise to find here and there in the work evidence of a French aristocratic and possibly royal provenance for Cleriadus et Meliadice)[8] and for the details of everyday life behind the ceremonial. Cleriadus, preparing to leave the port of Caradosse, having triumphed in a crusade, asks his subordinates to ensure that the army has no outstanding debts in the city; on another occasion a servant sets off to town to buy lances for Cleriadus who has exhausted his supply in a chivalric contest, the defence of la joyeuse maison (ff.57r–69v, f.89v).

The author's observation of contemporary life—the detail that supports and affirms his story[9]—is gratifyingly keen in matters musical. Throughout Cleriadus et Meliadice music generally follows the two main meals: first the disner, then the souper. It was often the custom in the later Middle Ages (in both France and England) for members of an aristocratic or courtly household to eat separately according to sex or rank, coming together after the meal to enjoy what came to be known as the esbatemens ('entertainments' or rather 'games'—implying participation by all).[10] Cleriadus et Meliadice incorporates a wealth of information about these esbatemens. In the opening pages of the romance Cleriadus and his father, the Count of Asturias, arrive at Windsor Castle while King Philipus of Grant Bretaigne (indiscriminately also called Engleterre) is at table (illus.1). Once the disner is finished Cleriadus enters the hall with his father's retinue; while the Count and Philipus fall into conversation he joins the company in the body of the hall:

les menestrers ... commencerent a corner. Vng grant seigneur de la court print la belle Meliadice. Cleriadus print vne des dames et

2 Cleriadus in his chamber attended by a surgeon and three kings (f.179v)

chascun chascune se prinrent a danser. La feste dura longue piece. Et quant il eubrent assez dansé les menestrers cesserent et se prinrent a chanter. La oyssiez hommes et femmes bien chanter. Or estoit Meliadice encoste Cleriadus et vng aultre cheualier de la compaignie du conte d'Esture. Si print Meliadice a dire a Cleriadus: 'Je vous prie que nous veulliez dire vne chanchon de vostre pays; vous auez assez oy de celles de ce pays'... Et lors commence Cleriadus vne chanchon tant bien que tous ceulx de la place l'escouterent moult volentiers. Et disoient tous que oncques mais n'auoyent oy si bien chanter. Et mesmes le roy leissa a parler pour l'escouter... (f.4v)

the minstrels began to play loud wind instruments. A great lord of the court took the fair Meliadice. Cleriadus took one of the ladies and all the men and women began to dance. The entertainment lasted a long time. And when they had danced their fill the minstrels ceased and they began to sing. There might you have heard men and women singing well! Now Meliadice was next to Cleriadus and another knight in the retinue of the Count. She said to Cleriadus: 'Pray sing a song from your country; you have heard enough songs from ours'... And then Cleriadus began a song so well that all those who were there listened to him gladly. They all said that they had never heard anyone sing so well. Even the king himself stopped talking to hear Cleriadus.

The *esbatemens* begin with the loud wind music of the minstrels. When the company tires of dancing, 'they' (apparently the 'men and women' of the court) begin to sing. Instruments are not mentioned. In these informal, but hardly intimate circumstances, Cleriadus is asked to sing; the company expects that young squires aspiring to *chevalerie* will be prepared to sing upon request. King Philipus and the Count have been talking during the other songs—so impromptu were the *esbatemens* on some occasions—but they both listen to Cleriadus. The *salle* does not—at least on this occasion—act like a modern concert hall; it is an arena for diverse and segregated pastimes. It is no surprise to read, in one 15th-century romance, that minstrels 'played in many places within the hall' *(juoient en pluissieurs lieux parmy la salle)*.[11]

The division of musical items into instrumental ones performed by minstrels and songs performed by courtly amateurs (with no reference to accompaniment) is maintained throughout *Cleriadus et Meliadice*. Almost invariably the minstrels play loud wind instruments, often for dancing (illus.3):

Les menestrez commencerent a corner et chascun se print a danser ... (f.18r)
The minstrels began to play loud wind instruments and everyone began to dance ...

3 Cleriadus and Meliadice, seated, watch dancers in the hall (f.159r)

Trompettes et menestrez estoient deuant qui cornoient.. (f.115r)
Trumpeters and minstrels went before playing loud wind instruments ...

trompettes sonnoyent, menestrez cornoyent, sans point cesser (f.122v)
trumpets sounded, minstrels played loud wind instruments, without ceasing.

menestrez, trompettes se prinrent a corner. (f.161r)
minstrels, trumpeters began to play loud wind instruments.

les trompettes et menestrez ... commencerent a jouer.. Lors le connestable commenche le basse danse (f.171v)
the trumpeters and minstrels ... began to play ... Then the *connestable* begins the *basse danse* ...

Les menestrelz commencerent a corner   deux seigneurs commencerent les danses . (f.190v)
The minstrels began to play loud wind instruments ... two lords began the dances ...

There are similar references in some other 15th-century fiction. In Antoine de la Sale's *Le Petit Jehan de Saintré*, a remarkable work which recounts the progress of its hero from the rank of page to higher things via success in the lists at home and on crusade abroad,

EARLY MUSIC OCTOBER 1982   443

there is a passage where minstrels play loud wind instruments and the courtiers dance, then sing:

menestrelz commencerent a corner, et les cuers joyeulz commencerent a dansser et puis a chanter . . .[12]

minstrels began to play loud wind instruments, and the joyous-hearted ones began to dance and then to sing . . .

There is a comparable reference in *Le livre des faits du bon chevalier Messire Jacques de Lalaing*, a prose narrative of the doings of an historical member of the Lalaing family in the 15th century which closely resembles a fictional romance (although a number of the more romantic exploits recounted in it are known to have taken place). Here we read that on one occasion minstrels played *trompettes* for dancing in the hall after the banquet, but then

chevaliers et dames se prirent de tous costés par la salle à danser, chanter et envoisier et faire feste . . .[13]

knights and ladies occupied every part of the hall in dancing, singing and celebrating . . .

At one point in *Cleriadus et Meliadice* there is an elaborate description of an *entremez* (an entertainment while the company is still seated at table) which shows how easily song found a place in the contexts of play and spectacle. Yet although the occasion is a festive one it is clear that only the voices of young ladies at court are heard. The professionals, the minstrels, who are playing various instruments as the *entremez* begins, are commanded to stop so that the voices may be heard. The event takes place in the courtyard of a palace where a large company is celebrating the marriage of Cleriadus and Meliadice:

Or est ainsi que auant qu'on leuast les tables apres les entremez, dont il y en eubt sans nombre, il y en vint vng vous orez quel. C'estoient xx. jeusnes enfans de .xv. ans et .xx. pucelles de cest eage. Les filz estoient montez sur lyons priuez bien sellez de selles de joustes et bien bridez, et tous couuers tant les enfans comme les lyons de pourpre, et les xx. pucelles estoient assizes sur licornes qui auoient moult belles selles et beaux harnas. Et estoient les pucelles vestues de pourpre de mesmez les valletons, tous leurs cheueulx gettez par derriere, et auoient chappeaulx vers sur leur teste Et chascune pucelle menoit son valleton par vne laisse de fil d'or et de soye. En cest estat arriuerent deuant la grant table et .xl. varlez auec eulx qui portoyent grant tourse de lances. Aussi tost qu'ilz furent arriuez les pucelles descendirent et les varletz prinrent les licornes, si se tirerent les pucelles a vne part et commencerent a chanter. Et pour leur beau chant fist on cesser les instrumens adfin de les mieulx oyr, et tous ceulx et celles qui les escoutoient disoient que oncques mais n'auoient oy mieulx chanter en leur vie Et tandis qu'ilz chantoient les valletons joustoient deuant la compagnie, et celuy qui estoit abatu se venoit rendre a le pucelle qui l'auoit amené, et celluy qui l'auoit abatu luy donnoit vne verge d'or pour sa renchon, *et puis il la donnoit a la pucelle. Et le pucelle la prenoit et luy donnoit le chapel qu'elle auoit sur sa teste, et puis le mettoit en sa main auprez d'elle et d'ung aultre. Et puis recommenchoient a jouster. Ainsi dura la jouste et la danse grant pieche.* (f.170r–v)

Now it happened that before the tables were raised after the countless *entremez*, another took place and you shall hear about it. It was performed by 20 young boys, each 15 years of age, and 20 girls of the same age. The boys were mounted on tame lions well saddled with jousting saddles and well bridled; both the lions and their young riders were completely clothed in purple. The 20 girls were mounted upon unicorns which were equipped with very beautiful saddles and fair harnesses. These girls were clothed in purple like the boys; their hair was thrown back and they had green hats upon their heads. Each girl led her boy by a lead of gold and silk. In this wise they arrived before the major table accompanied by 40 valets carrying a great bundle of lances. As soon as they were there the girls dismounted and the valets took the unicorns away; then the girls went off to one side and began to sing. Because of their beautiful song the instruments were commanded to be silent so that the girls might be better heard: all those who heard them, both men and women, said that they had never heard better singing in their lives. And while they were singing the boys jousted before the company. He who was beaten came to surrender himself to the girl who had brought him in, while the victor gave him a golden rod to ransom himself, then the loser gave it to the girl. In return the girl gave him the hat that she had upon her head and he put it in his hand beside her and another [?]. Then they began the joust again. Thus the dance and the joust lasted a long while.

Few passages better illustrate the intimate relation between chivalric literature and chivalric life in the 15th century. The essence of this description is exaggeration, not fantasy. The implication that the lions and unicorns are real is not a departure from realism, but an acknowledgement that in the remote and idealized past of the story some most difficult things were accomplished in the interests of ceremonial. Compulsive chivalric themes are on display here: the fascination with youth, *jeunesse*, so candid and precocious; the undying interest in images of sexual bondage and surrender; the attraction of everything implied by play—competition, display and reward. Song is a natural adornment for such an occasion; yet even though it contributes to the spectacle there is no accompaniment. Voices suffice.

Several times in *Cleriadus et Meliadice* a distinction is maintained between 'dancing to minstrels' and 'dancing to songs'—further evidence that the author wished to keep the instrumental music of the minstrels and the vocal, amateur performances of the courtiers distinct.

This opposition is brought out at the close of the following passage (which incidentally reveals the texture of courtly manners woven around the act of dancing the *basse danse*). King Philipus of *Engleterre* has arrived at the court of the Count of Asturias to fetch his daughter, Meliadice, whom he believed dead. Cleriadus is present, and there is a great celebration:

'Je feray venir les menestres pour festier la compagnie.' Le conte luy dit que ce seroit bien fait. Adonc Cleriadus fit venir trompettes et menestres qui ja auoi[en]t festié toutte la compaignie si commencent a jouer et Cleriadus a [MS: la] querir messire Domus, le quel estoit le plus grant seigneur de toutte la compaignie ... si la prent et la maine a Meliadice, et luy dist: 'Messire Domus, menez madame Meliadice vne basse danse.' Il s'agenoulle deuant Meliadice en s'excusant vng pou, disant que il ne sçauoit guerres danser; touttesfois Meliadice le pria qu'i[l] la [MS: qui la] menast, si fist son commandement et commencha la danse. Ceulx qui s'en sceurent entremettre prinrent dames et demoiselles tant celles de Meliadice que de celles de la contesse. Et Cleriadus print Romaine et la mena a la danse, car grant fain auoit de deuiser a elle. Et grant piece parlerent ensamble d'une chose et d'aultre. Ainsi fut la chose commencié[e] et bien entretenue tant de danser aux menestrez comme aux chansons. (f.112v)

'I will summon the minstrels to entertain the company.' The Count told Cleriadus that it would be a fine gesture. Then Cleriadus called in the trumpeters and minstrels who had already entertained the courtiers and they begin to play. Cleriadus sought Messire Domus who was the greatest lord in the whole company ... he takes him by the hand and leads him to Meliadice saying: 'Messire Domus, lead my lady Meliadice in a *basse danse*'. He kneels before Meliadice and excuses himself somewhat, saying that he knows little of dancing; however, Meliadice entreated him that he should lead her, and so he complied with her request and began the dance. Those who knew how to perform the dance took ladies and maidens, both those of Meliadice and those of the countess. Cleriadus took Romaine and led her to the dance for he had a great desire to converse with her. For a long while they talked together of one thing and another. Thus the entertainment was begun and well conducted, both in dancing to minstrels and in dancing to songs.

We find the same distinction later in the romance when Cleriadus and Meliadice are entertained by the French king—'the greatest and noblest of all Christians' —at his court in Paris after a series of jousts from which Cleriadus has emerged triumphant:

Les danses auoient longuement duré aux menestrez, car la feste estoit moult belle . Quant la compaignie fut traueillée de danser aux menestrelz ilz se prinrent a danser aux chanchons ... Le roy print Meliadice, et vne des dames de la royne, et commencha les danses aux chansons. Et la oyssiez hommes et femmes bien chanter. (f.127r–v)

The dancing to minstrels had lasted a long while, for it was a magnificent celebration ... When the company was tired of dancing to minstrels they began to dance to songs ... the king took Meliadice and one of the queen's ladies to begin the dancing. There might you have heard gentlemen and ladies singing well!

And again a little later during the same celebrations:

La feste aux chansons estoit ja faillie et redansoit on aux menestrez. (f.128v)

The festivity with songs was already over and the company was dancing to minstrels again.

Did amateur musicians combine vocal and instrumental music, accompanying themselves or others? *Cleriadus et Meliadice* incorporates many episodes where we might expect to find an answer to this question. It depicts a society in which instruments, like chessmen, can be called for whenever they are required to pass an hour or two.[14] Both Cleriadus and his lady are gifted harpists.[15] Contemporary illustrations sometimes show instruments stored in chambers ready for impromptu music-making. Yet 15th-century romances incorporate a number of references to segregation of voices and instruments. In *Pontus et Sidoine*, a romance dating from c1400 and unpublished in modern times, the hero is asked on one occasion to dance, to sing, and then to play the harp. This serves an obvious literary purpose for it emphasizes his talents by enumeration; yet each accomplishment is clearly self-sufficient:

Et apres se prindrent a chanter et a dancer Mais a paine peurent faire dancer le sourdit, et disoit qu'il ne sçauoit dancer Mais il fu a la dance et dança le mielx. Et apres aussi ne le pouaient faire chanter. Mais a la priere des filles du roy il chanta vne chançon le mieulx de tous. Apres ce qu'ilz eurent dancé le filz du roy et sa seur se prindrent a jouer de la herpe. Et quant ilz eurent vne piece herpé, prierent a Pontus qu'il herpast. Mais a paine le voulu faire. Et au fort herpa vng lay nouuel a merueilles bel ..[16]

And afterwards they began to sing and dance; yet they could scarcely persuade Pontus to dance, for he protested that he had no ability for it. However, when he joined the dance he danced the best. Nor could they prevail upon him to sing afterwards, but when the daughters of the king asked him he sang a song better than any. After they had danced the son of the king and his sister began to play the harp, and when they had harped a while they asked Pontus to play but they could barely persuade him to do so. But in the end he harped a lay that was new and wonderfully beautiful ...

There is more than a hint of such a separation of vocal and instrumental music in *Paris et Vienne* where the hero and his companion, Edardo, sing and *then* play beneath Vienne's window:

aloient de nuyt soubz la chambre de Vienne, faisant oubades de leurs chanssons, quar ilz chantoient souveraynement bien, et puys jouoyent de leur instrumens chanssons mellodyoses, comme ceulx qui de celluy mestier estoient les maistres.[17]

they were accustomed to go at night beneath Vienne's room using their songs as aubades, for they sang surpassingly well, and then they played melodious songs upon their instruments like ones who were masters of that craft.

Cleriadus et Meliadice contains some important evidence that may now be brought to bear upon this problem, for there are three occasions when music that is either possibly polyphonic (one instance) or definitely so (two instances) is performed by courtly amateurs. The first takes us to a chamber at the court of Wales where Cleriadus is recovering after wounds received in battle with a lion which had ravaged that country. He is abed, yet the setting soon loses its intimacy. Cleriadus (with four knights who keep him company) receives a visit from the King of Wales who brings a *priuee compaignie* (apparently two knights). The queen is sent for and she duly arrives together with her daughter, Cadore, and a party of waiting-women among whom there is 'a great wealth of beauties' (*grant foison de belles*). The occasion becomes a populous and convivial one and the king interprets it as ideal for a performance by Cadore, a precociously gifted singer:

Le roy demanda a Cleriadus: 'Volez vous oyr chanter ma fille?'. 'Oy, sire, s'il vous plaist.' Le roy appelle deux jeunes filz si leur commande qu'ilz chantent aueuc la fille. Adonc Cadore en commença a dire vne chanchon de si grant sentement et tant bien que Cleriadus estoit tout esmeruillié de l'oyr car elle n'auoit pas plus de sept ans . . . (f.38r)

The king asked Cleriadus: 'Would you like to hear my daughter sing?'. [Cleriadus replied:] 'Yes, please.' Then the king calls two young boys and commands them to sing with the girl. Then Cadore began to sing a song of such noble feeling, and so well, that Cleriadus was amazed to hear it for she was no more than seven years old . . .

The king calls two young boys (household pages perhaps) to sing with his daughter, but it can hardly be that one so talented needs moral support. Perhaps she performs a monophonic rondeau or some other refrain song that welcomes multi-voice performance? A particularly interesting possibility is that she performs the superius part of a polyphonic chanson while the two boys, possessing equivalent and slightly lower voices, perform the tenor and contratenor parts. There is no reference to the use of instruments.

There is some support for the 'polyphonic' interpretation of this passage in two further extracts from *Cleriadus et Meliadice*, both of them more explicit. In each one subordinate members of the household are called upon to perform in order to accompany a courtly amateur. The first incorporates an account of Cleriadus as a composer of secular polyphony—an episode unique, as far as I am aware, in 15th-century French literature. After his battle with the lion that had ravaged the kingdom of Wales Cleriadus sets out for the court of Philipus, King of *Engleterre*. He has been separated from Meliadice for a long while and during the journey he is pleased to see one of her valets riding towards him. The valet carries a love-letter containing a rondeau written by Meliadice:

Alez vous en mon desir amoureux
Deuers celluy pour quy souuent je veille;
Luy dire tout bas en l'oreille
Qu'aultre de luy je n'ayme si m'et Dieux.

Il est tant beau et si tres gracieux;
  Alez vous en mon desir amoureux;

Je ne quiers ne desire mieulx
Qu'a bien amer mon coeur sy appareille;
Dieu me doint oyr bonne nouuelle
Du plus leal qui soit desoubz les cieulx.

  [Alez vous en mon desir amoureux
  Deuers celluy pour quy souuent je veille;
  Luy dire tout bas en l'oreille
  Qu'aultre de luy je n'ayme si m'et Dieux]. (ff.49r–v)

'I am sending you a song', writes Meliadice in her letter enclosing this rondeau, 'and I pray you to compose music for it' (*je vous prie que la veulliez mettre en chant* [f.49r]). Cleriadus arrives at a town (*ville*) and finds lodgings so that he may begin work on the setting at once:

Si tost que Cleriadus fu descendu en son logeis il demanda incontinent vne harpe . . . Quant Cleriadus fut a par luy il commença a faire les notes de la chanchon que Melyadice luy auoit enuoyée, et le fit si bien que ceulx qui l'ouoient apres chanter disoient que jamais meilleur chant n'auoyent oy. Aprez la mist sur la harpe et joua longuement. Et puis, quant il eubt tout fait, il commença a faire vnes lettres a Meliadice. (ff.50v–51r)

As soon as Cleriadus entered his lodgings he demanded a harp at once . . . When he was all alone he began to compose the music for the song that Meliadice had sent him, and he succeeded so well that those who heard it sung afterwards said that they had never heard a better song. Afterwards he put it on the harp and played for a long time. When he had done everything he began to write a letter to Meliadice.

An illustration in the British Library manuscript of the romance shows Cleriadus harping in his chamber (illus.4). No writing materials are shown (and none is mentioned in the text) even though, as we later learn,

4 Cleriadus playing the harp in his chamber (f.51v)

the setting he composes is a polyphonic one in at least two parts. What are we to understand by the fact that he 'put [the song] on the harp and played for a long time'? His work on the song seems to involve two operations: composing the music, and 'putting' the music on the harp. In his reply to Meliadice, Cleriadus emphasizes that the second stage, the only one definitely involving a harp, has already (*desia*) been accomplished, as if it were not normally completed at the time of composition:

J'ay mis vostre chanchon en chant, non pas si bien que a la chanchon apertient veu le lieu dont elle vient, et si est desia mise sur le harpe, et la vous aporteray, se dieu plait, a heure dicte. (f.51r)

I have composed music for your song, though not so well as the song deserves considering from whom it comes, and also it has already been put upon the harp, and I will bring it to you, please God, at the said time.

There seem to be two possible interpretations of these events. The first is that Cleriadus composes the superius part and then, perhaps using the harp to help himself think harmonically and contrapuntally, he composes a line (or lines) to accompany it. The second possibility—and the one that I consider more likely—is that Cleriadus composes the whole piece, superius and (at least) tenor, and then produces a harp intabulation for Meliadice who is a skilled player upon that instrument (indeed the *varlet* who brings back Cleriadus's letter finds her playing the harp in her most private chamber).[18]

Despite the involvement of a harp, the leading 15th-century court instrument, in the above episode, Cleriadus does not use one when he is asked to perform his new composition in a hall of great splendour, purpose-built to celebrate a *pas d'armes* in which he has triumphed against all comers. King Philipus is present with many other noble ladies and gentlemen. The company is dancing:

Quant ilz eubrent longuement dansé aux menestrez ilz danserent aux chanchons Sy commencha Cleriadus que Meliadice auoit faicte. Vng escuier de sa compaignie luy tenoit la teneur, et pensez qu'il estoit bon a oyr, car il chantoit le mieulx que on auoit jamais ouy. Et quant il eubt fait il [la] bailla par escript en la main de Melyadice. (f.70v)

When the company had danced a good while to the minstrels they began to dance to songs. So Cleriadus began to sing what Meliadice had written. A squire from his retinue held the tenor part for him and you may believe that it was good to hear, for [Cleriadus] sang better than anyone had ever heard before. When he had finished he put a written copy of the song into the hands of Meliadice.

This provides our first piece of evidence in the romance that 'dancing to songs', discussed above, could involve polyphonic music, following the pattern, by now familiar, of professional instrumental music alternating with amateur vocal music during celebration. Cleriadus is clearly singing the superius, even though the poem it carries is written from a woman's point of view, and in addition there are strong reasons for believing that the squire who 'holds' the tenor is also singing, not playing an instrument (none is mentioned). Thus, for example, Mathieu d'Escouchy, in his account of the famous Feast of the Pheasant, says that the tenor of one polyphonic song was 'held' (*tenoit la teneur*); Olivier de la Marche, working from the same official account and referring to the same piece, records that the tenor was 'sung' (*chanta la teneur*); there is ample supporting evidence for this usage.[19]

Later in the romance Cleriadus composes another song which a *varlet de chambre* carries to Meliadice reporting that Cleriadus made it 'that very morning' (f.130v). Meliadice is preparing to set out to join the French royal court in a visit to the woods and it is during the return from such an expedition, while the company is in open country (*a plain champ*) on the way to Paris, that the French king asks Cleriadus to perform a song. After elaborately rhetorical and courteous preliminaries (in which Cleriadus, faithful to the chivalric demand for modesty in practising all the arts of peace, claims that he knows nothing of singing) Cleriadus arranges a performance of the song he has recently sent to Meliadice:

Cleriadus appella vng de ses pages (lesquelz estoient tous gentilz hommes) et si appella vng de ses escuiers pour tenir teneur a luy et a l'enfant. Adonc commence Cleriadus la chanson si bien et si gentement et d'une si belle voix et nette et haulte que le roy et la royne l'ouoient tant volentiers que c'estoit merueilles. Le plus de la compaignie vinrent au tour d'eux pour les oyr. Le chanson estoit moult bonne et de bon chant, et aussi la disoit bien Cleriadus et ceulx qui luy aidoient . . (f.133v)

Cleriadus called one of his pages (which were all of gentle status) and he also called one of his squires to hold the tenor for himself and for the child. Then Cleriadus begins the song so well and so nobly, and with such a beautiful, pure and loud voice that the king and queen heard it with marvellous willingness. The greater part of the company gathered around them to listen. The song was very good with beautiful music, and also Cleriadus and those who helped him sang it very well . . .

Once again subordinate members of the retinue are called upon to perform. A squire 'holds the tenor' as in the previous extract while Cleriadus sings. A *page* (also called *enfant*), presumably a boy of up to about 14 years of age, is also singing.[20] There is no mention of instruments and it seems clear that all the performers are singing: 'Cleriadus and those who helped him sang it very well'.

How must we assess the contribution of *Cleriadus et Meliadice* to our understanding of performance practice in 15th-century France? Can its details be trusted?

The British Library manuscript of *Cleriadus et Meliadice* was copied in an age when the relations between chivalric life and chivalric literature were so close that the modern reader 'may have difficulty in knowing whether many episodes . . . are based on facts heightened by fiction, or on fiction authenticated by facts'.[21] Aristocratic society tended to pattern its chivalric conduct on literary texts. The intimate relation of life and literature is readily apparent in the musical passages of *Cleriadus et Meliadice*. Consider the last extract quoted above. A performance of a polyphonic chanson takes place during a pause in a journey before royal personages and nobles of the highest degree; the performance involves amateurs (including a *page* drawn from the *gentilz hommes* of Cleriadus's retinue) one of whom is asked to 'hold' the tenor part; the author emphasizes that the king and the queen listen to the rendition *volentiers*. Now let us compare a well-known passage from an annalistic source, the memoirs of the Abbots of St Aubert, which relate how Philip the Good heard a polyphonic song performed at Cambrai in 1449. We are told that the performance took place during a pause before a journey and that two choirboys (probably from the cathedral) sang together while 'one of the gentlemen held the tenor' (*un des ses Gentils Hommes tint le tenure*); Philip is said to have listened to the performance *volentiers*.[22] There are many striking points of resemblance between this account and the passage from *Cleriadus et Meliadice*: the performance during a pause in a journey; the participation by courtly amateurs, including one of the *gentils hommes* who 'holds' the tenor; the assurance that the magnates for whom the performances are undertaken listen *volentiers*. The content, style and vocabulary of the two passages are so similar that we almost seem to be dealing with a literary topos, common to fiction and annal. The truth is rather that both types of writing, romance and record, endorse one another in support of a common assumption: that it is the nature of chivalric magnates to delight in musical performances, especially those involving courtier–amateurs, or *gentils hommes*, who are pleased to 'hold' a part, when they are called upon to do so, in circumstances all the more delightful for their spontaneity. Overriding the simplest concerns—a romancer's desire to celebrate his hero, an abbot's desire to celebrate the Cambrai choristers—there is a central tenet of medieval chivalry involved: that man's capacity for virtue 'seems inseparable from his desire for beauty and his pleasure in those forms of life and love governed by an ideal of aesthetic refinement'.[23]

Like many of the finest medieval romances *Cleriadus et Meliadice* supports its themes of love and chivalry by a mode of authenticating realism—'details from everyday life that lend the narrative an air of plausibility and that allow an audience to accept, or at least suspend its disbelief in, the improbabilities of the fiction'.[24] The musical references in this romance belong, I believe, to the author's exploitation of this mode. They are not structural, they do not advance the plot; each one participates in a realism designed to allow 15th-century readers at court to recognize their own experiences, and thus almost to recognize themselves, in the idealized world of the story. This they must do, for, as with much chivalric literature of the later Middle Ages, the moral world of this narrative is in earnest and readers must be manoeuvred into a position where they may appropriate it.

I propose that in these sections of *Cleriadus et Meliadice* we have three new pieces of evidence that in later 15th-century France polyphonic chansons could be—and perhaps generally were—performed by voices only. Everywhere in this romance we meet a distinction between vocal and instrumental music. One and the same piece may be played (as Cleriadus seems to play his setting of Meliadice's rondeau) or sung, which is how Cleriadus chooses to perform his setting at court. We must imagine these pieces performed by equivalent resources, not a voice and several disparate instrumental timbres. It is possible, of course, that singers differentiated their sounds to individualize their parts, yet this still leads to what is, by the standards of an instrumentally accompanied performance, a remarkable homogeneity, as experiment shows. It is surely time to reconsider some very basic notions about the performance of late medieval chansons.

Perhaps it is also time to reassess any sense of the 15th century that we may owe to an experience of its secular music in performance. The wedding of secular music to poetry, through the voice, now appears to have been an art often segregated from the candid, ingenuous sounds of harps and lutes and from the uncompromising asperities of trumpets and shawms; chanson performances, it would seem, did not necessarily have that 'partiality for brilliant things... shown by the naïve pleasure taken in tinkling or clicking sounds', or those 'naïve contrasts of primary colours' that Huizinga found to be so characteristic of the 'waning' Middle Ages.[25]

Summary of information on performance practice supplied by extracts from *Cleriadus et Meliadice*

(The song performed by Cadore and two boys is assumed to be polyphonic.)

Polyphonic song

1 Performing contexts
   Performed for listeners (always)
   In a chamber (? about 20 people present)
   In the hall
   For dancing
   Out of doors (a pause during a journey)
   Performed upon request

2 Performing forces
   Three voices (a seven-year-old girl and two boys)
   Two voices (Cleriadus and a squire who sings the tenor)
   Three voices (Cleriadus, a page, and a squire who sings the tenor)
   ?Harp intabulation of a ?two-part song

3 Composition of polyphonic song
   By Cleriadus; the text, a rondeau, having been written by Meliadice
   Use of the harp by Cleriadus ?during composition
   Written copy put into circulation by Cleriadus after composition
   Composition followed by performance

Monophonic song

1 Performing contexts
   In the hall at Windsor (a company of gentlemen and ladies present)
   In the hall as part of an *entremez*
   In the hall for dancing

2 Performing forces (the singers are invariably amateurs)
   Solo voice
   Groups of courtiers
   Groups of young girls

Instruments and instrumentalists

Minstrels invariably play loud instruments for dancing or ceremonial
Cleriadus plays ?intabulation of his polyphonic composition upon the harp
Minstrels are commanded to stop playing so that courtly amateur singers may be heard

---

[1] For a listing of some relevant bibliography see A. Hughes, *Medieval Music* (Toronto, 2/1980), items 1947ff. See also G. Reaney, 'Text Underlay in Early Fifteenth-Century Musical Manuscripts', *Essays in Musicology in Honor of Dragan Plamenac*, ed. G. Reese and R. J. Snow (Pittsburgh, 1969/R1977), pp.245–51; and J. T. Igoe, 'Performance Practice in the Polyphonic Mass of the Early Fifteenth Century' (PhD diss., U. of North Carolina at Chapel Hill, 1971).

[2] H. van der Werf, *The Chansons of the Troubadours and Trouvères* (Utrecht, 1972), p.19; L. Gushee, 'Two Central Places: Paris and the French Court in the Early Fourteenth Century', *Bericht über den Internationalen Musikwissenschaftlichen Kongress Berlin 1974*, ed. H. Kuhn and P. Nitsche (Kassel, 1980), p.143; D. Fallows, 'Specific Information on the Ensembles for Composed Polyphony 1400–1474', to appear in the proceedings of the New York conference on performance practice, October 1981 (Cambridge, in preparation) (I am most grateful to Dr Fallows for allowing me to see this paper before its publication); C. Wright, 'Voices and Instruments in the Art Music of Northern France during the 15th Century: A Conspectus', *Report of the Twelfth Congress [of the International Musicological Society] Berkeley 1977*, ed. D. Heartz and B. Wade (Kassel, 1981), pp.643–9; C. Page, 'Machaut's "pupil" Deschamps on the performance of music: Voices or instruments in the 14th-century chanson?', *EM* 5/4 (October 1977), pp.484–91

[3] J. Marix, *Les musiciens de la cour de Bourgogne au XVe siècle (1420–1467)* (Paris, 1937), p.xxi (my translation)

[4] See, for example, David Munrow's notes to his recording *The Mediaeval Sound* (Oryx EXP 46): 'The people of the Middle Ages and the Renaissance liked gorgeous colours in their clothes, sharp contrasts in their paintings, highly flavoured dishes at their table. In music they liked sounds which were bright and uncompromising.'

[5] J. Huizinga, *The Waning of the Middle Ages* (London, 1924), p.1. It would be a most worthwhile project to study the influence of Huizinga's ideas upon our conception of the sound-picture of medieval secular music. They exerted a crucial influence at an early stage; Rudolf Ficker, one of the first scholars who attempted to discuss in print the timbres and tone colours of medieval music, was indebted to Huizinga; see his study 'Polyphonic Music of the Gothic Period', *MQ* 15 (1929), pp.483–505. His concept of an 'autumn' of the Middle Ages (p.500) is directly derived from the original Dutch title of Huizinga's masterwork, and his views on the intensely coloured and brilliant quality of Machaut's music in performance seem to lead on from the notion that Machaut was a 'typical representative' of a 'moribund culture' (pp.500, 505). Signs of Huizinga's influence upon the writings of musicologists are everywhere, as for example in N. Bridgman, 'The Age of Ockeghem and Josquin', *New Oxford History of Music*, 3 (London, 1960), p.246, and H. Besseler, *Bourdon und Fauxbourdon* (Leipzig, 1950), p.207. For recent signs that *The Waning of the Middle Ages* is still casting its spell see L. L. Perkins and

H. Garey, eds., *The Mellon Chansonnier*, 2 vols. (New Haven and London, 1979), 2, p.63. For a penetrating examination of some of Huizinga's basic views see M. Vale, *War and Chivalry* (London, 1981), *passim*, esp. pp.1ff.

[6]*Jacobi Leodiensis Speculum musicae*, ed. R. Bragard, Corpus scriptorum de musica, 3 (Rome, 1955–73), i, p.54.

[7]All quotations here are taken from London, British Library, Royal 20 C.ii, a northern French or Flemish manuscript of the second half of the 15th century according to G. F. Warner and J. B. Gilson, *Catalogue of Western Manuscripts in the Old Royal and King's Collections*, 4 vols. (London, 1921), 2, p.371. For an inventory of other sources of the text, including early printed editions, see B. Woledge, *Bibliographie des romans et nouvelles en prose française antérieurs à 1500* (Geneva, 1954), and *Supplément 1954–1973* (Geneva, 1975), text no.42. For a recent survey of French prose *histoires* (and an excellent bibliographical guide) see R. Morse, 'Historical Fiction in Fifteenth-century Burgundy', *Modern Language Review*, 75 (1980), pp.48–64. I am most grateful to Dr Morse for valuable help and advice.

[8]The author speaks of the chivalry, the court and the King of France in the most flattering terms; see ff.117r, 129r, 167v.

[9]For further discussion of this point see below.

[10]Even in small households it seems to have been common for music to be reserved until after dinner. See, for example, P. Champion, ed., *Les cent nouvelles nouvelles*, 2 vols. (Paris, 1928), 1, p.132. This is perhaps the place to mention another interesting musical reference in *Les cent nouvelles nouvelles* which throws a little light on the vexed question of instrumentalists' repertory. In one story of the collection (2, p.211) a convict led to the gallows is saved by playing on his bagpipes a 'song that his companions knew very well and which began: *Tu demoures trop, Robinet, tu demoures trop*'. It is interesting that the anonymous virelai *Or sus vous donnés trop*, apparently dating from the second half of the 14th century, contains passages which seem to imitate bagpipes (an interpretation supported by the text at the relevant point: *Or tost, naquaires, cornemuses, sonnés*). The piece is edited in W. Apel, *French Secular Compositions of the Fourteenth Century*, Corpus mensurabilis musicae, 53 (n.p., 1970–72), iii, pp.42–5. Obviously there is no reason to assume that it is this very piece which is meant in the *nouvelle* (no bagpiper could play it all); what matters is the association of a certain kind of poem with a specific instrument and its idioms. Perhaps there are more such relationships to be discovered. Further information of this kind is badly needed.

[11]*Gilles de Chin*; text published in *Publications de la Société des Bibliophiles de Mons*, 4 (1837), extract quoted from p.17

[12]*Antoine de la Sale, Le Petit Jehan de Saintré*, ed. P. Champion and F. Desonay (Paris, 1926), p.86

[13]*Oeuvres de Georges Chastellain*, 8, ed. K. de Lettenhove (Brussels, 1866), p.64. This text is full of praise for the *esbatemens* at the Burgundian court (see pp.31, 41).

[14]Thus on f.60v of the romance *harpes, fleutres, jeux d'esches et de tables et de pluiseurs aultres gracieux jeux* are called for to entertain the hero, his lady and their company of friends in a chamber. Numerous sources attest to the fact that instrumental playing and singing bore the same social weight as playing board games. In the 15th century prose version of *La fille du Comte de Pontieu*, harping, playing *tablez* and *eschiés*, and singing are described as 'the three things in which gentlemen, ladies and maidens are accustomed to take great pleasure' (*trois chosez en quoy seigneurs, damez et damoisellez seulent prendre grand deduit*); see *La fille du Comte de Pontieu*, ed. C. Brunel (Paris, 1923), p.106.

[15]Meliadice learns to play the harp 'so well that she surpassed all others' (*si bien qu'elle en estoit maistresse par dessus touttes aultres*) (f.1v); for Cleriadus as a harpist see below. It is worth emphasizing here that musical skills were not always highly regarded in 15th-century French society. It is true that they belonged in the conception of courtly accomplishment that balanced violent activity such as combat and athletics by the indoor *gieux* such as chess, but the tone of courtly life in the prose romances and *ystoires* is overwhelmingly established by the pursuit of arms. According to a conservative author such as Antoine de la Sale 'the true lover–gentleman is not at all suited or disposed to the intellectual and holy sciences of theology, nor to decrees, laws or any other discipline of study save the very noble and illustrious science and trade of arms' (Champion and Desonay, eds., *op cit*, p.49). Since the conduct of war was so *artifficieuse et subtille* the way was open for *armes* to be regarded as a fulfilment of both the physical and ratiocinative ideals of life. Music might then be associated with the vice habitually bred at court and disastrous for the knight: sloth, or *oysiveté* (sometimes personified as a musician in 15th-century French art). It is the 'romantic' narratives such as *Cleriadus et Meliadice* where this stigma is most successfully removed from the readers' field of view. The hero of *Pontus et Sidoine* is an accomplished musician; see the text in British Library, Royal 15 E.vi, ff.209r–v, 213r (where Pontus composes a song), 217r (quoted on p.445) and 224v (where he disguises himself as a minstrel dancing to *chalumeaulx*). The hero of *Paris et Vienne* is a talented instrumentalist and singer; see R. Kaltenbacher, ed., 'Der altfranzösische Roman Paris et Vienne', *Romanische Forschungen*, 15 (1904), pp.394, 397–9, 405. The musical references in this text are discussed in H. M. Brown, 'Instruments and Voices in the Fifteenth-century Chanson', *Current Thought in Musicology*, ed. J. W. Grubbs (Austin, Texas, and London, 1976), pp.102f.

[16]British Library, Royal 15 E.vi, f.217r. For an inventory of the manuscripts of this text and of the early printed editions see Woledge, *op cit*, text no.124. [17]Kaltenbacher, ed., *op cit*, p.397

[18]F.52v. However, the references to the use of a harp in the composition episode have a complicated literary lineage and should not, at present, be pressed too hard for information of 15th-century relevance. For analogous material see R. Lathuillère, *Guiron le Courtois* (Geneva, 1966), pp.218–9, 229, 456.

[19]G. du Fresne de Beaucourt, ed., *Chronique de Mathieu d'Escouchy*, 3 vols. (Paris, 1863–4), 2, p.147; H. Beaune and J. d'Arbaumont, eds., *Mémoires d'Olivier de la Marche*, 4 vols. (Paris, 1883–8), 2, p.359. See also G. Vale, 'La cappella musicale del Duomo di Udine dal sec. XIII al sec. XIX', *Note d'archivio per la storia musicale*, 7 (1930), p.89; the chapter approves the appointment of Domenico da Buttrio on 2 May 1395, on the condition that 'the said priest Domenico must learn to hold the tenor in singing' (*dictus presbiter dominicus debeat addiscere cantum ad tenendum tenorem*). For another example of this usage, in the French vernacular, see M.-T. Bouquet, 'La cappella musicale dei duchi di Savoia dal 1450 al 1500', *Rivista italiana di musicologia*, 3 (1968), p.257, where Antonio Giunati is mentioned 'who holds the tenor with the said choristers' (*qui tient la teneur avecque lesdits innocens*) in 1470; the terminology of 'holding the tenor' also appears in the well-known extract from the memoirs of the Abbots of St Aubert which relates how Philip the Good heard a polyphonic chanson performed by three voices in 1449. For closely related terminology in Italian see N. Wilkins, *Music in the Age of Chaucer* (Cambridge, 1979), where musical references in Giovanni da Prato's *Il paradiso degli Alberti* (c1426) are most usefully quoted and translated (pp.51–2); in one extract, a ballate by Landini (*Or su, gentili spirti*) is said to have been performed by three voices: two girls and a man *tenendo loro bordone*. I owe this reference to the kindness of Dr Fallows.

[20]I am most grateful to Dr Malcolm Vale of St John's College, Oxford, for his advice on this point.

[21]J. Leyerle, 'The Major Themes of Chivalric Literature', *Chivalric Literature*, ed. L. D. Benson and J. Leyerle (Michigan, 1980), p.131

[22]Quoted in J. Marix, *Histoire de la musique et des musiciens de la cour de Bourgogne sous le règne de Philippe le Bon (1420–1467)* (Strasbourg, 1939/R1974), p.67

[23]E. B. Keiser, 'The Festive Decorum of *Cleanness*', *Chivalric Literature*, ed. Benson and Leyerle, p.65

[24]L. D. Benson, 'The Tournament in the Romances of Chrétien de Troyes and *L'histoire de Guillaume le Marechal*', *ibid*, p.13

[25]Huizinga, *op cit*, pp.248, 251

[17]

Texting in 15th-century French chansons: a look ahead from the 14th century

Lawrence Earp

It is commonly believed that the sources of 15th-century music are unclear in their presentation of text underlay, and that the editor is pretty much left to his own devices in establishing the correlation of syllables and notes.[1] This is understandable, since many editors of this repertory have approached the problem from a viewpoint that looks back from the 16th century. At some point, perhaps with the generation of Willaert and his followers, but not yet in the works of Crecquillon, Gombert and Clemens, the correlation between syllables and notes becomes unambiguous. Further, this texting corresponds to our ideas of proper word accentuation and text declamation. Manuscript and printed sources from the early part of the 16th century, as well as the entire 15th-century manuscript tradition, it is said, are notoriously more difficult to deal with.

I would like to approach specifically the 15th-century chanson sources from the other direction. The point that has not been recognized by many music historians is that the problem of text underlay first arises as a general problem in sources from the second half of the century. Now it is true that the basically clear representation of the correlation of word and music in sources prior to the mid-15th century may not correspond to the humanist's conception of good text accentuation and declamation, and perhaps this is why many editors still mistrust the sources and subject them to editorial emendation, even to the point of applying the ideals of Willaert to music composed 100 or 200 years earlier, or of calling on the precepts of a theorist of the 1570s for guidance in understanding a style of music by then long obsolete.[2]

Let us step back and view the situation in the 15th century from the 14th century forward. At the beginning of the 14th century, musical manuscripts, both for motet and chanson, were copied with the text first. It was the text scribe who was responsible for the overall layout of the manuscript, planning the pages and leaving blank spaces for the later insertion of staves and decorative initials. Judging from the spaces left by the staff ruler for initial letters at the beginning of lines and internally, the practice of entering the text before the ruling of staves obtained in the great motet and chanson collections of the 13th century, and continued in the de luxe manuscript of the *Roman de Fauvel* surviving as *F-Pn* fr. 146, in the Brussels *rotulus* (*B-Br* 19606), in the Machaut manuscripts, in most of the Cambrai fragments (*F-CA* 1328), in most of the Ivrea codex (*I-IVc* 115), and in the surviving portions of the Trémoïlle manuscript (*F-Pn* n.a.f. 23190). This procedure of copying music symbols directly over the syllables to which they belong did not change when, around 1340, the first examples of the new-style polyphonic chanson appeared. These works exhibit a highly melismatic cantus, the only voice to carry the text, and a very lengthy textless accompanying voice or voices. The extent of the melismas in the texted voice, as well as the length of the untexted parts were important stylistic innovations, and not easily copied using the old procedure. The text scribe now had to leave greater or lesser gaps for the notes of the melismas to be entered between syllables of text, and also had to indicate to the staff-ruler where the staves for the untexted voices were to be entered (illus.2). Indeed, the extension of the voice designation for the tenor into 'tenor or or or or or', seen in many 14th-century manuscripts, served to show the staff-ruler the length of the staves to be entered, in essence by giving an untexted part a 'text' over which to draw the staves.

This manner of copying music was very difficult and tedious when employed for the highly melismatic polyphonic chanson style. Even if the scribe were copying from an exemplar that was unambiguous, many factors could conspire to compromise what he produced. Exemplar and copy could be in a different format, and differences in column-width, or in the number of columns per folio, made the placement and length of melismas more difficult to predict.

In earlier sources, repeated phrases of music had always been written out in their entirety over a single line of text. Now, a double line of text, a new technique of copying the repeated sections of music for genres with *ouvert* and *clos* cadences, provided a distinct advantage

2 Machaut, 'Donnez, signeurs' (*F-Pn* fr. 1584, f.467r)

when dealing with highly melismatic music, since there was one less line of text to space out for the melismas. Even so, special skill was called for to space out the text at the *ouvert* and *clos* cadences. The new shorthand manner of dealing with *ouvert* and *clos* cadences for ballades and virelais was first applied to vocal music in the new style of the 1340s, and Machaut MS C (*F-Pn* fr. 1586, c.1350–5) is the first extant manuscript to employ the practice in vocal music. Of course the careful setting of notes over the text always relates to the top line of text; the declamation of the lower line was readily duplicated from the upper line of poetry, and an editor should not be surprised if the lower line of text appears askew (compare the ballade in illus.2).

It is evident that the process of music copying in the 14th century was a much more exacting procedure than the copying of text alone. Unless the scribe constantly referred to the exemplar for the exact spacing of each syllable, it was very easy for errors to occur. Later, when he returned to enter the music, he very likely found, on occasion, a syllable that should have been separated that was not, or some other infelicitous situation. This sort of inattention happened frequently as the central Machaut manuscripts were being copied, and various means were used to bring the copy back to the alignment shown more or less clearly in the exemplar, either by crowding the music symbols, or by drawing a diagonal line to indicate the proper co-ordination of syllable to note, or even by scraping and resetting a note or a syllable of text. Indeed, the majority of the hundreds of scribal corrections in the Machaut sources do not concern errors of pitch or rhythm, but rather what ought properly to be called the overlay of the music to the text. The scribes went to great trouble to indicate the correlation of text and music accurately.[3]

A slightly different but related manner of copying was practised in some purely musical *Gebrauchshandschriften*, whose staves were uniformly ruled before the text was entered. Here, a portion of text was entered, followed by the corresponding music above it, alternating back and forth, a procedure that guaranteed the correct disposition of melismas. Margaret Bent has shown that this very tedious and yet most exact manner of copying music was used for the Old Hall MS, and I believe the same could be demonstrated for parts of both the Ivrea codex and Oxford 213.[4]

Most significant for our purposes here is the fact that this technique of copying, when applied carefully, produced a largely unambiguous text setting, and that composers did indeed exercise imagination and choice in setting their texts to music. It was possible to indicate melismatic extensions of syllables, the desired treatment of the unaccented final '-e', and other aspects of texting. The result is not the texting of Willaert. He would certainly have considered it barbaric, as did Morley 50 or so years later, when he wrote in 1597, in a passage already cited by Margaret Bent: 'We must also take heed of seperating any part of a word from another by a rest, as som dunces have not slackt to do, yea one whose name is Iohannes Dunstaple (an ancient English author) hath not onlie devided the sentence, but in the verie middle of a word hath made two long rests . . .'[5]

I do not mean to imply that the manuscripts answer all the questions about text setting, but the fact that careful scribes were concerned about it, and that careful employment of the normal procedure of music copying most often ensured good and accurate results, is significant. Unfortunately, the correlation between text and music was the easiest, and probably the first, aspect of a composition to be corrupted by the repeated copying needed for wide circulation. For highly ornamental and melismatic music, including most late 14th-century rondeaux and the ornate ballades of the 1380s, many of the intentions with regard to texting are impossible to reconstruct with the sources at hand. Nevertheless, an editor who is aware of how a given manuscript was copied can interpret the evidence it contains in a way that resolves certain ambiguities.[6]

The generally wider circulation of music in the 15th century may have been one of the factors that promoted a manner of copying music that was simpler, quicker and more easily duplicated. In any case, the technical problems with this very exacting and time-consuming manner of copying music came to a head shortly before 1450,[7] when copyists on the continent finally gave up even the pretence of trying to show the correlation of word and music, and began to copy manuscripts music first, a much easier working method. The music symbols are placed equidistantly, and the text later underlaid below.

A hint of the new procedure is found just after the turn of the century, in some Italian manuscripts transmitting foreign repertory. John Nádas has reported that some sections—by no means all—of the Reina codex (*F-Pn* n.a.f. 6771) and Paris 568 (*F-Pn* it. 568) were copied music first, with notes separated for syllabic passages and crowded for melismas, and the words underlaid later.[8] I believe the same to have been the case in the copying of *ModA* (*I-MOe* 5.24). This procedure preserves the old distinction between syllabic and melis-

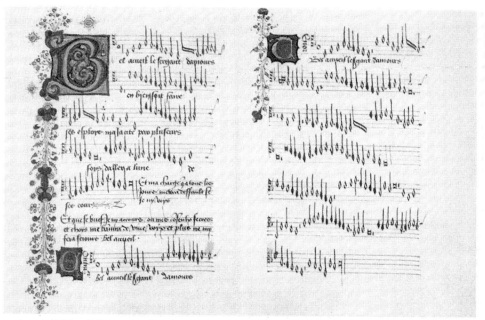

3 Busnois, 'Bel Acueil' (*US-NHy* 91, f.1v-2r)

matic passages, and although it is not as clear as music overlay, an editor aware of the practice might be able to make some good guesses as to the intentions lying behind passages that on the surface look confused. In any case, this type of underlay is far clearer than the practice of the mid- and later 15th century, in which all notational symbols are set equidistantly. Illus.3, from about 1475, provides a typical example of the practice of the last quarter of the 15th century. It should be compared with illus.2, a representative sample copied about 1375.

The actual point at which the old notational practices stop in France and Italy is not clear at the present state of research. The question of the preconditions and assumptions that go along with such a dramatic change in procedure is a complex one, and perhaps the picture will remain as difficult to clarify and as variable as the gradual change to white notation. It is noteworthy that one of the two scribes of *EscA* overlays music to text, while the other one underlays text to music.[9]

In practical terms, the difference in copying procedures means that the modern editor of repertories such as, for instance, Dufay chansons, is left with sources in which the clarity of the relationship between text and music varies from extremely clear, with the music overlaid (for example, the last section of the Reina codex), to extremely unclear, with the text underlaid (for example, any of the late 15th-century chansonniers). But the new technique of the mid-15th century, true text underlay, presumes that a style of music had developed in which there were clearly understood norms of performance practice that took care of the problem of text setting within bounds acceptable to the composer. This assumes that the new scribal practice was agreeable to composer and scribe alike—otherwise, we would have to believe that the composer suddenly had not the slightest interest in the projection of the text in his composition.

Let us review a few of the varieties of texting practices seen in the chanson before the mid-15th century, when it was still possible to be clear about the matter. Active from the 1340s to the 1360s, Machaut exercised a variety of preferences with regard to the placement of the final syllable of the poetic line, and of course he and his scribes were able to notate this. For instance, in his ballades, the penultimate syllable is usually extended at the internal *clos* and at the final cadence, but in a quarter of the 42 examples it is the final masculine syllable of the phrase that is melismatically extended.[10]

200 EARLY MUSIC MAY 1991

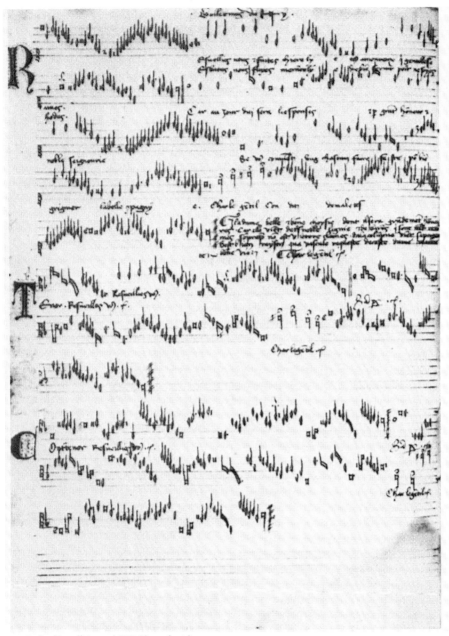

4 Dufay, 'Resvelliés vous' (*GB-Ob* 213, f.126v)

Melismatic extension of the final syllable is seen also in many works in Oxford 213, a repertory drawn largely from the early 15th century up to the mid-1430s. For instance, in two-thirds of the ballades in this source, the *clos* ending is treated as an extension, after the final text syllable has already been sung (cf. illus.4).[11] This is a new notational convention, not seen much in the Chantilly codex.

A further characteristic of text setting quite popular in the first quarter of the 15th century appears late in the previous century, the practice of beginning a song with a long untexted melisma.[12] There is but a single example of this striking new style in the Chantilly codex, the rondeau 'Va t'en mon cuer' by Gacian Reyneau of Tours,[13] where all three voices are texted (illus.5). By the time of Oxford 213, this practice had become common (Dufay's 'Ce jour de l'an' and 'Ce moys de may' are well-known examples).[14] The manuscripts present the first syllable and its initial inset, or the initial retains its usual decorative place at the edge of the music, and may be repeated when the text is properly supposed to begin. The placement of the initial at the edge of the page, illogical from the standpoint of texting, remains functional as a means of indicating the start of a new work, a means of finding one's way through the manuscript. Of the 46 secular works, French and Italian, ascribed to Dufay in Oxford 213, 16 (one third) begin with textless melismas. Of the 26 secular works ascribed to Binchois in the same manuscript, nine (again one third) begin this way.

Another stylistic feature common in the chansons of the first quarter of the 15th century is the appearance of one or several untexted internal melismas, separated from texted phrases by rests. This characteristic is met with in fully two-thirds of the Binchois chansons in Oxford 213 and one-half of those of Dufay. Sometimes the textless melisma provides a musical balance after an essentially syllabic phrase, and sometimes it has some other function. For instance, in Dufay's canonic 'Par droit je puis' (see illus.6 and ex.1) the alternation of syllabically texted and untexted phrases allows the declamation of the text in each of the canonic voices to emerge. Dufay's intent is perfectly represented in the manuscript. Note that after the first internal melisma, a diagonal ink line clarifies the placement of the text, which had not been adequately spaced out before the music was entered above (though not easily visible in illus.6, the hairline is quite clear in the original). Incidentally, texting the two lower voices does not seem to be an option here; the manuscript presentation of the work seems to be the most compelling one musically.

Untexted opening and internal melismas are but two examples of the possibilities that went out of fashion when, following a change of style in the music, texting practices were regularized and copying techniques changed in the mid-15th century.[15] In the chanson around 1450, one phrase of text almost always corresponds to one phrase of music, which exhibits generally syllabic declamation at the beginning of a phrase, followed by a melisma on the penultimate syllable. An analysis of the melodic lines for rhythmic patterns that fit the text may suggest whether it is syllabically or melismatically treated.[16] It must be emphasized that this procedure of texting, now assigned to the realm of performance practice, was a very recent one for the new-style repertory of the 1440s. Only a few years before it had been possible to indicate the correlation of text and music largely without ambiguity. The change of style is mirrored by a fundamental change in procedures of manuscript copying.

Can we assume that the first syllable of a phrase goes with the first note, and the last syllable, whether accented or an unaccented final '-e', with the last note? Such principles may seem obvious. And yet they are not, as we have seen from the variety of procedures used a short time before. The untexted opening melismas have gone out of fashion, and I think we can indeed place the first syllable with the first note.[17] I suspect that final syllables should generally be placed at the very end of a phrase, but a closer study is needed to determine if a uniform practice is discernible, or whether the variability seen in some manuscripts is intended. In the Chantilly codex the intention seems to be that the final syllable should fall at the end of a phrase, yet in Oxford 213, this is often not the case.[18] Whether a new uniform practice had emerged by 1450 is a question that cannot yet be answered.

Finally the question of the application of text to untexted parts of a chanson can be approached. In 14th-century France the position is quite clear, for there is virtually no evidence for such alternative texting of secular works. It was possible to notate the correlation of text and music unambiguously, with scribes going to great lengths to ensure the careful texting of the cantus voice, normally the only voice that was intended to carry text.[19] The few alternative textures are explicitly notated. All the voices are of course texted in polytextual works, but the same text is normally declaimed by two voices only in canonic works in the 14th century.[20] The type of chanson first witnessed by Gacian Reyneau's rondeau in Chantilly is a new departure, a uniform three-voice texure

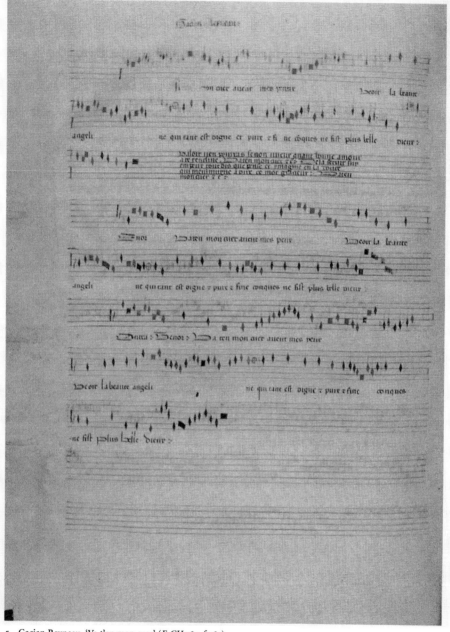

5 Gacian Reyneau, 'Va t'en mon cuer' (*F-CH* 564, f.56v)

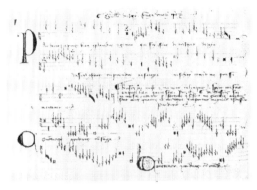

6 Dufay, 'Par droit je puis' (*GB-Ob* 213, f.18v)

ture clearly distinguishable from the layered texture—slow tenor and contratenor accompanying an active cantus—that was formerly the most usual.

It is for these reasons that the texting practice exhibited in the beautiful recordings by Gothic Voices (director Christopher Page) of 14th- and early 15th-century chansons seems to me unsatisfactory.[21] Regardless of texture, the text of the cantus is arbitrarily applied to all voices, a practice particularly annoying in older four-voice compositions, when the texting of the triplum inevitably and unfairly accentuates this subsidiary voice. The care bestowed—I believe by the composer—uniquely upon the texting of the cantus voice loses its effect.[22] If the untexted voices were intended to be texted

Ex.1 Dufay, 'Par droit je puis', ed. H. Besseler, CMM, i/6 (Rome, 1964)

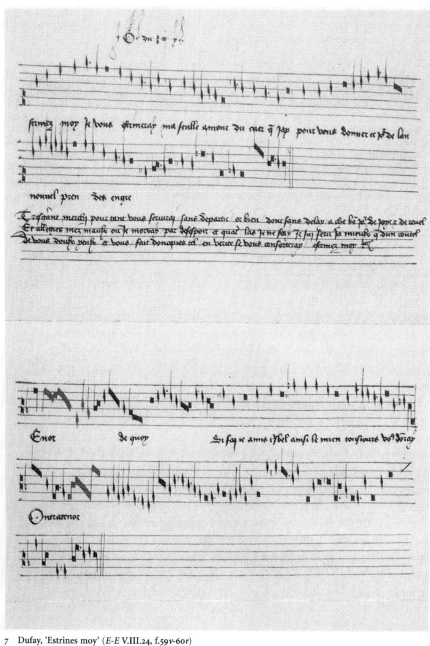

7 Dufay, 'Estrines moy' (E-E V.III.24, f.59v-60r)

in some arbitrary way, why was such care exercised in the application of the text to just a single voice? The care and effort expended by scribes in the first half of the 15th century make it unlikely that a chaotic setting of the upper voice's text to the lower voices, by breaking up ligatures, and so on, was left to performance practice.[23] When voices were to be texted, they were texted. Reyneau's 'Va t'en mon cuer', with its three voices explicitly texted in the source, is beautifully performed by Page's Gothic Voices in 'The Garden of Zephirus'.

But the clear stylistic distinction between this work and every other chanson in Chantilly should be respected in performance, just as the stylistic distinction between Dufay's 'Ce moys de may' (Besseler no.39) and 'Ce jour le doibt' (Besseler no.18) should be appreciated. Yet Page's own ground-breaking research on performance practice complements the picture given by the sources. We should begin to perform these works with voices on all lines—a scoring that Page's research shows to have been a normal one at the time—but without applying text where it was not called for. Instead, performers must experiment with vocalization of textless passages.[24]

This manner of performance makes the intention of the instances of partial texting in the sources clear.[25] Partial texting also provides some further evidence against the indiscriminate application of the full text to the other voices. Nobody puts down an instrument to sing occasional words (it has been suggested even quite recently that this was the practice), because one is already singing. Instances of isolated 'cucu's', or other fragments of text in imitation stand out in a logical way from their context. For instance, an example of partial texting that to my knowledge has gone unrecognized is provided by the imitative opening of Baude Cordier's rondeau 'Belle, bonne, sage'. The famous heart-shaped notation at the head of the Chantilly codex is extraordinarily carefully copied. The overlay of the notes of the tenor and contratenor to the opening two words calls for the partial texting of these voices. After the imitative opening gesture, the tenor and contratenor should continue by vocalizing.

Some examples of partial texting create marvellous artistic effects. For instance, in Dufay's famous dedicatory ballade of July 1423, 'Resvelliés vous' (illus.4),[26] after the typical untexted opening melisma, the tenor comes in with the first words of the text, 'Resvelliés vous' ('wake up'). But this is a playful ruse on Dufay's part, since the tenor actually serves only to awaken the cantus, which immediately responds with that text in imitation, as the tenor returns to his textless sustaining role. Later, all three voices join in the solemn intoning of the first words of the refrain, 'Charle gentil' ('noble Charles'). The addition of any more text to the lower voices would be destructive to the carefully-conceived changing textures of the work.

Another example from Dufay is the rondeau 'Estrines moy, je vous estrineray' (illus.7).[27] This work employs the normal French texture of a single texted voice over an untexted tenor and contratenor. But in the B section the tenor, representing the lady, answers the pleas of the lover. It only makes sense that this line was being vocalized all along, and that the cantus vocalizes as the tenor sings the poetic text. It is also impossible to imagine any further texting of the three voices: to do so would destroy the charming dialogue that is the point of the song.[28] Instances of partial texting should be interpreted literally.

I suspect that alternate texting is indeed a real possibility in the chansons of the latter half of the 15th century. These are works that often enjoyed a very wide circulation, susceptible to a great variety of local customs of performance.[29] It is probably no accident that the manner of copying the works is one that is faster and less prescriptive of performance options. Here we are free to experiment. Lessons drawn from earlier chansons would seem to indicate that instances of imitation were especially susceptible to texting in the accompanying voices (Busnois' 'Bel Acueil', illus.3, provides a familiar example).[30] On the other hand, if a lower voice returns to a non-imitative sustained texture, we should feel free to let it vocalize while the cantus projects the text. Other possibilities are available, clearly indicated in the chansons of a few years earlier. It is important to begin to look at the final flowering of this brilliant courtly music in terms suitable to it, and I believe that the sources themselves, if carefully examined, can provide a great number of answers.

Lawrence Earp is Associate Professor at the University of Wisconsin-Madison. He is currently finishing a book on Guillaume de Machaut (Garland).

[1] A version of this paper was read at the Twenty-Fourth International Congress on Medieval Studies at Western Michigan University (4–7 May 1989), with the title 'Alternate Textings: The Legacy of the Fourteenth Century'.

[2] The ample bibliography on text underlay in the 15th and 16th centuries is summarized in H.M. Brown, '"Lord, have mercy upon us": Early Sixteenth-Century Scribal Practice and the Polyphonic Kyrie', *Text: Transactions of the Society for Textual Scholarship*, ii (1985), pp.106-7, n.1. To the extensive bibliography in D. Harrán, *Word-Tone Relations in Musical Thought: From Antiquity to the Seventeenth Cen-*

tury, Musicological Studies and Documents, xl (1986), pp.472-89, should be added important studies by Margaret Bent, David Fallows, Frank Harrison, Christopher Page, Alejandro Planchart, Craig Wright, and most of the work of Howard Brown on this subject. The views of Margaret Bent are closest to those advocated in this article; see especially her 'Text Setting in Sacred Music of the Early 15th Century: Evidence and Implications', in U. Gunther and L. Finscher, eds., *Musik und Text in der Mehrstimmigkeit des 14. und 15. Jahrhunderts: Vorträge des Gastsymposions in der Herzog August Bibliothek Wolfenbüttel, 8. bis 12. September 1980*, Göttinger Musikwissenschaftliche Arbeiten, x (Kassel, 1984), pp.291-326.

[3]The question of text underlay in the Machaut manuscripts is treated at length in Earp, 'Scribal Practice, Manuscript Production and the Transmission of Music in Late Medieval France: The Manuscripts of Guillaume de Machaut' (PhD diss., Princeton Univ., 1983: University Microfilms International 8318466), pp.170-96 and 266-70. On diagonal lines drawn to clarify texting, see also. H. Schoop, *Entstehung und Verwendung der Handschrift Oxford Bodleian Library, Canonici misc.213*, Publikationen der schweizerischen musikforschenden Gesellschaft, Serie ii/24 (Bern and Stuttgart, 1971), pp.61-3; M. Long, 'Musical tastes in fourteenth-century Italy: notational styles, scholarly traditions, and historical circumstances' (PhD diss., Princeton Univ., 1981: University Microfilms International 8108092), pp. 168-70; J. Nádas, 'The Transmission of Trecento Secular Polyphony: Manuscript Production and Scribal Practices in Italy at the End of the Middle Ages' (PhD diss., New York Univ., 1985: University Microfilms International 8604074), p.110.

[4]For the Old Hall MS (*GB-Lbl* Add. 57950), see the example discussed by Bent in 'Text Setting in Sacred Music', *op cit*, pp.296-97. For Oxford 213 (*GB-Ob* 213), see G. Boone, 'Dufay's Early Chansons: Chronology and Style in the Manuscript Oxford, Bodleian Library, Canonici misc. 213' (PhD diss., Harvard Univ., 1987: University Microfilms International 8800749), p.6. Boone considers his example an isolated occurrence, but it may well be the scribe's normal procedure, revealed only because the work under consideration was left incomplete. The example of *I-Fn* Panc. 26 is discussed in Nádas, 'The Transmission of Trecento Secular Polyphony', *op. cit*, pp.64-9. Sometimes also the text was entered except for the final syllable, which the scribe then forgot to add after the music was copied. Examples from several manuscripts are noted in Earp, 'Scribal Practice', *op cit*, pp.258-9.

[5]T. Morley, *A Plaine and Easie Introduction to Practicall Musicke* (London, 1597), p.178, quoted in Bent, 'Text Setting in Sacred Music', *op cit*, p.302. For a modern edition, see T. Morley, *A Plain and Easy Introduction to Practical Music*, ed. R.A. Harman, (New York, 2/1963), p.291.

[6]See the comments in Bent, 'Text Setting in Sacred Music', *op cit*, p.294. The new edition of the Chantilly codex (*F-CH* 564) often interprets the manuscript text placement either too freely or too literally (G.K. Greene, ed., *French Secular Music: Manuscript Chantilly, Musée Condé 564*, 2 vols., Polyphonic Music of the Fourteenth Century, xviii-xix [Monaco, 1981-2]). The degree of accuracy of the texting in the Chantilly codex varies considerably from piece to piece, a factor that could perhaps be utilized to separate layers of transmission.

[7]Boone, 'Dufay's Early Chansons', *op cit*, has placed the final stages of the copying of Oxford 213, a manuscript with music overlay, that is, copied text first, at c.1436, while W.H. Kemp, 'The Manuscript Escorial V.III.24', *Musica Disciplina*, xxx (1976), pp.97-129, has placed the period of the copying of *EscA* (*E-E* V.III.24), a French manuscript in which only the second of the two scribes practised the new style of text underlay by copying the music first, at c.1430-45.

[8]See Nádas, 'The Transmission of Trecento Secular Polyphony', *op cit*, pp.213-4. For the practice in *Lo* (*GB-Lbl* 29987), see Long, 'Musical tastes', *op. cit.*, pp. 168-70.

[9]D. Fallows, 'Robertus de Anglia and the Oporto Song Collection', in *Source Materials and the Interpretation of Music: A Memorial Volume to Thurston Dart*, ed. I. Bent (London, 1981), p.105, reports that the Oporto manuscript (*P-Pm* 714), a Ferrarese or Bolognese source of the 1460s, displays extraordinary care in texting. Further study of this source, which is very accurately texted for a manuscript with music entered first, is called for. See facs. in H. Besseler, ed., *Guillaume Dufay, Opera omnia*, Corpus mensurabilis musicae [CMM], i/6 (Rome, 1964), p.lxxii.

[10]Two or more phrases are extended, by a few notes or by a melisma, in ballades nos.2, 6, 9, 10, 12, 14, 15, 16 (a case ambiguous in the manuscripts), 19 and 33 in F. Ludwig, ed., *Guillaume de Machaut Musikalische Werke*, vol. i (Leipzig, 1926/R1954). Only the *clos* cadence is melismatically extended in ballades 20 and 25. Less dramatic phrase extensions are seen in nos.5, 7, 8 and 18. Schrade (*The Works of Guillaume de Machaut*, Polyphonic Music of the Fourteenth Century, iii [Monaco, 1956]) removes almost all the final syllables to the final note of a phrase, whether the manuscripts show it that way or not; Ludwig's underlay more accurately reflects the sources.

[11]Of the 39 ballades in Oxford 213, 23 or 24 have the *clos* extension; 11 show some replacement music, in other words a true 'second ending'; three or four have no cadential differentiation between *ouvert* and *clos*; and Dufay's 'Se la face ay pale', no.19 in the Besseler edition, is through-composed.

[12]This practice is also seen in the Turin manuscript (*I-Tn* J.II.9): 5 of the 102 ballades, 7 of the 43 rondeaux, and 5 of the 21 virelais in this repertory have a textless opening melisma; cf. the comments in R.H. Hoppin, *The Cypriot-French Repertory of the Manuscript Torino, Biblioteca Nazionale, J.II.9*, CMM, xxi/4 (1963), p.ix.

[13]'Va t'en mon cuer' is edited by W. Apel, *French Secular Compositions of the Fourteenth Century*, CMM, liii/1 (1970), no.87 and by G. Greene, Polyphonic Music of the Fourteenth Century, xix, no.93. Reyneau was active at the Aragonese chapel from before 1398 until at least 1429, see H. Anglès, 'Gacian Reyneau am Königshof zu Barcelona in der Zeit von 139.. bis 1429', *Studien zur Musikgeschichte, Festschrift für Guido Adler am 75. Geburtstag* (Vienna, 1930 /R1971), pp.64-70. Vaillant's triple rondeau 'Tres doulz amis/Ma dame/Cent mille fois' has opening melismas in cantus 2 and tenor (misrepresented in Greene's edition, Polyphonic Music of the Fourteenth Century, xviii, no.12); perhaps the cantus 1 should also begin with a textless melisma.

[14]Nos.38 and 39 in the Besseler edition

[15]Very few pieces cross over the style boundary; some examples are Dufay's popular 'Se la face ay pale', Besseler no.19, and the anonymous 'Or me veult' (see below, n.17).

[16]Cf. D. Fallows, 'Robert Morton's songs: A Study of Styles in the Mid-Fifteenth Century' (PhD diss., Univ. of California at Berkeley, 1978: University Microfilms International 7904431), pp.3 and 22. See also the section on texting in Fallows's forthcoming edition of *Le Chansonnier de Jean de Montchenu*, the Chansonnier Cordiforme (*F-Pn* Rothschild 2973).

[17]The anonymous 'Or me veult', an old-fashioned work copied in the new manner in the Mellon chansonnier (*US-NHy* 91), f. 69v-71r, retains its opening melisma. See facs. and transcr. edited by L.L. Perkins, *The Mellon Chansonnier*, (New Haven and London, 1979), i, no.49. On the probable English origin of this work, see M. Bent, 'The songs of Dufay: some questions of form and authenticity', *EM*, viii (1980), pp.458-9.

[18]Schoop, *Entstehung und Verwendung, op cit*, pp.62-3, discusses text placement at the ends of phrases in Oxford 213. Although the scribal practice in the manuscript varies, he would have all final syllables separated and placed below the last note of the phrase. Even if his analysis is accepted, it should be emphasized that this is a feature of the style that was variable in chansons two generations earlier, and further that manuscripts of two generations earlier were explicit and reliable in their indication of it, and that Oxford 213 was copied in essentially the same manner as these earlier manuscripts.

[19]The strikingly different situation in Italy, highly variable according to the practice of individual scribes, is discussed in Nádas, 'The Transmission of Trecento Secular Polyphony', pp.110-7.

[20]V. Newes, 'The Relationship of Text to Imitative Techniques in

14th-Century Polyphony', in U. Günther and L. Finscher, eds., *Musik und Text in der Mehrstimmigkeit des 14. und 15. Jahrhunderts: Vorträge des Gastsymposions in der Herzog August Bibliothek Wolfenbüttel, 8. bis 12. September 1980*, Göttinger Musikwissenschaftliche Arbeiten, x (Kassel, 1984), p.128, discusses an interesting exceptional case.

[21]'The Mirror of Narcissus. Songs by Guillaume de Machaut (1300–1377)', Hyperion A66087 (1983); 'The Garden of Zephirus. Courtly songs of the early fifteenth century', Hyperion CDA66144 (1985); 'A Song for Francesca. Music in Italy, 1330–1430', Hyperion CDA66286 (1988)

[22]The results of the arbitrary texting of untexted voices is especially unfortunate for Machaut's 4-part ballade 'Dame de qui' and his 4-part rondeau 'Rose, lis' as performed in 'The Mirror of Narcissus'.

[23]Concerning sacred music, Margaret Bent suggests that singers may have been expected to adapt text to textless parts that included ligatures in 'New Sacred Polyphonic Fragments of the Early Quattrocento', *Studi musicali*, ix (1980), p.174–5. The scribal practice of alternative textings of early 15th-century Mass music has been discussed for the north Italian manuscripts *BL* (*I-Bc* 15) and *BU* (*I-Bu* 2216) in J. Widaman, 'Texted and Untexted Lower Voices in Early Fifteenth-Century Sources, or, A Few Words in the Defense of Scribes', a paper read at the Twenty-Fifth International Congress on Medieval Studies at Western Michigan University (10–13 May 1990).

[24]D. Fallows's review of 'The Mirror of Narcissus' in *Gramophone*, lxi (1983–4), p.898, urged vocalization of the textless parts. Vocalization of wordless passages (in this case, lower voices) was urged by F.Ll. Harrison in 'Tradition and Innovation in Instrumental Usage 1100–1450', in *Aspects of Medieval and Renaissance Music: A Birthday Offering to Gustave Reese*, ed. Jan LaRue et al (New York, 1966/R1978), pp.319–35; evidence for such a practice was adduced by C. Page, 'Machaut's "pupil" Deschamps on the performance of music: voices or instruments in the 14th-century chanson', *EM*, v (1977), pp.484–91 and 'The performance of songs in late medieval France: a new source', *EM*, x (1982), pp.441–50; C. Wright, 'Voices and Instruments in the Art Music of Northern France during the 15th Century: a Conspectus', *International Musicological Society, Congress Report Berkeley, 1977*, ed. D. Heartz and B. Wade (Kassel, 1981), pp.643–9; M. Bent, 'Text Setting in Sacred Music', *op cit*, pp.303–4; D. Fallows, 'Specific Information on the Ensembles for Composed Polyphony, 1400–1474', in *Studies in the Performance of Late Mediaeval Music*, ed. S. Boorman (Cambridge, 1983), especially pp.128–44; A.E. Planchart, 'Parts with Words and Without Words: the Evidence for Multiple Texts in Fifteenth-Century Masses', in *Studies in the Performance of Late Mediaeval Music*, ed. S. Boorman (Cambridge, 1983), pp.227–51, especially pp.231–7. For a recorded example of the kind of vocalization advocated here, cf. the 1983 performance of the pseudo-Dufay 'Je languis en piteux martire' (Besseler no.17) by the Medieval Ensemble of London, directed by Peter and Timothy Davies, in 'Mi Verry Joy: Songs of 15th-Century Englishmen', L'Oiseau-Lyre DSDL 714 (on the question of Dufay's authorship of this song, see M. Bent, 'The songs of Dufay', pp.458–9).

[25]Partial texting is discussed in G. Reaney, 'Text Underlay in Early Fifteenth-Century Musical Manuscripts', in *Essays in Musicology in Honor of Dragan Plamanec on His 70th Birthday*, ed. G. Reese and R. Snow (Pittsburgh, 1969), pp.245–51; Schoop, *Entstehung und Verwendung, op cit*, pp.87–91; M. Hasselman, 'The French Chanson in the Fourteenth Century' (PhD diss., Univ. of California at Berkeley, 1970: University Microfilms International 719830), pp.113, 147 n.1, 157ff; Newes, 'The Relationship of Text to Imitative Technique', *op cit*, pp.121–54.

[26]On the historical circumstances surrounding Dufay's famous ballade, see D. Fallows, *Dufay* (London, 1982), p.22.

[27]Besseler, no.58, which, following Oxford 213, is defective in that it lacks the partial texting in the tenor in the A section, visible in illus.7.

[28]Concerning illus.7, note that the first tenor words are under the wrong notes. This scribe, working in the more modern manner, underlays text to the previously-entered music, and such inaccuracies are typical. The example of 'Estrines moy' was also cited recently by T. McGee in 'Singing Without Text', a paper read at the Twenty-Fifth International Congress on Medieval Studies at Western Michigan University (10–13 May 1990), and concerned with a problem similar to that discussed here, but approached from 16th-century evidence of a continued practice of vocalization.

[29]For a study of later 15th-century sources that takes as its point of departure the richness and variety of the manuscript evidence, see L. Litterick, 'Performing Franco-Netherlandish secular music of the late 15th century: texted and untexted parts in the sources', *EM*, viii (1980), pp.474–85.

[30]Perkins, *The Mellon Chansonnier*, ii, p.138, sensibly suggests that all three voices of 'Bel Acueil' could be texted.

[18]

EMBELLISHMENT AND URTEXT
IN THE FIFTEENTH-CENTURY SONG REPERTORIES

by David Fallows

> When Josquin was living in Cambrai and a singer tried to add to his music *colores* or *coloratures* that he had not composed, he went into the choir and scolded him severely with everybody listening: „You idiot: Why do you add embellishment ? If I had wanted it I would have put it in myself. If you wish to improve completed compositions, make your own, but leave mine unimproved."

The famous anecdote of Josquin's fury at an over-confident singer survives only in a book published forty years after his death, in – as it happens – Basle.[1] This and Zarlino's related comments, published four years earlier,[2] may be the only clear statements against vocal embellishment from the years before 1600; apart, that is, from Guillaume de Machaut's passing and ambiguous remark in the *Voir-Dit* that Peronne should appreciate one of his songs „just as it stands, without adding or subtracting".[3]

As concerns the reliability of the Josquin anecdote, one could note that the book's compiler, Johannes Manlius, claimed to have received most of his information from Philipp Melanchthon, who had a close association both with the music publisher Georg Rhau and apparently with that most problematic of all witnesses to Josquin's life, Adrianus Petit Coclico.[4] As Helmuth Osthoff says, despite Coclico's demonstrable mendacity on several matters,

---

[1] Johannes Manlius, *Locorum communium collectanea a Johanne Manlio per multos annos, pleraque tum ex lectionibus D. Philippi Melanchthonis, tum ex aliorum doctissimorum virorum relationibus excerpta, & nuper in ordinem redacta*, Basle 1562, 542; the relevant passage is edited in Helmuth Osthoff, *Josquin Desprez*, vol. 1, Tutzing 1962, 222, with a German translation on p. 82.

[2] Gioseffo Zarlino, *Le istitutioni harmoniche*, Venice 1558, Terza parte, cap. 45 (p. 204): „Cantore . . . primieramente dee con ogni diligenza provedere nel suo cantare di proferire la modulatione in quel modo, che è stata composta dal Compositore; & non fare come fanno alcuni poco aveduti, i quali per farsi tenere più valenti & più savi de gli altri, fanno alle volte di suo capo alcune diminutioni tanto salvatiche (dirò cosi) & tanto fuori di ogni proposito, che non solo fanno fastidio a chi loro ascolta; ma commettono etiandio nel cantare mille errori." (In the widely available 1966 facsimile of the 1573 edition, it is in cap. 46, p. 239-40.) An English translation appears in Guy A. Marco and Claude V. Palisca, *Gioseffo Zarlino: The Art of Counterpoint*, New Haven 1968, 110.

[3] Paulin Paris, ed., *Le livre du Voir-Dit de Guillaume de Machaut*, Paris 1875, 69; the long-announced new edition by Paul Imbs is not yet published. The relevant passage is reprinted in Friedrich Ludwig, ed., *Guillaume de Machaut: Musikalische Werke*, vol. 2, Leipzig 1928, 55*: „Si vous suppli que vous le daigniez oÿr, et savoir la chose ainsi comme elle est faite, sans mettre ne oster."

[4] See Walter Blankenburg, „Melanchthon" in *MGG*, Victor H. Mattfeld, „Rhau, Georg" in *The New Grove*, and Marcus van Crevel, *Adrianus Petit Coclico*, The Hague 1940, passim.

there is a good case for believing that as a young boy he was indeed a pupil of Josquin.[5] Given Coclico's birth in about 1500, this can only have been at Condé, where Josquin lived from 1504 until his death in 1521. Coclico, about whose origins we know only his claim to have been Flemish, must definitely have been a choirboy somewhere, and that could well have been at Condé. It is easy enough to imagine the name of Condé being traduced to the more familiar Cambrai in the course of the story's transmission.[6] There seems a good chance, therefore, that the reminiscence reached Manlius from Coclico via Melanchthon and reflects an actual event.[7]

In any case, alongside its impied discouragement, it obviously offers evidence that some people did embellish polyphony in the sixteenth century. And there is plenty more, much of it relayed in the extensive secondary literature on the embellishment of sixteenth-century music. One of the most telling examples is Francisco Guerrero's ordinance for the instrumentalists at Seville Cathedral in 1586: he states that only one of the two players on the top line may embellish, but that when that line is resting the player on the next line down may „add all the glosses that he desires and knows so well how to execute on his instrument".[8] Evidently Guerrero was happy with embellishments from the instrumentalists, while the singers presumably sang the notes unadorned, but merely wanted them kept within certain bounds.

Most musicians today appear to have a deeply ambivalent attitude to embellishment. Whatever they may say in seminars and articles, they are noticeably reticent in practice. It is extremely uncommon to find performances or recordings that introduce embellishment as a matter of course – as

---

[5] op. cit., 83f. See also Adrianus Petit Coclico, *Compendium musices*, Nuremberg 1552, fol. B3: „Puer admodum tradebar in fidem nobilissimi Musici Josquini, ex quo cum levia illa artis nostrae praecepta, obiter tantum, nullo ex libro percepissem."

[6] The likelihood that Josquin ever lived in Cambrai seems minimal, even though it has recently become clear that we know considerably less about his life than was once thought, see Joshua Rifkin, „A Singer named Josquin and Josquin d'Ascanio: some problems in the biography of Josquin des Prez", forthcoming in *JRMA* and kindly shown to me by the author in advance of publication. I would reject the other conceivable corruption, namely that the city was indeed Cambrai but that the composer was in fact Dufay. It would have been much harder for Manlius to have access to an anecdote about Dufay. Moreover, as Osthoff argues, op. cit., 82, there is indirect confirmation from Glareanus of the next reminiscence in Manlius's book, which tells how Josquin made a practice of listening carefully to the choir as it tried out a new work of his and then telling them to stop so he could make changes.

[7] That Coclico, op. cit., fol. H3v, describes how to train a young singer in simple embellishments is no real contradiction of this hypothesis, since there is plenty of evidence that all choirboys were taught to embellish – though it could well explain why our story does not appear in Coclico's book.

[8] For an English translation of the entire ordinance, see Robert Stevenson, *Spanish cathedral music of the golden age*, Berkeley and Los Angeles 1961, 167. The original Spanish is in Robert Stevenson, *La música en la Catedral de Sevilla: documentos para su estudio*, 2nd edition, Madrid 1985, 72.

opposed to the occasional demonstrations that follow note-for-note the written decorative versions of the late sixteenth-century instruction books. Even in the simplest homophonic dance music of a Susato or a Praetorius, decoration these days is apt to be restrained and thin on the ground, in fact rather more so than it was thirty years ago.

A more surprising case is in performances of the English lute and keyboard music of the Elizabethan-Jacobean era. Here the sources are littered with ornaments of apparently good authority, but you rarely hear a performance that is not fairly selective in observing them.

That is not meant as an accusation. It merely underlines that ambivalent attitude. It draws attention to a current set of assumptions about Renaissance music and why people bother to perform it. Thirty years ago the music was in some ways primarily a vehicle for a colourful array of instruments. Embellishment was rife. In recent years, however, musicians have tended to move away from what is now sometimes called the toy-box mentality, partly because they became uneasily aware that these performances made one piece of music sound remarkably similar to any other. It is difficult enough at the best of times to distinguish the style of Josquin from that of Mouton, but it is infinitely more difficult if everything is covered with a mist of embellishment. The need to distinguish one work from another goes hand in hand with a feeling that the performance is wasted if it is not of top-flight music: the quality of the music is the mandate for the effort put into reproducing it.

The prejudice can be stated over-simply as follows: the better the music, the more damage is done to it by embellishment. Many people would probably prefer to reformulate that as: the more *sophisticated* the music, the more damage is done to it by embellishment. In simple homophony it can do little harm, but in complex or imitative polyphony it is a menace.[9] This is a prejudice that I share with many others, including probably most readers of this article and – if we believe the story – Josquin. Even so, comments like that in Guerrero's ordinance appear to suggest that – at least in Seville Cathedral – instrumental embellishment was normal in polyphony of some complexity, since his reference to passages where the top voice rests implies imitation of some kind. Fifteen years ago Howard Mayer Brown approached the problem by stating that many sixteenth-century elaborations were made in the worst of taste and remarking that bad taste should not be considered a prerogative of the twentieth century.[10] Yet his comment needs to be seen in the context of the early 1970s, when there was a tendency among historians to try to pretend that the issue did not exist.

---

[9] That view is in fact relayed in Juan Bermudo, *Declaración de instrumentos musicales*, Osuna 1555, fol. 29v (for vihuela music) and fol. 84v (for keyboard music).
[10] Howard Mayer Brown, *Embellishing sixteenth-century music*, London 1976, 73.

But it cannot be ignored. From the fifteenth century we have two massive sources of elaborated keyboard intabulations: the Italian Faenza codex, perhaps from the 1420s,[11] and the even larger German Buxheim manuscript from around 1460.[12] These, along with a handful of smaller tablature sources, offer plenty of evidence that the music was often decorated, at least when played on keyboard instruments; and they offer hints about possible embellishment in other circumstances. It is time to try again to broach the question of when and why, to try to see what can usefully be learned from the available sources.

*

Example 1 shows a song by Binchois that happens to survive in two different forms, one more florid than the other. Many other examples could be given. Several Italian trecento songs appear in two differently embellished versions, most famously Jacopo da Bologna's *Non al suo amante*; but the investigation here concerns the fifteenth century. There is also the mid-fifteenth-century song *Aime sospiri* which recurs in a heavily decorated form in one of the Petrucci frottola books;[13] here the chronological gap of fifty years between the two versions makes it hard to use as evidence of what the performer did or was expected to do when the song was first composed. But the Binchois song offers precious evidence, because the two versions were copied within about ten years of one another: the more florid version is in two sources copied late in the 1430s; the simpler version appears to be a decade or so earlier, to judge from its notation and its one surviving manuscript.[14] The version that

---

[11] Faenza, Biblioteca Comunale, Ms. 117; ed. in Dragan Plamenac, *Keyboard music of the late middle ages in Codex Faenza 117* = Corpus Mensurabilis Musicae, ser. 57, American Institute of Musicology 1972.

[12] München, Bayerische Staatsbibliothek, Mus. ms. 3725; ed. in Bertha Antonia Wallner, *Das Buxheimer Orgelbuch*, Kassel 1958-59 (Das Erbe Deutscher Musik, vols. 37-39).

[13] Walter H. Rubsamen, „The Justiniane or Viniziane of the 15th century", AMl 29 (1957) 172-84.

[14] The earlier source, given in ex. 1 as „Rei", is the final layer of the Reina Codex (Paris, Bibliothèque nationale, Ms. nouv. acq. fr. 6771, fol. 96v), a group of songs possibly copied around 1430; this group is edited complete in Nigel E. Wilkins, *A 15th-century repertory from the Codex Reina*, = Corpus Mensurabilis Musicae, ser. 37, American Institute of Musicology 1966. The later, „Ox", is in the first fascicle of that famous manuscript (Oxford, Bodleian Library, Ms. Canonici Misc. 213, fols. 9v-10) and probably written in about 1435.

provides the main text in example 1 is in the Reina codex and is in major prolation (with note-values quartered in the example). The florid version, taken from the Oxford Canonici manuscript, is in doubled note-values, that is, in perfect time with minor prolation; to make the two comparable, the notes are reduced to an eighth of their original value here. It is worth superimposing the versions, because the two separate transcriptions offered by Wolfgang Rehm in his edition of the Binchois songs rather disguise the simplicity of the relationship between them.[15] Moreover, aligning them demonstrates that all the sources contain a fair number of errors which can easily be eliminated.

Here and in the other examples I have taken several steps to prune down the information to what is strictly relevant for this inquiry. Not only are source errors quietly corrected (and there is obviously a certain subjectivity in that); ligature signs are also omitted, as are most accidentals and their variants. That is not to say that these matters are uninteresting or unproblematic; merely that their relevance to this topic is minimal. More controversially, texts are omitted: they may be directly relevant in some ways,[16] but they give rise to so many additional questions that they seemed better left out of the equation.

The example shows that the lower voices remain virtually the same in the two versions except at one point, in bar 17. New decoration is confined to the discantus. By and large this is a general pattern and fits curiously well with Guerrero's instructions to his instrumentalists. It is also the case in the Faenza intabulations and in all but the most heavily decorated of those in the Buxheim manuscript.

Both sources were written in the Veneto, which is to say some considerable distance from the Paris-Brussels axis in which Binchois appears to have spent these years. The other source of the later version, „Esc" (El Escorial, Biblioteca y Archivo de Música, Ms. V. III. 24, fol. 47), contains only the song's tenor: the facing page, which would have contained the discantus, is now lost; more puzzlingly, the contratenor is not added, even though the word „Contratenor" is entered below the first of two empty staves after the surviving tenor.

[15] Wolfgang Rehm, ed., *Die Chansons von Gilles Binchois (1400-1460)* Mainz 1957 = Musikalische Denkmäler, vol. 2, nos. 17 and 17a.

[16] Michael Morrow, who has given me the benefit of his views on this and much else over a period of some twenty-five years, believes that many of the embellishments in Buxheim can be used to derive hints about the correct alignment of text. But that would be hard to demonstrate clearly before there is a far fuller analysis of the various procedures and layers of activity concealed behind the blandly uniform script of the Buxheim manuscript.

Example 1: **Jamais tant** Binchois

In that context it is relevant that there is just one moment where embellishment of the discantus is entirely avoided, namely in bars 14-15 where there is unison imitation of all three voices. Two possible reasons can be offered. First, that any decoration in the discantus would need to be matched in the lower voices; and if that is the case it emphasises the pattern of avoiding embellishment in the tenor and contratenor. That in its turn may even be taken to suggest that embellishment is to be avoided in all imitative material of this kind. The other explanation could be the obvious musical one that the way the three lines circulate round a triad on middle-C, as so often happens in songs of this era, would be ruined by any embellishment. Apart from anything else, passages of this kind require particular care in balance, tone colour and phrasing; repeatedly in this repertory they present a moment of contrapuntal stillness that would be severely threatened by decoration.

For most of the discantus line the embellishment is of an extremely simple kind that anyone familiar with the repertory could easily have added. Bars 11 to 13 give the basic principles. At the beginning of bar 11 the two semiquavers

65

bridge the gap of a third, the next added note bridges a falling leap of a third, and the last note in the bar provides an anticipation of the next note. In the next bar the opening pattern simply fleshes out the cadence with a standard pattern. At the end of bar 12 there is something slightly more complex, a dip down to the *A*, evidently made necessary by the need to avoid interruption of the florid pattern at that point. The embellishments in bar 13 are equally simple and more or less inevitable in the context. Much of the rest can be seen in the same way.

Before examining the more difficult passages in *Jamais tant* and asking some of the questions the piece poses, it is worth turning to an entirely different document, shown in figure 1, a sheet of embellishment patterns in the British Library, Ms. Add. 70516, fol. 79.[17]

It contains a series of three-note tenors, each followed by four appropriate discantus patterns of increasing complexity, see example 2. No other document from the fifteenth century presents the material in quite this way. The German keyboard *fundamenta* in the Lochamer Liederbuch volume and in the Buxheim manuscript give similar kinds of information; so, reaching back to the 1320s, does the theory treatise of Petrus Dictus de Palma Ociosa, though that would appear to be an instruction book for composers, not performers.[18] But none of these presents a series of different patterns over the same tenor. None, in short, is quite so methodical. In fact there may be nothing comparable until Coclico (1552), Diego Ortiz (1553) and the Italian diminution manuals of the late sixteenth century.

---

[17] Its dimension are ca. 255 mm across and 216 mm up the right hand edge. This is an isolated leaf presumably taken from a binding in the Duke of Portland's collection, formerly at Welbeck Abbey. In 1947 the collection was deposited in the British Library (then the British Museum) as Loan 29, and this volume (devoted to early binding fragments) had the call-number Loan 29/333, under which the leaf is reported in Pamela J. Willetts, *[The British Museum:] Handlist of music manuscripts acquired 1908-67*, London 1970, 79. The collection became the British Library's property only in May 1987 and was subsequently given its present call-number. I am most grateful to Mr Francis Needham, formerly the Duke of Portland's librarian, for permission to photograph this leaf, to Dr. C. J. Wright of the British Library for assigning a foliation to the formerly unnumbered leaf, and to the British Library for permission to publish it. Additionally, I must thank Margaret Bent for checking and annotating my transcription at a time when I was many miles distant from London.

[18] This important and still undervalued treatise is edited from its only known source in Johannes Wolf, „Ein Beitrag zur Diskantlehre des 14. Jahrhunderts", *SIMG* 15 (1913-1914) 504-534.

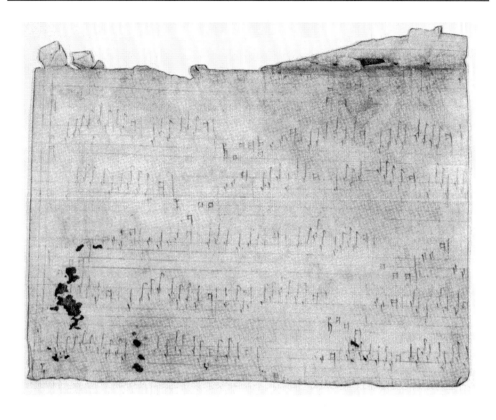

Figure 1: London, British Library, Ms. Add. 70516, fol. 79. By permission of the British Library

Example 2:

The London leaf is hard to date. It is of parchment (and, incidentally, written on only the flesh side: the hair side, though prepared, is entirely blank). The writing is evidently hurried, though comparable with some of the void notation material at the end of the Lochamer Liederbuch volume.[19] But it is written entirely in major prolation, which went out of use for normal purposes soon after 1430.[20] In this context it is eloquent that the florid version of Binchois' *Jamais tant*, as written in the late 1430s, is renotated in perfect *tempus* even though it contains nothing that is more complicated than the patterns on the London leaf. And it seems reasonable to suggest that the leaf may date from the first quarter of the fifteenth century.

To judge from its dimensions, we now have only the lower half of the sheet, which would originally have been around 38 by 28 centimeters in size with perhaps twelve staves on the page. With staves just over 20 millimeters deep, it would have been rather similar in size to the Chantilly codex or the Turin French-Cypriot manuscript, though it is obviously written in a much rougher hand.

Many details among these patterns are instantly familiar from the florid version of the Binchois. But it is fairly clear that this cannot be taken as direct evidence about the embellishment of the song literature. A glance at the tenor patterns and the two-voice counterpoint of the simplest versions shows very little that is appropriate to song performance. Only three of the eight tenors here actually descend to their final resolution on the octave – which is the almost invariable practice in the surviving secular polyphony. The remaining tenor patterns have extremely few cognates in the song repertory. Moreover there is an important clue in the fact that the tenors are presented in apparently indiscriminate *brevis* and *longa* values (which are difficult to transcribe in modern terms) whereas the corresponding values in the discantus lines are of a perfect *semibrevis*. This would suggest that the sheet is a demonstration of how to improvise over a chant tenor. There is in fact a series of early fifteenth-century fragments at Bourges, discovered and soon to be described by Paula Higgins, which includes extended workings laid out in precisely this way.[21] There the chants use the square notation current at the time; and the discantus lines are in major prolation with – precisely as in the London leaf – one perfect *semibrevis* for each note of the chant. Predictably, the three-note units of the London leaf tenors appear often in the Bourges fragments.

---

[19] Berlin, Staatsbibliothek Preussischer Kulturbesitz, Ms. Mus. 40613, p.88-92.
[20] Heinrich Besseler, *Bourdon und Fauxbourdon: Studien zum Ursprung der niederländischen Musik*, Leipzig 1950, revised version ed. Peter Gülke, Leipzig 1974, chapter VII; Charles E. Hamm, *A chronology of the works of Guillaume Dufay based on a study of mensural practice*, Princeton 1964.
[21] I am most grateful to Professor Higgins for having shared them with me prior to their formal publication.

But the London leaf is nevertheless relevant to a consideration of the song repertory for several reasons. It is a reminder, first of all, that most singers and composers in the fifteenth century (and later) were trained to improvise against a tenor with various degrees of diminution; so, apparently, were instrumentalists. The London leaf is the first clear evidence of the various ways in which they did so. And it is most particularly evidence of the kinds of variety that could be introduced. Until the last years of the fifteenth century, the singers of secular polyphony seem to have been almost invariably men or boys trained in the choirschools. This was their musical bread-and-butter. The leaf shows, in fact, that many of the differences between the two versions of *Jamais tant* were almost automatic for these musicians.

*

Returning now to the florid version of *Jamais tant*, it is time to make a few more observations about the two versions and ask some of the necessary questions.

First, it should be noted that the later version is no mere embellishment of the earlier, but in several respects actually a recomposition. There are places where the florid line changes the essential shape of the melody and improves it substantially. One could look, for example, at bars 8-9. In Reina the last two notes of the discantus in bar 8, the *A* and *F*, are both dissonant; bar 9 opens with parallel fifths between discantus and contratenor, followed by a leap from the *D* up a third to the dissonant *F*. Now none of these apparent anomalies is untypical of Binchois: part of the distinctive charm in his work is the way he can include unusual contrapuntal turns that succeed because of the music's linear grace and harmonic clarity. On the other hand, the new florid line is, contrapuntally speaking, infinitely stronger, quite apart from the success with which its fall from the high *C* reflects and resolves the fall in bar 7 from the high *D*.

Another case is in bar 17. Here the florid version has a substantial change in its inclusion of the high *F*, a note that does not appear in the simple version but occurs once earlier in the florid version, thus perhaps requiring its restatement before the final resolution of the piece. To include that note here, the reviser has added a rest – thereby establishing a parallelism between bars 16-17 and bars 1-2 (where a rest is also added). And by eliminating the falling triadic figure in bar 17 he has made it possible to replace a somewhat ugly version of the two lower voices with something that is undeniably stronger.

Or at least, it is contrapuntally more convincing, though one can easily see the attractions of the simpler version, in which both discantus and contratenor at this point echo the triadic figure already mentioned as one of the most delicate moments in the song. Perhaps it is also easy to see, however, that this was an idea that the composer could afford to lose, in view of the considerably improved strength of the climax thereby created in the rewriting of this passage.

That last sentence, of course, lets the cat out of the bag. It is very hard to resist the feeling that the more florid version of *Jamais tant* was by the composer himself, and a considered revision. It seems impossible to credit the changes in bar 17 to another hand. Or, to rephrase that, the adaptation of *Jamais tant* as a more floridly written song is so brilliantly done and so fundamental in several respects that it is difficult to imagine a lesser figure having the courage to attempt it on a work by one of the major composers of the age.

There are also changes that improve the counterpoint. At the very end of bar 18 the downwards move in the florid line may be primarily intended to continue and complete the grand fall of a tenth from the high F; and it may also work towards resolving the low C in bar 15 – that is, by including intermediate steps that help it to resolve towards the concluding G. But on a much more elementary level this change once again eliminates the parallel fifths between discantus and contratenor – again something that is not rare in Binchois' early works, but may well have seemed worth rewriting at a later stage.

Without wishing to prolong the detailed comparison of these two versions unduly, it is worth noticing two further points that suggest considerable refinement on the part of the rewriter. In the original, bar 11 of the discantus echoes bars 7-8 – a neat little idea that is common to the songwriters of the time, opening the *secunda pars* with material that takes off from what has just happened. In the more florid revision that echo is retained precisely. On the other hand, the discantus echo between bars 5 and 6 is now rejected. Or at least it is turned into something that still works around the same notes, and still has a hint of repetition, but turns the end of the phrase into something considerably more glorious and ambitious. And it is here that he introduces the high F that paves the way for the even more impressively treated high F mentioned earlier, the one in bar 17.

In any case, this all suggests that the rewriter was almost certainly Binchois himself. That may not initially have seemed the most likely conclusion, but in retrospect it is surely unavoidable; and it actually fits in well with other indirect evidence that Binchois had a hand in variants between the sources of some of his other works – albeit none of them quite so fundamental as in the case of *Jamais tant*. Given that a composer like Binchois is likely to have copied out little songs of this kind several times, it is easy enough to imagine him, some time after 1430, using one such occasion as an opportunity to transfer *Jamais tant* into the more current *tempus perfectum* notation: the contratenor contains many details that look fussy in the old *prolatio* notation. As he did so, he helped the discantus line to flow more easily by adding a few decorative details and at the same time tidied up a few patches that now seemed to him in want of adjustment.

This all obviously raises two questions that are interrelated. The first question may be impossible to answer but still needs asking. Namely, to what extent are the two versions to be performed at the same tempo ? Is it likely that the minima of *prolatio* notation in the 1420s is roughly equal to the semibrevis of *tempus perfectum* in the mid-1430s (assuming that to be the correct mensuration sign)? [22] Cutting a very long story short, there is evidence for several different conclusions. But the related question is more directly relevant to this inquiry. How far do the embellishments of the florid version in fact reflect performance practice of the time? That is, putting aside the places where the musical substance was actually recomposed, can the remaining patterns – found also in the London leaf – be applied to other songs of the time?

A first reaction to both questions is obviously that the innocent twentieth-century ear is inclined to hear the two versions as two entirely different pieces. That is how I viewed them when I first considered the song seriously, some fifteen years ago. But repeated absorption of this repertory over the intervening years has rather changed my mind. I now believe that major prolation music of that generation is usually performed rather too quickly. In fact it seems to me musically likely that the two versions would have had approximately the same speed and that this offers more general clues to the speed of the major prolation repertory. Along with that goes the related belief that these variants need to be taken to suggest an appropriate articulation for music of this kind. Just as keyboard players have learned to modify their articulation of slightly later music in the light of the knowledge that music was conceived indiscriminately for organ, harpsichord or lute, a performer of this song may do well to sing each version in a manner that minimises its differences from the other version.

Most of the smaller decorations in the discantus line prompt fundamental questions about the nature of embellishment.[23] There are many things a singer can do to vary a line without departing literally from the written notes. So much can be done by bending rhythms a little, by varieties of articulation, by degrees of portamento, by different gradations of tone colour and dynamics in the move from one pitch to the next, even by bending pitches – all of which can be virtually unconscious parts of a singer's art and are rarely notated. From that point of view, many of the differences between these two forms of Binchois' song may be almost academic.

---

[22] Neither of the perfect time sources has a mensuration sign; and there must always be a suspicion in such cases that the correct mensuration may be not *tempus perfectum* but *tempus perfectum diminutum*, which, by a more literal interpretation of some mensural theory, would result in a more exact equivalence of tempo between the two versions of this piece.

[23] Many of the ideas in this and the next paragraph, which represent the core of my argument, arose in the course of a discussion with Robin Hayward, at the time a second-year undergraduate in the Manchester University Music Department.

Moreover, in the course of a full rondeau performance the *prima pars* of the music will be heard five times. Most singers will introduce a certain amount of variety in any case. Perhaps this was the normal approach. The trouble with taking a literal paper view of the written variants is that it raises the question of what happens to the singer who begins with the Oxford manuscript, that is, with the more florid version. Is the singer then to add further embellishments to those already written ? (Or, to turn back to one of Arnold Schering's unfashionable but fascinating ideas, perhaps the singer in fact began with something rather simpler than the written notes, incorporating the fuller version – or allowing an instrumentalist to do so – as the song progressed.)[24] These are questions that tend to evaporate once the matter of embellishment is viewed in a less literal way and considered merely as a hint at some different kinds of articulation.

*

Plainly the question of *Urtext* raises its head here. It is has been debated many times in the past but needs to be reconsidered for fifteenth-century music. In the case of nineteenth-century music, the word *Urtext* was first used merely to denote an edition that returned to the original sources and refrained from the editorial additions and changes that had once been thought part of the editor's task. Yet it soon became clear that the notion of an „original" text was in most cases extremely misleading, not to say naive. Composers rarely left a work untouched after its first drafting; pieces often remained „work in progress" until the composer's death. For many nineteenth-century works, especially operas, it is now customary to accept several different versions of the work as equally „authentic", merely representing the composer's view of it at a particular stage in his life.

With medieval music the problem is far more difficult, mainly because we are dealing with an era in which aural transmission was as important as written. In literature, as in music, the sources are filled with errors that are most easily understood if we accept that the ear played a rather stronger role than the eye in the preparation of manuscripts. It was an age when literacy was still fairly rare (and in any case quite different from our own), an age in which even the most erudite retained the habits of listening and memory formed by centuries of unwritten culture.

---

[24] See, for example, Arnold Schering, *Studien zur Musikgeschichte der Frührenaissance,* Leipzig 1914, 70-81.

That is why, in the case of *Jamais tant*, it was necessary to separate two distinct features of the differences between the two surviving versions: actual recomposition of the work's substance; and the addition of florid elements. It is also why it is necessary to consider how far the fifteenth-century song repertory has a fixed text, and how far it must be thought subject to the freedoms that accompany the notion of an aural culture. Obviously, if it is really a mainly aural repertory without established texts, that could imply that the performer has a certain implicit invitation (or even an obligation) to decorate at will.[25]

Several early fifteenth-century works come to us in radically different versions. One particularly intriguing case is the anonymous rondeau *Une fois avant que morir*, which survives in two staff-notation versions that are radically different from one another, as well as a dozen copies, either incomplete or in tablature, which suggest that it circulated in several other discrete versions.[26] This is one of many songs with an apparently fluid identity, a song that hovers on the borderline between written and aural transmission.

Other works plainly did not, however. From the main body of the fifteenth century there is a very large number of songs that offer clear evidence of having had – in certain respects – a considered and definitive *Urtext*.

A case in point might be Dufay's rondeau *Le serviteur hault guerdonné*, which survives in fourteen staff-notation sources and is therefore the most widely distributed polyphonic song prior to the astonishing success of *De tous biens plaine*. *Le serviteur* was composed in the 1450s, and its sources come from various parts of France and Italy over the next forty years.

---

[25] See Howard Mayer Brown, „Improvised ornamentation in the fifteenth-century chanson", *Quadrivium* 12 (1971) 238-58. To a certain extent the argument that follows is an attempt to modify that view.

[26] This rondeau survives in a two-voice version in Paris, Bibliothèque nationale, Ms. nouv. acq. fr. 10660, fol. 47, and in a rather different three-voice version in London, British Library, Ms. Cotton Titus A.xxvi, fols. 4v-5; the tenor alone, in yet another version, appears in the Rostocker Liederbuch, fol. 22v (no. 23), see the edition and facsimile in F. Ranke and J. M. Müller-Blattau, eds. *Das Rostocker Liederbuch*, expanded reprint, Kassel 1987. To the nine intabulations in the Buxheim manuscript and the one in the Lochamer Liederbuch can now be added the incomplete intabulation in München, Bayerische Staatsbibliothek, clm 29775/6, fol. 1v, described (with facsimile) in Martin Staehelin, „Münchner Fragmente mit mehrstimmiger Musik des späten Mittelalters", *Nachrichten der Akademie der Wissenschaften in Göttingen: I. philologisch-historische Klasse* Jahrgang 1988, no. 6.

The main text in example 3 comes, bar one correction, from the Oporto Ms. 714, copied probably in Ferrara soon after 1460. The variants noted above and below ignore the differences in key-signature and accidentals, of which there are several, and they silently correct the fair number of obvious mistakes in the sources.[27] But they omit nothing in the way of decoration or essential musical differences apart from a wildly confusing passage in the Pavia manuscript at the end of the Contratenor. (Incidentally, it is a curious reflection on copying habits that very much the majority of source errors and of incomprehensible variants tend to come at the end of contratenor lines, at the point where the copyist's concentration evidently falls off.)

A casual glance at the sources rather tends to give the impression that there is an enormous variety of readings, particularly at cadences. But a diagram like this, once critically evaluated, tends to simplify the pattern enormously. If *Le serviteur* is a slightly special case in the consistency of its various readings, the results of an investigation of this kind are clear enough. They really do seem to confirm the view that many of the variants in other songs could stem from the composer but that Dufay at this stage in his life was inclined to regard a work as finished once it had been composed. After all, this work contains many details that copyists could, in a casual world, have been inclined to alter.

---

[27] Main source: Porto, Biblioteca Pública Municipal, Ms. 714, fols. 64v-65. Abbreviations used for the variants are mostly those found in the complete edition, Heinrich Besseler, ed., *Guillaume Dufay: cantiones* = Corpus Mensurabilis Musicae, ser. 1, vol. 6 (Rome, 1964), no. 92. Two sources are overlooked there: CG = Biblioteca Apostolica Vaticana, Ms. Cappella Giulia XIII. 27, fols. 77v-78; and Pix = Paris, Bibliothèque nationale, Ms. f. fr. 15123 (Chansonnier Pixérécourt), fols. 92v-93. In writing a new commentary for a revised and corrected reprint of Besseler's volume (in press), I have tried to categorise the source variants so that the apparent scribal slips, the ligature variants, the accidentals, and the actual different musical readings appear separately. There are no musical variants from Porto in two of the sources (BlnK and EscB). Perhaps I should add in passing that I find no virtue in Besseler's widely shared view that *Le serviteur* cannot be by Dufay; some reasons for accepting the song as authentic are stated in the new commentary to his edition.

Example 3: **Le Serviteur**

Dufay

1. There are many extremely simple sections in long notes which could have been subdivided; but the only variants here are in bars 20-21 where two manuscripts divide up notes in the tenor and two others divide a note in the contratenor, and in bars 5 and 7 where just one manuscript divides a note.

2. There are several intricate rhythms, such as the one in the last bar, followed identically by thirteen of the fourteen sources.

3. There are places where people may have wished to embellish a cadence, such as the peak in bar 28-29, where only the very late Chansonnier Pixérécourt has a variant that could have seemed more or less obvious to any reader or copyist: I imagine that its plain shape may have seemed important as echoing a similar shape at bar 11-12, a fourth lower but with similar counterpoints and a similar musical context. That kind of balancing is repeatedly important especially in Dufay's mature music.

4. There are also points where, on the principle of the Binchois *Jamais tant*, a copyist could have bridged a third or added an anticipation; but there are astonishingly few where any of the fourteen copyists involved here did so. In bar 7 just the Pavia manuscript adds one such in the discantus and one in the contratenor; in bar 8 just the Riccardiana manuscript does so in the contratenor; in bar 18 just the Seville manuscript bridges a gap; and in bar 20 two manuscripts do so.

5. Note values shortened to include a rest appear but they are few, very few, as in bar 9, tenor (leaving a nasty unsupported 4th, therefore presumably an error) and contratenor. A variant like that in the tenor at bar 6 must surely go back to scribal negligence. In the contratenor at bar 2 there are two variant readings, in one source each; and those do of course count as true embellishments. As for the three places where even quavers are replaced by dotted rhythms, all three must surely be scribal slips: the one in a single source at bar 11 contradicts the direct imitation in a passage that has three voices winding around a triadic figure, like the one in *Jamais tant* and many other songs, but more unusually based on G rather than C; the ones at bar 23 (one source for the tenor and two others for the discantus) are perhaps not so easily dismissed, since there are occasional hints of written-out *inégalité* elsewhere in the song repertory, but it is all the same difficult to take them seriously as alternative readings.

Actual variants, therefore, are confined to the cadential approaches in bar 8 and bar 14. These are obviously of the kind that look random and seem to support the case for free embellishment at such places. Equally, however, the bald figures tend to support the main text here – that is, at bar 8, eight sources as against two with one reading and four with another, and, at bar 14, six sources as against four with one reading, three with another and a single further version. But the search for musical reasons in support of that reading is always tempting and occasionally invigorating.

Starting with the second half of bar 8, it is easy to see that the main reading is unusual within the style, the kind of thing an unaware scribe would be tempted to change in precisely the ways found in the two variants, and the kind of thing that an editor ought to be inclined to accept on the principle of *difficilior lectio praestat*. I believe it is also relatively easy to agree that Dufay would prefer simple quavers here so as to let through the contratenor line, wlth its neat little 6/16 figure: the dotted figure in Cordiforme and Riccardiana simply confuses the texture; and the simpler crotchet in four other sources draws attention to itself by virtue of the suspension created. The majority version here has no dissonance until the final semiquaver. In bars 5-6, the earlier use of a 6/16 figure in the contratenor has similar rhythmic support, similarly dissonance-free.

If three quavers are the correct reading here, it seems necessary to have the two semiquavers on the previous note rather than the single quaver of four variant sources, because the anticipation of the *C* would put a stress on the second *C*, therefore encouraging performance of these last notes as a 3/8 group to support the 6/16 in the contratenor.

Turning to bar 14, the main point is of course that the majority version matches the final cadence of the piece in bar 32. It is less easy to offer purely musical reasons for rejecting the other three versions; that is to say, they would be so tentative as to be easily contradictable – after all, one could just as well argue that in bar 8 the reading in Perugia and Seville is the best in that it pre-echoes the imitated passage of bars 24-26.

But this discussion of the remarkably few visible variants among the large number of sources for *Le serviteur* has two main aims. The first is to suggest that the variants leave an almost unanswerable case for there really being an *Urtext* of this song. It concerns only the written notes, of course. Any decision about a „correct" reading for the accidentals, the ligatures and most particularly the text-underlay would be far harder to support in this way; and it is easy to agree with the growing number of musicologists who believe that those features of much music from the second half of the fifteenth century were indeed considered „accidental" by the composers of the time.[28] Particularly in that context, the relative fixity of the written notes is impressive.

Of course the second aim was to point, however sketchily, to a few of the ways in which every detail of this astonishing work is important. To start embellishing it seems almost sacrilege – which is of course the position from which we began, though the case here is based rather more on musical logic.

*

---

[28] For some of the considerations, as derived from probably autograph or near-autograph sources, see Joshua Rifkin, „Pietrequin Bonnel and Ms. 2794 of the Biblioteca Riccardiana", *JAMS* 29 (1976) 284-96, and Barton Hudson, „On the texting of Obrecht's Masses", *MD* 42 (1988) 101-27.

It is now time to turn to that most contentious of all fifteenth-century embellishment sources, the Buxheim keyboard manuscript. This extremely complicated source contains many different kinds of intabulation. Some are entirely undecorated, merely transferring into tablature the notes of the staff-notation version. Others bury the original discantus line under a welter of brilliant runs and flurries that are relevant to the performance of these songs on a keyboard instrument – or indeed any other instrumental ensemble, *mutatis mutandis* – but give no information that is likely to be relevant to how the songs were performed by vocalists. But there is an important middle category, with relatively sparse embellishment. It may well contain some of the clues about vocal embellishment that are so signally lacking elsewhere.

Another mature Dufay song can illustrate this. *Par le regard de vos beaux yeux* has twelve staff-notation sources and one for the contratenor line only. Among Dufay's songs, it is second only to *Le serviteur* in its wide source distribution. As with *Le serviteur*, the large number of sources makes it particularly suitable for this kind of inquiry.

Example 4 is rather more complicated than the other musical examples and may take a few moments to unpick. It again shows all the essential variants in the staff-notation sources. There are slightly more of these than in *Le serviteur*. But the diagram looks full because it seemed worth adding all details of the two Buxheim settings, including the surprisingly few differences in their intabulation of the lower voices.[29]

Example 4:   **Par le regard**   Dufay

[29] Again the main source is Porto, Biblioteca Pública Municipal, Ms. 714, fols. 61v-62. To the sources listed by Besseler (see note 27), no. 73, should be added Mü = München, Bayerische Staatsbibliothek, Mus. Ms. 9659, fols. 2v-3.

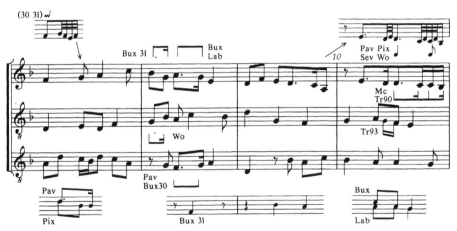

It shows that the two Buxheim settings are in fact almost identical – perplexingly enough. The line above the main discantus line represents the versions in both Buxheim no. 30 and no. 31 except where it is annotated with one of those numbers; where there is nothing on that line the Buxheim version is unadorned. The only real differences between the two are in bars 2-4; and these differences are, in all conscience, extremely slight. Later in the song there are two places where one Buxheim setting has embellishments while the other simply follows the undecorated form of the line.

A few points should be made about the staff-notation versions. Bar 1 is particularly interesting when seen after *Le serviteur*. In general it seems wise to view the division or tying of notes in fifteenth-century music as inessential. Notes are often divided to help the application of text, for example; there are innumerable cases similar to bar 1 of *Par le regard* and many later points in the song (though the larger number of sources in *Par le regard* makes the picture here more elaborate). Apparently these differences were perceived as having virtually no impact on the way the music was heard. That of course is another feature that may be directly relevant to how one should articulate the music.

The other variants are slightly more numerous than in *Le serviteur*, but not enormously so except in the sense that it would be rather more difficult to argue a purely musical case for the main version presented here being a defensible *Urtext*. That case would need to be mainly statistical, pointing out that most of the variants noted survive in only one source out of fourteen.

But there is one eloquent detail: the final cadence has identical readings in all sources apart from one of the Buxheim versions, and even that is unusually restrained. The reason is surely that the preceding two bars are so intricate that embellishment here would merely add confusion. Many similar cases can be explained on similar musical grounds. That is to say that examination of the variants and embellishments in Buxheim appears to suggest, at the very least, a strong and sensitive musical awareness in the intabulator. We may follow Howard Mayer Brown's attitude to the sixteenth-century embellishment literature in deploring its taste; but we also have to concede that the intabulator here reacted to the music as a musician.

It is almost certainly significant that bars 16-17 show no variants whatsoever, since this is again a point at which the three voices imitate and overlap, rather as they had done at the undecorated moment in *Jamais tant*. Of course it would also be more difficult for an organist to play a florid version of the discantus when the other two voices are overlapping it in the same range. But this is merely difficult, not impossible. Moreover, the Buxheim variant of the lower voices here in fact makes it easier to embellish the low A in the discantus, should the intabulator have wanted it. I suggest that in this case the musical context took precedence over the instincts prompted by digital technique.

I would think too that the relatively few embellishments found in the Buxheim versions are distinctively instrumental in nature, even digital.[30] Most of them could fairly easily be sung, of course: that is particularly true of the falling lines in bars 5, 10 and 19; but it is surely also just true of figures like those in bar 7, bar 12, bars 14-15, bar 18 and bar 22 – depending rather on how one proposes to interpret and articulate the ornament signs in Buxheim.

Returning to the discussion of the Binchois song in example 1, where many of the variants appeared to be merely elaborations of the bending, portamentos, articulations and gradations any singer might apply, it may be possible to go a little further. It is likely, for example, that the intabulated versions of *Par le regard* transfer a few of those details to a rather different medium, that of the keyboard which has so many fewer ways of varying the sound and the nature of the line. A sung performance of the literal details in Buxheim could be extremely exciting, though on balance it hardly seems sensible. But the broad picture does suggest that these details are likely to give some clue to the ways in which a singer could approach the art of bringing the line to life. If the more florid version of *Jamais tant* is to be considered an index of what happened, then the details of these two intabulations, and many like them, may be important for the interpretation of the repertory. But comparison of the surviving staff-notation sources emphatically confirms the view that literally elaborated singing is out of place.

So this all rather seems to lead to the conclusion that I originally offered as a mere prejudice. Particularly with a carefully crafted work, literal embellishment can only impede the communication of a song. Examination of the variants between staff-notation sources indicates that there was indeed a firm *Urtext* in many cases, that several of the differences between sources may stem from composers' second thoughts, and that for this repertory literal embellishment is to be avoided. That singers did often embellish may be seen as a consequence of a tradition in which they were trained, and which was part of their day-to-day practice, namely improvising counterpoints against a tenor. But there is little in the sources to justify actual interpolation in the written notes of the composed polyphonic repertory between about 1430 and the end of the century.

---

[30] Brown, „Improvised ornamentation in the fifteenth-century chanson" (see note 25 above), 248-50, offers a useful vocabulary of the simpler melodic embellishment figures in Buxheim.

That a few sources appear to suggest otherwise can be understood in the wider context of fifteenth-century music-making. When a song was adapted for purely instrumental performance the generating power and interest of the words and the inherent flexibility of the voice were no longer there; and adaptation inevitably followed. Here there was every opportunity for the musician to add – returning to Guerrero's words a century later – „all the glosses that he desires and knows so well how to execute on his instrument". Moreover, the polyphonic settings and adaptations of song tenors later in the century plainly show that it was becoming common, as an independent instrumental repertory emerged, to devise elaborate creations on the basis of received material. But as concerns the sung repertory of the polyphonic chanson, the evidence indicates that the written notes were what the composer expected to hear, albeit, perhaps, with a somewhat wider range of articulation than we normally hear today.[31]

---

[31] In addition to the help mentioned in notes 16-17, 21 and 23 above, I would like to record my thanks to Wulf Arlt and Alejandro Enrique Planchart, who offered perceptive comments after an earlier version of this paper was delivered in Basle in March 1989, as well as to Peter Reidemeister and Robert Crawford Young, who by inviting me to Basle on that occasion prompted me to examine and attempt to pin down an issue about which I had felt uncomfortable for some years.

Part VI
Other Matters

[19]

MUSICA RECTA AND MUSICA FICTA

MARGARET BENT

A twofold dilemma faces the editor of early music when he comes to supply accidentals. Firstly, he has insufficient evidence on which to base a definitive solution but must nevertheless specify what is to be performed; and secondly, such evidence as he does have appears to embody a conflict between the testimony of theorists and the evidence of manuscript accidentals. The present article attempts to set out a working hypothesis, presenting the main theoretical evidence relevant to the early fifteenth century; it arose as a by-product of the task of editing the music of the Old Hall manuscript.[1]

It is axiomatic of this hypothesis that theoretical testimony and manuscript evidence are in fact complementary, and that taken together they point clearly towards a practical solution. I take it as a pre-condition of any set of principles for the supplying of accidentals that it must be reconcilable with both available bodies of evidence. Some previous investigators in the field of *musica ficta* have tended to reject one in favour of the other. Those who have favoured the theoretical evidence have drawn up rules based on harmonic criteria,[2] while those who have favoured manuscript evidence have adopted melodic criteria.[3]

In establishing a set of principles I make one basic assumption: that the 15th-century singer had in front of him the sort of manuscripts that have come down to us (Old Hall shows clear signs of use by performers), and in particular that the accidentals written in such manuscripts were adequate visual clues for performance. In other words, the application of unwritten accidentals was essentially part of the medieval performer's art. Modern performers are no longer able to perceive instinctively the problems and choices involved: at the present time, the editor must still act for the performer, suggesting decisions which the medieval performer would have made himself. His task is

---

[1] The Old Hall Manuscript, ed. Andrew Hughes and Margaret Bent (Rome, 1969). The spur to the present formulation arose from extended correspondence with Andrew Hughes, after the decision to publish the edition jointly. It owes much to his initial criticism of and subsequent concurrence in its arguments, and he has developed many of the practical ramifications independently (*Manuscript Accidentals. Ficta in Focus, 1350-1450*, Musicological Studies & Documents 27, American Institute of Musicology, 1972). My husband's criticisms have been invaluable, and two articles, in particular, did much to suggest lines of thought: E. E. Lowinsky, "The Function of Conflicting Signatures in Early Polyphonic Music", *The Musical Quarterly* XXXI (1945), pp. 227-60, and R. H. Hoppin, "Partial Signatures and Musica Ficta in Some Early 15th-Century Sources", *Journal of the American Musicological Society* VI (1953), pp. 197-215.

[2] E.g. Hoppin, "Partial Signatures..."

[3] E.g. W. Apel, "The Partial Signatures in the Sources up to 1450", *Acta Musicologica* X (1938), pp. 1-13, and XI (1939), pp. 40-42.

to uncover the criteria of musicianship, the methods of teaching singing[4] and the theoretical principles which regulated chromaticism. These he must apply as far as possible to the actual situations he finds in the manuscripts; the main function of manuscript accidentals, in turn, is to guide the detailed application of theoretical principles.

There are two corollaries to this practical approach. In the first place, if the editor is to simulate a performance practice, then he should formulate practical rules of thumb which a singer could grasp and apply on the spot. Secondly, by its nature as a performing art, there must have been some room for flexible application of the rules, even after full allowance has been made for differing local traditions, and varying degrees of skill, conservatism, and contact with fresh or foreign ideas. We cannot expect, here or in any comparable performing technique, to uncover rules which would yield infallible results at first sight of a new piece, even for experienced singers working within a single tradition. But techniques which evolve practically and, in the final resort, instinctively, rarely lend themselves at any period of musical history to logical formulation in manuals of instruction, partly because contemporary writers take them for granted and have not themselves learned them by rote. There are bound to be equally acceptable alternatives, just as there are for the editor who realises a figured bass; spontaneous realisation is likely to incur discussion and mutual adjustment between players in rehearsal.

The operation of one or other of these two variables in the performance of medieval music is occasionally implied by the presence of conflicting written accidentals in two sources of the same piece, or of incompatible accidentals within a single source, representing two different layers of performing activity. Or in other circumstances, differences in written accidentals may be complementary and do not necessarily conflict. What the editor supplies, therefore, may be only one of several possible interpretations based on a single set of principles.

If the singer was responsible for applying accidentals, he must have done so in the first instance to the single part in front of him, and according to melodic criteria. Cadences and structural harmonic points can normally, in any case, be anticipated by identifying the characteristic cadential figures appropriate to each single line of the polyphony. The simultaneous result, the superimposition of each part upon the others, could then be adjusted in rehearsal to meet any overriding harmonic considerations which individual singers had been unable to anticipate. The fact that many of these additions and adjustments were not added to the manuscripts but retained in the memory need not tax our credulity: medieval singers were subjected to disciplines

---

[4] That much depended on teachers is suggested by Anonymous XI. See E. Coussemaker, *Scriptorum de Musica Medii Aevi: novam seriam Gerbertina alteram* (Paris, 1864-76) [henceforward referred to as CS], vol. III, p. 429.

which must have equipped them for life with enviable musical memories.

Individual theorists give relatively little help on the subject of *ficta*, and in order to assemble evidence in reasonable quantity it is tempting to draw it from a wide chronological range. It is hardly surprising when, in these circumstances, some results are at variance with others and with the musical situations they are applied to. Performance practices are always closely tied to stylistic and technical changes. Earlier teaching may be absorbed into later practice: thus, the writings of Jean de Muris are of great value in dealing with the Old Hall music a century later, when they were still respected and recopied. The Old Hall composers had been brought up on teachings dating from the fourteenth century or earlier. But since the teachings of Tinctoris and sixteenth-century theorists, however authoritative for their own period, can hardly have been an ingredient of their musical training, it is hardly surprising that some of them have been judged incompatible with music of earlier date. Only by stripping our minds of anachronistic teachings can we hope to see the problems and solutions through contemporary eyes and tackle them with contemporary tools. The case for adopting a similar restriction geographically is much less strong; I have found no major contradictions on the subject of *ficta* between theorists of different nationality.

The principles governing *musica ficta* are closely related to general contrapuntal rules. As the collisions of successive counterpoints, built around a tenor, gave way to something approaching accompanied melody, so angular chromaticism and false relations gradually yielded to smoother melodic contours and more euphonious chromatic inflections.

The value of theoretical evidence

Theoretical evidence has sometimes been set aside on the grounds that it deals primarily with harmonic reasons for chromatic inflection and refers to two-part progressions. The chief difficulty is to bridge the gap between this and the polyphony of the fourteenth and fifteenth centuries in three or more parts where each singer had only his own part in front of him. The answer to this lies, again, in the principle of successive composition. The author of the *Quatuor principalia* gives rules for three, four and even five-part writing:

> Qui autem triplum aliquod operari voluerit, respiciendum est ad tenorem. Si discantus itaque discordat cum tenore, non discordat [*recte* discordet?] cum triplo, et e contrario, ita quod semper habeatur concordantia aliqua ad graviorem vocem, et procedat ulterius per concordantias, nunc ascendendo, nunc descendendo cum discantu, ita quod non semper cum altero tantum. Qui autem quadruplum vel quintuplum facere voluerit, inspicere debet cantus prius factos, ut si cum uno discordat, cum aliis non discordat [discordet?], ut concordantia semper habeatur ad gravio-

rem vocem, nec ascendere vel descendere debet cum altero ipsorum sed nunc cum tenore nunc cum discantu, etc. (CS IV, p. 295) [5]

He who wishes to fit a third part to something must look to the tenor. If the discant is discordant with the tenor, it should not be discordant with the third part, and vice versa, so that there is always some concordance with the lower voice, and that if it [the lower part] proceeds by concords with the discant, rising and falling, there is not always only [consonance] with the other. He who wishes to compose a fourth or fifth part must look at the parts already written, and see that if it is discordant with one of them it is not discordant with the others, and that there is always consonance with the lower part; neither ought it to ascend or descend with any one part, but now with the tenor, now with the discant, etc.

This tells us that each added voice must always agree with at least one of the others, and that it should not be discordant with more than one other part at any one time. Above all, added parts must adjust to the lowest part; we have no indication that it is ever adjusted to them. To some extent an existing part, especially if it is a plainsong tenor, is regarded as fixed. This is confirmed in a chapter on *musica ficta* by Ugolino of Orvieto, where he determines the tenor progression, including its chromatic notes, before showing how the upper part must be made to fit to it by the rules of permitted consonance, and in these *musica ficta* plays an important part.[6] This means that where a chromatic inflection of the written pitch is demanded by the vertical relationship between the two parts, and where there is an equal choice between inflecting the top part, and inflecting the tenor or lowest voice, it is the upper, added part which should be modified.

In practice, the tenor should take priority for the application of melodic rules; its melodic integrity should be preserved even if other voices have to compromise theirs as a result. The lowest voice takes priority where harmonic considerations are concerned, and the other voices have to conform to it. This usually means the tenor, but another voice may cross below it, particularly in English descant, where the tenor plainsong is usually the middle part. The basic duet between the two lower parts is considered, in this style, before any adjustments are made to the upper part.

With these principles in mind, it is quite possible to apply all that the theorists have to say about *ficta* in two-part progressions to

---

[5] See also CS III, pp. 465-6 for an anonymous 15th-century directive on counterpoint in more than two parts.

[6] *Ugolino urbevetani declaratio musicae disciplinae*, ed. A. Seay (Rome, 1959-62), II p. 44.

MUSICA RECTA & MUSICA FICTA

polyphony in three or more parts, provided always that one is dealing with successively-composed music: the principles will have to be modified somewhat before they can be applied to the more vertically-orientated music of the mid-fifteenth century.

This removes one common objection to the using of theoretical evidence. The other, that theorists deal primarily with harmonic reasons for chromatic inflection, is ultimately not justified. Some of our most valuable evidence is given in purely melodic terms (see p. 89). In most other cases, the evidence of two-part progressions is, from the composer's or choirmaster's point of view, harmonic, but with melodic implications. From the standpoint of the individual singer, it is melodic, with harmonic implications. Most inflections affect cadential figures which are often recognisable melodically. The "harmonic" bias of most theorists must be related to the purpose of the treatise: for it is in manuals of counterpoint that *musica ficta* is usually given separate treatment, as part of the basic training not of singers but of composers. Lowinsky has drawn attention to the fact that "the composer of early music was faced by a problem with regard to accidentals when he was writing, as is the modern scholar when editing".[7] The writers of counterpoint treatises are concerned to prevent would-be composers from building impossible situations into their music. Of course, this does not guarantee that near-impossible situations will never confront the performer, but it does give many apparently difficult situations the stamp of normality. They provide the harmonic guidance we need for our singers' mutual adjustment in rehearsal, as well as incidental melodic hints derived from their chord progressions. Once we have admitted distinct functions in different treatises, we can see that many "contradictory" statements are in fact complementary. Prosdocimus' exhortation to be sparing in the use of *musica ficta* (CS III, p. 198) is often reckoned to be inconsistent with his own music examples, which show angular chromaticism. But if he is encouraging *composers* to avoid situations in which the *singer* would be forced to apply *ficta* where an alternative solution could be found, or if he is telling them not to *write* too many accidentals but to leave them to the performer, his advice is not relevant to singers, schooled orally in a performing art, nor to the modern editor who acts on the performer's behalf. Prosdocimus does not claim to help singers to solve problems; he tries to eliminate problems before the singer has to tackle them.

The procedure of applying melodic rules and supplementing them with harmonic adjustment has some theoretical support. Anonymous XI and several other theorists give rules for *ficta* in application to plainsong. It is in the plainsong section of the *Quatuor principalia* that the guidance on *ficta* occurs. But other theorists give strong hints that

---

[7] "The Function of Conflicting Signatures...", p. 238.

more *ficta* was needed for polyphony than for plainsong. Vitry, for example, makes the point in a word-play on *vera* and *falsa*:

> non falsa, sed vera et necessaria, quia nullus moctetus, sive rondellus sine ipsa cantari non possunt. (CS III, p.18)

> not false, but true and necessary, for no motet or rondellus can be sung without it.

John of Garland inserted the following well-known passage in his plainsong treatise, without giving any intimation that *musica falsa* is relevant to *cantus planus*:

> Videndum est de falsa musica, que instrumentis musicalibus multum est necessaria, specialiter in organis. Falsa musica est, quando de tono facimus semitonium, et e converso. Omnis tonus divisibilis est in duo semitonis, et per consequens signa semitonia designantia in omnibus tonis possunt amplificari. (CS I, p. 16)

> It should be observed of *falsa musica* that it is frequently necessary in performance [*musica instrumentalis* has this force in the Boethian classification, which recognises, besides, *musica mundana* and *musica humana*], particularly in *organa*. *Falsa musica* is when we make a tone into a semitone and vice versa. Each tone is divisible into two semitones, and consequently the signs designed for semitones can be extended to all notes.

Indeed, though it is never explicitly stated, there is a strong tendency to equate *ficta causa necessitatis* with harmonic reasons and *ficta causa pulchritudinis* with melodic reasons for chromatic inflection. The theoretical statement which most nearly supports this claim is from an anonymous Seville treatise[8]:

> Boecius autem invenit fictam musicam propter duas causas, scilicet causa necessitatis et causa pulchritudinis cantus. Causa necessitatis est quia non poteramus habere consonantias in omnibus locis ut supra dictum est. Causa vero pulchritudinis ut patet in cantilenis.

> Boethius contrived *musica ficta* for two reasons: because of necessity and because of beauty of song. It is "of necessity" because we were unable to have consonances in every place as stated above [i.e., harmonic necessity, the correction of vertical perfect intervals]. It is used for beauty as in cantilenas [melodic reasons].

[8] Biblioteca Colombina, MS 5.2.25, f.97. The manuscript is described and inventoried by F. Alberto Gallo, "Alcune Fonti Poco Note di Musica Teorica e Pratica" (Edizioni Centro Studi Sull'Ars Nova Italiana del Trecento), Certaldo, 1966, pp. 11-23. The portions used in this article are short anonymous treatises contained on ff. 56-56v and f. 97. There is no reason to assume any identity of scribe or author between these two items in a miscellaneous compilation. I owe my knowledge of the manuscript to Andrew Hughes.

MUSICA RECTA & MUSICA FICTA

Another possible interpretation of *causa necessitatis* and *causa pulchritudinis* is given by Lowinsky: "Necessity deals with rules pertaining to perfect consonances, beauty with rules pertaining to imperfect consonances".[9] This is apparently true for writers who give us only harmonic or contrapuntal guidance: the perfection of consonances is considered necessary. The two different interpretations of beauty, however, can easily be reconciled: the "colouring" of dissonances (or imperfect consonances: see p. 97 below) involves a two-chord progression and therefore a melodic consideration.

The role of solmisation

Perhaps the most important guidance we draw from the theorists is insight into the basic musical equipment of singers — and it was certainly through singing that a medieval musician acquired his fundamental training, terminology and musical thought processes. We need this insight before we can approach the manuscript accidentals through their eyes. For present purposes, the crucial part of this equipment is the solmisation system, whereby the notes forming the recognised total compass of music were represented in overlapping hexachords, and came to be shown mnemonically as finger-joints on a hand (the so-called Guidonian hand, although this particular device does not occur in Guido's surviving treatises) which was used throughout the middle ages for teaching singing. Its great value is that it enables the choirmaster to demonstrate to his pupils, and singers to signal to each other, where semitones occur, by pointing to the joints of his own fingers. The musical memory of the chorister is reinforced by verbal reminders (the solmisation names for the notes) and by the physical act of tracing out the steps on his own hand.

The notes included in this basic system of hexachords are called by the theorists *musica recta* or *vera*. They include the $b\flat$ below and the $b\flat$ above middle c, as well as the $b\natural$ adjacent to each, but not the $b\flat$ below those.[10] The system caters for the three most common semitone steps: b-c, e-f, a-$b\flat$. These are always solmised mi-fa, and mi-fa is always a semitone. Free transition between these hexachords was permitted, and the point of change was termed a mutation. The note on which the mutation was made had to have a solmisation name (*vox*) in both the old and the new hexachord. Which of the two names was actually sung is not always clear; sometimes both may have been used. In order to preserve the clear demonstration of semitones, mutation was not

---

[9] E. E. Lowinsky, Foreword to *Musica Nova accommodata per Cantar et Sonar Organi*, ed. C. Slim (Monuments of Renaissance Music, vol. I; Chicago, 1964), pp. viii-ix.

[10] This distinction has, of course, been recognised before, e.g. by Lowinsky ("The Function of Conflicting Signatures...", p. 254), but does not yet appear to have been used to support the conclusions drawn below.

permitted between mi and fa. Thus, *a b♭ c b♮ c* would be solmised mi fa sol/fa mi fa, with the mutation on *c*, where sol must yield to fa because of the semitone step which follows it.

In the course of the fourteenth century the system was extended by theorists to cater for an increasing amount of chromaticism, so that other chromatic steps could be indicated by the same mnemonics. This was achieved, according to the theorists, by the transposition of *recta* hexachords to "alien pitches", "unaccustomed places", where they classed as *musica ficta* or *falsa*. All chromatic notes so derived have their basis in *ficta* hexachords; the hexachord is created for the sake of the semitone step, mi-fa.

The term used by some theorists for this transposition process was *coniuncta*, the object of a recent study by Albert Seay.[11] The two main definitions he presents (in the words of Faxolis and Tinctoris) are anticipated almost exactly by an anonymous Paris treatise (of which the earliest known copy, dated 1375, is now at Berkeley):[12]

> Vel aliter coniuncta est alicuius proprietatis seu deductionis de loco proprio ad alienum locum secundum sub vel supra intellectualis transpositio.
>
> Est enim coniuncta quedam acquisita canendi actualis attributio in qua licet facere de tono semitonium & e converso... (p. 6)

In addition to these definitions, we find statements which seem to equate the *coniuncta* with *musica ficta*:

> Coniuncta, secundum vocem hominis vel instrumenti, est facere de tono semitonium et e converso...
> (Anonymous XI, CS III, p. 426)
>
> Est ficta musica quando de tono facimus semitonium, et e converso...
> (Vitry, CS III, p. 26)
>
> ...mutatio falsa, sive falsa musica
> (Anonymous II, CS I, p. 310)
>
> ...nisi forsitan intervenerit aliquis inusitatus cantus quem aliqui sed male falsam musicam appellant alii fictam musicam alii vero coniunctas eam nominant & bene... Et propterea invente fuerunt ipse coniuncte ut cantus antedictus irregularis per eas ad regularitatem quodimodo duci posset. (Paris anonymous, p.5)

[11] "The 15th-century Coniuncta: A Preliminary Study", in *Aspects of Medieval and Renaissance Music*, ed. Jan LaRue (New York, 1966), pp. 723-37. The quotations from Faxolis and Tinctoris mentioned below are on p. 730.

[12] See R. L. Crocker, "A new source for medieval music theory" *Acta Musicologica* XXXIX (1967), pp. 161-171 and M. Bent, "A postscript on the Berkeley theory manuscript", *ibid.*, XL (1968), p. 175. I am grateful to Mr. Oliver Ellsworth for his correction, used on p. 86 below, of a misreading contained in the latter.

MUSICA RECTA & MUSICA FICTA

We must emphasise again that all *b*♭s except the lowest one in the gamut count not as *musica ficta* but as *musica recta*. *It is therefore not correct to equate* musica ficta *with editorial accidentals.*[13] Manuscript accidentals and added accidentals each include both *recta* and *ficta* inflections, and are therefore not different in kind. The editor has to decide how many more of each sort to add to the handful of accidentals he finds in the manuscript. In so doing, he must assess whether the written accidentals were notated because they were in some way abnormal, or whether they constitute an arbitrary sample of normal treatment.

All this may seem unnecessarily cumbersome to the musician schooled in the key system and with reference to a fully chromatic, equally tempered keyboard. If all degrees of the chromatic scale were available (which is almost true by the late fourteenth century: *d*♯, *d*♭, *g*♯ and *a*♭ appear in Old Hall, *g*♭ in Chantilly), would not some system closer to our own have been more convenient, based on a chromatic division of the whole octave? Any idea of a set arrangement of tones and semitones for one composition must be rejected. *B*♭, *b*♮, *f*♮, *f*♯, *c*♮, *c*♯ may be used in one voice in fairly close succession, and the system of mutations was undoubtedly the most practical way of keeping in tune. Moreover, a careful distinction was observed in theory (and probably in practice by the meticulous) between major and minor semitones. Mi-fa, the normal semitone step, is always a minor semitone (e.g., *a-b*♭, *f*♯*-g*).

The solmisation of irregular melodic intervals presents another challenge to the theorists who pitted their ingenuity against an increasingly overburdened solmisation system. Intervals larger than the sixth fall into this category: Jacobus of Liège mentions sevenths and octaves, but excludes ninths and tenths "quia in cantu plano ecclesie nullus ultra dyapason ascendere debet immediate vel descendere".[14] He also includes the "semitritonus" (previously defined, in book II chapter 81, as containing two tones and two minor semitones), e.g. *B*♮*-F*:

> nec umquam extreme voces semitritoni ad eamdem pertinent solfationem. De hac vocum conjunctione parum aut nihil loquuntur a[u]ctores. (CS II, p. 294)

The Paris treatise discusses the solmisation of irregular melodic intervals and presents a device (or rather, an excuse) for coping with them: the *disiuncta*.[15] Major semitones, augmented seconds, tritones (of both kinds) and even minor sixths are among intervals which cannot

---

[13] The misconception is widespread. Hoppin writes: "...musica ficta, i.e., editorial accidentals" ("Partial Signatures...', p. 197).

[14] CS II, p. 294.

[15] I have not found this term in any other treatise: the word is however used in other contexts which invite analogy, e.g.: "ex conjunctione et disjunctione tetracordarum" (Odington, CS I, p. 215) and "possibile est perfectiones separari et disiungi, neque continuari" (J. de Muris, CS III, p. 296).

be solmised with regular mutation, as no one hexachord, whether *recta* or *ficta*, can contain both boundary notes of the leap. Yet all these intervals are explicitly used.

> Quia ab una deductione sepe sit transitus ad aliam in cantu quod absque mutatione vocum bono modo fieri non potest licet aliquis fiat per disiunctas. Est enim disiuncta vehemens transitus ab una deductione in aliam absque quacumque vocum mutatione ibi fieri possibile.
> (Paris anonymous, p.4)

The *disiuncta*, then, is a violent transition from one hexachord to another where no mutation is possible, i.e., when there is no pivotal note in the old and new hexachords.

B♭-b♮ and f-f♯ are major semitones, rare in practice, and not susceptible to regular solmisation. When, for harmonic reasons only, it was necessary to use major semitones, the hexachord was changed without mutation on a common note. The difference between the two semitone steps which fall within any one tone of *musica recta* (e.g., e♭-d♯) is the so-called comma of Didymus, or apotomy, which Marchettus designated as a fifth of a tone, but which later theorists (including Ugolino) more correctly recognise to be not an aliquot part of a tone. Each tone comprises one major and one minor semitone. Both semitone pitches are catered for in the sophisticated monochord tuning systems of Prosdocimus and Ugolino, but would be too unwieldy for a fixed-pitch performing instrument. The singer is not often concerned with pitching major semitones. Where he is, he is invariably helped by the vertical sonority of a perfect interval — the overriding harmonic factor which has forced the use of an irregular melodic interval. A case in point is the opening of Old Hall, no. 101, where the f♯ is in the manuscript:

In general, provided the choirmaster knew his way around the hexachord transpositions, the chorister still needed to bother only about the position of semitone steps, which he sang when his master pointed to the appropriate knuckle.

The system does indeed have limitations as a vehicle for advanced theoretical thought, but it was not designed for this. Why, then, should it concern us with music which must have been sung only by experienced singers? First, because all explanations by contemporary theorists concerning contrapuntal progressions, permitted intervals, melodic progressions, singing practices and *musica ficta* are given in terms of hexachords. An explanation couched in universally-understood terminology is more generally useful than one given in more sophisticated but less familiar terms. It is therefore vital to understand how the system worked, and where it was inadequate at any point in time, in order to understand the theorists' statements. Second, if we approach the manuscript situation with the medieval singer's training in mind, we are more likely to reason in his terms and approach his solutions.

Modes have no apparent relevance to *ficta* in the early fifteenth century. So long as the mode of a composition is open to dispute, it is more likely to prejudice than to help arguments based on modal assignations. The modes are fundamentally fixed arrangements of tones and semitones. If chromatic inflection can be superimposed on these arrangements without altering the modal definition, how can assignment to a mode help in the application of editorial accidentals? Theorists before Tinctoris rarely attempt to superimpose the modes onto polyphony. The anonymous treatise from Paris is one of the exceptions; but this short excursion into the modes and polyphony is not worked out in detail, nor is it applied to the exhaustive treatment of hexachords and mutations which precedes it. Without further guidance from contemporary theorists, it is not possible to apply the modes to any but the simplest polyphony. The solmisation system itself does not, of course, solve the problem of added accidentals. If any melody, however angular, can be solmised, we cannot assign accidentals on the basis of what is or is not susceptible of solmisation. By the late fourteenth century the system had, indeed, been extended to cope with all chromatic progressions. The theorists' explanations help us to fix priorities, tentative rules governing choice of hexachords, permitted harmonic and melodic progressions, and thus the accidentals to be applied. Having deduced the rules, the mnemonics are no longer necessary to us in fixing semitone positions: solmisation *ex post facto* is a superfluous chore.

The theorists of the fourteenth century imply *ficta* hexachords. They speak of "false mutation" (Vitry), "mental transposition" (Paris anonymous) and call a *ficta* sharp and its adjacent semitone mi and fa (Muris). But not until Ugolino is the full system of *ficta* hexachords exhaustively tabulated. For normal purposes, this full formulation cannot have been wholly necessary, and the flaws revealed by Ugolino's attempt were probably of no practical hindrance.

The primary rule for applying accidentals is that musica recta *should be used rather than* musica ficta *where possible.* Vitry, for example, writes:

Et ideo oritur questio ex hoc videlicet, que fuit necessitas in musica regulari de falsa musica sive de falsa mutatio, cum nullum regulare debeat accipere falsum, sed potium verum.   (CS III, p. 18)

And thus there arises the question, namely, why it was necessary in regular music to have false music, or false mutation, since nothing regular ought to accept what is false, but rather what is true.

The anonymous Seville author already quoted (see p. 78) reads:

Et ideo quando non possumus habere consonantias per rectam musicam tunc debemus recurrere ad fictam seu inusitatam et eam operari. (f. 97)

And therefore when we cannot have consonances by means of *musica recta*, we ought to resort to *ficta*, or the unusual, and apply that.

Prosdocimus allows the use of *musica ficta* "provided the consonance could not be coloured in any other way than by *musica ficta*" and says that it is never used "except where the context requires".[16] Ugolino tells us not to use *ficta* "except in places of cogent necessity".[17] *Musica ficta*, according to the theorists, is a last resort. However, many theorists were discontented with the terminology, being reluctant to call "false" or "feigned" something which was necessary to musical results. The above reference by the anonymous Seville theorist to the "unusual" is typical. *Recta* preference takes priority over most other rules, including that of plainsong preference, unless the *cantus prius factus* has a very strong melodic claim to use or to incur *ficta*, or if for some reason it is treated as immutable (as might be the case in certain imitative, canonic, isorhythmic or refrain-like repetitions). It may be impossible to use *musica recta*

1) if the use of a *recta* b♭ incurs the use of other more extreme *ficta* flats than a solution using just one or two *ficta* sharps;

2) if a manuscript accidental (perhaps representing the composer's decision) requires the use of *ficta*;

3) if the music has already been steered into *ficta* channels which it would be aurally perverse to abandon;

4) if it seems musically desirable to preserve exactly a close imitation, voice-exchange, a repeating or sequential figure, or to match one cadence to another in the same piece.

---

[16] In the *Tractatus tertius* of his *Tractatus de contrapuncto*: CS III, pp. 198-9.
[17] In chapter 34 of his *Declaratio musicae disciplinae*, ed. Seay, II, p. 45.

MUSICA RECTA & MUSICA FICTA

The interpretation of manuscript accidentals

Most theorists confine their explanations to two symbols: *b mollis* (♭) and *b durum* (♯ or ♮, usually interchangeable). Some, however, do observe a distinction between ♯ and ♮, but we can never be sure that this distinction applies to any particular source, which may use both indiscriminately.[18] The modern sharp sign may serve as warning of a major semitone. Marchettus says that this sign is peculiar to mensural music (GS III, p. 89); if he means polyphony, this will accord well with what we have already said about the use of the major semitone, that it is required only on vertical, harmonic considerations. This usage of the ♯ sign cannot be applied consistently, because if it were used for *f-f♯* in ex. 1 above, the ensuing minor semitone *f♯-g* would then be shown by ♯ instead of the normal *b durum* ♮. Scribes, possibly unaware of this distinction, may use exclusively one or other sign for *b durum*, or a hybrid form not clearly identifiable with either, or an apparently haphazard vacillation between the two forms, perhaps deriving from different layers of activity underlying the exemplars. The distinction may occasionally be meaningful, but we cannot depend upon it, and are forced to regard it as having more theoretical than practical importance. One distinct meaning of ♯ is to designate the hard hexachord on *g*, ♮ sometimes being used for the natural hexachord on *c*. According to the Paris anonymous:

> Unde cuiuslibet deductionis cantus habens originem in c cantatur per naturam, in f per ♭, in g per ♯. (p. 4)

> Whence, a melody in any hexachord starting on *c* is sung natural, on *f* soft, on *g* hard.

The sign ♭ is sometimes used for the *b* below middle *c*, a double-looped flat sign being reserved for the *b* an octave above. The latter is probably a survival of the use of a double row of letters (^b_b) for higher octaves. This would be a convenient means of distinguishing the only two *b*♭s available by *musica recta*, but here again the manuscript evidence is inconsistent. Often, as in the case of ♯ and ♮, we are faced with the confusion which results when one unthinking scribe has combined different practices. Other signs used in Old Hall, particularly by the second-layer scribes, include the letters c, f, g for the "soft" forms of those note-pitches, ♭ being reserved for *b* in the same pieces.

The universal rule for interpreting the manuscript symbols (here given in Prosdocimus' version) is:

---

[18] Prosdocimus, in CS III, p. 258, claims to have elucidated the difference in his counterpoint treatise, but no such passage occurs in the surviving sources; however, only one chapter of the *Tractatus tertius* survives.

Unde ubicunque ponitur b rotundum sive molle, dicere debemus hanc vocem fa, et ubicunque ponitur ♮ quadrum sive durum, debemus dicere hanc vocem mi, sive tales voces ibidem sint sive non; cuius ratio est quia in hac ditione b fa ♮ mi, in qua ponitur utrumque istorum B, immediate ante fa ponitur b rotundum sive molle, et tali voci fa famulatur; immediate vero ante mi ponitur ♮ quadrum sive durum, et tali voci famulatur mi; et ideo ad b rotundum sive molle dicimus fa, et ad ♮ quadrum dicimus mi. (CS III, p. 198)

Thus, wherever ♭ is placed we should give it the name fa, and wherever ♮ is placed we ought to give it the name mi, whether the *voces* are the same or not [i.e., whether or not they would normally have those solmisation names]. The reason for this is that in b fa ♮ mi, where either of these *b* can be placed, immediately before fa ♭ is placed and that note called fa, immediately before mi ♮ is placed and that note called mi; therefore we say fa when we see ♭ and mi when we see ♮.

Rarely do we find a direct admission that ♭ lowers a note or that ♮ raises it, though it is invariably possible to place that interpretation upon a theorist's statement. Of the theorists used in the present study, the Paris anonymous states this meaning most clearly:

Item ubicunque ponitur signum ♭ debet deprimi sonus verus illius articuli per unum maius semitonium & dici fa. Et ubi signum ♯ ponitur sonus illius articuli debet per maius semitonium elevari & dici ibidem mi. (p. 6)

Wherever the sign ♭ is placed, the *recta* sound of that note on the hand should be lowered by a major semitone and called fa.
Wherever the sign ♯ is placed the sound of that note on the hand should be raised by a major semitone and called mi.

But elsewhere he uses the signs simply to show the position of mi and fa. Prosdocimus words his definition with an ambiguity which may be deliberate:

1) in a rising interval ♭ diminishes the ascent and ♯ augments it;

2) these signs can add or subtract no interval other than the diatonic or major semitone. (CS III, p. 198)

To explore the ambiguity: the ascending interval is diminished by a ♭ but this may be effected by raising the lower note rather than by lowering the upper note. If the sign adds or subtracts an interval, it will be a major semitone (to place it a minor semitone away from its neighbour), but it may not be necessary to alter the *recta* pitch of the note. For example, the minor semitone between e and f may be reinforced by ♮ on e or by ♭ on f; neither pitch will be altered. The minor semitone $f\sharp$-g will normally be shown by ♮ on f, which will raise the pitch of that note by a major semitone. Less often, but equally legitimately, the same interval may be shown by ♭ on g, indicating fa, making mi a minor semitone below it, on f♯. The signs ♭ and ♯ locate the position of the semitone, causing inflection only if necessary. Sometimes both may be indicated, as in the examples given on p. 20 of the Paris treatise:

Ugolino indicates f♯ by placing a ♭ in the space above, on g. Thus, some care is needed when handling accidentals which are apparently placed carelessly on the stave. It would be wrong to treat every instance as meaningful, but some undoubtedly are. The context will usually determine whether or not the less usual interpretation of a symbol makes musical sense.

Each letter-name had not three pitches (♮, ♯, ♭) but only two, indicated by ♮ and ♭, and this was bound to lead to some ambiguity. Even where the ♯ sign does have a meaning distinct from the ♮, it cannot be equated with the modern distinction. D is normally the only ambiguous note in practice, but others are encountered in theoretical systems which try to cover all possibilities. These are the normal meanings:

| ♭ | b♭ | e♭ | a♭ | d♭/d♮ | g♮ | c♮ | f♮ |
| ♮ | b♮ | e♮ | a♮ | d♮/d♯ | g♯ | c♯ | f♯ |

However, when theorists attempt to cover both meanings in a single sequence, confusion arises. For example, when the Paris anonymous constructs a hexachord on a with the semitone position shown by c♯ and d♭, is he talking about the hexachord on a♮ with c♯, or the hexachord on a♭ with d♭, or both? Similar problems arise with the hexachords on b, e and d, which are available in ♮ and ♭ forms.

Several theorists tell us that accidentals need not be written in, even though their use is taken for granted.[19] We have already referred to Prosdocimus' admonition against using too much *ficta*, and suggested this as a possible interpretation. More clearly, the Paris anonymous says:

---

[19] Later, Tinctoris expresses the same view:
   Neque tunc b mollis signum apponi est necessarium, immo si appositum videatur, asininum esse dicitur, ut hic probatur. (CS IV, p. 22)
The musical example which follows requires b flats but has none written in.

Circa hec sciendum est quod in cantu inveniuntur duo signa scilicet signum b mollis & signum b quadrati demonstrantia ubi fa & mi debeant cantari & possunt poni in diversis locis manus ut patebit inferius de coniunctis: sed ipsa frequenter sunt in b fa ♮ mi virtualiter licet semper non signentur. (p. 3)

On this matter you should know that two signs are found in song, soft b and square b, showing where fa and mi should be sung, and they can be placed in various places on the hand, as we shall show below in dealing with *coniuncte*. But these are, legitimately, virtually never indicated in b fa ♮ mi [i.e., in practice you almost never find them marked in].

One exception is necessary in practice to the rule that ♭ always means fa and ♮ always means mi. If a more extreme flat or sharp in the same hexachord as an existing flat or sharp is either written in or required in performance, both cannot be called fa (or mi), as they will not both have an adjacent semitone step. Ideally, only the more extreme of these two sharps should be notated. This may, in fact, be one positive reason for the "failure" to notate all accidentals in early music. But in practice it was often more helpful to determine the hexachord by sharpening re if necessary. For a performer familiar with the procedures, there was no more need to mark in every accidental than there is for an accomplished executant to mark in his copy the bowing or fingering of every note — yet every note is played, and its bowing or fingering could be notated if necessary. In either case, there will be a tendency for markings to appear at points of possible ambiguity, irregularity or changes of "gear", but they will still not necessarily be full markings. It is in this direction, too, that we may seek an explanation for the early placing of accidentals in advance of the notes they affect. In some cases, at least, this practice serves as a warning of hexachord change; in order to solmise correctly, the singer needs to know in advance of the inflection itself. An excessive number of written accidentals may show that a piece has been used for teaching; conflicting accidentals in one piece may reflect the superimposed views of different performers.

This apparently casual attitude to written accidentals only makes sense in the context of performing reminders to the performer. To the singer learning his part without reference to a fixed-pitch keyed instrument, the placing of semitones was much more important than the precise pitch-names of the notes. His problems might be compared to those of the modern singer sight-reading a part in an unfamiliar transposition, clef or key, who locates his semitones as much by aural adjustment to the other parts as by accidentals marked in or absent from his own part. The medieval singer, however, was able to apply a series of rational principles when performing "blind" with others. Once a series of chromatic hexachords has been initiated, in performing a piece, there may be greater need to indicate that an uninflected note is required than to indicate all the inflections of the chromatic hexachords.

Melodic rules

The next concern is with the melodic rules relevant to *ficta* stated by the theorists. They are few and simple, and in most cases carry the harmonic implications of a cadence figure. The basic rule is stated by Jean de Muris:

> Quamdocumque [*recte* quandocumque] in simplici cantu est *la sol la*, hoc *sol* debet sustineri et cantari sicut *fa mi fa*, ut:

Whenever in a melody there is la sol la, this sol should be suppressed and sung as fa mi fa, thus:

> Quandocumque habetur in simplici cantu *sol fa sol*, hoc *fa* sustineri debet et cantari sicut *fa mi fa*, ut:

Whenever in a melody sol fa sol is found this fa should be suppressed and sung as fa mi fa, thus:

> Quandocumque habetur in simplici cantu *re ut re*, hoc *ut* sustineri debet et cantari sicut *fa mi fa*, ut: (CS III, p. 73)

Whenever in a melody re ut re is found, this ut should be suppressed and sung as fa mi fa, thus:

He instructs us to sharpen lower returning notes, and at the time he was writing this was normally applied only where the affected notes were *f, c* and *g*. However, in a previous example he uses a *d♯*.

The author of the *Quatuor principalia*, in the course of a section clearly addressed to singers, complains of two debasements of which modern singers were guilty:

> Intervalla etiam vocum perfecte pronuntientur, ut semitonium pro tono pleno non fiat, et e contrario. In hoc autem multi modernis temporibus sunt vitiosi, quoniam cum de *re,* per *fa,* in *sol* ascendunt, vix inter *fa et sol* semitonium ponunt. Insuper cum *sol, fa, sol* aut *re, ut, re* pronuntiant, semitonium pro tono mittunt, et sic genus diatonicum confundunt, ac

planum cantum falsificant. Interrogati quidem qua ratione sic semitonium pro tono pronuntiant, pro auctoritate enim atque ratione, cantores de magnatorum capellis allegant. Dicunt etenim eos non sic cantasse sine ratione, cum optimi sint cantores, sicque aliorum vestigiis decepti, et unus post alium omnes sequuntur errores (CS IV, p. 250)

Also the intervals of hexachord names should be correctly recited, so that a semitone is not sung instead of a whole tone, and vice versa. In modern times, however, many [singers] are at fault in this matter, for when they ascend from re to sol via fa, they scarcely ever place a semitone between fa and sol [as they should]. Moreover, when they *say* sol fa sol, or re ut re, they *sing* a semitone instead of a tone, and thus they throw the diatonic order into confusion, and falsify the chant. When asked for what reason they recite [the solmisation names for] a semitone instead of a tone, they allege that their reason and authority are the singers in magnates' chapels. And they say that *they* would not do this without reason, since they are the best singers, and thus deceived by the traces of others, they all follow one after the other into errors

The author is complaining here about singers who fail to sharpen melodic leading notes — they hardly ever sharpen the *f*, in which case it would not be called fa — and thus fail to apply *ficta* where they should. He also objects to singers who correctly sharpen lower returning notes, but use the wrong solmisation names. If they followed the rules of Jean de Muris they would know that these progressions have to be solmised fa mi fa.

Both authors are telling us to sharpen melodic leading notes. The same rule is given in harmonic terms (as "harmonised" leading notes) by Jean de Muris, Prosdocimus and Ugolino. Jean de Muris is particularly clear. His two-part examples stress the leading-note function of the melodic progression in the top voice (it is, after all, in his *Ars discantus*) as well as the interval progression.

To this rule must be added one provision, that of *recta* preference. The singer of the top part, in cadencing on *a*, may feel the lower part moving down to cadence on the *a* below, via *b*, and he may have to allow that part to exercise the *recta* preference and sing b♭, forgoing his own *ficta* g♯. The justification for this rule, which is surmised rather than stated, is that *ficta* is only used "where necessary", and where a satisfactory result could not be achieved by means of *recta* notes. It is surely possible that singers developed quite refined harmonic senses by learning to anticipate what their companions were about to do. Instead of merely interpreting their own lines regardless of others, and leaving all adjustments until afterwards, they may even have used some form of hand signals to indicate to their fellow-singers their own mutations, the direction of their own contrapuntal lines, and the *ficta* they were incurring. It is also possible that this is how singers reading from the same melodic line co-ordinated their efforts in choral performance, and this could be the explanation of the slightly raised hands seen in many pictures of medieval choirmen.[20]

Another anonymous Seville treatise gives a further melodic rule — one which is more often taken for granted by modern writers than stated by medieval theorists. The author is talking about the use of *b*, and adds to the *causa necessitatis* and *causa pulchritudinis* the *causa tritoni*:

> Causa tritoni tunc est quando cantus ascendit de f grave usque a [*recte* ad?] b acutum, et non ascendit amplius, et descendit in *f* grave, et tali modo cognoscitur quando b molle habetur causa tritoni, quod debemus vitare in mutationes sane intelligere boecius, quando ubique cantus habetur de f grave usque in b acuto... (f. 56)

> The reason of the tritone [for using *b♭*] is when the melody rises from *f* to *b*, ascends no further, and descends to *f*; and in this way you can tell when you should have *b♭* on account of the tritone, which [the tritone] we ought to avoid in our mutations, if we understand Boethius properly, when the melody moves from *f* to *b*.

The paragraph which follows is extremely obscure and apparently deficient. However, it deals with the progression *f b c* and appears to indicate that when the *b* serves as a leading note to the *c* it should be a semitone below *c* and therefore natural, the melodic tritone from *f* being permitted in this case. The melodic leading note function, with its harmonic implication, is the strongest melodic reason for inflection, and must be honoured before melodic tritones can be eliminated. The clearest theoretical justification for this is in Prodocimus' two notorious examples in the *Libellus monocordi* (notoriously misprinted in CS III, pp. 254, 256, *recte* below) and the single one in the *Tractatus de contrapuncto* (CS III, p. 199).
N.B.: pairs of semibreves in ligature are shown by joined quavers.

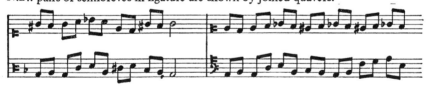

---

[20] For two easily accessible examples which may show such co-ordination see H. Besseler, *Die Musik des Mittelalters und der Renaissance* (Potsdam, 1931), plates I and XIV. Other depictions of singers, where hand signs are in evidence, may be as much concerned with the communication of solmisation as with the beating of time.

While the melodic tritone was tolerated in the interests of a leading note, it seems that it should be avoided (with or without intervening notes) where the tritone returns within its own confines in the same phrase. This will only be overruled in practice by the need to perfect a strong vertical consonance (see below). The same criterion, of returning within itself, may possibly apply also to certain other melodic intervals, such as the sixth: Prosdocimus, in the examples above, prescribes $b\flat$ where the melodic compass is bounded by b and d.

The adage *una nota super la semper est canendum fa*, although consistently referred to as a time-honoured statement of medieval theory, cannot be earlier than the abuses of solmisation which set in by the end of the fifteenth century.[21] It is taken to mean that $a\ b\ a$ should be performed $a\ b\flat\ a$. Even if sixteenth-century practice admitted la fa la as a proper solmisation of this progression (thus destroying the whole purpose of solmisation — the location of semitones), by the standards of the fifteenth and earlier centuries only mi fa mi could be used. When an upper returning note is flattened, as it frequently is and frequently has to be, the reason is usually either the avoidance of a melodic tritone outline, or the achieving of a correct "adhesion" between an imperfect and a perfect interval by the rules of Jean de Muris (e.g., $\genfrac{}{}{0pt}{}{a\ b\flat\ a}{f\ g\ d}$). But it may also result from purely aural considerations. What the singer hears happening around him may, in practice, be the strongest influence upon his own solution. In the absence of keyboard anchorage (with its simplification of the chromatic scale and primacy of white notes over black), and of any prejudice that b is to be sung natural unless marked flat, the singer is unlikely to persist with $b\natural$ if the lower parts are constantly using $b\flat$.

Rules for harmonic adjustment

The speculative reasoning which determined the intervals permitted in counterpoint also lay behind the harmonic reasons for chromatic inflection. These two considerations are, in any case, virtually inseparable. The most perfect intervals are those derived by the simplest ratios — the first few notes of the harmonic series in relation to the fundamental (octave 2:1, twelfth 3:1, fifteenth 4:1) and the fifth (3:2). Most theorists are somewhat reticent on the status of the fourth. Franco writes: *Consonantiarum tres sunt per se, et perfecte, scilicet: unisonus, diapason, et diapente*

---

[21] The sentiment, but not the wording, is widespread among 16th-century theorists, e.g. Rhaw, *Enchiridion* (edition of 1518): "Attamen in cantilenis primi & secundi tonorum, ultra la, ad secundam tantum procedendo semper fa canitur. Et hoc, si cantus mox relabitur ad F fa ut. Si vero non, mi cantetur, ut vides in Hymno, Ave maris stella."

(CS I, p. 154). Prosdocimus adds to these the third and sixth, calling them *combinationes consonantes sive concordantes*, while his list of *dissonantes, sive discordantes, sive dissonantias auribus humanis resonantes* includes the second, fourth, seventh and their octaves (CS III, p. 195). While the fourth has some claim to be classed as a perfect interval on mathematical grounds, it is not considered fit to stand on its own harmonically by the fifteenth century. This appears to be the dilemma: however, the fourth is never listed as a perfect interval for purposes of *ficta*.

The nearer an interval can be brought to perfection, the greater its quality becomes (in speculative terms), whether this be achieved by fair means (*recta*, the preferable way) or foul (*ficta*). If the interval cannot itself be made more perfect by chromatic inflection of either or both of the written pitches, then it can acquire some "virtue" from being as close as possible to the interval which follows it, and if that is already perfect, so much the better. In Ugolino's words, it gains *propinquiorem adhaesionem ad suam immediate sequentem consonantiam*. The final cadence of a phrase carried strong philosophical connotations of perfection, as the point to which all the intervals preceding it aspired.

The first essential harmonic rule (given full and lucid expression by Ugolino and Jean de Muris) is that vertical intervals such as unisons, fifths, octaves and their octaves should be perfect. If such an interval cannot be made perfect by *musica recta*, *ficta* is used. (The question of tenor precedence may then condition the choice of inflection.) The rule is usually stated in the form of a prohibition against sounding *mi contra fa* in perfect consonances:

> ...in combinationibus perfecte consonantibus nunquam ponere debemus *mi* contra *fa*, nec e contrario, quum statim ipsas vocum combinationes perfecte consonantes minores vel maximas constitueremus, que discordantes sunt, ut supra dictum est (Prosdocimus, CS III, p. 197).

> ...nullibi talibus perfectis concordationibus potest poni *mi* contra *fa*, cum insimul discordarent... Breviter dicendo in contrapunctu, super perfectas species nullibi contra *mi* potest poni *fa*, nec e contra, in contrapunctu, supra perfectas specias nullibi contra *fa* potest poni *mi* (from Jean de Muris' statement, CS III, pp. 71-2).

The qualification "in perfect consonances" and the strict application to vertical combinations (i.e., the usual force of *contra*) are of central importance. If *mi contra fa* were to apply to *imperfect* consonances we should always be forced, for example, to flatten the *b* in the progression $\begin{smallmatrix} a\ g\ f\sharp\ g \\ c\ b\ a\ g \end{smallmatrix}$ so that it could be solmised not $\begin{smallmatrix} \text{sol fa mi fa} \\ \text{fa mi re ut} \end{smallmatrix}$ but $\begin{smallmatrix} \text{sol fa mi fa} \\ \text{sol fa mi re} \end{smallmatrix}$, avoiding the *mi contra fa* of the sixth, *b g*, which is the only solmisation permitted by the placing of the semitones if *b♮* is sung. Clearly, a rule which permitted us to approach *g* only through *b♭* would be untenable against musical evidence, and the theorists do not call for it.

If mi and fa sound simultaneously in a perfect interval, this may be symptomatic of either of two faults. First, and most important, the interval which ought to be perfect may in fact be augmented or diminished. This must be put right. Second, even if the perfect interval itself is correct, it may be immediately preceded by an augmented or diminished interval. This could result from two simultaneous applications of accidentals which are incompatible, and the sounding of *mi contra fa* on the cadence chord, as Lowinsky pointed out, would serve (to the tone-deaf) as a warning that something had gone wrong. (The "closer adhesion" prescribed by Ugolino should thus not be taken too far.) Mi would incidentally sound against fa on the antecedent chord, but only because each was a semitone away from the final chord. Only the first of these faults is specifically illustrated by the theorists, but examples of how both arise include:

*This progression is actually written in Old Hall, no. 16; it must be the result of two incompatible alternatives finding their way onto a single copy. | *Recta* names are used above where available. No mutations are used in these examples.

It is clear from the examples given by the theorists that this rule applied to perfect intervals which have a cadence function, although this proviso is never explicitly stated. Simultaneous false relations do occur in the manuscripts in contexts where the conflicting accidentals seem well justified on linear grounds. In Old Hall, these instances invariably occur at weak points in the phrase (that is, not in the last interval of a cadential progression or the first of a phrase). The following examples are selected for their explicit manuscript accidentals:

Old Hall no. 27, bars 12 - 16 (Pycard)

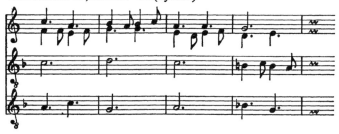

no. 36, bars 79 - 81, 91 - 95 (Cooke)

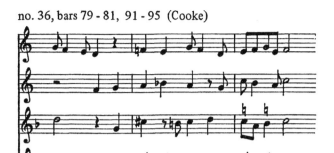

The conflict usually occurs between a leading-note function of the upper voice and tritone avoidance in the lower. Unless a melodic tritone is admitted as an adjunct to a leading note ($f\ b\ c$) or to avoid a vertical tritone or a false relation on a strong beat (the strength being to some extent a matter of subjective judgment), it should be avoided. Tritones and false relations are admissible as vertical intervals in auxiliary positions, more on the evidence of manuscript accidentals than of theoretical statements, though Tinctoris (CS IV, p. 127) gives later support to this principle. Clashes may be admitted between two voices, each of which has a correct relationship with the lowest part. In the progression $\begin{smallmatrix} e\,f\,e \\ c\,b\,c \\ c\,d\,c \end{smallmatrix}$ the imperfect fifth between f and b is allowable because each upper part behaves correctly with the tenor.

The other harmonic rule given by the theorists requires thirds and sixths preceding fifths and octaves to be major, where the upper note of the first interval rises a single step to the second one. Thirds preceding unisons or fifths should be minor if the top part descends one step. The clearest statement, again, is by Jean de Muris, and is accompanied by exhaustive examples (CS III, pp. 71-3). These can easily be adapted to apply to a lower part where the inflection of the upper is determined by manuscript accidentals, though the tenor is treated as a fixed part to which the others adjust, both in his exposition and in Ugolino's. If the tenor progression is governed by the priority of *recta* over *ficta*, as in $\begin{smallmatrix} g & a \\ b & a \end{smallmatrix}$, this will be applied instead of inflecting the upper part: in this case the lower part will have b♭ a, instead of g♯ a in the upper. Instead of having a discantus part proceeding by semitone step, we now have a tenor proceeding by semitone step, but the perfect octave is still preceded by a major sixth. The speculative basis of the rule is stated explicitly by Ugolino, who gives two reasons for applying *ficta* to imperfect intervals:

> Sed talem musicam etiam in consonantiis imperfectis sive dissonantiis colorandis fingimus, causa vero fictionis huiusmodi duplex est, scilicet, causa harmoniae dulcioris habendae, et causa propinquioris perfectionis acquirendae...　　　　　　　　　　　　(ed. Seay, II, p. 47)

But we must also feign such music [i.e., use *musica ficta*] to colour imperfect consonances or dissonances. *Ficta* is used here for two reasons: for the sake of achieving sweeter harmony and in order to gain closer proximity to perfection.

Prosdocimus gives a shorter but otherwise similar account of the detailed application of this principle, the main difference being one of terminology. Prosdocimus calls thirds, sixths, tenths etc. imperfect consonances, major or minor accordingly. Ugolino calls them imperfect consonances or dissonances, and usually refers to them as dissonances.

Chromatic inflection applied to these imperfect consonances or dissonances is often called "coloration" (*coloratio*) — i.e., a musical ornament, like the *chroma* of Marchettus. The notion that this is "ornamental" rather than "necessary" places this kind of inflection in the category of *causa pulchritudinis*. Prosdocimus gives the reason as "for the sake of sweeter harmony". The third preceding a fifth does not need to be made more perfect except for its own good: thus, its perfection classes as ornamental. Some confusion may arise from the constant distinction drawn between major and minor semitones. Ugolino, for example, says in his *Tractatus monochordi*:

> Nam potest intelligens organista maiore uti semitonio atque minore, altero quidem ad perfectionem, altero vero ad colorationem.
> 　　　　　　　　　　　　　　　　　　(ed. Seay, III, p. 252)

For the intelligent *organista* can use major and minor semitones, the one for perfection, the other for coloration.

MUSICA RECTA & MUSICA FICTA

This might legitimately be interpreted to mean that major semitones are used to perfect intervals which should be perfect, minor semitones to adjust the size of an imperfect interval proceeding to a perfect one. In fact, Ugolino makes it clear in the chapter *de ficta musica* in the *Declaratio* that he means: in order to perfect an interval (e.g. *b-f*), a major semitone must be added to one of the notes (i.e., *f-f♯* or *b-b♭*), while the "coloration" of an imperfect consonance, regarded as an ornament to the ensuing perfect consonance, is achieved by making one outer note of the imperfect interval a mere minor semitone away from the perfect interval (e.g., $\begin{smallmatrix} f & g \\ a & g \end{smallmatrix}$ requires *f♯*: although *f-f♯* is a major semitone, *f♯-g* is a minor semitone). Major semitones are occasionally required melodically for reasons of vertical perfection (see p. 82 above).

One important rider to the rule that imperfect consonances should be major when they proceed to perfect consonances concerns the application of the rule to successive part-writing. If each upper voice in the cadence figure shown below is considered only with the lowest voice, and each is made to form a major interval with the tenor, then the result, in combination, will be the so-called double-leading-note cadence; not because it is necessary to perfect the fourth between the upper parts but because *each* of the upper parts has a leading-note function. If the middle part fell cadentially to *e*, the *f* would be natural:

Prosdocimus extends the principle of "adhesion" to adjacent imperfect intervals. He justifies the *primam ♮ quadrum in cantu inferiori* in the third example quoted in ex. 6 thus:

> Quum talis sexta in sua minoritate minus distat a loco ad quem immediate accedere intendit, scilicet ab alia sexta immediate sequenti, quam in sua majoritate.
> (CS III, p. 199)

Clearly, as in the case of *mi contra fa*, this rule cannot be accorded universal application. To make all consecutive thirds major, or all minor, would incur numerous musical anomalies. But it may sometimes be used in the context in which Prosdocimus himself uses it; the pre-penultimate chord is made closer to the penultimate and thus to the final perfect interval. It could also be regarded as a leading note to a leading note.

Partial signatures

The problem of "key"-signatures has formed the starting-point for many recent articles devoted to *ficta*: no survey of *ficta* at this period can overlook them. One of the most far-reaching consequences of the distinction between *recta* and *ficta*, and the prior claims of the former, is its effect on the interpretation of these signatures. All that has been said so far is true for unsignatured parts. Absence of a flat signature would not restrain the application of b♭, since it forms part of the normal scheme for an unsignatured part, and may be sung flat or natural without prior claim by the uninflected form.

The normal solmisation procedure for any piece of music is by *musica recta*, giving a built-in system of priorities for applying editorial accidentals. What difference does a flat signature make? Having rejected a modal basis for early fifteenth-century polyphony, interpretations of signatures based on modal transposition are likewise excluded. There can be no question of applying a modern interpretation: the abiding problem of partial signatures is that a signature sometimes has to be overruled, while an unsignatured part sometimes requires flats. If b♭s can be freely supplied to a part without a signature, what significance can a b♭ signature have? If a b♭ signature were to eliminate b♮ as a *recta* note, only two *recta* hexachords would remain. If a signature of b♭ and e♭ were so interpreted, only one hexachord could be used without incurring *ficta*, and the entire balance of priorities would be upset because a *ficta* note (e♭) would be legitimised by the signature. Yet it is along these lines that the following suggestion is made: a flat signature serves to define the limits of *musica recta*, and the point at which *ficta* takes over.

The set of three hexachords on *c*, *g* and *f* represents a set of relationships. The terminology of natural, hard and soft reflects these relationships, for the arrangement of each individual hexachord is identical in terms of tones and semitones. Elimination of one or more of the *recta* hexachords would severely restrict the available mutations and the exercise of priority for *recta*, as well as producing a very different pattern of inflection for a part with a signature. If, however, we see "key signatures" as what might be termed "hexachord signatures", this effect is overcome, and the essential set of relationships preserved. By this reckoning, *flat signatures bring about a transposition of the basic* recta *system of three hexachords one degree flatwards for each note flattened in the signature*. Ficta involves the transposition of isolated hexachords for the purpose of creating chromatic notes, but transposition of *recta* implies that the whole structure is shifted, together with its built-in rules for applying accidentals. This interpretation solves a number of puzzling features. Signatured parts tend to occupy a pitch-range roughly a fifth lower (for one flat) than unsignatured upper parts in the same pieces, yet a bitonal interpretation of the total polyphonic sound is rarely palatable.[22] The hexachord

---

[22] This problem is discussed at length in Hoppin, "Partial Signatures...", Lowinsky, "Conflicting Views on Conflicting Signatures", *Journal of the American Musicological Society* VII (1954), pp. 118-204) and R. H. Hoppin, "Conflicting Signatures Reviewed", *ibid.*, IX (1956), pp. 97-117.

MUSICA RECTA & MUSICA FICTA

interpretation removes any need to suggest bitonality. A part with a one-flat signature has two *recta* hexachords in common with an unsignatured part on the one hand, and with a two-flat-signature part on the other, and it therefore shares a high proportion of actual *recta* preferences. Just as $b\flat$ is a legitimate *recta* note in an unsignatured part, $b\natural$ is a legitimate *ficta* note in a part with one flat, corresponding exactly to the status of $f\sharp$ in an unsignatured part. Similarly, $e\flat$ becomes a *recta* note in a part with a one-flat signature; and $a\flat$ is added to the *recta* range in a part with two flats, where $e\natural$ becomes a *ficta* note. (If the lower part of the cadence $\begin{smallmatrix} c & d \\ e & d \end{smallmatrix}$ is governed by a $b\flat$ signature, exercise of *recta* preference will favour $e\flat$ rather than $c\sharp$.)

Double-leading-note cadences are bound to be the normal result in successively-composed, unsignatured pieces (see p. 97 above). The same applies to a piece with two unsignatured upper parts and a flat signature in the lowest of three parts. Where both lower parts have a $b\flat$ signature, the middle part may tend more often to forego cadential patterns incurring extreme *ficta* sharps, and in this case single-leading-note cadences would be the logical result. It must be emphasised that the presence of a signature does not override the sharpening of leading notes.[23] *Recta* transposition is supported by Ugolino's discussion of a "double hand where all the solmisation name of *musica recta* and *musica ficta* are set out" and "another hand of *musica ficta* and *musica recta* starting a fifth below γ, on C, equivalent to the first hand except for its low pitch".[24]

No satisfactory explanation has yet emerged for the signature of $e\flat$ only, which occurs in Old Hall nos. 21 and 82. However, the clefless flat signatures found in some pieces in Bologna, Civico Museo Bibliografico Musicale, Q 15 and the Escorial *chansonnier* (Madrid, Biblioteca del Monasterio de San Lorenzo el Real de El Escorial, V III, p. 24) offer some comparison. *Tous deplaisir* (Escorial, ff.7v-8), for example, has a signature of two flats for each of the three parts, in each case on the second and fourth lines of the stave. C-clefs have to be assumed on the bottom line for the top part, on the middle line for the lower two. The flats therefore fall on *e* and *b* in the upper part, *a* and *e* in the lower two. The relationship is that of the signatures ♭ ♭♭ ♭♭, the placing one degree flatter.[25]

The distinction between a signature and an accidental is not always clear in manuscripts, and may not always have been clear to scribes. The flat signature functions as a kind of clef to the use of *musica recta*:

---

[23] The signature pattern of ♮ ♭♭ does, however, appear to supersede ♮ ♮ ♭ as traces of successive composition begin to weaken, and as single-leading-note cadences become more satisfactory on musical grounds.

[24] Ed. Seay, II, pp. 48-50.

[25] A signature involving more flats than conventional notation permitted was achieved by Pycard in a unique way. My solution to the double clefs of Old Hall, no. 76, is incorporated into the edition (see n.1) and explained in the commentary.

some accidentals may be treated as temporary signatures in this way. A manuscript accidental may be placed well in advance of the note it affects precisely for this reason or, as suggested above (p. 88), to warn of a single change of hexachord. In either case, early placing of an accidental may give prior warning of the intended solmisation and therefore of the intended inflections.

The principles outlined above provide a basis for practical guidelines. Accordingly, such guidelines are proposed in the introduction to the new edition of Old Hall, to which the present article serves as a background.

[20]

The Origin and Early History of Proportion Signs*

By ANNA MARIA BUSSE BERGER

Proportion signs, or, to be more specific, fractions in which a certain number of notes in the numerator are made equal to a different number of notes of the same type in the denominator, are probably found for the first time in Anthonello de Caserta's *Amour m'a le cuer mis* in the MS. Modena, Biblioteca Estense, M.5.24, compiled in Bologna in 1410 or 1411.[1] The earliest theoretical explanation of proportion signs is given by Prosdocimus de Beldemandis in his *Tractatus practice de cantus mensurabilis* of 1408 (1869, 218–19). It has long been established that they came into existence to override the minim equivalence of the French system (see in particular Bent 1980, 370), yet beyond that little is known. Where did this wish to override minim equivalence originate? Why did composers suddenly make use of proportions? Precisely how were proportions used in the late fourteenth and early fifteenth centuries? For example, it is generally assumed that two consecutive proportions are cumulative, since the great late fifteenth-century theorists Johannes Tinctoris[2] and Franchinus Gaffurius (1496, Bk. IV, Ch. 5) say they are. But was this also true in the early fifteenth century? Similarly, according to Tinctoris (1978, 53) and Gaffurius (1496, Bk. IV, Ch. 5) the mensuration within the proportion derives from the mensuration sign preceding the proportion and not from the proportion itself. Was this also the case in earlier times? For example, duple mensuration followed by *sesquialtera* proportion applied on the breve level can result in imperfect or perfect breves in the *sesquialtera* section, depending on whether the original duple mensuration of the breve is

---

* A shorter version of the paper was read at the fifty-third annual meeting of the American Musicological Society in New Orleans in October 1987.

[1] The French pieces in the source derive from "the largely French repertory of the courts of the schismatic popes Alexander V (elected in Pisa in 1409) and his successor John XXIII." Many of the pieces were, however, composed considerably earlier. See Günther 1980a and 1970.

[2] See Tinctoris 1978, where all horizontal proportional relationships are cumulative.

preserved (see Example 1a), or the triple mensuration of the *sesquialtera* takes over and is applied also on the breve level (see Example 1b). In the latter case the *sesquialtera* proportion changes the original binary mensuration of the breve resulting in two perfect breves rather than three imperfect breves. In other words, imperfect time becomes perfect. While this question is of little relevance for the performance of music, it was not only an important issue for fifteenth and sixteenth century theorists, but also played a major role in the development of proportion signs.

Example 1
(a) *Sesquialtera* proportion with imperfect breves

₵ □   □   = 3/2 □   □   □
  ◇ ◇ ◇ ◇   ◇ ◇ ◇ ◇ ◇ ◇

(b) *Sesquialtera* proportion with perfect breves

₵ □   □   = 3/2 □·   □·
  ◇ ◇ ◇ ◇   ◇ ◇ ◇ ◇ ◇ ◇

The present study investigates the use of proportion signs in the theoretical treatises and the most important musical sources of the late fourteenth and early fifteenth centuries. With every theorist or composition, it attempts to find answers to the following questions:

1. Which proportions are used?
2. How are they indicated?
3. Why are only certain proportions used and what is the reason for the great variety of signs used to indicate proportions?
4. Are proportions cumulative?
5. Is the mensuration derived from the proportion sign or rather from the preceding mensuration sign?

With regard to the first question, practically all late fourteenth- and early fifteenth-century theorists describe essentially the same set of proportions (see Table 1). Prosdocimus de Beldemandis (1869, 218–19) and Ugolino of Orvieto (1960, 210–11)[3] list the following five proportions: 2:1, 3:1, 3:2, 4:3, and 9:4. The fifteenth-century anonymous treatise *Iste sunt proportiones*[4] gives the same fractions, but adds 9:8 and 8:3. Other treatises that list all or some of the same

---

[3] Ugolino uses the same proportions in his compositions (Seay 1955, 152–66).
[4] Scb, f. 142r-v. The treatise shows both French and Italian characteristics. I would like to thank Professor Jan Herlinger for information on the treatise. See also Gallo 1984, 344–46, who provides an excellent summary of some of these treatises. Sca, f. 48v-56r in the same manuscript describes the same proportions.

proportions are: an English treatise from the early fifteenth century (Rvat), the Spanish treatise *Venerabiles domini* (SDI), the mid-fifteenth-century treatise by Georg Erber from Aibling (see Federhofer-Königs 1969), the anonymous *Regule proportionum in quantum ad musicam pertinet* (Vnm), the British manuscript London, British Library, Lansdowne 763 (Lbl), a little known fifteenth-century Provençal treatise written in Hebrew,[5] and the German Anonymous XI, copied before 1471.[6] The musical sources of the late fourteenth and early fifteenth centuries, in particular CH[7] and ModA (edited in Apel 1970), also only make use of precisely the same set of proportions: 2:1, 3:1, 4:1, 3:2, 4:3, 9:4, and 9:8.[8]

In the second half of the fifteenth century, Guilielmus Monachus still describes the same set of proportions (1965, 19–44), although he mentions in addition the inverted versions of all of these fractions. John Hothby's *Quid est proportio*[9] also lists the usual proportions, but in his motet *Ora pro nobis* he enlarges the rhythmic possibilities by including the fractions 5:2, 5:4, and 7:4 (HOb, ff. 26v-27 and Hothby 1964, 4–7). Johannes Tinctoris (1978) alone can be credited with

---

[5] Anonymous 1975. The author describes 5:4 (but the subsequent explanations make clear that he means 6:4) and the very unusual 17:8, *dupla sesquioctava*, indicated by ⊙, which is normally a sign of either *sesquialtera* on the minim level when set against O or *dupla sesquiquarta* when set against O; it is possible that the author meant either of those proportions. I would like to thank Talya Berger for having translated the treatise for me.

[6] Anonymous XI 1869, 474–75. He describes proportions 16:6 (which is the same as 8:3), and 9:6 (which is the same as 3:2). On p. 475 Anonymous XI gives another list which mentions only 2:1, 3:1, 4:1, 3:2, 4:3, and 9:8, saying that only these are used in performing music.

[7] For a detailed discussion of the Chantilly MS. see Ursula Günther, 1984, 87–118. Günther argues (1984, 107) that "the source of CH was written in Paris. It must then have been brought to Florence by a member of the Alberti family and copied there. If we leave aside all hypotheses, the probability remains that CH was not a southern French original but a testimony to the diffusion of the *Ars subtilior* in Italy and to the humanistic efforts of a Florentine patrician whose family found exile in France." As far as dating is concerned, Günther suggests that the manuscript is an early fifteenth-century Italian copy of late fourteenth-century music and gives the years 1393–95 as the earliest possible date. See also Günther 1980c, 663. A modern edition of the Chantilly manuscript is in Greene 1981.

[8] The following proportion signs are used in ModA: in Anthonello de Caserta's *Amour m'a le cuer mis* (ff. 32v-33r, Apel 1970:1, no.3) 9:6 and 4:2; in Comradus de Pistoria's *Se doulz espour* (f. 31v, Apel 1970:1, no. 15) 3 (that is, 3:2) and 2 (that is 2:3); the numbers 3 and 2, indicating *sesquialtera* and *dupla*, respectively, are also used in Johannes Simon Hasprois's *Ma douce amour* (f. 28r, Apel 1970:1, no. 41) and Bartholomeus de Bononia's *Que pena major* (ff. 37r-36v, Apel 1970:3, no. 301). In CH, Baude Cordier's *Belle, bonne sage* (f. 11v, Greene 1981:18, no.1) uses 8:9, Cordier's *Tout par compas* (f. 12, Greene 1981:18, no. 2) uses 3:1, 3:2, and 4:3.

[9] HOa, f. 26. The proportions listed earlier in the treatise do not refer to temporal measurements.

TABLE 1

Proportions in Theoretical Treatises, ca. 1400–1450

Theorist or Manuscript Siglum	2:1	3:1	4:1	3:2	4:3	9:8	9:4	8:3	unusual other proportions
Prosdocimus	x	x		x	x	x			
Ugolino	x	x		x	x	x			
"En alius tractatus" (Scb)	x	x		x	x	x	x	(x)	16:6 = 8:3
"Compilatio de proportionibus" (Sca)	x	x		x	x	x	x	x	
Rvat	x	x		x	x	x	x		
SDI	x			x	x	x			8:1; 9:1
Georg Erber	x	x		x	x	x	x		
Vnm	x	x		x					
Lbl	x	x	x	x	x	x			
Anonymous 1975	x	x	x	x	x	x			17:8
Anonymous XI	x	x	x	x	x	x	(x)		16:6 = 8:3, and 5:4

bringing the rhythmic proportions on a par with the harmonic ones. He describes twenty-five different proportions, all of which can, in addition, appear in inversion. Tinctoris's follower, Franchinus Gaffurius, perfected Tinctoris's system and included even more proportions.[10]

In addition to fractions, composers and theorists of the period used mensuration signs, coloration, and Italian note shapes to indicate proportions, often combining these devices to avoid ambiguity. Coloration and Italian note shapes have received considerable attention in the secondary literature,[11] and were used by composers and theorists alike to indicate the common proportions already enumerated: 2:1, 3:1, 3:2, 4:3, 9:4, and 9:8.[12] The practice of indicating proportions through mensuration signs, on the other hand, still awaits scholarly attention. In most cases a combination of different mensuration signs presupposes minim equivalence, as one might expect. Nonetheless mensuration signs were also used to indicate true proportions—that is, to override minim equivalence—often enough for us to conclude that such use represented an important practice in the late

---

[10] Gaffurius 1496, Bk. IV. See also Clement A. Miller's detailed discussion of Gaffurius's proportions (Miller 1968).

[11] E.g., Wolf 1904, 1:289–327; Apel 1953, 403–35; Gallo 1984, 336–39.

[12] See, for example, Philipoctus de Caserta's *En remirant* in ModA (ff. 34v-35r, Apel 1970:1, no. 79), which has a 9:4, 2:3, and 3:4 proportion. See also the *Tractatus figurarum*, formerly ascribed to Philippus de Caserta and recently edited in Schreur 1987.

THE EARLY HISTORY OF PROPORTION SIGNS

Example 2

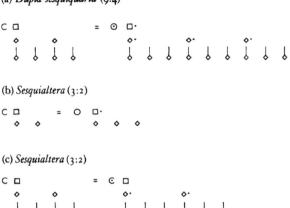

fourteenth and fifteenth centuries.[13] In many cases the mensuration signs are used without any additional explanations, in others a canon or coloration is added. Sometimes, too, mensuration signs are combined with Italian note shapes to remove ambiguity. It is important to stress that the proportional use of mensuration signs generally presupposes breve equality, that is, the lower note values are to be adjusted within an unchanging breve.[14] Marchettus (1961, 86, 66; Gallo 1984, 335) had already related the term *proportio* to one *tempus*. Similarly, the Hebrew treatise in Anonymous 1975 (58–76) enclosed all proportions within the central breve. As a result, the note values compared could vary: for instance, a 9:4 proportion will necessarily compare minims (see Example 2a), while a 3:2 proportion can either compare semibreves (see Example 2b) or minims (see Example 2c).

Table 2 lists all pieces which set perfect against imperfect time with the *sesquialtera* on the semibreve level, that is, presupposing breve equality as in Example 2b. All composers with the exception of Galiot use O to indicate *sesquialtera*. Galiot uses ⊙ instead (CH f. 37; Greene 1981:19, no. 53). Three of the pieces make use of a canon, obviously in order to avoid minim equivalence between the different mensurations.[15] Two use a red O to indicate the *sesquialtera* proportion.[16] Yet

---

[13] Berger 1986 describes the survival of this tradition in theoretical treatises in the fifteenth and early sixteenth centuries.

[14] The only sign which is not always associated with breve equality is ↄ. See below.

[15] Johannes de Janua in *Une dame requis*, (ModA, f. 12r, Apel 1970:1, no. 45, mm. 20, 32, and 65); M. de Sancto Johanne, *Je chante ung chant*, uses a red O set against C to indicate a *sesquialtera* proportion (CH, f. 16, Greene 1981:18, no. 9); Johannes

another piece uses both the sign of perfect time, major prolation against imperfect time, major prolation and red coloration to ensure that nine semibreves are set against six (see Example 3a).[17] The same piece uses coloration in the normal way for ₵: two perfect semibreves are replaced with three imperfect ones (Example 3b). In order to achieve the effect shown in Example 3a, the mensuration sign is absolutely necessary. On the other hand, the composer could not have used the sign without coloration, since he presupposes minim equivalence throughout the piece when perfect and imperfect time are set against each other. Finally, we have three pieces which indicate a *sesquialtera* proportion by O alone.[18]

Table 3 lists all pieces with imperfect time, minor prolation set against imperfect time, major prolation resulting in a *sesquialtera* proportion on the minim level when the breves or semibreves (there is no difference between breve and semibreve equality here) are equally long (as in Example 2c).[19] In three of the four cases the *sesquialtera* proportion is indicated by the mensuration sign alone; only Johannes de Janua's piece adds a canon.

The 4:3 proportion is shown by the reversed C (Ↄ), which can follow perfect time, minor prolation (see Example 4a) or imperfect time, major prolation (see Example 4b). While all other mensuration

---

Galiot, *Le sault perilleux*, (CH, f. 37, Greene 1981:19, no. 53, m. 19 in Contratenor and m. 22 in Cantus). Franchois Lebertoul indicates a *sesquialtera* proportion through O and a canon in *Depuis un peu un joyeux parlement* (Ob, f. 122v, Reaney 1959:2, 43, m.8).

[16] Cooke uses a red O in a Credo to signal a *sesquialtera* proportion (OH, ff. 78v-79, Hughes and Bent 1969:2: no. 92, m. 56); see also Damett, Credo, (OH, ff. 79v-80, Hughes and Bent 1969:2, no. 101); see also M. de Sancto Johanne, *Je chante ung chant*, (CH, f. 16, Greene 1981:18, no. 9, mm. 12, 25, and 40).

[17] Lyonel's Credo, (OH, ff. 70-71, Hughes and Bent 1969:1:2, no. 83, m. 47) also combines O with the red number 3 and coloration to indicate a *sesquialtera* proportion.

[18] Matheus de Perusio, *Dame que j'ayme*, (ModA, ff. 10v-11r, Apel 1970:1, no. 55, mm. 28, 51, and 71); *Ung lion say*, an anonymous piece in CH, f. 28v (Greene 1981:18, no. 35, m. 34) uses ⊙ in Contratenor and Cantus (but meaning O) against ₵ in the Tenor with breve equality only when no semibreves occur. Of particular interest is the piece *Salve mater salvatoris*, ascribed to both Dunstable (ModB, f. 116v-117, Dunstable 1970, no. 62, m. 51) and Leonel (Tr92, f. 193v-195). In ModB the scribe uses O alone to indicate the *sesquialtera* proportion, in Tr 92, ff. 193-195 O is combined with coloration, while Tr 92, f. 215 uses only coloration.

[19] The following pieces use C : ₵ as a *sesquialtera* proportion: Johannes de Janua in *Une dame requis*, (ModA, f. 12r, Apel 1970:1, no. 45, mm. 12, 39; in m. 66 O: ⊙ is used to show a *sesquialtera* proportion); Matheus de Perusio in *Le greygnour bien*, (ModA, ff. 32r-31v, Apel 1970:1, no. 51), Cantus and Tenor are written in C, contratenor in ₵ with equally long semibreves; the anonymous *Ung lion say*, (CH, f. 28v, Greene 1981:18, no. 35, m. 28ff.); Damett's Gloria, (OH, ff. 33v-34, Hughes and Bent 1969:2, no. 39, m. 72).

THE EARLY HISTORY OF PROPORTION SIGNS

TABLE 2

Sesquialtera on the Semibreve Level

ModA			
Johannes de Janua	*Une dame requis*	○ = C, with canon
Matheus de Perusio	*Dame que j'aym*	○ = C, without canon
Anthonello de Caserta	*Bauté parfaite*	⊙ = ₵, with coloration
CH			
M. de Sancto Johanne	*Je chant ung chant*	[○] = C, with canon
Johannes Galiot	*Le sault perilleux*	⊙ = C, with canon
Anonymous	*Ung lion say*	○ = C, without canon, but equal breve only when no semibreves are involved
OH			
Cooke	*Credo, ff.* 78v–79	[○] = C, without canon
Lyonel	*Credo, ff.* 70–71	and red notes = C
Damett	*Credo, ff.* 79v–80	[○] = C
ModB			
Dunstable	*Salve mater salvatoris*	○ = C, without canon

Square brackets indicate coloration; i.e., the symbols are written in red in the manuscript.

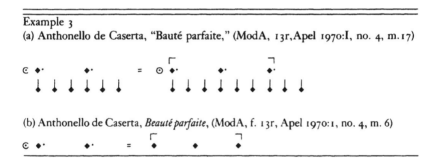

Example 3
(a) Anthonello de Caserta, "Bauté parfaite," (ModA, 13r, Apel 1970:I, no. 4, m. 17)

(b) Anthonello de Caserta, *Bauté parfaite*, (ModA, f. 13r, Apel 1970:1, no. 4, m. 6)

TABLE 3

Sesquialtera on the Minim Level

ModA			
Johannes de Janua	*Une dame requis*	C = ₵, with canon
Matheus de Perusio	*Le greygnour bien*	C = ₵, without canon
CH			
Anonymous	*Ung lion say*	C = ₵, without canon
OH			
Damett	*Gloria, ff.* 33v–34	C = ₵, without canon, but uses ₵ instead of C and C instead of ₵

EXAMPLE 4

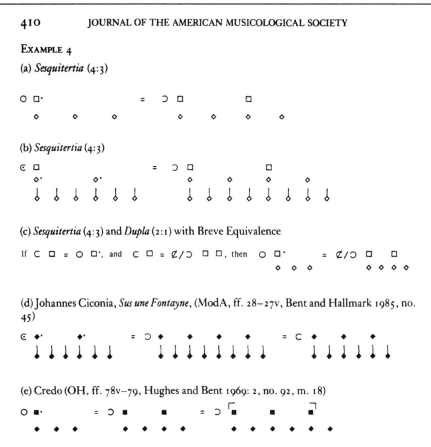

signs used as proportions presuppose breve equality, ⊃ does not necessarily do so in the late fourteenth and early fifteenth century.[20] Breve equality between ⊃ and ○ can be assumed only if ⊃ is also used in the same piece as a sign of *proportio dupla* (see Example 4c). I have been able to find only two pieces where ⊃ indicates a *proportio dupla*.[21] On the other hand, Johannes Ciconia's *Sus une Fontayne*, for example, combines ⊃ with C and ₵ (see Example 4d) in such a way that even though three minims of ₵ are set against four of ⊃, a minim of C is equal to a minim of ₵. We can thus conclude that ⊃ was not always associated with breve equality in the *ars subtilior*.[22]

---

[20] I would like to thank Dr. Wolf Frobenius who first brought this point to my attention.

[21] Matheus de Perusio's *Le greygnour bien*, (ModA, ff. 32r-31v, Apel 1970:1, no. 51, m. 21); and the anonymous *Par le grant sens* (Wolf 1904, 2:46-48).

[22] It is likely that from the early fifteenth century on ⊃ and ₵ were used interchangeably to indicate *proportio sesquitertia* and *dupla*. Alejandro E. Planchart has found in AO a version of a Gloria by Johannes Brasart that uses ⊃ to indicate a 4:3 proportion, while BL and Tr 90 and Tr 93 all use ₵ (Planchart 1981, 41-42).

THE EARLY HISTORY OF PROPORTION SIGNS 411

TABLE 4

Sesquitertia on the Semibreve and Minim Level

ModA		
Anthonello de Caserta	*Tres nouble dame*	O = ↃC, and C = ↃC, with canon
Johannes Ciconia	*Sus une Fontayne*	C = ↃC, without canon
Philippot de Caserta (Johannes Galiot)	*En atendant souffrir*	C = ↃC, without canon
Matheus de Perusio	*Dame souvrayn*	C = ↃC, without canon
Matheus de Perusio	*A qui fortune*	O = ↃC, without canon
Matheus de Perusio	*Se puor loyaulement servir*	C = ↃC, without canon
Anonymous	*En un vergier*	C = ↃC, without canon
CH		
Trebor	*Quant joyne cuer*	C = ↃC, without canon
Suzoy	*Prophilias*	C = ↃC, without canon
Philippot de Caserta	*Par le grant senz d'Adriane*	C = ↃC, without canon
Anonymous	*Je ne puis avoir plaisir*	O = ↃC, with Italian note shapes
Anonymous	*De tous les moys*	O = ↃC, with coloration
OH		
Anonymous	*Credo, ff. 62v–63*	O = ↃC, without canon
Bittering	*Credo, ff. 66v–67*	ʘ = ↃC, without canon
Power	*Credo, ff. 68v–69*	O = ↃC, without canon
Cooke	*Credo, ff. 78v–79*	O = ↃC, without canon

ↃC was used more often during this period than any other sign (see Table 4).[23] Because the sign was almost exclusively associated with the *sesquitertia* proportion, few composers found it necessary to clarify its meaning by additional signs: Anthonello de Caserta (*Tres nouble dame*) adds a canon; two pieces combine it with Italian note shapes[24] and one with coloration.[25] There are several pieces where the

---

[23] Anthonello de Caserta, *Tres nouble dame*, (ModA, f. 28v, Apel 1970:1, no. 8, m. 20); Johannes Ciconia, *Sus une fontayne*, (ModA, ff. 27r-26v, Apel 1970:1, no. 14, m. 1); Philippot de Caserta (Johannes Galiot), *En atendant souffrir*, (ModA, f. 20r, Apel 1970:1, no. 28, m. 48); Matheus de Perusio, *Dame souvrayne*, (ModA, f. 38r, Apel 1970:1, no. 56, m. 8); idem, *A qui fortune*, (ModA, f. 41r, Apel 1970:1, no. 61, m. 16); idem, *Se pour loyaulement servir*, (ModA, f. 43r, Apel 1970:1, no. 69, m. 26); Anonymous, *En un vergier*, (ModA, f. 18v, Apel 1970:2, no. 145, m. 1); Trebor, *Quant joyne cuer*, (CH, f. 31, Greene 1981:18, no. 40, m. 55); Suzoy, *Prophilias*, (CH, f. 35v, Greene 1981:18, no. 49, m. 11); Philippot de Caserta, *Par le grant senz d'Adriane*, (CH, f. 37v, Greene 1981:19, no. 54, m. 1); Anon., *Je ne puis avoir plaisir*, (CH, f. 24, Greene 1981:18, no. 25, m. 1); Anon., Credo, (OH, ff. 62v-63, Hughes and Bent 1969:1, no. 75, m. 72); Bittering, Credo, (OH, ff. 66v-67, Hughes and Bent 1969:1, no. 79, m. 164).

[24] Philipoctus de Caserta, *En remirant*, (ModA, ff. 43v-35r, Apel 1970:1, no. 79, m. 12); the anon. *Je ne puis avoir plaisir*, (CH, f. 24, Greene 1981:18, no. 25, m. 2).

[25] Anon. *De tous les moys*, (CH, f. 48, Greene 1981:19, no. 76, m. 32).

TABLE 5

Dupla Sesquiquarta (9:4) on the Minim Level

ModA			
Johannes de Janua	*Une dame requis*		C = ⊙, with canon
CH			
Cunelier	*Se Geneive, Tristan*		O = 🕒, with canon

TABLE 6

Sesquioctava (9:8) on the Minim Level

CH			
Johannes de Altacuria	*Se doit il plus*		⊃ = ℭ, with canon
Johannes Galiot	*Se sault perilleux*		⊙ = C, with canon; since the piece is diminished, semibreves are compared

combination of ⊃ with coloration results in a 2:1 proportion when related to the initial perfect time, e.g., in an anonymous Credo (see Example 4e above).[26]

Table 5 lists two pieces with *dupla sesquiquarta*, that is 9:4— ⊙ set against C gives a 9:4 proportion on the minim level (see Example 2a).[27] Both pieces use a canon.

Two pieces in CH use the sesquioctava proportion (see Table 6). In the first piece, Johannes de Altacuria's *Se doit il plus* nine minims of ℭ are set against eight of ⊃ (see Example 5). Again, the mensuration sign is elucidated by a canon. It is logical that the composer has compared ℭ to ⊃, since eight minims within one breve obviously

EXAMPLE 5
Sesquioctava (9:8) in Johannes de Altacuria's "Se doit il plus" (CH, 15v, Greene 1981:18, no. 8, m. 18)

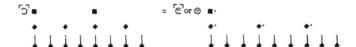

require diminution. What is surprising is that he did not use ⊙ or ⊙, even though three perfect semibreves are compared to four imperfect

---

[26] A similar situation obtains in *En albion de fluns*, (CH, f. 47v, Greene 1981:19, no. 75, m. 26).

[27] Johannes de Janua, *Une dame requis*, (ModA, f. 12r, Apel 1970:1, no. 45, m. 66) and Cunelier, *Se Geneive, Tristan*, (CH, f. 41v, Greene 1981:19, no. 63, m. 38).

ones. The other piece with *sesquioctava*, Galiot's *Le sault perilleux*[28] uses precisely this sign of perfect time with three dots (⊙). This piece also includes a canon.

Goscalch's *En nul estat* (CH, f. 39v, Greene 1981:19, no. 58) and Anthonello de Caserta's *Dame d'onour enqui* (ModA, f. 40v, Apel 1970:1, no.5) use two binary or ternary numbers on top of each other, the upper indicating prolation, the lower time. Johannes Wolf pointed out that such usage was described by Johannes Ciconia;[29] I have found it mentioned even earlier in the Berkeley Manuscript,[30] and then by Bartolomeus Ramis de Pareja (1901, 82) and Nicolaus Burtius (1975, 135). None of these theorists elaborate on this usage. However, from a study of the two compositions in which it appears makes clear that it was reserved for vertical and simultaneous combinations of different mensurations under breve equality. In Goscalch's *En nul estat*,[31] a breve of perfect time and major prolation ($\frac{3}{3}$) is made equal to a breve of perfect time and minor prolation ($\frac{2}{3}$) (see Example 6a), while imperfect time, minor prolation is always diminished by half—in other words, it substitutes ⊃ (see Example 6b). Precisely the same temporal relationships are found in Anthonello de Caserta's *Dame d'onour enqui* with the difference that Anthonello never uses perfect time, major prolation.

It will come as no surprise that theoretical treatises also make extensive use of mensuration signs as proportions. In a revision of the *Ars (musicae)* by Johannes Boen (1972, 44) we find a table (see Figure 1)

---

[28] CH, f. 37, Greene 1981:19, no. 53, m. 3. Since the piece is sung in diminution, semibreves and not minims are compared.

[29] Wolf 1904, 95–96. The text is printed in Anonymous de la Fage 1862, 387f. See also Wolf 1900, 202.

[30] "Ciphers of ternary and binary numbers are usually to be placed, one directly over the other. The lower signifies the tempus, the upper the prolation." ("Item solent poni cifre numeri ternarii et binarii, una sopra aliam directe. Inferior designat tempus, superior vero prolacionem." (In Goscalcus 1984, 170–71, "solent" is incorrectly translated as past tense.) The treatise is dated 1375 and therefore represents the earliest known discussion of these signs. It is striking that both the theorist, who is identified in the MS. Catania, Biblioteche Riunite Civiche e A. Ursino Recupero D 39 as "Goscalcus francigenus," and the composer identified in CH as Goscalch use these extremely rare mensuration signs. This lends further support to Klaus-Jürgen Sachs's hypothesis that the author of the Berkeley MS. was indeed the composer Goscalch (see Sachs 1974, 184). Ellsworth (Goscalcus 1984, 13–15) was able to add further evidence pointing to Goscalch's authorship, but was reluctant to decide firmly that Goscalch was the author. He seems to have been unaware that the composer and theorist both make use of these rare signs. According to Ursula Günther (1980b, 543–54) Goscalch, along with other composers represented in Chantilly, might have been a papal singer.

[31] See also Günther's perceptive discussion of this piece (Günther 1960, 283–85). A canon instructs the singer to sing some sections in augmentation or diminution.

Example 6

(a) Goscalch, *En nul estat*, (CH, 39v, Greene 1981:19, no. 58)

(b) Goscalch, *En nul estat*

to exemplify harmonic proportions. Yet the signs used by the scribe are exclusively associated with temporal mensurations. He uses ☉ as a sign of *proportio sesquioctava*, just as Galiot did in *Le sault perilleux* (CH, f. 3, Greene 1981:19, no. 53). The ℂ when related to the circle with three dots stands for *sesquialtera*, which is justified in view of the fact that time has been made perfect and three dots are used to show major prolation (see Example 7). ⊃ stands, as usual, for *sesquitertia*. Gallo suggests that "the working over of the treatise was connected with the theory and practice of *ars subtilior* between the end of the 14th and the beginning of the 15th century" (Boen 1972, 14).

Other theorists who use mensuration signs as proportions are: the anonymous author of an early fifteenth-century English treatise;[32] Ugolino d'Orvieto (in his compositions)[33]; the Hebrew author of Anonymous 1975[34], probably a student of Jean Vaillant who wrote

---

[32] Rvat, f. 51. The author uses ☉ for *sesquioctava* and ⊃ for *sesquitertia* proportion. I would like to thank Professor John Daverio for having made the microfilm available to me.

[33] Ugolino uses ☉ (when compared to ℂ) as a sign of *sesquialtera* on the minim level (see Example 2c) and ☉ (when compared to ℂ) as a sign of *dupla sesquiquarta* (see Example 2a) in his compositions. (Seay 1955, 152–66.) On the other hand, he also uses mensuration signs as proportions based on minim equivalence. For a detailed discussion, see Berger 1986, 17. It can well be imagined that a scribe placed the mensuration signs in Ugolino's compositions without Ugolino's knowledge, since we know that the composer preferred the use of fractions. See Ugolino 1960, 211, and p. 420, n. 45 below. For a discussion of Tinctoris's fractions, which suffered a similar fate, see p. 426ff. below.

[34] The author (pp. 55ff.) describes ⊃ as a sign of *sesquitertia* and ☉ as a sign of *dupla sesquioctava* (that is, 17:8; I think he meant 9:4, which is commonly associated with ☉), and ☉ for *sesquioctava* (that is 9:8). That the author was slightly confused can also be gathered from the fact that, on the one hand, he mentions a proportion *sesquiquarta* (that is 5:4), but on the other hand, gives an example where six and not five minims are set against four (ibid., 64–6).

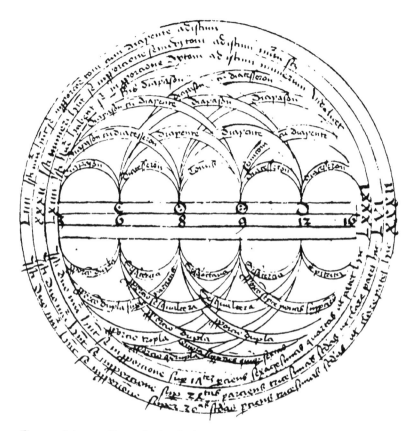

Figure 1 Johannes Boen, *Ars (musicae)*

down his treatise in the mid-fifteenth century; Coussemaker's Anonymous XI, whose treatise probably dates from the same time;[35] John

---

[35] Anonymous XI lists ↄ for *sesquitertia*, ☉ for *proportio sesquioctava*, that is, 9:8, and ↈ for an 8:3 proportion, which is, again based on breve equality when compared to ○ (see Example 8).

Example 8

Dupla superbipartiens tertias, 8:3

He also gives ↄ as a sign of *proportio sesquiquarta*. Neither the sign nor the proportion are mentioned anywhere else (Anonymous XI 1869, 471–75). For dating see Gushee 1980, 444.

Example 7
Sesquialtera

Hothby;[36] and the anonymous fifteenth-century author in Ccc.[37] I have traced a number of late fifteenth-century theorists who still use precisely the same set of mensuration signs to indicate proportions based on breve equality (Berger 1986). Thus, the anonymous author of PEc makes consistent use of mensuration signs as proportions, always presupposing breve equality. For example, ⊙ is used after C to produce a 9:4 proportion between minims (f. 80r, see Example 2a), and ⊙ is used after O to produce a 9:8 proportion between minims[38] (see Example 5).

Tinctoris, on the other hand, is extremely critical of composers who use mensuration signs to indicate proportions. But he is clearly fighting a popular tradition of indicating, for example, a *sesquialtera* proportion through the sign of major prolation or a *sesquitertia* by ⊃. "But I pray them to spare me, since these signs are so frivolous, so wrong, and so far from all appearance of reason that I have not believed them worthy of example."[39] Ironically, the scribe of one source of *Proportionales musices* signals *sesquialtera* through a mensuration sign, namely imperfect time, major prolation with coloration (Fl, f. 8v). However, this does not necessarily mean that the scribe did not understand what he was writing. Tinctoris's critical remarks on the use of mensuration signs as proportions appear only towards the end of the treatise (Bk. III, Ch. 3), while the *sesquialtera* example occurs in Book I, Chapter 2. One can well imagine that the scribe realized his mistake, but was reluctant to do any corrections in order to keep a clean copy.

---

[36] Hothby describes a ℭ for *sesquialtera*, ℭ for *subsesquialtera*, ⊃ for *sesquitertia* and ⊙ for *subsesquitertia*, and the very unusual ⌒ for *sesquioctava* and ⌒ for *subsesquioctava* (HOa, f. 26r).

[37] The manuscript gives ⊃ for *sesquitertia*, ⊃̇ for *dupla sesquitertia* (7:3), ⊙ for *dupla sesquiquarta*, and ⊙ for *subsesquioctava* (8:9), ff. 12–13.

[38] PEc, f. 79r. In the manuscript C is not cut, either because of an error, or in deference to English usage.

[39] "Sed mihi deprecor parcant quoniam haec signa adeo frivola, adeo erronea adeoque ab omni rationis apparentia sunt remota, ut nec exemplo digna crediderim." (Tinctoris 1978:2a, 48; trans. Tinctoris 1979, 36.) Similarly, Gaffurius 1496 (Book IV, Ch. 2 and Ch. 5) disapproves of mensuration signs to indicate proportions.

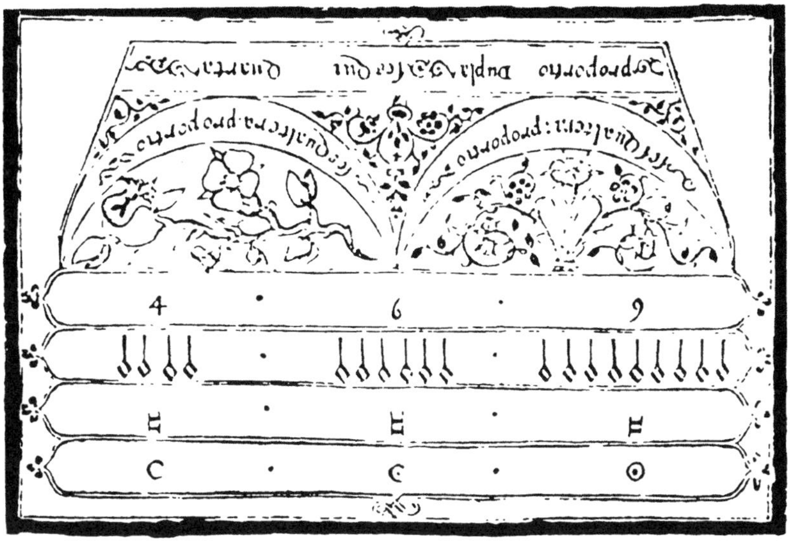

Figure 2 Diagram of mensural proportions from Chapter 16 of Spataro's *Tractato di Musica* (1531)

Giovanni Spataro inserted a diagram in his *Tractato di musica* of 1531 (Ch. 16) in which mensuration signs still have the same proportional function (see Figure 2): on the assumption of breve equality, the *sesquialtera* relationship on the prolation level is found between minims of C and ₵, and on the *tempus* level between ₵ and ⊙, while the *dupla sesquiquarta* (9:4) relationship is found between minims of C and ⊙. Similarly, Pietro Aaron states in his *Lucidario in musica* of 1545 (f. 12v) that the circle after the semicircle indicates a *sesquialtera* proportion.

In sum, we have seen that there is a tradition of indicating proportions through mensuration signs in both practical and theoretical sources, which proportions result from a combination of basic mensuration signs, without or with the stroke of diminution, and presuppose that the duration of the breve remains constant.

We have further seen that early theorists and composers, with very few exceptions, used only those proportions listed in Table 1. Why did early theorists and composers use only these proportions and not the other ones later described by Tinctoris? What do the proportions in Table 1 have in common? Fourteenth- and fifteenth-century theorists certainly never restricted the number of ratios when describing the intervallic system, but instead presented the whole set as found in Boethius. One might suppose that the temporal proportions chosen corresponded to the most important harmonic intervals, but this does not explain the prominent occurrence of 9:4. Nor could one claim that these proportions were selected because they were the easiest to perform. All of the fractions described by the early theorists do have one feature in common: they, and only they, are the proportions that can be shown as a combination of mensuration signs with breve equality assumed. The fact that the earliest theorists mentioned only those proportions that can be indicated by means of mensuration signs, and that they listed all proportions that can be thus indicated, cannot be mere coincidence. I propose that proportion signs were introduced not only to override the minim equivalence of the French notational system, but also to provide an arithmetically precise notation to circumvent the ambiguity that arises from the combination of different mensuration signs.

When and where did this happen? Gallo (1984, 334–36) has described how Franco, Marchettus, and Johannes de Muris used the term *proportio* when comparing different note values with each other. In the narrower sense described above the idea can be traced back to the writings of Johannes de Muris, who, in the second book of his *Notitia artis musicae*, written in 1321, advocated division of the breve into anywhere from two to nine semibreves of equal duration :[40] "A song will be made of 2, 3, 4, 5, 6, 7, 8, 9 equal semibreves of the same shape."[41] Another source of the concept was, of course, the Italian notational system which permitted *sesquitertia* and *sesquialtera* proportions by combining different mensurations (see Gallo 1984, 304–27 and Long 1981, 54–97). Yet the Italian notational system could not allow the occurrence, say, of a 9:4 proportion, since the imperfect time had to be one-third shorter than the perfect one, there being no provision for equality in the breve between perfect and imperfect time.[42]

In short, it can well be imagined that composers in the second half of the fourteenth century were inspired to use proportions by the writings of Johannes de Muris and, in part, by the Italian notational

---

[40] See Michels 1970, 106–8 and Gallo 1984, 272–78.

[41] "Fiet igitur cantus ex 2, 3, 4, 5, 6, 7, 8, 9 semibrevibus equalibus eiusdem figurae." Johannes de Muris 1972, 104. Michael P. Long (1981, 35–47) has suggested a different reading of this passage: he believes that de Muris is describing semibreves which have the same shape rather than length. However, I believe that de Muris states clearly two different things in this sentence: first, that the semibreves are equal (and with this he can only refer to their length), and second, that they do have the same shape. See also Ristory (1987, 98) who also argues that the semibreves are equally long.

[42] Gallo 1984, 312–14. I would also like to thank Professor Leeman L. Perkins for a stimulating letter on this subject.

system. But why did they select only certain divisions of the breve from de Muris's system, ignoring the division into five and seven equal semibreves entirely? The answer can be found in the notational system of the period: before the introduction of the fractions in the early fifteenth century, there was simply no method available to indicate, let us say, a 5:3 or 7:4 proportion. Composers were forced to use only those proportions which they could indicate, either through mensuration signs, different note shapes, or coloration. The author of the late fourteenth-century treatise *Tractatus figurarum*, attributed in some sources to Philip de Caserta, describes precisely this struggle to find an adequate notational tool for the technique of combining various mensurations under breve equality:

> And granted the masters instructed us in these note shapes [duplex long, long, breve, semibreve, and minim] and also in the four principal mensurations; namely, in perfect time of major prolation and in imperfect time of the same, in perfect time minor prolation and in imperfect time of the same. Yet they did not teach us how we should discant perfect time of minor prolation against imperfect time of minor prolation, and visa versa, and so on for the individual *tempora* which will clearly be shown one-by-one below. Because it would be very incongruous that it which can be performed could not be written and to show this clearly, I took care to organize this little treatise.[43]

The author of this treatise sought to overcome this problem by developing various note shapes which allow to indicate precisely the same set of proportions discussed above. But these note shapes were never used with much consistency (see von Fischer 1956, 118–21; Gallo 1984, 336–9). Walter Odington describes the situation perhaps best when he says: "There are as many inventors of new note shapes as there are writers of music." ("Quot [sunt nota]tores tot sunt novarum inventores figurarum." Odington 1970, 42.) The author of the revised Boen manuscript and the composers in CH and ModA took another path, associating mensurations signs with proportions. But the use of mensuration signs to indicate proportions was problematic, since mensuration signs were usually combined with minim

---

[43] "Et licet magistri instruxerunt nos in his figuris ac etiam in quatuor mensuris principalibus, videlicet in tempore perfecto majoris prolationis et in tempore imperfecto ipsius, in tempore perfecto minoris prolationis et in tempore imperfecto ipsius. Tamen non docuerunt quomodo super tempus imperfectum minoris discantare deberemus perfectum minoris, et e converso, et sic de singulis temporibus quod clare singulariter inferius patebit. Quia esset multum inconveniens quod illud quod potest pronuntiari non posset scribi et clare ostendere tractatum hunc parvulum ordinare curavi." Schreur 1987, Ch. 2.4–2.6.

equality. Some of the problems inherent in the use of coloration (Apel 1953, 126–44) were perceptively discussed by the author of the Berkeley Manuscript:

> From this, it can be deduced that sometimes the tempus alone is diminished by varying the colors, sometimes only the prolation, and sometimes both together. If one wishes to indicate diminutions by changing colors (for example), let him take care to accomplish it without becoming involved in a contradiction.[44]

Precisely because mensuration signs, note shapes, and coloration could all be interpreted differently, they were often combined with each other and with canons in the hope of eliminating any ambiguity.

It is clear that theorists were troubled by the lack of a notational device to indicate proportions unambiguously. The binary and ternary numbers written on top of each other, the upper denoting prolation and the lower time, as described by the author of the Berkeley Manuscript, Ciconia, Ramis, and Burtius, can be seen as another attempt for combining mensuration signs under breve equality, since they are exclusively reserved for showing proportional relationships. Considering all these confusing and ambiguous methods to indicate proportions, it is not astonishing that fractions were greeted with enthusiasm by Prosdocimus de Beldemandis (1966, 141–42) and Ugolino, the latter of whom saying: "And there is no shortcoming in them [fractions], but in the others [mensuration signs] there can occur error and ambiguity . . . We like the numbers better, because through them proportions can be shown better."[45] As we know, this did not prevent Ugolino or the scribes who notated his music from using mensuration signs to indicate proportions in his compositions.

The Turin Manuscript (Tn), completed in the second decade of the fifteenth century, provides further proof for the hypothesis that the introduction of the fraction resulted in the use of proportions not naturally inherent in the mensural system, that is, numbers not

---

[44] "Item ex hiis potest elici quod quandoque tempus solum diminuitur variando colores, quandoque prolacio tantum, et quandoque ambo simul. Caveat igitur diminuere sic voluens sub variacione colorum, ut exemplum, sibi non implicet contradiccionem." Goscalcus 1984, 30–31.

[45] "In eis namque nulla deceptio, in his autem ambiguitas cadere potest et error . . . nobis plus placet cifrarum positio qua proportionum clarior ostenditur demonstratio." Ugolino 1960, 211.

divisible by two or by three.[46] The collection includes several pieces with fractions which include the numbers five and seven, unheard of in the earlier repertory.[47]

How were all of these fractions related to one another? Were the proportions cumulative or rather related to the original mensuration sign? If the hypothesis is valid that fractions were introduced as an improved substitute for mensuration signs, it would seem logical that fractions would not be cumulative, just as mensuration signs could not be cumulative. A study of all numerical proportions encountered in ModA and CH supports this view: none of the proportions appear to be cumulative. We must distinguish between two kinds of numerical signs: first, a single number standing for a multiplex or superparticular proportion, for example 2 indicating a 2:1 proportion, or 3 indicating a 3:2 proportion; and second, a fraction. Both types occur in ModA and CH—the former often with a canon,[48] and the latter always without a canon,[49]—and both types are always related to the preceding mensuration sign, never to another proportion. Similarly, fractions in Ugolino's and Hothby's compositions are never cumulative.[50] (Neither of the two composers discusses the problem in their treatises.) The top voice of Anthonello de Caserta's *Amour m'a le*

---

[46] A similar expansion in the number of used proportions has been traced in the development of architecture of the fifteenth and sixteenth centuries by Naredi-Rainer (1985, 149–78, see in particular 162–67). Leon Battista Alberti, for example, uses 6:5 proportions in the façade of the Palazzo Rucellai in Florence, built around 1455, even though proportions based on the number five are only legitimized as canonic in Andrea Palladio's *Quattro libri dell'architettura* of 1570. According to Naredi-Rainer the prominence of the 5:4 (equivalent to the major third) and 6:5 (equivalent to the minor third) proportions derives from the description of the triad in music theoretical treatises of the time.

[47] See for example the ballade *Puisque ame* (Hoppin 1963:3, no. 26) which makes use of a 5:2 (m. 58) and 7:3 (m. 67) proportion. See also Hoppin 1957.

[48] Conradus de Pistoria in *Se doulz espour*, (ModA, f. 31v, Apel 1970:1, no. 15, m. 12) uses the number 3 to show *sesquialtera* and the number 2 (m. 17) to show *dupla*; he does not add a canon; the same numbers occur with a canon in Johannes Simon Hasprois' *Ma douce amour*, (ModA, f. 28r, Apel 1970:1, no. 41, m. 8 and m. 12) and Bartholomeus de Bononia's *Que pena major* (ModA, ff. 37r-36v, Apel 1970:3, no. 301, mm. 10, 24, 42, 54)

[49] Anthonello de Caserta's *Amour m'a le cuer mis*, (ModA, ff. 32v-33r, Apel 1970:1, no. 3, mm. 8 and 13); Baude Cordier's *Belle, bonne sage*, (CH, f. 11v, Greene 1981:18, no. 1, m. 44) uses an 8:9 fraction after the number 3 which is not cumulative; Cordier's *Tout par compas* (CH, f. 12, Greene 1981:18, no. 2) makes use of fractions which are always alternated with mensuration signs.

[50] For Ugolino's compositions see Seay 1955. For Hothby see HOb, ff. 26v-27 and Hothby 1964, 4–7. Similarly, the proportions indicated by a single number in the early fifteenth-century anonymous treatise in Rvat (f.51) are not cumulative. This treatise is also particularly interesting because fractions and mensuration signs are used interchangeably in the musical examples.

Example 9

Anthonello de Caserta, *Amour m'a le cuer mis*, (ModA, ff. 32v-33r, Apel 1970:1, no. 3)

cuer mis (see Example 9), perhaps illustrates the problem best. The piece starts out in perfect time, minor prolation. After the 9:6 proportion in m. 8, nine minims are equivalent to six. When in m. 13 a 4:2 proportion is written, it is not related to the immediately preceding section—that is, not multiplied with the 9:6 fraction, as would be arithmetically correct— but related to the initial mensuration sign of perfect time, minor prolation.

Example 10

PEc, f.90v (cf. Tinctoris 1978, 54, m. 1-5)

In contrast, all examples in Tinctoris's *Proportionale musices* are cumulative. He cautions the reader that proportions can be related "by comparison to the preceding number in one and the same voice, or . . . by comparison to the notes of the other part".[51] In one of his examples (see Example 10) the discant has a 2:1 proportion followed by a 3:2 proportion.[52] The 3:2 proportion is not related to the initial perfect time, but to the 2:1 proportion, resulting in a 3:1 proportion.

Gaffurius gives perhaps the clearest description of how successive proportions are to be performed:

> Various proportions following each other in succession are reckoned according to the proportion directly preceding. If, for example, *proportio tripla* follows *proportio dupla*, *proportio sextupla* will result from reckoning the *tripla* with the first number preceding the *dupla*, as is seen in these two numbers, 1:2:6.[53]

Thus, we can conclude that even though fractions were introduced in order to provide musicians with accurate and less ambiguous

---

[51] "Per relationem ad numerum praecedentem in una et eadem parte . . . per relationem ad notas alterius partis . . ." Tinctoris 1978:2a, 13; trans. Tinctoris 1979, 3-4.

[52] I am indebted to Dr. Bonnie Blackburn for calling my attention to the fact that Albert Seay's transcription (Tinctoris 1978, 54) is incorrect. I should like in turn to propose an emendation to Dr. Blackburn's solution. In order to avoid "the parallel ninths which are not sanctioned in Tinctoris's rules of counterpoint" (Blackburn 1981, 42, n. 31) her first sentence should be corrected to "Seay's transcription of the first measure of the discantus should be amended to begin with a breve imperfected *ad partes* (four minims)" rather than "imperfected *ad totum* (six minims)", which would result in a 20:9 proportion rather than 18:9, that is 2:1 proportion. My transcription is based on the PEc, f. 90v).

[53] "Diverse proportiones sese invicem consequentes varias subsequentium notularum ad precedentes sana consyderatione ducunt habitudines. Namque si (exempli causa) tripla proportio in notulis immediate *duplam* fuerit subsequuta: sexcupla illico proportio ex numerositate notularum ipsius triplae descriptae ad priorem notularum numerum qui scilicet ante *duplam* ipsam dispositus fuerit: resultabit: quod his numeris sane percipitur 1.2.6." Gaffurius 1496, Bk. IV, Ch. 13; trans. Gaffurius 1968, 234.

notational symbols to indicate proportions, it took almost one hundred years for musicians to learn to use the fractions in an arithmetically correct way, and to forget their origin as a substitute for mensuration signs. As in many other aspects of the mensural system, the great theorist-reformers Tinctoris and Gaffurius were the ones who initiated this change and emancipated the fraction from the mensuration sign.

This point is closely related to the last question: is the mensuration in a proportion derived from the proportion itself or from the preceding mensuration sign?[54] It would seem a logical assumption that those theorists who use proportions interchangeably with mensuration signs also determine the mensuration in the proportional section from the proportion sign itself. Since mensuration signs from which the proportions presumably derived can alter the original mensurations, proportions can do so as well. Statements by both Prosdocimus and Ugolino indicate that our assumption is indeed correct. Prosdocimus says:

> Likewise you must know that these notes so diminished must be brought back to the mensurations mentioned above in the first chapter . . . for the diminished notes which are sung in *sesquialtera* proportion, that is, three for two, must be brought back to perfections of mensurations, and can be perfected, imperfected, emptied out [a black note, made white], altered, and, in short, all occurrences which can be permitted for the notes having a true perfection of mensuration can be allowed.[55]

Ugolino (1960, 210) makes a similar statement. Thus, it is not surprising that in Hothby's motet *Ora pro nobis*[56] the 6:4 section which follows a passage in C makes the semibreves perfect.

Guilielmus Monachus also makes clear that the mensuration is derived from the preceding proportion sign. In his comments on the performance of *sesquialtera* he states:

---

[54] Willi Apel (1953, 150) is the only scholar to recognize the problem. He assumes that the proportional mensuration always takes precedence over the original one.

[55] "Item scire debes, quod iste figure sic diminute habent reduci ad mensuras superius in primo capitulo nominatas, . . . nam figure diminute que in proportione sexquialtera cantantur, sicut tres pro duabus, habent reduci ad perfectiones mensurarum, et possunt perfici, imperfici, evacuari, alterari, et breviter omnes passiones pati quas pati possunt figure recte perfectiones mensurarum habentes." Beldemandis 1869, 219.

[56] Hothby 1964, 4–7, m. 55. Hothby often avoided confusion concerning mensurations after proportion signs by using mode signs (O2 , C 2, and OO2 etc.) which not only diminish but also show the precise mensuration on every level. See Chapter 4 of Berger forthcoming.

THE EARLY HISTORY OF PROPORTION SIGNS

Sesquialtera in perfect minor [perfect time, minor prolation] requires that the minims be counted in threes as the minims of imperfect [time] major [prolation] are counted, and in the same way the minims are altered before semibreves, and, just as there, the semibreves are imperfect before minims, and three minims are placed for a single *mensura* of the common semibreve . . .[57]

In other words, the mensuration is changed from minor to major prolation and the semibreve becomes perfect.

The earliest author to state explicitly that in proportions the original mensuration must be preserved is the same theorist who emancipated fractions from mensuration signs—Johannes Tinctoris, in his *Proportionale musices* of ca. 1473–4:

It must be noted that in any proportion we ought to consider in what modus, in what tempus, and in what prolation it is made, for certain proportions are binary, as duple, quadruple, etc., certain ternary, as triple, sesquialtera, etc., certain both, as sextuple, sesquiquinta, etc., certain neither, as sesquiquarta, superbipartiens tertias, etc. They, however, cannot change the nature of the quantities in which they are made. Regardless whether any proportion be either binary, ternary, or both, or neither, always the notes must be computed according to their perfection or imperfection in respect to the modus, tempus, and prolation signature under which they fall.[58]

In other words, he advises the retention of the original mensurations under proportional signs, and stands therefore in opposition to all

---

[57] "Sexquialtera super perfecto minore exigit ut minimae numerentur ternae uti numerantur minimae temporis imperfecti maioris, et eodem modo minimae alterantur ante semibreves, et ut ibidem semibreves sunt imperfectae ante minimas ponunturque tres minimae pro singulo ictu pausae communis semibrevis, . . . " Guilielmus 1965, 21. According to Wolf Frobenius (1971, 4), Guilielmus's term for *mensura* is *ictus pausae* or *ictus pausationis*. *Pausare mensuram* must be translated as "making the rhythm of a *mensura*." He adds further that it is unclear why the word *pausa* was used in this meaning.

[58] "Deinde notandum est quod circa quamlibet proportionem debemus considerare in quo modo, in quo tempre et in qua prolatione fiat. Nam quaedam proportiones binariae sunt, ut dupla, quadrupla, etc., quaedam ternariae, ut tripla, sesquialtera, etc., quaedam utraque, ut sextupla, sesquiquinta, etc., quaedam neutrae, ut sesquiquarta, superbipartiens tertias, etc. Non tamen naturam quantitatum in quibus fiunt immutare possunt. Immo qualiscumque proportion sit sive binaria, sive ternaria, sive utraque, sive neutra, semper notae iuxta perfectionem aut imperfectione earum per respectum signi modalis, temporalis et prolationalis, sub quo consistunt computandae sunt . . . " Tinctoris 1978, 53; trans. Tinctoris 1979, 41.

Example 11

(a) cf. Tinctoris 1978, 13, m. 1-3

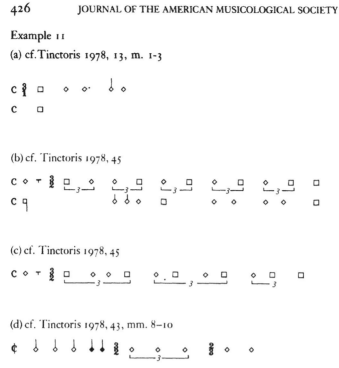

(b) cf. Tinctoris 1978, 45

(c) cf. Tinctoris 1978, 45

(d) cf. Tinctoris 1978, 43, mm. 8-10

earlier theorists.[59] However, several of Tinctoris's own examples do not follow the rules he has outlined. In *proportio tripla* (see Example 11a) he can easily retain the original mensuration, since the triple mensuration places three imperfect breves against one imperfect breve. However, in *sesquialtera* following C it is considerably more difficult to preserve the original mensuration. Before Tinctoris, theorists and musicians usually replaced two semibreves of C with three semibreves of *sesquialtera*, but this resulted in perfect time. The only way to preserve the original mensuration is to replace two imperfect breves with three. This is Gaffurius's solution, as will be seen shortly. However, both of Tinctoris's examples of C followed by $\frac{3}{2}$ make the breve perfect, as can be seen clearly from the way the *sesquialtera* section is aligned with the C in the other voice (see Example 11b). If the examples were regrouped into imperfect sesquialtered breves (see Example 11c), the last triplet would not be complete. Similarly, the preservation of the original mensuration is impossible in Tinctoris's example of ₵ followed by the *sesquialtera* (see Example 11d). Since the theorist uses only three semibreves (or one

---

[59] It is striking that this wish to retain the original mensuration in proportions is formulated at about the same time as is the rule of preserving the original mensuration under diminution. See Berger 1987.

perfect breve), we must interpret the *sesquialtera* as perfect time. In sum, we can conclude that Tinctoris did not preserve the original mensuration consistently in his examples, even though he advocated the practice in his text. It is possible that he felt unable always to follow his rules, because the pull of the traditional and current practice was too strong.

Tinctoris's most important follower, Franchinus Gaffurius, also demands that the original mensuration be preserved in a proportion. He is more consistent than Tinctoris in applying his rules to imperfect time:

> I also do not approve of the improper practices of many composers who, in showing *sesquialtera* by a number three, think that alteration and perfection are an augmentation of notes, and who write *tempus imperfectum* instead of *tempus perfectum* (which is absurd), and *prolatio minor* instead of *prolatio maior*, while *sesquialtera* is easily understood as a proportional diminution . . . . For a perfect breve and an altered semibreve are only found in *tempus perfectum*, whose proper sign is a circle; a perfect semibreve and an altered minim are only found in *prolatio perfecta* or *maior*, whose proper sign is a dot within the sign of *tempus*. In *tempus imperfectum*, which is shown by a semicircle, a breve always contains just two semibreves, whether normal or in *proportio diminuta* (unless a dot of augmentation is used), and a semibreve never increases in value through alteration. In the same way a semibreve of *prolatio minor* cannot become perfect nor a minim be altered.[60]

In other words, "when *proportio sesquialtera* occurs in imperfect mensurations, all notes and rests are imperfect."[61] This is shown clearly in Example 12a. Whenever Gaffurius intends a perfection

---

[60] "Neque assentio complurimorum coruptellae: qui quum solo ternarii numeri charactere sesqualteram describunt in notulis *tempus* imperfectum (quod absurdum est) pro perfecto: atque pro maiore prolatione minorem posuere: alterationem & perfectionem in notulis consyderantes quo facile conspicitur ex diminutione proportionis deductum esse in notulis augmentum . . . . Brevis enim perfecta & semibrevis alterata in solo tempore perfecto disponitur: cuius proprium signum est circulus. Semibrevem vero perfectam ac mininam alterabilem sola maior sive perfecta prolatio confert: huius proprium signum est punctus in signo temporis affixus. In tempore autem imperfecto quod semicirculus declarat: brevis notula duas tantum semibreves semper possidet sive recta: sive quavis Proportione diminuta: nisi punctum augmentationis susceperit: sed neque in eo semibrevis unque alterationis suscipit incrementum. Atque idcirco eodem sensu neque semibrevis in minori prolatione perfectionem acquiret: neque minima poterit alterari." Gaffurius 1496, Bk. IV, Ch. 5; trans. Gaffurius 1968, 182.

[61] "Si autem proportio sesquialtera disposita fuerit in notulis imperfectae quantitati subiectis omnes tunc notulae & pausae semper erunt imperfectae." Gaffurius 1496, Bk. IV, Ch. 5, trans. Gaffurius 1968, 182.

Example 12

(a) Gaffurius 1496, Bk. IV, Ch. 5, (cf. Miller 1968, Ex. 80)

(b) Gaffurius 1496, Bk. IC, Ch. 5 (cf. Miller 1968, Ex. 79)

within a *sesquialtera* proportion in imperfect time, he adds the circle to the proportion sign (see Example 12b).[62]

In sum, we have been able to trace the following development in fifteenth-century theoretical treatises: at first, the mensuration following the proportion sign was determined by the fraction, since the fraction substituted for a mensuration sign. The first theorists to differentiate clearly between the functions of mensuration signs and fractions were Tinctoris and Gaffurius, both of whom explained that the function of the fraction was to indicate not the mensuration but only the level of diminution. Closely correlated with this reform was, of course, their novel idea that proportions should be cumulative.

In conclusion, I want to postulate the following scenario. The idea of dividing the breves into two to nine equal parts was introduced by Johannes de Muris in 1321. This suggested to musicians who wanted to use in one piece several of the four *Ars nova prolationes* that they could relate them to one another with the breve retaining constant duration. Indeed, theorists and composers of the second half of the fourteenth century picked only those divisions of the breve which could be shown by a combination of various mensuration signs with the assumption of breve equality. The other proportions were not used because musicians lacked a notational tool to express them. The use of fractions to indicate rhythmic proportions represented a true innovation. It allowed not only a less ambiguous notation of already used proportions, but also the gradual inclusion of the proportions not naturally inherent in the mensural system of the time. However, in

---

[62] Gaffurius 1496, Bk. IV, Ch. 6, Example 79. Gaffurius does not preserve the original mensuration in major prolation. For a detailed discussion of Gaffurius's, Giovanni Spataro's, and other theorists' view on this subject see Ch. 5 of Berger, forthcoming.

the first half of the fifteenth century fractions were used as if they actually *were* mensuration signs—that is, like their predecessors, the mensuration signs, they were not cumulative and they determined mensuration in their own right. It took theorists of Tinctoris's and Gaffurius's stature to emancipate fractions from mensuration signs and to use these fractions in an arithmetically correct way. As a result, they were able to enlarge the number of proportions to include those which did not result from combination of various mensuration signs under breve equality, so that the system of rhythmic proportions could become as rich as that of harmonic proportions. It is puzzling that composers wrote music which made use of elaborate proportions only in the late fourteenth and early fifteenth centuries, at a time when they were still searching for a notational tool to indicate them unambiguously. Once the fraction had been associated with proportions, composers lost interest in writing music with elaborate proportions and the whole matter became a theoretical issue.

University of California, Davis

List of Works Cited

Manuscript Sigla

AO	Aosta, Biblioteca del Seminario Maggiore, MS. A.1.D. 19.
BL	Bologna, Civico Museo Bibliografico Musicale, MS. Q 15.
Ccc	Cambridge, Corpus Christi College, MS. 410.11.
CH	Chantilly, Musée Condé, MS. 564.
Fl	Florence, Biblioteca Medicea-Laurenziana, MS. Plut. XXIX, 48.
HOa	John Hothby. *Quid est proportio*. London, Lambeth Palace, MS. 446, ff. 19–30.
HOb	———. *Ora pro nobis*. Faenza, Biblioteca Comunale, MS. 117, ff. 26v-27.
Lbl	London, British Library, MS. Lansdowne 763, ff. 117–23.
ModA	Modena, Biblioteca Estense, MS. M.5.24.
ModB	Modena, Biblioteca Estense, MS. lat. 471 (X1,11).
Ob	Oxford, Bodleian Library, MS. Canonici misc. 213.
OH	London, British Library, MS. Add. 57950 (olim Old Hall, St. Edmund's College, Ware, Herts.).
PadA	Padua, Biblioteca Universitaria, MSS. 684 and 1475, as well as Oxford, Bodleian Library, Can. Pat. lat. 229.
PEc	"Regule de proportionibus. Cum suis exemplis." Perugia, Biblioteca Comunale Augusta, MS. 1013, ff. 78–123.
Rvat	Rome, Biblioteca Apostolica Vaticana, MS. Regina lat. 1146, ff. 48–51.
SDI	Saint-Dié, Bibliothèque municipale, MS. 42, f. 131.

Sca   Siena, Biblioteca Comunale degli Intronati, MS. L.V.30, ff. 48v-56r.
Scb   Siena, Biblioteca Comunale degli Intronati, MS. L.V. 30, f. 142r-v.
Tr 90   Trent, Museo Provinciale d'Arte, MS. 90.
Tr 92   Trent, Museo Provinciale d'Arte, MS. 92.
Tr 93   Trent, Museo Provinciale d'Arte, MS. 93.
Tn   Turin, Biblioteca Nazionale Universitaria, MS. J.II.9.
Vnm   Venice, Biblioteca Nazionale Marciana, MS. lat. VIII 85 (3579), f. 69.

Printed Editions of Primary Sources

Aaron, Pietro. *Lucidario in musica*. Venice, 1545.

Anonymous 1975. Florence, Biblioteca nazionale centrale, MS. Magl. III 70. Ed. Israel Adler. *Hebrew Writings Concerning Music*. Répertoire Internationale des Sources Musicales, Series B, vol. 9/2, 55–67. Munich, 1975.

Anonymous XI. *Tractatus de musica plana et mensurabili*. Ed. E. de Coussemaker. Scriptorum de musica medii aevi, 3:416–75. Paris, 1869.

Anonymous de la Fage. *Essais de diphtérographie musicale*. Paris, 1862.

Apel, Willi. *French Secular Compositions of the Fourteenth Century*. Corpus mensurabilis musicae, no. 53. [Rome], 1970.

Bent, Margaret, and Hallmark, Anne, eds. *The Works of Johannes Ciconia*. Polyphonic Music of the Fourteenth Century, no. 24. Monaco, 1985.

Boen, Johannes. *Ars (musicae)*. Ed. F. Alberto Gallo. Corpus scriptorum de musica, no. 19. [Rome], 1972.

Burtius, Nicolaus. *Florum libellus*. Ed. Giuseppe Massera. Historiae musicae cultores biblioteca, no. 28. Florence, 1975.

Dunstable, John. *Complete Works*. Ed. Manfred Bukofzer, Margaret Bent, Ian Bent, and Brian Trowell. Musica Brittanica, no. 8. London, 1970.

Gaffurius, Franchino. *Practica musicae*. Milan, 1496. Trans. Clement A. Miller. Musicological Studies and Documents, no. 20. [Rome], 1968.

Goscalcus [attr.] [*Tractatus secundus*]. *The Berkeley Manuscript, University of California Music Library, MS. 744*. Ed. and trans. Oliver B. Ellsworth. Greek and Latin Music Theory, no. 2. Lincoln, Nebraska, 1984.

Greene, Gordon K., ed. *French Secular Music, Manuscript Chantilly, Musée Condé 564*. Polyphonic Music of the Fourteenth Century, nos. 18 and 19. Monaco, 1981.

Guilielmus Monachus. *De preceptis artis musicae*. Ed. Albert Seay. Corpus scriptorum de musica, no. 11. [Rome], 1965.

Hoppin, Richard H., ed. *The Cypriot-French Repertory*. Corpus mensurabilis musicae, no. 21. [Rome], 1963.

Hothby, John. *The Musical Works of John Hothby*. Ed. Albert Seay. Corpus mensurabilis musicae, no. 33. [Rome], 1964.

Hughes, Andrew and Bent, Margaret, ed. *The Old Hall Manuscript*. Corpus mensurabilis musicae, no. 46. [Rome], 1969.

Johannes de Muris. *Notitia artis musicae*. Ed. Ulrich Michels. Corpus scriptorum de musica, no. 17. [Rome], 1972.

Marchettus de Padova. *Pomerium*. Ed. Joseph Vecchi. Corpus scriptorum de musica, no. 6. [Rome], 1961.

Odington, Walter. *Summa de speculatione musicae.* Ed. Frederick Hammond. Corpus scriptorum de musica, no. 14. [Rome], 1970.
Prosdocimus de Beldemandis. *Expositiones tractatus practice cantus mensurabilis magistri Johannis de Muris.* Ed. F. Alberto Gallo. Antiquae musicae italicae scriptores, no. 3. Bologna, 1966.
——. *Tractatus practice de cantus mensurabilis.* Ed. E. de Coussemaker. Scriptorum de musica medii aevi, 3:200–28. Paris, 1869.
Reaney, Gilbert, ed. *Early Fifteenth-Century Music.* Corpus mensurabilis musicae, no. 11. [Rome], 1959.
Ramis de Pareja, Bartolomeus. *Musica practica.* Bologna, 1482. Ed. Johannes Wolf. Leipzig, 1901.
Spataro, Giovanni. *Tractato di musica.* Venice, 1531.
Tinctoris, Johannes. *Proportionales musices.* Ed. Albert Seay in *Opera theoretica.* Vol. 2a. Corpus scriptorum de musica, no. 22. [Rome], 1978.
——. *Proportions in Music.* Translations, no. 10. Colorado Springs, 1979.
Ugolino of Orvieto. *Declaratio musicae disciplinae.* Ed. Albert Seay. Corpus scriptorum de musica, no. 7, vol. 2. Rome, 1960.

Secondary Literature

Apel, Willi. *The Notation of Polyphonic Music, 900-1600.* Cambridge, Mass., 1953.
Bent, Margaret. "Notation." *New Grove Dictionary.* London, 1980.
Berger, Anna Maria Busse. "The Relationship of Perfect and Imperfect Time in Italian Theory of the Renaissance." *Early Music History* 5 (1986): 1–28.
——. "The Myth of *diminutio per tertiam partem.*" Paper read at the Colloquium on Performance Practice in the Fourteenth and Fifteenth Centuries, Kloster Neustift, Bressanone (Brixen), Italy, August 19–26, 1987.
——. *Mensuration Signs and Proportions in Italian Theory of the Renaissance* (forthcoming).
Blackburn, Bonnie. "A Lost Guide to Tinctoris's Teachings Recovered." *Early Music History* 1 (1981): 29–116.
Federhofer-Königs, Renate, ed. "Ein Beitrag zur Proportionenlehre in der zweiten Hälfte des 15. Jahrhunderts." *Studia musicologica Academica scientiarum Hungaricae* 11 (1969): 145–57.
Fischer, Kurt von. *Studien zur italienischen Musik des Trecento und frühen Quattrocento.* Publikationen der Schweizerischen Musikforschenden Gesellschaft, ser. 2, no. 5. Bern, 1956.
Frobenius, Wolf. "Tactus" (1971). *Handwörterbuch der musikalischen Terminologie.* Ed. Hans Heinrich Eggebrecht. Wiesbaden, 1971- .
Gallo, F. Alberto. "Die Notationslehre im 14. und 15. Jahrhundert." In *Die mittelalterliche Lehre von der Mehrstimmigkeit.* Geschichte der Musiktheorie, no. 5. Ed. Frieder Zaminer. Darmstadt, 1984.
Günther, Ursula. "Der Gebrauch des tempus perfectum diminutum in der Handschrift Chantilly 1047." *Archiv für Musikwissenschaft* 17 (1960): 277–97.
——. "Das Manuskript Modena, Biblioteca Estense, M.5.24." *Musica Disciplina* 24 (1970): 17–67.

———. "Anthonello de Caserta." *New Grove Dictionary.* London, 1980. (1980a)
———. "Goscalch." *New Grove Dictionary.* London, 1980. (1980b)
———. "Sources." *New Grove Dictionary.* London, 1980. (1980c)
———. "Unusual Phenomena in the Transmission of Late Fourteenth-Century Polyphonic Music." *Musica Disciplina* 38 (1984): 87–118.
Gushee, Lawrence. "Anonymous XI." *New Grove Dictionary.* London, 1980.
Hoppin, Richard H. "The Cypriot-French Repertory of the Manuscript Torino, Biblioteca Nazionale, J.II.9." *Musica Disciplina* 9 (1957), 79–125.
Long, Michael P. "Musical Tastes in Fourteenth-Century Italy: Notational Styles, Scholarly Traditions, and Historical Circumstances. Ph. D. diss., Princeton University, 1981.
Michels, Ulrich. *Die Musiktraktate des Johannes de Muris.* Beihefte zum Archiv für Musikwissenschaft, no. 8. Wiesbaden, 1970.
Miller, Clement A. "Gaffurius's 'Practica Musicae': Origin and Contents." *Musica Disciplina* 22 (1968): 105–28.
Naredi-Rainer, Paul von. "Musiktheorie und Architektur." In *Ideen zu einer Geschichte der Musiktheorie.* Geschichte der Musiktheorie, no. 1. Ed. Frieder Zaminer. Darmstadt, 1985.
Planchart, Alejandro E. "The Relative Speed of *Tempora* in the Period of Dufay." *Royal Music Association: Research Chronicle* 17 (1981): 33–51.
Ristory, Heinz. "Ein Abbreviationstraktat im Umfeld der franconischen und post-franconischen Compendia." *Acta Musicologica* 59 (1987): 95–110.
Sachs, Klaus-Jürgen. *Der Contrapunctus im 14. und 15. Jahrhundert. Untersuchungen zum Terminus, zur Lehre und zu den Quellen.* Beihefte zum Archiv für Musikwissenschaft, no. 13. Wiesbaden, 1974.
Seay, Albert. "Ugolino of Orvieto, Theorist and Composer." *Musica Disciplina* 9 (1955): 111–66.
Schreur, Philip E., ed. *The Tractatus figurarum: Subtilitas in the Notation of the Late Fourteenth Century.* Ph. D. dissertation, Stanford University, 1987.
Wolf, Johannes. "Der niederländische Einfluss in der mehrstimmigen gemessenen Musik bis zum Jahre 1480." *Tijdsschrift der Vereeniging voor Noord-Nederlands Muziekgeschiednis* 6 (1900): 197–217.
———. *Geschichte der Mensuralnotation.* 3 Vols. Leipzig, 1904.

Abstract

In the late fourteenth and early fifteenth centuries rhythmic proportions were indicated through coloration, Italian note shapes, mensuration signs, and fractions. Even though Johannes de Muris had introduced in 1321 a division of the breve into from two to nine equal parts, theorists and composers used only those proportions which could be indicated by a combination of various mensuration signs with the assumption of breve equivalence: 3:2 shown by ○:C or ₵:C; 4:3 by Ↄ:O or Ↄ:₵; 9:4 by ○:C; 9:8 by ○:₡; 2:1 by C:₡; 8:3 by ₡:₵. Other proportions were not used because musicians lacked adequate signs to indicate them. The invention of the fraction to show rhythmic proportions presented, therefore, a true innovation because it permitted the indication of proportions not naturally inherent in the mensural system. However, fractions were used until the late fifteenth century as if they were mensuration signs, that is, they were not cumulative and they determined the mensuration of the following section. It was not until the late fifteenth century that Johannes Tinctoris and Franchinus Gaffurius emancipated proportions from mensuration signs and used fractions in an arithmetically correct way.

[21]

Jerome of Moravia on the *Rubeba* and *Viella*

CHRISTOPHER PAGE

JEROME of Moravia's *Tractatus de Musica* is the most important written source for the history of Western stringed instruments before the 15th century. At a time when musical theorists were inclined to say little if anything about instruments Jerome gives three tunings for the *viella* and one for the *rubeba*, specifying the fingering of each and, in the case of the *viella*, describing a virtuoso technique. Hitherto only extracts from this work have been made available in English, many of which incorporate serious errors in translation.[1] It is perhaps because of this that few of the many authors who have quoted the tunings have managed to get them right; the notes of the strings are variously back to front, an octave too high or low, in the wrong order, or simply incorrect. Worse still, they have been tacitly rearranged to fit various prejudices and preconceptions. The purpose of this article is to provide a text that is closely based upon the original manuscript (Pls. XX–XXII), accompanied by a translation that is as literal as possible in the hope that these errors, once exposed, will evaporate.

JEROME OF MORAVIA AND THE *TRACTATUS DE MUSICA*

The unique manuscript of the *Tractatus de Musica* is preserved in the Bibliothèque Nationale at Paris. It is our only source of information concerning Jerome's life: a note at the end of the treatise refers to him as a Dominican monk from Mähren.[2]

The work was probably composed in the city of Paris, for the manuscript was circulating in university circles there not long after its completion (see below), while certain aspects of its make-up show that it is an official copy made for the inspection of university authorities before the text was released for publication.[3]

The date of the work can not be precisely determined. In the seventh chapter Jerome quotes from a treatise of Thomas Aquinas completed in 1272, and thus a firm *terminus a quo* can be fixed. Yet it is possible that this terminus may be brought forward by at least a decade or so, since Franco's *Ars Cantus Mensurabilis* is one of the treatises that Jerome includes in his compilation; recently a date of *c.* 1280 for this text has gained influential support.[4] A *terminus ad quem* is established by the death of Pierre de Limoges (1306) who bequeathed the manuscript to the Sorbonne.[5] In all probability therefore Jerome's *Tractatus* was composed sometime during the last two decades of the 13th century, and not *c.* 1250 as has so often been stated.

As it stands in the manuscript the text of the *Tractatus de Musica* is a most complicated affair. In addition to the columns of main text there are corrections in various hands for which at least two different readers are responsible (the initials of two names, both correctors, appear in marginal notes in the manuscript[6]). We cannot avoid the questions these corrections and annotations raise since they incorporate material of the highest interest.

In the section on the *rubeba* and the *viella* (see Plates) we may detect three hands: (1) the hand of the main text; (2) the hand who supplies material omitted by the first hand in Pl. XX (far-right margin) and Pl. XXI (same place); (3) the hand responsible for various notes and comments in Pl. XXI (far-right margin top, and bottom margin); also in Pl. XXII (far-left margin and bottom margin). We need not consider the work of the second hand, since he only adds material which should have been in the text but was omitted. The work of the third hand is far more important, since it includes a long note on the use of the *bordunus* at the bottom of Pl. XXII which is one of the most important pieces of evidence in the whole text.

Two crucial questions must be answered: (1) when were the notes by hand 3 added? (2) If they were added at an early date, were they intended as corrections to be incorporated in future copies of the text made from this exemplar? Fortunately new evidence has come to light which removes most of the uncertainty surrounding these additions.

A note in the manuscript at Paris reveals that the *Tractatus* was bequeathed to the Sorbonne by one Pierre de Limoges (*ex legato magistri Petri de Lemovicis*). Pierre was a Master of Arts associated with the Sorbonne. He died in 1306, leaving more than a hundred books to the University of which sixty-seven still rest in Paris at the Bibliothèque Nationale. Madeleine Mabille has shown that Pierre annotated a number of his manuscripts in a small, cramped hand quite unlike the main text hand of each manuscript concerned.[7] At my request François Avril, Conservateur at the Bibliothèque Nationale, compared the manuscripts annotated by Pierre with the notes at the close of the *Tractatus de Musica* (the originals of all the relevant manuscripts were

78

at his disposal). He concluded that, in spite of minor differences in the hands (possibly due to the varying space into which Pierre had to cram his annotations) the notes in all the manuscripts were written by the same person.[8] Thus we may assume that the identity of hand 3 has been established: these notes were written by Pierre de Limoges sometime before 1306, and not in the late 14th century as has often been assumed.[9]

The question remains whether Pierre wrote these notes in some official capacity so that they might be included in future copies from this exemplar. It is actually most unlikely that they are anything more than personal annotations. They are not corrections; they explain and amplify the text. In the far right margin of Pl. XXI, Pierre notes that a string referred to by Jerome as the *secunda* is actually first on the instrument (*que est prima vielle*); similarly he notes at the bottom of the same page that the D string, now running over the fingerboard, produces two stopped pitches which Jerome does not bother to specify. The private character of the notes is fully revealed in Pl. XXII (far-left column): here Pierre comments in the first person that he does not understand how *b acutum* can be produced with the third tuning; *sed non video*, he writes, *quomodo b acutum formetur* ('but I do not see how b♮ may be formed').

Why did Jerome include a section on the *rubeba* and *viella* in his treatise? It is at least clear that the material in the chapter was designed to be used; it is far removed from the purely theoretical treatises on the organistrum and monochord. Jerome's desire that the student should grasp the rudiments of the instruments cannot be mistaken, and several of his remarks bring us as close to the actual business of instrumental tuition in the Middle Ages as we are ever likely to get. An almost intimate, conversational tone prevails. 'Having reviewed these things and committed them to memory', Jerome assures his reader, 'you will be able to encompass all the art of *viella* playing'. To this end he gives variant tunings for the *viella* and specifies the letters of the notes produced by each of the stopping positions used at the time.[10] The reader is clearly intended to work through the tunings as Jerome describes them, familiarising himself with the note names (probably in conjunction with a copy—or at least a good mental picture—of the Guidonian hand). Details of fingering are not overlooked; we are told that the *rubeba* must be held 'in a natural position in the left hand, between the thumb and the first finger', while some fingers must be applied 'bent' and others 'naturally . . . which is to be done with all the other fingers on the *rubeba* and the *viella*'.

79

Clearly therefore Jerome envisaged a readership of well-educated persons trained to learn by studying pages of Latin and anxious to acquire the rudiments of the *viella* and *rubeba*. We know from his introduction to the *Tractatus* that the work was intended for the 'brothers of our order or another' (*fratres ordinis nostri vel alii*),[11] but if the treatise achieved any success in Paris its circulation was probably wider than this. We do not know whether our manuscript was ever used for the purposes for which it was intended prior to its acquisition by Pierre de Limoges. But assuming the whole project of copying out the exemplar led to something rather than to nothing whatsoever, then the separate sections (*pecia*) of the manuscript would have been hired from the stationers of Paris by masters, pupils, or scribes acting on their behalf.[12] It would therefore have been at large in Paris, at the disposal of anyone who both wished and was able to read it.

There are numerous indications in other sources that a literate class of *viella* players existed, the class for whom Jerome compiled his chapter. In an arresting passage the theorist Lambertus (pseudo-Aristotle), a contemporary of Jerome, states that a good student of *musica mensurabilis* should be able to transcribe musical handwriting in such a way that 'however much any music has been diversified to the limit, it may be made consistently manifest by means of [musical handwriting] in the manner of a *viella*'.[13] This fascinating and enigmatic passage seems to suggest, at the very least, that some *viellatores* performed from notated music, and may even imply the existence of a form of *viella* tablature hitherto unsuspected. That fiddlers existed who practised their art in relation to the rules of *musica* as a literate skill is clear not only from Jerome's text, but also from Albertus Magnus's distinction between fiddlers who play *ex arte* and those who play *ex usu*.[14] It is presumably the type of fiddler playing *ex arte* which Johannes de Grocheio has in mind when her refers to the '*bonus artifex in viella*', while praising the instrument above all others.[15]

Another French theorist, Elias of Salomon, writing his *Scientia Artis Musice* (1274) 'in curia Romana', gives the *viella* a place in the world of the trained *cantor*. He inveighs against the singer who is ignorant of the Guidonian hand (an aid to advanced *viella* playing according to Jerome) and 'does not know how to adjust his voice to singing the kind of song which would best be sung with a wooden instrument, a *viella*'.[16] Elias joins Jerome and Johannes de Grocheio in praising the versatility of the instrument,[17] but he is only concerned with literate players: the singer who plays the *viella* and knows the Guidonian hand is a *cantor* but anyone who does not know the hand is merely a *ioculator seu iauglator*

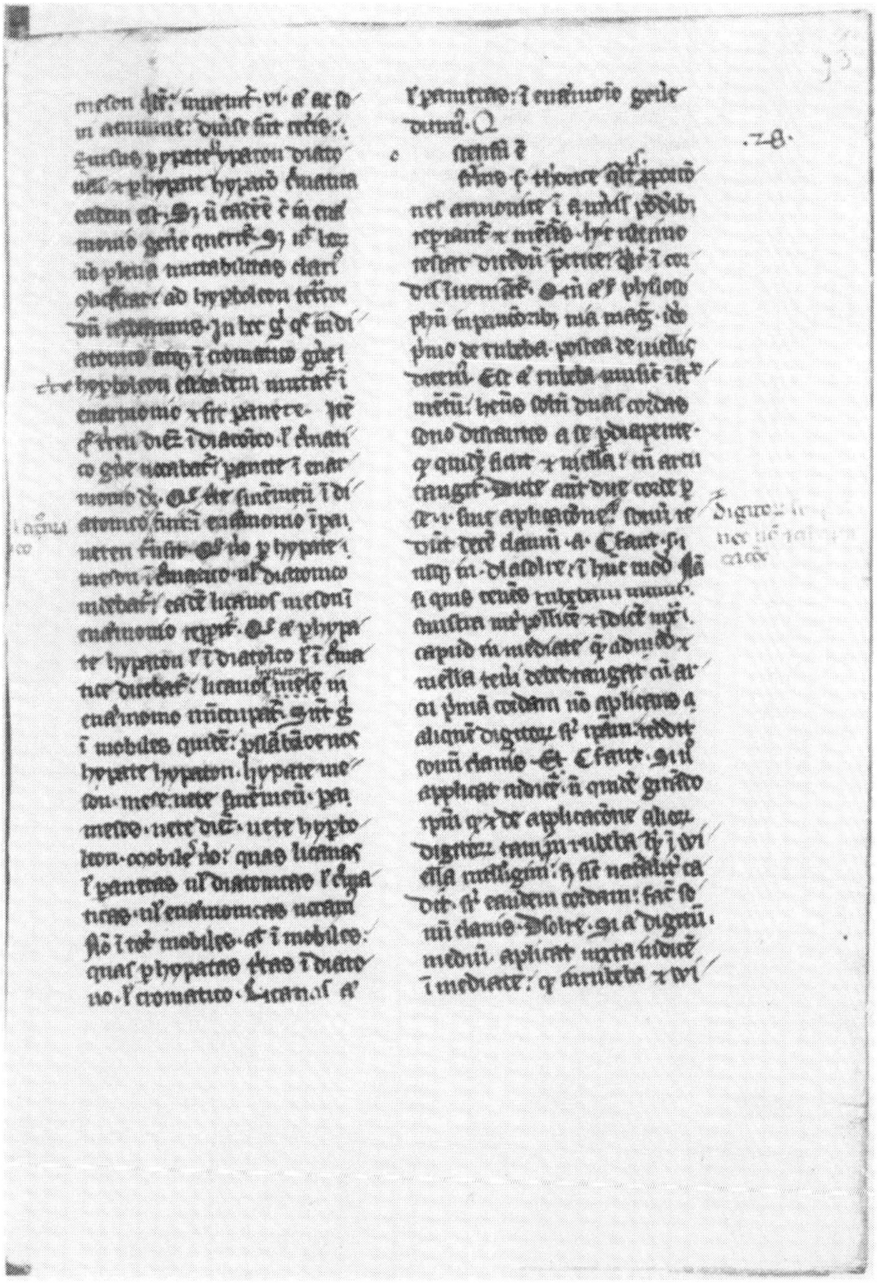

PLATE XX

Paris, Bibliothèque Nationale, MS. Lat. 16663, fol. 93r. Opening of Jerome's chapter on the rubeba *and* viella

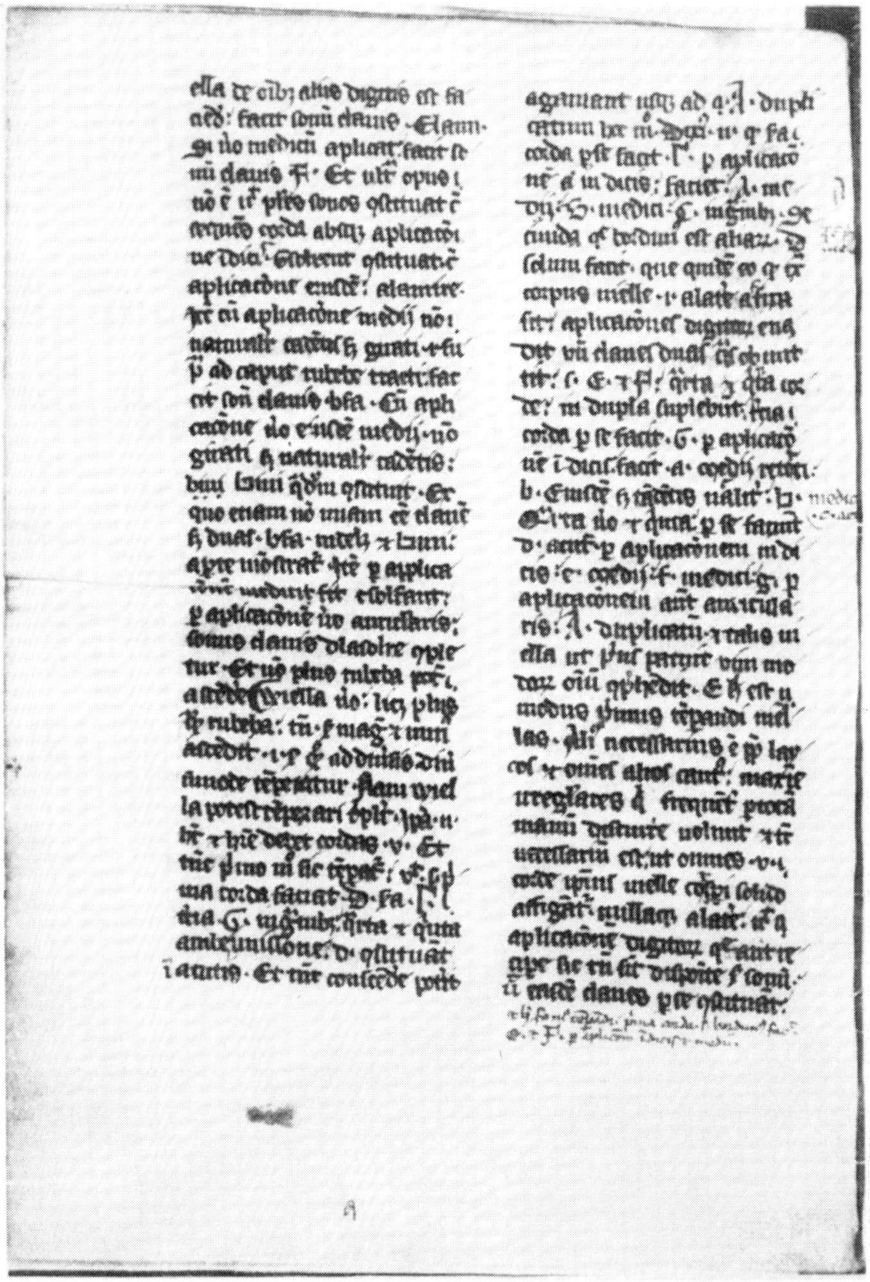

PLATE XXI

Paris, Bibliothèque Nationale, MS. Lat. 16663, fol. 93v.

in his estimation.[18] This distinction between literate musicians and *ioculatores*—found in other treatises including the *De Musica* of John 'Cotton'[19]—should put an end to any suggestion that Jerome is concerned with the world of 'amateurs and minstrels'. This phrase (an inaccurate translation of Jerome's *laycos cantus* which can be traced to Hortense Panum and probably further[20]) has been widely quoted and, given the general vagueness of the term 'minstrel', has served to obscure the fact that the real milieu from which Jerome's chapter is derived is that of well-educated Parisian circles, and primarily that of *cantors* amongst the secular and regular clergy.

Considering this evidence, we must ask whether it is likely that Jerome was the only pedagogue of the Middle Ages who catered for the instrumental needs of this readership. Did he set out upon his chapter as a pioneer without models or precedents of any kind? It is more probable that the aspirations of such musicians were catered for by a now vanished genre of Latin technical writing dealing with the rudiments of stringed instruments. These documents would have been instrumental tutors in effect, probably taking the form of a few folded leaves. Jerome's chapter on the *viella* and *rubeba* may be such a tutor taken over wholesale and inserted into the *Tractatus*; this would be in keeping with the nature of the treatise which is essentially a compilation of pre-existing materials. The fact that other 'tutors' do not survive need cause no surprise; where are the tutors that could be purchased from English minstrels in the late 15th century?[21] It is in the nature of such documents to be literally thumbed out of existence.[22]

However, enthusiasm for this hypothesis must not be allowed to obscure the literary tradition in which Jerome's chapter belongs. His introduction presents the material as a formal, practical demonstration of theoretical points already studied. The guiding principle is the same as that enunciated by Regino Prumensis several centuries earlier: any discussion of music must end with *musica artificialis*, including instruments, so that the invisible may be finally demonstrated by means of the visible;[23] thus Jerome's chapter on instruments stands at the end of his work, so that all may close *practice ... in cordis*. The practice of referring to current secular instruments (rather than purely pedagogical ones such as the monochord) in order to make theoretical points can be traced to the *De Institutione Harmonica* of Hucbald (d. 930) where remarkable use is made of the six-stringed European lyre.[24] Similar, but briefer references occur in a number of minor works, including a treatise once attributed to Odo of Cluny which refers to the octave range of the *fidula*—perhaps a bowed instrument.[25]

It is certain that by the 13th century the practice of referring to current instruments to make theoretical points was widespread. Lambertus (pseudo-Aristotle) advises the novice to mark the letters ΓABC on the neck of a '*cythara, viella* or *citole*',[26] and the same injunction may be found in the anonymous *Quatuor Principalia Musica* (1351) where *vielle, cistolle* and similar instruments seem to be recommended as monochord substitutes.[27] In the light of these texts Jerome's chapter appears as a rather less amazing document, and one written within a well-established tradition of theoretical practice.

VIELLA AND RUBEBA

Of the two instruments which Jerome describes the *viella* is the easiest to identify. This five-stringed bowed instrument may be encountered in many French manuscript illustrations and carvings of the 13th century (Pl. XXIII). It is often shown with the lateral bourdon string that Jerome describes.

The *rubeba* presents more serious problems.[28] The source of this word itself is clearly Arabic *rabāb* which today, in various forms, denotes a host of stringed instruments all over the Arabic-speaking world. The *rabāb* of Morocco, shown in very much its modern form in the celebrated *Cantigas* manuscript (Seville?, 1280–3, see *GSJ* XXI, Pl. XVII*d*), is one plausible candidate that has been suggested for Jerome's *rubeba*.[29] This instrument is bi-chordic (a relatively rare phenomenon in medieval Europe), and is tuned to a fifth. In both respects it corresponds to Jerome's *rubeba*, but its pitch is particularly interesting (approximately *c g* like the two bottom strings of a modern viola),[30] for Jerome's *rubeba* is tuned *C fa ut/G sol re ut* (i.e. *c g*) which is a much lower pitch than we are accustomed to associate with medieval names built on an *r-b* stem such as *rebec, rebebe* etc. This Moroccan instrument was widely distributed in the Middle Ages,[31] and there are several representations of it in northern European sources. As far as I am aware no example has been found contemporary with Jerome, though a 12th-century French example has recently come to light.[32]

THE TUNINGS

The tunings given by Jerome have often been misrepresented. They are:
rubeba viella
c g d Γg d′d′   d Γg d′ g′   ΓΓ d c′c′

The arrangements shown here preserve the sequence of the notes exactly as they are given by Jerome, but grouped into probable courses which Jerome does not specify. The most important observation to be made is that the second tuning for the *viella*—the one said by Jerome to be best for secular melodies—is *not* the constantly ascending series it has so often been said to be (i.e. it is not Γ-d-g-d'-g'). It is simply the first tuning with the top string taken up a fourth. Far from being a continuous series it is (1) re-entrant, and (2) the Γ and g form in all probability an octave course. With regard to (1), Jerome's Latin is abundantly clear: '[the strings of the second tuning] should be so arranged in pitch (*sic tamen sint disposite secundum sonum*) that they make the same notes as in the method of the first [*viella*]; this is true of the first, second, third and fourth strings, but not of the fifth, which is not in unison with the fourth but is said to make sesquitertia [4:3, i.e. a fourth]; thus it is placed at g among the *superacutae*. The phrase *secundum sonum* might be rendered 'according to pitch' and taken to mean that the strings are rearranged on the fingerboard in ascending order of pitch, but this conflicts with Jerome's unequivocal assertion that strings 1–4 produce exactly the same notes as in tuning 1.

The next important aspect of the tunings is the placement of the lateral bourdon string. Jerome's remarks in this regard have often been muddled with those of the later annotator, Pierre of Limoges. According to Jerome, only *one viella* tuning, the first, uses a lateral bourdon string. He is quite specific that all the strings run over the fingerboard in the second *viella* tuning, and he says nothing at all with respect to the third. It is Pierre de Limoges who, in an extensive note at the close of the chapter (Pl. XXII, bottom), says that there is a gamma *bordunus* in the third tuning.

The fact that Jerome notates the *viella* tunings with gamma as the lowest note has prompted the view that the instruments he knew were actually tuned in the region of modern G at the bottom of the bass clef. There are a number of reasons for rejecting this idea. It is quite clear that in the Middle Ages the gamut was an infinitely moveable framework of pitch nomenclature and musicians put it where it was required.[33] The actual pitch of gamma for example was a matter of indifference to the authors of the monochord treatises who worked by proportion, not by measurement from a standardised quantity.[34] The implication of the passage from the *Quatuor Principalia Musica*, alluded to above, is that the lowest pitch of any *viella* might be labelled gamma by the student using the instrument in place of the traditional monochord. Given the relatively short string-length employed on most medieval bowed instruments it is inconceivable that any but the very largest examples were capable of reaching down to G with the gut of the period.[35]

The danger of drawing conclusions about instrumental pitch from the use of gamut letters can easily be illustrated by the case of medieval chime-bells or *cymbala*. The numerous treatises that survive on the manufacture of these bells frequently employ a series beginning on C *fa ut* (i.e. c) to denote the pitches of the bells. Yet as they are shown in medieval art *cymbala* are quite small, and probably sounded at least two octaves higher than c.[36]

Jerome had no choice but to notate the *viella* tunings from gamma upwards. We must remember that he specifies the stopped pitches as well as the open ones, and the second *viella* tuning with the especially wide compass covers a range of two octaves and a fifth. Since the complete compass of the gamut in the 13th century did not exceed two octaves and a sixth, Jerome was compelled to begin with the lowest degree; had he started any higher he would simply have exhausted the range of signs available to him. From this it follows that all the *viella* tunings must be notated in this range for, as Jerome is most careful to specify, the tunings are very closely related to one another. The second is simply the first with the top string taken up a fourth, and the last is 'the opposite of the first'. Using a standard pitch notation for all three tunings these relations are apparent; a change in the notational basis would obscure them. Thus the relation between d Γg d'd' and d Γg d' g' is clear; similarly the fact that the third tuning begins with an inversion of the opening intervals of the first is clear from the notation d Γg d'd' and ΓΓ d c'c' (dΓg/ΓΓd).

The *Tractatus de Musica* has generally been regarded as the only 13c. source for the tuning of bowed instruments. In fact there is a second, almost exactly contemporary source, which confirms the type of tuning given by Jerome. This anonymous text, the *Summa Musicae*, was written between 1274 and 1307, most probably in France, and possibly in Paris.[37] The author divides stringed instruments into those which have 'no greater continuous [intervals] than tone and semitone', including *citharae* (harps), and *psalteria* (psalteries), and those 'which are tuned in the consonances of octave, fourth and fifth; by variously stopping with the fingers the players of these make tones and semitones for themselves'.[38] These are clearly fingerboard instruments tuned in very much the same way as Jerome's *viella*. Bowed instruments are by far the most common examples of the lute class in French iconography of the period 1274–1307, and the author was undoubtedly thinking of *vielle* among other instruments when he wrote. Thus Jerome of

Moravia's testimony can be safely accepted as a wholly reliable guide to the tuning of the *viella* and the *rubeba* in late 13th-century Paris.

NOTES TO THE ABOVE INTRODUCTION

[1] Jerome of Moravia's treatise on the *viella* and *rubeba* first attracted attention in 1828, when Perne published a French translation and commentary (*Revue Musicale*, II (1828), 457–467, 481–490). The text was first published by Coussemaker (CS, I, p. 152–3). An English paraphrase of the material was published by J. F. R. Stainer in 1900 ('Rebec and Viol', *Musical Times*, September 1, 1900, p. 596–7). A text with Italian translation (but no critical commentary to speak of) was published by Anna Puccianti in 1966 (*Collectanea Historiae Musicae*, IV, p. 227f); Puccianti did not use the complete edition of the *Tractatus de Musica* published by S. Cserba in 1935 (*Hieronymus de Moravia O.P. Tractatus de Musica*, Regensburg, 1935).

Jerome's chapter is mentioned in a host of secondary sources, but many of these have little value because of their inaccuracies. The only modern work which deals with the tunings and is genuinely worth mentioning is Werner Bachmann's *Origins of Bowing*, trans. Norma Deane, 1969, *passim*.

[2] See plate XXII. For an account of the materials pertaining to Jerome's life see Cserba, *op. cit.*, xix f.

[3] That is to say that the manuscript is made up of *pecia*, or free sections, to be hired and copied individually by scribes. This system was used at the university of Paris in Jerome's day. See Jean Destrez, *La Pecia dans les Manuscrits Universitaires du XIIIe et du XIVe siècle*, Paris, 1935, and Cserba, *op. cit.*, lxxxii. See also M. B. Parkes and A. G. Watson, *Medieval Scribes Manuscripts and Libraries*, 1978, p. 145f.

[4] See G. Reaney and A. Gilles, eds., *Franconis de Colonia Ars Cantus Mensurabilis*, American Institute of Musicology, *Corpus Scriptorum de Musica*, 18 (1974), p. 10–11.

[5] For the date of Pierre's death I have followed Madeleine Mabille, ('Pierre de Limoges, copiste de manuscrits', *Scriptorium*, 24 (1970), p. 45–47). Cserba (*op. cit.*, xix) gives the date as 1304, not 1306.

[6] Cserba, *op. cit.*, lxxix, gives the details.

[7] Mabille, *op. cit.*, *passim*.

[8] Private communication, 4 October, 1978.

[9] The date assigned to them by Cserba, *op. cit.*, p. 291.

[10] That is to say he does not go beyond the first position. It is quite certain that some stopping positions were used which Jerome does not specify. See the commentary below.

[11] Cserba, *op. cit.*, xvii.

[12] The operation of the *pecia* system is described in Destrez, *op. cit.*, p. 5f. But cf. Parkes and Watson, *op. cit.*, *passim*.

[13] CS, I, p. 269.

[14] *Ethica*, ed. A. Borgnet, Paris, 1891, p. 165.

[15] E. Rohloff, ed., *Die Quellenhandschriften zum Musiktraktat des Johannes de Grocheio* (Leipzig, 1972), p. 134–7.

[16] GS, III, p. 61.

[17] *Ibid.*, p. 26, 'in viella et similibus in quinque chordis totus cantus potest compleri'.

[18] *Ibid.*, p. 23.

[19] Jos. Smits van Waesberghe, ed., *Johannis Affligemensis De Musica cum Tonario*, American Institute of Musicilogy [AIM], *Corpus Scriptorum de Musica* [CSM], I, Rome, 1950, p. 51. See also *idem*, *Aribonis de Musica*, AIM, CSM 2, 1951, p. 47.

[20] Hortense Panum, *Stringed Instruments of the Middle Ages*, 1940, p. 388. Panum also gives the title of the treatise incorrectly (p. 385).

[21] See Alison Hanham, 'The Musical Studies of a Fifteenth Century Wool Merchant', *Review of English Studies*, NS viii (1957), p. 271. The merchant George Cely pays a harpist 3s and 6d (a remarkable sum) for a 'byll ffor to lerne to tevne the levt'.

[22] See H. S. Bennet, 'Science and Information in English writings of the Fifteenth Century', *Modern Language Review*, 39 (1944), p. 2, remarks upon treatises upon hawking: '. . . probably manuals were more frequent than the existing number would suggest, for it is most likely that their constant use made it inevitable that they fell to pieces sooner or later, literally thumbed out of existence'.

[23] GS, I, 236.

[24] See M. Huglo, 'Les Instruments de Musique chez Hucbald', *Hommages à André Boutemy*, ed. Guy Cambier, Brussels, 1976, p. 178-96.

[25] GS, I, 271.

[26] CS, I, p. 257-8.

[27] See *GSJ* XXXI, p. 53.

[28] See *GSJ* XXX, p. 10.

[29] Anthony Baines, 'Jerome of Moravia', *FoMRHI Quarterly*, April, 1977, p. 25.

[30] I am grateful to Jean Jenkins for information on this point.

[31] For an excellent collection of illustrations see I. Woodfield, *The Origins of the Viol*, Dissertation, University of London, 1977.

[32] Information provided by Laurence Wright.

[33] I am grateful to Professor Joseph Smits van Waesberghe and Dr. Gaston Allaire for corresponding with me on this subject.

[34] See C. Adkins, 'The Technique of the Monochord', *Acta Musicologica*, xxxix (1967), p. 34f.

[35] I am grateful to Dr. Ephraim Segerman for several long and informative letters on this topic.

[36] This observation was kindly confirmed by Mr. Hughes of the Whitechapel Bell Foundry Ltd., London.

[37] To judge by the forms *flaiota* and *flauta* which the author uses, he was French. Jos. Smits van Waesberghe (*Johannis Affligemensis De Musica*, p. 33) surmises that the treatise was written in Paris or Liège.

[38] GS, III, p. 214.

PREFACE TO THE TEXT

The text follows the manuscript as closely as possible. The absolute minimum of editorial changes have been made, all of which are indicated in the apparatus and explained in the notes which follow. MS. v for w and w for v have been reproduced by w and v respectively (thus *viella* for MS. *wiella*, *ut* for MS. *vt* etc). The MS. punctuation has been discarded in favour of a system following modern practice. The additions (generally corrections in the form of insertions) by hand 2 are contained in round brackets and inserted in the text, as are the annotations of hand 3, Pierre de Limoges. The hand responsible for the material is specified in each case. The contractions in the script—involving well over three quarters of the words in the text—have been expanded without italicising the interpolated letters. Letters introduced for the purposes of emendation are placed in square brackets. The purpose of the apparatus is to account for every stroke in the original manuscript; errors deleted by the scribe and others missed by him and his correctors are noted by line number.

Note: Jerome uses the standard gamut and hexachord notation Γ (gamma) A B C D E F G a b♭ b♮ c d e f g a b♮ c d, with each letter identified by its solmisation syllables. Nominally Γ corresponds to G (at the bottom of the bass clef).

THE TEXT

[In tetracordis et pentacordis musicis instrumentis, puta in viellis et similibus per consonancias cordis distantibus mediis vocum invencionibus]

[fol. 93r col. 2] Ostensum est superius theorice qualiter scilicet proporciones armonice in numeris ponderibus reperiantur et mensuris. Hic ultimo restat dicendum practice qualiter in cordis inveniantur. Quoniam autem secundum philosophum in paucioribus via magna, ideo primo de rubeba, postea de viellis dicemus.

Est autem rubeba musicum instrumentum habens solum duas cordas sono distantes a se per diapente. Quod quidem, sicut et viella, cum arcu tangitur. Dicte autem due corde per se, id est sine aplicacione (*hand 2* digitorum super ipsas nec non et cum aplicacione) sonum redunt decem clavium a C fa ut scilicet usque in d la sol re in hunc modum.

Nam si quis tenens rubebam manu sinistra inter pollicem et indicem iuxta capud immedi[t]ate, quemadmodum et viella teneri debet, tangat cum arcu primam cordam non aplicans aliquem digitorum super ipsam, reddit sonum clavis C fa ut. Si vero applicat indicem non quidem girando ipsum, quod et de applicacione aliorum digitorum tam in rubeba quam in viella intelligimus, sed sicut naturaliter cadit super eandem cordam, facit sonum clavis D sol re. Si autem digitum medium aplicat iuxta indicem immedi[t]ate, quod in rubeba et vi[*fol. 93v col. 1*]ella de omnibus aliis digitis est faciendum, facit sonum clavis E la mi. Si vero medicum aplicat facit sonum clavis F. Et ultra opus non est, ut plures sonos constituat, cum sequens corda absque aplicacione indicis G sol re ut constituat; cum aplicacione eiusdem a la mi re. Item cum aplicacione medij non naturaliter cadentis sed girati, id est supra ad caput rubebe tracti, facit sonum clavis b fa. Cum aplicacione vero eiusdem medij non girati sed naturaliter cadentis, ♮ mi quadrum constituit. Ex quo etiam non unam esse clavem, sed duas, b fa videlicet et ♮ mi, aperte monstratur. Item per applicacionem medici fit c sol fa ut; per applicacionem vero auricularis sonus clavis d la sol re completur. Et non plus rubeba potest ascendere.

88

TRANSLATION
(N.B. 'hand 3': Pierre de Limoges)
[Concerning four- and five-stringed instruments of music, especially *vielle* and such, for the sake of consonances on strings separated by intervals, with the performance of notes between.[1]]

It has been shown above theoretically how the harmonic proportions may be obtained in harmonious weights and quantities.[2] Here at the end [of the work] something remains to be said of how they may be practically found upon strings. Since, according to the philosopher, 'the true way lies among smaller things',[3] therefore we will speak first of the *rubeba*, and afterwards of *vielle*.[4]

The *rubeba* is a musical instrument having only two strings standing a fifth apart. It is played with a bow just as the *viella*.[5] The said two strings by themselves, that is without the application (*hand 2*: of the fingers upon them as well as with their application) give the sound of ten letters, namely from *C fa ut* up to *d la sol re* in the following manner.

If one holds the *rubeba* next to the peg box, in a natural position[6] in the left hand between the thumb and the first finger in the way that the *viella* must be held, and touches the first string with the bow, not applying any of the fingers to it, it gives the sound of the letter *C fa ut*. If, however, one applies the first finger—but not by twisting it; this is a caveat we so observe for the other fingers as much on the *rubeba* as on the *viella*—but just as it falls naturally over the same string, it makes the sound of the letter *D sol re*. If one applies the second finger naturally next to the first—which is to be done with all the other fingers on the *rubeba* and *viella*—it makes the sound of the letter *E la mi*. If, however, one applies the third finger, it makes the sound of the letter *F*. There is no further need that it produce more notes, since the following string may make *G sol re ut* without the application of the first finger, and with the application of the same [may make] *a la mi re*. Similarly, with the application of the second finger not naturally falling but bent—that is drawn towards the pegbox of the *rubeba* above[7]—it produces the sound of the letter *b fa*. With the application of this same second finger not bent, but naturally falling, it makes ♮ *mi quadrum*. Thus it is clearly shown that there are two letters here, not one, that is *b fa* and ♮ *mi*. Similarly, by the application of the third finger *c sol fa ut* is made, and by the application of the fourth finger the sound of the letter *d la sol re* is accomplished. The *rubeba* may ascend no more.[8]

Viella vero licet plus quam rubeba, tamen secundum magis et minus ascendit, id est secundum quod a diversis diversimode temperatur. Nam viella potest temperari tripliciter. Ipsa enim habet, et habere˙debet, chordas v. Et tunc primo modo sic temperatur: ut scilicet prima corda faciat D; secunda Γ; tertia G in gravibus; quarta et quinta ambe unissone d constituant in acutis.

Et tunc conscendere poterit [*col. 2*] a gamma ut usque ad $\overset{a}{a}$ duplicatum hoc modo. Diximus enim quod secunda corda per se facit Γ; per aplicacionem autem indicis faciet A; medij B; medici C in gravibus. Secunda, que bordunus est aliarum (*hand 3* que est prima vielle) D solum facit. Que quidem eo, quod extra corpus vielle, id est a latere, affixa sit, aplicaciones digitorum evadit. Unde claves duas quas obmittit, scilicet E et F, quarta et quinta corde in dupla suplebunt. Tertia corda per se facit G; per aplicacionem indicis facit a; medij retorti b; eiusdem sed cadentis naturaliter ♮; (*hand 2*: medici c acutum). Quarta vero et quinta per se faciunt d acutum; per aplicacionem indicis e; medij f; medici g; per aplicacionem autem auricularis $\overset{a}{a}$ duplicatum. Et talis viella, ut prius patuit, vim modorum omnium comprehendit.

Et hic est modus primus temperandi viellas.
Alius necessarius est propter laycos et omnes alios cantus, maxime irregulares, qui frequenter per totam manum discurrere volunt. Et tunc necessarium est ut omnes v corde ipsius vielle corpori solido affigantur nullaque a latere, ut aplicacionem digitorum queant recipere. Sic tamen sint disposite secundum sonum ut easdem claves per se constituant (*hand 3*: et hoc secundo modo temperandi prima corda, scilicet bordunus, facit E et F per aplicacionem indicis et medii) [*fol. 94r col. 1*] quas modo prime, et prima corda, secunda, tertia et quarta sed non quinta que non unissona cum quarta sed sesquitertia fieri dicitur, id est in g collocata superacuto.

Et tunc dicta corda quinta per applicationem indicis faciet $\overset{a}{a}$; medij retorti $\overset{b}{b}$; eiusdem sed naturaliter cadentis aliud $\overset{♮}{♮}$; per applicationem medici $\overset{c}{c}$; per applicationem vero auricularis $\overset{d}{d}$. De reliquis cordis sicut prius.

90

The *viella* is more highly valued than the *rubeba*, yet it ascends both more and less completely;[9] that is, according to how it is variously tuned by different players. For the *viella* may be tuned in three ways. It has, and must have, five strings. According to the first manner it is tuned as follows: the first string should make D; the second Γ; the third G—all among the *graves*,[10] and the fourth and fifth strings should form two unisons at d among the *acutae*. Then it will be able to ascend from *gamma ut* up to $\overset{a}{a}$ in the following way. We have said that the second strings makes Γ by itself; however, with the application of the first finger it will make A; of the second B; of the third C—all among the *graves*. The second string,[11] which is the *bordunus*[12] of the others (*hand 3*: which is the first of the *viella*) only makes D. This string, because it must be fixed outside the body of the *viella*, that is, to the side, escapes the contact of the fingers. The two notes which it omits, namely E and F, will be supplied by the fourth and fifth strings in unison.[13] The third string by itself makes G; by application of the first finger a; of the second finger bent ♭; of the same but naturally falling ♮; (*hand 2*: of the third [finger] high c). The fourth and fifth strings by themselves make high d; by the application of the first finger e; of the second f; of the third g, and of the little finger $\overset{a}{a}$. Such a *viella* as just described encompasses the material of all the modes.[14]

This is the first manner of tuning *vielle*.
Another [tuning] is necessary for secular songs[15] and for all others—especially irregular ones—which frequently wish to run through the whole hand. Then it is necessary that all the five strings of this *viella* are fixed to the real body of the instrument, not to the side, so that they may be able to receive the application of the fingers. However, they should be so arranged in pitch that they make the same notes as in the method of the first [*viella*] (*hand 3*: and in this second manner of tuning the first string, namely the *bordunus*, makes E and F by the application of the first and second finger). This is true of the first, second, third and fourth [strings], but not of the fifth, which is not in unison with the fourth but is said to make *sesquitertia* [4 : 3 ie a fourth], thus it is placed at g among the *superacutae*. Then the said fifth string will make $\overset{a}{a}$ by the application of the first finger; $\overset{b}{b}$ by the second finger bent; $\overset{♮}{♮}$ by the same naturally falling; by the application of the third finger $\overset{c}{c}$, and by the application of the little finger $\overset{d}{d}$. The remaining strings [produce stopped notes] as before.

Tertius modus oppositus est primo, eo scilicet, quod prima et secunda corda facit Γ; tertia D; quarta et quinta c. Et in hoc quoque modo tercio voces medie inveniuntur modo superius
70 prenotato (*hand 2*: sed non video quomodo b acutum formetur).

Quibus visis et memorie commendatis totam artem viellandi habere poteris arte usui aplicata. Finaliter tamen est notandum hoc quod in hac facultate est difficilius et solempnius meliusque, ut scilicet sciatur cum unicuique sono ex quibus unaqueque
75 melodia contexitur cum bordunis primis consonanciis respondere, quod prorsus facile est scita manu secundaria, que scilicet solum provectis adhibetur et eius equante que in fine huius operis habetur (*hand 3*: scilicet in pagina sequenti).

(*hand 3*: Quod D bordunus non debet tangi pollice vel arcu nisi
80 cum cetere corde arcu tactu faciunt sonos cum quibus bordunus facit aliquam predictarum consonanciarum scilicet diapente, diapason, diatessaron etc. Prima enim corda, scilicet superior exterior, que dicitur bordunus, secundum primam temperacionem facit D in gravibus, secundum terciam facit Γ, id est gamma. Per
85 manum autem sequentem scitur cum quibus litteris hae due faciunt consonanciam).

APPARATUS CRITICUS

Title: lacking. Supplied from prologue list of chapter headings.
1 Ostensum] o *in margin*, superius] superius .s. *with* .s. *deleted*. *2* in numeris] in a numeris *with* a *deleted*. *10* scilicet] scilicet *with following superfluous descender deleted*. *13* iuxta] iuxta *with following superfluous descender deleted*. immedi[t]ate] in mediate. *14* aplicans] aplicans a *with* a *deleted*. *15* clavis C fa ut] clavis El C fa ut *with* El (E l[a mi]) *deleted*. *20* immedi[t]ate] in mediate. *22* opus] opus *with following superfluous descender deleted*. *23/4* aplicacione] aplicacōi/ne *with second* i *deleted*. *25* non] nōi *with* i *deleted*. *26* facit] fac/cit. *28* cadentis, ♮ mi quadrum] cadentis bmi ♮ mi quadrum] *with* bmi *deleted*. *30* medici] medicit *with* t *deleted*. *34* a diversis] ad diversis. *37* secunda Γ] secunda Γ *with following superfluous descender not deleted*. *39* ã] a ã *with first* a *deleted*. *40* secunda] secunda *with following superfluous descender deleted*. *46* Tertia] tertiai *with second* i *deleted*. *52* est] est u *with* u *deleted*. *55* v] v c *with* c *deleted*. *56* ut] ut a *with* a *deleted*.

62 collocata] collaocata *with first* a *deleted*. d *in left margin*. *63* ã] ã A *with* A *deleted*. *67* est primo] est primus primo *with* primus *deleted*. *68* tertia] tertiam *with* m *deleted*. hoc] hoc *with following superfluous descender deleted*. *79* D] d. *84* D] d.

92

The third manner [of tuning] is the opposite of the first, by virtue of the fact that the first and second strings make Γ, the third D, and the fourth and fifth c.[16] In this third tuning the [stopped] notes in between are found in the manner discussed above (*hand 3*: but I do not see how b♮ may be formed).

Having reviewed these things and committed them to memory you will be able to encompass all the art of *viella* playing by joining art to practice. However, one thing must be finally noted, namely that which is most difficult, serious[17] and excellent in this art: to know how to accord with the *borduni* in the first harmonies any note from which any melody is woven. This is certainly easily known from the suitable second hand, which is only used by advanced players, and from its equivalent which is to be found at the end of this work (*hand 3*: that is to say on the following page).

(*hand 3*: Because the D *bordunus* must not be touched with the thumb or bow, unless the other strings touched by the bow produce notes with which the *bordunus* makes any of the aforesaid consonances namely fifth, octave and fourth etc.[18] For the first string, namely the upper outer one which is named *bordunus*, according to the first tuning makes D among the *graves*, and according to the third makes Γ, that is, *gamma*. By the following hand it may be known with which letters these two make consonance).[19]

COMMENTARY ON THE TRANSLATION

[1] This reference to *tetracordis* . . . *instrumentis* ('four-stringed . . . instruments') is puzzling, since this description fits neither the *rubeba* nor the *viella*. It is also noteworthy that Jerome's promise to deal with '*vielle* and such' implies rather more than he actually supplies. Both of these instances in which the chapter heading is not fully consonant with the content of the text suggest that, if this chapter was in circulation before Jerome, then it originally contained more (or at least somewhat different) material. Galpin (*Old English Instruments*, p. 61) seems to have taken the reference to four strings as an indication that the *rubeba* had double courses. Sibyl Marcuse's statement that this *rubeba* tuning is confirmed by Pierre Picard (*A Survey of Musical Instruments*, Newton Abbot and London, 1975, p. 484) is based upon an over-hasty examination of Coussemaker's edition; the twenty-eighth chapter of Jerome's *Tractatus de Musica* is not part of Pierre of Picard's *Ars Motettorum Compilata Breviter* (see the edition of F. Alberto Gallo, *Corpus Scriptorum de Musica*, 15 (1971), p. 11f.

As for the pitch of the tuning Werner Bachmann has notated Jerome's *C fa ut*/*G sol re ut* (nominally $c\ g$) as $c'\ g'$ (*Origins of Bowing*, p. 134) This conflicts with his transcription of the *viella* tunings, and has presumably been done because $c\ g$ is a lower pitch than Bachmann associates with instruments whose names are built upon *r–b* stems. Two suggestions may be made: (1) that the *rubeba* known to Jerome was actually tuned low like the two-stringed Moroccan *rabāb* (see Anthony Baines, 'Jerome of Moravia' in *FoMRHI Quarterly*, April, 1977, p. 25); (2) that Jerome wished to designate the *rubeba* pitch as being roughly a fifth above *viella* pitch (which was defined, for Jerome's purposes, by notational consideration—see above).

[2] Jerome's original Latin here alludes to a biblical passage, *Sapientia* II: 21.

[3] The aphorism '*in paucioribus via magna*', which is presumably intended to say something about the relative characteristics of *viella* and *rubeba*, is a mystery. It is not recorded in H. Walther, *Carmina Medii Aevi Posterioris Latina, Proverbia Sententiaeque Latinitatis Medii Aevi*, 5 vols., Göttingen, 1963-67, nor in J. Werner, *Lateinische Sprichwörter und Sinnsprüche des Mittelalters*, Heidelberg, 1966. The *philosophus* should be Aristotle, but no likely source comes to mind. I am grateful to Dr David Rees for the conjecture that *via* should be *vis* (thus: 'in smaller things great strength'); this might then be an allusion to Plato, *Republic*, Bk. IV, where it is suggested that a small city may gain strength from its cohesion, whereas a large one may be disunited. Jerome would then be making a comparison between the virtues of

94

the compact, two-stringed *rubeba* which has the advantage of smallness, and those of the *viella*, a larger and more diversified instrument.

⁴ The use of the plural *vielle*, both here and in the chapter heading, clearly indicates that Jerome does not imagine all the *viella* tunings as *scordatura* for a single instrument and a single set of gut strings.

⁵ In view of the fact that *rubebe* seems to have been a new word in the French language when Jerome wrote (see *GSJ* XXX, p. 10) it is striking that he feels compelled to define the *rubeba* as 'a musical instrument' and to assure his readers that it is 'played with a bow'. Generally speaking he discusses the *rubeba* in terms of the obviously more familiar *viella* whenever he can. Thus we are told that the *rubeba* is bowed 'just as the *viella*'; that it must be grasped 'in the way that the *viella* must be held', and that the first finger must be applied naturally 'as much on the *rubeba* as on the *viella*'. Possibly this part of the treatise incorporates material originally written in a country where the *rubeba* was more familiar; Spain perhaps?

⁶ The translation 'in a natural position' is based upon my emendation of the manuscript *in mediate* (for *immediate*, 'immediately, without intermediary') to *immedi[t]ate* 'naturally, unstudied' which gives better sense (compare Jerome's insistence that fingers be placed down *naturaliter*). Since the interval of a tone is not accomplished by placing one finger *immediately* next to another, the emendation to *immedi[t]ate* seems best in line 20 also where the manuscript again has *in mediate*. If Jerome had wished to refer to such 'immediately' adjacent placement of fingers, he would surely have recommended it for the semitone rather than the tone.

⁷ Jerome is compelled to explain what he means here since he has already forbidden that the fingers be twisted when they are applied.

All Jerome's fingerings are diatonic; the index finger stops the first tone after the nut, the second finger stops the minor and major thirds, and the third finger stops the interval of a fourth. The little finger is only used on the highest string. All his stopped notes are *musica vera*; he specifies no stoppings that produce notes not found in the Guidonian hand.

⁸ In no case does Jerome exceed the resources of the first position.

⁹ This statement that the *viella* may sometimes have a more narrow compass than the *rubeba* presumably refers to *viella* tuning 3 (ΓΓ d c'c'), thus indicating that this tuning is a drone block ΓΓd with a melodic facility running from the subdominant of the chord to the tonic (c'–g'), giving it an effective melodic range of a fifth as opposed to the *rubeba*'s ninth.

¹⁰ The *graves* ('low notes'), the *acutae* ('high notes') and the *superacutae*

('above the high notes') are the three divisions of the gamut (Γ-G. a-g, $\overset{a}{a}$-$\overset{e}{e}$).

[11] Jerome gets into a muddle here by referring to the first string on the fingerboard (Γ) and the lateral *bordunus* (D) as both being the 'second' string. Pierre de Limoges has sorted out the confusion with a marginal note.

[12] *Bordunus* is a word with an extremely complicated history. I have heeded the warning of Anthony Baines (*op. cit.*, p. 25) and resisted the temptation to translate it as 'drones' for this technique is not actually implied in the treatise.

[13] These notes are, of course, actually supplied an octave *higher*. This reflects Jerome's indifference to octave transposition which was certainly a common resource of medieval string players.

[14] This tuning certainly comprehends all the modes, since all the modal material is contained within an octave. However all the modes cannot be played if the instrumentalist restricts himself to the stopping positions which Jerome describes. This point may be simply demonstrated by placing the modal interval sequences below the sequence produced by the tuning:

```
       Γ  A  B♭ B♮
       G  a  b♭ b♮ c  d  e  f  g  a
```

Notes of tuning	T	S	S	S	T	T	S	T	T
Dorian	T	S	T	-	T	T	S	T	
Hypodorian	T	-	S	T	T	S	T	T	
Phrygian		S	T	-	T	T	S	T	T
Hypophrygian			S	T	T	S	T	T	[T] beyond range
Lydian			T	-	T	T	S	T	T	[S] beyond range
Hypolydian				T	T	S	T	T	[T S] beyond range
Mixolydian	T	T	-	S	T	T	S	T	
Hypomixolydian	T	S	T	-	T	T	S	T	

[15] Here Jerome's Latin may be construed in two ways, both equally correct: (1) *laycos* may be taken as an adjective ('secular') governing *cantus*, thus the full phrase would be rendered 'another is necessary for secular songs'; (2) *laycos* may be taken as a noun ('laity') thus: 'another is necessary for the laity and all other types of song'. The difference between the two renderings is not, perhaps, as significant as it may first appear; Jerome describes this tuning as specially appropriate for secular music in one, and for secular musicians in the other. The most interesting implication of the Latin, however it is translated, is that secular melodies formed only a part of the *viella* repertory. The

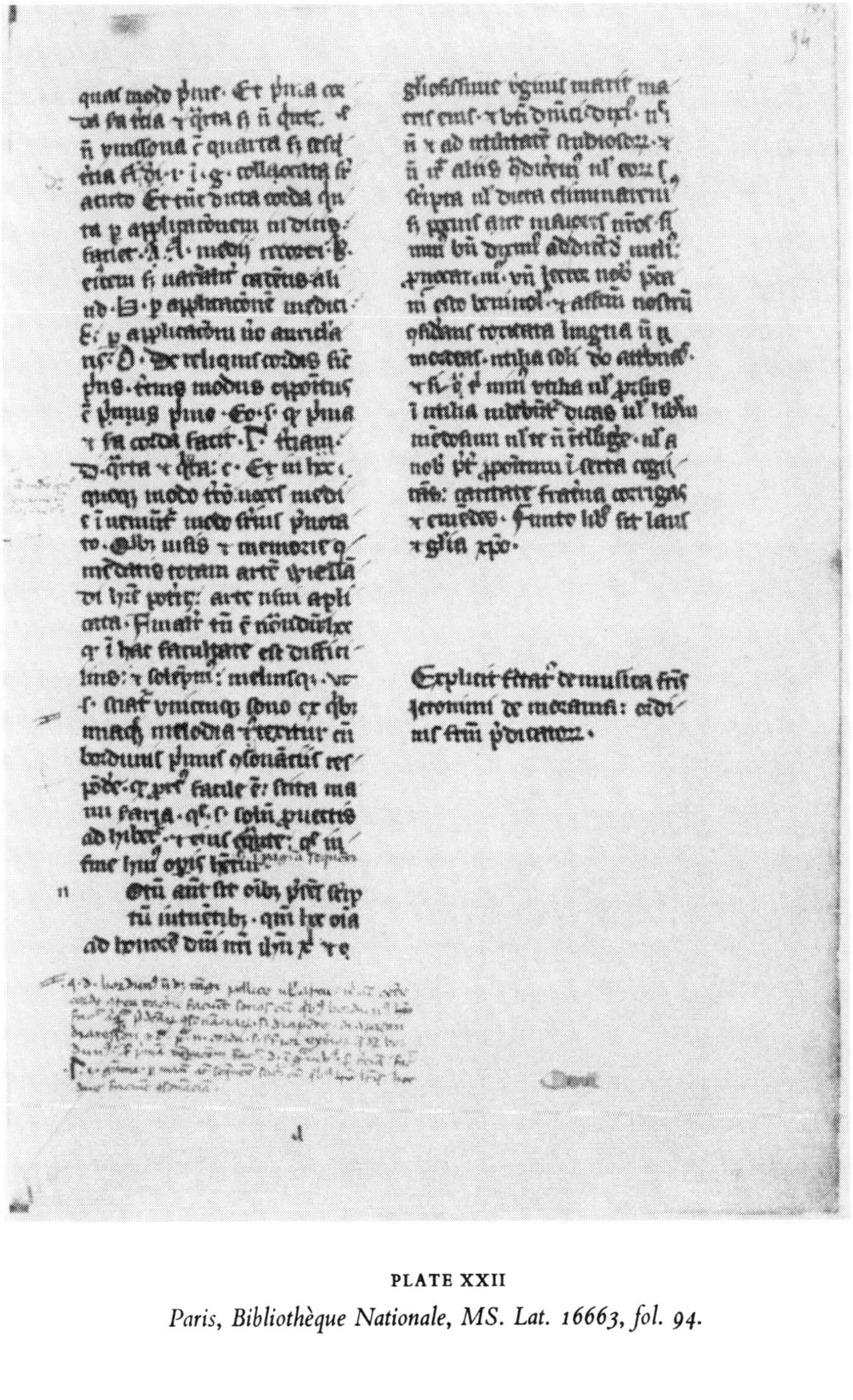

PLATE XXII

Paris, Bibliothèque Nationale, MS. Lat. 16663, fol. 94.

PLATE XXIII

Fiddle player (the lateral bordunus *is clearly shown). New York, Pierpont Morgan Library, MS. 638, fol. 17r, illustration to Judges 21: 21. French (?Paris), 13c.*

special reference to lay music (or lay musicians) suggests that some of Jerome's material is relevant to the other social group implied by this distinction—the clergy, and to their music.

It is by no means clear what these 'irregular' melodies are that 'frequently wish to run through the whole hand', i.e. two octaves and a sixth in Jerome's day. The monophonic repertories of the period rarely exceed a twelfth and the polyphonic motets rarely exceed two octaves. Possibly Jerome is thinking of certain special performance techniques which involved rendering material in different registers, or to certain conventional preambles in which it was customary to exploit a wide range.

It should be noted that this tuning is reentrant and, given the likelihood that Jerome's Γ and G form an octave course, does not give an unbroken linear ascent throughout its compass. The instrument's sound picture would have been rich in octave ambiguities, concealed by the incorrect way the tuning has been presented in many modern works. This means that when the player ran through the compass of the instrument it sounded not thus:

but thus:

```
         1  2  3   4   5
courses  D  ΓG  d'  g'
```

[16] This tuning is the 'opposite of the first' because it begins with ΓΓd, whereas the first began with dΓg.

[17] *solempnius* might be rendered in a variety of ways in addition to my 'more ... serious'. 'More established' or 'more customary' would

also be possible, but neither of these convey the clearly superior character of the technique Jerome wishes to describe. 'Serious' implies a keen and studious devotion to the more artistic aspects of fiddling, and I take it that this is what Jerome means. One might also translate 'more eminent', and this suits the context.

[18] A discussion of this technique must, unfortunately, be reserved for treatment elsewhere.

[19] The hand in question is a normal Guidonian hand.

ACKNOWLEDGEMENTS

This article represents some of the results of six years interrupted work on Jerome, and during that time I have incurred many obligations. Nicholas Ostler, Bernard Barr and J. W. Binns read and checked the translation at various stages. I am myself responsible for any errors that remain. François Avril, Conservateur at the Bibliothèque Nationale, Paris, never failed to answer my queries promptly, personally and in detail. Professor Jos. Smits van Waesberghe, Dr Gaston Allaire, Dr Richard Rastall, Dr Ephraim Segerman and Prof. D. Randel answered many of my enquiries with encouraging letters representing a most generous sacrifice of their leisure. Editors of numerous unpublished Latin Dictionaries—too numerous to specify I fear—sent me their citations for *rubeba* and *viella*.

Above all I am grateful to Professor Howard Mayer Brown, with whom I corresponded on this subject during 1977.

[22]

The "Arabian Influence" Thesis Revisited

By Shai Burstyn

The Eastern influence on medieval European music was a hotly debated topic in the musicological literature from the early 1920s through the 1940s.[1] Interest in the "Arabian Influence" thesis has reawakened in recent years and appears to be slowly but surely gathering momentum again.[2] Firmly convinced that the origins of Western chant were rooted in Eastern sources (Byzantine, Syriac, and ultimately Jewish), chant specialists made efforts to uncover East-West links in the first Christian centuries—efforts

---

[1] Some of the landmarks in the debate include Henry G. Farmer, "Clues for the Arabian Influence on European Musical Theory," *Journal of the Royal Asiatic Society* (1925): 61–80 (republished by Harold Reeves [London, 1925]); idem, *Historical Facts for the Arabian Musical Influence* (London: Reeves, 1930); Kathleen Schlesinger, "Is European Musical Theory Indebted to the Arabs?" *The Musical Standard* 2 (16 May 1925; republished by Harold Reeves [London, 1925]); Julián Ribera, *Music in Ancient Arabia and Spain* (Stanford: Stanford University Press, 1929); Otto Ursprung, "Um die Frage nach dem arabischen bzw. maurischen Einfluss auf die abendländische Musik des Mittelalters," *Zeitschrift für Musikwissenschaft* 16 (1934): 129–41; Marius Schneider, "A propósito del influjo árabe," *Anuario musical* 1 (1946): 31–141; and idem, "Arabischer Einfluss in Spanien?" *Gesellschaft für Musikforschung: Kongress-Bericht, Bamberg 1953* (Kassel: Bärenreiter, 1954), 175–81. For a comprehensive bibliography of the manifold aspects of the question, see Eva Perkuhn, *Die Theorien zum arabischen Einfluss auf die europäische Musik des Mittelalters* (Walldorf-Hessen: Verlag für Orientkunde, 1976).

Throughout this article I use the general, somewhat vague geographical designation "Eastern" for lack of a more precise term. "Islamic" is inappropriate as it now comprises millions of Muslims who live outside the cultural orbit of my concern. Likewise, the term "Arabic" is at once too general as a national designation and too narrow as a linguistic indicator, for that culture includes speakers of languages other than Arabic. Nevertheless, the religion of Islam and the Arabic language are the two crucial factors which lent unity and cohesion to medieval Islamic culture. This culture "was a collective achievement, and not only of Arabs and Persians, but also of Copts, Aramaeans, Jews, Byzantines, Turks, Berbers, Spaniards, and not even excluding contributions from Africans and Indians" (Hamilton Gibb, "The Influence of Islamic Culture on Medieval Europe," *Change in Medieval Society*, ed. Sylvia L. Thrupp [New York: Appleton-Century-Crofts, 1964], 156; originally published in *Bulletin of the John Rylands Library, Manchester* 38 [1955]: 82–98).

[2] See, among others, Alexander Ringer, "Eastern Elements in Medieval Polyphony," *Studies in Medieval Culture* 2 (1966): 75–83; idem, "Islamic Civilization and the Rise of European Polyphony," *Studia Instrumentorum Musicae Popularis* 3 (1974): 189–92; Don M. Randel, "Al-Fārābī and the Role of Arabic Music Theory in the Latin Middle Ages," *Journal of the American Musicological Society* 29 (1976): 173–88; Habib H. Touma, "Was hätte Ziryāb zur heutigen Aufführungspraxis mittelalterlicher Gesänge gesagt," *Basler Jahrbuch für historische Musikpraxis* 1 (1977): 77–94; idem, "Indications of Arabian Musical Influence on the Iberian Peninsula from the 8th to the 13th Century," *Revista de Musicología* 10 (1987): 137–50; Ernst Lichtenhahn, "Begegnung mit 'andalusischer' Praxis," *Basler Jahrbuch für*

that were usually deemed legitimate.³ Far less acceptable to many music scholars was the proposition of a second wave of Eastern influence on medieval European music, based on eight centuries of Arabic presence on the continent and on the close contact with the East during the Crusades. Still echoing the eighteenth-century contempt for non-European music, a marked Euro-centrist musicological penchant reacted to the "Arabian Influence" thesis in a variety of ways, ranging from vehement rejection of any influence whatsoever to disregard of the topic as if the question itself were not legitimate. These reactions form an interesting chapter in the recent historiography of Western music.

There is little question that the most knowledgeable and effective advocate of the "Arabian Influence" thesis was Henry George Farmer. For some fifty years, from 1915 until he died in 1965, Farmer flooded the musicological literature with studies of Arabic music and its contribution to Western music. His most cogent arguments are found in the book *Historical Facts for the Arabian Musical Influence*.[4] He amassed a wealth of information which he presented as facts "proving" the Arabic influence on medieval European music. He drew up an impressively long list of musical instruments of Eastern origin which found their way to Europe, followed by an even longer list of Latin, French, Spanish, and English words relating to music, of Arabic origin.

Many of Farmer's interpretations make good sense. Others are open to question. From a distance of six decades, Farmer still impresses with his powerful, often insightful advocacy of the "Arabian Influence" thesis. Obvious strengths of his writings are their grounding in medieval Arabic written sources of music theory, and their coverage of pertinent Latin

---

historische Musikpraxis 1 (1977): 137–51; Joseph Kuckertz, "Struktur und Aufführung mittelalterlicher Gesänge aus der Perspektive vorderorientalischer Musik," *Basler Jahrbuch für historische Musikpraxis* 1 (1977): 95–110; Hans Oesch, "Zwei Welten—erste Gedanken und Fragen nach der Begegnung mit andalusischer Musik aus Marokko," *Basler Jahrbuch für historische Musikpraxis* 1 (1977): 131–51; Stefan Ehrenkreutz, "Medieval Arabic Music Theory and Contemporary Scholarship," *In Theory Only* 4 (1978): 14–27; George D. Sawa, "The Survival of Some Aspects of Medieval Arabic Performance Practice," *Ethnomusicology* 25 (1981): 73–86.

[3] Hucke rejects Idelsohn's view that Gregorian chant derives from Jewish tradition (Abraham Z. Idelsohn, "Parallelen zwischen gregorianischen und hebräisch-orientalischen Gesangweisen," *Zeitschrift für Musikwissenschaft* 4 [1921/2], 515–24) and claims that "The forms of Western chant were developed in the West, even if they were sometimes stimulated from the Orient" (Helmut Hucke, "Toward a New Historical View of Gregorian Chant," *Journal of the American Musicological Society* 33 [1981]: 439).

[4] The book grew out of an extended scholarly argument between Farmer and Kathleen Schlesinger, who in her "Is European Music Theory Indebted to the Arabs?" sought to rebut Farmer's "Clues for the Arabian Influence."

sources. But, for all his usual caution, his strong convictions sometimes led him to read more into the evidence than was warranted. Indeed, some of his less credible "facts" seem to result from excessive zeal to show derivations at all cost. Despite his diligent spade-work and sharp intuition, Farmer's writings remain the work of a maverick who failed to leave an indelible mark on medieval musical scholarship. In order to have argued his thesis more convincingly, Farmer would have had to construct his arguments on information and methodology which were not fully available to him. In my opinion they are not available even today. Reviewing the voluminous literature on the thesis leads one to the conclusion that most attempts to assess Eastern influences on medieval European music—however interesting and ingenious they may be—stumble over one or more obstacles. The following are the most troublesome issues that must be sorted out prior to meaningful investigation of the topic:

1) The lack of sufficient knowledge about non-learned music traditions. This aspect of medieval music is of crucial importance to our subject, as it was very likely a meeting ground for oriental and occidental musicians in the Middle Ages. The concept of medieval European music as part of an essentially oral culture is largely undefined, and many questions remain unanswered, including the nature and role of improvisation in medieval musical practice, the applicability of the modal system in that musical culture, and the relationship between music theory and practice.

2) The lack of sufficient understanding about important aspects of Arabic music in general and its medieval theoretical and practical features in particular. A prime example is the concept of *maqām*, which, for all its centrality in Arabic music, remains a controversial topic even among specialists.

3) The methodological difficulty of dealing with oral musical practices, Eastern and European, which took place a millenium ago. To what extent can the extant written medieval musical repertory, cultivated by the Church and the upper classes, be taken to reflect non-learned oral practices? How much similarity can be conjectured between contemporary Eastern musics and their medieval predecessors? Without means to overcome these methodological obstacles, the "Arabian Influence" question remains largely moot.

122 Festschrift for Ernest Sanders

4) The absence of a comprehensive theory of the musical influence of one culture on another. For all the progress made in recent years in acculturation studies, they fail to provide firm guidelines for understanding what happens when two cultures come into contact. Ethnomusicologists have studied many isolated cases of music acculturation, mostly relating to specific situations in well-defined non-European and non-Western locales. Historians of Western music, however, have rarely availed themselves of either general tentative theories of acculturation, or specific ethnomusicological findings as tools for understanding musical European processes.[5] Thus, no attempt has been made to date to approach the "Arabian Influence" thesis from the standpoint of musical acculturation, although this approach offers a sorely lacking conceptual tool.

Even though definitive answers to these and related questions are presently unavailable, I shall address some of them as a necessary preamble to re-evaluating the "Arabian Influence" thesis.

The starting point for any investigation of the "Arabian Influence" thesis must be the recognition that Eastern music was in the Middle Ages, and still is today, an oral phenomenon. While one could never guess it from reading current textbooks on medieval music, this is also the salient feature of monophonic European music of the same period.[6] As Pirrotta aptly put it, "The music from which we make history, the written tradition of music, may be likened to the visible tip of an iceberg, most of which is submerged and invisible. The visible tip certainly merits our attention, because it is all that remains of the past and because it represents the most consciously elaborated portion, but in our assessments we should always keep in mind the seven-eighths of the iceberg that remain submerged: the music of the unwritten tradition."[7]

---

[5] See Klaus Wachsmann, "Criteria for Acculturation," *International Musicological Society: Report of the Eighth Congress, New York 1961*, 2 vols. (Kassel: Bärenreiter, 1961–62), 1:139–49.

[6] Charles Seeger chastised "the majority of musicologists [who] are not primarily interested in music, but in the literature of the European fine art of music, its grammar and syntax (harmony and counterpoint), and have dug neither deeply nor broadly enough even in that rich field to find either oral tradition or folk music, except in some rather superficial aspects" (Charles Seeger, "Oral Tradition in Music," *Funk & Wagnalls Standard Dictionary of Folklore, Mythology and Legend* [New York, 1950], 825).

[7] Nino Pirrotta, "The Oral and Written Traditions of Music," *Music and Culture in Italy from the Middle Ages to the Baroque* (Cambridge: Harvard University Press, 1984), 72.

It stands to reason that the submerged seven-eights of oral musical tradition in medieval Europe is fertile ground for examining possible Eastern influences. Because our only remaining link with it is through the extant manuscripts, we must recognize the strong oral residue in those written documents, and see them as potentially reflecting oral musical practices.[8] Nevertheless, for all its instructiveness and ingenuity, the act of forcing medieval written musical documents to yield information pertinent to vanished oral practices is a research technique of at best limited prospects.

The only other course open to the medieval historian is to study contemporary oral musical practices. This approach rests, of course, on the assumption that the changes in musical practices of the contemporary oral cultures have been small enough to allow meaningful comparisons with the European Middle Ages. This is indeed the course of action advocated, or at least implied, by Schneider, Bukofzer, Anglés, Wiora, Sachs, Harrison, and Apfel, to mention only a few.[9] Justifying this method is the apparent need of oral cultures to preserve their conceptualized knowledge through frequent repetition, which establishes, according to Walter Ong, "a highly traditionalist or conservative set of mind that with good reason inhibits intellectual experimentation."[10] Corroborating this view is Bruno Nettl's observation that oral cultures, due to their special nature, must depend on certain mnemonic devices such as repetition of melodic and rhythmic units, melodic sequence, predominance of a single tone, drone and parallel polyphony.[11] Alex Lomax agrees and finds that

---

[8] See Leo Treitler, "Oral, Written, and Literate Process in the Transmission of Medieval Music," *Speculum* 56 (1981): 471-91.

[9] Marius Schneider, "Kaukasische Parallelen zur mittelalterlichen Mehrstimmigkeit," *Acta musicologica* 12 (1940): 52; idem, "Klagelieder des Volkes in der Kunstmusik der italienischen Ars nova," *Acta musicologica* 33 (1961): 162-68; Manfred Bukofzer, "Popular Polyphony in the Middle Ages," *Musical Quarterly* 26 (1940): 31-49; Higinio Anglés, "Die Bedeutung des Volksliedes für die Musikgeschichte Europas," *Gesellschaft für Musikforschung: Kongress-Bericht, Bamberg 1953*, 181-84; Walter Wiora, "Schrift und Tradition als Quellen der Musikgeschichte," *Gesellschaft für Musikforschung: Kongress-Bericht, Bamberg 1953*, 159-75; idem, "Ethnomusicology and the History of Music," *Studia musicologica* 7 (1965): 187-93; Curt Sachs, "Primitive and Medieval Music: A Parallel," *Journal of the American Musicological Society* 13 (1960): 43-49; Frank Ll. Harrison, "Tradition and Innovation in Instrumental Usage 1100-1450," in *Aspects of Medieval and Renaissance Music: A Birthday Offering to Gustave Reese*, ed. Jan LaRue (New York: Norton, 1966), 319-35; Ernst Apfel, "Volkskunst und Hochkunst in der Musik des Mittelalters," *Archiv für Musikwissenschaft* 25 (1968): 81-95.

[10] Walter J. Ong, *Orality and Literacy: The Technologizing of the Word* (London and New York: Methuen, 1982), 41.

[11] Bruno Nettl, *Theory and Method in Ethnomusicology* (New York: Free Press, 1964), 236. The same view is expressed by Alan Merriam in *The Anthropology of Music* (Chicago: Northwestern University Press, 1964), 297.

"musical style appears to be one of the most conservative of cultural traits."[12]

There are no set criteria for determining the relevance of various contemporary oral cultures to the problem at hand, although geographic proximity and historical links are the more obvious possibilities.[13] Some scholars draw the line for relevant "control groups" within Europe, while others extend the scope to non-European cultures.[14] As for using contemporary Arabic music as a reliable model for medieval Arabic musical practices, several studies indicate sufficient grounds for comparison, provided caution is exercised. Beyond the slow rate of change generally assumed for the musical practices of oral cultures, the tonal materials used in contemporary Arabic music are thought to conform largely to those of medieval Arabic music.[15] Moreover, the writings of medieval Arabic theorists contain important points of contact with contemporary Arabic practices. Al-Fārābī (d. 950) and al-Isfāhānī (d. 967?), among others, are important theoretical sources for establishing continuity in customs relating to the social functions of music, and even more significantly, for particular improvisatory and ornamental techniques.[16] This is the raison d'être behind experiments such as the "Woche der Begegnung—Musik des Mittelmeerraumes und Musik des Mittelalters," in which the Schola Cantorum Basiliensis brought together Moroccan professional musicians with Western colleagues specializing in research and performance of me-

---

[12] Alex Lomax, "Folk Song Style," *American Anthropologist* 61 (1959): 930.

[13] For corroborating his analysis of Homer's *Iliad* and the *Odyssey* in terms of formulaic epithet technique, Milman Parry turned to the still living oral tradition of Yugoslavian poet bards (Adam Parry, ed., *The Making of Homeric Verse: The Collected Papers of Milman Parry* [Oxford: Clarendon Press, 1971]). Albert B. Lord refined and further developed Parry's theories in his field studies of Serbo-Croatian epic singers (*The Singer of Tales* [Cambridge, Mass.: Harvard University Press, 1964]). And in medieval musicology Nino Pirrotta was able to establish links between contemporary Sicilian folk songs and compositions from the Codex Reina ("New Glimpses of an Unwritten Tradition," *Words and Music: The Scholar's View*, ed. Laurence Berman [Cambridge, Mass.: Harvard University Press, 1972], 271–91).

[14] Such comparative approaches are at least tacitly gaining legitimacy in medieval musical research, as evidenced by, for example, the Round Table "Eastern and Western Concepts of Mode" which took place at the 1977 IMS congress (*International Musicological Society: Report of the Twelfth Congress, Berkeley 1977*, ed. Daniel Heartz and Bonnie Wade [Kassel: Bärenreiter, 1981], 501–49).

[15] Sawa, "Medieval Arabic Performance Practice," 80–83; idem, "Bridging One Millenium: Melodic Movement in al-Fārābī and Kolinsky," *Cross-Cultural Perspectives on Music*, ed. Robert Falck and Timothy Rice (Toronto: University of Toronto Press, 1982), 117–33.

[16] Lois Ibsen al-Faruqi, "The Nature of the Musical Art of Islamic Culture: A Theoretical and Empirical Study of Arabian Music" (Ph.D. diss., Syracuse University, 1974), 78.

dieval music.[17] At the same time we are cautioned that Arabic music has continuously changed as a result of contact with other cultures, and that the interpretation of medieval Arabic theoretical sources is fraught with difficulties.[18]

Assuming that enough information about medieval Arabic musical practices can be gleaned from the theoretical sources, the researcher must then devise a methodological framework for dealing with the "Arabian Influence" thesis in the context of music acculturation. But there is no universally accepted definition of acculturation, because anthropologists and sociologists constantly shift the emphasis and therefore the meaning of the term. We may start with the 1936 definition put forth in the so-called "Memorandum for the Study of Acculturation": "Acculturation comprehends those phenomena which result when groups of individuals having different cultures come into continuous first-hand contact, with subsequent changes in the original culture patterns of either or both groups."[19] There is disagreement about the nature of the cultural contact implied in this definition: does it have to be continuous? does it have to be first-hand? In any case, acculturation clearly comprises phenomena such as cultural borrowing, diffusion, assimilation, and rejection. Moreover, the study of acculturation examines the process of change that cultural elements undergo as they are integrated into their new setting. Here we can consult the ethnomusicologists who have studied cases of music acculturation and attempted theoretical summations of this complex question.

Bruno Nettl, in his recent book on the Western impact on world music, enumerates the following factors relevant to the study of the response of the borrowing culture: "general character of a culture, its complexity, geographic proximity to Europe or North America, relative similarity to that of the West; relative complexity and similarity of a musical style and of its system of musical conceptualization, institutions, behavior, transmission processes in relation to the Western [style]; a society's attitude towards music, towards change and cultural homogeneity; type and length of exposure to Western music."[20] Mutatis mutandis, these factors are applicable to the "Arabian Influence" thesis.

---

[17] Wulf Arlt, ed., *Basler Jahrbuch für historische Musikpraxis* 1 (1977): 11–151.

[18] Amnon Shiloah, "The Arabic Concept of Mode," *Journal of the American Musicological Society* 34 (1981): 19–20.

[19] Robert Redfield, Ralph Linton, and Melville Herskovits, "Memorandum for the Study of Acculturation," *American Anthropologist* 38 (1936): 149.

[20] Bruno Nettl, *The Western Impact on World Music* (New York: Schirmer, 1984), 23.

126 Festschrift for Ernest Sanders

If there is any one singularly weak area in the voluminous literature on the "Arabian Influence" thesis, it is the treatment of the subject from the standpoint of acculturation—general, or musical, or both. In fact, most writers have not even identified the problems to be addressed. Farmer, for example, assumed that musical influence was proven by establishing etymological links between Arabic and European terms and names, and by tracing the migration of musical instruments from point A to point B. Current ethnomusicological studies show, however, that various reactions to the transplantation of a foreign musical instrument are possible. For example, Persian classical music adopted the Western violin to such an extent that it became its most popular instrument. With the violin came the tuning, playing and bowing styles, pizzicato, vibrato, and other typically Western playing techniques. Nettl observes that "more than his colleagues playing traditional instruments, [the Persian violin player] tends to alter the traditional scales, with their 3/4 and 5/4 tones, in the direction of the closest Western equivalents."[21] In south India, on the other hand, the violin was also taken over, but stripped of its Western techniques. It was made to fit Indian style in playing position, sound production, and all other essential performing aspects. George List cites the adoption of a crude version of the Western fiddle by the Jibaro Indians of the Ecuadorian and Peruvian Amazon as an example of a type of hybridization "which parallels neither indigenous nor European forms."[22]

Even assuming that the physical transfer of Eastern musical instruments to medieval Europe is a proven fact—as indeed it is in many cases—questions arise which Farmer never dealt with. When Europe adopted the Eastern musical instruments, did it also adopt stylistic traits of their indigenous music? and if so, to what degree? How much did European musicians accommodate the Arabic instruments to their own stylistic preferences? Relevant here is Jack Westrup's rebuttal of the claim that the European presence of Eastern instruments shows their influence in the songs of the troubadours and trouvères: "It is not conclusive in itself any more than the French origin of the saxophone has determined the character of the music written for it."[23]

Studying the contact between African and New World Negro musics, Richard Waterman attributed the resultant high degree of syncretism to

---

[21] Ibid., 47–48.

[22] George List, "Acculturation and Musical Tradition," *Journal of the International Folk Music Council* 16 (1964): 20–21.

[23] Jack A. Westrup, "Medieval Song," *New Oxford History of Music*, vol. 2, ed. Dom Anselm Hughes (London: Oxford University Press, 1954), 229.

several musical features of the two cultures.[24] Alan Merriam generalized from this and other case studies and hypothesized that "when two human groups which are in sustained contact have a number of characteristics in common in a particular aspect of culture, exchange of ideas therein will be much more frequent than if the characteristics of those aspects differ markedly from one another."[25] Nearly all subsequent ethnomusicological writings on acculturation have taken this statement as their point of departure. Nettl refined the notion of basic stylistic compatibility as a plausible explanation of musical syncretism by differentiating between the transfer of actual compositions and stylistic features, and speculated that one could possibly be transmitted without the other.[26]

The amount and type of material adopted by a borrowing culture are factors relevant to students of the "Arabian Influence" thesis. Margaret Kartomi argued that "transculturation occurs only when a group of people select for adoption whole new organizing and conceptual or ideological principles—musical and extramusical—as opposed to small, discrete alien traits."[27] But however modest the status and potential cumulative influence of the latter, it should not be neglected, as "the borrowing of single elements is much more frequent than that of trait complexes."[28]

The adoption of a borrowed alien element always entails some degree of change, for that element must be integrated into the borrowing culture. Some scholars argue that the mutation acculturated elements undergo could make their identification more problematic if they belong to the aesthetic rather than the technological sphere. A borrowed technology is "culture transferable" in the sense that the adopting culture tends to change its uses, not the technology itself.[29] On the other hand, "no structural aesthetic element can be effectively transferred to another culture

---

[24] Richard A. Waterman, "African Influence on the Music of the Americas," *Acculturation in the Americas*, ed. Sol Tax, Selected Papers of the XXIXth International Congress of Americanists, vol. 2 (Chicago, 1952; repr., New York: Cooper Square Publications, 1967), 207–18.

[25] Alan P. Merriam, "The Use of Music in the Study of a Problem of Acculturation," *American Anthropologist* 57 (1955): 28.

[26] Bruno Nettl, "Speculations on Musical Style and Musical Content in Acculturation," *Acta Musicologica* 35 (1963), 37.

[27] Margaret J. Kartomi, "The Processes and Results of Musical Culture Contact: A Discussion of Terminology and Concepts," *Ethnomusicology* 25 (1981): 244. Kartomi distinguishes between the processes and results of culture contact and advocates the employment of the term transculturation to describe the former.

[28] Ralph Linton, *Acculturation in Seven American Indian Tribes* (Gloucester, Mass.: Peter Smith, 1963), 485.

[29] Norman Daniel, *The Cultural Barrier: Problems in the Exchange of Ideas* (Edinburgh: Edinburgh University Press, 1975), 4–5.

unless in the process of transference it is adapted to the aesthetic tastes and requirements of the recipients."[30] This suggests that even if European medieval music were influenced by Eastern elements, the direct search for the latter in cantigas, troubadour chansons, and other medieval compositions would probably be unproductive. By the same token, the failure to demonstrate specific Eastern motives, melodies, or stylistic features in medieval music may not necessarily stem from their absence, but rather from inadequate methodology.

Analyzing the influence of Islamic culture on medieval Europe, Gibb drew "a fairly clear distinction...between 'neutral' borrowings from the Arabic-Islamic culture and the 'shaded' influences or adaptations. In the neutral sphere of science and technology, the medieval Catholic world took over everything that it could use. In the intellectual and aesthetic spheres, it is very remarkable that all the elements taken over into western culture prove to be either elements of European origin adopted into the Arabic-Islamic culture, or elements with very close relations in western culture."[31] While Gibb's view is essentially correct, it may be too restrictive in view of the tremendous medieval enthusiasm and sensitivity to color, shape, and texture. According to Schapiro, "there is in western art from the seventh to the thirteenth century an immense receptivity matched in few cultures before that time or even later; early Christian, Byzantine, Sassanian, Coptic, Syrian, Roman, Moslem, Celtic, and pagan Germanic forms were borrowed then, often without regard to their context and meaning."[32] Schapiro's telling examples of European adaptations of Arabic objets d'art squarely place this aesthetic preference at the center of medieval mentality. It affirms the "amazing openness of the medieval European mind to borrowings from alien cultures" that Lynn White observed mainly, but not exclusively, in the field of technology. "Europe's capacity to exploit and elaborate such borrowings far beyond the level achieved in the lands that generated them"[33] is highly suggestive to musicologists contemplating European adaptations of Arabic musical instruments, and even more so of coloristic drone effects turned in the West to structural purposes.

The aesthetic borrowing of medieval Europe from other cultures was not indiscriminate. Europe was oblivious to origin and context of those items whose aesthetic flavor it found compatible with its own. Compatibility in general, and aesthetic compatibility in particular, significantly influ-

---

[30] Gibb, "The Influence of Islamic Culture," 165.

[31] Ibid., 166–67.

[32] Meyer Schapiro, "On the Aesthetic Attitude in Romanesque Art" (1947); repr. in his *Romanesque Art* (New York: Braziller, 1977), 16.

[33] Lynn White, "Cultural Climates and Technological Advance," *Viator* 2 (1971): 182.

ence the extent of acculturation. It seems to me that a well-made case for the basic compatibility between Western and Eastern musics in the Middle Ages could prove useful to investigators of the "Arabian Influence" thesis.

* * *

Middle Eastern musical tradition was recently delineated by the following characteristics, common to all regional dialects: "The vocal component predominates over the instrumental; the musician is both a composer and a performer; there are no time limits and no fixed program in the performance; rather the performance is a display of soloist virtuosity and the performer is permitted, and indeed encouraged, to improvise spontaneously; in this he is helped by the continuous interplay between himself and a limited, often intimate audience, which confronts him directly, without any formal barriers; the music is orally transmitted."[34]

All these points describe central features of medieval music, Eastern as well as Western. Apart from possible historical influences, the striking similarity in basic musical attitudes of these musics stems above all from their orality. A comparison of passages from al-Fārābī and al-Isfāhānī with the socio-musical behavior of contemporary Middle Eastern audiences points to a continuity of customs, such as shouting words of praise and requests for popular songs.[35] No comparable theoretical evidence exists for medieval Europe before the thirteenth century, due to the inferior status of low class music and its itinerant performers. But the musical treatises of Johannes de Grocheo and Hieronymous de Moravia document a dramatic change in attitude towards secular music and dancing. Grocheo's novel "sociological" division of musical genres and Moravia's detailed viella tunings intended for playing secular music reflect the newly acquired prestige of low class genres, which seem to have newly enjoyed great popularity. Henri Bate's musical reminiscences of his student days in Paris (ca. 1266–70) provide but one example of numerous literary references attesting to the great predilection for popular music, and the distinctly informal nature of performer-audience rapport.[36] Oral perform-

---

[34] Amnon Shiloah and Erik Cohen, "The Dynamics of Change in Jewish Oriental Ethnic Music in Israel," *Ethnomusicology* 27 (1983): 229.

[35] Sawa, "Medieval Arabic Performance Practice," 75–78.

[36] For information on informal music making in medieval Europe, see Walter Salmen, *Der fahrende Musiker im europäischen Mittelalter* (Kassel: Hinnenthal, 1960). The relevant passage from Bate's treatise *Nativitas magistri Henrici Mechliniensis* appears in Christopher Page, *Voices and Instruments of the Middle Ages: Instrumental Practice and Songs in France 1100–1300* (Berkeley and Los Angeles: University of California Press, 1986), 59–60.

ers tailor their renditions to the specific audience they confront by improvising verbally and musically pertinent changes. Capturing the attention and participation of the audience is essential. According to Ong, "in oral cultures an audience must be brought to respond, often vigorously."[37] As to the orality of musical contents, the fact that medieval monophony was written down does not necessarily make it a product of literate culture. Rather, numerous written-out chants and secular songs have the earmarks of documented performances. The constraints oral culture imposed on the performer in the musical traditions under discussion here may be elucidated by assessing the role of melodic formulas in medieval Western and contemporaneous Eastern musics.

It has long been recognized that melodic formulas are found in a great deal of medieval monophony. But the formulaic phenomenon is not generally viewed from the performer's side, and its importance as an aid to a unified composition-performance act, as well as its function in a given piece, may therefore be missed. The positioning of formulas is most often syntactically oriented. Analyzing the nearly 300 extant troubadour melodies, Halperin isolated 130 recurrent formulas: 56 are employed at the openings of 60 percent of all phrases, 41 final formulas are found in almost 70 percent of the phrases, and 33 internal formulas appear in 39 percent of the phrases.[38] These initial, internal and final formulas are often linked together by ascending or descending seconds. A typical pattern of phrase structure in a troubadour chanson is constructed from an initial formula, one or two internal formulas, and a cadential formula. Nevertheless, the resulting music is far from being a mechanical stringing together of formulaic clichés, and at their best troubadour melodies display great flexibility and variety in their formulaic application.

The formulaic phenomenon has been studied extensively in the realm of plainchant, especially by Peter Wagner, Paolo Ferretti, and Willi Apel.[39] All three scholars interpreted the phenomenon according to a theory of centonization. As in the Jewish *Te'amim*, practiced to this day, from which centonization technique in Christian chant is possibly derived, the formulaic phenomenon makes great sense from a practical point of view:

---

[37] Ong, *Orality and Literacy*, 42.

[38] David Halperin, "Distributional Structure in Troubadour Music," *Orbis musicae* 7 (1979–80): 19.

[39] Peter Wagner, *Gregorianische Formenlehre: eine choralische Stilkunde* (Leipzig: Breitkopf & Härtel, 1921; repr., Hildesheim: Olms, 1930); Paolo Ferretti, *Estetica gregoriana, ossia Trattato delle forme musicali del canto gregoriano* (Rome: Pontifico istituto di musica sacra, 1934; repr., New York: Da Capo Press, 1977); Willi Apel, *Gregorian Chant* (Bloomington: Indiana University Press, 1958).

the purpose of centonization is "to facilitate the task of the singer by reducing the melodies to a limited fund of formulae that can be memorized and applied according to the requirements of the texts." The tracts of the eighth mode are "a perfect example of centonization, a unified aggregate of eight elements variously selected and combined."[40]

Faulting centonization theory for its static approach, Treitler urged an alternate view, taking as his starting point the dynamic, "inexorable forward movement of the process" of oral composition.[41] The idea of a fixed "frozen" collection of pitches and durations that the literate mind is in the habit of identifying as a specific "piece" is foreign to the musical conception of the oral mind. Rather than reproducing a totally preconceived opus committed whole to memory, a singer in oral tradition literally constructs the song, creating it as he performs. He is guided in this creative process by a "formulaic system," a pattern of the general direction the melody is to follow, with strategic points outlined along the way. Formulas, on the other hand, are stereotyped melodic figures which gradually crystallized through repeated performances guided by a formulaic system. As already observed in the case of troubadour melodies, formulas tend to be context-bound and are especially expedient at strategically important melodic points, above all at beginnings and endings of phrases.[42]

Once the general melodic configuration of a chant, outlined and signposted by structural tones (*initium, flexa, mediatio, terminatio*), is known to the singer, he can proceed to pad out the melodic skeleton with formulas whose last (i.e., central) tones fit those of the melodic outline. That this is a realistic description of the process of musical reproduction under the constraints of oral music making may be seen not only by analysis of plainchant, but, more instructively, by observing living Middle Eastern traditions. The musical practice of the Christian Arabs is of particular interest here because it comprises stylistic traits of both the Byzantine Church and Arabic music based on the *maqāmāt*. Analysis of recorded

---

[40] Apel, *Gregorian Chant*, 316.

[41] Leo Treitler, "'Centonate' Chant: *Übles Flickwerk* or *E pluribus unus?*" *Journal of the American Musicological Society* 28 (1975): 12–13.

[42] For a detailed exposition, see Leo Treitler "Homer and Gregory: The Transmission of Epic Poetry and Plainchant," *Musical Quarterly* 60 (1974): 352–53. One could speculate about several stages in a process leading from a formulaic system to a relatively stable song. These would include the gradual formation of stereotyped melodic formulaic families, and later of specific formulas; the association of certain formulas with particular syntactical melodic functions; the growing tendency of some formulas to become contiguous and appear together in pairs or even in larger aggregates; and finally, the "settling down" of these elements together with the brief intervallic links connecting them into a permanent shape, a song having a specific musical identity. Variants among different renditions of the song will depend on the stylistic latitude permitted in the musical culture in question.

132 Festschrift for Ernest Sanders

performances of Christian-Arab music reveals not only the centrality of melodic formulas, but also their largely fixed position in the melody. Some formulas are "mobile," however, and can be employed in different contextual positions. Of special interest is the "Resurrection Hymn" in the third *lahan* (i.e., mode-*maqām*) as rendered by nineteen different singers.[43] While no two performers position all ten formulas of this melody in the same way, the differences do not seriously affect the melodic contour. This is because the variations involve mainly formulas ending on the same tones, making them capable of fulfilling identical functions. Even more telling is the finding that in repeated performance some informants interchange the position of several formulas. Here, too, mostly formulas ending on the same tone are interchanged, indicating that what is important is not the formula per se, but the function it fulfills in the melodic pattern.

Melodic pattern, then, is the key concept in the three oral repertories surveyed. This conclusion fully agrees with Lord's account of the training of oral epic singers in twentieth-century Yugoslavia:

> Although it may seem that the more important part of the singer's training is the learning of formulas from other singers, I believe that the really significant element in the process is rather the setting up of various patterns that make adjustment of phrase and creation of phrases by analogy possible. This will be the whole basis of his art. Were he *merely* to learn the phrases and lines from his predecessors, acquiring thus a stock of them, which he would then shuffle about and mechanically put together in juxtaposition as inviolable, fixed units, he would, I am convinced, never become a singer. He must make his feeling for the patterning of lines, which he has absorbed earlier, specific with actual phrases and lines, and by the necessity of performance learn to adjust what he hears and what he wants to say to these patterns. If he does not learn to do this, no matter how many phrases he may know from his elders, he cannot sing.[44]

---

[43] Dalia Cohen, "Theory and Practice in Liturgical Music of Christian Arabs in Israel," *Studies in Eastern Chant* 3 (1973): 25–26.

[44] Lord, *The Singer of Tales*, 37.

The overriding importance of pattern over detail partially explains variants among concordances in the medieval monophonic repertory. It also provides a bridge with the compatible attitudes towards the composition, performance, and transmission of Eastern music.[45] The skeletal tones of which melodic patterns are created reflect the infrastructures that organize the tonal material available to the performer. These infrastructures, in our case, are the modes and the *maqāmāt*, two systems that have long resisted satisfactory explanation, let alone definition. Difficulties compound when mode and *maqām* are approached from a performance-oriented rather than from a purely theoretical viewpoint. The general Western tendency to interpret modes as scales was adopted by Middle Eastern music theorists as a model for classifying the bewildering assortment of *maqāmāt*.[46] This, however, has had the unfortunate result of slighting, and even disregarding, central *maqām* features other than scalar construction. It is ironic that the contemporary Eastern movement away from its real nature towards a scalar interpretation of the *maqāmāt*, coincided with the growing Western tendency to interpret the medieval modes as melodic types rather than mere scale formations. Harold Powers's suggestion to locate modal phenomena on a continuum spanning the poles of "particularized scale" and "generalized tune"[47] may profitably be applied to an analysis of medieval modal conception and its compatibility with essential traits of the *maqām* phenomenon.

In his mid-ninth-century *Musica disciplina*, Aurelian of Réôme discusses the various modes in terms of their melodic formulas.[48] The syllables attached to these formulas (*ANNANO, NOEANE, NONANNOEANE*, etc.) are derived from the *enēchēmata*, the Byzantine intonation formulas of the *oktōēchos*. They also appear in the same context in other medieval treatises, among them the *De harmonia institutione* of Regino of Prüm and the later, probably tenth-century *Commemoratio brevis* whose author writes that "*NOANE* are not words signifying anything but syllables suitable for study-

---

[45] Although I am concerned in this article mainly with medieval monophony, the tenaciousness of orality in written and even literate culture (Ong, *Orality and Literacy*, 115) should explain the pertinence of musical traits observed here in monophonic genres to the polyphonic repertory. In addition to melodic formulas, rhythmic modes, various isorhythmic constructions and *formes fixes* are obvious manifestations of the central position of schemata in medieval music. The drawings of Villard de Honnecourt (ca. 1240), among others, should remind us that schema is a pervasive phenomenon, indeed an ingrained habit, of medieval mentality.

[46] For a report on the 1932 Cairo Congress on Arabic music, see *Recueil des Travaux du Congrès de Musique Arabe* (Cairo, 1934).

[47] Harold S. Powers, "Mode," *New Grove Dictionary of Music and Musicians* (1980) 12:377.

[48] Aurelian of Réôme, *Musica disciplina*, ed. Lawrence Gushee, Corpus scriptorum de musica, no. 21 (n.p.: American Institute of Musicology: 1975), 82–84.

ing melody (investigandam melodiam)."[49]

The seemingly meaningless *NOEANE* syllables bear striking resemblance to the "nonsense" syllables employed by Samaritans in their singing to this day.[50] The Samaritans' jealous guarding of their ancient traditions makes this link with the formative oral stage of Western chant all the more plausible and intriguing.

Hucbald also mentions the *NOEANE* syllables in his *De harmonica institutione* and applies Greek letters to the neumes in an attempt to fix their pitches. He intends the neumes and the letter-named pitches to remain joined, apparently "because then the subtle instructions to the performer embodied in neumes, intimating duration, tempo, tremulant or normal voice, grouping or separations of notes, and certain intonation of cadences are preserved."[51] Hucbald's position reflects a crucial turning point. His desire to preserve the neumes and all they signify reflects strong ties with Eastern, especially Byzantine origins. His efforts to establish clear tetrachordal structures and to determine their intervallic makeup clearly indicate a move away from the melody-type pole of the modal continuum towards a scalar system with its rational classification of chant melodies. The developing notational system allowed new chants to be composed that were less dependent on the Eastern formulaic procedures and more keyed to the tonal selection of the diatonic modes.

It must be remembered that the modal system emerged amidst attempts to impose a theoretical framework upon an existing repertory of chants formed according to melodic principles at variance with those of the new theory. For all the theorists' ingenious strategies, the resultant chant theory never managed to cover all cases. The persistent efforts of Carolingian theorists to modify problematic chants—especially through transposition—significantly narrowed the gap between practice and theory; but many inconsistencies and modal ambiguities remained, mainly in conflicting modal assignments of the same chants.[52]

The struggle to accommodate ex post facto the existing plainchant melodies to the forming Western theory, which was itself replete with

---

[49] *Hucbald, Guido, and John on Music: Three Medieval Treatises*, trans. Warren Babb and ed., with introductions, by Claude V. Palisca (New Haven: Yale University Press, 1978), 6–7. On the transfer of the Byzantine *enēchēmata* to Western musical theory, see Michel Huglo, "L'Introduction en occident des formules Byzantines d'intonation," *Studies in Eastern Chant* 3 (1973): 81–90.

[50] Ruth Katz, "On 'Nonsense' Syllables as Oral Group Notation," *Musical Quarterly* 60 (1974): 187–94; Eric Werner, "The Psalmodic Formula *NEANNOE* and Its Origin," *Musical Quarterly* 28 (1942): 93–99.

[51] Palisca, *Hucbald, Guido, and John*, 10.

[52] Apel, *Gregorian Chant*, 166–78; Powers, "Mode," 382–84.

Byzantine elements, is a fascinating case study in music acculturation. It is also an index of the increasing severence from Eastern roots of the developing theoretical framework which was to inform Western music for centuries to come.

If the modal system fails to explain plainchant practice comprehensively, its application to the troubadour and trouvère repertories further exposes its inadequacy. Attempting to account for the plethora of discrepancies between concordant trouvère melodies, Hendrik Van der Werf posited the crucial position of the interval of the third, using it as a common denominator for grouping the Mixolydian, Lydian, and Ionian modes under "medieval major" scale types, and the Dorian, Phrygian and Aeolian modes under "medieval minor" scale types.[53] Halperin's analysis of the entire troubadour repertory showed a distinct preference for the major mode; Ernest Sanders repeatedly emphasized the strong English predilection for the interval of the third in general, and for the major mode in particular; and Curt Sachs long ago urged us "to get rid of our modal obsession" and pointed to "The Road to Major."[54] In addition to locating many major melodies, a recent modal analysis of the *Cantigas de Santa Maria* came up against melodies that resisted rational explanation in terms of contemporary modal theory.[55] These studies strongly corroborate Johannes de Grocheo's statement that secular music does not follow the rules of the ecclesiastical modes.[56] Nor is Grocheo the only medieval theorist to insist that secular music does not obey the strictures of the modal system. At the end of his *Tractatus de musica,* Jerome of Moravia describes three alternate tunings for the viella. While the first "encompasses the material of all the modes,"[57] the second "is necessary for secular and all other kinds of songs, especially irregular ones, which frequently wish to run through the whole [Guidonian] hand."[58] It is not surprising that no medieval instrumental music spanning the range of two octaves and a

---

[53] Hendrik Van der Werf, *The Chansons of the Troubadours and Trouvères* (Utrecht: Oosthoek, 1972), 57–58.

[54] Halperin, "Distributional Structure," 17; Ernest H. Sanders, "Tonal Aspects of 13th-Century English Polyphony," *Acta musicologica* 37 (1965): 22, 27; Curt Sachs, "The Road to Major," *Musical Quarterly* 29 (1943), 381–82.

[55] Gerardo V. Huseby, "The 'Cantigas de Santa Maria' and the Medieval Theory of Mode" (Ph.D. diss., Stanford University, 1983), 270–89.

[56] "Non enim per tonum cognoscimus cantum vulgarem, puta cantilenam ductiam, stantipedem.... Dico etiam cantum ecclesiasticum, ut excludantur cantus publicus et praecise mensuratus, qui tonis non subiciuntur" (Ernst Rohloff, *Der Musiktraktat des Johannes de Grocheo* [Leipzig: Reinecke, 1943], 60).

[57] "vim modorum omnium comprehendit" (trans. Page, *Voices and Instruments,* 64).

[58] "necessarius est propter laycos et omnes alios cantus, maxime irregulares, qui frequenter per totam manum discurrere volunt" (ibid., 64–65).

sixth has been preserved, since that repertory was most likely improvisatory in nature and drew on oral musical idioms. While Jerome's secular genres are irregular because of their excessive range, an anonymous fourteenth-century treatise speaks of "irregular music [which] is called rustic or layman's music...in that it observes neither modes nor rules."[59]

It stands to reason that medieval secular monophony would exhibit considerable deviation from the theoretical mainstream, not being nearly as tightly grounded in modal theory as plainchant and by nature more receptive to external influences. Numerous discrepancies between concordant troubadour and trouvère melodies involve B versus $B\flat$, F versus $F\sharp$, and C versus $C\sharp$. Could these possibly be the only notational solutions the diatonic system afforded the scribes who, in fact, attempted to record tones located *between* these intervals? In other words, "did the scales used for the melodies of the troubadours and trouvères contain some intervals that were larger than a minor second but smaller than a major second?"[60] The theorists clearly document that microtonal intervals were an integral part of the tonal materials used in the early stages of plainchant. Early neumatic notation, intended as a mnemonic aid outlining melodic direction rather than discrete pitches, was ideally suited to the Eastern-derived portamento performance of chant. The diastematic neumes, developed in the quest to fix the notation of individual pitches, contradict in principle the *in campo aperto* nature of earlier notation. Looked at from the angle of future Western development, they certainly represent an important breakthrough. But the ability to notate well-defined pitches was gained at the expense of the ability to notate the very melodic qualities cherished in the East. Guido d'Arrezzo teaches us that the new notational developments reflected changing aesthetic preferences. He writes at the end of chapter 15 of his *Micrologus:* "At many points notes 'liquesce,' like the liquid letters, so that the interval from one note to another is begun with a smooth glide and does not appear to have a stopping place en route.... If you wish to perform the note more fully and not make it liquesce, no harm is done; indeed, it is often more pleasing."[61]

In the interim period when liquescence and other ornaments were still practiced but had to be notated diastematically, scribes faced a "notational crisis" typical of periods of stylistic change, but in reverse. The new

---

[59] "Irregularis autem dicitur cantus rusticanus sive laycalis...eo quod neque modis neque regulis constat" (*Tractatulus de cantu mensurali seu figuratio musicae artis*, ed. F. Alberto Gallo, Corpus scriptorum de musica, no. 16 (n.p.: American Institute of Musicology, 1971), 12. Quoted in Page, *Voices and Instruments*, 257 n. 22).

[60] Van der Werf, *Chansons of the Troubadours and Trouvères*, 57.

[61] Palisca, *Hucbald, Guido, and John*, 72–73.

notational system was inappropriate for certain melodic turns previously covered by neumes such as the *salicus, oriscus, trigon,* and *quilisma.* The notational decisions scribes were forced to make compromised musical reality, whether they wrote down *E* or *F,* for what they lacked was a means to notate the indeterminate pitches they heard in between. Numerous variants among concordant chant sources can be shown to stem from such notational constraints.[62] The eleventh-century tonary of Mass chants from Dijon (MS Montpellier H 159) is particularly revealing. A comparison between its nondiastematic neumes and the letter notation inserted directly under them show how special signs had to be used in the latter to indicate microtonal situations in the former.[63]

The eight estampies and the saltarello from *Lo* (London, British Library, Additional 29987) differ markedly in their melodic style and phrase structure from all other known fourteenth-century music, and at the same time show a strong affinity to certain Middle Eastern genres. McGee finds a close resemblance between the tonal structure of *Ghaetta* and *Chominciamento di Gioia* and that of the Turkish ritornello form *peşrev.*[64] The manner and order in which these medieval pieces gradually unveil their structural pitches show their close association with the Turkish *maqāmāt rast* and *uzzal,* respectively.[65] Other elements in the two pieces bear striking resemblance to Middle Eastern idioms, including the unusually long (for Western music) and asymmetrical phrase structure, and a particular kind of pervading sequential patterning typical of Middle Eastern *taqsīm* improvisations on the *ūd* (example 1).[66]

---

[62] David G. Hughes, "Evidence for the Traditional View of the Transmission of Gregorian Chant," *Journal of the American Musicological Society* 40 (1988): 394.

[63] See, among others, Joseph Gmelch, *Die Vierteltonstufen im Messtonale von Montpellier* (Eichstätt: Seitz, 1911); Johannes Wolf, *Handbuch der Notationskunde,* 2 vols. (Leipzig: Breitkopf & Härtel, 1913–19; repr., Hildesheim: Olms, 1963) 1:44–46; Apel, *Gregorian Chant,* 110–23; Hughes, "Transmission of Gregorian Chant," 395–98.

[64] Timothy McGee, "Eastern Influences in Medieval European Dances," in Falck and Rice, eds., *Cross Cultural Perspectives on Music,* 79–100. The area comprising modern Turkey participated in regional political developments long before the fall of Constantinople in 1453. Likewise, Turkey partook in Middle Eastern culture from the time of its conversion to Islam in the tenth century and throughout the rule of Seljuk and Ottoman dynasties. During these centuries, linguistic, poetic, and literary influences of Arabic and Persian origin found their way into Turkish culture, as have the musical components of what was referred to above as the Great Tradition. The still dominant instrumental form *peşrev* is considered to be "especially old" and is ascribed to Sultan Veled (1226–1312). See Kurt Reinhard, "Turkey," *New Grove Dictionary of Music* (1980) 19:268.

[65] The equivalent Arabic *maqāmāt* are *mutlaq fi majra al-wusta* and *khinsir fi majra al-binsir.*

[66] For the music see McGee, "Eastern Influences," 81–88. The *taqsīm* from which the musical examples are taken was performed in Tel-Aviv on 17 July 1988 by Mr. Taysir Elias. I would like to take this opportunity to thank him for his kind assistance. For additional

138 Festschrift for Ernest Sanders

Example 1. A comparison of melodic sequences from the medieval European *Ghaetta* and *Chominciamento di gioia* with sequences from a contemporary Eastern *Taqsīm*.

1a. *Ghaetta,* mm. 18–20.

Taqsīm.

1b. *Ghaetta,* mm. 95–99.

Taqsīm.

1c. *Ghaetta,* mm. 82–85.

Taqsīm.

1d. *Chominiciamento di gioia,* mm. 163–66.

Taqsīm.

These nine instrumental pieces of *Lo* can in no way be explained as indigenous European music. Their distinctly Eastern character is easily discernible.[67] If these estampies are indeed of Eastern origin, it is likely that their Italian scribe—in his attempt to write them down—introduced

examples of similar sequences in *taqāsīm* see Bruno Nettl and Ronald Riddle, "Taqsīm Nahawand: A Study of Sixteen Performances by Jihad Racy," *Yearbook of the International Music Council* 5 (1973): 31–33, 37–89. For similar sequences in a *peşrev*, see Karl L. Signell, *Makam: Modal Practice in Turkish Music* (Seattle: Asian Music Publications, 1977), 93–94 *et passim.*

[67] Criticizing the "modern Arab manner" of some recorded performances of these estampies, Frederick Crane rates the probability of their fourteenth-century performance in that style "near zero" ("On Performing the *Lo estampies,*" *Early Music* 7 [1979]: 31).

some formal modification better to mold them to the formal requirements of the estampie. In addition, he probably changed some notes for the closest substitutes he could find in the notational system at his disposal.[68] Alternately, these instrumental pieces could be original Western imitations of Eastern models, but this seems less likely on stylistic grounds. We may note that the estampie is among the secular forms Grocheo specifically cites as not following the modal system. In either case, we are afforded a rare glimpse of a case of fourteenth-century musical acculturation involving the transfer of entire pieces, or of salient stylistic traits.

The foregoing discussion of indeterminate intervals in both sacred and secular repertories of medieval monophony suggests that intervals smaller than a minor second, and intervals lying between a minor and major second, were part of the European soundscape throughout the Middle Ages. It is difficult to assess how widespread the microtonal phenomenon was, partly because it could not have been recorded in conventional notation, and was probably confined to popular genres which were almost never written down.[69] The partial coverage by the modal system of extant medieval monophony, the strong tendency to formulaic construction, and the evidence of microtonal intervals add up to a stylistic stance that has important compatibility with Eastern music, especially as revealed in the *maqām* phenomenon. I shall restrict the following discussion to points amplifying the *maqām*'s compatibility with genres of medieval monophony.

Microtonality has been one of the most striking and constant characteristics of *maqāmāt* throughout the centuries. Medieval Arabic theorists may present the scalar formations of various *maqāmāt* in different, even conflicting ways, but they all agree about their microtonality.[70] For example, Safi-al-Dīn (d. 1292), the founder of the so-called Systematist school of music theory, divides the 9:8 whole tone of 204 cents into two equal

---

[68] Interestingly, this very solution can be observed even today in Rumanian music, where surviving Turkish influences calling for microtonal performance are compromised when performed on European instruments tuned to the tempered scale. Ses Robert Grafias, "Survivals of Turkish Characteristics in Romanian Musica Lautareasca," *Yearbook for Traditional Music* 13 (1981): 105.

[69] Although it occurs in the context of discussing polyphonic music, Marchettus de Padua's curious argument in his *Lucidarium* for dividing the whole tone into five parts gives some indication that the idea was conceivable to him in the realm of musical practice. See Jan W. Herlinger, ed., *The Lucidarium of Marchetto of Padua* (Chicago: University of Chicago Press, 1985), 131–37; F. Alberto Gallo, "Marchetto da Padova," *New Grove Dictionary of Music* (1980) 11:662.

[70] For the theoretical systems developed by Arabic medieval theorists, see Liberty Manik, *Das arabische Tonsystem im Mittelalter* (Leiden: Brill, 1969).

limmas of ninety cents and a comma of twenty-four cents. His normal division of the octave is into two conjunct tetrachords and a whole tone, or into one tetrachord and a conjunct pentachord. The two-tetrachord method, with its resultant seventeen-tone division, is schematized in figure 1.[71]

Figure 1.

Since musical practice and not abstract theory concerns us here, we must note that the degree to which Safi-al-Dīn's three theoretical treatises reflect musical practice is uncertain, "since they result from passing the raw material of practice through a filter of theoretical presuppositions about the nature of consonance."[72] The exact relationship between theory and practice has been scantily explored in contemporary Arabic music as well, but comparisons of medieval Arabic theory and current practices indicate that "most of the tones used by the contemporary musicians are identical or accord very closely with those of the classical theorists."[73]

Contemporary Arabic theory divides the octave into twenty-four equal parts, out of which the actual intervals in the various *maqām* scales are formed. We will focus on the combinations of two quarter tones (minor second), and four quarter tones (major second). The tetrachord (*jins*) has been the basic scalar formation of Arabic theory from its earliest stages to the present.[74] Figure 2 shows the identity of the tetrachords of medieval modes and the tetrachords of *maqāmāt* that use only major and minor seconds. To these affinities of theoretical thinking should be added other mode-defining concepts such as ambitus, finalis, and confinalis.

Figure 2.

$$Ajam = 1 - 1 - \tfrac{1}{2} = \text{Mixolydian}$$

$$Nahawand = 1 - \tfrac{1}{2} - 1 = \text{Dorian}$$

$$Kurd = \tfrac{1}{2} - 1 - 1 = \text{Phrygian}$$

---

[71] See O. Wright, *The Modal System of Arab and Persian Music*, A.D. *1250–1300* (Oxford: Oxford University Press, 1978), 34.

[72] Ibid., 2.

[73] al-Faruqi, "Musical Art of Islamic Culture," 77.

[74] For al-Fārābī's account of tetrachordal division in his *Kitāb al Mūsīqī al Kabīr*, see Rodolphe d'Erlanger, *La musique arabe*, 6 vols. (Paris: Geuthner, 1930–59), 1:55–61.

While the intervallic demonstration of basic diatonic alliance between elements of medieval modes and *maqāmāt* is revealing, the compatibility of the two systems can be shown to be more profound yet. Earlier, we discussed the functioning of the modal system in the context of oral musical culture, and the roles played by composition-performance patterns, formulaic systems, and melodic formulas. We now need to apply this approach to the *maqām* system.

The term *maqām* variously refers to a particular scale, to that scale plus its central tones, or according to some, to the latter and characteristic melodic formulas. The precise relationship between a *maqām* and the *taqsīm* based on it is more troublesome yet. The perennial argument over the alleged presence of melodic motives or formulas, either typifying specific *maqāmāt* or changeable among them, tends to confound the subject even more and to steer it away from what I take to be its central issues.

In addition to its ambitus and tetrachordal arrangement, the *maqām* is further defined by a tonic (*qarār*), a "dominant" (*ghammāz*, often, but not always, a fifth above the tonic), a starting tone (*mabdá*), a "leading tone" (*zahīr*), and tones of secondary importance (*marākiz*). The strong functional nature of these tonal degrees attenuates the scalar notion of the *maqām* and underlines its essence as a structural model to be realized. Linking the various tonal stations of the *maqām* during its musical realization, the performer follows the *uslūb* ("method"), a procedure for melodic progression through its structure.[75] The term *sayr al amal* ("progress of the work"), and indeed the very term *tarīqah* (way, road), synonymous with *maqām*, clearly indicate the prescriptive nature intended: in order to create a *taqsīm* (an instrumental improvisation-composition), the performer follows a musical plan for actualizing the structural tonal ingredients latent in the *maqām*. (There are no equivalent durational requirements; the rhythmic-temporal aspect of the *taqsīm* is entirely free and may be shaped according to the wishes of the performer.)

The elements to be realized in a *taqsīm* can be summarized as follows: (1) A *taqsīm* is made up of several segments clearly marked off by silences (*Waqfāt*). (2) A segment is a melodic passage controlled by one of the tones central to the *maqām* on which the *taqsīm* is based. (3) A central tone has "satellite" tones of secondary importance to which the performer may temporarily digress.[76] (4) The *taqsīm* player usually presents the segments

---

[75] al-Faruqi, "Musical Art of Islamic Culture," 100.

[76] For an interesting attempt to shed light on the enigmatic "borrowed notes" in ancient Greek theory (i.e., notes that digress from their assigned *tonos*) by correlating them with the living practices of Turkish and Persian music, see Nancy Sultan, "New Light on the Function of 'Borrowed Notes' in Ancient Greek Music: A Look at Islamic Parallels," *Journal of Musicology* 7 (1988): 387–98.

in a gradually ascending order, reaches a peak, and descends to the main tonal center. (5) This gradual exposition of central *maqām* tones is worked out within the framework of the *ajnās* in a way designed to bring out their typical tetrachordal structure.[77]

This scheme suffices to demonstrate a major point: under the constraints of oral performance-composition, the Arabic musician playing a *taqsīm* certainly does not "freely improvise"; nor does he improvise on the basis of some vague procedures. On the contrary, he is following a tightly structured pattern, binding in its general plan. The instrumentalist enjoys considerable flexibility within the overall indispensable framework. For example, he may decide the number, length, and complexity of segments, whether to modulate temporarily to another *maqām*, and if so, to which one and for how long.

Nettl and Riddle studied sixteen *taqāsīm* on *maqām* Nahawand and posited "the existence of certain principles that are characteristic in the macrocosm and the microcosm of performances, and at points between these extremes. In certain parameters or elements of music, the performer carries out the same kind of musical thinking in bits of melody hardly more than a second in length, in longer segments of melody, in sections, and in entire *taqāsīm*. The structural integrity of these improvisations is thus considerable, and we again learn that in those cultures in which improvisation plays a major role, it provides freedom for the musician to invent only within a rigorous and tightly-knit system of structural principles."[78]

In order to be able to play a *taqsīm*, a young performer must acquire the skill of breathing musical life into the overall formal pattern. He applies to that pattern his familiarity with the structural tones of the *maqāmāt* and their tetrachordal arrangements, initially creating short, relatively simple *taqāsīm* that satisfy the minimum requirements of the general pattern. Gradually he tries more daring performances, weaving a complex net of subsidiary tonal relations, venturing farther from the main route but never losing sight of its structural signposts. His musical predilections will eventually stabilize into an individual style. It is likely

---

[77] Touma minutely analyzed *taqāsīm* on *maqām* Bayati and graphed them second by second. According to him, the various phases are organized in larger sections he called *anfās*. A *nafas* may contain one or more phases. His analysis stresses the central tones of the *maqām* scale and disregards tetrachordal structures. Habib Hassan Touma, *Maqam Bayati in the Arabian Taqsim: A Study in the Phenomenology of the Maqam* (International Monograph Publishers, 1975).

[78] Nettl and Riddle, "Taqsīm Nahawand," 29.

Example 2. Idiomatic figures in *ūd* and *qānūn taqāsīm*.

that certain melodic turns and short motives heard elsewhere, or originated with him, will become part of his personal vocabulary and appear from time to time in his performances of *taqāsīm*. Some of these melodic formulas probably originate in the idiomatic language of the performer's instrument: for example, the figures shown in example 2 are melodic clichés associated with *ūd* and *qānūn*, but not with *nāy* performances.[79] Other melodic, rhythmic, or melodic-rhythmic motives may occur and contribute to the typically repetitive nature (*takarrur*) of the *taqsīm*. Their individual profile is usually rather low as they are not intended to transcend their cliché quality. It is their very nondescript profile which renders them so useful to the performer-improviser by providing him with the handy, tiny flexible tonal aggregates he needs at his fingertips to propel the performance forward. Despite the definite presence of these formulas, the *taqsīm* cannot be explained as a process of centonization. Idelsohn's interpretation, as well as its numerous echoes, correctly identified the presence of formulas in *taqāsīm*, but misinterpreted their role.[80] Formulas of various kinds may indeed be part of a *taqsīm*; their raison d'être is explained by the improvisatory nature of the performance. As far as the structural pattern of the *taqsīm* is concerned, formulas fulfill an incidental and not a salient function.

---

[79] Interestingly, example 2b appears in al-Fārābī's *Kitāb al Mūsīqī al Kabīr* (ed. Ghattas Abd-el-Malek Khashaba and Mahmoud Ahmed el Hefny [Cairo, 1967], 972) in his discussion of various melodic patterns. Translated in al-Faruqi, "Musical Art of Islamic Culture," 430. This figure also appears in the *taqsīm* notated in Nettl and Riddle, "Taqsīm Nahawand," 41.

[80] Abraham Z. Idelsohn, *Jewish Music in Its Historical Development* (New York: H. Holt & Co., 1929; repr., New York: Schoken, 1967), 24–25.

144 Festschrift for Ernest Sanders

The instrumental improvisation-performance of the *taqsīm* has an exact vocal counterpart in the popular *layālī*. The *qasīdah* is another related vocal type based on classical Arabic poetry. The centrality of pattern in these essentially improvisational genres, and the operational procedures followed in their realization, must have been of great interest to European oral performers who were working with similar techniques. Moreover, Western musicians found a broad aesthetic common denominator with Eastern music; after all, meandering, unpredictable melodies often made up of loosely defined motivic cells are eminently present in both plainchant and secular monophony. This melismatic, essentially nondirectional, nondevelopmental style has been often traced back to Eastern origins. Like so much Eastern music, ornamentation in this medieval style is the very essence of melody and not an optional feature. Alongside these prominent Eastern tendencies, European musicians gradually evolved a different melodic style marked by clear tonal teleology. Goal-directed melodies exhibiting this trend evince symmetrical, often antecedent-consequent phrase construction, and utilize the tetrachord-pentachord division of the modal octave to their structural advantage.[81] Ernest Sanders clearly demonstrated the carefully planned and well balanced phrase structure of cantilenas and early motets. Moreover, it was his particular achievement to have defined and set in historical perspective the special concern for tonal unity which marks thirteenth- and fourteenth-century English polyphony.[82]

When combined in a centonate fashion, predetermined melodic aggregates yield brief transitory directionality, but this procedure limits the options for tonal combinations that would enhance overall organization. Thus, the development of long-range tonal articulation required breaking precompositional units into discrete components.[83] Syllabic melodic passages, especially when further delineated by measured rhythm, better define individual tones and enhance tonal directionality more effectively than melismatic unmeasured passages. Viewed from this angle, texting the upper voices of discant clausulae contributed to a better tonal defini-

---

[81] Leo Treitler, "Musical Syntax in the Middle Ages: Background to an Aesthetic Problem," *Perspectives of New Music* 4 (1965): 75–85.

[82] Ernest H. Sanders, "The Medieval Motet," *Gattungen der Musik in Einzeldarstellungen: Gedenkschrift Leo Schrade*, ed. Wulf Arlt et al. (Bern: Francke Verlag, 1973), 497–573; idem, "Tonal Aspects," 19–34; idem, "Die Rolle der englischen Mehrstimmigkeit des Mittelalters in der Entwicklung von Cantus-firmus-Satz und Tonalitätsstruktur," *Archiv für Musikwissenschaft* 24 (1967): 24–53.

[83] Dalia Cohen, "'Separation' and 'Directivity' as Guiding Principles in the Comparison between Eastern and Western Music," *Proceedings of the World Congress on Jewish Music* (Tel-Aviv, 1982), 147.

tion of the incipient motet. Likewise, Garlandia's description of copula as falling "between discant and organum"[84] underlines the gradual shift from the unmeasured, essentially nondirectional organum, through the symmetrical, antecedent-consequent structure of the copula, with its modally rhythmic upper voice and unmeasured lower voice, to the discant where both voices are modally rhythmicized. Compositions mixing organal, copula, and discant styles are therefore transitional pieces, combining old and new tendencies within the same work.[85] A good deal of thirteenth-century theoretical activity can be seen as efforts to define and regulate the implications inherent in the new tendencies. Franco of Cologne, for example, in his *Ars cantus mensurabilis*, attempted to wrest individual durations from their context-bound rhythmic modes by assigning them individual notational symbols.

At this juncture in the evolution of Western musical styles, melodic and rhythmic formulas, melismatic delivery, and improvisational approaches must have become stylistic liabilities rather than assets. The further European music proceeded along the path of long-range tonal planning, the less it needed those Eastern stylistic traits that had served it for centuries. The stylistic transition was neither quick nor straightforward. Old and new tendencies lived side by side for centuries. They are found in the same genres, mixed in the same manuscripts, even within the same pieces. Goal-directed motion is present in Alleluia melismas,[86] in the *ouvert-clos* structure of many a troubadour and trouvère chanson, and very clearly in the *Cantigas de Santa Maria*. On the other hand, strong residues of Eastern practices are not hard to detect even in fourteenth-century polyphony. The main reason why thirteenth-century theorists were apparently not interested in translating al-Fārābī's *Kitāb al-Mūsīqī al Kabīr* was that they no longer found its practical stylistic discussion expedient for their

---

[84] Erich Reimer, *Johannes de Garlandia: De mensurabili musica*, 2 vols., Beihefte zur Archiv für Musikwissenschaft, nos. 10–11 (Wiesbaden: Steiner, 1972), 1:88.

[85] Ernest Sanders noted that "even the three sources of the *Magnus liber* available to us all still contain passages whose notation is so unpatterned, so truly organal, as to make it inadvisable—indeed, virtually impossible—to transcribe them with unequivocal indication of durational values or of any definite time frame for the constituent phrases. To a limited extent variant transcriptions could be equally legitimate" ("Consonance and Rhythm in the Organum of the 12th and 13th Centuries," *Journal of the American Musicological Society* 33 [1980]: 274). For the process of syllabication of melismatic organum, see Sanders, "*Sine Littera* and *Cum Littera* in Medieval Polyphony," *Music and Civilization: Essays in Honor of Paul Henry Lang*, ed. Edmond Strainchamps and Maria R. Maniates (New York: Norton, 1984), 215–31.

[86] Leo Treitler, "On the Structure of the Alleluia Melisma: A Western Tendency in Western Chant," *Studies in Music History: Essays for Oliver Strunk*, ed. Harold S. Powers (Princeton: Princeton University Press, 1968), 59–72.

purposes. Farmer calls this treatise "the greatest contribution to the theory of music up to his time."[87] But, in actual fact, theorists limited their borrowing from al-Fārābī to the methodological remarks in his *De scientiis* (*Ihsā' al-ulūm [Classification of the Sciences]*). This is not, however, as Randel suggests, because "much of what al-Fārābī had written about music did not bear on their personal experience."[88] For it is clear that a great deal of thirteenth-century European music exhibits strong stylistic affinities with Eastern techniques and contents. Rather, they might have sensed that the theoretical interests of the emerging tonal teleology were taking a different direction.

In the previous pages I have revisited the "Arabian Influence" thesis mainly from the viewpoint of music acculturation and confined the discussion of compatible traits to Western monophony. Other topics that could not be covered here certainly deserve study, including the extent to which stylistic findings in the monophonic literature are relevant to contemporary polyphony,[89] the function drone techniques played in organum and later polyphony, the position of Spain as the hub of medieval Eastern influences, and the actual process of transmitting and disseminating Eastern musical characteristics in the medieval West. That the future development of Western music lay away from Eastern traits does not belittle the latter's centrality in Europe's early music history. Rather, it hones the perspective for future study.

---

[87] Henry G. Farmer, *The Sources of Arabian Music* (Leiden: Brill, 1965), 28.

[88] Randel, "Al-Fārābī and the Role of Arabic Music Theory," 188.

[89] Ernest Sanders reminded us that "certainly in the first several centuries of Western *Mehrstimmigkeit* an 'organized' melody, whether it was a chant or a paraliturgical versus, was not thought of as a musical opus of distinct stylistic specificity, but as an elaborated version of that melody" ("Consonance and Rhythm," 264).

Series Bibliography

Adorno, T.W. (1967), 'Bach Defended against His Devotees', in T.W. Adorno, *Prisms*, London, pp. 133–46.

Aldrich, Putnam (1957), 'The "Authentic" Performance of Baroque Music', in *Essays on Music in Honor of Archibald Thompson Davison by His Associates*, Cambridge, MA: Department of Music, Harvard University, pp. 161–71.

Bank, J.A. (1972), *Tactus, Tempo, and Notation in Mensural Music from the 13th to the 17th Century*, Amsterdam: Annie Bank.

Blades, James and Montagu, Jeremy (1976), *Early Percussion Instruments: From the Middle Ages to the Baroque*, London: Oxford University Press.

Boulez, Pierre (1990), 'The Vestal Virgin and the Fire-Stealer: Memory, Creation, and Authenticity', *Early Music*, **18**, pp. 355–58.

Brett, Phillip (1988), 'Text, Context and the Early Music Editor', in Nicholas Kenyon (ed.), *Authenticiy and Early Music*, Oxford: OUP.

Brown, Clive (1999), *Classical and Romantic Performing Practice 1750–1900*, Oxford: Oxford University Press.

Brown, Howard Mayer *et al.* (2001), 'Performing Practice', in Stanley Sadie and John Tyrrell (eds), *The New Grove Dictionary of Music and Musicians* (2nd edn), 29 vols, London: Macmillan, vol 19, pp. 349–88.

Brown, H.M. and Sadie, S. (eds) (1989), *Performance Practice* (2 Vols), The New Grove Handbooks in Music, London: Macmillan.

Butt, John (2002), *Playing with History: The Historical Approach to Musical Performance*, Cambridge: Cambridge University Press.

Careri, E. (1993), *Francesco Geminiani 1687–1762*, Oxford: Oxford University Press.

Copeman, Harold (1990), *Singing in Latin or Pronunciation Explor'd*, Oxford: Harold Copeman.

Covey-Crump, Rogers (1992), 'Vocal Consort Style and Tunings', in John Paynter *et al.* (eds), *Companion to Contemporary Musical Thought*, Vol. II, London and New York: Routledge, pp. 1020–50.

Dart, Thurston (1954), *The Interpretation of Music*, London: Hutchinson's University Library.

Davies, S. (1987), 'Authenticity in Musical Performance', *British Journal of Aesthetics*, **27**, pp. 39–50.

Davies, S. (1988a), 'Transcription, Authenticity and Performance', *British Journal of Aesthetics*, **28**, pp. 216–27.

Davies, S. (1988b), 'Authenticity in Performance: A Reply to James O. Young', *British Journal of Aesthetics*, **29**, 373–76.

Donington, Robert (1963), *The Interpretation of Early Music*, London: Faber, and New York: St Martin's Press; 4th edn 1989.

Dreyfus, Laurence (1983), 'Early Music Defended against Its Devotees: A Theory of Historical Performance in the Twentieth Century', *Musical Quarterly*, **69**, pp. 297–322.

Druce, Duncan (1992), 'Historical Approaches to Violin Playing', in John Paynter *et al.* (eds), *Companion to Contemporary Musical Thought*, Vol. II, London and New York: Routledge, pp. 993–1019.

Dulak, Michelle (1993), 'The Quiet Metamorphosis of "Early Music"', *Repercussions: Critical and Alternative Viewpoints on Music and Scholarship*, **2**, pp. 31–61.

Garratt, James (2002), *Palestrina and the German Romantic Imagination: Interpreting Historicism in Nineteenth-Century Music*, Cambridge: Cambridge University Press.

Goehr, Lydia (1992), *The Imaginary Museum of Musical Works: An Essay in the Philosophy of Music*, Oxford: Clarendon Press.
Greenberg, Noah (1966/1978), 'Early Music Performance Today', in Jan LaRue (ed.), *Aspects of Medieval and Renaissance Music: A Birthday Offering to Gustave Reese*, New York: W.W. Norton, pp. 314–18; reprint edn, New York: Pendragon Press, 1978.
Grout, Donald Jay (1957), 'On Historical Authenticity in the Performance of Old Music', in *Essays on Music in Honor of Archibald Thompson Davison by His Associates*, Cambridge, MA: Department of Music, Harvard University, pp. 341–47.
Harper, John (1991), *The Forms and Orders of Western Liturgy from the Tenth to the Eighteenth Century: A Historical Introduction and Guide for Students and Musicians*, Oxford: Clarendon Press.
Haskell, Harry (1988), *The Early Music Revival: A History*, London: Thames and Hudson.
Haynes, Bruce (2007), *The End of Early Music: A Period Performer's History of Music for the Twenty-First Century*, Oxford: Oxford University Press.
Higgins, P. (1993), 'From the Ivory Tower to the Marketplace: Early Music, Musicology, and the Mass Media', *Current Musicology*, **53**, pp. 109–23.
Hudson, R. (1994), *Stolen Time: The History of Tempo Rubato*, Oxford: Oxford University Press.
Jackson, Roland (1988), *Performance Practice, Medieval to Contemporary: A Bibliographic Guide*, Music Research and Information Guides 9, Garland Reference Library in the Humanities 790, New York and London: Garland.
Kenyon, Nicholas (ed.) (1988), *Authenticity and Early Music: A Symposium*, Oxford and New York: Oxford University Press.
Kenyon, Nicholas (1997), 'Time to Talk Back to Treatises!', *Early Music*, **25**, pp. 555–57.
Kerman, Joseph, Dreyfus, Laurence, Kosman, Joshua, Rockwell, John, Rosand, Ellen, Taruskin, Richard and McGegan, Nicholas (1992), 'The Early Music Debate: Ancients, Moderns, Postmoderns', *Journal of Musicology*, **10**, pp. 113–30.
Kivy, Peter (1995), *Authenticities: Philosophical Reflections on Musical Performance*, Ithaca, NY and London: Cornell University Press.
Lawson, Colin and Stowell, Robin (1999), *The Historical Performance of Music: An Introduction*, Cambridge: Cambridge University Press.
Le Huray, Peter (1990), *Authenticity in Performance: Eighteenth-Century Case Studies*, Cambridge: CUP.
Leppard, R. (1988), *Authenticity in Music*, London: Faber and Faber.
MacClintock, Carol (ed.) (1979), *Readings in the History of Music in Performance*, Bloomington, IN and London: Indiana University Press.
Marcuse, Sibyl (1975), *A Survey of Musical Instruments*, New York: Harper and Row.
Mertin, Josef (1986), *Early Music: Approaches to Performance Practice*, trans. Siegmund Levarie, New York: Da Capo.
Milsom, David (2001), *Theory and Practice in Late Nineteenth-Century Violin Performance: An Examination of Style in Performance 1850–1900*, Aldershot: Ashgate.
Morrow, Michael (1978), 'Musical Performance and Authenticity', *Early Music*, **6**, pp. 233–46.
Neumann, F. (1982), *Essays in Performance Practice*, Epping: University of Rochester Press.
Neumann, F. (1989), *New Essays on Performance Practice*, Ann Arbor, MI and London: University of Rochester Press.
Philip, Robert (1992), *Early Recordings and Musical Style*, Cambridge: Cambridge University Press.
Philip, Robert (2004), *Performing Music in the Age of Recording*, New Haven, CT and London: Yale University Press.
Potter, John (1998), *Vocal Authority: Singing Style and Ideology*, Cambridge: Cambridge University Press.
Remnant, Mary (1978), *Musical Instruments of the West*, London: B.T. Batsford.

Rosen, Charles (2000), 'The Benefits of Authenticity', in Charles Rosen, *Critical Entertainments*, Cambridge, MA and London: Harvard University Press, pp. 201–21.

Rosenblum, Sandra (1991), *Performance Practices in Classic Piano Music: Their Principles and Applications*, Indiana: Indiana University Press.

Sachs, Curt (1953), *Rhythm and Tempo: A Study in Music History*, New York: W.W. Norton.

Sadie, S. (1990), 'The Idea of Authenticity', in J.A. Sadie (ed.), *Companion to Baroque Music*, London: OUP, pp. 435–46.

Saint-Saëns, Camille (1915a), 'The Execution of Classical Works: Notably Those of the Older Masters', *Musical Times*, **56**, pp. 474–78.

Saint-Saëns, Camille (1915b), *On the Execution of Music, and Principally of Ancient Music; a Lecture by M. Camille Saint-Saëns, Delivered at the ... Panama-Pacific International Exposition. Done into English with Explanatory Notes by Henry P. Bowie*, trans. Henry P. Bowie, San Francisco, CA: The Blair-Murdock Company.

Segerman, Ephraim (1996a), 'A Re-examination of the Evidence on Absolute Tempo before 1700 – I', *Early Music*, **24**, pp. 227–48.

Segerman, Ephraim (1996b), 'A Re-examination of the Evidence on Absolute Tempo before 1700 – II', *Early Music*, **24**, pp. 681–89.

Sherman, Bernard D. (1997), *Inside Early Music: Conversations with Performers*, New York and Oxford: Oxford University Press.

Stevens, Denis (1972), 'Some Observations on Performance Practice', *Current Musicology*, **14**, pp. 159–63.

Stevens, Denis (1980), *Musicology: A Practical Guide*, London: Schirmer Books.

Stowell, Robin (1985), *Violin Technique and Performance Practice in the Late-Eighteenth and Early-Nineteenth Centuries*, Cambridge: Cambridge University Press.

Strahle, G. (1995), *An Early Music Dictionary: Musical Terms from British Sources, 1500–1740*, Cambridge: CUP.

Taruskin, Richard (1982), 'On Letting the Music Speak for Itself: Some Reflections on Musicology and Performance', *Journal of Musicology*, **1**, pp. 338–49.

Taruskin, Richard et al. (1984), 'The Limits of Authenticity: A Discussion', *Early Music*, **12**, pp. 1–25.

Taruskin, Richard (1988), 'The Pastness of the Present and the Presence of the Past', in Nicholas Kenyon (ed.), *Authenticity and Early Music: A Symposium*, Oxford and New York: Oxford University Press, pp. 137–207.

Taruskin, Richard (1995), *Text and Act: Essays on Music and Performance*, New York and Oxford: Oxford University Press.

Vinquist, Mary and Zaslaw, Neal (eds) (1970), *Performance Practice: A Bibliography*, New York: W.W. Norton, 1970. Supplements in *Current Musicology* (1971), **12**, pp. 129–49 and (1973), **15**, pp. 126–36.

Walls, Peter (2002), 'Historical Performance and the Modern Performer', in John Rink (ed.), *Musical Performance: A Guide to Understanding*, Cambridge: CUP, pp. 17–34.

Walls, Peter (2003), *History, Imagination and the Performance of Music*, Woodbrige, Suffolk and Rochester, NY: Boydell.

Williams, Peter (1992), 'Performance Practice Studies: Some Current Approaches to the Early Music Phenomenon', in John Paynter et al. (eds), *Companion to Contemporary Musical Thought*, Vol. II, London and New York: Routledge, pp. 931–47.

Winternitz, Emanuel (1979), *Musical Instruments and Their Symbolism in Western Art: Studies in Musical Iconology* (2nd edn), New Haven, CT and London: Yale University Press.

Wistreich, Richard (2002), 'Practising and Teaching Historically Informed Singing – Who Cares?', *Basler Jahrbuch für historische Musikpraxis*, **26**, pp. 17–29.

Wray, Alison (1992), 'Authentic Pronunciation for Early Music', in John Paynter et al. (eds), *Companion to Contemporary Musical Thought*, Vol. II, London and New York: Routledge, pp. 1051–64.

Young, J.O. (1988), 'The Concept of Authentic Performance', *British Journal of Aesthetics*, **28**, pp. 228–38.

Name Index

Aaron, Pietro 437
Abelard, Peter 195
Adémar de Chabannes 24
Adenet le Roi 87
Adler, Guido 212
Albertus Magnus 458
Alexandre de Bernay 34
Al-Fārābi 486, 491, 507, 508
al-Isfāhānī 486, 491
Allaire, Gaston 480
Altacuria, Johannes de 432
Anderson, Gordon A. xx, xxi, 210
Anglés, Higinio 485
Anthonello de Caserta 423, 431, 433, 441
Apel, Willi 210, 440, 492
Apfel, Ernst 485
Appel, Carl 57
Aristotle 97, 181, 193, 197, 199, 474
Armand de Belvezer 247
Arnold, Denis 290
Arnold, I. 75
Atkinson, Charles M. xx, xxi, 165–90
Aquinas, Thomas 268, 455
Aubry, Pierre xviii, 29, 36, 211
Augustine (Saint) 51, 181–4
Aurelian of Réôme 10, 495
Avril, François 456

Bachmann, Werner 474
Bacon, Roger 183, 184
Baines, Anthony 474, 476
Barr, Bernard 480
Bartsch, Karl 64, 83
Bate, Henri 491
Beck, Jean xviii, 29, 36
Beethoven, Ludwig van xiv, 63
Bent, Margaret xxiv, 355, 395–422
Berger, Anna Maria Busse xxiv, 423–53
Berno of Reichenau 6
Berruguete, Pedro 285
Berry, Mary 3, 5, 12, 13
Besseler, Heinrich 10, 327, 328, 362
Binchois, Gilles 358, 368, 369, 375–8, 384, 390

Binns, J.W. 480
Blackley, R. John 9
Blondel de Nesle 37, 60
Boe, John 38
Boen, Johannes 433, 434
Boethius 180, 183, 195, 197, 198, 437
Boorman, Stanley xi, xv
Borges, J.L. 26
Borromeo, Carlo 290
Boulez, Pierre xv
Bouquet, Marie-Thérèse 289
Bowers, Roger xxiii, 293–324
Bozon, Nicole 108, 109
Brahms, Johannes 159
Brenet, Michel 286, 289
Briquet 326
Brown, Howard Mayer xi, xxiii, 292, 367, 389, 480
Brunner, Lance W. xvii, 3–14
Bukofzer, Manfred 210, 485
Burstyn, Shai xxv, 481–508
Burtius, Nicolaus 433, 440

Caccini, Giulio 163
Camilla of Aragon 288
Campin, Robert 279
Cardine, Eugène (Dom) xvii, 3, 5–7, 10, 13, 21
Caserta, Philip de 439
Cassiodorus 180
Catullus 181
Cervantes, Miguel 26
Cesaris, Johannes 327
Chandos, John (Sir) 88
Charlemagne 15, 16, 42, 127
Chaucer, Geoffrey 242
Chrétien de Troyes 71
Chrodegang of Metz 19
Cicero 181
Ciconia, Johannes 430, 433, 440
Clemens non Papa, Jacobus 353
Clement of Lessay 122, 126
Coclico, Adrianus Petit 365, 366, 372
Colombe, Jean 280

Cordier, Baude 362
Cotton, John 461
Couperin, Louis 149
Coussemaker, Edmond 191, 248, 435
Crecquillon, Thomas 353
Crocker, Richard xx, 7
Czerny, Carl 224

D'Accone, Frank 290
Dalglish, William xvi
Danjou, Félix 19
Dante 34
De Van, Guillaume 12
Deschamps, Eustache 335–9
Didymus 404
Dietricus 221
Dorfmüller, Kurt 31
Dositheus 197
Dragonetti, Roger 29, 35, 36
Dufay, Guillaume 279, 291, 330, 356, 358, 362, 380, 381, 384–6
Duffin, Ross xi
Duns Scotus 198
Dunstaple, Iohannes 355

Earp, Lawrence xxiv, 353–64
Eleanor (Queen) 285
Ellinwood, Leonard xxi
Erber, Georg 425
Eude de Sully 150
Everist, Mark 250, 255
Eyck, Jacob van 279
Eyck, Jan van 279

Fallows, David xi, xxiii, xxiv, 255, 365–91
Farmer, Henry George 482, 483, 488
Fauré, Gabriel 57
Faxolis, Florentius 402
Federhofer-Königs, Renate 425
Ferretti, Paolo 492
Fibonacci, Leonardo 34
Fischer, Kurt von 439
Fletcher, Shane 255
Foerster, W. 71
Fothergill, Marmaduke 322
Francis I 285
Franco of Cologne 38, 52, 151, 152, 158, 159, 165–79 *passim*, 182, 183, 185–9, 216, 222, 414, 438, 456, 507
Froissart, Jean 87, 107, 108
Fuller, Sarah xx

Gace de la Buigne 99, 338
Gaffurius, Franchinus 423, 426, 443, 444, 446–9, 453
Gajard, Joseph (Dom) xvii, 5
Galiot, Johannes 427, 434
Gall, Philippe 286
Gallo, F. Alberto 427, 434, 438, 439, 474
Galpin, Francis W. 474
Gautier de Coinci 98
Gennrich, Friedrich xviii, 238
Gerbert de Montreuil 96
Gibb, Hamilton 490
Gilson, Etienne 183
Goldschmidt, Adolph 266
Gombert, Nicolas 353
Gosalch 433
Greene, Gordon K. 427, 434
Gregory IX 270, 271
Gregory of Tours 18
Gregory the Great 18
Grocheio, Johannes de xix, 51, 52, 55, 56, 61, 121–3 *passim*, 140, 144, 185, 216, 217, 241, 242, 458, 491, 497, 501
Grossin, Estienne 326, 329
Grout, Donald xiv, xv
Guéranger, Prosper (Dom) xvii, 19, 20
Guerrero, Francisco 366, 367, 369, 391
Guido of Arezzo 6, 498
Guilielmus Monachus 425, 444
Guillaume d'Amiens 63
Guillaume de Lorris 74
Guntram 18

Haines, John xxv
Halperin, David 492, 497
Harrison, Frank Ll. 10, 289, 291, 313, 320–2, 485
Haydn, Joseph 163, 224, 300–303
Heinen, Hubert xviii
Hellauer, Susan xi
Hibberd, Lloyd xxi, 338
Higgins, Paula 375
Hildegard of Bingen xvii
Hiley, David xvii
Hoffmann, E.T.A. 261
Hofhaimer, Paul 285
Hothby, John 425, 436, 441, 444
Hucbald 461, 496
Hughes, Andrew 57
Huizinga, J. 343, 351
Huot, Sylvia xix, 69–119

Husmann, Heinrich xviii, 37

Isidore of Seville 11, 18, 180

Jackson, John-Paul Christopher xi
Jackson, Roland xi
Jacopo da Bologna 368
Jacques de Liège 186, 187, 250, 343, 344, 403
Jammers, Ewald xvi, xviii, 3
Jausion (Dom) 19
Jean duc de Berry 82, 278, 279, 282
Jerome of Moravia xxv, 151–3, 158, 163, 167, 176, 177, 179, 455–8 *passim*, 461–5, 474–6, 479, 480, 491, 497, 498
Johannes de Garlandia (John of Garland) 52, 151, 160, 168, 170, 171, 173, 174, 176, 177, 179, 183, 184, 188, 191, 193–5, 199, 201–204, 206–208, 212, 213, 215, 216–8, 220, 221, 223, 400, 507
John of Dacia 194
John the Deacon 16, 24
Josquin des Prez 365–7

Kaltenbacher, R. 90
Karp, Theodore xx
Kartomi, Margaret 489
Kenyon, Nicholas xv
Ker, Neil 321
Kilwardby, Robert 189
Kippenberg, Burkhard 49, 238
Knapp, Janet xx, xxi
Knighton, Tess xi
Kroyer, Theodor 261

Lambertus 215–8, 222, 458, 462
Landini, Francesco xxi
Lasso, Orlando di 286
Le Huray, Peter 289
Leech-Wilkinson, Daniel xxi, 255
Legge, Dominica 321, 322
Leichentritt, Hugo 261
Leonin 149, 220
List, George 488
Livljanić, Katarina 15–26
Lockwood, Lewis 290
Lomax, Alex 485
Long, Michael P. 438
Lord, Albert 494
Lowinsky, E.E. 401, 416
Ludwig, Friedrich xviii, 209–11, 325

Mabille, Madeleine 456
McGee, Timothy xi, 499
Machaut, Guillaume de 65, 79, 82, 109, 325, 330, 335–8, 343, 353, 355, 356, 365
McKinnon, James W. xxii, 261–92
Maddrell, J.E. xviii, xix
Mahler, Gustav 224
Maillart, Jean 96
Manlius, Johannes 365, 366
Marche, Olivier de la 349
Marchettus of Padua 404, 407, 418, 427, 438
Marcuse, Sibyl 474
Marguerite of Valois 290
Marie de France 78
Marius Victorinus 180
Marix, Jeanne 289, 343
Martin of Dacia 193
Mathieu d'Escouchy 349
Matthiassen, Finn 42
Maximilian I 286
Meiss, Millard 278
Melanchthon, Philipp 365, 366
Menard, Pierre 26
Merriam, Alan 489
Miélot, Jean 271, 272
Mocquereau, André (Dom) xvii, 5, 61
Mölk, Ulrich 29, 30, 43–5
Montagu, Jeremy xv
Monterosso, Rafaello xviii, 57
Moreschi, Alessandro 25
Morrow, Michael xv, 11
Mouton, Jean 367
Mowbray, Lord John 310
Mozart, Wolfgang Amadeus 57, 159
Muelich, Hans 286
Muris, Johannes (Jean) de 255, 397, 405, 411, 412, 414, 415, 417, 438, 439, 448, 452

Nádas, John 355
Nero 181
Nettl, Bruno 485, 487, 488, 489, 504
Niccolò da Bologna 272
Noble, Jeremy 292
Notker of St. Gall 16

Odington, Walter 151, 158, 216, 222, 223, 439
Odo of Cluny 461
Ong, Walter 485, 492
Ortiz, Diego 372
Osbern 323

Osthoff, Helmuth 365
Ostler, Nicholas 480
Oswald von Wolkenstein 30

Page, Christopher xi, xviii, xix, xxi, xxiii, xxiv, xxv, 66, 90, 95, 121–45, 241–57, 335–52, 360, 362, 455–80
Panofsky, Erwin 270, 276
Pérès, Marcel xi
Péronne d'Armentières 335, 365
Perotin 149, 151, 161, 215, 220, 225
Perrin d'Angecourt 113
Peter of Spain (Petrus Hispanus) 193, 195, 199
Petrus Dictus de Palma Ociosa 372
Philip the Fair 289
Philip the Good (Duke of Burgundy) 271, 350
Phillips, Elizabeth xi
Pierre de Limoges 456–8, 463, 467, 469, 476
Pierre de Palude 241, 242
Pierre of Peckham 320
Pierre of Picard 474
Pippin 16
Pius X 3, 4, 12
Pixérécourt, René Charles Guilbert de 384
Planchart, Alejandro Enrique xvii
Plato 474
Polk, Keith 290
Pothier, Joseph (Dom) xvii, 4, 19
Powers, Harold 495
Praetorius, Michael 367
Priscian 197
Prosdocimus de Beldemandis 404, 406–09, 412, 413–5, 418, 419, 423, 424, 440, 444

Quantz, Johann Joachim 149, 163
Quintilian 181

Raimbaut de Vacqueiras 62
Ramis de Pareja, Bartolomeus 433, 440
Randel, D. 480, 508
Rastall, Richard 480
Rayburn, John xvi
Raynaud, Gaston 338
Reaney, Gilbert xx, xxi, xxii, 325–31
Reckow, Fritz 165, 167, 173, 174, 192, 200, 203
Rees, David 474
Regino Prumensis 461, 495
Rehm, Wolfgang 369
Reimer, Erich 171, 177, 204, 220
Renart, Jean 76

Restori, Antonio xviii
Reyneau, Gacian (of Tours) 358, 362
Rhau, Georg 365
Riddle, R. 504
Riemann, Hugo xvi, 29, 261
Robert de Castel d'Arras, 36
Robertus de Sabilone 151
Roesner, Edward xx, xxi, 149–64, 167, 172, 175–7, 180, 188
Rohloff, Ernst 123
Rokseth, Yvonne 247
Rudel, Jaufre 31, 39, 42, 43
Ruffo, Vincenzo 290
Rufinus 181

Sachs, Curt 12, 41, 210, 485, 497
Sadie, Stanley xi
Safī-al-Dīn 501, 502
Salomon, Elias of 245, 255, 458
Sanders, Ernest H. xx, xxi, 209–39, 497, 506
Sappler, Paul 29, 31
Schapiro, Meyer 490
Schering, Arnold 261–3, 379
Schneider, Marius 485
Schneyer, Johann Baptist 122
Schrade, Leo 210, 325
Schubert, Franz 57, 224
Schumann, Robert 224
Seay, Albert 121, 402
Sedulius, Caelius 323
Segerman, Ephraim 480
Seneca 128
Sforza, Constanzo 288
Sherman, Bernard xi
Smits van Waesberghe, Jos. 480
Spartaro, Giovanni 437
Stäblein, Bruno 7
Stevens, John 57
Stevenson, Robert 290, 291
Stradanus, Johannes 286
Strunk, Oliver 165, 172, 175, 180
Summerly, Jeremy 255
Susato, Tielman 367

Taruskin, Richard xv
Tavernier, Jean 272
Thibaut, Anton 261
Thomas d'Angleterre 93
Thornton, Barbara xi
Tinctoris, Johannes 402, 405, 417, 423, 425, 426, 436, 437, 443–9, 453

Tischler, Hans xviii, xix, xx, 29–47
Treitler, Leo xx, 22

Ugolino of Orvieto 398, 404, 406, 409, 412, 415, 418, 419, 424, 434, 440, 441, 444

Vaillant, Jean 434
van der Werf, Hendrik xviii, xix, 29, 31, 34, 37, 39, 41, 42, 49–67, 238, 497
van Doorslaer, G. 289
Viollet le Duc 20
Vitry, Philippe de 335, 400, 405
Vollaerts, J.W.A. xvi
Von Ramm, Andrea 11

Wagner, Peter xvi, 492
Waite, William G. xx, 155, 192
Walther, H. 474

Walther von der Vogelweide 31, 39, 42, 43
Waterman, Richard 488
Werner, J. 474
Westrup, Jack 488
White, Lynn 490
Willaert, Adrian 353
William of Aquitain 38
Wiora, Walter 485
Wolf, Johannes 433
Wolfzettel, Friedrich 29, 30, 43
Wright, Craig xxiii, 290, 291

Yudkin, Jeremy xx, xxi, 167, 191–208

Zachara, Antonio 328
Zarlino, Gioseffo 365